Fremdsprachen
in Geschichte und Gegenwart

Herausgegeben von
Helmut Glück und Konrad Schröder

Band 15

2015
Harrassowitz Verlag · Wiesbaden

Nicola McLelland

German Through English Eyes

A History of Language Teaching
and Learning in Britain
1500–2000

2015

Harrassowitz Verlag · Wiesbaden

Cover illustration:
The illustrated map of Germany used on the cover is by A R Whitear for Sprich Mal
Deutsch, vol. 2 by William Rowlinson (OUP, 1967) and is reproduced by permission
of Oxford University Press.

Printed with financial support from the Faculty of Arts Dean's Fund,
University of Nottingham.

Bibliografische Information der Deutschen Nationalbibliothek
Die Deutsche Nationalbibliothek verzeichnet diese Publikation in der Deutschen
Nationalbibliografie; detaillierte bibliografische Daten sind im Internet
über http://dnb.dnb.de abrufbar.

Bibliographic information published by the Deutsche Nationalbibliothek
The Deutsche Nationalbibliothek lists this publication in the Deutsche
Nationalbibliografie; detailed bibliographic data are available in the internet
at http://dnb.dnb.de.

For further information about our publishing program consult our
website http://www.harrassowitz-verlag.de

ISSN 1860-5842
ISBN 978-3-447-10148-6

This book is dedicated to the German teachers and lecturers who shaped my view of German as a pupil and student in the 1980s and 1990s: Mrs Janssen, Miss Watts, Mr Mannell, John Clifton-Everest, Manfred Pienemann, and Brian Taylor. Also to the memory of Vivien Law, who first introduced me to the history of linguistics at Cambridge.

Contents

Chapter 1

Writing a history of foreign language learning in the UK 1

1.1 Introduction: 1 – 1.2 The history of modern language teaching and learning in the British Isles: 3 – 1.3 Research on the history of German teaching and learning in the British Isles to date: 8 – 1.4 The History of German as a Foreign Language: 9 – 1.5 The history of foreign language teaching methodologies in Great Britain and Ireland: 10 – 1.6 A textbook-based history of foreign language learning and teaching in the British Isles: 11 – 1.7 Approaches to textbooks: 13 – 1.8 A caveat: the story in history and my selection of textbooks: 16

Chapter 2

**The birth of a subject: the first hundred years of German
as a Foreign Language in England (1615–1715)** 19

2.1 The earliest evidence of learning German as a foreign language in Europe: the ninth to sixteenth centuries: 19 – 2.2 The first beginnings of learning German in seventeenth-century England: 24 – 2.3 The early eighteenth century under the House of Hanover: Johann König's *Royal Compleat Grammar* (1715): 44 – 2.4 Conclusion: 48

Chapter 3

Learning and teaching German in the 'long' nineteenth century 51

3.1 Introduction: 51 – 3.2 The eighteenth century – before the institutionalization of German: 52 – 3.3 Why learn German? Changing motivations from the 1770s: 56 – 3.4 Early evidence of German in schools, and the birth of the "exercise": 68 – 3.5 Reflections on language and method: 74 – 3.6 The establishment of German in schools and universities: 78 – 3.7 The emergence of the "method" and didactic progression in modern language teaching: 84 – 3.8 Teaching to the test: 97 – 3.9 Philology in textbooks of German: 103 – 3.10 The new science of phonetics and the Reform Movement: 109 – 3.11 Excursus: learning German in the United States in the nineteenth century: 134 – 3.12 Conclusion: 136

Contents

Acknowledgements

I have greatly enjoyed writing this book, but that enjoyment was only made possible by the help of a great many other people. I owe a great debt to my colleagues in the Department of German at the University of Nottingham. They not only endured me holding forth on the subject of this book, both formally and informally; more importantly, they shouldered my load while I had the luxury of a year's research leave in 2010–11, during which almost all of this book was written. Warm thanks to them all. It was an early conversation of Judith Still that opened my eyes to the potential of a germ of an idea; Peter Yeandle pointed me in the right direction at a very early stage in my forays into this history of education in Britain. I also benefited greatly from the expertise of Fredericka van der Lubbe on early grammars of German. Richard Smith saved me weeks of labour by giving me a crash course on the Reform Movement and key primary and secondary sources and by generously allowing me to borrow several books for months on end, and has provided advice ever since. Michael Byram read a draft of Chapter 4, Franziska Meyer gave me very useful comments on a draft of Chapter 6, and Magnus Brechtken was also helpful on the history of Anglo-German relations. John Flood – who, as ever, turned out to have been there before me – more than once pointed me in the direction of useful secondary literature. Anne Simon read the entire manuscript in draft and made many very constructive suggestions. Any remaining weaknesses are, of course, my own.

I am very grateful to a number of archivists around the country, whose ability to know what questions I ought to be asking them was invaluable. At the head of these is Gillian Cooke at the Cambridge Assessment archives, who was a great help on two visits there. Jessica Womack at the Institute of Education, Rachel Bond at Eton College, Rusty MacLean at Rugby, James Cox at Gonville & Caius College, Cambridge, and Annabelle Gardiner at Queen's College were all equally helpful. Helmut Glück and his colleagues were wonderful and generous hosts during my ten-day stay at the University of Bamberg in 2010, and allowed me rich use of the Taylor Collection of textbooks. Special thanks to Professor Glück's secretary Barbara Heger, without whose gentle prodding I might never have got myself organized to get there in the first place. It was ironic that I viewed this collection in Bamberg, for its donor, Brian Taylor, had taught me German at the University of Sydney 1988–1991, and he continued to answer numerous queries, not to mention sending additional textbooks, from Sydney.

In 2009 I made a first terrified appearance on Radio 4's *Making History* to talk about the *German Through English Eyes* project – my thanks go to the producer Nick Patrick and presenter at the time Vanessa Collingridge for somehow making sense of what I was trying to say. The result was a massive response from the public. Many people shared their reminiscences, and donated or lent textbooks that they had held onto for decades,

Acknowledgements

to an extent that absolutely transformed the scope of the research that I was able to undertake. The many, many people who got in touch are too numerous to mention individually here, though I have tried to acknowledge some of them at the appropriate points in the book itself, but I must single out Patsy Hans, who first drew my attention to the delightful 1930s *Brush up Your German* series, and Richard Taylor, who sent a crate-load of books from Bootham School in York. Many people also responded to a request for interviewees – my thanks to Paul Coggle, Robert Kirk, Karin Reekie, Richard Shaw, Duncan Sidwell, Richard Stokes, and Colin Wringe, as well as others who chose to remain anonymous, for giving up their time to be interviewed, and thanks too to numerous others whose recollections, sent in by email, I also drew on for this book.

The preliminary research for the book was funded by the University of Nottingham's Research Strategy Fund, which allowed me to employ Katherine Bennett and then Sally Brailsford as research assistants for some of the bibliographic donkey work at the start of the project. Both were immensely helpful and worth their weight in gold. My thanks to the British taxpayers, in the form of the Arts and Humanities Research Council, who funded half of the year's research leave that went into writing this book. I hope some of them, at least, get some pleasure from reading it.

Nottingham, March 2015   Nicola McLelland

Image credits

Every effort has been made to trace the holders of the copyright of the images reproduced in this book. Please contact the author for more information. I gratefully acknowledge the following for kind permission to reproduce copyright material:

Figure 1.1 *Schachzabelbuch* image by kind permission of the Bildarchiv Foto Marburg. Figure 2.1 Frontispiece of Martin Aedler's *High Dutch Minerva*, Figure 3.1 and Figure 5.7 (both from Beiler 1731), Figure 3.2 (from Bachmair 1771), Figure 5.1 (from Noehden 1800), by permission of the Bodleian Library. Figures 5.2 and 5.10 (from Wendeborn 1797b) by kind permission of the British Library. Figure 3.4 (from Render 1804), Figure 3.8 (from Otto 1864), Figure 3.9 & 3.10 from Eysenbach & Collar (1887), Figure 5.13 (from Bernays 1832), and Figure 5.15 (from Woodbury 1851) all by kind permission of New York Public Library. Figures 3.5, 3.11 (examination papers) by kind permission of Cambridge University Library, Figure 3.12 by kind permission of Rugby School Archives. Figures 3.14, 3.16 and 5.11 (all from Brandt 1888) by kind permission of the University of Michigan. Thanks to the Sammlung Taylor (at the University of Bamberg) for permission to reproduce Figures 3.18, 6.40, 6.41 (from Trotter 1898), Figures 3.19 and 3.20 (both from Ungoed 1912), Figures 4.8 and 5.6 (both from Orton 1959), Figure 4.11 (from Ripman 1921), Figure 5.5 (from Koischwitz 1938), Figure 5.8 (from Rosenberg 1938), Figure 5.14 (from Ollendorff? n.d.), Figure 5.17 (from Oswald 1940), Figure 6.2 (from Beresford Webb 1903), Figure 6.4 (from Althaus 1916), Figures 6.15 and 6.19 (from Scholle & Smith 1909), Figure 6.29 (from Fenn & Fangl 1954). The photo of Rippmann in Figure 3.22 is reproduced by kind permission of Queen's College, London. Figures 4.4 and 4.5 (lino cuts by Hertha Kluge-Pott) courtesy Hertha Kluge-Pott and Australian Galleries. Figures 4.6, 4.7, 4.9, 5.20, 6.16, 6.31 (from Rowlinson 1967, 1969, Smith 1985) and Figure 6.19 (from Bates & Smith 1992) by permission of Oxford University Press. Figures 4.10 and 4.65 (photos which appeared in Hammond 1969) by kind permission of the German Embassy in London. Figures 4.14 and 4.15 (from McNab 1969) by kind permission of Ealing Council. Figure 5.3 (from Render 1799) by kind permission of the National Library of Ireland. Figure 6.13 (from Barker 1941) by kind permission of Heffers. Figure 6.39 by kind permission of the DOSB (Deutscher Olympischer Sportbund). Figure 6.24 Maps from *Berlin in Early Cold War Army Booklets* used with permission.

About the Author

Nicola McLelland is Professor of German and History of Linguistics at the University of Nottingham. She studied in Sydney, Bonn and Cambridge before taking up her first post in German at Trinity College, Dublin. She began her academic career as a specialist in German medieval literature, and her first book was on a less-known version of the Lancelot story, Ulrich von Zatikhoven's *Lanzelet*. Her second book, on the first major grammar of German, a 1500-page work which its author Schottelius called a "Comprehensive work on the German language", was published in 2011. The volume *Germania Remembered: Remembering and Inventing a Germanic Past* (1500–2009), co-edited with Christina Lee, appeared in 2012. She is editor of the journal *Language and History*.

Glossary of terms
specific to the English / British education systems

A-level (General Certificate of Education, Advanced level) –
examinations taken at age 18, introduced in 1951. Pupils usually have three or four A-level subjects.

College of Preceptors (since 1998 the College of Teachers) –
established by Royal Charter in 1849, one of the first bodies to provide formal examinations for pupils, from 1851, as well as for teachers, from 1846.

comprehensive school –
state-funded secondary school catering to pupils of all backgrounds and ability ranges, established from the late 1950s and 1960s.

CSE (Certificate of School Education) –
examinations taken at age 16, introduced in 1965 for pupils in secondary modern schools or comprehensive schools, to provide a an alternative qualification to O-levels for pupils not expecting to proceed to A-levels and further study. The range of subjects was wider than for O-levels and included vocational subjects. CSE and O-level examinations were merged into the GCSE system from 1986.

elementary school –
the first schools funded by taxation, providing education for children between the ages of 5 and 14 between 1870 and 1944. In some areas older children were educated in separate Higher Elementary Schools. Many of these schools became primary schools after 1944.

GCE (General Certificate of Education) –
see *A-level* and *O-level*.

GCSE (General Certificate of Secondary Education) –
examinations taken at age 16, introduced in 1986 to replace O-levels and CSE examinations.

grammar school –
academically selective secondary school, for those pupils scoring in the top 25% of the "11+" examination; the remainder went to a secondary modern school. Some schools with *Grammar School* in their title are private schools, however.

higher grade elementary school –
(in the late nineteenth and early twentieth century) school for older and more able pupils who had passed the equivalent of Year 6 in elementary school, the end of today's primary education.

Glossary of terms specific to the English / British education systems

HSC (Higher School Certificate) –
examinations taken by pupils at age 18 between 1918 and 1951, when the HSC was replaced by A-levels.

O-level (Ordinary level) –
subject examination taken at age 16 as part of the General Certificate of Examination, introduced in 1951. Pupils would take up to 10 O-level subjects, sometimes more.

private school (or independent school) –
a school where fees are charged for pupils to attend.

Public School –
despite the name, the term Public School refers to the older, more exclusive and more expensive fee-paying private secondary schools in Britain.

School Certificate –
examinations taken by pupils at age 16 (between 1918 and 1951, when the certificate was replaced by O-levels).

secondary modern school –
a school for the majority of pupils, those not achieving scores in the top 25 % of the "11+" examination. Replaced by comprehensive schools in most parts of Britain.

Chapter 1 –
Writing a history of foreign language learning in the UK

1.1 Introduction

Much of the business of educationalists is, inevitably, to identify weaknesses in existing approaches and materials in the light of the latest pedagogical insights (see, for example, the analyses in Byram's edited volume from 1993 measuring textbooks according to how they integrate "intercultural" awareness in language education). We tend to assume that our current theory and practice of language education represent an "improvement" in absolute terms on the "deficiencies" of what went before. Yet "improvement" is hard to measure and, perhaps, equally hard to achieve. Despite over a century of concerted attention from educational experts, modern foreign language teaching is still often perceived to be in crisis, exactly as many practitioners claimed it was at the end of the nineteenth century. Even though the *Common European Framework of Reference for Languages: Learning, teaching, assessment* (CEFR) has been widely adopted in Europe and beyond, fundamental questions about foreign language education are still the subject of continued debate: questions about the purpose of foreign language learning in the UK and elsewhere; the importance of foreign language skills (whether to the individual learner or to society as a whole); and the question of which languages and which skills are needed, at what level. The venerable British Academy, for example, launched a four-year programme in 2011 "to demonstrate the value of language-learning in the humanities and social sciences and build capacity", and has since published a report, *Languages: The State of the Nation* (2013).[1] Informed experts and practitioners with vested interests may be utterly convinced of the importance of foreign language competence, but British society at large is not. The same holds true of many of the other English-speaking countries. In other parts of the world (including much of Europe), the importance of learning English is unquestioned, but there is less agreement about the status of other languages.

We seem, then, to be little closer today than we were at the dawn of the twentieth century to answering the questions that lie at the very foundations of language teaching: who should learn a foreign language, why learners learn, what they need to learn, and what we want to teach them – answers that we need before we can consider *how* we want to teach. This book does not answer those questions, but it is intended to help us to take "the long view" of them, providing a historical perspective in the shape of an

---

1 See the British Academy webpages, http://www.britac.ac.uk/policy/Languages.cfm and http://www.britac.ac.uk/policy/State_of_the_Nation_2013.cfm (= Tinsley 2013), accessed May 2013.

interdisciplinary history of German language learning and teaching in the British Isles. I hope that this "long view" will, amongst other things, help us make explicit what assumptions we tend to make in debates about falling or rising 'standards'. When we say that pupils have been learning 'German' or another language (or *not* learning it to our satisfaction), what is it, exactly, that they (should) have been learning? German is not – either historically or currently – the first foreign language in Britain. That place belongs, and has always belonged, to French (albeit now facing stiff competition from Spanish). Nevertheless, the learning and teaching of German in the British Isles is a particularly rewarding case study for tackling such questions because German history, and British relations with Germany, have been complex and subject to major shifts, especially over the past century.

This book is not, primarily, a history of language teaching methodology, of *how* language has been taught, but instead an examination, in its historical context, of *what* has been taught: both 'the language' and 'the culture' (both rather monolithic concepts which will be unpicked below, especially in Chapters 5 and 6). It tells the story of teaching and learning German not 'from above' – not as a history of the educational theories that filter down to practice. Instead, this history of language education is told 'from below', told primarily through the textbooks that were used by teachers and learners – for the period up to 1850, they are in any case almost our only sources. While I have certainly also drawn on a wide range of other sources where available – including statements of pedagogical theory, policy documents, correspondence in professional journals, and personal testimonies – it is textbooks that are at the heart of the study. Although textbooks are by definition codifications of the supposedly essential 'facts' in a discipline, they are as yet an almost entirely untapped resource for investigating historical representations in Britain of our own and other cultures. A notable exception to this is a recent flurry of work by historians on how history textbooks have represented both changes in international relations, and conceptions of the nation more generally, in Britain, Germany and indeed in Europe as a whole.[2] Chapter 6 of this study includes an investigation of such themes in textbooks of German. Ultimately, the findings there should be compared with the treatment of the same themes in popular culture or in history curricula, an area in which there has been recent work.

Less obvious than the shifting tides of international cultural and political relations, but arguably just as relevant to the daily experience of both native speakers and language learners alike, are the changes that all languages undergo over time. In whatever way we choose to present language to foreign language learners, their competence can only ever be as good as the linguistic input that they receive. Chapter 5, therefore, addresses the changes in how linguists have analysed, described and represented German to learners, both in the light of developing grammatical and linguistic theories and in an ongoing

---

2   A project at the Institute for Historical Research on History in Education largely focuses on the history of teaching of British history in Britain (http://www.history.ac.uk/projects/history-in-education). See also Schissler (1987), contributions in Schissler & Soysal (2005), including Soysal et al. (2005), Dierkes (2005); Rodden (2006, 2007), Yeandle (in prep.); and the project *EurViews: Europe in Schoolbooks* starting at the Georg-Eckert-Institute in Brauschweig. See also below.

game of 'catch-up' with changes in the language itself. The chapter extends recent sociolinguistic research on national standard languages (e.g. Mattheier & Radtke 1997, Linn & McLelland 2002) and language prescription (e.g. Beal et al. 2008; Percy & Davidson 2012); looking at what non-native speakers are taught provides a counterpoint to the study of *native* German speakers' beliefs about what constitutes the standard language (see e.g. Davies & Langer 2006, Wagner 2009). Such questions are especially pertinent for a 'pluricentric' language like German (Clyne 1995), which is the language of (for a time) two Germanies, Austria, and German-speaking Switzerland, each with their own standard varieties.[3]

Chapters 2, 3 and 4 provide the foundation for chapters 5 and 6. Chapter 4 provides an overview of how, why and by whom German was learnt, taught and assessed in the course of the twentieth century. Chapters 2 and 3, however, are devoted to the more distant history of German language teaching and learning, from ca. 1600 to 1900. I make no excuse for going so far back in time. That history has not been written. It is time to write it, and, as we shall see, it raises many of the same questions that will later concern teachers and learners of the twentieth century: why and how to learn a language, and what to learn. As for the remainder of this first chapter, I set out below some preliminaries: the current state of research (1.2 to 1.6); some methodological considerations (1.7); and some brief theoretical reflections on the historiography of ideas about language (1.8). Those sections will not be of equal interest to all readers. For the reader simply keen to learn about the rich history of German language learning in the British Isles, it will be as well to take the plunge straight into Chapter 2.

1.2 The history of modern language teaching and learning in the British Isles: the current state of research

All researchers like to begin by pointing out a research gap, but in the case of the history of teaching and learning foreign languages in the UK it is more than a mere topos. Stern (1983: 76) noted the 'paucity of studies' in the history of second language teaching and regretted the inevitably 'short memory' of language teaching theory that is its result – and little has changed since 1983. Two studies of the learning of German in Britain, by Ortmanns (1993) and Wegner (1999), are important contributions, to which I return below. In contrast, Hüllen (1995: 1), writing about the history of English-learning in Germany, might lament that "hardly any research has been done on English textbooks", but he was nonetheless able to turn to a 522-page book on learning English in Germany in the period 1700–1900 (Klippel 1994) and a three-volume history of the methods of teaching English in Germany from 1800–1960 (Macht 1986–1990). Several volumes by Konrad Schröder provide bibliography and studies of the history of English teaching in Germany up to 1900 (Schröder 1975; and 1969 for English at universities to

---

3   Of course German is also the language of at least some members of other neighbouring states, including Luxembourg, Denmark, and Italy, but these do not possess their own standard variety to which speakers orient themselves in the sense that Clyne means it.

1850) as well as comprehensive bibliography of the history of the wider teaching of modern foreign languages in the German-speaking countries (Schröder 1980–1985; 2nd ed. Schröder 2014). For the period 1700–1945, there is also comprehensive documentation, in seven volumes, of the official state guidelines and prescriptions on the teaching of modern languages in Germany (Christ & Rang 1985). We should note too Manfred Görlach's annotated bibliography of nineteenth-century grammars of English (Görlach 1999), and a number of monographs on various aspects of the history of teaching and learning foreign languages in Germany.[4] For the history of modern foreign language teaching in Britain, the equivalent bibliographical foundations are almost entirely lacking. It is still true today to say with Stern (1983: 76) that 'the current state of historical documentation is far from satisfactory'.[5]

Stern outlined a list of desiderata for researching the history of language teaching and learning which bear reviewing here, thirty years later (Stern 1983: 113–114). I summarize Stern's desiderata below, and for each I indicate to what extent they have been met:[6]

1. 'detailed and well documented studies of language teaching and learning in given periods in particular countries', both within the European language tradition and outside Europe (and both before and after contact with the European tradition). For Europe, we can note here Maréchal (1972) for a history of language teaching in Belgium up to the early twentieth century; Puren (1998, 1994) for France; Schröder (1980, 1982, 1983, 1985) and Hüllen (2005) for Germany; Hammar (1991) for the learning of French in Sweden before 1807; Kibbee (1991) for French in England up to 1600, and publications by Kok Escalle for French in the Low Countries (including Kok Escalle 1999, Kok Escalle & Strien-Chardonneau 2010). An important recent addition is the substantial study by Kuhfuß (2014) of French learning in early modern Germany, while Rjéoutski & Tchoudinov (2013) focusses in particular on the learning of French in Eastern Europe from the seventeenth to nineteenth centu-

---

4 These include Tintemann (2006) on Karl Philipp Moritz's Italian grammar for Germans (1791), and a number of dissertations supervised by Friederike Klippel in Munich: Doff (2002) on the teaching of English to girls in the nineteenth century, Riedl (2004) on the reform figure Hermann Breymann, Franz (2005) on English manuals for Germans emigrating to America, Ostermeier (2012) on modern languages in Prussian schools 1859–1933, Kolb (2013) on the teaching of culture in English teaching, 1975–2011, and Ruisz (2013) on the teaching of English in post-War Bavaria. See also Doff (2007) on the teaching of English in the Federal Republic, 1949–1989.

5 The relative lack of attention paid to the history of foreign language learning in the British Isles compared to Germany reflects both the relatively lower status of foreign language learning anyway, and the fact that in Germany teacher training is spread out over a number of years, rather than undertaken in a single intensive year, as in the British Postgraduate Certificate of Education (PGCE). Both factors mean that the pool of teacher-trainers who might typically research such topics is smaller in the UK. Equally, the history of teaching any of the major European languages is likely to pale into insignificance behind the attention paid to the history of the booming business that is English as a Foreign Language teaching (e.g. Howatt & Widdowson 2008).

6 My numbering here differs from that in Stern (1983), as I have treated his points 1. and 9., and 2. and 3. together.

ry.[7] Watson's survey of the *Beginnings of Modern Subjects in England* (1909) includes sections on the modern languages, and is, as already noted in the 1971 reprint, "the basic source work […] yet to be superseded" (p. v). Amongst (somewhat) more recent work, the survey by Hawkins (1987) is the closest to an overview of the history of modern language teaching for the British context, and is particularly useful for its discussion of the late nineteenth-century reform movement and its limited impact on teaching (Hawkins 1987: 117–153). Ortmanns (1993) deals specifically with the history of German teaching in Great Britain up to the year 1985. Both are important contributions, but neither is concerned with the primary material for the business of teaching and learning. Hawkins aims rather to provide a survey of developments in educational philosophy, policy and curriculum design, while Ortmanns gives a very useful 'institutional' history of German, tracing evidence for the presence of German in school curricula, the provision of teachers, and numbers of pupils learning German. Wegner (1999) is a uniquely valuable study, comparing the history of German as a foreign language in France and England in the twentieth century. Crucially, Wegner also compares developments in didactic theory with the evidence of textbooks themselves (see especially Chapter 4 below). Muckle (2008a, b) provides a history of the Russian language in Britain, a "historical survey of learners and teachers". While Muckle's primary focus was not the history of the processes of teaching and learning, so much as the changing status of Russian as a foreign language in Britain, some of his analysis – particularly for the twentieth century – provides a useful point of comparison for the status of German.

Stern himself (1983: 75–116) still offers the best review and summary of earlier surveys of the teaching of foreign languages including Titone (1968) and Kelly (1969). Wheeler's *Language Teaching Through The Ages* (2013) is an engaging book of thirty-odd short features on key figures and movements in the history of language learning, including the grammar-translation method (with a focus on Ahn and Ollendorff), Thomas Prendergast, François Gouin and Harold Palmer, and language teaching to the armed forces in World War II (see Chapter 3.7 and 4.6 below). However, Wheeler's volume in many ways merely underlines our lack of knowledge: most of his chapters on the pre-modern era deal with materials for teaching Latin, or with other topics in the history of linguistics that have little immediate connection to the teaching of modern foreign languages (e.g John Wilkins's rational language, Robert Lowth and Lindley Murray's grammars of English).[8] Wheeler does not draw on the very useful research in the German sphere (noted above) that would have filled some of the gaps; still, it is no exaggeration to say that the research foundations for a complete history of language learning, especially for English-speaking learners, are simply lacking.

---

7 Note also the much older study of the teaching of French in Tudor and Stuart times by Lambley (1920).

8 The same applies to a lesser extent for the more recent period, where topics include the development of Esperanto and of Basic English.

For non-European traditions, the field appears to be largely untouched, though some snippets can be gleaned from surveys of the history of linguistics of the various traditions (e.g. in Auroux et al, 2000–2006, Vol. I) or in the now burgeoning field of the history of missionary linguistics.[9] For example, del Valle (2000: 234) discusses Arabic grammars of Hebrew; Sasse (2000: 67, 70) notes materials for the learning of Chinese by Korean speakers, including Korean glosses of Chinese from the fifteenth century onwards, as well as for the learning of Japanese, Mongolian and Manchurian; Kaiser (2000: 82) documents growing interest in Japan in learning Korean, with the first textbooks for learning Korean dating to 1729; Scharfe (2000: 131) notes the emergence of textbooks for teaching Sanskrit as a foreign language from the fourth century onwards. As for European influence, from the eighteenth century onwards numerous grammars of Indian languages were written by and for Europeans (Shapiro 2000: 178; cf. also n. 9 above on missionary linguistics); Vos (2000) notes the influence of Dutch grammar on Japanese language study, and Pellin (2011) that of the British phonetician and philologist Henry Sweet's ideas (whether directly or indirectly) on twentieth-century Chinese language study, citing Zhang (2002).

2. 'studies of major trends or events in the recent history of language teaching'. An important contribution to meeting this need is the five-volume documentation of the Reform Movement in language teaching in the late nineteenth and early twentieth centuries by Howatt & Smith (2002); the work by Gilbert (published in a series of articles 1953, 1954, 1955) remains the most comprehensive overview of the Reform Movement (see Chapter 3 below for more information on the traces of this movement in the teaching of German in Britian). Puren (1994) is a history of 'eclecticism' (the watering down of reform ideas in France in the second quarter of the twentieth century). For the most part, however, the studies of the kind Stern would like to see are lacking.

3. 'in-depth studies of particular aspects of language teaching' (for which Kelly's 1969 monograph might provide a model, since it is structured according to such themes, rather than being purely chronological). Caravolas (1994, 2000), like Kelly, documents reflections on particular aspects of language learning up to the end of the eighteenth century, including the role of memory, the role of the first language, the role of grammar, error correction, the role of teacher and learner, learning vocabulary, how to read, write, speak and pronounce in the foreign language. Guthke (2011) examines the gradual emergence of literature in textbooks of German in Britain between 1770 and 1830. Apelt (1967) is a critique of the teaching of culture as part of the *kulturkundliche Bewegung* in Germany, while Risager (2007) examines the more recent history of teaching 'culture' in the foreign language classroom (cf. chapter 6 below). Reinfried (1992) offers a history of visual media in the teaching of French

---

9   For an impression of the field of missionary linguistics, see the series of conference proceedings *Missionary Linguistics* (Amsterdam: Benjamins), of which the most recent volume (IV) is Zwartjes et al. (2009). For recent surveys of the study of 'exotic' languages by Europeans, see articles 126–136 in Auroux et al. (2000).

as a foreign language (and in so doing also provides an excellent general history of developments in language teaching theory). Again, however, these are lone flags in a large field.

4. 'biographical and critical studies of the personalities, ideas, and influence of great language teachers and thinkers'. There remains a great deal to do here. Van der Lubbe (2007) is the first book-length work to provide such a biographical study for the history of German in Britain, devoted to the author of the first grammar of German (Martin Aedler, 1680); Flood (1999) presents the biography of Adolphus Bernays (1794–1864), a German appointed to teach German at King's College London in 1831.[10] Brief biographies of Otto Siepmann and Walter Rippmann (two very influential figures in British modern language teaching in the early decades of the twentieth century; see 3.10 below) are provided by Whitehead (2004) and McLelland (2012c); see also Paulin (2010) on Karl Breul. Other figures who would certainly merit closer study for German in Britain are Magda Kelber (author of the innovative *Heute Abend* and *Heute und Morgen* series used before, during and after World War II), A. S. Macpherson and Paul Strömer, the authors of the very widely used series *Deutsches Leben* at about the same period, and the Russons, whose 'Complete German courses' were likewise extremely widely used for half a century after World War II (and were still used by some pupils taking A-levels in 2000; Michael White, p.c.). Many, many others, of whom we know only what their textbook title pages reveal, would reward closer study too.

5. 'historical studies of language *learning,* based on a systematic review of historical biographies and autobiographies' following the suggestion in Fraenkel (1969). Here the volume *Fremde Sprachen in frühneuzeitlichen Städten* (ed. Häberlein & Kuhn, 2010) is worth noting for the range of methodologies its contributors variously try out in order to trace the history of foreign learning languages in the early modern period, in particular the exploitation of archive material, from town records to ego-documents. Finally, Stern would like to see

6. both 'a critical review of historical introductions to writings on language teaching' and 'a well-documented, research-oriented critical general history of language teaching and learning.' As to the former, Stern's own lucid survey (1983: 75–116) remains the best available. As to the latter, despite surveys such as Caravolas (1994: 66–120; 2000: 3–40) and Hüllen (2005a), it will be impossible to provide such a survey that takes into account the British context until more of the groundwork has been achieved. Indeed, Caravolas's (2000) chapter on foreign language learning in nineteenth-century England contains two paragraphs on the learning of German, as Caravolas writes that his information is 'limited' and notes just one of more than a dozen grammars of German available in the eighteenth century, Bachmair (1751). (Caravolas was clearly not aware of Carr (1935), discussed below.)

---

10 Note also Flood (to appear). Beyond German studies, note Smith (2009) on the French teacher Claude Marcel (1793–1876), and Linn (2008) on the emergence of what he calls an Anglo-Scandinavian 'school' of applied linguists in the late nineteenth century.

The present book is intended to help lay the groundwork for meeting Stern's desiderata by setting out some lines of enquiry for the history of foreign language learning in the British Isles. As its case study, the book takes the learning and teaching of German since 1600. German is a major foreign language in the British Isles; there is very little research indeed on German in Britain thus far; and to write a complete history of French – another obvious candidate – is to tell a much longer and more complicated story, in its early phases at least.[11]

1.3 Research on the history of German teaching and learning in the British Isles to date

Two articles by Charles Carr provide a map to some of the territory to be explored: Carr (1937) describes the textbooks of German available in England from 1680 to 1750, while Carr (1935) examined changes in grammatical description in fourteen grammars of German in English printed over the period 1750 to 1834. Carr's two articles remain the two most comprehensive surveys to date. More recently, Blamires (1990) is an investigation of the knowledge of German in England prior to the very first grammar of German in English, Martin Aedler's *High Dutch Minerva* (1680). Guthke (2011) is, as already noted above in 1.2, an important overview of the place of literature in the teaching of German for the period 1770–1830. One of only two monographs on the history of German teaching in the UK, by Fredericka van der Lubbe, is devoted to Aedler's grammar (Van der Lubbe 2007a), and also goes beyond Blamires to provide further useful background on the social and intellectual climate which prompted Aedler to write his work.[12] Van der Lubbe (2007b) is a brief but useful investigation of seventeen grammars of German for English learners published from Aedler (1680) to 1800, with a focus on the shift from German as a language of utility to a "language of culture" (Van der Lubbe 2007b: 144). (For comparison, Hüllen finds that there are 27 text-books of English for Germans for a slightly shorter period, 1700–1770; Hüllen 1995: 1). Van der Lubbe (2008) explores the representation of the German nation in the same group of texts. Proescholdt (1991) documented the early beginnings of German teaching in English universities (from the 1830s, though it should be noted that at Trinity College, Dublin, a Chair of German had already been established in 1775; cf. Raraty 1966; Sagarra 1999), in public schools (from the mid-nineteenth century, beginning with Harrow in 1839), and in primary schools (from the 1870s; cf. Bayley 1989). Flood (1999) fleshes out the bare bones of the history of German at universities sketched by Proescholdt, with a bi-

---

11 The history of French learning in Britain is both longer and less straightforward than that of German, because for centuries after the Norman Conquest, there existed amongst the elite a French-English diglossia, or even French-English-Latin triglossia, where – at least to begin with – some speakers were more at home in French than in English. Even once England became more monolingual, French had in the eighteenth century the status as a *lingua franca* in European court circles. On the status and teaching of French in England, 1000–1600, see Kibbee (1991). On the teaching and learning of Latin in the Middle Ages in England, see Hunt (1991).

12 The other monograph is Ortmanns (1993). See below.

ographical study of the kind Stern calls for, outlining the career, works and educational philosophy of Dr Adolphus Bernays (1794–1864), a German appointed to teach German at King's College London in 1831. Jaworska, writing on the place of the German language in British higher education, begins with an overview of twentieth-century developments in language pedagogy in Britain (Jaworska 2009: 6–47).[13] For the twentieth century, however, when the number both of textbooks and of learners really takes off, not even the first steps towards a bibliography of German language learning textbooks have been taken (let alone for foreign languages as a whole, as in Schröder's bibliography), although the study by Wegner (1999, noted above) is a very useful first foray into the field. Three volumes produced to reflect the "state of the discipline" of German in the 1970s, 1980s and early 1990s are now also useful historical documents (CILT 1976; CILT 1986; Tenberg & Jones 1993).

The dearth of studies devoted to the history of German language learning specifically is somewhat offset by a small number of studies on the history of foreign language teaching and learning in Britain more widely (e.g. Bayley 1991, Bayley & Yaworsky Ronish 1992, Bayley 1998, Cohen 2001, 2002), but these too are patchy. Most are surveys that are not specific to the British Isles, and, in the absence of further scholarship, there is a tendency for certain favourite British names to recur, typically Roger Ascham, John Locke, and, if the survey extends to the turn of the twentieth century, Henry Sweet and Harold Palmer, giving a very incomplete picture: thus Titone (1968), Kelly (1969), Germain (1993), Caravolas (1994); Hüllen (2007).[14] Hüllen (2005a) deals with Germany; Puren (1988; 1994) is chiefly restricted to France, while Maréchal (1972) is on Belgium. Specific to the British context is Hawkins (1987), but he does not examine textbooks, so much as provide a survey of developments in policy and curriculum design. Stern (1983: 75–116) offers both a lucid review of earlier surveys and presents a summary of. his own.

1.4 The History of German as a Foreign Language

Another approach to the history of German language learning in Britain might be expected to come from the field of German as a Foreign Language (GFL or, to give it its usual German label, *Deutsch als Fremdsprache*, abbreviated to DaF; cf. Helbig et al. (2001)), but that is itself a young – though burgeoning – field. Krumm (1999: 123–124) reports that in 1986, 61.2 % of DaF learners in a Goethe-Institut survey said they did not like their textbook; in a study of learners of German in Japan reported on by Slivensky in 1996, only 3.1 % said they had learnt "a lot" from their textbook; two-thirds said they had learnt "not very much". Such depressing statistics surely give DaF practitioners a further spur to reflect on the nature of textbooks in the history of language teaching.

---

13 For an evaluation of the status of German at British universities in the early 1990s, see also Kolinsky (1993), Tenberg (1993).

14 A survey in English of foreign language teaching in Europe 1748–1750, based on Hüllen (2005a: 1–72); a very short survey in German of the history of language teaching and learning in Europe is Schröder (2000).

Two substantial international handbooks devoted to DaF – Helbig et al (2001) and Krumm et al. (2010) – each contain a half-dozen pages surveying German in schools and universities in Britain: these overviews, by Rösler (2001) and Reershemius (2010), are most useful for the further references they provide on the history of DaF, updating Stone (1978); Fischer (2001) provides a similar overview for the Irish context.

For the history of DaF, however, much remains to be done. Glück's survey of the history of German as a Foreign Language is a pioneering study, and devotes a section to the study of German in the British Isles (Glück 2002: 323–337; see also Glück 2011), but necessarily relies on the scanty previous work in the area, and goes only as far as 1700; a second volume, tackling the eighteenth century, has just appeared (Glück 2013). Koch (2002) is a very rich study of the history of German language education in eighteenth-century Russia; Budziak (2010) does the same for Poland, for the period from 1500–1800; see now also Extermann (2013) on the history of German as a foreign language in Romance-speaking Switzerland. The informative study by Ortmanns (1993) of the "external" history of German learning in Britain – with facts and figures about teachers, learners, examinations and curricula – was already noted above, as was Wegner (1999). Other small contributions have been made in the context of the history of German grammars: Langer (2002) and McLelland (2008) both compare developments in foreign grammars of German with grammars written for German native speakers, and McLelland (2012a) examines the treatment of a small number of grammatical points in a selection of textbooks for British learners from 1680 to the late twentieth century. As already noted, a major impediment thus far has been the lack of bibliography of the textbooks that one might wish to examine. While a project led by Helmut Glück in Bamberg has now yielded a number of annotated bibliographies of German language learning materials in Bohemia (Glück et al. 2002), Poland (Glück & Schröder 2007), Russia and the Baltic countries (Glück & Pörzgen 2009), there is as yet nothing comparable for the British Isles. The bibliography in the present volume is intended as a first step in the right direction, but it will certainly not be found to be exhaustive.

1.5 The history of foreign language teaching methodologies in Great Britain and Ireland

As for the history of language teaching methodology, or at least of theories of modern language teaching in Britain, we are not quite so poorly served. This is in large part because while the history of foreign language learning in the British Isles is decidedly neglected, the same cannot be said of the history of English Language Teaching. English Language Teaching (ELT) has become a global industry, and its prominence is matched by the work that has gone into tracing its history and the history of 'applied linguistics' more widely, most notably in the multi-volume collections of primary sources in Howatt & Smith's *Foundations of Foreign Language Teaching* (2000, devoted to major figures of the nineteenth century) and their five-volume series *Modern Language Teaching. The Reform Movement* (Howatt & Smith 2002), with a useful general introduction (Vol. I xi–xliii) as well as introductions to each of the individual volumes. The Reform Movement (ca. 1882 to 1909) was driven both by university academics and by many very engaged, practising language teachers,[15] and this, together with the fact that it had its roots in Germany, means that the ideas of teachers of German in Britain of this period have received somewhat more attention than for other eras. Walter Rippmann, for example, rates a mention in Titone's survey (Titone 1968: 38–39), and for once the bibliographical situation is somewhat better thanks to the bibliographies of reform-literature of Hermann Breymann (1895, 1900), now available in a reprint from 2002 (Howatt & Smith 2002). Still, as far as I am aware, the riches that they contain have barely begun to be investigated. Wegner (1999) is an important advance, as she explicitly compares pronouncements *about* language teaching and learning with selected textbooks used *for* language teaching and learning, but much remains to be done. Fischer (2000) examined Irish views of Germany over the period (1890–1939); his chapter 7, on the role of education in shaping these views, is particularly relevant to this study.

1.6 A textbook-based history of foreign language learning and teaching in the British Isles. Theoretical and methodological considerations

One might wonder why it is worth devoting any time to the history of language teaching and learning, for the more one studies it, the more it becomes clear that there is nothing new under the sun. As Kelly (1969: 363) observed more than forty years ago, "The total corpus of ideas accessible to language teachers has not changed basically in 2,000 years. What have been in constant change are the ways of building methods from them, and the part of the corpus that is accepted varies from generation to generation, as does the form in which the ideas present themselves." One might add that the new ways in which certain principles are put into practice are very often determined by what is technically, practically possible. When printing made it possible to rely on a written text rather than on memory alone, the catechistic, question-and-answer form of Donatus's *Ars Minor* (for centuries every pupil's introduction to Latin; cf. Law 2003), structured so as to aid oral memorization and recall, looked dry; humanists took advantage of innovations in printing to set out paradigms in tables for the first time (Puff 1995, 1996). At the same time stand-alone grammars were found wanting, and came to be supplemented by more or less lively dialogues (of which Erasmus's *Colloquia* and those of Luis de Vives are the best-known); eventually, as images became affordable, books without illustrations looked dull, and in the later nineteenth century the question of how best to use pictures (a question hovering in the background of language teaching at least since Comenius' *Orbis Sensualium Pictus* of 1658)[16] gained new relevance and remains topical today (e.g. Skorge 2008; Hecke & Surkamp 2010). Pronunciation had been a concern of the ear-

---

15 The close contacts between (some) university professors and school language teachers would astonish many today on both sides of the fence – Karl Breul, lecturer at Cambridge and later Schröder Professor of German at Cambridge, and author of *The teaching of modern foreign languages and the training of teachers* (Breul 1898) is a case in point. See Paulin (2010), Howatt & Smith (2002), and Chapter 3 below, especially 3.6.2.

16 As described for example in Hüllen (2002); see also Reinfried (1992: 33–55).

liest foreign language manuals; as students of foreign languages could be assumed to know others, sounds could be described by comparisons with these – for German, often French alongside Latin and Greek – and, once textbooks became tailored to learners with a particular first language background, contrasts could also be made with the first language or by using the spelling conventions of the first language to describe the sounds of the language to be learnt.[17] However, there is no question that the ability to record speech from the late nineteenth century onwards, and later the invention of the portable tape recorder, changed what was possible in the language classroom more fundamentally than many centuries of textbook sections on pronunciation had ever done. It is an overstatement, but not a ludicrous one, to say that it is technology that has changed language teaching more than any amount of reflection on teaching and learning itself.

Quite aside from reflecting on method or theory, the study of the history of modern language teaching and learning is an important source of information about our own society and its relations with other societies. The value of textbooks as *socio-cultural artefacts* is increasingly being recognized, particularly as a means of investigating representations of European identities.[18] Beyond the field of education, constructions of Germany's past remain an important focus in German cultural studies and in studies of historiography (cf. the historians' dispute or *Historikertreit* about National Socialism) and the construction of memory,[19] and recent work has also examined the history of Anglo-German relations and British images of Germany (Birke & Brechtken 2000, Nicholls 1997, 2005; Robbins 1999). Textbooks are a largely neglected yet highly influential resource to add to our understanding of British views of Germany's past and its culture.[20]

Studying the presentation of the target language in textbooks for foreign learners can also add to the history of the target language and how it was perceived outside its "native" grammatical tradition. It can also deliver new insights into German grammatography (i. e. how German grammar has been described), for which the period up to 1850 is well understood. For the period since 1850, far less is known, and about grammar for non-native speakers little is known at all, despite a few individual historical studies by Langer (2008, for nineteenth-century US grammars), Van der Lubbe (2007, 2008, on seventeenth- and eighteenth-century grammars) and Durrell (2005, for four twentieth-century textbooks). Key surveys of the history of German grammar make no reference at all to grammar-writing for non-native speakers.[21] Indeed, in research on

---

17 For example, the first grammar of German for English speakers renders the first line of the Lord's Prayer *un-ser vàuter, dare doo bist im him-le* (Aedler 1680: 45).
18 See for example Anklam & Grindel (2010), and Eurviews (a project based at the Georg-Eckert Institute for International Schoolbook Research in Braunschweig: http://www.eurviews.eu/en/home. html).
19 This is now a vast field. For a first orientation, see Erll & Nünning (2008).
20 Though not historical, a collection of studies of the representation of Germany in early 1990s British textbooks is worth noting here: Byram (1993).
21 I am thinking here of Naumann's history of German grammar between 1781 and 1856 (Naumann 1986), and a survey article by Knobloch et al. which extends up to the mid-twentieth century

language prescriptivism internationally, this remains a major gap whose existence is only now being noticed.

It is important to remember too just how important textbooks were for centuries in defining a society's knowledge. We have so quickly become used to finding whatever we want to know about anything via Google that it is easy to forget how hard it was to come by knowledge about another culture until only very recently. Learners were very dependent on their textbooks, and textbooks in the language classroom were the main, and in many cases, the only source of information about the target language and target culture.[22] As sociologists of education such as Michael W. Apple have demonstrated (Apple 1979, 4th ed. 2004, Apple 1992), curricula express social control, and school textbooks are "crucial organs in the process of constructing legitimated ideologies and beliefs" – as we shall see in Chapter 6 below. They may therefore be "sites of considerable educational and political conflict" (Crawford 2003: 1). Crawford continues,

> the manufacture of textbook content is [or at least *may be*, NMcL] the result of competition between powerful groups who see it as being central in the creation of collective national memory designed to meet specific cultural, economic, ideological and social imperatives.

Textbooks codify what is 'known', or rather what is accepted knowledge, and they are highly selective, concentrating on the supposedly 'essential' knowledge for the learner (Issitt 2004). For precisely these reasons, textbooks – carrying great authority for large numbers of learners in the classroom – must be included in the critical historiography of Modern Foreign Language (MFL) teaching and learning, in the history of language codification, in social history more widely, and in cultural studies. This book models an approach that will contribute to all these disciplines.

1.7 Approaches to textbooks

Besides drawing on archives and interviews where possible, this study relies above all on textbooks as its source material. It is worth pausing to clarify just what is meant by that term: "textbook". A traditional classification of language textbooks might distinguish elementary primers, grammars, dictionaries, readers, and translation exercises, while Hammar (1992) offers a far more fine-grained categorization. Certainly it is possible

---

(2005). There are, of course, synchronic analyses of foreign-language textbooks from the perspective of educational theory, for example Watts (2000).

22 The emergence of holiday programmes, town twinnings and exchange programmes in the twentieth century were all efforts to address this fundamental problem of limited exposure. Still, in surveys conducted in the years 1985–1988, 90 % of British and 96 % of American school pupils learning German identified their German lessons as one of their main sources of information about Germany (pupils were permitted to select up to three answers from a given list). Television was in second place for British pupils (71 %) and in third place for American pupils (48 %). Only a small minority of British pupils identified history and geography lessons as important sources (each 7 %), a result which contrasts markedly with American pupils, for whom history lessons came in second place (56 %) and geography in fifth place (28 %). (See Fritz 1991: 57).

to classify more finely, but any classification is in a sense already a history. At the start of the German language learning tradition, we find a pure grammar (Aedler 1680); the next stage is a grammar with dialogues (Offelen 1786); then comes the addition of reading passages; gradually exercises are added (an innovation beginning with Meidinger). By the late nineteenth century, authors increasingly sought to include most if not all of the above in their books, with a grammatical section, some reading and conversation material, and a vocabulary at the back of the book. Meanwhile, the presentation of grammar was gradually moving away from the centuries-old order of material (beginning with letters and pronunciation, then parts of speech and syntax), sequencing the introduction of grammatical rules in new ways intended to make learning easier – does it at this point become a "course-book"? Is not the level for which the work is intended just as important as the type of work? To do justice to all these considerations would yield such a complicated classificatory system that it would cease to be useful. The approach taken here, then, is a very pragmatic one: any kind of book that one might learn German from is a textbook, including 'readers' of selected material (but not mere editions of German literature). Dictionaries are not textbooks.[23] Nor are phrasebooks, to the extent that they are merely dictionaries whose entries are phrases rather than single lexemes.[24] The corpus of textbooks for this study is drawn from COPAC, the catalogues of the British Library and the Institute of Education (London), the Institute for Germanic and Romance Studies, and the Taylor collection held at the University of Bamberg; a small number of titles are also listed in the John Trim collection held at the European Centre for Modern Languages (ECML) in Graz; digital copies of many older titles are available through ECCO (Eighteenth Century Collections Online) and through the Hathi Trust.[25] There is no doubt that the kind of close study of individual biographies of authors that Van der Lubbe was able to devote to Aedler can bear fruit. Where known, then, limited biographical information about the authors is included in the bibliography as a spur to further research.

There is as yet no standard approach to *historical* textbook analysis, although the *UNESCO Guidebook on Textbook Research and Textbook Revision* (Pingel 2010, 1st ed. 1999, published under the auspices of the Georg-Eckert Institute) includes very basic guidance on developing quantitative and qualitative methods in the analysis of textbooks as "instruments of education towards international understanding" (pp. 7, 67–79); an overview by Nicholls (2003) draws on Pingel as well as Mikk (2000) and Bourdillon (1992). Kast (1994) suggests a template for evaluating textbooks for the teaching of

---

23 Even here an exception must be made: Minsheu (1617) is a dictionary, but still merits discussion in Chapter 2. Other dictionaries will be noted in passing. For the pre-1700 history of dictionaries including German and English, see the relevant entries in the lexicographical bibliography of W. J. Jones (2000).

24 There is unfortunately as yet no study of the phrasebook genre.

25 In many cases, I have been able to work from my own copies of texts kindly donated by former and current learners and teachers of German. I am most grateful for their generosity. ECCO is at http://gale.cengage.co.uk/product-highlights/history/eighteenth-century-collections-online.aspx. Hathi Trust is at http://www.hathitrust.org/. The ECML is at www.ecml.at.

foreign languages. In the case of *historical* textbook analysis, the textbooks analysed may be the chief or only source of information about the history of language teaching and learning, but it remains essential to situate textbooks as far as possible in their full context (following Christ 2005: 149–50):

1. the authors, their opinions and experience, including interconnections between authors, or between authors and practitioners, between authors and theoreticians, and the recognition that in some cases an author may be all three)
2. the contemporary historical context (particularly pertinent for twentieth-century teaching and learning of German in the British Isles)
3. the geographical context (proximity to a border with the target culture may affect attitudes and approaches to the language)
4. the intellectual context, including political ideologies, and views of history, of the role of literature and indeed of the purpose and method of education itself (for example, the importance of language learning to early modern merchants, to the Grand Tour of the eighteenth century, or to the aspiration of European integration after World War II).
5. the specific context in which foreign language learning takes place: in school and/or privately, and under what conditions, and for what reasons?

In many cases, and at the risk of circularity, we must rely on the textbooks themselves to tell us most about the context in which they were written and used, especially authors' prefaces. In other case, we may be able to draw on other sources. Up to the middle of the nineteenth century, almost our sole source for the history of language learning is the books that teachers and learners themselves used, occasionally supplemented by anecdotes or opinions from writers whose ideas have, serendipitously survived. No doubt archival research will enrich the picture, as in a recent project based in Bamberg on the history of foreign language acquisition in late medieval and early modern German cities.[26] The case of Martin Aedler, author of the first grammar of German in English, is an exceptional case where meticulous archival work has already substantially enhanced our knowledge of the circumstances in which particular works were written (Van der Lubbe 2007a). In the absence of such groundwork, however, it is the books that must speak for themselves – both the teaching materials and the prefaces, where clues as to practice are often found.

From about the middle of the nineteenth century – when German became institutionalized as a school subject (Oxford and Cambridge Boards of Examinations offered German from their first year of operation, in 1858) – the bureaucracy of teaching and assessing set in, and it becomes possible to refer to the archives of examining boards and of schools themselves. For this study, I have used the University of Cambridge and Cambridge Assessment archives of syllabi and examination papers since 1858, as well

---

26 *Fremdsprachenerwerb und Fremdsprachenkompetenz in deutschen Städten des Spätmittelalters und der Frühen Neuzeit* at the University of Bamberg (cf. Glück, Häberlein, Schröder 2013; cf. also Häberlein & Kuhn 2010).

as examinations and staff meeting notes preserved in the archive of Rugby School.[27] In addition, for the twentieth century, I have been able to draw on methods from oral history and ethnography to obtain information from current and former teachers, learners and textbook authors.[28] These additional sources can tell us how textbooks were used in practice; how long they were used for after their publication; which ones were most widely used; and, indeed, which parts of them stick in the learners' mind decades later. From the time of the Reform Movement onwards, and with the emergence of teacher training programmes, we may compare textbooks with explicit theoretical reflections on how best to teach languages. Although – as already stated – this book is not intended to be a history of teaching methodologies, such an approach is taken in parts of Chapter 3 and in much of Chapter 4. Overall, my methodology is deliberately eclectic, and this is particularly the case in Chapter 6, where I trial a number of different approaches to analysing representations of culture and history in textbooks of German, including Critical Discourse Analysis and – though this remains the exception – some limited quantitative analysis of topic coverage. These approaches are introduced more fully in Chapter 6.

1.8 A caveat: the story in history and my selection of textbooks

Having accumulated source material for a history of language learning, one must order it to write that history, and the result is a *narrative*, a "reconstruction" of the past that is already an interpretation of the sources (cf. Schlieben-Lange 1989; Schmitter 2003; Hüllen 2005b for reflections on the writing of the history of linguistics). The issues that arise here – at the crossroads of the history of education and the history of linguistic ideas – are the same that arise for any historian. They include the validity of any periodization; the desire to identify continuities or discontinuities at the risk of overlooking others; the presentation of texts as a series whose authors may or may not have perceived themselves to be part of any such series. Difficult, too, is the selection of certain texts that will inevitably be taken as representative – ironically the same problem of selection that faces any textbook author (Issitt 2004). The selection is to some extent already made for us, by accidents of history; we add to it when – from the later nineteenth century onwards – we select examples from an overwhelming body of material. Klippel (1994) was able to select the 300 English textbooks for German learners that she examined for the period 1746–1900 from a pre-existing bibliography of 560 titles (Schröder 1975). In his

---

27 I have used Rugby School simply because it was the first school to respond to inquiries that has a suitable archive. Future research should certainly widen the pool, in particular by looking at a grammar school rather than a major public school. The Cambridge Assessment archive is untouched as far as the materials relating to German are concerned, although Shaw & Cooke (2009) use the archives in a similar way to explore changes in history examinations.
28 Those interviewed were selected from among the many who responded to my appeals via teachers' and academics' mailing lists, to appeals at teacher conferences, and to an appeal on Radio 4's *Making History*. Many others supplied information in writing. To all of them, I am very grateful. Gardner (2003) on the use of oral history in education guided my reflections on how to conduct and evaluate the interviews.

study of representations of France and Germany in German and French language-learning textbooks (1950–1980), Krauskopf (1985) claimed to have examined over 90 % of the textbooks published in that period, and some of his findings are quantitative (the amount of space devoted to particular topic, for example); nevertheless, the selection of examples for discussion will always remain a subjective one, shaping our chosen narrative.[29] How we shape that narrative will depend on what questions we want to answer: are we interested in tracing sources and influences? in a teleological approach ('how did everything that went before bring us to here?') or in documenting a change in how a particular topic of grammar – such as the adverb, say – was understood? (cf. McLelland 2008).

The dangers inherent in selecting, representing, reconstructing and re-telling are all the greater in the present project, where there is so little other work to provide a counter-balance. For the case of textbooks of German for English-speaking learners, I have been able to include most of the relatively few works published between 1600 and the mid-nineteenth century. Thereafter, I have chosen works that were either widely used, or that are illustrative of a particular development, or that are striking in some way. With few exceptions, I have examined only textbooks published in the UK, the overwhelming majority of which were published in England; exceptions are noted where they occur. In common with Krauskopf (1985: 23), for the twentieth century I have excluded those works published *in* Germany, as being part of a separate, though of course no less interesting, tradition. The history of German teaching and learning – and *a fortiori* the history of language learning in Britain – presented here is just *one* such history, neither comprehensive nor definitive. It does no more than demonstrate some lines of enquiry. I very much hope it will be followed by others.

---

29 In her otherwise excellent study of French and English twentieth-century German textbooks, Wegner (1999) unfortunately provides no information on how she selected the textbooks that she analysed.

Chapter 2 –
The birth of a subject: the first hundred years of German as a Foreign Language in England (1615–1715)

2.1 The earliest evidence of learning German as a foreign language in Europe: the ninth to sixteenth centuries

> *Stulti sunt Romani, sapienti sunt Paioari, modica est sapienti[a] in Romana plus habent stultitia quam sapientia.*
> *Tole sint uualha, spahe sint Peigira; luzie ist spahi in uualhum, mera hapent tolaheiti denne spahi.*

> 'The Romans [i.e. Romance-speakers] are foolish, the Bavarians are wise. Amongst the Romans wisdom is little, they have more foolishness than wisdom'

This evidence that stereotypes are nothing new comes from the earliest surviving materials for the learning of German as a foreign language (GFL). The word-lists and phrases from which it is drawn are found, written by several different hands, in a manuscript written produced near Regensburg in the first quarter of the ninth century, a manuscript that also contained theological arguments and material intended for priests. Cited by Helmut Glück (2002: 68) in his history of German as a Foreign Language in Europe, these are the so-called Kassel Glosses, word-lists and phrases that might have been used by a Romance-speaking traveller, perhaps an Italian, in Bavaria, in the south of the German-speaking lands. Besides short phrases, the Glosses also contain simple bilingual word-lists, including for parts of the body (*stomachus – mago* 'stomach' *latera – sitte* 'side' *costis – rippi* 'rib') and animals (*boves – ohsun* 'oxen' *vaccas – choi* 'cows' *pecora – skaaf* 'sheep' etc.; cf. Braune & Ebbinghaus 1994). The glosses were probably aimed at relatively high-status individuals, as indicated by phrases that a master might use to his servant (*gimer min ros* 'give me my horse'; Penzl 1984). At any rate, these earliest materials for learners of German are purely practical in orientation and deal with everyday spoken language. Another example is offered by the 'Paris Glosses' of ca. 900 (so-called because one of the two manuscripts is preserved in Paris in the French National Library).[1] The Paris conversations are clearly the work of a French speaker not familiar with the written

---

1   Hellgardt (1996) believes both sets of glosses are based on a much older tradition of using conversation in language teaching represented by the so-called *Hermeneumata pseudodositheana* of ca. 200 A.D., which contained models of Greek conversation for speakers of Latin.

German of the time – the manner of jotting down in the margins and spaces certainly suggests copying from an earlier original. The French origin of the scribe is betrayed by the dropping of *h* in *erro* (*Herr* 'master') and the use of the French *gu* to render the unfamiliar German *w* as in *guillis willst du* ('do you want') (Jolles 1968). Individual words and phrases with their translation are followed by two self-contained conversations set in an inn, and further fragments of dialogue, in German with Latin translations. The language is the kind needed to arrange food and accommodation and to make conversation with strangers. The conversations also model techniques for evading direct questions and for dealing with suppressed hostility, as Jolles noted in his article "The Hazard of Travel in Medieval Germany" (Jolles 1968).

> Vndes ars in tino naso *i. Canis culum in tuo naso*
> Guer ist tin erro.*i. Ubi est senior tuus?*
> Ne guez.*i. Nescio*
> Guaz guildo.*i. Quid vis tu?*
> Erro guillis trenchen guali got guin *i. si uis bibere bonum vinum?*

> 'Dog's bottom in your nose.
> Where is your master? I don't know.
> What do you want?
> Does my lord want to drink good wine?'

By the fifteenth century at the latest, texts such as these for those travelling to Germany were certainly a well-established tradition, in particular for Italian cloth-merchants travelling from Venice to the southern German cities (Pausch 1972, Busch 1992).[2] Such manuals often consisted of two parts: a word-list section and a dialogue section. The earliest preserved exponent of the tradition dates from 1424, and we have evidence of a Venice language school run by a certain Master George of Nuremberg (Rossebastiano Bart 1983, 1984a, b; Höybye 1956, 1964, 1974); a version of Italian-German language manuals attributed to Adam von Rottweil was printed in 1477 in Venice (ed. Giustiniani 1987). Like the Paris conversations from centuries earlier, the dialogues are lively exchanges. Besides some implicit focus on form (frequent use of imperatives of verbs, comparative and superlatives of key adjectives like *good* and *bad,* numerals needed for naming prices) and key specialist vocabulary particularly relevant to the cloth trade, the dialogues could also model the pragmatics of commercial interactions, especially the art of haggling (McLelland 2004: 212–215).

---

2 On German merchants in Italy see also Glück (2002: 246–250).

— Zaig her den parchant fon der chron.	— *Show me the 'barchent' [a type of mixed cotton-linen cloth produced in Nuremberg]³ with the crown on it.*
— Ich mag euch chain pösen zaigen, also helff mir Got. Ich bird in euch allsampt zaigen und ir bert nemen den der euch aller paz gefelt. Und den der euch aller nutz sey ze furn.	— *I won't show you any bad one, so help me God. I'll show them all to you and you take the one which pleases you best of all. And the one which will be of most use to you to carry.*
— Du sagst wol, do mogst nicht poz sagen. Hastu gueten falessi und gueten bochasin	— *You speak well, you cannot speak better. Do you have good 'falessi' and good 'bochasin'?*
— Han ich euch nicht gesagt? ich han den aller pesten der in diser stat ist.	— *Haven't I said so? I have the very best there is in this town.*
— Pring her! Lass in sehen!	— *Bring it here! Let me see it!*
[there follows a discussion of price]	*[...]*
— Du peucz in zetewr. Ich mag in wol anderswo leichter haben.	— *You are offering it at too high a price. I can surely get it more easily elsewhere.*
— Ez ist mir liebt ob er alz guet ist als der.	— *That's fine by me if it is as good as this here.*
— Ich gelaub er sey noch pesser zwen auff ein zentar.	— *I think it is better still at two [ducats] per hundredweight.*

An extract from Cod. it. 261, cited in Höybye (1974: 174ff.). The original is German and in Italian; here I have replaced the Italian with my own English translation.

The strategy identified by Jolles in the earlier glosses of avoiding direct answers to questions is incidentally also still modelled here:

— Wo seit ir alz lang gebesen daz ich [*supply*: euch] niht han gesehen?	— Where have you been so long, that I haven't seen you?
— Hier und her an fil enden	— Here and there in many places

(cf. McLelland, 2004: 214)

The Italian-German cloth trade was just one of the important trade routes in the Middle Ages. There was intensive trade too between Germany and England. By the late thirteenth century, the Hanseatic League – a trading alliance of North German cities – had branches in London, Boston, Ipswich, Hull, Yarmouth and King's Lynn, and by the fourteenth century there were colonies of German craftsmen settled in London (Glück 2002: 323). However, perhaps because the primary organizational impetus for trade came from the Hansa based in Germany, rather than from English merchants, there is no evidence of Eng-

---

3 See the Nuremberg *Stadtlexikon*: http://online-service.nuernberg.de/stadtarchiv/rech.FAU?sid=6E6B18478&dm=2&auft=0, accessed May 2013.

Figure 1:
Cod. poet. 2⁰ 2: *Schachzabelbuch*, 1467.
Folio 244 (held by the Stuttgart
Landesbibliothek)
© Bildarchiv Foto Marburg

lish speakers learning German for the trade (Flood 1991). On the other hand, German merchants coming to England apparently had to learn English; Glück cites evidence of Hamburg merchants of the thirteenth century knowing English, and of a system of German apprentices at the London Hansa base being sent to a clothmaker in the country to learn English (Glück 2002: 325). On the other hand, when the Hansa disbanded in 1552, and after the Hansa merchants were ejected in 1598, the English took over the trade routes to German ports (see Schnurmann 1991). They would have needed to know Low (i. e. northern) German, and increasingly High German, the southern variety, too, as it emerged as Germany's supraregional language and so replaced Low German as the language of correspondence in north German cities by about 1650 (Gabrielsson 1932/33); Low German would still have been the spoken language long after the switch was made in writing. There is no evidence of English-German language learning materials before the seventeenth century, however.

By the sixteenth century, contacts between England and Germany went beyond trade to shared intellectual and religious interests, particularly among Protestant reformers. Some English Protestants fled to Germany and Switzerland during the rule of Queen Mary (1553–1558), including John Knox, who went to Frankfurt am Main.[4] There is also evidence of English people travelling to Germany, including English theatre groups playing in Germany in the early seventeenth century. Yet there is still no evidence of any organized teaching of German in Britain at this time. There were occasional English people skilled in German, however: Blamires lists prominent reformers like William Tyndale and Martin Coverdale, as well as Thomas Cranmer. Harald Jantz's examination of late sixteenth-century matriculation books of German universities indicates "a steady stream of English students coming over", and Jantz claimed – unfortunately without further details – that his "list of prominent Elizabethans who definitely knew German is an impressively long one" (Jantz 1952: 152; cited by Blamires 1990: 106), even if Queen Elizabeth I's German was judged by a contemporary as "not good" (Blamires

---

4 Frankfurt and Frankenthal were home to refugee Reformed communities. Brücker's *Deutsche Grammatic* (1620) may have been written with this community of adult learners of German as a second language specifically in mind (McLelland 2005).

1990: 108).[5] The English poet Sir Philip Sidney certainly made an effort to learn German, as a passage from a 1574 letter to a friend (cited by Glück 2002: 33) makes clear. In it, Sidney wrote that he despaired of ever learning German, even just to understand it, because it had "all kinds of difficulties" – not the last time we will find evidence of this perception.[6] Overall, the English do not seem to have believed that Germany and the Germans had a great deal to interest them: a 1575 travelogue says of the Germans:

> The Germane hath ye gesture of a Cutter or Ruffian, the gate [i. e. gait] of ye cock, a firce looke, a manly voice, rude behaviour, variable apparell, and nothinge hansome [...] The Germans are harshe and harde in their speech, and simple [...] Towardes straungers the Germans are roughe and inhospitable [...] In conversation the Germanes are imperious and intolerable [...] The German weeman [are] variable and foolish

> (cited by Guthke 2011: 166, also Glück 2002: 330, from an English translation of Hieronymus Turler's *De peregrinatoine et agro Neapolitano libri II*).

While such stereotypes certainly cannot have helped the profile of German in England (any more than they do today; cf. Chapter 6.9), the lack of interest in language learning in sixteenth-century England appears to have been more general, with the possible exception of learning French.[7] Visitors from the continent appear to have been unimpressed with the English lack of skill and interest in foreign languages (*plus ça change...*). Van der Lubbe quotes from a dialogue in an Italian textbook for English learners (1578) by John Florio, a writer, translator and teacher of Italian to Queen Anne (cf. Caravolas 1994: 96), in which he appears to lament the lack of interest of the English in other languages:

> [...] fewe of these English men delight to haue their children learne diuers languages, whiche thing displeaseth me. When I first arriued in London, I coulde not speake Englishe and I met aboue fiue hundred persons, afore I coulde find one that could tel me in Italian, or French, where the Post dwelt.

> (Van der Lubbe 2007a: 25, n. 4).

One suspects that Florio's search might have taken him into the thousands had he been looking for a German speaker. More evidence for the lack of knowledge of German

---

5 It is known that she prided herself on being able to greet visitors in their language, but a short primer of Irish (Nugent 1564? http://www.isos.dias.ie/libraries/Farmleigh/Irish_Primer/irish/catalogue.html) which it is assumed was presented to Elizabeth in the 1560s (thus Pádraig Ó Macháin http://www.isos.dias.ie/english/index.html) perhaps indicates the level she was expecting/or was expected to reach: to read the alphabet, and to recognize a dozen words and a half-dozen phrases (all that the 12-sheet volume contains), including *Speak Latin* and *God Save the Queen of England*.
6 See 4.6.4. According to Watson (1921: 693), Philip Sidney's brother spoke rather better German; so too did Bishops Hooper and Parkhurst.
7 On the history of French language study in Britain, see Kibbee (1991), Streuber (1914 and 1962–1964), Lambley (1920). See also Cohen (1999).

comes from translation activity. Blamires (1990: 104–5) cites as typical the case of Henry Watson's *Shyppe of Fooles* (London, 1509), which was translated not from the German original of Sebastian Brant (1494), but from a French intermediary. Equally, where we know there *were* translations from German – versions of the *Fortunatus* and *Faust* tales, for example – "the invisibility of translators presumably means that there was no fame to be gained from advertising one's command of German" in the sixteenth and seventeenth centuries. Such private teachers as there were concentrated on French, then Italian and Spanish (Blamires 1990: 103, citing Charlton 1965: 270–71). And, it must be said, English was likewise of little interest to the continent. It was only in 1535 and 1576 respectively that English was added to two widely distributed families of multilingual textbooks that had been going for a couple of centuries, beginning with Adam von Rottweil in 1477 (see above) and Noel de Berlaimont (Hüllen 2002a: 249; Hüllen 2005a: 50–62). The British Isles were – not just literally – still quite insular.

From the second half of the sixteenth century onwards, however, as Latin lost its status as lingua franca, and as English travellers realized that English got them nowhere once they left England, interest in foreign languages – and no longer just French – increased. Van der Lubbe notes the effect of the Enlightenment, the growth of the middle class and merchant education, the Grand Tour (which began from about 1660, but where Germany did not feature as a destination before about 1714: Van der Lubbe 2007a: 36), and greater need and opportunities for travel, including to the New World, which brought with it a general broadening of horizons. Van der Lubbe summarizes that "the production of new language texts can be associated with three phenomena: firstly, an upturn in compelling practical reasons for an increased usage of modern languages on the part of the English; secondly, a decline in the importance of Latin, and thirdly, an accompanying rise in the status of the English language."

2.2 The first beginnings of learning German in seventeenth-century England

The early seventeenth century yields some hints of a marginally increased interest in the German language. The British Library lists 26 entries for the text-type known as "Noel van Barlement" or a *Parlament* – i. e. a language manual with conversations, the genre taking its name from the Antwerp language teacher Noel der Berlaimont (d. 1531; cf. Hüllen (2005: 55–57)), confused with the word *Parlament*. Only two of these 26 were printed in England, in 1637 and 1639:

> 1637 *The English, Latine, French, Dutch, Schole-master. Or, an Introduction to teach young Gentlemen and Merchants to travell or trade. Being the onely helpe to attaine to those languages, etc.* London: A. G. for Michael Sparke, 1637. (BL 1568/2818.)
> 1639 *New Dialogues or Colloquies, and, A little Dictionary of eight languages. Latine, French, Low-Dutch, High-Dutch, Spanish, Italian, English, Portugall, etc. (Colloquia & dictionariolum octo linguarum, etc.) [By Noel van Barlement.]* London: E. G. [Edward Griffin] for Michael Sparke junior, 1639 (BL 629.a.3.)

Still, the publication of these two in London within two years of each other suggests a growing interest in language learning in England. The title of the first suggests a market not just of merchants but of "young Gentlemen" travellers, and it is this market of leisured travellers that grows stronger over the coming decades (the 'Grand Tour').[8] Significant too is the fact that in the second of these editions, the publisher has added "High-Dutch", i. e. German.[9]

Likewise in the 1630s, German *may* have been taught in an "academy for nobles", the Musaeum Minervae, apparently set up by the writer and courtier Sir Francis Kynaston (1587–1642) in 1635 at his house; at any rate the proposal including costing a teacher of German at £26 per annum (Ortmanns 1993: 20).[10] Sir Balthazar Gerbier tried again to set up an academy in 1649 for young nobles before travel abroad. The academy soon closed, but at least the *proposal* to offer German at these two academies "indicates that German was of some interest to the cultural elite" (Van der Lubbe 2007a: 36).

The very first means of learning German in England, however, predates the 1630s. It is John Minsheu's *Guide into Tongues* (1617).

2.2.1 John Minsheu's *Guide into Tongues* (1617)

Even before hints of an awakening interest in German in the 1630s, the year 1617 had aleady seen the publication of a completely new work for language learners that also included German: John Minsheu's *Guide into Tongues*. The Royal Society appears to have acquired a copy, since a first edition of the work is listed in its library of 1825, along with two dictionaries of German: one German-Latin (Dufflau 1599) and one German-French-Latin (Duez 1664). (There was, however, no German grammar, even though there were grammars of several other languages: Van der Lubbe 2007a: 39). The full title of Minsheu's *Guide into Tongues* runs as follows:

---

8 In fact there is as yet little to interest the gentleman traveller here – the emphasis is on buying and selling, calling in a debt, writing a receipt, and the like. See below (2.2.3 and 2.4) for the emergence of dialogues catering to the Grand Tourist. On the evolution of the Grand Tour, see Chaney (1998).

9 High Dutch, by contrast with Low Dutch, was the common term in English for what we now call High German, *Hochdeutsch*, which began as a regional label (the German of the southern uplands rather than of the northern low-lying areas) but came to refer to the standard language emerging in the seventeenth century, based on these varieties. (On the history of this term and its use, especially in the eighteenth century, see Faulstich 2008). Blamires (1990: 103), following the OED, suggests that *German* was not used to refer to the language until 1748, but it is already found in Minsheu's 1617 *Guide into Tongues* (see below), where the abbreviation *T.* is glossed at the front of the work (contents page), using the three synonyms "Teutonick, high Dutch, or the German tongue".

10 A similar academy had already been proposed around 1570 by Sir Humphrey Gilbert; it too envisaged a teacher of German alongside masters for French and Italian – the latter were expected to need an usher in support (Watson 1909: xxxii–xxxiii). Guthke (2011: 167) rightly emphasizes the lack of evidence that German was actually taught at Kynaston's academy, despite its frequent mention as the starting point of German language learning in Britain.

> The guide into the tongues: with their agreement and consent one with another, as also their etymologies, that is, the reasons and deriuations of all or the most part of wordes, in these eleuen languages, viz. 1. English. 2. British or Welsh. 3. Low Dutch. 4. High Dutch. 5. French. 6. Italian. 7. Spanish. 8. Portuguez. 9. Latine. 10. Greeke. 11. Hebrew, &c.: which are so laid together (for the helpe of memory) that any one with ease and facilitie, may not only remember 4. 5. or more of these languages so laid together […]/ by the industrie, studie, labour, and at the charges of Iohn Minsheu published and printed. anno 1617.

> Cum gratia & priuilegio Regiae Maiestatis, & vendibles extant Londini: Apud Ioannem Browne Bibliopolam in vico vocato little Brittaine…, 1617.
> Parallel publisher's statement on title page: And are to be sold at Iohn Browne's shop a Book-seller in little Brittaine in London.

> (Minsheu 1617, rpt. 1978)

Described in the Cambridge University Library catalogue as "an etymological dictionary of the English language", Minsheu's substantial work (500 pages folio in its first edition) was intended to be much more than that by its author, who described himself in an earlier work (a 1599 dictionary and grammar of Spanish) as a "Professor of Languages in London" (see Salmon 2003). Its structure is that of a dictionary: entries are listed alphabetically by English headword, with the translation given in ten other languages, sometimes also including (Anglo-)"Saxon" for comparison. On the one hand, then, it is a learned work for those interested in comparing languages, as suggested by the "learned Latin preface, a certificate by the University of Oxford and an impressive list of subscribers [over 400] that includes most of the illustrious names of the day from King James to John Donne" (Schäfer 1978: v; see also Schäfer 1973). On the other hand, however, the author clearly also hoped that it would serve for those seeking to learn a language for practical use, as "a practical guide for merchants 'that are in person to traficke in forreien Countreys and Tongues' " (Schäfer 1978: vii, citing from the full title of the work). As the English address to the 'common reader' explains at some length, Minsheu regarded his etymologies and the linguistic comparison that they made possible "primarily as a mnemonic aid in learning foreign languages. His basic didactic device of 'laying the [words of those] languages so together, that are of one sound', i.e. juxtaposing cognate Germanic or Romance words, successfully exploits the dual origin of English vocabulary; whenever this method fails, etymological analysis will serve to establish a connective" (Schäfer 1978: xi). Schäfer does not indicate what the sources of Minsheu's German material might have been, though elsewhere he considers his German "remarkably idiomatic" (Schäfer 1973: 35); he notes that Minsheu did draw on John Baret's *Alvearie or triple dictionary in englishe, latin and French* (1573) and international polyglot dictionaries such as Adrianus Junius's *Nomenclator* which first included English in a 1577 edition, and further notes that "even by the standards of the Renaissance" he must be "considered an arch-plagiarist" (Schäfer 1978: xiv).

The intention that the work be practically usable is underlined by the fact that the 1625 edition dropped two of the more 'obscure' languages, Welsh and Portuguese, as well as the two long learned prefaces, as well as by the fact that much pruning of the etymologizing was undertaken, so that this edition is only 380 folio pages instead of 543 (Schäfer 1978: xvii). Since the work marketed itself as being of practical use, it is worth undertaking a little "experimental language-learning" by analogy with experimental archaeology, to reconstruct what the result might have been. Let us suppose that I, a speaker of English, wish to say "My name is Nicola' and 'Can you show me your best room?'– the latter a common request in the colloquy/ phrase-book tradition, where asking to see 'best cloth' is also frequent. Looking up the individual words and noting their equivalents, which took about twenty minutes, yielded the following results:

> i. My name is…
> mine (*my* note listed) = Meyn
> Name T. Namen, nam, antiq. namo
> Is or It is T. er ist
> Result: My name is = *Meyn namen er ist*, or, assuming I realize the pronoun must be dropped, *Meyn Namen ist*.

> The second foray was less successful:
> ii. Can you show me your best room / cloth?
> [I] Can = Ich kan
> you = Ihr
> your = Ewer
> [to] Shew = Schawen
> me = Mich [no mention of *mir*]
> Best of all = Gar wol
> [a] Roome = Raum
> Result: *Kan Ihr schawen Mich Ewer gar wol Raum*

Here the verb does not agree with the subject, and accusative *Mich* should be dative *mir*; *gar wol* is adverbial *best*, not adjectival (for which no option is listed), *Raum* is the wrong word-choice but comprehensible, and *Schawen* means to look, not show. The word order is of course also distinctly odd, and the overall result would perhaps be just about comprehensible with goodwill of the listener and assuming the pronunciation was somehow intelligible.

The conclusion is hardly a surprising one. Impressive though the work is in its size and scope – and it includes quite technical terms (legal and botanical, for instance), it is virtually useless for learning a language, if by that is meant more than learning individual lexical items for scholarly comparison. That is worth emphasizing given that the work ran to four issues by 1627. Clearly good numbers of people did want this work – but not for everyday communicative needs. Minsheu's work sums up well the status of German in the early decades of the seventeenth century. Though tiny numbers evidently did learn German, some of them very well, it was still only of marginal but perhaps slowly growing interest to the population as a whole, but increasingly of interest to scholars.

Van der Lubbe (2007: 37) concurs with the evidence of Minsheu that some interest in German was driven by growing interest in Old English, in which interest exploded in the seventeenth century. William Nicholson (1655–1727), an Oxford scholar, went to Leipzig to learn German and Scandinavian languages in 1678. Another key figure in this burgeoning comparative philology was Thomas Marshall (1621–1685) – a pupil of Franciscus Junius (the Younger, who was a pioneer in the study of Gothic and Anglo-Saxon), and later Cambridge University librarian as well as Chaplain of Trinity College. A keen philologist of Germanic and oriental languages, Marshall spent twenty-two years as a chaplain to the Merchant Adventurers in Holland, where he was able to mix with Low Countries scholars of language, exploring the relationships between languages (cf. Van Hal, 2010a). It is telling that Marshall owned one of the first copies of the *High Dutch Minerva* by Martin Aedler (1680), alongside some German theological works. Likewise, the library of Sir Isaac Newton (1643–1727) contained at his death only *one* book in German, but again it was Aedler's *High Dutch Minerva* (Proescholdt 1991: 93–94). This *High Dutch Minerva*, owned by both these leading scholars of their day, was the very first grammar of German in English, and so a very significant step in the history of German as a Foreign Language (GFL) in the British Isles.

2.2.2 Martin Aedler's *High Dutch Minerva* (1680)

Published anonymously in 1680, the *High Dutch Minerva* was the first grammar of German for English speakers. For comparison, the first grammar of English for Germans had appeared in 1664: Telles' *Grammatica Anglica* (Glück 2002: 336; cf. Caravolas 1994: 163); the first specifically German-English dictionary, that of Christian Ludwig, was to appear in Leizpig in 1716 (Glück 2002: 336). The earliest language manual to include English at all alongside other European languages – dialogues and dictionary in Flemish, English, German, French, Spanish and Italian – dates from 1576 (Anon. 1576), according to Flood (1991: 258). The title *Minerva* assumed a learned audience, capable of understanding the allusion to the goddess of Wisdom, likewise its references to the Royal Society, to matters of theology and to Old English (cf. Van der Lubbe 2007: 117). However, when the remaining unsold copies were bought up in 1685 by the bookseller William Cooper, he gave it a new title page, calling it *High-Dutch Grammer* [sic], which suggests an attempt to reach a less learned audience (Van der Lubbe 2007: 73).

Although published anonymously and still said by Glück (2002: 334) to be of unknown authorship, the *High Dutch Minerva* was in fact written by Martin Aedler (1643/44–1724), as Van der Lubbe has shown (Van der Lubbe 2007). Aedler was a German from Saxony, who may have studied at Jena and then possibly lectured there in Oriental languages (Van der Lubbe 2007). He is known to have been a member of the German language society, the *Deutschgesinnte Genossenschaft* ('German-spirited Society') founded by the poet, purist and spelling reformer Philip von Zesen (1619–1689). As Van der Lubbe notes (2007: 61–62) "membership of this society was […] admission to an élite club of capable and educated people, the vast majority of whom were from the middle

Figure 2:
Frontispiece of Martin Aedler's
High Dutch Minerva (1680); the shield
reads, with Aedler's own preferred spelling,
*des Adelen hohteutshe Sprahkonst für die
Englishen*, where *des Adelen* 'of the Noble
one' is a play on his name Aedler,
in the style of the nicknames used by
members of the German language
society, the *Fruchtbringende Gesellschaft*
(Fruitbearing Society).

class: lawyers, pastors, teachers, writers"; he may also have been a member of another such language society, the *Fruchtbringende Gesellschaft* ('Fruitbearing Society') – at the very least he got as far as having a draft motto, society name, and poem of recommendation (dated 1677), possibly in the handwriting of Philip von Zesen. It may be that Aedler was never formally registered or accepted because by the summer of 1677 he was in England. Van der Lubbe (2007a: 75–76) argues plausibly that having just sought membership of the Fruitbearing Society and being still registered in the tax records as an inhabitant at a house in Jena in 1679, Aedler did not intend to stay in England, but in fact he remained there, scraping a living by teaching Hebrew and other Semitic languages at Cambridge – but bemoaning the poor standards and the lack of students – until his death in 1774 (Van der Lubbe 2007a: 78–88).

It is not clear why Martin Aedler went to England in the first place, although it was typical for scholars to spend some time abroad (very often in the Low Countries, as did Schottelius (1612–1676), the German grammarian to whom Aedler's own grammar is heavily indebted; see below). Van der Lubbe (2007a: 70) cites evidence that there was a formal programme of sending "young German divines" to Oxford and Cambridge from Halle, so Aedler's foray to England would not have been so very unusual. Aedler's expertise in oriental languages would certainly have made him sought-after in seventeenth-century England.

Van der Lubbe (2007a: 71) summarizes the *High Dutch Minerva* as "a mixture of practical grammar rules and idioms on the one hand, but with a great deal of commentary on contemporary linguistic issues on the other, some of which have political overtones." The work is a three-part grammar with the typical structure for grammars of this era: the first part dealt with letters, sounds and syllables (*grammatologia*); the second part was the *etymologia* (declension and conjugation of the parts of speech); the third part dealt with syntax (here called *orthologia* and *idiomatologia*). For whom was the volume intended?[11] It is dedicated to Prince Rupert of the Palatinate (1619–1682), German by birth but also member of English royalty and living in England, and a patron of the Royal Society, presumably in the hope of generosity to impecunious scholar (Van der Lubbe 2007a: 113–114). Aedler says in correspondence that he published the *Minerva* "at the request of certain friends" (Van der Lubbe 2007a: 74; cf. also 107).

Three groups of addressees can be envisaged:

1. Fellow champions of German back home in the German language societies: By providing the English with the means to learn German, Aedler "would help raise the status of German and in turn help to convince its native speakers to take pride in their language, and to use it in preference to French; moreover, it would encourage speakers of other languages to respect German and perhaps force them to learn German in an effort to communicate with native Germans" (Van der Lubbe 2007a: 122). Aedler did indeed publish his book under his society pseudonym of *Der Aedle* 'the noble one'; his criticism of foreign borrowings and his use and advocacy of a reformed spelling system can be seen as contributions to the specifically German intellectual context.[12] His comparison of the need for spelling reform with the necessity of the Protestant Reformation incidentally makes plain his Protestant convictions in common with most members of the largest language society, the *Fruchtbringende Gesellschaft* ('Fruitbearing-Society') and seventeenth-century German grammarians, including Schottelius.

2. Van der Lubbe summarizes that "Aedler intended his work to be used as a text for the purposes of imparting German to the English intellectual elite – specifically, academics and members of the Royal Society; thus to some extent this work must be considered a pedagogical grammar with some kind of practical use" (Van der Lubbe 2007a: 145). Certainly, the Royal Society, which already owned Minsheu's *Guide into Tongues*, was still eager for information about German, and its members were apparently eagerly awaiting a dictionary of German, said to be being undertaken by Fruitbearing-Society.[13] The German writer Martin Kempe (1637–1683) was asked to make enquiries about it on the Royal Society's behalf (Van der Lubbe 2007a: 39).[14] Like Minsheu, Aedler's work seems to assume interest in German on the Part of scholars of English. He makes many references to *Angle-Saxonick* (or *AS*), as well as

---

11 Van der Lubbe (2007: 107–109) rightly dismisses Gottsched's suggestion that the work was written for a colony of English merchants living in Germany, a surmise formed without any evidence in its favour and without any knowledge of Aedler's biography in England.

12 Aedler desired an economical spelling that avoided unnecessary letters, hence his preference for <h> rather than <ch> for the palatal and velar fricatives in words like *ich, machen*, resurrecting a spelling found in Old High German texts, and *sh* for *sch*. See 5.4 below.

13 On the plans of some Fruitbearing Society members for such a dictionary, see McLelland (2011: 216–17, 237–40).

14 An earlier attempt at a dictionary of German reached only one volume, up to the letter G, before its author died (Henisch 1616). See Considine (2008: 135–38).

remarking that one needs some German to understand the English tongue (Aedler 1680: 158; Van der Lubbe 2007a: 109–110). He gives parallel examples of language change in Old English and German, and refers to Méric Casaubon's treatise on Hebrew and Old English (*De quatuor linguis commentationis, pars prior: quae, de lingua Hebraica: et, de lingua Saxonica*, 1650) in a way that assumes a scholarly reader familiar with it. Furthermore, there are oblique references to the Royal Society, such as the references to the works of Royal Society members: John Wallis's English grammar of 1653 (Aedler 1680: 82–83), and John Wilkins's universal language scheme (though Wilkins is not mentioned by name (Van der Lubbe 2007a: 112). Most tellingly, perhaps, Aedler dedicated his work to the Royal Society's Patron, Prince Rupert of the Palatinate. Of the fourteen copies known to survive, five are held in Cambridge, and three of the fourteen belonged to high-ranking clergy (Van der Lubbe 2007a: 14). As already noted, the very title *Minerva* assumes a familiarity with the classical allusion; we can assume too from what we know of his connections in Germany and from his intolerance of low scholarly standards at Cambridge that Aedler's 'certain friends' for whom he claims to have written – whether German, English or both – would have been relatively well educated.

3. It seems likely that Aedler also hoped that his book – which he took on the costs of printing himself and which was to be sold, the title page states, in the public house Rabbets & Harrow in Blackfriars, near the wharves – would be of use to travellers to Germany (Carr 1937: 456; Van der Lubbe 2007a: 71 asserts that it was not that unusual for booksellers to sell through public-houses). Aedler quotes on p. A3 from Francis Bacon's essay (1561–1626), 'Of Travel': "he that travelleth into a countrie, before he hath some entrance into the language, goeth to school and not to travel", which reads in this context like an admonishment to those "Younge Gentlemen and Merchants" preparing "to travel or trade" addressed by works such as the 1637 London Barlement edition. The fact noted above, that the unsold copies of the *Minerva* were re-issued under the more transparent title of *Grammer* (sic; Van der Lubbe 2007a: 73), certainly suggests an attempt to reach a less scholarly audience.

In reality, it seems that of these three groups, English scholars interested in German for comparison with their own language and its earlier stages were Aedler's prime concern, just as for Minsheu. Whatever the audience, "to some extent this work must be considered a pedagogical grammar with some kind of practical use" (Van der Lubbe 2007a: 145). Certain pedagogical adjustments as well as genuine efforts to explain how to use the language are evident. The first and most obvious is Aedler's effort to explain the pronunciation by giving a phonetic rendering using English spelling conventions – the first of a great many such attempts in the history of German as a foreign language for the English.[15] Aedler uses the Lord's Prayer and the Articles of Faith as his sample texts (the Lord's Prayer as a sample text of unknown languages already had a long tradition,

---

15 A twentieth-century equivalent is Rosenberg (1938). On pronunciation in textbooks, see Chapter 5.5 below.

as for example in Gesner's *Mithridates* (1555) (cf. Colombat & Peters 2009), also found in the German grammar of Schottelius (1663: 130–131). In the excerpt below, the first line illustrates Aedler's preferred spelling – note in particular his preference for <-h> rather than <-ch> for the fricatives /ç, x/ and <sh> rather than <sch> for /ʃ/. The second line is Aedler's attempt to give a phonetic rendering using English spelling conventions (cf. 5.5 below on the teaching of pronunciation in textbooks of German).

> ih glaube an Gott den va-ter all-maehtig-en shoepfer des himm-els und der erd-en.
> ig ghlòu-wey aun Gut dane vàuter, oll-maghᵗ-e-ghen, shoepf-er das him-mels und dare arden.

Second, under Rule 4, the 'construction of the verbs', Aedler dwells at some length on forms of address depending on the addressee, by far the most explicit lesson in German pragmatics that I am aware of in the whole GFL tradition to that time; below is an extract:

> Children and our own servants, as well as beasts: second person singular; for the servants of others, "and other common sort of people as peasants and tradesmen are" 2ⁿᵈ ps. Pl; to a Gentleman or Gentlewoman and upwards, in the third person singular, and a magistrate of authority (though a single person) in the third person plural"

> (Aedler 1680: 169)

This is followed by advice on what to call the person: *Heinrich, or Meister Heinrich, or mein geneigter Herr, der gnaedige Herr,, ewere Fürstliche Durhlaeuhtigkheit hat or haben…*

Third, an early problem for those preparing materials of German was the use of black letter or Gothic type (see 5.3 below). Minsheu's *Guide* presents not just German, but also English and Dutch in what he calls Saxon type, so as an aid to the reader Minsheu lists the letters with their antiqua equivalents on the contents page at the front of his volume; Aedler, on the other hand, considered it pedagogically advisable to use the more familiar antiqua.

A final pedagogical innovation concerns Aedler's use of the notion of the rootword. Aedler is the first GFL grammarian at all to be able to draw on the first theoretically underpinned grammar of German, that of Justus-Georg Schottelius (1663; McLelland 2010, 2011 and further references there).[16] Schottelius's chief innovation and key theoretical notion underlying every aspect of the grammar was the notion of what he considered to be the typically German and always monosyllabic 'rootword' (*Stammwort*), to which prefixes and suffixes could be added, and which, together, could be combined to

---

16 Schottelius's *Ausführliche Arbeit von der teutschen Haubtsprache* (1663) was a 1500-page compendium of current knowledge about the origin, structure and use of the German language. It included a grammar and ten orations in praise of the German language (which had already been published as his *Teutsche Sprachkunst* in two editions of 1641 and 1651), as well as a poetics and a treatise on translation. See McLelland (2011).

form compounds (e.g. *schuld, verschulden, wiederverschulden, unwiederverschuldet* 'debt, owe, owe back, not owed back', Schottelius 1663: 176). For verbs, the rootword was always the second person imperative (*Trink! Geh!* 'Drink! Go!').[17] Martin Aedler, a 'veritable Stammwort-enthusiast' (Van der Lubbe 2007a: 185), used the terms *Radix* and *primitive* for the concept of rootword in English, and used the notion (like Schottelius) as a guiding principle in his orthography. He also drew on it to explain intonation and the German rule of first-syllable stress on native words:

> Every true both High- and Low-dutch Radix has its tonick accent, (and that either soft when the syllable is long, or sharp when the syllable is short), in the first syllable, where it still remains both in derivativs [sic] and compounds'.

(Aedler 1680: 30, cf. also 34)

However, contrary to Schottelius's view that the root was the second-person imperative, Aedler presented the root as the verb 'in the first person', arguably a more salient form for learners. In practice, though, Aedler described derivation from verbs as proceeding by removing -en from the infinitive, so that he did not adhere to his own definition of the root (Van der Lubbe 2007a: 186). For Aedler, then, the root of *gehen* 'to go' would be *geh* rather than *gehe*, the first person singular form that he seems to specify. The approach was less theoretically rigorous than that of Schottelius, but perhaps more accessible for the learner.

Aedler was also less rigorous than Schottelius in his discussion of suffixes, though very obviously indebted to him. Of the 23 German *Hauptendungen* ('derivational suffixes') that had been identified by Schottelius, Aedler did not include -*ei*, and, more importantly, he added several of his own that would not have qualified for Schottelius as endings. Some of these were, in Schottelius's view, not suffixes but rootwords in their own right (-*los, -voll, -arm, -rei[c]h* '-less, -ful, -poor, -rich'; Van der Lubbe 2007a: 186) so that they should properly be treated under compounding. Others were not monosyllabic, but were, strictly speaking, already derived, consisting of rootwords with a derivational ending added (-*haftig, -sühtig, -girig* 'containing __, seeking __, desiring __', all with -*ig* added to a root noun). In short, Aedler sacrificed the niceties of theoretical, principled distinction between rootwords and derivational endings, and the Schottelian belief that they must be monosyllabic. Instead, he used the notions of rootword and affix as handy but flexible explanatory tools, to emphasize the "close relationship between German and English, which will allow the learner to apply principles of English word-building to German" (Van der Lubbe 2007a: 188; Aedler 1680: 131–62). In comparing German and English word-formation, he presented learners with productive affixes. Like Minsheu, then, Aedler used explicit comparison between languages as a means to learning them.[18] Moreoever, although his is the only grammar in the English

---

17 On the history of the rootword in the German language tradition see McLelland 2010, also McLelland (2011b).

18 "The basic educational technique of the High Dutch Minerva rests on a comparative technique",

tradition to show the direct influence of Schottelius, it is early evidence of the value of the transfer between theoretical reflection on German and pedagogical grammars for foreign learners.[19]

Aedler's grammar is also somewhat unusual, in the European tradition of foreign language grammars, in what it *lacks*: conversations. The practice of using model dialogues had deep roots in foreign language learning and pre-dated explicit grammars of the vernacular languages by many centuries (as we saw in 2.1 above), and would be a fixture in many grammars of German after Aedler's, including that of Aedler's near-contemporary Heinrich Offelen (as we shall see in 2.3 below). Yet the *High Dutch Minerva* contains no such conversations. Given his chiefly scholarly orientation, Aedler's omission of everyday conversations is not entirely surprising; perhaps he did not realize initially that such dialogues might be thought desirable by language learners. The justification that he gives for the omission of dialogues has an interesting theoretical basis, however. He held what is known as a "universalist view" of language: i.e. the assumption that there is a universal grammar that is common to all languages. Now, any authors who used the grammatical structure and categories of Latin grammar to describe French, English or any other language in effect made an implicit assumption about shared, universal grammar, even if they were not always conscious of doing so. There was, consequently, a recurring obsession with finding six cases in German to match the six cases of Latin, from the very first grammarian of German, Albertus (1583), into the nineteenth century. (Besides the nominative, accusative, genitive and dative familiar to today's learners of German, authors came up with forms for the vocative and ablative too (*O Vater!, von dem Vater* 'oh father! from the father'; cf. McLelland (2009: 62)). However, Aedler's universalist conviction ran deeper than this. So convinced was he of the basic structural similarity of languages that he felt model dialogues would be superfluous, for they would contain too much that intelligent readers could already assume from their reading of the grammar, or that they could safely deduce by assuming German to be the same as English: "other common talk knowne already to everyone before, as well as by his own language".

Idioms, however, constituted one area of the language that did vary unpredictably between languages, Aedler believed, and so he provided a list of idioms as the chief features that are unique to any one language. He was confident that by observing these, "the chiefest and sometimes uncouth phrases" listed by him, "the beginner will certenly by this help be better and sooner instructed in the knowledge of either of our tongues, than by any other books made for that purpose" (Aedler 1687: 177). Aedler's idioms are loosely alphabetically arranged by English keyword (suggesting that Aedler was working from an English dictionary of some kind?): *account, abuse, acquaintance, ago, agreed, alive, alone, angry, ask, awe, back, bad, baits, balked, bargain, bar, bate, clap*. However,

---

as Van der Lubbe has pointed out (Van der Lubbe 2007a: 168). The comparative technique in language learning was far from new to the British Isles at this time, however; comparisons are already made between Old Irish and Latin in ninth-century glosses See Russell (2012).

19 While Aedler illustrates a watering down of Schottelius's theoretical tenets to pedagogical ends, Kramer (1694) provides a refinement of Schottelius's account of word-formation. See McLelland (2010), McLelland (2011a, Chapter 7).

the lack of system in the alphabetical list would have made it rather unsuitable as a reference work, and Aedler does not draw attention to this organizational principle at all. The intention was, presumably, that the reader should work through the idioms from beginning to end. The idioms were indeed "sometimes uncouth": *er hat di Franzosen or die Venus-krankheit* 'he has a clap or the French pocks'; *snauze dih du garstiger sakk!* Or *puze di nase du unflat* 'blow your nose you slut you' (Aedler 1680: 181, 185).

Despite its importance today as the first grammar of German for English learners, the *High Dutch Minerva* caused little stir in its day. William Cooper's reissue of it in 1685 with a new title page shows that copies remained unsold five years after its publication; and most, though not all, copies that survive today are in pristine, unused condition (Van der Lubbe 2007a: 195–196). As for the author, Aedler in effect bankrupted himself to pay for the printing of the grammar; he was ultimately forced to marry an elderly widow to whom he was in debt, and the marriage was not a happy one. He died alone and in poverty at the age of 81 (Van der Lubbe 2007a: 72, 104).[20] It was, in sum, not a particularly auspicious start to the history of German textbooks for English learners.

2.2.3 Heinrich Offelen's *Double Grammar* (1687)

It seems that Aedler and Minsheu had their books printed in Little Britain (modern London EC1) (Van der Lubbe 2007a: 71; Carr 1937: 456; see Cambridge catalogue record for Minsheu 1617); both took the financial risk upon themselves; and both appear to have plunged themselves into debt as a result.[21] One gains the impression that the scholarly interest in learning other languages – and specifically German – was growing sufficiently for two individuals to have a go at catering to that market; but not yet sufficiently for either to make any money out of it. However, within two years of Aedler's grammar being re-issued in 1685, the next work for English learners of German had appeared: Heinrich Offelen's *Double Grammar* (1687). Its full title runs as follows:

> A double GRAMMAR for GERMANS to learn *ENGLISH* AND FOR ENGLISHMEN to Learn the *GERMAN*-tongue: *Wherein all* Latine *Words, belonging to the* Grammar, *are translated both into the* German *and* English *tongue.*
> Treating besides of the Derivation of the *English* tongue, with all Grammatical Rules, and Dialogues, Treating of all necessary matters that daily may be spoken of. *AND*
> Especially what is to be seen for a Stranger at *Versailles* in *France*; and *England*; with a *Compendium* of the Estate of the *German* Empire.
> Composed and set forth by Henry Offelen, Doctor in Laws and Professor of Seven languages, *(viz.) English, French, Spanish, Italian, Latin,* and High- and *Low-Dutch*

The author describes himself as a "Professor" of seven languages. He is also the author of *Devises et emblemes anciennes et modernes* (Amsterdam 1691, and later editions in-

---

20 See Van der Lubbe (2007a: 49–104) for Aedler's decidedly unhappy personal biography.
21 On Minsheu's difficulties, see Schäfer (1978).

cluding 1692, 1693, 1699) in seven languages, an edition of a book of "emblems" by Daniel de la Feuille (cf. Saunders 2000: 86), where the motto corresponding to each emblem is translated into six other languages, including English and German. Such emblem-books – consisting of symbolic images, or "emblems", accompanied by explanatory text – were extremely fashionable in the seventeenth century in the Low Countries and Germany (Strasser & Wade 2004; Westerhoff 2001), and their use by a practical language teacher as an additional source of language practice, rich in proverbs and idioms, gives an indication of the kind of learner he anticipated: well-educated and fashionable.

Glück's description of Offelen's grammar as "in a sense the first contrastive grammar of English and German" (Glück 2002: 332, my translation) is somewhat misleading, as the two parts of the book – that aimed at German learners and that aimed at English learners – are in separate halves of the book, rather than on facing pages. Here I shall consider only the German grammar for English learners and the additional bilingual dialogue material that could have been used by both sets of learners. In Offelen's own words, he wrote the grammar for "friends of the arts and sciences" (the German text here reads simply *wissenschaften*; 'To the beloved German reader', unnumbered first page, with German version on facing page), and in particular for the Lübeck-born portrait artist Gotfrid Kneller (1646–1723) (see Bayer-Klötzer 1979), who moved to England in 1676, where he painted members of the Royal Family and dominated portrait-painting for forty years. In his address 'To the English reader', Offelen states that he has tested this method in private teaching at Rome, Vienna, and "especially at Paris" and "I am sure it will be well received by the Nobility, Schollars and all Well-bred People". The work is dedicated to the ruling British King James II's son-in-law, Prince George of Denmark, who had married Anne (who would be Queen Anne form 1702) in 1683. Although the title page states that the book was printed in London, Carr (1937: 465) takes the view that it was actually done in the Low Countries, as the German title page ends in Dutch: "Tot London, gedruckt vor den Autheur, en zijn te koop by Nathanial Thompson in den ingangh van Old Spring Garden by Charing Cross. 1689". Carr suggests that Aedler's grammar was also printed in the Netherlands, because of an apparently typically Dutch spelling of Blackfriars on the title page (Carr 1937: 456). This seems surprising in both cases since both authors are known to have lived in England – perhaps a Dutch printer was operating in London who dealt with printing in the unfamiliar German language more readily that an English printer?

The mention of Kneller, the fact that the German part of the grammar comes first, and the fact that the information on England given in dialogue XV is far more detailed and practical in nature than that given in dialogue XVI on the state of Germany all suggest that Offelen wrote first with German learners of English in mind.[22] Neverthe-

---

22 The state of Germany well may be modelled on a passage which clearly dates back to 1685, but which I came across in a 1720 French grammar, catalogued as Anon. but very possibly by König (discussed below), *The Royal French GRAMMAR*: "A Discourse upon the Estate of France, as it is now govern'd under Lewis the XIVth in the Year 1685" (Anon (König?) 1720: 301). This is evidence of the extent of cross-fertilization of language teaching methods and materials between instructors of differing languages in England at this time (see also the discussion of König and Kramer, footnote 29 below). The same grammar incidentally contains a dialogue lamenting the death of William III who died

less, the grammar of German is a full one. Like Aedler's and like most foreign language grammars up to that time, Offelen's grammar in effect follows the standard model of Latin grammar, proceeding from a treatment of letters and pronunciation, then etymologia, then syntax, in three parts. However, the table of contents lists separate chapters, rather than these three divisions, which might suggest that the intention was to treat one chapter per lesson. Although clearly indebted to Aedler in many regards (Van der Lubbe 2007a: 201), unlike Aedler, Offelen opts for using black letter because it is that "which most German Authors and Books are of" (Part II, unnumbered first page of 'To the English Reader'). How, when and where to introduce readers to black letter or 'Gothic type' remains a dilemma that is discussed by textbook authors in their prefaces well into the middle of the twentieth century (see 5.3).

Carr (1937: 469), in his examination of early grammars of German, is clearly not impressed by Offelen: "On the whole this grammar shows little advance on the Minerva and in some parts is even inferior to it. It certainly cannot be called 'gründlich, wissenschaftlich und praktisch', as Schaible does" (Schaible 1885). Yes this is a rather harsh assessment of a text whose author makes a real effort to take the learner with him. No fan of the direct method, Offelen states the importance of grammar in his "To the German reader": "no man is able to learn a Language perfectly without the knowledge thereof". However, he makes allowances for those who may not have encountered grammar already (or who perhaps have forgotten it since childhood?), beginning by translating all grammatical terms from Latin into English and explaining them (Offelen 1687: Part II, 1–12):

> Pronomen. A Pronoun is a Noun implying a Person and not admitting the sign *a.* or *the.* before it […] .

(Offelen 1687: Part II, 4)

(There follow definitions of the various categories of pronouns, a point to which we shall return). This use of "signs" for recognizing parts of speech goes back to Humanist pedagogical reform to improve the teaching of Latin to young boys in the fifteenth and early sixteenth centuries (see Puff 1995: 228–244). Their use here is interesting evidence that pedagogical strategies for teaching Latin to children were now, in the seventeenth century, being used for teaching grammar to adults as a prelude to learning a foreign language, even if many of Offelen's definitions might not quite satisfy us:

> Phrasis. A Phrase is a Sentence composed of Several Words. Ex. I am your most humble Servant.

(Offelen 1687: Part II, 1)

---

on March 8th, 1702. The habit of describing systems of government is in turn highly reminiscent of the genre of the urban topography, or *chorography*, that flourished particularly in the seventeenth century (see Verbaan 2011, in Dutch but including an English summary).

For comparison with Aedler I shall consider briefly some examples of the treatment of pronunciation, etymologia, and syntax. It is Offelen's guide to pronunciation which most exercises Carr, who calls it "faulty and incomplete" (Carr 1937: 466). Carr singles out Offelen's descriptions of German *s* as soft, but this was and is both a widespread pronunciation (in the south) and no impediment to communication. Carr notes Offelen's remark that *o* is pronounced like "oa in English" in German, with the example *Wort* (Offelen 1687: Part II, 16). Certainly German *o* does not rhyme with *oa* in *road*, but I wonder whether that *oa* was Offelen's attempt to account for vocalization of *r* after *o* in *Wort*, which is standard for *r* after vowels in German today: /woɐt/, perhaps better *Wo-art*. This would certainly be an overgeneralization of *o* before *r* to all instances of *o*, but it was possibly a perceptive observation. Of greatest concern to Carr is the plain error that suggests that "ee. is pronounced as thus. Seel, read Seal Soul" (Offelen 1687: Part II, 17). This is without doubt incorrect: the *ee* in German *Seel* (modern German *Seele*) is a long /e:/, and not a long /i:/ which the English *Seal* would suggest. Presumably the error is a result of Offelen's inadequate grasp of English pronunciation. On the other hand, of *ü*, Offelen states that "ü is a little more melting than ee in English", giving "Müntz, read Meentz". While "melting" could mean anything, recognizing the affinity between /i/ and its rounded counterpart /y/ (ü) is impressive at this time, hundreds of years before the birth of phonetics in the nineteenth century.

If Offelen's account of pronunciation is wanting, then in the etymologia he scores better in some areas, at least. He does deal with the prepositions, which Aedler did not. He lists 49 prepositions in alphabetical order (Offelen 1687: Part II, 117–120), with none of the reluctance that we find among later grammarians to recognize certain prepositions derived from other parts of speech such as *wegen* 'because of' or *ungeachtet* 'regardless of' as "true" prepositions (see 5.9.3, note 43, below; McLelland 2012a), although *trotz* 'in spite of' is not included. In some instances the case indicated is surprising: *gegen* is said to take either dative or accusative, though this might reflect the older usage of *gegen* 'against' with dative (the example given is with the accusative); on the other hand, the claim that *bey* can take accusative as well as dative has no basis in reality that I am aware of (Offelen 1687: Part II, 118). Even Carr (1937: 467) concedes that Offelen's treatment of pronouns is very systematic, grouping them into personal, reciprocal, demonstrative, possessive, relative, and interrogative pronouns (Offelen 1687: Part II, 59–64). This is an innovation in the German grammatical tradition – in German grammars for native speakers, a class headed personal pronouns does not appear until Longolius (1715) (see Jellinek 1914: 273). Under comparison of the adjective, Offelen continued an oddity that goes back to the obsession of Schottelius (1663) with finding prefixes and phrases that can convey similar meanings to grammatical processes. Like Schottelius, then, he treated intensifying adverbs (*ser, gar, fast, wol* 'very, completely, very, well') and prefixes like *erz, haupt* ('arch-, chief-') under the heading of comparative and superlative because, like the comparative and superlative, they can indicate degree (McLelland 2011a: 101). Presumably Offelen is following Aedler here: Carr (1937: 460) traces two examples *hauptperl, hauptstatt* through both Aedler (1680: 65) and Offelen (1687: 38). Aside from such oddities, though, Offelen's basic exposition of the degrees of comparison is admirably clear:[23]

> The degrees of comparison are formed as in English you add in the Comparative (er.) and in the Superlative este, or ste. *As for Example* if you will know what signified Rich in English you will find in the Dictionary Reich, Rich: being the Positive. In the Comparative, you add only er. *As* Reicher, Richer. And in the superlative, est or ste. *As,* Reicheste or Reichste, Richest, only you must observe here again that the Characteristick Letter, a. and the Bi-vowel, au, as also o. and u. of the Monosyllabick Positives, are changed in their Comparisons. a into ae. au into aeu. o into ö and u. into ü.
>
> *Note.* That in the Comparatives and Superlatives, the same Rule must be observed, that we have given of the Positives. As,
>
> Ein großer Mann, a tall Man.
> Ein größerer Mann, a taller man.
>
> (Offelen 1687: Part II, 37)

This is clearer than the statement in the Schottelius's grammar (1663: 246–249). Incidentally, it is not clear what dictionary Offelen might have intended his reader to use here – a full German-English dictionary was not available until Ludwig (1715), but perhaps Minsheu's work might have done service here? On the other hand, his own work includes lists of vocabulary grouped onomasiologically, i. e. by semantic field/ topic (Part 3, 159–188) – clearly superior to an alphabetical listing by one language if either language may be the target language, depending on the user.

Carr considers Offelen's treatment of the verb to be quite inferior to Aedler's (Carr 1937: 468), for Offelen was "quite behind the times" in his use of the notion of the optative mood (though still used by Ritter 1616, it had disappeared by Schottelius). In fact Offelen has so little to say about the optative or subjunctive (there is just a brief note of the first person forms of the "optative" through all tenses, thus in effect covering both optative and subjunctive, Offelen 1687: Part II, 66) that it is hard to take offence at the use of the term. Carr (1937: 469) is also dissatisfied with the one line on the passive. One can hardly deny that Offelen's terse statement "Some say *ich wurde geliebt*, others *ich war geliebt*" is incomplete, but it is does at least recognize the variation between the two competing auxiliaries; it is thus clearer than either Aedler or Schottelius, both of whom switch confusingly but apparently unconsciously between listing *werden* and *sein* as passive auxiliaries. For the historian of the German language, this is one of the clearest metalinguistic statements on the variation in formation of the German passive of the

---

23 Compare Aedler (1680: 63): "R.1 the degrees of comparison are formed as in English either in adding some certain syllables to the positiv [sic] viz. to the absoluyte (or as it stands after a verbe without any substantiv [sic] or article) in the absolute comparativ ER, and in the absolute superlativ ESTE (to which is added an N, if precede [sic] the particle am) [...]".

time.[24] For the history of language teaching, one is inclined to think that one clear page that could be expanded on by a teacher might be superior to pages of confusion.

As for syntax, Carr is again underwhelmed by Offelen's account of German word order, but to the present reader it has the benefit of clarity. It begins:

> You are to understand that every Verb Active or Passive governs the same Case which they govern in English, though some are excepted, which you shall see afterwards, when we speak of the Syntaxis of Verbs; Only *Observe* that he that does the Action, is put always in the Nominative case, and what is done in the *Accusative. As for example* Mein Vatter liebt meine Schwester, My Father loves my Sister. Mein Vatter, is put in the *Nominative Case*, because he does the Action of Love. Meine Schwester, is the *Accusative*, because it is She that he loves.
> Here follows a Compendium of eight lines, containing the whole Syntaxis.

(Eight sentence types follow: affirmative, negative, interrogative and negative-interrogative, each in present and perfect tenses.)
Most impressively, Offelen succeeds in describing inversion clearly – and this is a considerable improvement on, for example, Schottelius (1663) (see McLelland 2008 for further discussion of early attempts to describe inversion, and see Chapter 5.8 below).[25]

> The accusative goes regularly after the verb, but sometimes before the verb in this language, and then the Nominative must go after the verb especially if we speak of a thing with Emphasis [...] The same holds if an Adverb is put in the beginning of a Phrase.

> (Offelen 1687: 96)

One might compare this with Aedler (1680: 167): "R[ule].2 when the verbe stands betwixt two nouns, the worthiest (that is either the first or the second) goes before it and the third follows, e.g. *ih bin es* I am it."

Offelen's grammar proper is preceded by some comparisons between German and English, "How an English Man may derive from the English Tongue German Words" – the chapter of two and a half pages covers certain systematic regularities accounted for by the High German sound shift (though this is not alluded to), including *th vs d* or *t; p vs f* or *pf, t vs s, k vs ch, b vs p, d vs t, t vs ts*. This is not dissimilar to the kind of comparisons made by some textbook authors in the later nineteenth century under the influence of the comparative philology of the day; see 3.9 below. However, such regularities relating to the High German sound shift are arguably obscured in Offelen's book by others (e.g. *f vs b wife-Weib*) as well as by far less systematic correspondences concerning the vowels, and finally by others that are mere spelling conventions. For example, English *d* at the begin-

---

24 On grammarians' accounts of the passive at this time, see Jellinek (1914: 306–308).
25 Inversion is the requirement in German that the verb must come in second position in a main clause. If something other than the subject occupies first position, the subject and verb must then be "inverted" to allow the verb to take second position: e.g. *Ich schreibe heute* vs *Heute schreibe ich* ('I write today, today write I').

ning of a word is said to correspond with German *th* (e.g. *do* – *Thun*, modern German *tun*); English <*sh*> "changed" into <*sch*>. In this last case, the two sounds are the same, and the only difference is one of spelling; recall that Aedler had even preferred to use <*sh*> rather than <*sch*>. Still, despite its faults, Offelen's attempt at systematic comparison was new; it represents an attempt to generalize correspondences that were implicit in Minsheu's 1617 "laying together" of cognate words (as Minsheu's title page put it).

The two grammars for English and German in Offelen's book are followed by a third part, usable by both groups of readers: vocabulary grouped by topic, and then sixteen dialogues with German and English in parallel (English on the left) (Offelen 1687: Part 3, 189–269). Their titles are given on the left of Table 2.1. For comparison, the second column gives the title of dialogues from a popular twentieth-century text aimed at adult learners of German which also (still!) used the method of parallel German and English dialogues, *Brush Up Your German* (Grundy 1931, discussed in Chapter 6 below).

Table 2.1: Sixteen dialogues in Offelen (1687) with counterparts in Grundy (1931)

Offelen (1687)	Grundy (1931)
Between a Sea-man and a Gentle-Man	Cf. 2. On Board the Ostend Steamer
To Ask the Way	18. Asking the Way
Being in an Inn	42. In the Hofbräuhaus at Munich
With a Merchant about a Bill of Exchange	9.-10. In the Bank
About taking a Lodging	5. Arriving at the Hotel
Of Eating and Drinking	15.-17. Lunch
Of Buying and Selling [cloth]	(several shops; see also discussion of cloths in 20. A question of clothes)
With a Taylor	29. Herr Meyer calls at his Tailor's
With a Shooe-maker	47. In the Boot-Shop
With a Coach-man	–
With a Horse-courser	11. Her Meyer hires a Baby Car.
Between a Sick Gentleman, his Servant and a Physician.	35. The Doctor's Visit
With a La[u]ndress	–
Between to Gentleman of strange Countries, and first of France.	–
Of England.	–
About the present State of Germany.	–

Offelen's last three dialogues – which have no counterpart in Grundy (1931) – read like additions aimed specifically at the Grand Tour market containing (as the titles already indicate) conversation on the sights of Versailles, of London and England more generally, and brief background on Germany.[26] Together with Offelen's multilingual emblem-book, they are further evidence of the growing interest in German (and vice versa) amongst fashionable society. In dialogue XV on England, we learn about London (the various parks, Whitehall, Westminster, London Bridge, St Paul's, the Law courts, Tower, Monument), as well as about Oxford, Cambridge and Windsor as worthy of a visit; about coffee, tea, and chocolate; about smoking habits in England; about Clubs (whether of scholars or of tradesmen); the post-days for Germany (Tuesday and Friday); public holidays. The dialogue devoted to Germany concentrates not on sights, but on history and governance: how the emperor is elected; Hansa cities; the Teutonic Order; religion (three permitted: Catholic, Lutherans [sic] and Protestants) and background to Luther; war with the Turks; what people drink in Germany; praise for German friendliness to strangers if they be honest; German sincerity generally, and an assertion that they love "Sciences and strange Languages", so that if one has not travelled one is not esteemed. Significantly, rather than rehearsing negative stereotypes (as in the *Stulti sunt Romani* gloss I cited at the start of this chapter, and in the travelogue cited above), such comments prepare Grand Tourists to bridge the hostility that might be felt in dealing with strangers of a different culture. (Similarly, the French are described as noble and civil to strangers: Offelen 1687: 213). What one might want to see in Germany is described in very general terms: various courts, two fairs a year in Frankfurt, three at Leipzig; and a new one at Brunswick (Offelen 1687: 267–269). Finally, Hungary is noted as worth a visit, with pleasant climate and wine.

While the majority of the dialogues are stock-in-trade topics for travellers of all kinds (including information on laws and prices, and a warning against well-dressed pickpockets, pp. 213–214), dialogues XIV and XV in particular suggest the growing importance of language-learning for the Grand Tour, as the dialogue participants compare their knowledge of different parts of Europe:

> – In good truth if that is so as you say, this Nation has many Vertues and good
>   Qualities, but I have known a great many, who have not been so as you say.
> – It is true, I do not speak of all, I do but speak of the greatest part; I have
>   known myself several Young Gentlemen, who were sent by their Parents in
>   strange Countries, to learn Languages, and other Nobles Exercises, but in-
>   stead of executing their Parents Will and Mind, they lookt for bad company"

(Offelen 1687: 267, in the dialogue about Germany)

---

26 As Caravolas (1994: 165) observes, "En effet, la France est partout, même dans le manuel que les Allemands utitlisent pour apprendre l'Anglais." Partly this is the result of recycling dialogue material from other manuals, but more than this, French culture still evidently carries the highest prestige – German will not be begin to compete until the late eighteenth century. See Chapter 3.

Of the first thirteen dialogues in Offelen (1687), listed in Table 2.1, only that dealing with laundry has no counterpart at all in Grundy (1931), aimed at twentieth-century business travellers to Germany. At the sime time, the discussion of buying and selling cloth also has a history going back centuries in Europe, as we saw evidenced in the Italian-German dialogue cited in 2.1 above – with the same haggling over price.

> What will you buy, Sir?
> Have you got any good Cloath, Ribbands, good Hats, good Gloves, or Stockings?
> Yes Sir, the best in Town.
> Shew me a piece of good Cloath.
> Black or Coloured?
> There's a Cloth for you Sir, if you like the Colour.
> What's this a Yard?
> Twenty Shillings.
> How! Twenty Shillings, you take me for a Stranger I see.
> No Sir, we are not in France here.
> We sell no dearer to a Stranger in this Countrey, than to an Englishman.
> Well, I will give you sixteen Shillings.
> Upon my word, it costs me more.
> There's seventeen Shillings.
> Truly Sir I cannot afford it under nineteen
> Well, I will not stand with you [*nicht drauf stehen*]; I hope you will be my Customer another time.
> I will with all my heart Sir.
> Will you have it carried home?
> Yes Sir if there's ever a porter here about.
> Here Honest man go along with the Gentleman to his Lodging.
> I am very much beholding [*sic*] to you Sir
>
> (Offelen 1687: 267–269; I cite only the English for reasons of space)

Carr (1937: 466) concludes on Offelen's work, "Certainly the setting out of the rules and paradigms is clearer than in the Minerva", but "in many cases Offelen is less up to date and certainly not so accurate". Offelen's inaccuracies are those of a non-native speaker (note besides the problems with pronunciation the unidiomatic *I will not stand with you* rendering the German idiom *nicht drauf stehen* in the exchange quoted above). Still, pedagogically his text is a considerable improvement on Aedler's.

2.3 The early eighteenth century under the House of Hanover: Johann König's *Royal Compleat Grammar* (1715)

The final work to consider in the first hundred years of German as a Foreign Language in Britain is Johann König's *A royal compleat grammar, English and High-German Das ist: Eine Königliche vollkommene grammatica, in Englisch-und Hochteütscher Sprach… Durch John King,…* (London, 1715). This "royal" grammar (a play on the author's name) is the first German grammar of the eighteenth century in Great Britain.[27] The author states in his preface that this grammar is a revised version of his *Englischer Wegweiser* or *Complete English Guide* from some years earlier (1706, in fact: Carr 1937: 470), by then out of print (though it was in fact later edited by other authors after his grammar appeared). Carr notes that the grammar was reprinted for the tenth time in 1782, and Hüllen (1995: 1) counts twelve editions by 1802, making it "the most successful text-book for English as a foreign language in the eighteenth century" (similarly Klippel 1994: 67; Klippel discusses König pp. 67–73; see also Driedger 1907). The following discussion is based on the 1715 edition, dedicated to King George of the German House of Hannover, who had ascended the British throne in 1714 after the death of Queen Anne (as her closest living Protestant relative). Hüllen (1995: 1) notes that the 1715 edition was revised by König based on his experience and so considers that König viewed it as "the ultimate version of his didactic ideas". Like Offelen's work, the book is clearly aimed predominantly at a German market, but it was printed in England, where König evidently lived and taught German visitors to the country. Thirty-six pages deal with pronunciation; thirteen deal with homophones, polysemous words (e.g. *alone*, meaning both *allein* 'alone' and *zufrieden* 'content, in peace' as in 'leave me alone') and idioms; 91 pages deal with grammar, including word order (seven pages) and word formation (44–50 for nouns and adjectives). 39 pages then present word-lists, followed by 37 pages of *Gemeine Gespraeche* (actually lists of idiomatic expressions rather than 'conversations'), followed by sixteen short dialogues (189–216) and reading material (217–262). In fact, the grammar, though bilingual, is "not a German grammar at all, but an English one with the examples translated into German" (Carr 1937: 469). Certainly one could not learn any German grammar from it. For example, König lists prepositions in English and German, in no particular order, including "about, wegen", but he explains that they *regieren aber eigentlich keinen gewissen Casum* 'actually don't govern any particular case' (König 1715: 110). Even if the translation of English examples into German shows normal case usage (*wegen* with the genitive, for example, König 1715: 114), there is no presentation of German grammar for a learner of the language.

As a supplement to an existing grammar, however, the *Royal Compleat Grammar* is certainly of potential interest to English learners of German because of the supplementary material following the grammar, which was equally suited to language learning in either direction. For immediately following the grammar is a dictionary of 2,429

---

27 Glück (2002: 332) notes a 1702 work by Daniel Franz Pastorius aimed at the children of German migrants to the U.S.A.

entries over 39 pages, which Hüllen considers a substantial list in a book of this size; it is certainly far more extensive than Offelen's list. The words are arranged by topic, a practice of which Jan Amos Comenius (1592–1670) is perhaps the best-known exponent and which rests on an assumption that "a 'natural' arrangement of words, which follows the 'natural' order of things, is helpful for the memory of the language learner" (Hüllen 1995: 3; on the onomasiological dictionary tradition, which more or less collapsed as an independent genre after 1700, cf. Hüllen 2002: 89–101). König's classification is as follows: God, the elements, time (i. e. the world as a whole); Man, society; body, senses, clothes, food; family relationships; offices; war; arts, professions; church, court; tools; house, husbandry; school; metals; animals; precious stones; agriculture, plants; countries, towns; measures, numbers. The choice of semantically related words betrays some basic (neither sophisticated nor innovative) assumptions about the order of the world typical of the later seventeenth century,[28] but it also reflects König's belief of what is useful in learning a foreign language. As Hüllen points out, "If we assume that the grammatical rules and examples in the previous parts of the book were presented in order to be learned, we can also assume that John King assembled these semantic word-groups for the same purpose. He must have thought that an arrangement in semantically cohesive clusters would facilitate memorisation for the learner" (Hüllen 1995: 3). Indeed, a dialogue in Beiler (1731), discussed in Chapter 3.2 below, refers explicitly to learning off such word-lists. It should also be noted that from a marketing point of view such a grouping also made the lists usable as a reference for learners of either language, whereas any alphabetical listing implicitly defines one language as the target language.

Following the word-lists come *Gemeine Gespraeche*, lit. 'common conversations': these consist of parallel columns of idioms in English and German (179–188), followed by sixteen short dialogues (189–216).[29] The context is clearly that of a German traveller in England. Besides the dialogues – which make specific reference to approaching the English coast, getting directions to London and the dangers of English highwaymen – there is also a guide to the sights of London (217–262; Oxford, Cambridge and Windsor are also mentioned – all also noted in Offelen 1687: 220) – and models of familiar letter-writing (including love-letters) apparently taken from the best authors (263–273).[30]

---

28 It is reminiscent, for example of John Wilkins' 1668 *Essay Towards a Real Character and a Philosophical Language*. Here Wilkins presented a classification scheme that sought to divide reality up systematically into categories and sub-categories (with overarching categories including "Concerning God", "Of Elements and Meteors", "Of Plants", Concerning Animals", etc.), and then assigned to each thing and concept in the system a unique name.

29 Klippel (1994: 71) notes many similarities – including word-for-word correspondences – between König's work and Kramer (1746), which is in turn an adaptation of a much earlier book for Dutch learners of English, Sewel (1705, first published as an appendix to a dictionary in 1691). It is almost certain that König took some of his material from Sewel – the dialogues contain several references to Amsterdam and Holland (p. 214, 215), as well a reference to William and Mary as the King and Queen of England (p. 234: Queen Mary died in 1694, William in 1702).

30 Here the copy digitized for EEBO (*Early English Books Online*) contains a handwritten note observing in German that the German translations are rather literal, but that this is deliberate for the benefit of the German learner of English.

From pp. 274–303, the text is of no value to the learner of German, as it switches to English only: pp. 274–290 offer letters in English only taken from the 'best' English authors as well as others apparently translated into English from French, followed by Aesop's fables (apparently from Phillip Ayres, *Methodologia Ethica*), which are intended for those who can now read and pronounce English well: these short fables *können gelesen und expliciret werden* 'can be read and explicated" (König 1715: 291).

Even if the form of the grammar, the focus on English sights, and the material in English only, makes much of the book of no interest to a potential learner of German, the language of the dialogues certainly is of interest, for the language presented is that of the nobility on its Grand Tour, and this is the very first text to offer any means of teaching young Englishmen German of this register, beyond the small step already taken in that direction by Offelen's dialogues XIV to XVI. The *Gemeine Gespraeche* presented on pp. 179–188 are short phrases in parallel translation, grouped under headings such as "of complaining, of hoping and of despairing", "of affirming, granting, believing and denying", "to ask advice", "of threatening and assaulting" – and, amusingly, "of lying", but this turns out to be an error in translation for *Von Leugnen*, i. e. disputing an assertion (König 1715: 183). This grouping of useful phrases according to *function* is new,[31] and indicates that Anglo-German contact is perceived here as a matter of communicating, developing and sustaining personal relationships, according to strictly defined social etiquette, just as native speakers also needed to master the rules of these etiquette-bound communicative genres (Linke 1988, 1996). The goal was evidently not merely mastery of 'survival' language for practical travel needs and trade. The number of dialogues that follow – sixteen – might lead one to expect overlap with Offelen, and there are indeed some similarities. Here too we find conversations about negotiating a price for lodgings, coming to an inn, arranging to take a ship to England, and dealing with a merchant about a bill of exchange. But many of the topics and the language used in König's dialogues are very specific to the class of the travelling gentlemen whose chief concern is to pass the time in social intercourse:

> 'Pray make my compliments to him' *Ich bitte euch, meine Complimenten bey ihm abzulegen*'
> 'Sir I come to pay my humble Respect to you. *Ich komme mein Herr, meine unterthänige Aufwartung bey euch abzustatten*'
> 'Bring us some long pipes. And the best Tobacco you have. *Bringt uns lange Pfeiffen und von dem besten Taback, den ihr habt*'
>
> (König 1715: 190, 193, 198)

The dialogues model linguistic tasks such as paying a call, the art of making small talk over the news and weather, taking one's leave, politely refusing or accepting an invitation to dine or to have supper; recommending reputable tradesmen (in this case a watchmak-

---

31 My use of the term *function* here is of course anachronistic. On the introduction of functions to twentieth-century textbooks, see 4.6.2–3 below.

er), and being chaffed over being in love (one can learn the phrase *the fair sex* or *ehrliche Frauenzimmer* König 1715: 202).[32]

König's work is also worth pausing over for the insights it gives into teaching methods that were being used by a language teacher resident in London. (König describes himself in his preface as a *Sprachmeister* who had lived in London for about thirty years.)[33] As Hüllen observes, "King's special merit seems to be the bringing together of all these traditional ways of teaching in the sequence in which they appear. His is not a book on grammar, lexis, etc. but a text-book. This, together with the natural appeal of his style, may account for his success" (Hüllen 1995: 5). König notes in the preface to the reader that the fact that he is a non-native speaker of English is if anything an advantage, because he could not have his English *mit der Mutter Milch nicht einflissen* 'flow in with his mother's milk' (König 1715, Vorrede p. 8); and after all *Man kann unglaublich besser das jenige andern communiciren, was man ordentlich und bey mehrerm Verstand gelernet und begriffen hat* 'One can communicate to others unbelievably better what one has learnt and grasped in an orderly way and using more reason' (Vorrede p. 9) rather than if one had just picked up the language by habit. König notes that there are other methods to learn a language but is critical of all of them, including the method of learning by translating through a third language, or of teaching by showing (which he considers to be *miserabel* and *eitel* with adults ('wretched' and vain', p. 10 of Vorrede), or by going to the countryside out of London where one will only hear English, but which is no good because the dialect one learns will not be understood (a criticism of the 'direct' method). It is better to lay a foundation in London first. Still others want to hear nothing of grammar but would rather learn by routine – but they are 'those who abandon the easy, short and pre-cleared way through a thicket and want to find themselves another

---

32 Similar language, though less sophisticated, can also be found in Gonzaga's *The Eloquent Master of Languages* (Gonzaga 1693). Both König and Gonzaga's dialogues include implied criticism of those who make too many "compliments" (Gonzaga 1693: fourth page of the second Dialogue between two friends; König 1715: 198). Gonzaga's work, which was printed in Hamburg, is worthy of a footnote here as another work aimed squarely at the Grand Tour market; the author writes in his preface that "chiefly I have endeavoured to bring together what may serve most to the more fluent Instruction in the said four Languages" so that "with fundamentall rules taken from the best Authors of this time" [...] "as with the thread of Ariadne you may pass through the most principal Townes and Countries of Europe" (Gonzaga 1683: preface p. 2). *The Eloquent Master* presents a variety of material in the four "principal" languages (*Haupt-Sprachen*) French, German, Italian and English: there are grammars of French (in French, German and English in parallel); of English (in English, German and French), and of Italian (in Italian and German only), as well as assorted word-lists, phrases, two German-English dialogues, some "General rules of Vertu" (in English, German and French) and the Rodomontades in Italian, German and French. The one constant is German, and there is no grammar of German, so that – despite a multilingual title page – it is clearly for German learners.

33 König calls himself a *Sprachmeister*, a title which, Hüllen (1995: 7, n.14) remarks, "placed them in line with other teachers of practical skills, like riding, fencing and dancing (*Reitmeister, Fechtmeister, Tanzmeister*). They were altogether a different social category from professors." This may be so, but the differences between Offelen (who called himself a Professor) and König are not immediately evident from the texts that they produced.

way according to their own ideas' (*die jenigen, die den leichten, kurtzen und vorgebahnten Weg durch ein Gebüsche verlassen, und nach ihrem eigenen Sinn sich einen andern erfinden wollen* Vorrede p. 11). Like Offelen, then, this man who lived by teaching others was at pains to emphasize that "second language instruction does make a difference."[34] He calls his method *klahr, naturell und exact* 'clear, natural and exact" (Vorrede p. 12) and has a clear plan of progress. After two months, learners will be able to take part in conversations. After two [more?] weeks, they will be able to read papers with the help of a good teacher. After [a further?] six weeks, they will be able to "explain" an author (Vorrede p. 14) (recall the fables to be "read and explicated' in König 1715: 291).[35]

2.4 Conclusion

What do these works tell us about the teaching and learning of foreign languages in the seventeenth and early eighteenth centuries, and of German in particular? It is striking that the works discussed have little in common with the names from the sixteenth and seventeenth century who are commonly cited in surveys of the history of foreign language didactics, for example by Titone (1968: 8–16). This is perhaps not surprising since after all, those commentators were still commenting on how to teach Latin – this is the case with figures such as Roger Ascham (1515–1568), William Bath (1564–1614), and Michel de Montaigne (1533–1592). There are two exceptions in the seventeenth century, however, where some coincidence of ideas – if not influence – is worth noting. The two figures in question are the German Protestant educational reformer Wolfgang Ratke (1571–1635) and the Czech educator Jan Amos Comenius (1592–1670).

Wolfgang Ratke's reform agenda was not limited to language teaching, but one of his language teaching principles was a belief in a universal grammar underpinning all languages, and he was the author in 1619 of a "general grammar" or *Allgemeine Sprachlehr* for children (cf. McLelland 2005b; Ising 1959). As we have seen, that belief in a common, universal basis to all languages can be found still in Martin Aedler's general assumption that a certain amount of the target language will be obvious from a shared universal grammar (cf. Van der Lubbe 2007a: 145–194). On the other hand, another of Ratke's principles, his rejection of learning by heart, was certainly not adopted by Aedler. Any overlap in method with Ratke is likely to be largely coincidental, in any case, though it is not impossible that Aedler was exposed to broadly Ratichian ideas, for instance perhaps through the Pietist movement based in Halle (cf. Van der Lubbe 2007a: 70).[36]

The second exception is the Czech Jan Amos Comenius, cited by Titone (1968: 13) as a "pioneer of the 'direct method'" in language teaching – i. e. (broadly) teaching the target language *through* the target language. Comenius's *Orbus Pictus*, intended for the

---

34 That is the claim that applied linguistics of the twentieth century and beyond has also being trying to argue. Cf. for example the article "Second Language Instruction Does Make a Difference" of Catherine Doughty (1991).

35 It is unclear from the passage whether the periods of two weeks and six weeks are to be understood as following the first two months, or as being stages in the two months.

36 On Pietist educational ideas see Neumann & Sträter (2000).

teaching of Latin, envisaged a direct method of language teaching-by-showing using pictures (see e.g. Reinfried 1992: 41–47). König, as we have seen, was emphatically *not* a fan of such a direct method 'by showing', as envisaged by Comenius, or at least not for the adults who were his target market, for whom he considered it a waste of time. It is worth noting that König used onomasiological groupings of the kind advocated by Comenius, but it should be remembered that this practice had roots teaching back to Classical Hermeneumata (third century) or, in the British Isles and Germany specifically, to glossaries of the eighth to tenth centuries.

A third figure often cited on the topic of language teaching in the seventeenth century is the Enlightenment philosopher John Locke (1632–1704). He is therefore worth noting here precisely for the marked *difference* between his view and that of the experienced language teachers Offelen and König. Locke was an advocate of allowing the pupil to "pick up" the language from natural exposure in conversation, or – failing that – by reading, making as literal a translation as possible, and writing the Latin words over the top: "If grammar ought to be taught at any time, it must be taught to one that can speak the Language already; how else can he be taught the Grammar of it? (cited by Titone 1968: 16, citing Locke's *Some Thoughts Concerning Education* of 1683). Yet Locke was neither a teacher, nor surely anything like an average pupil in his ability – and furthermore his idea of literal translation with the Latin words written over the top is scarcely an advance on what we find in glossed elementary grammars of Latin centuries earlier (see Ising 1970). What is more, at the time of Locke's death there was not one book in German on the shelves of his library (of which two fifths were in Latin, and a fifth in French, the rest English (Proescholdt 1991: 93). Clearly his interest did not extend to German. The relevance of his remarks to the teaching of German is therefore marginal. Far more relevant, in fact, are the views of practitioners like König, discussed in 2.3. The history of reflections on language learning is not to be confused with the history of teaching practice.

Rather, the early history of texts for the study of GFL in the UK over the first century of its existence, from 1617–1715, can be summarized as follows:

1. The history begins with Minsheu (1617), a scholarly but word-based comparative approach, where the aim was probably and the outcome was certainly at most an awareness of the equivalent of English words in German (and other languages) for the purposes of academic study, not fluency in speaking.
2. The inclusion of German in Minsheu's *Guide* was followed two decades later by the addition of German to a 1639 London edition of Barlement's colloquies, but the very first text devoted to German for English learners exclusively is Aedler (1680), which is evidence of an interest in learning German that was still rather scholarly than practical, albeit now in a format that would at least be recognizable in the European tradition as a text through which one might conceivably learn a language, a grammar. Despite the scholarly discussions, there are some clear efforts to aid learning: by avoiding black letter; by giving a guide to pronunciation that might give the learner the general idea even if a teacher was not there; by including key idioms, not forgetting some very down-to-earth ones; and by devoting some space to the socially cru-

cial question of correct forms of address, possibly for the very first time in GFL. Finally, Aedler's grammar – drawing on, but then making more didactically useful, a current dominant theoretical notions (in this case the rootword) – is the first example of a long history of fruitful exchange between theoretically sophisticated grammars of German and practical teaching grammars for foreign learners.

3. Offelen (1687) marks the beginning of a much more practical and less scholarly approach. Offelen is the first writer of GFL materials whose experience in teaching seems to shine through, despite some errors: he uses a combination of grammar accessibly explained in the mother tongue (assuming no prior knowledge of grammar, yet taking for granted its importance) with simple parallel dialogues on everyday topics. Significantly, Offelen drew on a Humanist pedagogical tradition for teaching Latin – the use of "signs" to recognize parts of speech – to teach a vernacular language to adults. Meanwhile, alongside new headway in grammatical exposition, the dialogues – particularly the long-lived of exchange on buying cloth – continued a tradition in GFL that reaches back into the Middle Ages (and indeed centuries further still in foreign language learning more widely in Europe). Offelen's work also demonstrates how foreign-language grammars may arrive at clearer explanations than those produced by the native expert grammarians: in his presentation of pronouns, prepositions, the passive, and word order, Offelen was actually ahead of the German native tradition of his time. We shall in Chapter 5 see that this phenomenon can be found again and again in the history of German grammatography.

4. Finally, the expansion of German as a Foreign Language into the training of gentlemen on their Grand Tour is attested by the very different language modelled in König (1715). There are two points of interest here. First, on method, if König's text was used for learning German at all, then it can only have been the parallel conversations in German and English that were of any use to English learners – which could mean, if they did not have access to a grammar, that their method of learning was not a whit further advanced on the earliest glosses we have recorded from eight hundred years earlier. More importantly, on the language, we must note that the care with which different functions of language are identified – from insulting to paying compliments – shows that Anglo-German cultural exchange had gone beyond the mere desire to achieve a basic level of understanding, and now required pragmatically successful communication in socially varied and complex situations, including avoiding faux pas such as too much "complimenting".

Taken all together, the first century or so of materials for English speakers to learn German are evidence of interest in German i. as a language to be studied by scholars in comparison with others; ii. as a language for practical everyday communication; and iii. as a highly differentiated language as a social tool and an expression of one's class. There is not yet a hint of interest in German "high" culture, however. That was to come in the later decades of the eighteenth century, as we shall see in Chapter 3.

Chapter 3 –
Learning and teaching German in the 'long' nineteenth century

3.1 Introduction

The 'long' nineteenth century was defined by Erich Hobsbawm as stretching from the French Revolution to World War I (1789–1914). In the history of linguistic ideas, we might choose a slightly different timespan: from William Jones's speech to the Asiatic Society in Calcutta in 1786 (in which Jones first pointed out the connection between Sanskrit and the Germanic and Romance languages, thus laying the foundation for historical-comparative Indo-European philology), to the posthumous publication of Ferdinand de Saussure's *Cours linguistique* (1915), a milestone in the synchronic study of language. Such developments in linguistics did impinge to some extent on what children – initially still mainly boys – learnt in the language classroom of the nineteenth century. In the history of teaching and learning modern languages, meanwhile, the long nineteenth century can be summed up as the century of the institutionalization of the subject. For German, we might reasonably define it as stretching from 1775 to 1918: from the first Chair of German (founded at Trinity College, Dublin, in 1775; cf. Raraty 1966) to the introduction of a spoken language element in School Certificate examinations which – after a century of largely different priorities – marked a new valuing of the spoken language in the early decades of the twentieth century: 1888 for the Cambridge Syndicate's short-lived commercial language examinations, but only 1902 for the Syndicate's standard school examinations. Or, if we look instead at the materials with which learners were presented, we might argue for 1774 to 1899: from the earliest textbook recommendations of German literature, marking a decisive change in how German was viewed in Britain (Wendeborn 1774), to the appearance of phonetic script in a British textbook of German (Rippmann 1899), one of the very obvious effects of the new, synchronic study of speech – speech science – on the practice of language learning and teaching. However defined, it is this long nineteenth century, broadly, that is the subject of this chapter. Below, however, I begin with an overview of developments in the eighteenth century.

3.2 The eighteenth century – before the institutionalization of German

The earliest known reference to a language school teaching German dates from 1748 (Sir Balthasar Gerbier's Academy in Bethnal Green, London), even if French, Italian and Spanish were clearly already better established (Proescholdt 1991: 94). By 1748, as Blamires notes, "Great Britain had had kings of German birth and language for some thirty-odd years", since George I had inherited the crown in 1714 after the death of Queen Anne. Blamires claims that German was already "coming to be thought of as a language of culture and not merely utility" (Blamires 1990: 103) on the strength of this royal connection, but the evidence for that claim is uncertain. True, Johann König's *A royal compleat grammar, English and German* (1715) had already been dedicated to the husband of the future Queen Anne, but the fact that the House of Hanover ruled Britain from 1714–1837, did not, in Glück's view, make German and the Germans "more popular" (2002: 329). Similarly, evidence gathered by Percy (2012) suggests that George's first priority in England was English: he seems to have pressured his German bride Charlotte to learn English as swiftly as possible, beginning with their marriage ceremony in that language, a language she did not yet speak (Percy 2012: 286); English was clearly the dominant language of their children, and although they were all taught German, the King noted the Prince of Wales' imperfect study of German (Percy 2012: 290).

In fact, the first statements in praise of the culture of German date not from the start of the Hanoverian period, but from the 1770s, and it is telling that Boehning's documentation of the reception of German literature in England begins only with the 1760s (Boehning 1977). At any rate, it is true that there was a growing interest in German, reflected both in an increase in the number of texts produced for learners, and in the fact that they start to run into more than one edition. That interest may have ben assisted to some extent by the fact that Britain was now ruled by German kings, but certainly also the growth in popularity of the 'Grand Tour' meant there were far greater numbers travelling between Britain and Germany (though with Italy typically as the ultimate goal), increasing both the number of intercultural contacts and the numbers of those with the desire, leisure and resources to learn some German.[1] Indeed, in Ireland, the first University Chair of German in the world, at Trinity College, Dublin, was founded in 1775 to help reduce the expense of the Grand Tour, so that "young gentlemen of Fortune [are able] to finish their education at home" (Raraty 1966).

The first generation of textbooks of German after the ascent of George I to the throne were very similar to what had gone before. When Benedictus Beiler, who, as the Clerk to the German Church in Trinity Lane, London, had taught small numbers of private learners, published a grammar with accompanying dialogues (Beiler 1731, 1736), it remained very similar in general layout to Offelen's work of nearly half a century earlier.

---

1   It seems likely too that the increased number of Germans resident in Britain, especially London, might also have played a role in raising the profile of the language. In London there were, by 1800, between 16,000 and 20,000 German speakers, which – when one considers that Berlin had only 80,000 inhabitants and Cologne more like 40,000 – is a significant population (Jefcoate 2000: 27).

Its greatest point of interest is that it contains a dialogue which seems first to have appeared in Thomas Lediard's *Grammatica Anglicana Critica* (1725), and which deals with the practicalities of language learning before the institutionalization of the subject.[2] Since it is the earliest and most explicit discussion of language learning that would have been available to English learners of German, Beiler's version of it bears reproducing here (below, Figure 3.1). For a learner who could read with indifferent pronunciation, who knew the formation of the auxiliaries and regular verbs, and who had learnt the irregular verbs by heart ("a good thing", apparently), Beiler's (or Lediard's) language instructor recommended 16 hours a month, at a cost of two ducats per month,[3] with the first half hour spent reading modern comedies, where one will encounter the "most concise, beautiful and expressive phrases", "and explaining at the same Time" (a method which recalls the fables to be "read and explicated" in König 1715). The second half of each lesson was to be spent learning grammar and syntax ("Etymology and Construction of the different Parts of Speech"), as well as correcting independent work. That work would consist first in learning the vocabulary, then the phrases, and then the dialogues, as well as learning grammatical rules with their examples, before proceeding to translation into the target language. Here, then, we seem to have a half-way house between earlier methods – which, to judge from the books on the model of Offelen, appear to have viewed grammar and conversation as the twin pillars of language learning – and later methods that were to place far more emphasis on reading and translating written prose. For comparison, it is worth noting that around this time John Tompson's *English Miscellanies,* "Pieces in Prose and Verse, taken out of some of our best Authors",[4] were published for the benefit of German learners of English and enjoyed great success, with four editions between 1737 and 1766, evidently catering to a similar desire for suitable reading material for learners (Finkenstaedt 1992).

Twenty years after Beiler, John Bachmair's grammar (1751, 1752, 1771; American editions 1793, 1811) marked a decided step further towards encountering German as a literary language, even if Carr's assessment of the grammar itself was that it is "despite its popularity […] woefully inadequate" since "Bachmair is […] a century behind the times", showing little advance on the *Minerva* or on Offelen's work in many areas (Carr 1937: 470).[5] As well as idioms, proverbs, and sample personal and commercial correspondence, Bachmair gave greater emphasis to reading connected prose, including short extracts from German news-

2 The dialogue is printed in facsimile in the preface to Konrad Schröder's edition of Viëtor (1882) (Schröder 1984: 11–16, who notes p. 42 that similar dialogues can be found in the late seventeenth and eighteenth century), and it is also discussed elsewhere by Schröder. See Klippel (1994: 88).

3 Two ducats, or around 9s 4d in 1725, would equate to about £29.70 (RPI) or £379 (average earnings) in today's money. Using the average earnings comparison, £379 for 16 hours would work out at over £23 per hour today – at the lower end of today's private tutoring market. My thanks to David J. Appleby for this information.

4 Thus Tompson's own description in a report cited by Finkenstaedt (1992: 62).

5 Carr made two exceptions to this damning judgement: Bachmair was the first Anglo-German grammar to give an account of the subjunctive, and he deserves considerable credit for his treatment of word order, where he gave "accurate and well-arranged rules for the order of words, with copious examples". See Chapter 5 below.

The German Grammar. 283

Ich werde die Ehre gewärtig seyn.	I shall expect the Honour.

Das siebenzehnde Gespräch. — *The XVII. Dialogue.*

Zwischen einen Teutschen der die Englische Sprache lernet und seinem Sprach-Meister. — Between a German learning English and his Master of Languages.

Haben sie mich holen lassen / mein herr?	Did you send for me, Sir?
Ja / mein herr / ich hätte gern etwas Anweisung in der Englischen sprache.	Yes, Sir, I should be glad of some Instruction in the English Tongue.
Haben sie eine übrige stunde?	Have you a spare Hour?
Ja / mein herr / diese stunde / von 11 biß 12.	Yes, Sir, this Hour from 11, to 12.
Wie viel muß ich ihnen des Monahts geben?	What must I give you a Month?
Zwey Ducaten.	Two Ducats.
Wie oft kommen sie die Woche?	How often do you come a Week?
Ich rechne 16 stunden auf einen Monaht.	I reckon 16 Hours a Month.

O o 2   Ich

284   The German Grammar.

Ich will ihnen geben was sie fordern / ich bitte aber fleißig zu seyn.	I'll give you your Price, but pray be diligent.
Ich hoffe sie werden mit mir zu frieden seyn.	I hope I shall give you Satisfaction.
Wenn wollen wir anfangen?	When shall we begin?
Jetzund wenn es ihnen beliebig ist.	Now if you please.
Womit wollen wir anfangen?	What shall we begin with?
Können sie etwas Englisch.	Can you speak any English?
Ich habe vor einigen Jahren einen Anfang gemacht.	I made a Beginning some Years ago.
Ich bitte / lesen sie mir etwas vor.	Pray let me hear you read.
Wie gefält ihnen meine Aussprache?	How do you like my Pronunciation?
So/ so/ haben sie durch Regeln gelernet?	Indifferent, did you learn by Rule?
Ohne Regeln.	By Rote.
Ein gemeiner Fehler der meisten sprachmeister.	The common Fault of most Masters of Languages.
Wissen sie etwas von der Englischen Grammatic.	Do you know any Thing of the English Grammar?
Sehr wenig / ich kan nur die Verba auxiliaria	Very little, I can only repeat the auxiliary liaria

The German Grammar. 285

liaria repetiren / und ein Verbum activum formiren.	Verbs, and form a regular Verb Active.
Und denn kan ich die Verba Irregularia auswendig.	And then I know the irregular Verbs by Heart.
Sie haben einen guten Anfang gemacht.	That is a good Beginning.
Wissen sie etwas von der Syntaxi und dem Gebrauch der Casuum und der Temporum?	Do you know any Thing of the Use and Construction of the Cases and Tenses?
Gantz und gar nichts.	Nothing at all.
Noch von dem besondern Gebrauch gewisser Verborum?	Nor the particular Use of sundry Verbs?
Nein/ mein herr/ ich weiß nichts als was ich ex Usu gelernt habe.	No, Sir, I know nothing but what I have learn'd by Rote.
Nun ich weiß wie weit sie gekommen sind / kan ich mich desto besser darnach richten.	Now I know how far you are advanc'd, I can the better tell what Method to take.
Welcher Methode wollen wir uns bedienen?	Pray, what Method shall we make Use of?
Wir wollen die erste halbe Stunde im Lesen und zugleich	We will spend the first half of our Hour in Reading, im

286   The German Grammar.

im Expliciren zu bringen.	and explaining at the same Time.
Was für ein Buch soll ich lesen?	What Book shall I read?
Weil sie bereits was gelesen zum Theil verstehen/ sollen sie mit den neuesten Comedien anfangen.	As you already in part understand what you read, you shall begin with modern Comedies.
Da werden sie die kürtzeste / zierlichste und nachdrücklichste Redens-Arten der Englischen Sprache finden.	There you will find the most concise, beautiful, and expressive Phrases of the English Tongue.
Wie wollen wir die übrige Zeit anwenden?	How shall we employ the Remainder of our Time?
Die nöthige anmerckung/ über die Etymologie und Syntaxin der unterschiedenen Partium orationis zu machen.	In making the necessary Observations upon the Etymology and Construction of the different Parts of Speech.
Und bißweilen mit der Corrigirung und Examination dessen was sie in meiner Abwesenheit thun werden.	And sometimes in correcting or examining what you do in my Absence.
Was soll ich in ihrer Abwesenheit thun?	What shall I do in your Absence?

Lernen

The German Grammar. 287

Lernen sie erst das Vocabularium auswendig.	First learn the Vocabulary.
Als denn die kurtze familiere Phrasen.	Then the short familiar Phrases.
Diesen nach die Sprich = Wörter und familiere Gespräche.	Afterwards the Proverbs and familiar Dialogues.
Zuweilen die Regel der Construction, und derselben Exempeln.	At Times, the Rules of Syntax and their Examples.
Und darnach kommen sie zu der Übersetzung.	And then proceed to Translation.
Was soll ich übersetzen?	What shall I translate?
Einige kurtze Italiänische oder Frantzösische Briefe.	Some short Italian or French Letters.
Warum nicht Teutsche.	Why not German?
Weil die andern/ besonders aber die Frantzösische/ mit dem Englischen stylo epistolari am besten übereintreffen.	Because the other, especially the French, are more adapt to the English Epistolary Style.
Worin bestehet die Zierlichkeit des Englischen Brief-Styli?	Wherein consists the Beauty of the English Epistolary Style?

Das

288   The German Grammar.

Daß es kurtz/ natürlich/leicht/ kräftig/ und ausdruckend sey.	That it be short, natural, easie, pithy, and expressive.
Ich werde in allen ihren Raht folgen.	I shall follow your Directions in every Thing.
Ich will Morgen wieder aufwarten.	I'll wait on you again to Morrow.
Sie werden mich obligiren.	You'll oblige me.
Ihr gehorsamer Diener / mein herr. Adieu.	Your humble Servant, Sir. Farewel.

Das achtzehende Gespräch. — *The XVIII. Dialogue.*

Zwischen einem Medico und einem Krancken. — Between a Doctor and his Patient.

Ich habe mir der Freyheit bedient / meinen herrn holen zu lassen;	Sir, I took the Liberty of sending for you;
Und bin verbunden daß sie so gleich eingefunden.	And am oblig'd to you for your ready Attendance.
Das ist dj wenigste meiner Schuldigkeit.	It is the least part of my Duty, especially

Figure 3.1: Dialogue "Between a German learning English and his master of languages" (Beiler 1731: 283–288)

Figure 3.2: Bachmair (1771: 263–264)

papers (see figure 3.2) and sample letters (personal and commercial), with literal English translations (preserving German word order), and longer moral pieces (running to several pages, without translations) – as well as poetry (albeit simple fables, as in König 1715).[6]

Nearly contemporary with Bachmair's book, an anonymous *True Guide to the German Language* (1758) is a curious work. In one regard, it provided a welcome update on what had hitherto been available, for, as stated in the preface, its author largely followed the authoritative grammar of the German literary giant Gottsched (1748), whose *Grundlegung der deutschen Sprachkunst* had, despite its failings (cf. Jellinek 1913: 229–244), now replaced Schottelius (1663) as the leading authority in Germany.[7] In what it offered in addition to the grammar, however, it was similar in pattern to works of half a century earlier, and was itself rather a hotch-potch, with letters, as well as word-lists, dialogues and idioms borrowed from König, all supplemented, as an apparent afterthought, by a description of London in German, complete with a "P.S." that this "may serve the English Learner of the German Language to exercise his Skill in translating it into his Mother-Tongue" (Anon, 1758: 432).

---

6 Van der Lubbe (2008: 269) notes that Beiler "recommends the use of literature and particularly modern comedies as a learning strategy (1731: 286)", but her reference is to the dialogue clearly recycled from Lediard's text-book for German learners of English, so advocates English comedies to learn "Phrases of the <u>English</u> tongue" (my emphasis).

7 There were five editions of Gottsched's grammar between 1748 and 1762, and it was translated into Russian and French during his lifetime, and into Latin, Dutch and Hungarian after his death (Jellinek 1913: 244).

3.3 Why learn German? Changing motivations from the 1770s

The *True Guide* still emphasized the practical need for German: "It is to be wondered at, that the English have been so long without a faithful Guide to this copious Language, considering the extensive and advantageous Commerce they carry on with Germany, and the Necessity many are under to converse daily with German, of whom a vast Multitude reside in this Metropolis" (Preface, p. [1]).[8] A textbook by Heinrich Christoph Albrecht (1762–1786), published in Hamburg in 1786, made similar arguments: his preface still claimed that "the want of a Short German Grammar" was felt by Englishmen who were "chiefly induced by a commercial intercourse with the trading towns of Germany, to apply themselves to that language." After all, since the second half of the sixteenth century, English merchants could operate the trade routes between Germany and England no longer controlled by the Hansa, so that the English had by now certainly joined the ranks of those foreigners who had been learning German for trade since the Middle Ages (see Chapter 2.1). So, Albrecht tells his readers, his work is kept short, "calculated for the use of men of business"; and gives few rules on syntax, even though most grammars would contain twice as many "for a language that is not simple at all in its constructions". However, Albrecht was at pains to emphasize, "there is a vast difference between learning a language, to speak and to converse in it, and studying a language by the rules laid down in Universal Grammar.[9] The former is what the man of business does"; the latter, in Albrecht's view, was for the philosopher. With this remark, Albrecht was the first to comment explicitly on what has been a tension in modern foreign language study ever since – that between language learning as a practical skill and language learning for the scholar.[10] Apparently with no leanings to theoretical linguistics, Albrecht announces that "No book is ever read with more reluctance, than a Grammar; it is hardly read at all; the reader will pass by, what can be passed by." While "The Nature and Genius of a language may be explained by curious researches," Albrecht continued, "the speaking a language will be learnt by rote; and even to speak it right requires more of care and habitual attention than thorough knowledge of rules." For those who liked rules, Albrecht referred his readers to Adelung, "justly revered", whose German grammar had appeared in 1781 and had promptly superseded that of Gottsched.

---

8 This claim that there were no guides to German of course rather misrepresents the facts. The author does acknowledge Bachmair, at least, but considers him "deficient [...] in the precepts of pronunciation".

9 The reference to universal grammar in particular reflects the fact that the second half of the eighteenth century saw a blossoming of German grammars that tackled their subject as part of universal grammar (deemed to be common to all languages), ultimately under the influence of the universal grammar of Lancelot & Arnauld (1660), but beginning in Germany with the grammar of Johann Werner Meiner (1781), and also evident in Adelung's German grammar. See Naumann (2000).

10 Macht describes this tension as one between "realists" and "idealists" (Macht 1992: 111); the situation in Britain parallelled that elsewhere in Europe: cf. Macht's overview of the situation in Germany in "Practical skills or mental training? The historical dilemma of foreign language methodology in nineteenth and twentieth century Germany" (Macht 1994).

Like the *True Guide*, Albrecht's book contains both letters and tales in parallel German and English, but also a longer prose passage in German, without translation. In addition, an extract from "one of the best German comedies (that may particularly serve to shew the style of a familiar German discourse with all its Idioms) has been added, to exhibit a Specimen of a different German Style," namely an early version of Goethe's *Stella* (first published 1775, but reworked as a tragedy in 1803–1805, and published in that form in 1816). Albrecht was clearly putting into practice the suggestion in Beiler's grammar of 1731 (and Lediard 1725), that learners should read "modern Comedies" as good linguistic models (Beiler 1731: 286) – and it is surely no accident that the passage from *Stella* concerns the arrival of passengers at an inn, dealing with luggage, seeking food and accommodation, and incidentially also illustrates the different forms of address between intimates, strangers, and servants (see 5.7 below). Along with the practical value of the chosen extracts, though, Albrecht's learners were also being introduced to a leading German literary figure of their day. The key development in German studies in eighteenth-century Britain was without a doubt the process by which German was increasingly styled as a literary language alongside French.

3.3.1 Learning German as a language of literature

Gebhard Wendeborn (1742–1811), Minister for the German chapel on Ludgate Hill, was the first to treat German explicitly as a language of literature and culture (but still using Gottsched's rather than Adelung's grammar).[11] In the preface to his *Elements of German grammar* (1774), Wendeborn commented that "[T]he Germans have lately made great improvements, both in their language and their manner of writing" (1774: [1]), so that even the French were now taking an interest in their literature, and the English would no doubt follow suit:

> The French, who in general are thought to be rather partial to their own productions, have lately begun to study the German language, and to think favourably of German literature; against which they formerly entertained great prejudices. Among the English the German has been hitherto very little known; but there is reason to expect, that within a few years, even in this country, so famous for the improvement and patronage of the arts and sciences, the language and the literature of the Germans will no more be looked upon with indifference.

(Wendeborn 1774: viii)

Like Albrecht (1786), Wendeborn seems to have believed that over-long grammars had contributed to putting learners off German ("It is true, the language has its difficulties [...] Voluminous grammars have also contributed to deter people from learning it", p. ix), so that Wendeborn kept his grammar comparatively short, at just 158 pages. Unlike Albrecht, however, Wendeborn deliberately omitted dialogues and vocabulary,

---

11 As an example of Wendeborn's debt to Gottsched, Wendeborn follows him in his remark that *die grossen Männer* is correct, rather than South German *die grosse Männer* (Carr 1935: 493).

"since they are not constituent parts of grammar", but noted that if his grammar were well-received, he would write a short practical grammar with exercises added, as a certain Louis Chambaud had done for French.[12] In keeping with the growing interest in German culture, Wendeborn's 1774 edition reproduced two chapters of Tacitus's *Germania* in German and literal English translation (pp. 143–148): "[t]o show the difference between German and English Construction, I shall give here a mere literal and grammatical translation of the first two chapters of the Treatise of TACITUS, on the situation, customs and people of Germany" (1774: 143); it was followed by "A specimen of German print. Gellert's lectures on morality" (1774: 149–152).

A revised edition of Wendeborn's grammar in 1790 did indeed integrate some dialogues of the pattern familiar since Offelen as "A Practical Part of Grammar, to facilitate the learning of the language" (1790: 165–187, here 165).[13] These were supplemented by further reading: an extract from *Der Freigeist* by Lessing (1749) (Wendeborn 1790: 185–192); an extract from Gellert, *Moralische Vorlesungen* (1770) (as already in 1774, but with a different passage selected, 1790: 193–196); letters in German (which Wendeborn had translated himself from the English *Spectator*) (1790: 197–201); and poetry: two verse fables by from Gellert (in German, with vocabulary given as footnotes), and one by Friedrich von Hagedorn (1708–1754), taken from *Oden und Lieder*, book 5 (1757, posthumous). Wendeborn's choice of Gellert in particular here reflects the early reception of German writings in England. Searching the English short-title catalogue, the online national bibliography for the English-speaking world to 1800, for the terms "German" and "translated" yielded no relevant entries at all for the period 1740–1800 that were printed in the UK, and just 24 printed in Germany, the earliest of which are a translation of a work on German commercial correspondence (Smith 1768) and a medical work (Madai 1784). The remaining 22 entries – which do include works by Goethe and Schiller – all date to the 1790s.[14] But Gellert was already being translated from the 1750s; Klopstock, Gessner and Jerusalem all from the 1760s; Wieland from the 1770s.[15] – Render (to

---

12 Chambaud published several popular works for learning French, including *The Treasure of the French and English Languages* (1750), and *Elements of the French Language* (1762), which presumably provided the inspiration for Wendeborn's own title.

13 The topics covered in the dialogues are: 1. the arrival of a foreigner in London; 2. on London; 3. a conversation between some friends (health, weather, tea); 4. on dress (with tailor and hatter); and 5. on letter-writing. Incidentally Wendeborn also switched in 1790 to German type, evidently with some reluctance as he had deliberately not used it in 1774. He commented in the preface (p. 2) to the 1790 edition that since many wished to have the book in the "common German types", "I have, after some hesitation, thought proper to submit to it". His recommendations for reading highlight two authors whose works were available printed in Roman type, Gesner and Kleist.

14 Jefcoate (2000: 32, n. 32) lists some of the earliest translations of German works from 1795 onwards.

15 Jefcoate (2000: 27) points out that a search of the *English short Title Catalogue* using the search terms "High Dutch" or German, and "translated" yields some 800 titles, but that he would expect the number of English works translated into German by that date to be ten times as large, for the reception of English works in Germany had started some decades earlier and was correspondingly more intensive at this time. However, since many items that are translated from German do not come up in the ESTC under the search term "translated", Jefcoate's figure may be misleadingly low.

whom I turn below) wrote in the preface to his grammar that "among persons of taste", Gellert "will always be much admired" (Render 1799: vi).

Wendeborn's grammar was reviewed in 1775 in the *Critical Review* (reprinted in Boehning 1977, Vol. I, 266), and the reviewer commented, "As German literature is at present of much greater consequence than is commonly apprehended, we join with the author in wishing, that it were more attended to, and that this Grammar may be an inducement and a help to the study of it, for at present we know scarce anything of it, excepting through the medium of French translations."[16] Of particular interest in this climate of hunger for German literature is Wendeborn's "Catalogue of Some of the best German modern writers" (1774: [153]-[156]), which he updated and expanded in a volume of *Exercises* published separately to accompany the third edition of the grammar (Wendeborn 1797: 196–200; see Table 3.1).[17] The catalogues are headed as follows: 1774: "A Catalogue of some of the Best German Modern Writers, Whose Work, on account of the Purity and Elegance of the Style, will improve the reader in the Language, and at the same Time afford him some agreeable Entertainment. They may be had, together with a Variety of other Books, in various Languages, of C. Heydinger, Bookseller, No. 274, Strand." 1797: "A Catalogue of some modern German books. Without reading some of the best books, that are published by esteemed authors, in their native language, it is impossible to acquire that difficult art of writing and speaking a foreign language, with propriety and elegance. I shall, therefore, here subjoin a small catalogue of some modern German books, whose authors have acquired celebrity. Many of them are, at this time, still living; and some, whom I have mentioned, though they are of a more remote date, will, however, in my opinion, never lose their merit. – The books mentioned are in Octavo, and some of a smaller size." The small size presumably made them relatively affordable. In view of this long list of practical recommendations, Guthke's criticism of Wendeborn for not including literary excerpts himself seems harsh. Guthke claims that Albrecht's readers (whom Guthke characterizes as *englische[n] Kaufleute in deutschen Territorien*, "English merchants in Germany territories", since the book was published in Hamburg), would have received a more literary education than Wendeborn's pupils – recall that Albrecht included an extract from Goethe's *Stella* (Guthke 2011: 176). Many of the items in Wendeborn's list have an explicitly religious, devotional or moral subject, in line with Jefcoate's observation that it was German views on religious matters, especially Protestantism and the Pietist movement, that most influenced English-language culture

---

16 An article in the *Speculator* (1790, reproduced in Boehning 1977: Vol. I: 282–288) likewise lamented the lack of attention paid to German literature thus far, blaming it both on bad early translations and on "an idea of the difficulty almost insuperable, annexed to the acquisition of the language of the Germans", which together have "tended to produce an indifference to their literature". (Recall Philip Sidney's complaint that German had "all kinds of difficulties" cited in Chapter 2.1 (and by Glück 2002: 33). The author notes that "Fortunately for the extension of English letters, these opinions have not been mutual. The language of England makes in Germany a part of education, and is even regularly taught by the professor of an university" (Boehning: 1977: Vol. I, 285).

17 First noted by Van der Lubbe (2007: 149).

in the eighteenth century (Jefcoate 2000: 27).[18] Over half of the authors whom Wendeborn listed were still alive at the time Wendeborn was writing. They included Goethe (aged 48 in 1797) and Schiller (aged only 38), both new additions in the 1797 list.

Table 3.1: Wendeborn's recommendations for reading in German (1774, 1797)[19]

1774	1797	Periodicals recommended
Y	N	*Bibliothek (die Allgemeine Deutsche)*; "the Universal German Library, being a Review of all the new German Publications. 21 vol. 8vo. Berlin, 1765–74 (is continued)"
Y	N	*Bibliothek (die), der schönen Wissenschaften und freyen Künste*; "the Library of Belles-Lettres and liberal Arts, a periodical Work; 12 vols. 8vo, 1768–74 (is continued)."
Y	N	*Der Gesellige*, the sociable Man, a weekly Publication. 6 vols. 8vo Halle, 1764.
Y	N	*der Jüngling, eine moralische Wochenschrift*; the young man, a Moral Weekly Publication; containing Miscellaneous Pieces, completed in 2 vols, 8vo. Königisberg, 1768.
Y	N	*Der Mensch*; the Man, a weekly Publication, 12 vols. 8vo. Halle, 1767.
Y	N	Unzer, Johann August (physician, 1727–1799*), der Arzt, eine Medicinische Wochenschrift*; the Physician, a Medical Weekly Publication, completed in 6 vols. 8vo. Leipzig, 1770.

1774	1797	Authors recommended
Y	Y	Abbt, Thomas (philosopher and writer, 1738–1766). [1774] *Vermischte Werke* "Miscellaneous Works: containing, an Essay on Merit; on the Death for One's Native Country; a Fragment of the History of Portugal; and Familiar Letters; 3 vols. 8vo. Berlin 1768–1771. [1797]: *Vermischte Werke*, Berlin. 1790. "The first volume contains a treatise on Merit, which has met with a most favourable reception."
N	Y	Bartels, Johann Heinrich (mayor of Hamburg, lawyer, travel-writer, 1761–1850). *Briefe* über *Calabrien und Sicilien*, 3 Bde., Göttingen 1787–92.
N	Y	Beckmann, Johann (technologist, 1739–1811). Beiträge zur Geschichte *der Erfindungen*, 5 Bde., Leipzig 1780–1805.

---

18 The only German items in Eton College library that date to before 1800 were, with one exception, all bequeathed by the theologian Nicholas Mann (*bap.* 1680?, *d.* 1753), who had attended the school. His bequest included a 1568 copy of Luther's Bible, a Latin-German-Polish dictionary, a Latin-Swedish-German dictionary, and Wachter's German-Latin dictionary (Wachter 1737). As in the previous century, then, interest in German seems to have been largely driven by religious interests – the only pre-eighteenth century German book held by Eton is a German work recommended by Wendeborn, Wieland's *Goldener Spiegel* (1772). I am most grateful to Rachel Bond, Eton College, for this information.

19 The life-dates and descriptions given here are taken from the NDB/ADB portal: http://www.biographie-portal.eu. The works named are as specified by Wendeborn.

1774	1797	Authors recommended
N	Y	Bürger, Gottfried August (writer, poet, 1747–1794). *Gedichte*, 1789, 3 Vols. "The author died about two years ago. His Leonora is translated into English."
N	Y	Campe, Joachim Heinrich (pedagogue and publisher, 1746–1818). "*Sammlungen von Reisebeschreibungen für die Jugend*, in many volumes. *Die Entdeckung von Amerika*, Braunschweig, 1791. 3 vols. *Theophon, oder der erfahrne Rathgeber, für die unerfahrne Jugend*, Braunschweig, 1790. Robinson der Jüngere, 1779, 2 Vols."
Y	N	Cramer, *Johann Andreas (religious writer, Lutheran theologian, 1723–1788).* Fortsetzung des Bossuets *Einleitung in die Geschichte der Welt und der Religion*; Continuation of Bossuet's Introduction to the History of the World, &c. 6 vols. 8vo. Leipzig, 1765.
Y	Y	Cronegk, Johann Friedrich Freiherr von (writer, 1731–1758). [1774] Works, containing Plays, &c. 2 vols. 8vo. Leipzig, 1757–72. [1797] *Sämmtliche Schriften*, Leipzig, 1762. 2 Vols.
Y	Y	Dusch, Johann Jakob (writer, 1725–1787). *Moralische Briefe zur Bildung des Herzens*, Leipzig, 1762. 2 Vols.
N	Y	Fischer, Friedrich Christoph Jonathan (professor of law, and cultural historian, 1750–1797). *Geschichte des deutschen Handels*, Hannover, 1793.
N	Y	Garve, Christian (philosophical writer, 1742–1798), *Abhandlung über die menschlichen Pflichten, in drei Büchern, aus dem Lateinischen des Cicero*, Breslau, 1792. 2 Vols. "This is an elegant and masterly translation, of Cicero's three books, *de Officiis*."
Y	Y	Gellert, Christian Fürchtegott (writer, 1715–1769). [1774] *Werke*. Works, containing Fables, Sacred Poetry, Lectures on Morality, Familiar Letters, Plays, and Miscellaneous Pieces, 8 vols. Leipzig, 1770. [1797] *Sämmtliche Schriften*, 10 vols. "Gellert's writings, of which there are many editions, will always remain classical, in the German language, in spite of those, who think them to be out of date and out of fashion."
Y	Y	Gesner, Salomon (writer, painter, illustrator, 1730–1788) [1774] *Schriften*; "Works, containing the Death of Abel, Idyls, &c. (N. B. Printed in Roman characters." 5 vols. 8vo. Zürich, 1770–1773. [1797] Sämmtliche Schriften, Zürich, 1775. 5 Vols. "Several of Gesner's writings are translated into English".
N	Y	Gleim, [F. W. error for J. W.?] Johann Wilhelm Ludwig (writer, 1719–1803)? *Sämmtliche Schriften*, 1780, 7 Vols.
N	Y	Goethe, Johann Wolfgang von (writer, 1749–1832), *Sämmtliche Schriften*. "Many volumes are published already, and perhaps many more are still to come. The sorrows of Werther have made this author known in England."
Y	Y	Hagedorn, Friedrich von (poet, 1708–1754) [1774] "*sämtliche poetische Werke*, Poetical Works: 3 vols. 8vo. Hamburg, 1769." [1797] "*Sämmtliche poetische Werke*, Hamburg 1769, 3 small vols. A specimen of his poetry I have given in my Grammar, p. 206."

1774	1797	Authors recommended
Y	Y	Haller, Albert / Albrecht von (1708–1777, writer, natural scientist, statesman). [1774] *"Usong, eine morgenländische Geschichte*; Usong an Oriental History, (N.B. This Work has been translated into English, by Desire of her Majesty.) 8vo. Bern, 1771." [1797] *"Gedichte*, Göttingen, 1762. They make only a small volume, but his poem *the Alps* and his Ode *on Eternity* have great merit."
N	Y	Hermes, Johann Timotheus (Protestant theologian, author of novels, 1738–1821), *Sophiens Reise von Memel nach Sachsen*, 1778, 6 Vols. "A romance very well written."
Y	N	Iselin, Isaac (historian, 1728–1782), *über die Geschichte der Menschheit;* on the History of Mankind; 2 vols. 8vo. Zürich, 1770. *Vermischte Schriften*; Miscellaneous Works, 2 vols, 8vo, ibid., 1770.
Y	N	Jerusalem, Johann Friedrich Wilhelm (Lutheran theologian, Enlightenment thinker, schoolman, 1709–1789), *Betrachtungen über die vornehmsten Wahrheiten der christlichen Religio*n; Considerations on the Principal Truths of Religion; 8vo, Braunschweig, 1770; *Sammlung einiger Predigten*; Collection of Sermons; 2 vols. 8vo, ibid., 1760.
Y	Y	Kleist, Ewald Christian von (writer, officer, 1715–1759). [1774] *"Werke*; Works (N.B. Printed in Roman characters.) 2 vols. 8vo. Berlin, 1766." [1797] *Sämmtliche Werke*, 1760. 2 Vols.
Y	Y	Klopstock, Friedrich Gottlieb (writer, 1724–1803). [1774] *Messias*; the Messiah, 3 vols, 8vo. Halle, 1760–69. [1797 adds] "This poem and likewise his *Death of Adam*, a tragedy, have been translated into English, many years ago."
Y	Y	Lessing, Gottfried Ephraim (writer, 1729–1781) [1774] *Lustspiele*; Comedies, 2 vols 8vo, Berlin, 1772. *Trauerspiele*; Tragedies, ibid. 1772. *Vermischte Schriften*; Miscellaneous Works, 8vo, ibid., 1772. [1797] "No less than thirty volumes of this author have been published after his death, but I would recommend, to a beginner, only his Comedies, and his Tragedies, which are published separately" (editions as above).
Y	N	Meier, Georg Friedrich (philosopher, 1718–1777), *Philosophische Sittenlehre*; Philosophical Lectures on Morality; 5 vols. 8vo. Halle, 1762–66.
N	Y	Meiner, Christian (cultural historian and polyhistor, 1747–1810), Briefe über die Schweiz, Berlin, 1790, 4 Vols. "These letters give a very entertaining and faithful account of Swisserland."
N	Y	Meißner, August Gottlieb (writer, 1753–1807), *Bianca Cavello*, 1785; his *Skizzen* (Sketches) 10 vols. 1786; and his *Alcibiades*, 4 Vols. are, among many other productions of this author, much read.

1774	1797	Authors recommended
Y	Y	Mendelssohn, Moses (philosopher, 1729–1786), *Phäden, oder über die Unsterblichkeit der Seele*, Phaedon, or on the Immortality of the Soul; 8vo. Berlin., 1760. *Philosophische Schriften*; Philosophical Writings, 2 vols. 8vo. Berlin, 1771. [1797 lists only the latter and adds:] "are written with great solidity and, at the same time, great accuracy of language."
Y	N	Miller, Johann Peter (Protestant theologian, pedagogue, 1725–1789), *Historisch-moralische Schilderungen zur Bildung des Herzens*; Characters, Moral and Historical.
Y	N	Mosheim, Johann Lorenz (Protestant theologian, historian, 1694–1755), *heilige Reden über wichtige Wahrheiten der Religion*; Sermons on various Important religious Subjects; 3 vols. 8vo. Hamburg, 1765.
N	Y	Posselt, Ernst Ludwig (historian and jurist, 1763–1804), *Geschichte der Deutschen*, 1789, 2 Vols. *Geschichte Carls des Zwölften, Königs von Schweden*; "likewise his *Geschichte Gustavs 3, Königs von Schweden*, are written in a fine historical stile, though, perhaps, too florid."
Y	N	Rabener, Gottlieb Wilhelm (satirist, 1714/1717–1771), *Satiren*; Satirical Writings, 4 vols. 8vo. Leipzig, 1770.
Y	Y	Ramler, Karl Wilhelm (writer, 1725–1798), *Lyrische Gedichte*; Lyric Poems; 8vo. Berlin, 1772; [1774 only:] *Lieder der Deutschen*; a Collection of the best German Songs, 8vo. ibid, 1769.
Y	N	Reimarus, Hermann Samuel (Protestant theologian, philologist, teacher, 1694–1768), *Gedanken von der natürlichen Religion*; Thoughts on Natural Religion; 8vo. Hamburg, 1766. *Allgemeine Betrachtungen über die Triebe der Thiere*, general Observations on the Instincts of Animals; 8vo. ibid. 1762.
N	Y	Riesbeck, Johann Kaspar (writer and translator, 1754–1786), *Briefe eines reisenden Franzosen über Deutschland*, Zürich, 1784. "These letters are translated into English."
N	Y	Salzmann, Christian Gotthilf (pedagogue, 1744–1811). *Carl von Carlsberg, oder über das menschliche Elend*, Leipzig, 1783, 6 Vols. "This is a good national romance, written by Mr. Salzmann, in which the character and the manners of the time are well sketched.
N	Y	Schiller, Friedrich von (writer, philosopher, historian, 1759–1805), *Don Carlos, Infant von Spanien*, Leipzig,1787. *Geschichte des dreißigjährigen Krieges*, 2 Vols. *Der Geisterseher*, 1789, "and several of his plays, are extremely well written."
Y	N	Spalding, Johann Joachim (Protestant theologian and philosopher, 1714–1804), *Predigten*; Sermons; 2 vols. 8vo. Berlin, 1770. *Von der Bestimmung des Menschen*; on the Destination [sic] of Man, 8vo. Leipzig, 1768.
Y	Y	Sulzer, Johann Georg (mathematician, philosopher [et al.], 1720–1779), *Theorie der angenehmen und unangenehmen Empfindungen*; Theory of agreeable and disagreeable Sensations; 8vo. Berlin, 1762. *Philosophische Schriften*; Philosophical Works, 2 vol. 8vo. ibid, 1770 [but not listed in 1797]. *Unterredungen über die Schönheiten der Natur*; Dialogues on the Beauty of Nature. 8vo. ibid. 1770.

1774	1797	Authors recommended
Y	Y	Uz, Johann Peter (poet, 1720–1796), *Poetische Werke*; Poetical Works, 2 vols. 8vo. Leipzig, 1768.
N	Y	Voß, Johann Heinrich (poet, 1751–1826), *Gedichte*, 1785. *Luise, eine ländliches Gedicht, in drei Idillen*, 1795, "is translated into English."
N	Y	Weber, Veit = Wächter, Georg Philipp Ludwig Leonhard (writer and historian, 1762–1837), *Sagen der Vorzeit*, Berlin, 1794. 6 Vols.
Y	N	Weiße, Christian Felix (writer, editor, 1726–1804), *Beiträge zum deutschen Theater*, a Collection of Plays; 5 vols. 8vo. Leipzig, 1767. [1794 mistakenly lists the name as Weise, Joh. W.] [1797 adds:] "*Sämmtliche Trauerspiele*, 3 Vols. *Comische Opern*, 3 Vols. *Lustspiele*, 3 Vols. *Neuere Gedichte*, 2 Vols. His *Kinderfreund* is a periodical paper, much esteemed."
Y	Y	Wieland, Christoph Martin (writer, 1733–1813) [1774] *Poetische Schriften*, Poetical Works, 3 vols. 8vo, Zürich, 1770. *Proaische Schriften*; Prosaic Works, 2 vols. 8vo. ibid., 1771. *Geschichte des Agathon*; The History of Agathon, (N. B. Is translated into English and French.) 2 vols. 8vo. ibid, 1770. *Die Abendtheuer des Don Sylvio von Rosalva*, the Adventures of Don Sylvio de Rosalva, (N. B. Is also translated into English and French.) 2 vols. 8vo. Leipzig, 1772. *Der goldene Spiegel; oder, die Geschichte der Könige von Scheschian,* the golden Mirror, or, the History of the Kings of Sheshian, 4 vols. 12 mo. Leipzig, 1772. [1797] "*Werke*, of which above a dozen volumes are printed, and, perhaps, as many are still to follow. Most of them may be had in single volumes of former editions, as *Sammlungen Poetischer Schriften*, 3 Vols, *Prosaischer Schriften*, 2 Vols. *Amadis*, 2 Vols. Agathon, 4 Vols. *Die Abderiten*, 2 Vols. Likewise his *Oberon – Idris – Musarion* &c."
Y	Y	Zachariae, Justus Friedrich Wilhelm (poet, 1726–1777) [1774] *sämtliche Werke*; whole Works, 9 vols. 12 mo. 1765. [1797] *Gedichte*, 2 Vols. *Sämmtliche poetische Werke*, 6 Vols. "They contain, among others, a translation of Milton's Paradise Lost."
Y	Y	Zimmermann, Johann Georg (physician, philosopher, 1728–1795), [1774] *Erfahrungen in dern Arzneykunst*; Practice of Physic, 2 vols. 8vo. Zürich, 1764. *Vom Nationalstolze*; an Essay on National Pride, (N. B.. Is translated into English.) 8vo. ibid. 1768. [1797] *Über die Einsamkeit*, Leipzig, 1785. "This work is translated into English from a French translation! [sic]. Several other works of this author are also translated."
Y	Y	Zollikofer, Georg Joachim (Reformed theologian, writer, 1730–1788), *Predigten*; Sermons, 2 Vols. 8vo 1769–71. [1797 cites a 1784 ed. of the same work, and adds:] "These sermons are justly esteemed."

In addition to this reading list, Wendeborn also recommended the grammars of Aichinger (1754) and Gottsched (1762), and dictionaries by Arnold (1770)[20] and Ludwig (1765). In 1797, the grammars were no longer listed, but in addition to the dictionaries already mentioned Wendeborn included a second edition of Adelung's dictionary (1797) ("This new edition is corrected and improved by the author, and it can justly be said, that this dictionary may rival any of its kind, among other European nations. – Mr. Adelung has likewise just published a very useful Abridgement of this greater dictionary, in 4 Vols."), and that of Ebers (1793–1794), "composed chiefly after the German dictionaries of Mr. Adelung and Mr. Schwan" (Wendeborn 1797: 199).[21]

The growth in prestige of German was very rapid from 1774 onwards – something which is documented by the steep increase in the reception of German literature in England, for which Boehning (1977) provides evidence, but so too does another catalogue for learners of German by a certain Reverend William Render, teacher of the German language at the University of Cambridge (according to Render 1799: x). Render published his own *Concise practical grammar of the German tongue*, based on his experience of teaching both at Oxford and Cambridge, and of teaching "fine families" in London for over eight years.[22] Like Wendeborn's, Render's grammar falls clearly into the group of those teaching German not for its practical utility, but for its intellectual interest. Lamenting in his dedication to his royal patron Prince Frederick (Duke of York and second son of George III), that "hitherto there has been no complete practical German grammar published in this kingdom", Render continued that "This is the more to be wondered at when it is considered that German is an original language, having no relationship to the Celtic; that it is one of the most ancient, the most copious, and the most energetic languages of the world; and that it has a particular claim to the attention of the literati in England, from its striking affinity to their own tongue" (Render 1799: v–vi).[23]

---

20 Theodor Arnold had also published a successful grammar of German for English learners in 1736, of which there were 16 new editions or adaptations up to the year 1838 (Klippel 1994: 168).

21 Although the history of lexicography is beyond the scope of this book, it should be noted that hand in hand with the growth in numbers of learners of German (and indeed of German learners of English), a number of German-English dictionaries became available, including Arnold (1770), Bailey (1783, 1801), Rabenhorst (1800), Noehden (1814 and later revisions, itself a revision of Rabenhorst), Lloyd (1836), Kaltschmidt (1837), and Flügel et. al. (1841).

22 Carr observed that in some sections – but not all – Render followed Wendeborn closely: his treatment of the noun is independent of him, but "the section on the verb simply repeats Wendeborn" (Carr 1935: 482). In the area of the noun, Render went his own way, presenting noun plural endings as quite separate from noun declension, and claiming "There is but one declension in the German language, and that very simple." Though Carr (1935: 491) patently considered Render's approach insanity, it is clear enough its own ways. In America, however, Charles Follen, whose grammar drew on both Noehden and Rowbotham, was critical of Noehden on certain points in the preface, including on the subject of his system of noun declensions (Follen 1828: xi), as well as his claim that Luther could be considered the father of the German language (vii). Three-quarters of a century later, Keane (1873) took up and discussed Render's approach in his *True Theory of the German Declensions and Conjugations*.

23 Render's praise of German as "original" (not related to Celtic), "ancient", and "copious" (i. e. having a rich word-stock) rehearses standard arguments made by German language patriots to assert

Notwithstanding the very eighteenth-century description of the language as "energetic", we are back in a sense to Aedler's scholarly defence of German as an object worthy of study.

In accord with this scholarly inclination, Render published in 1804 *A complete analysis of the German language, or A philological and grammatical view of its construction, analogies, and various properties*, which, as its title suggests, is decidedly more scholarly its entire approach (Render 1804, discussed below). Unike Aedler, Render could now state with confidence, "It is, I believe, generally allowed, that no country has produced a greater variety of Authors than Germany: and it is well-known that many of them have obtained a distinguished reputation in the various branches of literature" (p. vii). Render went on to name a good many writers, across many fields of endeavour, including the following (I have used italics to indicate figures who were also cited by Wendeborn): for philosophy, Johannes Kepler, Leonhard Euler, Gottfried Wilhelm Leibniz, and Christian Wolff; *Albrecht von Haller,* Friedrich Hoffman, Lorenz Heister, Johann Christian Polycarp Erxleben, Johann Georg von *Zimmerman,* and Lorenz Florenz Friedrich von Crell in chemistry and medicine; Samuel Freiherr von Puffendorf, Georg Püttner, and Melchior Dethmar Grollman in law and natural philosophy; Johann David Michaelis, *Johann Lorenz von Mosheim, Johann Joachim Spalding, Georg Joachim Zollikofer,* and Johann August Ernesti in Divinity and polemic criticism; *Christian Fürchtegott Gellert* and Johann Kaspar Lavater in morality, *Gottlieb Wilhelm Rabener* for satire; *Friedrich Gottlieb Klopstock,* Salomon Gesner, Gottfried August Bürger, Johann Wolfgang von Goethe, Ewald Christian von Kleist, Gottlieb Konrad Pfeffel, Aloys Blumauer, Christian Friedrich Daniel Schubart, and Count Friedrich Leopold Stolberg for poetry; and *Friedrich von Schiller, Gottfried Ephraim Lessing,* August Wilhelm Iffland, August von Kotzebue, and Johann Christian Brandes for drama. (Render, p. vii, refers the reader to "a catalogue of the best German writers at the end of this work", which, with over 130 names listed, repeats many of those given here (Render 1799: [227]–[229]; see Table 3.2).[24] Thus, Render concluded, "I think it will be obvious to every reader, that an acquaintance with the German language must be of great utility; in order to peruse the works of German writers in the original; to have, as it were, free and unconstrained access to the treasures of knowledge, which the industry of the German has successfully been accumulating for a considerable time" (Render 1799: viii–ix). As for Render's choices, Guthke suggests with some disdain that Render's recommendation of Kotzebue's *sentimentale und krasse Dramen* "sentimental and crass dramas" and works of the young Schiller (in places similarly flawed, according to Guthke) do not speak for Render's good taste; the educated elite of England were, according to Guthke, already screwing up their noses at such works (see Guthke 2011: 178 and 194, n. 45).

---

the status of German among the world's languages since the seventeenth century. See McLelland (2011: 220–226).

24 Unlike Wendeborn, who specified works and even editions, Render merely listed names under various headings. See also the list given by Render (1804: 349–51), which is much more extensive still, both adding names under existing headings and adding recommendations under new headings, including education.

Table 3.2: Render's recommendations by topic (Render 1804: 349–351)

Subject area (the order of subjects is that of Render himself)	Number of authors listed
Divinity, Polemic, Criticism	57
Reformation	4 (all sixteenth-century authors)
Ecclesiastical History	8
Moral Philosophy	20
Law of nature, Jurisprudence	24
Education	17
Astronomy, Mathematics	11
Geography, Statistics	17
Natural Philosophy, Natural History, etc.	28
Agriculture, Economy	6
Commerce, Manufactures, Police	5
Medicine	26
General History	22
Poetry	22
Drama	14
Miscellaneous Works	33
Writers on the German language	8
Novels	10
Antiquities, mythology	5
Politics	5
Travel	9
Military Publications	7
Freemasonry	5
TOTAL (in which those authors listed by Render under more than one heading are counted multiple times)	363

Noehden (1800) is the first textbook author who Guthke considers to have "finally" (*endlich*) made a serious attempt to do justice to the best literature of the period, with ten pages of short extracts from Wieland, Herder, Goethe, and Schiller, although Noehden removed the extracts in all later editions. However, it is George Crabb (1778–1851), apparently a teacher of classical languages at Carlisle House School,[25] and seemingly the first non-native speaker of German to attempt a textbook of German, whom Guthke

25 This according to Watson (1921: 694). A riding school was established in London in the 1750s at

credits with really introducing the best of German literature to his learners, in the first anthologies of German literature for English learners: his *Easy and entertaining selection of German prose and poetry. With a small dictionary, and other aids for translating* (Crabb 1800b) and the revised version, *German Extracts from the Best Authors* (Crabb 1811), which ran to eight editions.[26] The first edition, written by Crabb at the age of 22, began with a grammar; the following five sections offered fables, stories, letters, readings about "nature", and poetry, and seems to have been largely taken from pre-existing collections. The revised edition, though largely still taken from others' collections, shows signs of an improved literary consciousness and taste, but Guthke concludes that overall there are as many "lesser" author as there are great authors of the *Goethezeit*; Schiller is given most room, but no more than Kotzebue (Guthke 2011: 200, 207), who remains just as prominent as he was in Render's book.

Whether or not German learners were exposed to the "right" literature by Guthke's criteria, by 1832, Rowbotham (1832: iv) was able to declare: "The Germans hold so high a rank in literature, science and the arts, and their authors of eminence are so numerous in every department of human knowledge, that the study of their language has now become, not merely desirable as a matter of taste, but, in some degree, necessary to every person who has the slightest pretensions to an acquaintance with European literature." At the same time, too, "Its utility, in a mercantile point of view, cannot be doubted." By this date, German had begun to be offered in British public schools, as we shall see below.

3.4 Early evidence of German in schools, and the birth of the "exercise"

Render's assertion of the "utility" of German was, in 1799, about utility in a new sense, couched not in terms of travel and commerce, but within the framework of the needs of an educated elite. For parallel with the growing status of German as a prestigious language of culture, the end of the eighteenth century also saw German – along with French – becoming part of school curricula. Direct evidence of where German was taught before the 1830s is hard to come by. Although it appears that French was widely taught in private schools catering to the emerging middle classes, German seems to have been taught only in the so-called Dissenting Academies of non-conformist Protestant groups in the eighteenth century, where modern languages were taught alongside Latin, Greek, English, Mathematics and a science (Ortmanns 1993: 21, following Watson 1921: 694). The number of these and similar schools increased after 1779, when non-conformists were legally allowed to be teachers. Many other pupils would have learnt German with a private tutor.

Carlisle House in Soho, London. An 1820 image of Carlisle House School, Westminster Bridge Road, Lambeth, exists. I have been unable to ascertain any more about the school.

26 See Guthke (2011: 208–11). For a detailed account of what is known of Crabb's biography, see Guthke (2011: 181–185). The contents of Crabb's readers are discussed in detail by Guthke (2011: 185–208).

At any rate, the evidence of the textbooks themselves speaks for there being a market from the 1790s for materials that focussed on drilling grammar, so-called 'practical grammars', in the context of the Neo-Humanist approach to language learning as inherently valuable mental training.[27] Indeed, the term "practical grammar" in the title of Render's 1799 grammar work had an almost technical meaning, the very reverse of "practical" in the sense that one might have called eighteenth-century manuals like Offelen's practical. Macht (1986, vol. I, p. 19) equates the word *practical* in the title with an allegiance to the method of Johann Valentin Meidinger (1756–1822), whose "practical" *Practische Französische Grammatik wodurch man diese Sprache auf eine ganz neue und sehr leichte Art in kurzer Zeit gründlich erlernen kann* (1783) had set a fashion in modern language teaching.[28] The approach of Meidinger and his ilk must be seen in the context of a Neo-Humanist approach to school education at the end of the eighteenth century, according to which modern languages were now valued not as practical communicative tools, but only to the extent that they could contribute to the "mental training of pupils", part of the overarching aim of education to develop pupils' intellectual rigour; "every thought of promoting practical skills that might be of immediate use in everyday life had to be discarded. The sole aim of language teaching was to be the improvement of the mind" (Macht 1994: n.p.; cf. also Macht 1992). Certainly the word "practical" (*praktisch*) began to crop up in the titles of textbooks from the late 1780s onwards.

Render's "practical" grammar was typical of the genre. It included exercises after the exposition of each grammatical point, and this was the key innovation: pupils could now *practise* applying grammatical rules, rather than just memorizing and being presumed to thereby somehow absorb how to use them. In Render's book the exercises begin with an exercise in pronunciation, which takes the form of a dialogue (with parallel English translation) apparently from Kotzebue's *Die Verschwörung in Kamtschatka* (1791).[29] The tradition of the 'practical' grammar in the Anglophone German-learning begins a little before Render, with John Uttiv's *Complete practical German grammar* (1796; cf. Klippel 1894: 142 for the parallel phenomenon in German textbooks of English). In many ways Uttiv's work was very similar to its eighteenth-century predecessors, including for example sixteen dialogues, of which the eleventh is an abridged version of the Lediard conversation with a language teacher (pp. 310–388), but 'practicality' meant including exercises devoted to specific points of grammar. In this task Uttiv explicitly stated that he had "chiefly followed: and indeed often strictly copi'd" the "truly excellent" method of Meidinger (Uttiv 1796: Preface A2). For example, the first exercises, which are on the first declension, begin (p. 28): *The father of the master. The proprietor of the garden. The*

---

27 *Neo-Humanism* here refers to the German Humanism of ca. 1790–1840, which shared with international Latin Renaissance Humanism of the fifteenth and sixteenth centuries its focus on education as the formation of the individual, as well as the prominence given to Latin and Greek antiquity. Its founder was Wilhelm von Humboldt. See below, and Landfester (2012).

28 On Meidinger, see Kuiper (1961: 73–118).

29 August von Kotzebue was apparently "by far the most popular German author in London around 1800", and his dramas "dominated the London stage for a few seasons in the latter part of the 1790s" (Jefcoate 2000: 28).

brother of the gardener. the looking-glass of the sister. The chamber of the girl. The daughter of the mother. The sword of the governor. The exercise is followed by the nouns needed, listed in two columns, beginning: *The father, der Vater The master, der Lehrer.* Uttiv's exercises were judged by an anonymous reviewer in the *Allgemeine Literarische Zeitung* (Anon. 1797) to be fade[n]" ('dull'), and "ganz nach der Meidingerschen Manier" 'completely in the Meidinger manner' – interesting evidence that this practical approach had its critics from the very outset.[30]

Perhaps spurred on by Uttiv's 1796 publication, but at any rate in keeping with the 'practical' development in language teaching, Wendeborn – now living in Hamburg – also issued a book of exercises to accompany the third, 1797, edition of his grammar, responding, he said, to the "wish of many" for exercises "illustrating his Grammar and giving, to a beginner, an opportunity of putting the rules, which are laid down there, into practice" (Wendeborn 1797b: preface, p. 1). The exercises followed the order of the grammar (and the two works cross-reference each other), so that they were grouped by part of speech,[31] and generally alternated between German to be translated into English and English to be translated into German (for all the exercises require translation). Wendeborn apologized that the style of his exercises was not as "neat and elegant", nor as "connected and interesting" as in other types of writing. Rather, "[t]he author's chief aim was to combine, in each line of an Exercise, as many words as could be well joined, to elucidate the particular rules for which they were intended […]". Wendeborn did indeed contrive to string together lots of words in a single sentence, resulting in a highly stilted style. For example, an exercise on the definite article, to be translated into German, runs: "The cunning fox, that killed the hen of the poor woman, who sold the eggs to the wife of the butcher, has been seen near the cottage, which is not far from the meadow, where the cows and the sheep of the farmer are grazing" (Wendeborn 1797: 8–9). Besides requiring eleven definite articles which between them cover all three genders, singular and plural, and all four grammatical cases, this sentence plainly incorporates a good number of syntactical complexities that would be far beyond the reach of the learner at the start of studying the grammar. Similarly, the first exercise for translation into English (p. 7) runs: *Ein Habicht, der eine Taube verfolgte, sah ihr mit einem scharfen Auge nach, und schoß, von einer großen Höhe, auf sie herab: allein, ein Jäger rettete sie, indem er, mit einer Flinte, dem Raubvogel eine Kugel in die Brust schoß.* ("A hawk, which was chasing a dove, followed it with a sharp eye, and shot down at it, from a great height; but a hunter rescued it, by shooting the bird of prey in the breast with a bullet from his shotgun"). The sentence does indeed illustrate the indefinite articles in three cases, but, even with all the vocabulary supplied in a list below the sentence, its syntax would still have posed

---

30 Uttiv's grammar – unlike all the others since 1750 – did not contain any literature (Van der Lubbe 2008: 70), and the reviewer also noted this lack of materials containing historical, moral or factual matter, which would have been *unstreitig nützlicher und zweckmäßiger* 'indisputably more useful and to the purpose". Most of the review, however, is taken up with listing perceived Germanisms and other errors in the English of the grammar.

31 To be precise, syntactical points were also treated under the relevant part of speech, so that there are no separate exercises for syntax.

a considerable challenge to the beginning learner (with two subordinate clauses and separable verbs, for example, not to the mention the differences in idiom). While the addition of targeted exercises was an innovation, and the layout on the page was clear and generous, making them at least look manageable, little thought had yet been given to the grading of the exercises.

Render's exercises were scarcely more inviting than Wendeborn's. Like Wendeborn, Render's grammar proper began with the article, and Render's first exercise – combining both definite and indefinite articles – runs as follows, a nice expression of late eighteenth-century ideas about the solid foundation of the state: *Die Mutter, der Vater, das Gesinde und die Kinder machen in einem Hause eine kleine Gesellschaft aus, die durch eine gute Einrichtung den ersten Grund zur Wohlfahrt eines Staates liefert* ("The mother, the father, the servants and the children make up a small society in the house, which, through its good organization, lays the first basis for the commonwealth of the state." Render 1799: 20).[32] Not until John Rowbotham's grammar of 1824 did anything approaching the notion of "graded" exercises emerge.[33] In it, Rowbotham observed – in what would be a very fair assessment of Wendeborn and Render at least – that "the great disadvantage is, that, in most or all of those [grammars] which have been published, the first exercises begin with long sentences, which require the application of all the rules of syntax, and that, in some instances, more rules are requisite than the writers themselves have given". But "In this grammar, every rule or important note is followed by easy exercises, or by suitable examples; the exercises increase in difficulty by regular and almost imperceptible gradations, commencing with the articles and nouns, which are sufficiently difficult for beginners" (Rowbotham 1824: iv-v). The exercises are, indeed, more manageable, if rather dry:

> So, for exercise, decline.
> *der Bogen*, the bow. *die Tochter*, the daughter
> *der Bruder*, the brother. *der Vogel*, the bird
>
> (Rowbotham 1832: 9)

From around 1800, grammars of German for English learners come thick and fast. Only a year after Wendeborn's third edition of 1797, Franz Berg – based like Albrecht and Wendeborn in Hamburg, where he taught German and English – published his own contribution, acknowledging Albrecht's influence, though with no mention of Wendeborn. Faced with writers "of high repute", "pure in their diction and sublime in their style", yet "differing as well in those, as in the Orthography of their words and in the structure of their Periods and Sentences", and with even "eminent grammarians […] far from agreeing", Berg reported that he could do no more than follow the best authori-

---

32 The English translations of each word are given in footnotes to each word.

33 I have used the 1832 edition. The preface is dated Marlborough Place Academy, Walworth [in London], 1832. Rowbotham is also noteworthy as being one of the first textbook authors who was not, to judge by his name, a native speaker of German.

ties – in his case, "Mr. Adelung, as the first in the list of German Grammarians" (Berg 1798: iii–iv). Berg's appendix consisted "but of a few exercises", progressing from passages "taken from some German authors" accompanied by close English translation (a dialogue from Karl Friedrich Kretschmann (1738–1809) including such lines as "Who can eat, when such divine Symphony is performing?") and extracts from Johann Karl Christoph Nachtigal (1753–1819); then exercises entirely in German for translation into English (Nachtigal again, and Johann Friedrich Schink, 1755–1835); and, in a third set, passages in English for translation into German (Swift and Pope).

Henry Noehden – who had been living in England since 1793 – also took Adelung as his authority in his grammar of 1800, though he was not afraid to take issue with some of his pronouncements (cf. Noehden 1800: 9). In his grammar, with editions in 1816, 1818, and 1832,[34] and which Carr (1935: 483) called "the most important and most influential grammar published in this period", Noehden was at pains to emphasize in his preface that his grammar differed from its predecessors, though in overall structure it was entirely traditional, consisting of an *etymologia* arranged according to the eight parts of speech, and a syntax. It did, however, include a survey of the history of High and Low German, indebted to Adelung, and a very lengthy discussion of pronunciation (Noehden 1800: 28–78).[35] Noehden did not include any exercises specific to grammatical points, although he claimed to have only "practical utility" in view (p. 9), and his appendix offered extracts from Wieland, Herder, Goethe,[36] and Schiller (Noehden 1800: 419–427), "as conspicuous for their learning and genius, as they are distinguished by the purity and elegance of their language" (1800: 417), together with translations.

In a break with centuries of tradition in foreign language grammars, Render (1799) had dispensed altogether with a separate section on syntax, and merely noted syntactical points under the relevant part of speech as they were treated in turn. For example, the section on the adverb contained both notes on the *formation* of adverbs (with a list of common suffixes) and *syntactical* notes on their placement in the sentence. Combining information about the forms of parts of speech and about how to actually use them may

---

34 Other grammars that followed the "Adelung-Noehden tradition" according to Carr are those of John Rowbotham (1793?-1846, who, besides his German grammar of 1824, also published a French grammar); Bramsen (1834), whose account of the adverb Carr however considered "quite senseless" (Carr 1935: 494); Tiarks (1834); and Troppaneger (1836) (Carr 1935: 483).

35 From this point in the history of German learning and teaching it is no longer possible to discuss all the works published. Carr (1935) discusses the works of Wendeborn, Render, Noehden, Fischer (1819, devoted to the classification of the nouns only), Jehring, Boileau, Rowbotham, Becker, Skene, Klattowsky, Bernays, Bramsen, Tiarks, and Troppaneger. Guthke (2011: 198–99) also considers Wendeborn, Render, Noehden, Crabb and Troppaneger, as well as Schoeler (1830), Eulenstein (1839) and Apel (1840). Jehring's grammar of 1820 is notable as apparently being the first German grammar published in Scotland; otherwise it is chiefly memorable for Jehring's "many mistakes and inaccuracies", which "it would be risky to [attribute] to any reputable German grammarian", though on word order it represented an improvement compared to some of its predecessors (Carr 1935: 483, 498). Carrs's assessments are generally reliable, though inevitably incomplete. On the treatment of some aspects of word order in the history of German grammars, see 5.8 below.

36 Goethe and Noehden were correspondents; see for example Richter et al. (n. d.).

strike us as obviously sensible, but in doing so Render was breaking with a centuries-old tradition of treating forms and usage of parts of speech in completely separate sections (*etymologia* and *syntax*) – a significant innovation. Render also offered "some Extracts from our best writers, with an English translation, that the reader, by comparing the two languages, may be able to perceive in what respect their idioms differ" (Render 1799: 194). As for dialogues, which had been a mainstay of German grammars right up to Wendeborn (who had himself still felt compelled to add a few to the second edition of his grammar in 1790, after initially omitting them), Render was dismissive. They brought "more danger than utility", he believed, for the learner who relied on them would be either "trite and vulgar" or "bombastic and ridiculous" (1799: 194–195) – a damning assessment of the carefully constructed small-talk of the dialogues for those on the Grand Tour. Rather, one should learn viva voce from the teacher. Render therefore replaced dialogues with a few extracts from German authors (with translations, not quite literal) so that the reader "will be able to see the beauty of the German language": the extracts chosen are from Kotzebue's *Die Verschwörung in Kamtschatka* (1791), and Schiller's *Kabale und Liebe* (1784) and *Die Räuber* (1781) (Render 1799: 196–201; 202–219; and 220–226).

Like Render, George Crabb attached importance to reading. As we saw above, he published not only a grammar – which was a translation and adaptation of Adelung's grammar – but also a separate anthology, *An easy and entertaining selection of German prose and poetry* (Crabb 1800a, b). On the other hand, he also felt the need for *Elements of Conversation* (Crabb 1800c).[37] Crabb stated in his preface to the latter his belief that the "subject of language" could be divided into three: reading, composition, and conversation. The utility of conversation, Crabb underlined, was "not so much the learning by rote of the simple sentences which are given, as in collecting a stock of words, and of acquiring the faculty to combine other sentences more complex. This application of it is, however, seldom made in teaching, and never appears to be the object of any writer on this subject" (Crabb 1800c: [iii]). Crabb was – apparently without realizing it – reinventing the wheel, for his lists of vocabulary according to topic area and simple parallel sentences in German and English merely reverted to a tradition going back centuries, and were new only in being adapted to formal schooling (the work appeared under the publisher Boosey's heading *Books for the Use of Schools*). New too, though, was Crabb's idea of including some translation exercises: English dialogues to translate into German, using vocabulary lists supplied. Though this *could* have been done with the dialogues given in parallel from Offelen onwards, here it was explicitly required.

Such exercises are in keeping with Crabb's desire to produce English speakers who were able to read German to further their intellectual development. Crabb took an active interest in the question of education: his *The Order and Method of Instruction Children, with Strictures on the Modern System of Education* was published in 1801; in a

---

37 Crabb also published a *Neue praktische englische Grammatik* for German learners (Frankfurt, 1803), which, as the keyword *Praktisch* suggests, followed the Meidingder approach and was very successful; an eighth edition was published in 1850 (Klippel 1994: 169).

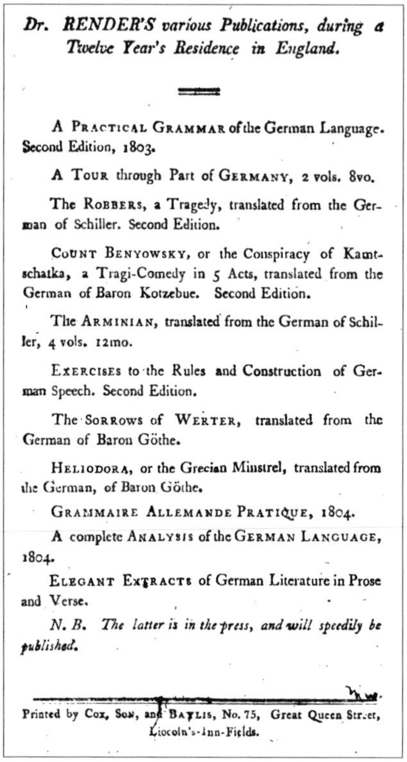

Dr. RENDER'S various Publications, during a Twelve Year's Residence in England.

———

A PRACTICAL GRAMMAR of the German Language. Second Edition, 1803.

A TOUR through Part of GERMANY, 2 vols. 8vo.

The ROBBERS, a Tragedy, translated from the German of Schiller. Second Edition.

COUNT BENYOWSKY, or the Conspiracy of Kamtschatka, a Tragi-Comedy in 5 Acts, translated from the German of Baron Kotzebue. Second Edition.

The ARMINIAN, translated from the German of Schiller, 4 vols. 12mo.

EXERCISES to the Rules and Construction of German Speech. Second Edition.

The SORROWS of WERTER, translated from the German of Baron Göthe.

HELIODORA, or the Grecian Minstrel, translated from the German, of Baron Göthe.

GRAMMAIRE ALLEMANDE PRATIQUE, 1804.

A complete ANALYSIS of the GERMAN LANGUAGE, 1804.

ELEGANT EXTRACTS of German Literature in Prose and Verse.

N. B. The latter is in the press, and will speedily be published.

———

Printed by Cox, Son, and BAYLIS, No. 75, Great Queen Street, Lincoln's-Inn-Fields.

Figure 3.3:
Render's works as advertised
in Render 1804: [352].

section "On Languages" he reflected on the degree to which "difference of language" is a barrier to communication, and thus a limit on our knowledge, for "The sentiments of others are more than three parts of our knowledge. How confined must the observation of any individual be, unaided by the rest of mankind! [...] The application of these opinions to the study of languages is evident. The substitute of translations is very imperfect. It serves to convey information, but it shuts the door against general communication" (Crabb 1801: 176–178, cited by Guthke 2011: 185). By practising translation, learners would ultimately, become readers of German, rather than translators, and so overcome the limits of that "difference of language".

With his separate grammar and exercises, Wendeborn was in the 1770s at the head of a new trend which is itself indicative of a growing market: the tendency for authors to publish multiple volumes, each offering different types of material. As already noted, Render, also published a separate volume of exercises an anthology of German prose and poetry (though I have been unable to locate copies of either) beside his practical grammar, and translations of two works by Goethe, two by Schiller and one by Kotzebue – see Figure 3.3), as well as a more scholarly German grammar (1804).

3.5 Reflections on language and method

Render was already teaching German at Oxford and Cambridge around 1800, and five years after his practical grammar of 1799, he also published a work that is the first since Aedler (1680) that seems intended for a more scholarly audience, *A complete analysis of the German language, or A philological and grammatical view of its construction, analogies, and various properties* (1804), a work that Render somewhat surprisingly dedicated to the 27-year-old Russian Emperor Alexander I, perhaps in recognition of the educational reforms he introduced – Alexander was also married to a German, Louise of Baden. Having conversed with "scholars", Render reported that "I found they all sincerely lamented the neglect of the modern German language at our public seminaries;

for they maintained, with the greatest confidence, that it was utterly impossible for an English writer to be quite pure in his native language, without having previously some comparative knowledge of the *Anglo-Saxon*, or *modern* German" (Render 1804: xix; emphasis in original). Elsewhere, he commented on the value of modern German as a bridge to studying the ancient, including "Maeso-Gothic" and Anglo-Saxon (p. xviii) – evidently the seventeenth-century English scholarly interest in German noted above in Chapter 2.2–2.3 had not abated. Render commented in the preface on "the uncommon popularity of German literature in England, which has increased to such a degree, as to render even the translation of a translation acceptable", echoing the comments made by the reviewer of Wendeborn's grammar that the English tended to encounter German literature via French (vii). Render hoped that the present work might "tend to render German literature henceforth read in their native dress" (viii). Not only was Render critical of translations of translations, he was also at pains to point out the dangers of an inadequate mastery of the language in those who did take the trouble to translate directly from the German, who "by making *one* small mistake, have at times perverted the sense of a whole translation" (Render 1804: xix). It was apparently not unheard of for language learners not just to use translation as a means to learn the language, but to go on to publish those translations: an extreme case of learning by doing whose results could be of very variable quality (see Klippel 1994: 52). Render went on to criticize a contemporary (unidentified) translation of Schiller's *Kabale und Liebe,* where the failure to recognize the double meaning of *Ihr* (your/ her) caused problems, and where the translator had furthermore added material "of his own fancy" (Render 1804: xxiii).

Render's 1804 work is also of interest for its philosophy of education, which smacks strongly of the Enlightenment. Of his method, Render commented, "The plan adhered to in the subsequent work is strictly conformable to the operation of nature; a progress which ought to be invariably observed in a grammar of any language whatsoever". The learner needed first to "be first grounded in the radical principles of the language which he is about to learn" (and not "extraneous details"). Render was therefore critical of the growth in popularity of the reading method: "It is, in fact, the same with extensive reading, where a quantity of information and of knowledge is accumulated and stored up in the mind without the power of arranging the various parts, so as to be adapted for those occasions in which it is requisite to be called into action. [...] In the present work, the learner will be led gradually from the most obscure (of what may be termed *animal articulations*) to absolute and clear ideas of rational signs of representations" (like a "new-born infant") (Render 1804: viii). Render continued:

> It may undoubtedly be said, that a new-born infant possesses the power of ex-pressing external sensations of joy, fear, or sorrow; his next progression is to articulate words; afterwards, in proportion as the powers of perception and com-bination expand, he next learns to unite those simple ejaculations into certain sentences or phrases, and thus regularly proceeds, till he becomes enable [sic] to embrace a larger sphere of ideal exertion and communicates his thoughts in appropriate language. Such is the progress of nature; and shall we, her children,

> in teaching her own method, presume to deviate, and build, by the shallow aid of metaphysical reasoning, a fanciful structure without any solid foundation?

(Render 1804: ix)

There are strong echoes here of the typically eighteenth-century German anthropological view of the evolution of language in humans as having run parallel to language acquisition that can be observed in the individual child – proceeding from inarticulate cries to words and sentences (cf. discussion and documentation in Neis 2003, including of course Herder). This very Enlightenment-inspired approach goes somewhat beyond what the explicitly philological title of Render's work might lead us to expect, but what is interesting is that Render did indeed – for the first time in the teaching of German as a foreign language, as far as I am aware – break with the absolutely standard tradition of ordering grammar according to the eight parts of speech, starting with the article. Instead, Render's 1804 work progressed from a chapter on the individual sounds ("Of Letters and their Sound"), to "the Formation of Words" (syllables, words and their derivation, then their composition and "junction" in sentences), and thence to the "Accent or Tone of Words" (Chapter III). This First Part was followed by a Second Part *Of Words, as Parts of Speech and their Flexions*, in which the parts of speech were treated in order in the usual way, and a Third Part, *Of the Syntax*, beginning "Of the Combination of Words." With the exception of Chapter II, the structure is not that revolutionary: it boils down in essence to the sounds followed by the parts of speech and a syntax – but the rationale is significantly different.

In his more scholarly approach to German, Render (1804) was joined by Daniel Boileau, whose *Nature and Genius of the German Language* (1820) was not a grammar, but a work dealing with questions of German style, and also begins to integrate findings from philology (mentioning the relationship of German to Greek and Persian as evidence for a possible Scythian ancestral language, p. 1).[38] Boileau also used the long-popular image of the German language as a tree with roots in order to extol its capacity for forming new and transparent compounds from existing roots. In asserting the superiority of German, as well as in the imagery and arguments used, the influence from Schottelius's image of the language-tree is still palpable two and a half centuries later.[39] The image itself – as used by Schottelius's disciple Kaspar Stieler on the frontispiece of his grammar and dictionary of 1691 – is in Figure 3.4:

---

38 On the so-called Scythian hypothesis, whose origins go back to the early seventeenth century, see Van Hal (2010b) and Considine (2010), as well as Metcalf (1974). Boileau is also of interest as the author of *The linguist: a complete course of instruction in the German language* (2nd ed. 1840), which took an inductive, reading-based approach to learning German. It begins by presenting one of Gellert's fables, and then commenting on points of grammar as they present themselves in the passage. The volume proceeds in the same way with further reading passages.

39 Cf. McLelland (2002) for discussion of the tree image in Schottelius's grammar of 1663, and McLelland (2010) for the long-lasting influence of the image.

Figure 3.4:
The German language-tree (a banyan or Indian fig-tree, with aerial roots descending from its branches so that the tree can spread out over a huge area), as shown on the frontispiece of Stieler (1691).

"The German language, although its affinity with the Greek and Persian languages seems to point at a common Scythian origin, is yet in every respect a primitive language. It has been aptly compared to a tree, which, having been transplanted with all its roots, has continued to thrive on its new soil, and increased the luxuriance of its branches and foliage, without having ever been grafted with any exotic twig. […] The German compound words are all formed out of these well-known roots of the language, without the interference of any other idiom; they are formed according to familiar analogies, and instantly become perfectly intelligible to the meanest capacity. It is this circumstance which raises the German so far above the English and the French languages."

(Boileau 1843: 3, 5)

Boileau pointed out that nine "compound verbs" could be formed from *greifen* by means of prefixes, while the corresponding English verb allowed none; likewise 28 verbs and corresponding derived nouns could be formed on the root of *setzen*, all of which are "immediately intelligible to the individual acquainted with the radical verb setzen" (Boileau 1843: 7). Like Render, too, Boileau pointed out finer points of German, for example the use of the article by comparison with English, with examples taken from literature.

By the dawn of the nineteenth century, then, German had undergone a rapid change in status in Britain, and the nineteenth century saw more dramatic changes. First, German had become recognized as a prestige language of great literature and philosophy as well as of the natural sciences. Second, German (along with the other modern languages) now found itself part of a Neo-Humanist school curriculum across Europe which privileged the study and explicit practice of grammar and the reading of great authors over "mere" practical utility of a modern language. With that, a tension between utility and intellectual worth was set up which continues in foreign language learning in the UK to the present day. Third, as a consequence of that inclusion of modern foreign languages in some kind of standardized education (rather than arrangements between private masters and individual learners), the first timid efforts were made to didacticize material, whether in the targeted grammatical exercises of Uttiv, Wendeborn and Render, under the broad influence of Meidinger; in loosely graded reading exercises; or, in Noehden, in efforts to arrange the material innovatively. Parallel to this, the grammarians also kept pace with developments in the native German grammatical tradition, turning first to Gottsched and later to Adelung as their authorities (cf. Carr 1935).

3.6 The establishment of German in schools and universities

The first third of the nineteenth century saw a continuing steady stream of German grammars, some of them at least continuing to follow the latest grammars published for native speakers in Germany, as Wendeborn had earlier followed Gottsched, and Noehden had later turned to Adelung. Amongst the eleven grammars discussed by Carr (1935) for the period between 1801 and 1836, Becker's (1830) was an English translation of his own grammar published in German a year earlier, and Klauer-Klattowsky (1831) was a manual for both French and English learners that was a "slavish copy" of Heyse's grammar for German schools (1816, 1822) (Carr 1935: 483).[40] We should also note the grammar of Karl Benjamin Schade (b. 1771), published in Leipzig in 1805 and again 1817; 1822, 1828), a very traditional and substantial (560-page) grammar that – beyond being in English – made few concessions to the English learner, beginning like Wendeborn with definitions of grammar and letters. Even Schade's English was uninviting, being rather Germanic in style: "Only to words, which have more than one accent, the verbal accent does refer" (Schade: 1828: 20). G. L. M. Strauss (1807?-1887), who in his memoirs called himself "an old bohemian" (1883), likewise published a grammar of the German language in London "adapted for the use of English students from Heyse's Theoretical and Practical German grammar" (1852), as well as a reader (1859).

The status of German – though historically always second to French as a foreign language – was enhanced, no doubt, by the example of Queen Victoria, who came to the throne in 1837. Queen Victoria employed a German governess for her own children, and that royal example meant that from the 1840s "an increasing number of well-to-do families in England wanted their children to be taught German by a native speaker (Hardach-Pinke 2000: 25). From the 1830s, it also became possible to learn German in an institutional setting too. Languages could be learnt at colleges for the training of governesses, including Queen's College (see 3.6.2 below). German began to be offered in major public schools; the first may have been the newly founded University College School (founded as part of University College London, established in 1826), whose prospectus issued in 1830 indicated that boys would "enter the German class" as soon as they were "sufficiently master of the French language"; the study of German was "introduced for the specific purpose of enabling the pupil to avail himself of the valuable assistance afforded by the labours of German Philologists towards the right study of Classical Literature", and five hours a week were to be devoted to French and German combined

---

40 Wilhelm Klauer-Klattowsky also published two literary readers for learners of German "[with] a translation of all unusual words and difficult passages and with explanatory notes" (1834, 1837). Like Boileau, Klauer-Klattowsky also touched on the resemblance between German and Persian, and quoted Voss' opinion, that Greek is derived from German. He also mentioned Gothic as "the mother of Franconian, Saxonic, and the Northern languages" (Carr 1935: 485).

in the third to sixth classes (Usher et al. 1981: 13). Others followed: Shrewsbury (1837), Harrow (1839) and Winchester, King's School Canterbury, Marlborough and Uppingham all following suit in the 1840s (Proescholdt 1991: 95; Ortmanns 1993: 28). Like Eugene Oswald (1826–1912), who took up the post of assistant master at University College School in 1856, teachers were generally still, as they had almost always been in the history of learning German in Britain, native speakers from Germany.[41] At Rugby, under Thomas Arnold, French and German were apparently even compulsory for pupils not taking a science (Ortmanns 1993: 27; see also Hope Simpson 1967: 7). In 1855 tests in German were introduced both for the Civil Service and for the Military Academy at Woolwich. (Woolwich had had German lecturers for artillery and fortification from the founding of the academy in 1741 until the mid-nineteenth century. Prussian field exercises were translated for use in Britain in 1757 and again in 1888: see Prussia 1757; Glünicke & Wood 1888).[42] German had been made compulsory at Wellington Military Academy (founded 1853) by the mid-1860s (Ortmanns 1993: 31–32). By 1858, German was sufficiently established – along with French – to be included in the syllabus of the University of Cambridge Syndicate examinations first offered to pupils in that year (see 3.8 below).[43]

3.6.1 German in higher grade elementary schools, and experiments in commercial German

In 1851, only 3.8 % of public day schools "catering to the poorer classes"[44] (though certainly not the poor) offered a modern language (Bayley 1989: 58). Meanwhile, the higher grade elementary schools (i. e. schools for the older and more able pupils who had passed the equivalent of Year 6, the end of today's primary education) began to offer German, once it attracted government funding from 1880 (French had been eligible since 1872). By 1894, the Bryce Report found that French was taught in virtually all 32 higher grade and organized science schools surveyed (listed in an appendix to the report), catering between them to 22480 children; eleven of the 32 offered German as well as French. These schools also entered children for the Oxford and Cambridge Local examinations, the College of Preceptors examinations, the University of London examinations and the

---

41 Oswald was, as Flood reports (2005), "tireless in promoting German literary studies and in fostering Anglo-German relations generally." After the retirement of Bernays from King's College London (see below), Oswald applied unsuccessfully for that Chair; he was a founder member of the English Goethe Society, established in 1886. See also Flood (2000: 243–44).

42 The numbers taking German for entrance to the Woolwich military academy were not large, however. For the period 1886 to June 1888, 49 of 360 successful candidates passed in German; for the period November 1888–1890, 125 out of a total of 325 successful candidates passed in German – in both cases about half the number of those who passed in French. See Ortmanns (1993: 53–54).

43 Examinations were offered at two levels, for those under the age of 16 (Junior), and for those under the age of 18 (Senior), by the University of Cambridge Local Examinations Syndicate from 1858. Similar examinations for school pupils were introduced by the University of Oxford Delegacy of Local Examinations in the same year. See Watts (2008).

44 The student body at higher grade schools would usually consist of "a few pupils from well-off families, the rest from the ranks of skilled workers, minor professionals, and tradesmen" (Bayley 1989: 59).

like (Bayley 1989: 15).[45] However, the numbers were small – of 18449 children who took examinations in "specific" subjects in ten London boroughs in 1885, there were only 423 passes in French, and none at all in German (Bayley 1989: 62). There was a strong need felt for German for commercial purposes – something not remotely reflected in the types of examinations for which pupils were prepared, nor indeed in the Elementary Code which governed the curriculum of such schools. "Clearly, French and German were often learned not for cultural enrichment but for securing berths as clerks and agents in commercial houses. It was generally felt that the schools were failing in this mission. They were regularly criticized in the press, chambers of commerce, and Parliament for being 'lamentably deficient' in this respect" (Bayley 1989: 62). An item in the *Educational Times* noted a report by the London Chamber of Commerce, which had found that "the number of foreign clerks employed by leading firms steadily increases" August 1, 1887, p. 301; cf. also December 1, 1887, p. 466). In this climate, the Cambridge Syndicate introduced a commercial examination in 1888 with a foreign language element,[46] at which German could be offered as a subject. Manuals of Commercial German were produced too: the *German Commercial Correspondence* of Joseph T. Dann, who had experience as an assistant master at University College School, offered sample letters in German and in English for translation (Dann 1888); F. Coverley Smith's *Introduction to Commercial German* (1892), whose author was assistant master at my local independent Nottingham High School, took a more pragmatic approach. As Coverley Smith's headmaster noted in a foreword, it was neither desirable nor affordable "wholly to separate boys intended for commerce from those intended for professions"; nor could such boys be expected to stay at school longer in order to acquire the specialist knowledge of commecial German, and in any case "Few boys have experience or imagination enough to enter intelligently into the higher commercial technique", which was therefore "best left to the practical training of the office". Under such circumstances, a compromise was necessary, recognizing that "all boys may gain working knowledge of German by means of a more useful vocabulary and a less complicated grammar than that usually presented" (p. vi). Accordingly, Coverley Smith's book is a straightforward grammar, though with an effort made to include some core business vocabulary (e.g. *Kaufleute, Geschäft, Kommis*), and introducing simple business letters in the later chapters.[47]

The results of the Cambridge commercial examinations were unimpressive. In the first year, only eight out of 49 candidates were awarded Commercial Certificates (1888 Report of the Local Examinations and lectures Syndicate to the Senate of Cambridge Univer-

---

45 The College of Preceptors (since 1998 the College of Teachers) was established by Royal Charter in 1849; it was one of the first bodies to provide formal examinations for pupils, from 1851 (as well as for teachers, from 1846).

46 The College of Preceptors had been offering such an examination for many years, but without a foreign language requirement, as a piece on the new Cambridge certificate noted in the *Educational Times* (December 1, 1887, p. 408).

47 Another such volume, by Bally (1896) was reviewed in the *Educational Times* (January 1, 1897, p. 34), and judged to be "in general… useful" to "young Englishmen anxious to supersede the ubiquitous German clerk".

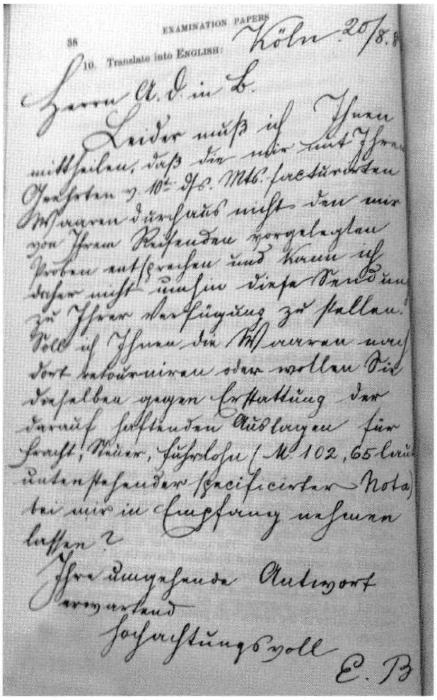
38 EXAMINATION PAPERS

10. Translate into ENGLISH:

Köln 20/8. 8

Herrn A. D. in L.

Leider muß ich Ihnen mittheilen, daß die mir mit Ihrem Schreiben v. 10. d. M. facturirten Waaren durchaus nicht den mir von Ihrem Reisenden vorgelegten Proben entsprechen und kann ich daher nicht umhin diese Sendung zu Ihrer Verfügung zu stellen. Soll ich Ihnen die Waaren nun dort retourniren oder wollen Sie dieselben gegen Erstattung der darauf haftenden Auslagen für Fracht, [illegible], Fuhrlohn (M 102,65 laut untenstehender specificirter Nota) bei mir in Empfang nehmen lassen?

Ihrer umgehenden Antwort entgegensehend

Hochachtungsvoll E. B

Figure 3.5:
A German business letter to be translated into English; taken from the Cambridge Commercial Certificate German examination, December 1888

sity, p. 5), and in German, "the most ordinary rules of German grammar seemed to be unknown to most of the candidates […] No candidate was able to write a German business-letter on a given subject" (p. 9). "In German Conversation [not compulsory] two of the seven candidates who presented themselves passed" (p. 10). The 1892 report for German was no more positive: "No candidate gave evidence of being able to write a correct and idiomatic German letter (p. 8). The numbers presenting for the Commercial Certificate remained low, as did the rate of success: 24 (6 passes) in 1889; 29 (with 12 passes) in 1890; twelve (with 4 passes) in 1891; 17 (with seven passes) in 1892; and eight (with five passes) in 1893; as a result the examination was discontinued (Report of the Local Examinations and lectures Syndicate to the Senate of Cambridge University, 29 January 1895). Although the 1900 Minute of the Board of Education stipulated that there should be instruction in one foreign language in Higher elementary schools (by now a much reduced group of schools, since many had not met new standards recently introduced), by 1906 the Board of Education was discouraging the teaching of a modern language because it "doubted it could be properly taught' in higher elementary schools" (Bayley 1989: 67).

3.6.2 German at university

Parallel to its establishment in schools, German also began to gain recognition as a subject to be studied at university. Render had evidently already been teaching German at Oxford and Cambridge around 1800, but it is to University College London that the honour goes of the first appointment to a Professorship of German Language and Literature in Britain, in May 1828. The professor appointed, Ludwig von Mühlenfels, left only three years later, in 1831, which was apparently "no great loss" (Flood 1999: 105, n. 12),[48]

48 A reviewer of Mühlenfels's *Introduction to a Course of German Literature* (1830) objected strenuously to Mühlenfels's "mischievous views", to his "fanciful parallels between the conditions of nations and the stages of human life", and to much that is "astoundingly absurd". The review concluded that "it rests entirely with Dr. Mühlenfels to become a useful and interesting lecturer; but he has much to unlearn and lay aside" (Boehning 1977: 289–291). On the other hand, a second, short

and in the same year Adolphus Bernays was appointed as Professor of German Language and Literature at King's College London (Flood 1999), where he remained until 1863.[49] Bernays himself had already published two works for learners of German – a poetical anthology (1829; later eds. 1831, 1837) and a short grammar (1830), to which exercises and a key appeared the following year (1831), and he continued to publish works of various kinds for students until 1855.[50] For the record, the first professor of German at Oxford was appointed in 1845;[51] Karl Breul (1860–1932) was appointed the first lecturer in Germanic language and literature at Cambridge University in 1884; in 1910 he was appointed the first Schröder Professor of German at Cambridge.[52] It was possible to take a full degree course in German at Cambridge from 1886. At Oxford, the defeat of a proposal to introduce a School of Modern Languages in 1887 was welcomed by the *Educational Times* (December 1 1887, p. 469), first because it was felt that there was no

---

review considered that "these Lectures are highly creditably to his zeal and talent as a literary in- quirer, and as a professor in the new institution to which he belongs" (Boehning 1977: 309).

49 Flood (1999) offers a detailed account of Bernays' life and works.

50 Bernays's grammar had reached nine editions by 1855, the Exercises their eleventh by 1855 (Flood 1999: 108). He also published a reader (1833; six editions by 1855), a historical anthology (1835; 2nd ed. 1855), poetry for beginners (1837), a "word-book" comparing German and English vocabulary (1852), a conversation-book (1853), and annotated versions of Schiller's *Wilhelm Tell* (1847) and *Maria Stuart* (1855). The poetical anthology of 1829, called a "judicious and elegant selection" by a reviewer in the *Monthly Magazine*, received only a lukewarm review in the *Edinburgh Literary Journal*: "On the whole, we are inclined, from our inspection of this book, to regard its author as a man of education rather than natural talent. From the sphere of teaching into which he seems to have got, we are inclined to believe him well-qualified for that profession. His book is well adapted for a text-book; and had it made no higher pretensions, should have been allowed to pass; but it is held forth, at the same time, as a 'literary guide' to more advanced students; and to have bestowed upon it, in this point of view, more unqualified approbation than we have done, would have been gross flattery" (Boehning 1977: 274–275; 279).

51 Actually, the German Francis Henry Trithen was appointed to a chair in modern European lan- guages. See Ortmanns (1993: 68). He was succeeded in 1854 by Friedrich Max Müller (1823– 1900), who according to Ortmanns (1993: 73) – but not according to the *Dictionary of National Biography* (Fynes 2007) – also somehow managed to find time to teach at Rugby from 1854 on- wards (see below). Watson (1921: 694) states that German was taught at Oxford by the Taylorian lecturer from 1868 onwards.

52 For a biography of Breul, see Paulin (2010) and AIM25 (Archives in London and the M25 area) http://www.aim25.ac.uk/cgi-bin/vcdf/detail?coll_id=5879&inst_id=31&nv1=search&nv2=basic. See also *Who was Who 1931–1940*. As Paulin notes, Breul arrived at Cambridge in 1884, and "With great energy Breul threw himself into the teaching of Germanic philology (in which Gothic, Old Saxon, and Old High German featured prominently) at Cambridge. With his German train- ing he saw no contradiction in equipping future teachers of German with these skills. Tirelessly he pursued teacher training, contacts and exchanges, and women's education, above all taxing the educational establishment with its indifference towards things German. This was part of a ceaseless campaign for Anglo-German understanding at a cultural and even popular level. He encouraged Germans to come to Cambridge, but also wrote the university's own non-official handbook of study. He lobbied – unsuccessfully – for a German institute in London and a British counterpart in Berlin. He was prominent in the Modern Language Association (serving as its president in 1910), the English Goethe Society, and the Anglo-German Friendship Committee."

demand for such a degree (candidates for the degree at Cambridge apparently having outnumbered the examiners in 1886–87), and second because the proposed school at Oxford would have "compassed the teaching of Modern Languages colloquially," which could better and more easily be done on vacation tours. A full degree in German could not be taken at Oxford until 1903 (Flood 2000: 29).

The inaugural lecture of Bernays (given in November 1831) is discussed by Flood 1999: 105–110); in it, Bernays sketches the history of the language, and outlines the advantages of learning it, and offers some remarks on its "nature and genius" (Bernays 1831: 4). In 1849, Bernays also delivered a "lecture on the German language" at Queen's College, an institution founded for the education of women founded in 1848, particularly for the training of governesses. In his lecture, Bernays reflected on the two competing methods: the "fancy, that languages are best learnt without a grammar" by which "you will neither understand, nor be understood" (Bernays 1849: 100), and the method, to which Bernays was firmly inclined, "to let the pupils carefully and attentively go through the rules, write exercises on each, and by committing such exercises to memory when corrected, and by constantly referring to the same rules while reading, so to fix them in the memory through practice [...] from mere habit, and without at the time being conscious that they are following any rules whatsoever (Bernays 1849: 112). This sympathetic account of the grammar-translation method places as much faith in "unconscious" and by implication therefore relatively effortless learning as accounts of behaviourist-inspired methods would do a century later.

Bernays' lecture provides further evidence for the changed status of learning German, as Bernays re-stated the now familiar Neo-Humanist arguments that learning a modern language was – like studying the Classics – an intellectual and character-forming education, though here, before a female audience, he added that modern languages lend themselves to the education of women in particular:

> Every one knows [...] what a powerful instrument for the training of the minds of boys is the study of the classical languages. Every faculty is called into play: especially memory and judgement, [...] Now the German language may be used in the same manner, as a formative vehicle with the ladies; with the particular advantage for them, that we have a great variety of works, in every branch of literature, which we may read with them with safety, profit, and pleasure, and many more they may afterwards read for themselves; while the Greek and the Latin languages contain but few works suitable for Christian women of the nineteenth century.

(Bernays 1849: 107–8, also cited by Flood 1999: 111)

The career of Bernays in many ways sums up the status of the subject in the mid-nineteenth century. His publications – a wide variety of different texts to cater to the different aspects of language learning and language study – continued the tendency towards expanding the range of textbook types already found at the close of the eighteenth century. His reflections on language learning in his lecture to the Queen's College governesses-to-be express the tension between utility and intellectual pursuit that emerged in the eighteenth century; and his methodological reflections, with their sympathetic account of grammar-translation (of which more below) are also of their time.

3.6.3 A note on foreign language education for women and girls

Bernays's series of lectures at the newly founded Queen's College in 1849 was quite possibly the first time that young women were exposed to the Neo-Humanist approach to foreign language education that dominated the education of boys. Very often girls whose brothers went to public school were themselves educated entirely in the home by native-speaker governesses (in accordance with the "fancy", roundly dismissed by Bernays, "that languages are best learnt without a grammar"). Even when girls did go to school, very different expectations and patterns of education for girls and boys resulted in differing outcomes in language education. The seventeen-year old Ginevra Fanshawe's summary of her achievements in Charlotte Brontë's novel *Villette* (1853) is probably typical (even if her insistence on totally ignorance is somewhat overstated!): "I know nothing – nothing in the world – I assure you; except that I play and dance beautifully, – and French and German of course I know, to speak; but I can't read or write them very well. Do you know they wanted me to translate a page of an easy German book into English the other day, and I couldn't do it" (*Villette*, OUP 2000 edition, p. 54). The remarks on teaching methods in 3.7 below, then, are less applicable to female education than to male education, at least for the first half of the nineteenth century. In the later nineteenth century, however, forward-looking educational institutions could become the laboratory for reformers like Walter Rippmann to try out their new ideas in language teaching methods (see 3.10.2 below).

3.7 The emergence of the "method" and didactic progression in modern language teaching

> In our great schools […] French and German are taught by the help of 'Messrs Otto, Ollendorf [sic] and Ahn' in a haphazard empirical style, which is of practically no educational value whatever […]
>
> W. Stuart MacGowan [French master at Cheltenham College and founder of the Modern Language Association][53] (1893: 31), cited by Ortmanns (1993: 43)

With the growth of modern language teaching in nineteenth-century British schools, a number of competing "methods" emerged for the hard-pressed and in many cases far from expert teacher (for many teachers were classicists by training who were then required to turn to the modern languages alongside the classics). Francis Storr – teacher at Merchant Taylor's School (London) and also active on the council of the College of Precep-

---

53 See Gilbert (1954: 16) on MacGowan.

82	LIST OF AFFIXES.

10.—icht.

Resembling in shape, colour, texture, taste, etc.

From	Comes the Derivative Adjective	
Haar hair	haaricht	resembling hair.
Holz wood	holzicht	„ wood.
Kupfer copper	kupfericht	„ copper.
Wolle wool	wollicht	„ wool.

(See "*N.B.*, Comparison of -en or -ern, -icht, -ig," page 84.)

11.—ig.

Corresponding to the Engl. *-y* [see L. of Ch. 10, *b*]: it means *possessing, abounding in, full of*.

In Compounds it may be translated by *-ed*: as lang long, Haar hair, and langhaarig long-haired.

ENGL. EQUIV.:— *-y, -ful, -ous, -ed.*

From	Comes the Derivative Adjective
Bedacht thought, deliberation	bedächtig deliberate, cautious, thoughtful.
Blume [bloom] flower	blumig flowery.
Blut blood	blutig bloody.
Durst thirst	durstig thirsty.
ein one, Falte fold	einfältig simple [Lat. *sim-plic-single-fold*], silly.
Freude joy	freudig joyful, joyous.
Geschwätz babble	geschwätzig full of babble, babbling.
Gewalt power, force, violence	gewaltig forcible, powerful.
Gnade grace	gnädig gracious.
Grimm wrath, fury	grimmig wrathful, furious.
Haar hair	haarig hairy; langhaarig longhaired.
haben to have } heben to heave }	heftig violent, vehement.
Heil [heal] health, wholeness	heilig holy.

Figure 3.6:
The interlinear method applied to Goethe's "Erlkönig", the first text to be read in Sonnenschein & Stallybrass (1857: 92).

tors[54] – reportedly said of his own experience of teaching German, "We nearly all of us learn modern languages by teaching them" (cited by Ortmanns 1993: 46).[55] In his short survey, Titone (1968) highlighted the methodological reflections of figures including Johann Bernard Basedow, James Hamilton, and Joeseph Jactotot around the turn of the eighteenth to nineteenth century. According to the German Basedow (1723–90), "Languages were to be taught be speaking and then by reading, and grammar was not to be introduced until late in the course" (thus Titone 1968: 19).[56] In Britain, James Hamilton (1769–1831), whom Titone dubbed the English "spokesman of […] educational reform", drew on his own experiences in learning German for his method of teaching by interlinear translation, reading aloud to the pupils and translating word by word. Pupils should then repeat the exercise themselves, until they could write or speak a perfect translation of the whole text (described in Hamilton 1816; cf. Titone 1968: 21). Klippel reports that Hamilton was the first to *market* his method. Although Hamilton was not involved in school education, the internlinear translation method did grow in popularity (Klippel 1994: 226): examples for English learners of German include Otto (1864: 16) and Sonnenschein & Stallybrass (1857) (see Figure 3.6 for an example from the latter).[57] The method of the Frenchman Joseph Jactotot (1770–1840) was both popular and then controversial in France. Titone (1968: 23) described the method as follows:

---

54 Storr is listed as a council member in a report of a meeting of the College of Preceptors on December 12, 1896 (*Educational Times*, January 1, 1897). He also published Storr (1897). See also 3.8 below.

55 The phenomenon of being a lesson ahead of the class was, regrettably, not limited to the nineteenth century, as teachers asked to retrain to teach another modern language in the twentieth century will attest.

56 Render's "catalogue of celebrated German authors" listed Basedow as recommended reading under the heading of education (Render 1804: 350).

57 The only other example I am aware of in German textbooks for English learners is Brenkmann (1885), *Hossfeld's New Practical Method for Learning the German Language.*

> The usual starting point was a basic reader [...] Here the original text is faced by a literal translation. The pupil sets out to memorize a long passage and repeats it as often as needed. With the aid of the literal translation, he comes to graps the meaning of each word, while his analysis of the whole sentence enables him to deduce certain implicit grammar rules. Of course, this procedure demands a great number of oral and written exercises in which the pupil imitates, summarizes, and compares the texts. Everything that the pupil acquires in this fashion must be linked to the preceding notions by his comparing similarities and differences between the new and the old.

Common to these three very different developments was the shift away from taking grammar as the natural starting point. However, as Titone (1968: 24) puts it in rather partisan fashion, this "good tradition" of the late eighteenth century was to be "spoiled" in the nineteenth century, when "textbook compilers were mainly determined to codify the foreign language into frozen rules of morphology and syntax to be explained and eventually memorized. Oral work was reduced to an absolute minimum." (Titone 1968: 26). Germans were the leading exponents of this new approach, and at their head stands Meidinger, already mentioned above, whose new method was – typically – first applied to French. Probably Germany led the way simply because the need was felt earliest in Germany, where language learning was embedded in the Neo-Humanist curriculum of the *Gymnasien* – thanks to the guidelines set out by Wilhelm von Humboldt in Prussia in 1809 – earlier than in the school systems of other countries. Prominent exponents after Meidinger were Johann Heinrich Friedrich Seidenstücker (1785–1817),[58] Johann Franz Ahn (1796–1865), Heinrich Gottfried Ollendorff (1803–1865), and Karl Plötz (1819–1881). In Kelly's view, it is really the last in this line, Karl Plötz, whose French grammar was published in 1847, 36 years after Seidenstücker's (cf. Hüllen 2005: 96), who bears the blame for the bad reputation of the so-called grammar-translation method of Meidinger and his successors. If in Ollendorff's method "as yet the content of the course was not unreasonable," in Plötz's system, "which was basically that of Ollendorff, the disciplinary and analytical value of language study was paramount, and the linguistic aims quite secondary. The growing exactness of philological studies was reflected in the increased formalism of his grammatical description. [...] Language skill was equated with the ability to conjugate and decline" (Kelly 1969: 52, 53).

While mention of Seidenstücker or Plötz by name is rare in texts used in Britain,[59] both Ahn's and Ollendorff's "methods" were extremely widely used (and were later

---

58 Although Titone (1968: 27) remarks that in Seidenstücker's texts "the sole form of instruction was mechanical translation", Klippel offers a more positive assessment, considering that Seidenstücker's innovation consisted in distinguishing between beginners and advanced, with different methods for each, using an inductive approach for beginners, as already advocated by John Locke, rather than with explicit grammar teaching from page one (Klippel 1994: 347).

59 Eve lamented in the preface to his German *Grammar for Schools*, "I have not been able to meet with any book by a non-German which does for German what Holder, Plötz, Bernhard Schmitz & c. do for French" (Eve 1880: v). Ploetz's epitome of history, first published in English in 1883, appears to

fiercely criticized during the Reform Movement by Bahlsen 1905). Kelly (1969: 52) considered them the "best known Grammar-Translation texts". Ollendorff's *New method of learning to read, write, and speak a language in six months: adapted to the German: for the use of schools and private teachers* appeared in 1838, apparently translated from an earlier French edition.[60] Ollendorff's work went through 22 issues or editions between 1838 and 1876, complete with a *Key* (itself re-published several times), and there were also popular versions for English learners of French, Italian, Spanish and Russian.[61] A measure of the popularity of Ahn's method in Europe is provided by Klippel's figures for his textbook of English for German learners, of which there were 40 editions between 1856 and 1885, and altogether 61 editions up to 1937, i. e. over 81 years all told (Klippel 1995: 405–406). I am aware of eleven editions of his method for learning German between 1849 and 1888.

Ollendorff's *German Method* (1st ed. 1838)[62] certainly stood for explicit and through rote learning of grammar. His books for the different languages were "essentially translations of each other", with "the same grammar, the same examples, and even the same translation sentences" (Wheeler 2013: 115). The second edition (1850) opens with an anecdote headed "The sea-compass" in which a young sailor is asked by a monk aboard ship if he knows his prayers as well as his sea-compass. "No, replied Jack, "for I can tell you, father, that I know my sea-compass a great deal better than even you know your prayers". For the monk can only say his prayers forwards, not backwards, unlike Jack, who can recite the points of the compass forwards, backwards, and "a thousand ways". Ollendorff (1850: vi) concludes, "Jack has just told us how a language ought to be learnt and known". But Ollendorff has perhaps received more criticism than is strictly deserved. Though guilty as charged of using artificial sentences in order to illustrate a rule (Titone 1968: 28), Ollendorff was innovative in his time in developing further the "practical" grammar of Meidinger. Each lesson consisted of a grammatical point followed by model sentences in with English on the left, German on the right, and then sentences for

---

have been much more widely known in Britain and the USA than his language textbooks, to judge by the many copies held on COPAC and Hathi Trust.

60 King's College London holds a copy whose title reads "translated from the fifth French edition, by G. J. Bertinchamp", suggesting that the French original was some years earlier, but I have been unable to discover a copy earlier than 1838. Titone's and Kelly's reference to a 1783 edition of the work is presumably an error, given that Ollendorff's life-dates are everywhere given as 1803–1865 (Titone 1968: 121; Kelly 1968: 442).

61 Ollendorff was evidently aware of many imitations of his works. On the reverse of the title page to his second edition (Ollendorff 1850), we read, "As to the spurious editions of my works, after having carefully examined all of them, I am bound to state, that they are bad, incorrect and incomplete, and so far from assisting the learner, they are calculated to make him adopt erroneous principles of German. They have, in fact, nothing in common with my works, but the titles; and any one possessing a knowledge of German, will, in looking into them, soon discover that they are so many impositions. Each copy of the only genuine edition has its number and my signature." In the copy I consulted, the text is indeed accompanied by a handwritten *No. 1014* and signature.

62 The battered copy which I consulted in the Taylor Collection is undated.

translation.[63] Merely the attempt to break down the material into lesson-sized chunks, divided up in the Table of Contents into a course over five months, and so making a course-book rather than a grammar, was an innovation. Likewise the attempt to progress within each lesson from presentation, to exemplification, to practice and revision was innovative. Symptomatic of increasing reflection on educational method, Ollendorff included detailed instructions for the teacher on how to use the book:

> Each lesson should be dictated to the pupil, who should pronounce every word, as it is dictated to him. After this, the teacher should exercise the pupil by putting questions to him in every possible way. Each lesson, with the exception of the fourth, will comprise three divisions: the Professor commences examining the pupil by putting such questions to him as are given in the exercises; next, he will dictate to him the following lesson; lastly, he will put to him new questions on all the preceding lessons. According to the different degrees of competency of the pupils, one lesson may be divided into two, two lessons into three, or three lessons combined into one.

> (Ollendorff n. d.: 5–6)

Note – given the common charge that methods like Ollendorff's gave no opportunity for the pupil to practise speaking – the instruction that the pupil "should pronounce every word" and should answer questions put to him. The final lesson of the 1850 second edition contains a passage for translation into German with the following exchange between pupil and master:

> Master: If I were now to ask you such questions as I did at the beginning of our lessons (viz.) Have you the hat which my brother has? Am I hungry? Has he the tree of my brother's garden? &c., what would you answer?
> The Pupils: We are obliged to confess that we found those questions at first rather ridiculous; but full of confidence in your method, we answered as well as the small quantity of words and rules we then possessed allowed us. We were, in fact, not long in finding out that these questions were calculated to ground us in the rules, and to exercise us in conversation, by the contradictory answers we were obliged to make. But now that we can almost keep up a conversation in the energetic language which you teach us, we should answer […]

> (Ollendorff 1850: 416)

It is clear that in Ollendorff's conception, at least, if not always in practice, his was a method aiming at conversation.

---

63 Note that this book is one of the last whose author still seems (in part) to have in mind the individual learner taught by a private tutor, rather than a whole class, an impression supported by the subject of a dialogue given for translation (p. 381). Headed "Dialogue between a Father and mother on the welfare (*das Wohl*) of their children", it is in fact between a Count and Countess on the subject of a suitable match for their daughter.

Ahn's *New [...] Method of learning the German language* was published in 1849, translated from a French original (1843; cf. Ahn/ Pfeiffer 1868: preface), which was in turn published after Ahn's *Praktischer Lehrgang* for learning French (cf. Macht 1992: n. p.).[64] It is the earliest for which I have a concrete evidence of use (see below), in the incarnation of Ahn (1868), a *First German Course* published in London as part of the series of Allman's Popular Elementary Series of Works for Learning Foreign Languages, ten years after the first board examinations for pupils learning German at school. Macht (1994: n. p.) described Ahn's method as

> [a] remarkable modification of Meidinger's simple grammatical pattern [...] Ahn's innovation consisted mainly in the fact that in the first volume of the manual he replaced Meidinger's elaborate grammatical rules by lists of model sentences intended to illustrate the grammatical items that were to be practised. The model sentences were then followed by sentences in the mother tongue as practice material. Ahn does not furnish the learner with the explicit rules of grammar until the second Part of the volume.

Despite Ahn's innovative intentions and the popularity of his works, Macht continues that "The memories attached to them seem to be mainly unpleasant, probably due to the drudgery of having to learn by heart large numbers of totally unconnected model sentences void of any real meaning, e.g., *You always interrupt me when I am speaking. You were coming from the tailor's as I was going to the shoemaker's. Your nephew is always smoking when we call to see him. While the house was burning, the people were running to fetch water and could not get any* (Ahn 1834: Vol. 1, p. 48). Certainly Bahlsen – who had been taught by Plötz – was no enthusiast, writing of "a barren waste of insipid sentence translating" (Bahlsen 1905: 10).

The 1868 edition of the *Ahn's New Practical and Easy Method of Learning the German Language* held in the Taylor Collection in Bamberg is inscribed with a name and dated "May fourth /70", so is evidence of the book's being in use in 1870, presumably in Australia, since the collection was donated by the Australian academic Brian Taylor, al-

---

64 Ahn's method was first developed for French (Ahn 1834), and was then both translated (e.g. Vallés (1800) and adapted to new languages, including Italian (Filippi 18–?) as well as German and English. It was extremely popular through the nineteenth century and spawned many imitators, and the original text for learning French (Ahn 1834) had 207 re-editions or re-prints over fifty years (Macht 1994: n. p.). Klippel (1994: 405) counts 30 editions of his textbook for learning English between the first edition in 1856 and 1885. Macht (1992: n. p.) lists some of the imitators of Ahn's methodology as James Aubry, *Elementarbuch zur Erlernung der englischen Sprache* (Hamburg, 1836); Gerhard van den Berg, *Praktischer Lehrgang zur schnellen und leichten Erlernung der englischen Sprache* (Hamburg, 1847); F. H. Hedley, *Praktischer Lehrgang zur schnellen, leichten und gründlichen Erlernung der englischen Sprache* (Wien, 1847); Karl Gräser, *Praktischer Lehrgang zur schnellen und leichten Erlernung der englischen Sprache* (Leipzig, 1856); Robert Westley Erster *Unterricht im Englischen* (Leipzig, 1859). As a marketing tool, Ahn's name lived on even after his death, for example in a phrase-book badged as *Ahn's Manual of Conversation* printed in New York in 1871 (Grauert, 1871). As the very opening sentence of the "editor"'s preface makes clear – "The very idea of a living language presupposes oral communication" – its philosophy was quite different from that of Ahn.

though the provenance of the items is not always clear – some were evidently purchased from second-hand shops). In the inside flyleaf is written what appears to be a plan for a week's teaching:

Tues	Fri
Exercise Learn verb Vocabulary Reading Gram.	Exercise Grammar Vocabulary Translation Dictation [illegible]

While it is difficult to re-construct much from this, there is at any rate a notable absence of conversation.

The much-maligned authors of supposedly arid grammar-translation methods were in fact more ambitious, in intention at least. For Ahn shared with Seidenstücker the idea of *not* beginning with explicit grammar – something which was already advocated by Basedow. Ahn's method *New, Practical and Easy Method* as revised by Johann Pfeiffer (1868) begins with some simple words and phrases. One may criticize the tedium of the exercises like those quoted by Macht in his discussion of Ahn's English grammar such as *Are you the daughter of that Indian woman? I am not the friend of this liar (fem.)*, which can easily be matched by examples from Ahn (1868: 17). But it must be conceded that Ahn nevertheless made a concerted effort to allow the pupil to progress from easier to more complex material. The simple sentences like "The father is tall. Is the mother tall?", with key adjectives like *big, small,* and *good* introduced on the first page (see Figure 3.7), were surely somewhat closer to the concrete experience of children, and translating or speaking them was surely more achievable for the beginner that the first exercises in Render (1799) and Wendeborn (1797) had been. Parts I–III of the book build up gradually to longer and more complex passages, with only brief grammatical observations interspersed. The explicit grammar part is reserved to the final part, Part IV. The book concludes with exercises devoted to practising particular grammar points (beginning with the regular verbs *glauben, sagen*), followed by short tales with a moral for translation, with vocabulary listed below. Last come "easy dialogues" (pp. 116–128) on the following everyday topics: 1. Eating and drinking; 2. going and coming, 3. Questions and answers, 4. The age, [sic, i. e. asking and saying one's age] 5. The hour [i. e. telling the time], 6. the weather, 7. greeting 8. The visit 9. Breakfast 10. Before dinner 11. The dinner 12. the tea. To be fair to Ahn, then, if in practice usage of his book apparently degenerated into grammar and translation, the book itself offered scope to do much more than this. In an undated copy of Ahn's Method revised by Drielsma, who was German Master at Regent Street Polytechnic, London, Drielsma commented, in good faith, that "Ahn's method may now fairly be considered 'the quickest and pleasantest way to learn a language'".[65]

---

65 The quote is not attributed.

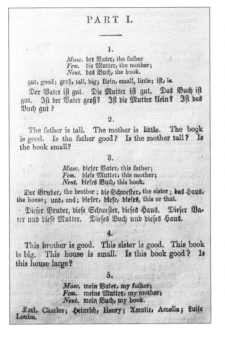

Figure 3.7:
Ahn & Pfeiffer (1868: 5)

The apparent dominance of the grammar-translation method also needs relativizing in the light of a third nineteenth-century champion of a "method", Emil Otto (1813–?), whose method gave considerable weight to speaking. Otto's *German conversation-grammar* was, again, published after the success of an earlier version by him for French, and following a model pioneered by Thomas Gaspey in his *Englische Konversationsgrammatik* (1851; cf. Klippel 1994: 405). Otto's preface (reproduced in Otto, revised Lange 1890), outlined the method:

"The '*German Conversation-Grammar*' [...] combines the grammatical and logical exposition of the German language with the constant application of the different forms and rules to *writing* and *speaking*.
The book is divided into Lessons, each complete in itself, and containing, in a methodical arrangement, a portion of the grammar followed by a German *Reading exercise* in which the different grammmatical forms are applied to whole sentences. An *Exercise for translation* into German comes next: the lesson being concluded by an easy *Conversation*, re-embodying the matter introduced in the previous exercises.
The most practical method of acquiring and developing the faculty of *speaking* German is for the student to be questioned in German on subjects already familiar to him by translation. In a short time the ear becomes familiarized to the foreign accent, the teacher is understood, and the tongue at the same time acquires a fluency that cannot be attained by any other method. This success if solely due to the *conversational* exercises the advantage of which is evident.
In respect of the mode of employing this Grammar, the author begs to be allowed to offer teachers and pupils a few suggestions: The rules with their examples and the 'Words' should be first learned by heart, and the German 'Reading Exercise' read and translated into English. This done the Exercise for translation (*Aufgabe*) into German should at first be translated *vivâ voce* and then be written down and corrected *vivâ voce*. For the next lesson a fair copy of it should be written out. Finally the '*Conversation*' should be carefully read out and the pupils be questioned in German on its contents. The Reading lessons and the easier poems in the 'Appendix' should be done when the student has gone through about one half of the first Part."

— 22 —

Aufgabe (Exercise for translation). **2.**

1. The king and the queen. The son and the daughter. The father and the mother. The child has the book. The daughter has the book. The man has the (*Acc.*) stick. I have the wine. The man has the water. This father. This woman. This house. The king has the castle. The queen has the book. Which book? Which house? Which pen? That book; that pen. Every man. I have the (*Acc.*) dog.

2.*) I have not the stick. The child has the stick. That wine and this water. This man has not the book. Which castle has the (*Nom.*) king? He has that castle. That mother has the child. The house of the woman. **) The castle of the queen. Hast thou the book? Which plates (*Teller*)? These plates. Those plates. The son of the queen. The pen of the daughter.**) Every mother. Every book.

Sprechübung (Conversation).

Habe ich die Feder?	Ja, du hast die Feder.
Hast du das Buch?	Nein, ich habe das Buch nicht.
Hat der Vater den Wein?	Er hat den Wein.
Hat die Frau die Katze?	Ja, sie hat die Katze.
Welche Katze hat sie?	Sie hat die junge (young) Katze.
Hat das Kind den Stock?	Nein, der Vater hat den Stock.
Welches Schloß hat die Königin?	Sie hat dieses Schloß.
Hat diese Frau das Kind?	Nein, jene Frau hat es (it).
Hat der Mann den Hund?	Der Mann hat den Hund nicht; er hat die Katze.
Welches Buch hat der Sohn?	Er hat das Buch der Mutter.
Hat die Mutter das Buch?	Nein, die Tochter hat das Buch.
Welche Feder hat das Kind?	Es hat die Feder der Frau.
Hat der Vater Wasser?	Nein, er hat Wein.
Welches Haus hat der Mann?	Er hat das Haus der Mutter.

*) Most of the Exercises are divided into two parts. The second part need not be translated until the pupil repeats, which should be done after 10 or 12 lessons have been gone through.

**) Feminine nouns have all the cases in the singular like the nom^ative; thus only the article is declined.

Figure 3.8:
Otto (1864: 22)

The front cover described the author Emil Otto as "Professor of modern languages, Lecturer at the University of Heidelberg". Though Otto's text is fairly traditional in its form, beginning with information and an exercise on pronunciation before progressing to grammar (which starts as usual with the definite article), there are some innovations besides the emphasis on conversation. First, the grammar begins with an overview of all ten parts of speech and an explanation of the four cases (nominative, accusative, dative and genitive). Under the heading of the definite article, Otto takes the opportunity to introduce already the demonstrative pronouns *jene, jede, welche, diese*, because they are declined in the same way. Beyond such adjustments in presentation of content, the greatest novelty is found in the structure of the lessons, which, like Ahn's, are clearly intended to proceed from the easier to the more difficult, but with explicit rather than implicit introduction of grammar from the start. As the passage cited above outlines, the lessons begin with the exposition of the grammar, which is followed by examples, words to be learnt, a reading exercise based on the vocabulary just introduced, an exercise for translation from English to German, and – hence the title of the book – a *Sprechübung*, the first of which is reproduced in Figure 3.8. The conversation exercises are not wildly imaginative, nor particulary authentic, but they do appear to be written with pair-work amongst the pupils in mind, as the use of the *du*-form indicates (cf. *Habe ich die Feder? Ja, du hast die Feder* in Figure 3.8), and presumably they could be varied.

Otto's publisher Julian Groos was an aggressive marketer of the method. In 1890, the 25th edition of the *Conversation-Grammar*, revised by Franz Lange (Otto/ Lange, 1890) contained the warning:

> The method of Gaspey-Otto-Samer is my own private property, having been acquired by purchase from the authors. The text-books made after this method are incessantly improved. All rights, especially the right of making new editions, and the right of translation for all languages are reserved. Imitations and fraudulent impressions will be persecuted according to the law. I am thankful for communications relating to these matters.
> Heidelberg.   Julius Groos.[66]

---

66 The same warning is found in Otto (1889).

Lange published a *Progressive German Examination Course* of his own which explicitly included materials for "dictation, extempore, conversation" (Lange 1888: title page). Julian Groos also published a number of other "books for the study of foreign languages", a list of which appears at the front of Otto (1883) with the following explanation, paraphrasing Otto's preface, cited above:

> Most of the books contained in the following list have been composed after D. Otto's "CONVERSATIONAL METHOD OF TEACHING LANGUAGES", either by himself, or by other eminent professors. This method combines the grammatical and logical exposition of the rules with their constant application to SPEAKING and WRITING. [...] It is impossible to conceive a more practical method of acquiring the art of SPEAKING a modern language, than that adopted in these books: the teacher questioning the pupil on subjects already familiar to him by translation, and the pupil endeavouring to give a fitting reply. In a short time the EAR becomes so familiar with the strange sounds, that he teacher is understood, and meanwhile the TONGUE acquires a fluency which can hardly be attained by any other method.

By 1875, Otto had come to the conclusion that a separate textbook was necessary for conversation, albeit only as far as "Geläufigkeit im Englischsprechen überhaupt auf Schulen erreicht werden kann" 'to the extent that fluency in English speaking is at all achievable in schools' (Otto 1864 V, VI.; cf. Klippel 1994: 341). In his *German-English Conversations* (Otto 1883; 1st ed. 1875, following the *Englisch-deutsches Gesprächsbuch* (1864) (cf. Klippel 1994: 341; cf. also Otto & Wright 1889),[67] he sought in particular to improve upon the conversations inherited from the eighteenth century between gentlemen and their tailors, and the like. Accordingly Otto's conversations included topical matters such as a relative who emigrated to America in 1869 "um sein Glück zu machen" (to make his fortune) or the composition of the English fleet under Nelson.

As Otto wrote in the preface to his conversation book, "The frequent intercourse between English and Germans or Americans have made the study of the German language so universal, that good books written to this purpose always find a good reception," such that his grammar had already reached its nineteenth edition, but Otto felt a need for a separate book for those wishing to

> perfect themselves *in speaking German*. On examining the existing dialogue-books, I find that they are only intended mechanically to be learned by heart, and that they are wanting in method.
> To learn to speak a foreign language, four elements are required: 1) a store of words; 2) a number of easy short phrases; 3) subjects fit for the purpose; and 4) a series of regular conversations and dialogues in good German.
> The present manual is the first book which contains these four elements in logical succession, as a look into the contents will show.

---

67 Groos lists texts for learners of English, French, Spanish, Italian, Portuguese, and Russian.

The advantage of such special *conversational exercises* is evident. Whoever has occupied himself with the practical study of a modern language, is aware that one of the most difficult things is to *comprehend* the foreign idiom. Accustomed therefore at first to understand the easy questions the teacher addresses to him and which, besides, he has before his eyes in the book, and then to answer in the same language on easy and interesting subjects, the learner exercises equally his *ear* and *tongue*, so that he will, in a short time, be enabled to express his thoughts fluently and correctly in the foreign language.

The present book contains therefore: 1) Easy questions with answers in both languages [= Part I, pp. 1–50, German on the left, English on the right]. 2) Questions in English, with answers in German [= first part of Part II, pp. 51–67]. 3) Questions in German, with answers in English, to be turned into German by the pupils. [= 2ⁿᵈ part of Part II, pp. 68–91; in addition the Third Part 92–107 contains word lists on various semantic fields, beginning with *Weltall, Pflanzen, Familie* etc., and including 15. *Vom Unterricht*, in each case followed by about a dozen questions in German], 4) 32 regular conversations on amusing and instructive subjects, drawn from daily life, from history, geography, physics, astronomy, etc., the first 15 of which have, for better understanding, the English text on the opposite page, [= pp. 108–143 of Part IV, the remainder without English translations, pp. 144–168] which may be covered, if advisable.

By this method, the pupil not only acquires a great store of words, but learns also to form questions and answers in German, which are the chief form of talking."

Otto extended his method even to his *Materials for Translation* (1866; 6ᵗʰ revised ed. Otto & Wright 1889), which were, despite the title, still intended to give practice in conversation. The volume consisted of two parts: one, graded passages for translation, and a second part – which need not wait till after the first part was completed – of "English dialogues for translating into German with notes and a vocabulary and which has been prepared for the purpose of practising conversational style" (Preface to 1889 edition by J. Wright).

Other authors who emphasized the importance of being able to *speak* German include Hermann Huss and William Eysenbach.[68] Huss published a *System of Oral instruction* in German that was "intended to assist the instructor in teaching beginners to speak German with the constant guidance of the grammar, and is an attempts to include that which is vital in the two methods which hitherto have been making war against each other, viz. the 'grammatical' and the so-called 'natural' method" (Huss 1888: [iii]).[69] It consisted of a theoretical Part (i.e. grammar) and "material for conversation" in which the rather stultifying and utterly disconnected sentences "are meant to be *memorized* by the student, to serve afterwards as material for conversation" (Huss 1888: theoretical

68 Sachs's *German conversational grammar* (1894) should also be noted; I have not been able to inspect a copy.
69 The copy I inspected was owned by Emil Trechmann (see below).

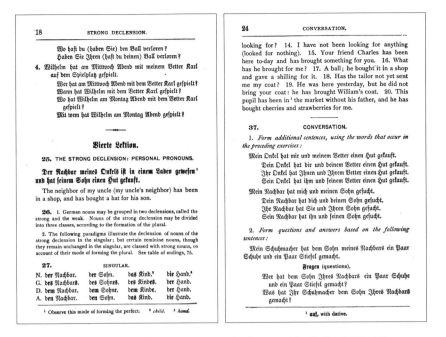

Figure 3.9 (left): The start of lesson IV in Eysenbach, revised by Collar (1887: 18)
Figure 3.10 (right): The end of lesson IV, ending with "Conversation", in Eysenbach revised by Collar (1887: 24)

part, p. 1). Eysenbach's *Practical grammar of the German language and introduction to conversation for the use of schools and private students*, published by Wigand in 1885, was a more successful attempt to marry features of the 'natural' method with the study of grammar. The author – who noted in his preface his thirty years of experience teaching German "privately and in classes both in England and Germany," having been Junior Principal of Charlton High-School, Manchester, and "later Director of an Educational Establishment for Young Englishmen at Darmstadt" – believed he had found the means by which "the peculiar difficulties which the English student faces in the study of German" might "in great measure be removed and *time* and *labour* economized." (One is struck here by the language of the industrialized economy!) Eysenbach had "two objects in view: first to simplify and facilitate the study of the [sic] German grammar, secondly to enable the student to express himself correctly and with fluency on topics of general conversation" (1887: iii). Eysenbach's "leading principle" was that "The language is to be acquired as much as possible in the same manner, as the child would learn his native tongue in his own country, or the vernacular tongue in a foreign one." The method involved beginning with a model sentence, as in Figure 3.9 – see also Figure 3.10 for how the lesson built up to conversation.

There were many editions of Eysenbach's grammar over the following fifteen years or so, including two separate revised editions in 1887: one by A. C. Büttner (London: H. Grevel & Co.), one in America by William C. Collar (Boston: Ginn & Co.). In fact Collar, in his revision, considerably reduced the emphasis on oral skills. Collar wrote (1887: iv), "It was Eysenbach's object to write a grammar that should equip the faithful student for understanding, speaking and writing German with the utmost economy of time and labor". But Collar himself felt the neglect of reading, and so to make room for the reading lessons, "not a few conversational exercises [...] have been eliminated." (p. v). While calling Eysenbach's book "admirably suited to a purely oral method", Collar found it "deficient in scientific [i. e. philological, NMcL] spirit and method" (p. vii), and made a number of changes. For example, Collar put both nouns and verbs into two classes, strong and weak, a classification "more scientific (p. v); he put together the account of the pronouns, which Eysenbach had "scattered" through the book, a little at a time. Collar considered his method the "method of observation, comparison, imitation, and induction, which long experience has taught me is the really 'natural method', as well as the most interesting and fruitful" (p. vi). On the model of the *Beginner's Latin Book*, Collar's aim was to reduce the burden on memory by using intellect and understanding more, for while one might get a long way in language learning by imitation and memorization, "According to American notions, the Germans are inhuman in their demands upon the memory" (vi). "The object, of course, is not to make philologists, but to quicken interest and intelligence, and to form an intellectual habit of great value" (p. vii). I return to the influence of philology on textbooks below.

It is in such a climate as this that a statement in 1851 by Adolph Heimann – "PhD. Professor of the German language and literature in University College, London" according to the title page of his *Materials for Translating from English into German* – about the relative *neglect* of translation into the target language, compared to spoken fluency, becomes understandable:

> A proficient scholar in German ought to be able to do four things well: to explain the structure of the language; to read a German book; to speak with some fluency; and to write a letter, or to translate a part of an English book into German without the assistance of Dictionary and Grammar. The greatest number of pupils master the first three points, but very few succeed in the last.

> (Heimann 1889; preface dated preface dated 1851)

Evidently – at a time when German had begun to be offered in British public schools and universities – at least some teachers felt that it was not speaking, but translation, that needed support.

3.8 Teaching to the test

As already noted, in 1857–1858 Oxford and Cambridge had introduced local school examinations at Junior (under 16) and Senior (under 18) levels, so that from 1858 onwards we have available for research not just the textbooks that pupils and teachers used, but also the examinations for which pupils were prepared; the syllabi (in the form of the regulations for the examinations and lists of set texts); the examinations themselves; examiners' reports; and some other archive material.

The first year of examinations set by the Cambridge Syndicate included passages from Lessing (fables, prose and verse) (for the Juniors, lower level), Bürger (for the Juniors, higher level) and Schiller (*Revolution of the Netherlands*) and Goethe (*Hermann und Dorothea*) for the Seniors, as well as Voß's *Luise*, which had already featured on Wendeborn's list of recommended reading in 1797. The papers required translation from German to English, questions on grammar and parsing (Junior, lower level), and translation from English to German (Junior, higher level). The Seniors sat two papers, both including translation from German to English. The first also contained "historical and geographical questions" relating to the set text. The second paper at Senior level contained a translation of a certainly very difficult passage from John Locke from English to German, and "Grammatical questions". (See Figure 3.11.)

Table 3.3 shows the set texts for the Cambridge Junior and Senior German examinations from 1858–1912. In 1858, the grammatical questions in the Senior paper were certainly very dry grammatical ones (for example, pupils were required to give the first person singular present, imperfect indicative, and imperfect subjunctive of the verbs *befehlen, heissen, empfangen, friern, bergen*," as well as the requirement to identify "unidiomatic constructions" in the satirical poem "Der Neudeutsche" by Stiegler. In 1867, the paper had shown some philological influence: candidates were required to supply English cognates for given German words and to "infer hence a rule which regulated such consonantal changes", though such questions did not feature in the later papers that I sampled (1877, 1884, 1887, 1888, 1889). In 1884, German morphology appeared to have become a point of interest: pupils were asked to "translate or explain" compounds such as *Majestätsbeleidigung, Parforcejagd, Rathskeller*. The emphasis is indeed on grammar and translation, but one can see the thinking behind the questions. Part of the paper required mere regurgitation of grammatical forms, bearing in mind the view, as stipulated in the regulations (e.g. 1877, 1885, for example), that "Without a fair knowledge of Accidence, a Candidate cannot pass". There were then slightly more thought-provoking grammatical questions which required some ability to analyse or explain German forms, as in *How is a purpose and how is a wish expressed in German?* (1877 Seniors) or *State with examples when the verb is placed before the subject and when it stands at the end of the clause* (1888). Presumably – despite the seemingly terrifying level of the English-to-German translation as exemplified in Table 3.5 – it was only the very best candidates who performed anything like creditably in the translation.

Certainly examiners' reports include the plaint that

"The translation by many candidates of a sentence not included in the paper, though occurring in the immediate context of one of the extracts set, shewed that the preparation of these candidates had been of a bad mechnaical type."

(Cambridge Syndicate Local Examinations Examiners' report, German Juniors 1896, p. xxxix)

The papers changed very little right up to the end of the nineteenth century, and, not surprisingly, school-internal papers appear to have followed closely the model of the external examinations. See Figure 3.12 for an 1890 German paper at Rugby School. For example, questions in the Cambridge examinations of the form "Distinguish between der *Erbe* and *das Erbe, der See* and *die See,* and between *die Gesichter* and *die Gesichte, die Männer* and *die Mannen*" (Senior, 1884) or "What is the German for two – thirty-three – four hundred and twenty-nine?" (Junior, 1877) have counterparts in Rugby's papers, with questions like "Write down in German words 10, 80, 54, 101 [...]" and "Distinguish between: *bitten, bieten; können, kennen; fliegen, fliehen* [...]". As for this last variant, the fact that such a question could even be asked underscores how little German was really spoken: minimal pairs in pronunciation seem here to have been of purely theoretical interest. Internal school papers and external syndicate examinations seem to reflect the Neo-Humanist view of language education, as already expressed by Bernays in 1849, and faithfully restated in subsequent pronouncements by influential figures like the Modern Languages Professor at Oxford, or, fifteen years later, the Headmaster of University College School, Henry Weston Eve (d. 1910), to the Headmasters' Conference in 1879: *Your first object is to discipline the mind; your second to give a knowledge of French or German* (cf. Hawkins 1987: 113).

The phenomenon of teaching to the test, and examiners' habits of including traps to catch the unwary (note the irregular *dreiunddreißig* required in the Junior 1877 paper) resulted in teachers devising menomonic tricks, including rhymes. A tour de force in this dubious genre is *German Declensions and Conjugations By Help of Reason and Rhyme,* a sixpence pamphlet of 28 pages published in 1891 by Francis Storr, a teacher at Merchant

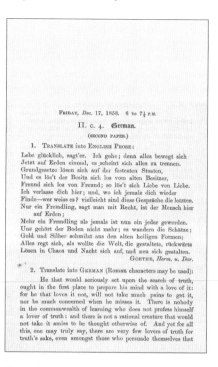

Figure 3.11a:
The second of two Senior German papers set by the Cambridge Local Examinations Syndicate in 1858 (University of Cambridge 1858 [rpt. 2008], p. 95

96   EXAMINATION PAPERS.   [*Senior*

they are so. How a man may know whether he be so in earnest, is worth inquiry: and I think there is this one unerring mark of it, viz. the not entertaining any proposition with greater assurance, than the proofs it is built upon will warrant.

LOCKE.

3.   Grammatical Questions.

(1) What cases are respectively governed by the following verbs: reuen, ärgern, träumen, pflegen, zahlen, bezahlen, lehren? and what by the following prepositions: um, mit, nach, ohne, nebst, zu, in, auf, halben, wegen?

(2) What is the full force of the line (in § 1), "Gold und Silber schmilzt," &c.? Of the verbs, gehen, ruhen, fallen, schlafen, rufen, schicken, kommen; which are construed with sein, and which with haben? With which is schmelzen construed?

(3) Give (a) the Present and (b) Imperf. Indicative, and (c) the Imperfect Subjunctive, of the first person sing., as also (d) the Imperative sing., of the verbs, befehlen, heissen, empfangen, friern, bergen.

(4) Give the different meanings, with the gender in each case, of each of the following nouns: Mensch, Thor, Erbe, Band, Geissel, Hut. Give Baum with the Adj. grün and the definite article, in the Nom., Gen. and Dat. both sing. and pl.

(5) When is a compound verb said to be separable, and when inseparable; and how is the conjugation of the verb affected by the difference? What is the force of the particles er, ver, zer, ent, anheim?

4. Point out (without translating into English) the unidiomatic constructions in the following lines:

Der Neudeutsche.

Mit dem prosaischen Geschwätz
Was wollt Ihr, dem gemeinen?
Von mir nur an nehm' ich Gesetz'
Und sonst von Andern keinen.

Candidates.]   EXAMINATION PAPERS.   97

Was ob Ihr durch Autorität
Auch Euren Satz vertheidigt,
Schiert mich? hat die Majorität
Ja stets genarrentheidigt.

Ist bei der Jetztwelt gleich mein Stil
Geworden noch nicht Mode,
Erreichen ganz gewiss mein Ziel
Werd' ich nach meinem Tode.

Denn endlich doch in dieser Welt,
Die alte, wie die junge,
Jedwed' Autorität zerfällt,
Auch die der Adelunge.   STIEGLER.

THURSDAY, *Dec.* 16, 1858. 9 to 11½ A.M.

II. D.   **Euclid and Conic Sections.**

1. DEFINE a superficies, an angle, adjacent angles, parallel straight lines.

If two triangles have two sides of the one equal to two sides of the other, each to each; and have likewise the angles contained by those sides equal to each other, they shall be equal in every respect.

Construct a triangle of which the base, the sum of the other sides, and the vertical angle are given.

2. If a side of any triangle be produced, the exterior angle is equal to the two interior and opposite angles, and the three interior angles of every triangle are together equal to two right angles.

At what angles are the sides of a regular duodecagon inclined to each other?

3. If a straight line be divided into two equal, and also into two unequal parts; the squares of the two unequal parts are together double of the square of half the line, and of the square of the line between the points of section.

If the sum of the squares of the distances of a point *P* from two fixed points is constant, the locus of *P* is a circle.

Figure 3.11b: The second of two Senior German papers set by the Cambridge Local Examinations Syndicate in 1858 (University of Cambridge 1858 [rpt. 2008], pp. 96–97

Taylor's School, notwithstanding the author's knowledge that "I am laying myself open to the jibes and jeers of the New Learning" (Storr 1891: v). For example, a rhyme for "neuters ending in -er all umlauted" begins:

*The **Dach** of a **Dorf** and the **Aas** of a **Rind**,*
*The **Haupt** of a **Kalb** and the **Kleid** of a **Kind**,*
*The **Nest** of a **Huhn** in a **Loch** with **Eier**,*
*The **Wörterbuch**'s **Blatt** and a **Scheit** for the fire*
[18 more lines in this vein]
All in -ER their plurals make,
And all umlauted vowels take.

(Storr 1891: 19).[70]

---

70 Notwithstanding this doggerel, Storr was a sensitive appreciator and translator of German, as a highly positive review of his translation of Heine in the *Educational Times* (March 1, 1887) indicates.

99

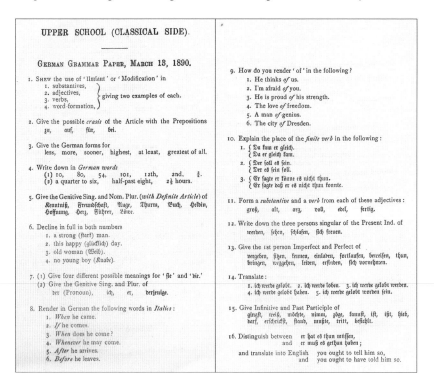

Figure 3.12: An examination paper from Rugby School, 1890

Wesselhoeft (1904) also included such *Merkreime*, for example for genitive prepositions:

> Unweit, mittels, kraft und während,
> laut, vermöge, ungeachtet,
> oberhalb und unterhalb,
> innerhalb und außerhalb,
> diesseit, jenseit, halben, wegen,
> statt, a u c h längs, zufolge trotz,
> stehen mit dem Genitiv,
> doch ist hier nicht zu vergessen,
> daß bei diesen letzten drei
> auch der Dativ richtig sei.

Besides local examinations, teachers also had an eye to the civil service and military examinations which their pupils might go on to sit. So, for example, in the general preface to Siepmann's German Series (Advanced), a series of annotated texts published by Macmillan, Otto Siepmann observed that "some knowledge of word-building and derivation is [...] constantly demanded in our military and other examinations", so that a short chapter on these has been added to the advanced texts (Voegelin 1900: ix). Volumes like Becker (1891) or Hohnfeldt (1887) contained sample examination papers; others provided sample passages for unseen translation, such as Lechner (1885; according to the title page, Lechner was Senior Master of Modern Languages, Modern School, Bedford); others advertised themselves as specifically suitable for examinations, such as Meissner's *Practical Lessons in German Conversation. A companion to all German grammars and a Manual for Candidates for the Civil and Military Service Examinations* (Meissner 1888: title page). These were first introduced in 1855. Though even by the 1880s the numbers taking German at such examinations were small, both by comparison with the overall number of successful candidates (about a seventh of these) and by comparision with candidates for French (about half as many) (cf. note 43 above), textbook authors who had direct experience of such examinations advertised the fact on their title pages: Dr Franz Lange was Professor of German at the Royal Military Academy, Woolwich (Otto & Lange 1890: title page) and was an examiner to the College of Preceptors, as well as in the German language and literature "at the Victoria University, Manchester" (Lange 1888: title page). Alfred Oswald was examiner to the the Civil Service Commission, London, as well as to the University of London (Oswald 1912: title page).

*Table 3.3: Cambridge Syndicate Local Examinations set texts for German 1858–1895 (where * "denotes that an edition has been issued in the Pitt Press Series").*

Titles (sometimes short forms, with idiosyncratic capitalization) are as in the original. The list is taken from French and German set books for 1858–1892 held by Cambridge Assessment Archive. From 1875 onwards, an effort seems to have been made to use texts issued in the Pitt Press Series for school use.

	Juniors	Seniors
1858	Lessing, Fables, Prose and verse	Schiller, Rev. of the Netherlands; Goethe, *Hermann und Dorothea*
1859	Schiller, W. Tell	Schiller, Rev. of the Netherlands; Goethe *Iphegenie*
1860	Schiller, W. Tell	ditto
1861	Fouqué, Sintram	Schiller, Thirty Years War, iii, Goethe *Iphegenie*
1862	Andersen, Bilderbuch ohne B.	Dahlmann, History of Engl. Rev. iii–vii; Schiller, Turandot i, ii
1863	Schmid, die Ostereier	Dahlmann i–ii, Schiller Turandot as above
1864	Schiller, Der Neffe als Onkel	Dahlmann, Histo of Engl. Rev. iii–vii; Schiller, Wallenstein i
1865	Fouqué, Undine	Pauli, Bilder aus alt-England i, ii, xii; Gellert, Fabeln i

	Juniors	Seniors
1866	Schiller, W. Tell	Pauli, Bilder aus alt-England viii, x, xi, Goethe H und D
1867	Bielfeld. German ballads 103–end	Heine, die Harzreise, Schiller, Maid of Orleans
1868	Ditto	Fouqué, Sintram; Goethe *Iphegenie*
1869	Uhland, Gedichte pp. 191–300	Schiller, *Wallenstein's Tod* und *der Dreissigjährige Krieg* iv
1870	Heyse, Novellen i. pp1–89	Brugsch, Aus dem Orient i; Lessing, Nathan der Weise
1871	Fouqué, Undine	Schiller, Rev. of the Netherlands; Goethe, Egmont
1872	Hauff, Das Wirthshaus im Spessart	Juniors subject + Goethe, H und D
1873	Fouqué, Die b. Hauptleute, Aslauga's R.	Juniors subject + Schiller, die Piccolomini
1874	Hauff, Die Karavane	Juniors subject + Goethe, Iphegenie
1875	Kohlsrausch, das Jahr 1813*	Juniors subject + Schiller, W. Tell
1876	Goethe's boyhood (arranged by Wagner)*	Juniors subject + Goethe, H und D*
1877	Freytag, Der Staat Friedrichs d.g.*	Juniors subject + Freytag, Bilder aus d. D. Vergangeheit
1878	Von Raumer, der erste Kreuzzug*	Juniors subject + Dactylic poetry (arranged by Wagner)*
1879	Immermann, der Oberhof*	Juniors subject + Lessing, Minna von Barnhelm
1880,	Hauff, Das Wirthshaus im Spessart*	Juniors subject + Goethe, Iphegenie
1881	Goethe's Boyhood (arranged by Wagner)*	Juniors subject + Gutzkopf, Zopf und Schwert*
1882	Uhland, Ernst, Herzog von Schwaben*	Juniors subject + Freytag, Der Staat Friedrichs d.g.*
1883	Von Raumer, der erste Kreuzzug*	Juniors subject + Schiller, die Piccolomini
1884	Riehl, Culturgeschichtliche Novellen*	Juniors subject + Goethe, H und D
1885	Hauff, Die Karavane*	Juniors subject + Schiller, Maria Stuart
1886	Hauff, Das Wirthshaus im Spessart*	Juniors subject + Lessing, Minna von Barnhelm
1887	Lessing and Gellert, Selected Fables*	Juniors subject + Gutzkopf, Zopf und Schwert*

	Juniors	Seniors
1888	Benedix, Dr Wespe*	Juniors subject + Mendelssohn, Selected letters*
1889	Hauff, das Bild des Kaisers*	Juniors subject + Goethe, Iphigenie
1890	Riehl, Culturgeschichtliche Novellen*	Juniors subject + Schiller, Wilhelm Tell*
1891	Goethe's Boyhood*	Juniors subject + Freytag, die Journalisten
1892	Hauff, Die Karavane*	Juniors subject + Goethe, Hermann und Dorothea*
1893	Hauff, Das Wirthshaus im Spessart* (omitting Said's Schicksaa[sic]le);	Juniors subject + Schiller, Maria Stuart
1894	Klee, die deutschen Heldensagen	Juniors subject + Gutzkopf, Zopf und Schwert*
1895	Riehl, Geschichte aus alter zeit: Die Gauerben, die Gerechtigkeit Gottes	Juniors subject + Hackländer, Der Geheime Agent

3.9 Philology in textbooks of German

If Collar's aim was "not to make philologists", other authors of textbooks in the nineteenth century, the very heyday of historical-comparative scholarship, took a different view. This is perhaps not surprising. In the early stages of the institutionalization of the subject, there was evidently a good deal of cross-fertilization. Both Professors Bernays and Müller were – on paper, at least – teachers at Rugby in the mid-nineteenth century;[71] Bernays had already been teaching German before his appointment at King's College London; and Bernays was not alone as a university don in writing textbooks. The Oxford and Cambridge Local Examinations were set and marked by university dons. In short, there was plenty of potential for insights from German philology to penetrate school textbooks. Here I consider some examples where they did so, to a greater or lesser extent.

This is not the place to rehearse the history of nineteenth-century philology,[72] but some key dates given in Table 3.4 (gleaned from Robins 1997) may serve as useful milestones. Of fundamental importance was Jacob Grimm's statement in 1822 of the "first" sound shift, often called Grimm's Law, which distinguished the Germanic languages from the remaining Indo-European languages (ca. 500 B.C.) and which explains regular consonant alternations in cognates like *piscis* and *fish*; and of the "second" or "High

---

71 A Monsieur Bernays is recorded as having briefly taught German at Rugby in the mid-nineteenth century (Hope Simpson 1967: 28); Max Müller, was likewise recorded as a teacher there from 1854 (Ortmanns (1993: 73). Presumably – given their commitments elsewhere – they were visiting teachers rather than the main instructors of German.

72 See, for example, Davies (1998).

German" sound shift, which separated High German from Low German and other Germanic languages (ca. 500 A.D.), explaining consonant alternations between standard German *Pfeife* and the English cognate *pipe*. Grimm also introduced the terms *Ablaut* to describe regular vowel changes to mark tense and other functions in Germanic verbs (as in *sing, sang, sung*) and *Umlaut* for other vowel changes that were originally phonetically conditioned but now often have a grammatical function (for example marking plurals, e.g. *Vater, Väter* father(s)). Grimm distinguished too between "strong" verb conjugation (those reliant on *Ablaut* for tense marking) and "weak" or regular verb conjugations, and applied the same terms, strong and weak, to the two patterns of adjectival declension found in German. In 1875, Karl Verner was able to explain some of the exceptions to Grimm's Law as the result of a process that came to be known as Verner's Law.

Table 3.4 Some key dates in the history of linguistics to 1880

1786: William Jones's paper to the Royal Asiatic Society in Calcutta making the connection between Sanskrit and the Germanic and Romance languages
1814: *Indo-European* first used in English (1823 *indogermanisch*)
1822: Jacob Grimm, *Deutsche Grammatik* (2nd ed.): strong & weak conjugation and declension, *Ablaut, Umlaut, Lautverschiebung*, later known as Grimm's Law (the first sound shift; already stated by Rasmus Rask)
1848: Alexander John Ellis, *Essentials of Phonetics*
1854– Grimm, *Deutsches Wörterbuch* (-1960)
1867: Alexander Melville Bell, *Visible speech: the science of alphabetic*
1875: Karl Verner's statement of "Verner's Law", which explained the regularity behind some apparent exceptions to the First Sound Shift.
1876: Wenker's dialect questionnaire (*Wenker-Sätze*)
1876: Eduard. Sievers, *Principles of Phonetics*
1877: Henry Sweet, *Handbook of Phonetics* (distinctive vs non-distinctive features)
1878: Neogrammarians' manifesto of language change as 'exceptionsless laws' published by Hermann Osthoff and Karl Brugmann
1880: Hermann Paul, *Principles of the history of language*

Only a few years after Grimm's comparative grammar of 1822, Becker's German grammar for English speakers (1830) – a translation of his grammar published a year earlier in German – already shows the influence of Grimm, dividing the nouns and verbs into the "ancient" and "modern" declensions and conjugations respectively, corresponding to "strong" and "weak" (Carr 1935: 490, 496);[73] Strauss (1852) already used the terms

---

73 I cannot find evidence for Carr's claim that Bernays (1830) followed Becker in distinguishing "ancient" and "modern" declensions and conjugations (Carr 1935: 491, 496). The terms "ancient" and "modern" are still found in Whitney's grammar of 1869. It should be noted that although the distinction between strong and weak verbs may appear self-evident now, it had taken several centuries of German grammar-writing to arrive at that distinction; cf. McLelland (2009).

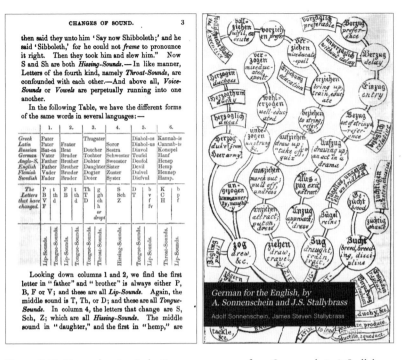

Figure 3.13: Figure showing Indo-European cognates from Sonnenschein & Stallybrass (1857: 3), here placed alongside the front cover of the volume, highly expressive of a philologist's view of what learning German was all about in the mid-nineteenth century

"strong" and "weak". Becker's "philological bias" was followed by Skene (1831) and Bernays (1830), though it was, according to Carr (1935: 484), in some measure "not beneficial […] particularly in Becker's attempt to class the German strong verbs according to the original vowel of the infinitive". The categorizations strong and weak were relatively quickly established – see Eysenbach & Collar (1887) in Figure 3.9 above for an example.

The use of the categories strong and weak had obvious value in making the grammar of German clearer. However, even more "hard-core" philological insights find a place in at least some teaching of German in schools. Rugby's examination papers include, for example, in July 1890, Upper School German Fifth set, some plainly comparative philological questions:

> Give the English cognate forms of: *Taube, Vogel, Düne, Kessel, Schmiede, Säbel, sieden, heulen, schaufeln, die liebe lange Nacht*
> And the Latin cognate forms of: *Kerker, Insel, Acker, heute, Spelunke*
> Trace the word *Apotheke* in Greek, French and English.

Such questions incidentally have no counterpart in the Cambridge local examinations around the same time, but if Müller really was engaged at Rugby in some capacity in the mid-nineteenth century, then a philological bias is perhaps not entirely surprising.[74] Other textbook authors made even higher demands on their pupils. As early as 1857, Sonnenschein & Stallybrass included a table in their German for the English which set out cognates across the Indoeuropean language family (Figure 3.13). This book was aimed squarely at "pupils" (not adults!) and even claimed inspiration (p. iii) from the leading educationalist of the time, the Swiss Johann Pestalozzi (1746–1827), for his principle of proceeding from the known to the unknown (p. iii). The belief in progressing from the known to the unknown was, for example, the motivation behind the attention that Sonnenschein & Stallybrass paid to sound changes, such that the learner realizes that "far the greater part of these words [i. e. new words to be learnt in the foreign language] are not 'strangers' to him, but old acquaintances in disguise".

Another interesting example is Henry Weston Eve, whose dictum at the Headmasters' Conference in 1879 was already cited: "Your first object is to discipline the mind; your second to give a knowledge of French or German" (cf. Hawkins 1987: 113), making quite clear his allegiance to the Neo-Humanist view of language learning as mental training.[75] The newest insights into the history of the German language provided fertile territory for such training (and Eve mentioned Sonnenschein's book as "a book which no teacher can read without pleasure and profit" (Eve 1880: vii). So in the preface to his *School German Grammar*,[76] Eve evangelized that "A teacher cannot begin too soon to point out the changes of letters in passing from English to German and *vice versa*; in fact, to keep Grimm's Law, and other simple rules, always before his pupils" (1880: vii). Advanced pupils should be made to write down etymologies "in a full and systematic way". As a model, Eve gave:

> **Vermessenheit**, *presumption*, from 1. **sich vermessen**, *to measure oneself amiss*, and hence *to presume beyond one's powers or rights*. 2. **Heit** a termination equivalent to *head* or *hood*, forming an abstract noun.

> (Eve 1880: vii)

---

74 Müller's statement to the Clarendon (Public Schools) Commission in 1864 on the purpose of foreign language study has been oft-quoted: *"I would aim principally at securing an accurate knowledge of grammar and secondly a sufficient amount of reading – but I should not attempt fluency in conversation"*.

75 As the comment suggests, Eve was a teacher of both French and German (as well as Maths and Chemistry), who had perfected his German while studying chemistry in Heidelberg. He had first taught at Wellington military academy, and his *Wellington French Primer* (1870), written with his Swiss colleague de Baudiss – who joined him at University College School in the late 1870s (Usher et al. 1981: 30, 37) – ran into many editions. An abridged version of the *School German Grammar* in 1884, with a set of *First German Exercises* to accompany it, was also published (*A Short German Accidence and Minor Syntax*), and *Second German Exercises* (also with F. de Baudiss), to accompany the full grammar. Eve was the Dean of the College of Preceptors – the first professional body of teachers – from 1884.

76 The third edition of Eve's grammar was reviewed in the *Educational Times* (December 1, 1886, p. 433), where the reviewer judged the text to be "correct and reliable", and welcome to "drive out of the school-room such unsystematic manuals as Otto, Ahn, &c.", though noting that some of the vocabulary was a little archaic and not very useful.

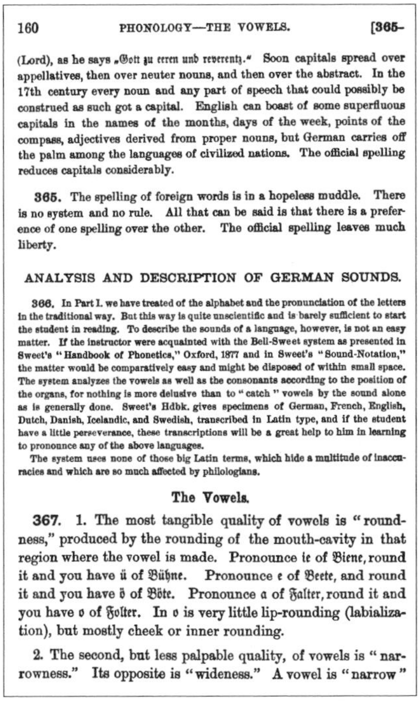

Figure 3.14:
Brandt (1884: 182)

160   PHONOLOGY—THE VOWELS.   [365-

(Lord), as he says „Gott zu erren und reverrentz." Soon capitals spread over appellatives, then over neuter nouns, and then over the abstract. In the 17th century every noun and any part of speech that could possibly be construed as such got a capital. English can boast of some superfluous capitals in the names of the months, days of the week, points of the compass, adjectives derived from proper nouns, but German carries off the palm among the languages of civilized nations. The official spelling reduces capitals considerably.

365. The spelling of foreign words is in a hopeless muddle. There is no system and no rule. All that can be said is that there is a preference of one spelling over the other. The official spelling leaves much liberty.

ANALYSIS AND DESCRIPTION OF GERMAN SOUNDS.

366. In Part I. we have treated of the alphabet and the pronunciation of the letters in the traditional way. But this way is quite unscientific and is barely sufficient to start the student in reading. To describe the sounds of a language, however, is not an easy matter. If the instructor sees acquainted with the Bell-Sweet system as presented in Sweet's "Handbook of Phonetics," Oxford, 1877 and in Sweet's "Sound-Notation," the matter would be comparatively easy and might be disposed of within small space. The system analyzes the vowels as well as the consonants according to the position of the organs, for nothing is more delusive than to "catch " vowels by the sound alone as is generally done. Sweet's Hdbk. gives specimens of German, French, English, Dutch, Danish, Icelandic, and Swedish, transcribed in Latin type, and if the student have a little perseverance, these transcriptions will be a great help to him in learning to pronounce any of the above languages.

The system uses none of those big Latin terms, which hide a multitude of inaccuracies and which are so much affected by philologians.

The Vowels.

367. 1. The most tangible quality of vowels is "roundness," produced by the rounding of the mouth-cavity in that region where the vowel is made. Pronounce i of Biene, round it and you have ü of Bühne. Pronounce e of Beete, and round it and you have ö of Bötte. Pronounce a of Falter, round it and you have o of Folter. In o is very little lip-rounding (labialization), but mostly cheek or inner rounding.

2. The second, but less palpable quality, of vowels is " narrowness." Its opposite is "wideness." A vowel is "narrow"

Eve continued to update the editions of the grammar; he revised his account of Grimm's Law in 1890, adding the account of Verner's Law then, and revised these paragraphs again in the fifth edition (cf. preface 1903), to expand on the description of the "First Shifting", of Verner's Law and the "Second Shifting." The explanation – very early in the textbook – made few concessions to the age and prior knowledge of the pupils, as the terse account of the sound shift illustrates. Classes already familiar with Latin and Greek might, admittedly, have included some quite sophisticated learners, and teachers may themselves had added a good deal of explanation; still, it is hard to imagine all pupils grasping these rules with ease.

"VERNER'S LAW. There are, however, certain words in which the Indo-European tenues p, k, t, become not aspirates, as Grimm's Law would require, but medials, b, g, d. Such are *heben* compared with *capio* [other examples follow, NMcL] It is found that this change takes place only in words in which the main accent follows the tenuis."

(Eve 1903: 7)

One textbook included Verner's law a mere nine years after Verner had published on it. Its author H.C.G. Brandt was, according to the title page of his grammar, "Professor of German and French at Hamilton College, N.Y. Formerly of John Hopkins University, Baltimore", and his grammar was published in both New York and London, with the title *A Grammar of the German Language for High Schools and Colleges. Designed for Beginners and Advanced Students* (1884).[77] Brandt had published an account of Verner's Law in the first volume of the *American Journal of Philology*, which had been founded in 1880, and, unlike Collar, he apparently did seek to make philologists out of his readers, both beginners and advanced students at American high schools and colleges. Brandt described his

---

77 There were several later editions. Brandt's grammar was reviewed very positively in the *Educational Times* (March 1, 1885, p. 128) as an "excellent book" which "bridges the gap between our best German Grammars and the present state of philology", though the reviewer judged that Verner's Law and a number of other points should have been treated "much more fully".

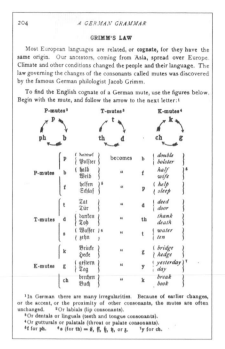

Figure 3.15:
Using Grimm's Law to find cognates
(Ball 1908: 204)

book as "an attempt to treat German grammar with regard to the present stage of Germanic philology" and "the scientific analysis of German sounds and accent". It covered the *Ablautreihen*, Grimm's Law, and Verner's Law, and included a "Historical Commentary upon Accidence". Brandt specifically stated in the preface to a later edition that these sections were "not intended to be [...] for teachers and specialists only" (Brandt 1893: iii). Figure 3.14 shows the start of his account of Grimm's Law. Brandt's work is an impressively early reception at school level of the latest research in German philology; it is several years ahead of, for example, Emil Trechmann's 1891 English translation of Otto Behagels' *History of the German language* (or in Karl Breul's words, in his *The Teaching of Foreign Languages in our Secondary Schools* "an adaptation of it, which is not free from slips" (Breul 1898: 69–70).[78]

Within a few years, these recent findings from philology had begun to be made more digestible to learners. Ball's *German grammar for schools and colleges* (1908) offers a summary of Grimm's Law that does not describe the actual processes of the sound shift at all (in which, to simplify greatly, voiced stops became voiceless). Instead, Ball set out diagrammatically what the learner must do to get from the German word to its English cognate – which in effect meant reversing the direction of the sound shift, from voiceless stops to voiced ones (hence *p > b, t > d, k > g* in Figure 3.15), such that *doppel* "becomes" *double*. (In fact, in the sound shift, it was the form containing an original *b* that became *p*). By this time, however, textbooks authors' interest in historical linguistics was already waning (cf. McLelland 2013a); educators' interests were taken by the applicability of a new linguistic science, phonetics, to language teaching, as we shall see in the next section.

---

78 See Taylor (to appear in *Biblionews*), according to whom Trechmann (b. 1856?) studied at Leipzig, Heidelberg and then Oxford, and was the first lecturer in Modern Languages at University College, Bangor, a post which he left in 1888 to take up a similar position at the University of Sydney, where he was responsible for teaching German and French from 1889 to 1903. Presumably for his students at Sydney, Trechmann, who owned a copy of Lechner's unseens, published his own *Passages for Translation into French and German for use in University and school classes* in 1899.

3.10 The new science of phonetics and the Reform Movement

The following is the figure content (a reproduction of a page):

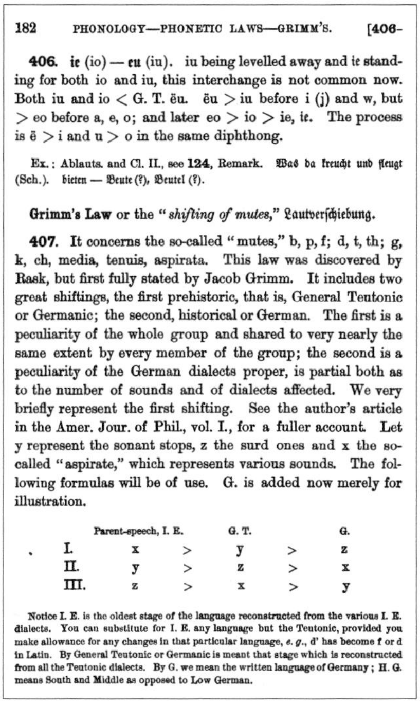

182   PHONOLOGY—PHONETIC LAWS—GRIMM'S.   [406-

406. ie (io) — eu (iu). iu being levelled away and ie standing for both io and iu, this interchange is not common now. Both iu and io < G. T. ëu. ëu > iu before i (j) and w, but > eo before a, e, o; and later eo > io > ie, ie. The process is ë > i and u > o in the same diphthong.

Ex.: Ablauts. and Cl. II., see **124**, Remark. Was da freucht und fleugt (Sch.). bieten — Beute (?), Beutel (?).

Grimm's Law or the "*shifting of mutes*," Lautverſchiebung.

407. It concerns the so-called "mutes," b, p, f; d, t, th; g, k, ch, media, tenuis, aspirata. This law was discovered by Rask, but first fully stated by Jacob Grimm. It includes two great shiftings, the first prehistoric, that is, General Teutonic or Germanic; the second, historical or German. The first is a peculiarity of the whole group and shared to very nearly the same extent by every member of the group; the second is a peculiarity of the German dialects proper, is partial both as to the number of sounds and of dialects affected. We very briefly represent the first shifting. See the author's article in the Amer. Jour. of Phil., vol. I., for a fuller account. Let y represent the sonant stops, z the surd ones and x the so-called "aspirate," which represents various sounds. The following formulas will be of use. G. is added now merely for illustration.

	Parent-speech, I. E.		G. T.		G.
I.	x	>	y	>	z
II.	y	>	z	>	x
III.	z	>	x	>	y

Notice I. E. is the oldest stage of the language reconstructed from the various I. E. dialects. You can substitute for I. E. any language but the Teutonic, provided you make allowance for any changes in that particular language, *e. g.*, d' has become f or d in Latin. By General Teutonic or Germanic is meant that stage which is reconstructed from all the Teutonic dialects. By G. we mean the written language of Germany ; H. G. means South and Middle as opposed to Low German.

Figure 3.16:
Brandt makes reference to Bell and Sweet (1884: 160)

"He talked of pedagogics, and this was natural enough; but he had much to say of modern theories in Germany [...] the old masters were still in their places but a good many changes had taken place notwithstanding their stubborn resistance [...] Though the form-masters still taught French to the lower school, another master had come, with a degree of doctor of philology from the University of Heidelberg and a record of three years spent in a French *lycée*, to teach French to the upper forms and German to anyone who cared to take it up in place of Greek."

W. Somerset Maugham, *Of Human Bondage* (Vintage Classics Edition, pp. 64, 66, from Chapters 15 and 16)

Somerset Maugham's semi-autobiographical account of the effect of a new headmaster on the teaching of modern languages at a minor English public school in the late 1880s (based on his experiences at King's School, Canterbury) captures the growing, sometimes grudging recognition of modern languages in the curriculum in the late nineteenth century, together with the appetite for new teaching methods under the influence of German theories – including Wilhelm Viëtor, of whom more below. For, contemporary with the definitive statements of neogrammarian approaches to historical comparative philology (Verner 1975, Osthoff & Brugmann 1878, Paul 1880), a major shift in language study was beginning to make itself felt, in a series of publications outlining the science of speech, including Alexander Melville Bell's *Visible speech: the science of alphabetic* (1867), Eduard Sievers' *Grundzüge der Phonetik* (Principles of Phonetics, 1876), and Henry Sweet's *Handbook of Phonetics* (1877). These new approaches were swiftly adopted by textbook authors. For example, Brandt – whose adherence to philology was just noted above – was equally up to date with developments in phonetics:

> From the works of Osthoff, Sievers, Paul, Kluge, Braune and Sweet I have appropriated most of the new results and methods, which are accepted and popularized only two slowly

(Brandt 1884: iii)

Brandt's account of the German sounds made reference to Bell and Sweet by name. The notion of distinctive features – expounded by Sweet – is already in practice here, as, for example, Brandt guided the reader from the familiar long *i* to the less familiar rounded front vowel represented by German <ü> simply by adding the feature of rounding (Figure 3.16).

However, the place of phonetics in language teaching – and the focus on the spoken language more widely – soon became caught up in the wider "Reform Movement" or *Neuere Richtung* which gathered momentum in the last two decades of the nineteenth century.[79] The reform is usually said to have been sparked off by the pamphlet of the German Wilhelm Viëtor, *Der Sprachunterricht muss umkehren* ('Language teaching must change', 1882), in which Viëtor asked why, with so much time devoted to modern language teaching in the German schools, the outcome was so poor. With reference to Charles Sayce's *How to learn a language* (1879) Viëtor found the answer in the methods adopted, which placed so much emphasis on the dry learning of grammar and translation of highly artificial sentences (as in the "methods" discussed above) at the expense of the living language. Already by the 1880s there is a noticeable increase in the number of textbooks that explicitly place emphasis on speaking the language. Huss (1884), Lange (1890) and Eysenbach (1885) were noted above (besides the older method of Otto). Meissner – professor of German at Queen's University Belfast and author of several textbooks of German[80] – commented in his *Practical Lessons in German Conversation* that

> The ultimate object of learning a living language is to be able to speak it [...] It is true, the systematic teaching of the spoken language has been greatly neglected of late years. This has been an unavoidable result of the manner of conducting examinations in modern languages [...] But [...] now several of the English Examining Boards not only require a proficiency in the use of the spoken language, but even refuse to give credit for the written examination when the candidate fails to satisfy the examiners in the oral examination. Conversation has, therefore, to be studied as much as any other subject of examination.

(Meissner 1888: vii–viii)

Where the examination format was unchanged, the frustration with the inadequacies of traditional methods, particularly with the lack of attention paid to spoken language, can be sensed too in 1890s examiners' reports contained in the Cambridge Assessment Archives:

---

79 See Gilbert (1953–1955) and Bayley (1998) – drawing heavily on Gilbert – for overviews of developments in this period. Howatt & Smith (2002) offer a treasure trove of primary sources.

80 Meissner's textbooks included his *Public School German Grammar* (1886, key 1887), still widely used in Ireland in 1909–1910, alongside editions of Otto's *German-Conversation Grammar* (1857), Siepmann's *Public School German Primer* (1896), and Spanhoofd's reader of 1910. See Fischer (2000: 471).

As in the preceding year, there were occasional indications of merely mechanical use of text-books, as also of the *insufficient importance attached in some schools to the oral side of language teaching.*

(Cambridge Local Examinations, 1895 German Juniors report, p. xxxix, my emphasis)

In conclusion the examiner wishes to express once again his strong conviction that in a great many schools a complete reform of the teaching of elementary German is required. Unless more time and greater attention are given to the careful teaching of the elements of the language, and *unless German is taught from the very beginning as a living and spoken language by duly qualified teachers, the results of the teaching of German will remain eminently unsatisfactory*, and the aim of modern language teaching will be completely missed.

(1898 German Seniors report , p. xli, my emphasis)[81]

Many voices adopted the call for the teaching of modern languages as *living* languages, no doubt in part because it was taken up by prominent scholars like Henry Sweet and Karl Breul.[82]

The reform was a broad church. While some laid the emphasis on speaking the target language in class – for which some phonetic training of teachers, if not of the pupils, was obviously valuable – others were more concerned with wider developments in pedagogy, which, in the nineteenth century, was now drawing on insights into child psychology. The "natural" method – concentrating on using the language as much as possible in class – appealed to those who believed second language acquisition should proceed following the natural process by which children learn their mother tongue, even though Bernays had pointed out as early as 1849 that to adopt such a method strictly implied having to "wait as long as the child" to learn the language, a child, moreover, who also had the benefit of "practice of many hours from their earliest infancy" rather than just a few hours a week (Bernays 1849: 111).

---

81 For 1898, the examiners listed include both Karl Breul and Walter Rippmann (of whom more below). It is not clear to me who would have written the German section of the 1895 report, as no examiner for German is listed, though Breul was listed for 1894.

82 According to Gilbert (1954: 15), the German reform movement was first mentioned in England by the philologist and phonetician Henry Sweet in a paper to the Philological Society in 1884 on the "Practical Study of Languages" (cf. Sweet 1899); Wiliam H. Widgery, Assistant Master at University College School, was instrumental in popularizing its ideas through a series of articles in the *Journal of Education* (afterwards published as a pamphlet: Widgery 1888) and in lectures. Note also Colbeck (1887) *On the Teaching of modern languages,* and Karl Breul, *The Teaching of Modern Languages in Our Secondary Schools* (1899) (Breul was a University Lecturer in German at Cambridge at the time, and one of the regular examiners for the Cambridge Syndicate Local Examinations). A very influential publication was the English translation of the Dane Otto Jespersen's *Sprogundervisning*, which appeared as *How to teach a foreign language* in 1904. For a history of the reform movement, see the introductions and documentation in the five volumes of Howatt & Smith (2002).

Others were attracted in particular to the idea of the "object lesson", a teaching method developed by the Swiss educationalist Johann Pestalozzi, who sought to make educational experience follow the general process of concept formation in children, which, he believed, began with sensation, with impressions from which concepts are formed. Pestalozzi designed graded "object lessons" in which children were guided to examine minerals, plants, animals and man-made objects, in a sequence that progressed from the simple to the complex, the easy to difficult, and from the concrete to the abstract.[83] Sonnenschein & Stallybrass (1857: iii) had cited Pestalozzi's dictum of moving from the known to the unknown together with Eduard Bacon's approach (who described his own practice of giving "objective and conversational lessons" in the preface to his own textbooks: Bacon 1879: iv).[84] In the United States, a set of primers by Conrad Witter, aimed at the children of German migrants in Missouri (heritage speakers, more or less bilingual),[85] also made use of the object lesson. An example is given in Figure 3.17, where the pupils were asked to consider the similarities and differences between a rose and a carnation. In Britain, Elizabeth Mayo's *Lessons on Objects as given to children between the ages of six and eight in a Pestalozzian School at Cheam, Surrey* (1830) were widely used and ran into many editions, and the object lesson was then soon adapted to foreign language learning too, particularly for young children. In 1898, the method of the object lesson was adapted specifically to foreign learners of German. Trotter's 1898 volume was adapted from Alexander Cran's set of object lessons for French. It combined with Pestalozzi's pedagogy the reformists' view that "the first lessons in a living language should be given orally, with the help of a blackboard and of pictures, the object being to associate the name with the thing seen" (as Cran wrote in the preface: Trotter 1898: iii). Trotter's is one of the earliest books to rely in its pedagogy on illustrations, which were evidently now becoming affordable.[86] Already in the 1880s, a set of wall pictures show-

---

83 On the history of the object lesson in education, see Carter (2010).

84 The object lesson was also central to another influential method in the United States, that associated with Maximilian Delphinius Berlitz, who founded his first 'Berlitz School' in Providence in 1878, but whose method spready rapidly – the *Berlitz method for teaching modern languages: English Part* (New York/Berlin, 1888) was sold in large numbers (241st reprint in 1936). As Macht (1994: n.p.) notes, Volume I of the *Berlitz manual* was distinguished by the emphasis on 'object teaching', i.e. object-related conversations between teacher and students. On developments in the United States – beyond the scope of this book – see the brief Excursus under 10.3 below.

85 On the history of German migrants to Missouri, see Olson (1980), Burnett & Luebbering (1996).

86 Another early example, Lowe's *First German Primer*, likewise aimed at young beginners, relies heavily on high-quality engravings, with short simple sentences: *Der Löwe ist grimmig; Das Rhinoceros hat ein dickes Fell*, etc. (Lowe 1903: 12–13). Of course, the potential of pictures or objects to support language learning had a much older history in Europe – Comenius's *Ianua Linguarum* (Gateway to Languages, 1631) and *Orbis sensualium pictus* (The Visible World in Pictures, 1658) were highly innovative in their time, and one of Comenius's key aims was to allow children to learn through objects rather than through words. It is no accident that Comenius's 300th anniversary was celebrated enthusiastically in 1892, in the midst of the reform movement. Hawkins (1987: 102–109) outlines Comenius's ideas on language education in simple terms; Reinfried (1992: 33–55) gives a more detailed account. See also Murphy (1995) and, from the perspective of the history of lexicography and onomasiology, Hüllen (2002c).

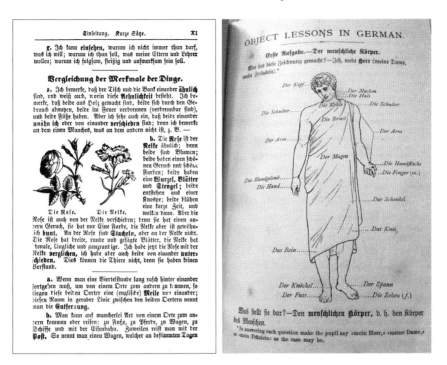

Figure 3.17 (left): Conrad Witter, *Deutsch-Amerikanisches Lesebuch*, Schlussstufe (1865: XI)
Figure 3.18 (right): J. J. Trotter, *Object Lessons in German*, 1898

ing the four seasons, produced by the publisher Eduard Hölzel in 1885, had begun to be used in foreign language teaching, beginning with the Swiss reform teacher Sines Alge, and used by Walter Rippmann in his adaptation of Alge's work in the *First French Book* and *First German Book* (1898, 1899, discussed in section 3.10.2 below).[87] These are relied on too in *First Steps in German* by Scholle & Smith (1902): "The linguistic matter is provided by object lessons, based on Hölzel's pictures of Spring and Winter and on class surroundings, to enable the learner to connect the German word directly with the object it represents" (Scholle & Smith 1902: 1).[88] Scholle & Smith outline in some detail how, "in our view", lessons should be taught, taking Lesson 1 and 20 as their examples:

---

87 The series of wall pictures had originally been commissioned by an Austrian association of elementary school teachers, and drawn by Marie and Sophie Görlich (Vienna: Hölzel, 1885). See Reinfried (1992: 106–113), including reproductions of the four seasons pictures pp. 110–113; Byram (2004: 269).

88 Scholle & Smith's book was still in use at Canterbury Boys' High School, Sydney, Australia, in 1945, as a name entered in the flyleaf of the copy held in the Taylor collection indicates. The owner, G. Bradshaw, was in class 2A – one might surmise that, in the top stream (A), he was starting German as his second foreign language in his second year of secondary school.

> Lesson 1. – The picture is hung up before the pupils. The books of the pupils remain shut. The teacher pronounces: *der Vater, die Mutter, das Kind, der Garten, das Haus*, etc., pointing at the same time to the respective person or object in the picture, and ascertaining whether the pupils have understood the meaning of the words. The class in chorus or the pupils individually pronounce the words after him. When this treatment of the first part of the lesson has been continued until the pupils are quite familiar with the sounds, the teacher points again to the respective persons and objects, asking: *wer ist dies?* (or *das?*), *was ist dies?* (or *das?*), demanding the full answer: *dies (das) ist der (ein Vater)*, etc. After, finally, the questions of the second part have been gone through a few times, the books are opened, and it will be found that the pupils are able to read the German words straight off. To demand any spelling at this stage, whether orally or in writing, would be but a waste of time.

(Scholle & Smith 1902: 11)

Trotter and Cran's volume of object lessons begins with the familiar – the human body, illustrated by a figure modestly clothed in a Roman toga (Figure 3.18), followed by familiar everyday objects: slate and pencil, a petroleum lamp. Trotter's volume also contained a Reader (77–101) on familiar topics beginning with *der Mensch*, moving on to topics such as circulation and digestion, and then the home and garden.

Related to the belief that the value of pictures was that they allowed the pupil to connect new lexical items directly with the concept, another feature of the reform movement was the importance attached by some, including Viëtor himself, to *Realia*. Mary Brebner cites Breul's definition of *Realia* as "illustrative facts and studies, comprising a study of foreign life and thought, customs and institutions at different periods, to be partly acquired by personal examination" (Brebner 1898: 34). *Realienkunde* implied both teaching *facts* about the culture (German *Landeskunde*, in effect), and encouraging inspection of *objects* themselves, where possible. It enabled pupils to become more aware of the language as a living language – whether by talking about real objects in the classroom, or by learning about the culture of those who spoke the target language. (Such a focus on what would later be called the "target" culture had arguably only become necessary in the nineteenth century, once modern languages had begun to be taught to many who would *not* be going on a Grand Tour themselves to experience the culture first-hand). Mary Brebner was a graduate of the Cambridge Training College for Women Teachers, and her account of a visit to Germany in 1897 to observe language teaching practices in Germany, funded by a £50 Travelling Scholarship for Women Teachers, was reprinted many times. In it, Brebner described the new technique of using *Realia* instigated by Professor Gustav Wendt in Hamburg, who had taken great pains to assemble a collection of materials from England for the learning of English (Wendt 1892).[89]

---

89 Breul (1899: 81) noted that Kron's book on German daily life would meet a similar need in England (cf. Kron 1916; see Chapter 6).

114

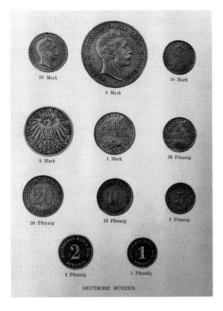

Figure 3.19:
Ungoed (1912) facing page to title page:
German coins

Brebner described an English lesson for German pupils which took British coins as its starting point:

"On another occasion he [the teacher, a certain Professor Heim] showed the class different English coins, asking various questions about their value, appearance, etc. The difference between the old and new "pennies" led to the description of Britannia and the Union Jack, and the different flags that had been united to form the latter. Questions were asked, in this connection, about the dates of the union of England with Ireland and Scotland respectively. [...] The students were interested and animated throughout."

(Brebner 1898: 35).

Ungoed, in his *First German Book on the Direct Method* (and accordingly entirely in German) (with two editions in 1912), was possibly directly inspired by Brebner's account to include a full-page illustration of German coins that could be used by any teacher for a discussion like that reported above (Figure 3.19; similarly Rippmann 1917: 92). Describing the currency for learners has a long history, stretching at least two and half centuries from an anonymous *Royal French Grammar* of the early eighteenth century (Anon. 1720: 259–60, possibly by John König with *Royal* being a play on words) to the illustrations of coins and notes in *Einfach toll* 1 (Smith 1985: 32, 35).

Brebner commented that there was certainly a place for realia-based teaching, but that she had more than once heard German teachers comment that it could be overdone: "'What do German boys want to know about English football, etc.?' [...] Nevertheless, wherever I came across the teaching of *Realien*, I always noticed that it increased the interest and zeal of teacher and pupils alike" (Brebner 1898: 34). The reference to sport in particular finds a counterpart in *Bell's First German Course* (1907), written by L. B. T. Chaffey, M. A, Assistant Master at Eton, one of the earliest textbooks to includes photos, the first two of which show a tennis team (p. 4) and German football teams (p. 16).[90] The second of these accompanied a dictation exercise, itself an innovation, with its focus on recognizing German sounds): "the advantage this has of fixing the sounds and symbols of a language like German as well as the meaning of words can hardly be overestimated" (p. viii). Innovative too (even if it had first been tried by

90 Baumann (1902) includes two photos; cf. Chapter 6.2.

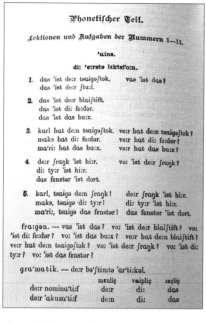

Figure 3.20:
The start of lesson one in phonetic script in Ungoed's *First German Book on the Direct Method* (1912: 88)

Aedler in 1680) was the use of Roman rather than Gothic type "to render the early work more easy" (p. ix), until the last few stories. Chaffey was clearly putting into operation some of the ideals of the reform movement. Interestingly, however, "Pages to elucidate pronunciation, though once written, have been cut out, since experience seems to show that pupils do not look at them" (p. vii).

Chaffey may well have been right, but other textbooks in the early years of the twentieth century did include phonetic script to help teach pupils correct pronunciation, following Rippmann's early example in his *First German Book* (1899, discussed below in section 3.10.2). Ungoed's text is one such example. Although aimed at "pupils who begin to study German at an early age" (Ungoed 1912: v), several lessons were reproduced at the back of the book in phonetic script, as in Figure 3.20, and with specific references to the pronunciation norms set by Viëtor and Theodor Siebs (1898) (See also Egan 1913). Contemporary with Ungoed, Meyer's *Deutsche Gespräche. Mit phonetischer Einleitung und Umschrift* likewise used phonetic script, in this case on the facing page to the text itself (Figure 3.21). As the preface stated, it aimed to do for German what Franke's *Phrases de tous les jours* and Jespersen's *True Spoken English* had already done for French and English. In her *First German Book* for A. & C. Black, Althaus (1916) took the view that only the teacher needed the phonetic script, and published a separate edition of the first thirty lessons in script, "strongly recommended to the notice of the teacher" (Althaus 1916: iii). She emphasized that there could be no "slackness in exacting the utmost effort from the pupil" in articulating sounds. They would be unable to distinguish shades of sound, for example in forming the German tense vowels, but would be able to see that their cheeks were stretched out sufficiently far. Only once their organs are in the right position should the teacher allow the children to make a sound (Althaus 1916: iv).

The relationship between Reform Movement discussions swirling throughout Europe over some three decades and what actually changed in textbooks and classrooms, at a time when many of the voices in the debate were themselves classroom teachers and textbooks authors, is still very little studied, and that gap cannot be filled here – though Hawkins (1987: Chapter 5) gives a spirited survey; see also Bayley (1998) and Gilbert

<table>
<tr><td>

— 46 —

Ihnen. — Sie sind sehr gütig. — (Das' ist) sehr liebenswürdig von Ihnen, daß Sie mich (mal) besuchen.

11. Machen Sie keine Umstände. (Machen Sie keine Geschichten!)

Bitte, machen Sie sich keine Umstände meinetwegen. Lassen Sie sich durch mich ja nicht stören. — Störe ich? O bitte, nicht im geringsten. — Entschuldigen Sie¹) (, wenn ich Sie belästige). O bitte! — Pardon! Bitte! — Entschuldigen Sie, ich hab's nicht absichtlich getan [es war nicht meine Absicht]. — Verzeihen Sie, wenn ich Sie unterbreche. — Verzeihen Sie, gnädige Frau, ich glaube, Sie sind im Irrtum. — Erlauben Sie, das ist *mein* Regenschirm.

12. Sprechen Sie französisch? Ja, etwas. Ich kann grade genug, um mich verständlich zu machen. — Er spricht es leidlich, geläufig. — Er kann [—schreibt] französisch wie seine Muttersprache. — Ich verstehe besser als ich spreche.

Man merkt ihm in der Aussprache den Ausländer fast gar nicht an. — Sie haben eine sehr korrekte Aussprache. — Prosa lesen Sie recht gut, aber Verse können Sie noch nicht lesen. Das ist Mangel an Übung.

Wo haben Sie Ihr Deutsch gelernt? Seit wann treiben Sie es?

11. ¹) *Entschuldigen Sie mich* gebraucht man.

</td><td>

— 47 —

iˑnn. — zi zɪnt zeˑɹ ˈgyːtɪç. — (das ɪst) zeɹ ˈliˑbmsvɹrdɪç fɔn iˑnn, ˌdas zi mɪç (mal) bəˈzuːxn.

11. maxn zi ˈkaenə ˈʔʊmʃtɛndə. (ˌmaxn zi kaenə jəˈʃɪçtn!)

bitə ˌmaxn zi zɪç ˈkaenə ˈʔʊmʃtɛndə maen(ə)tˈveˑjən. ˌlasn zi zɪç durç mɪç ˈjaˑ nɪçt ˈʃtøːrən [ˈʃtøːɹn]. — ˈʃtøːrə ɪç? o ˈbitə, nɪçt ɪm jəˈrɪŋstn. ɛntˈʃʊldjən ziˈ (, vɛn ɪç ziˈ bəˈlɛstjə). o ˈbitə! — parˈdɔŋ! ˈbitə! — ɛntˈʃʊldjən zi, ɪç haps nɪçt apˈzɪçtlɪç jətaːn [ɛs ˌvaˑr nɪçt maenə ˈʔapzɪçt]. vɛn ɪç zi untɹˈbrɛçə. — fɹˈtsaeˑ(ə)n zi gnæˑdjə frao, ɪç ˈglaobə zi zɪnt ɪm ˈʔɪrtuˑm. — ɛrˈlaobm zi, das ɪst ˈmaen reˑjnʃirm.

12. ʃprɛçn zi franˈtsøːzɪʃ? ˈjaˑ, ˈʔɛtvas. ɪç kan ˌgraˑdə jəˈnuːx, um mɪç fɹˈʃtɛntlɪç tsu maxn. — ʔɔ kan [— ˈʃraept] franˈtsøːzɪʃ vi zaenə ˈmutɹˈʃpraˑxə. — ɪç fɹˈʃteˑə bɛsɹ als ɪç ˈʃprɛçə.

man ˌmɛrkt iˑm m dɹ ˈʔaosʃpraˑxə den ˈʔaoslɛndɹ fast ˈgaˑr nɪçt ˈʔan. — zi haˑbm aenə zeɹ kɔˈrɛktə ˌʔaosʃpraxə. — ˈproːza leˑzn zi rɛçt ˈguˑt, abɹ ˈfɛrzə kɛnn zi nɔx ˈnɪçt leˑzn. ˈdas (ɪ)st ˌmaŋəl an ˈʔyˑbuŋ.

voˈ ˌhaˑbm zi iɹ dɔytʃ jəˈlɛrnt? ˌzaet van ˈtraebm zi ɛs?

wenn man durch ein Geschäft oder dergleichen plötzlich abgerufen wird und weggehen muß.

</td></tr>
</table>

Figure 3.21: Meyer's *Deutsche Gespräche* (1912) with facing page phonetic transcription, pp. 46–47; the first edition of the work was six years earlier, in Uppsala, 1906

1953–1955.[91] The *Educational Times* (the periodical of the College of Preceptors) and *Modern Language Teaching* (the organ of the Modern Language Association, which had been founded in 1892) of the 1890s and the first two decades of the twentieth century attest to the lively discussions amongst the first generations of professional modern language teachers.[92] By way of illustration of how the reform movement affected the teaching and learning of German, I give an overview below of two stalwarts of the Modern Language Association, whose obituaries appeared alongside each other in *Modern*

---

91 The tenor of Hawkins's survey can be gleaned from his concluding remarks to Chapter 5: "It is impossible to reflect on this outcome of the movement […] without a feeling of sadness that so much generous endeavour should be disappointed. Of course much was gained. Language classes, at least for a select minority of able grammar school pupils, were challenging, exciting and enjoyable places in the 1930s, 1940s and 1950s. The methods used, however, owed little to Sweet and Jespersen. Phonetics and direct method were mere echoes from an old song, except in a very few schools" (Hawkins 1987: 150–51).

92 Two examples that are of particular interest for the history of applied linguistic theory and of classroom practice respectively are: 'The importance of intonation in the pronunciation of foreign languages' (*Modern Language Teaching* 10 (1914): 201–2–5), and A. W. Pegrum's contribution on 'The oral teaching of German: an actual lesson and a suggestion' (*Modern Language Teaching* 10 (1914): 206–212).

Figure 3.22:
Walter Rippmann.(Reproduced by kind permission of Queens College, London.)

Language Teaching 28: 3 (September 1947), p. 117: Otto Siepmann (1861–1947) and Walter Rippmann (later Ripman) (1869–1947). Both were very active as teachers, as textbook authors, and as editors of major publishers' modern language series, but, as we shall see, Rippmann was a more radical proponent of reform than was Siepmann.[93]

3.10.1 Walter Rippmann (later Ripman) (1869–1947): a wholehearted reformer

Walter Rippmann was a more prominent figure in the modern language teaching scene than Otto Siepmann, even if unlike Siepmann he does not yet feature in the *Oxford Dictionary of National Biography*; the most complete account of his biography is that of Flood (2000: 246–247). Born at 18 Bowerie Road, Stoke Newington on January 22nd, 1869, the son of Christiane Rippmann (née Daumiller) and commercial clerk Hugo Rippmann (b. 1843),[94] he attended Dulwich College, before being admitted on October 6th, 1887 to Gonville & Caius College, Cambridge, to read Medieval and Modern Languages, with an entrance scholarship of £50.[95] In December of 1887, aged eighteen, he was awarded the only First Class B. A. in German for that year by the University of London, for which he had studied as an external student, having already obtained the prize at the Intermediate Examination the previous year (*Educational Times* 1888, Jan. 1, under "University and College Intelligence"). He passed the "Previous Examination," parts I and II, at Cambridge in December 1887, and was exempted from Additional Subjects (German) by the Oxford and Cambridge combined schools examination certificate. He obtained a First Class result at the Intercollegiate Modern and Medieval Languages examination in June 1888, and his scholarship was raised to £60. The following year, 1889 he took a II.2 in Part I of the Classical tripos. He graduated in 1890 in the Modern and Medieval Languages Tripos

---

93 The biographical details and textbook comparison below were first published in McLelland (2012c).

94 Hugo's address at the time of Walter's birth was Rockbank, Overhill Road, Lordship Lane, London SE; by the time of 1901 census, Hugo Rippmann was a naturalised British subject.

95 I am grateful to Mr James Cox, archivist at Gonville & Caius College, for his assistance in obtaining much of the biographical detail given here. According to those archives, Rippmann was also senior lecturer in French and German at Wren's for the period 1897–1915, but I have been unable to find out any more about this institution. My thanks are also due to Ms Annabelle Gardiner (Queen's College archivist), who likewise supplied valuable details on Rippmann's career.

with First Class honours and with a distinction in spoken German; his scholarship was extended for a year and raised to £70, and he received an additional prize of £5. Clearly both a high achiever and something of a collector of qualifications, Rippmann went on to obtain a second class degree in classics in 1891, and second class in oriental languages in 1892. His MA was conferred in 1894.

Rippmann remained at Gonville & Caius until 1896 as an Assistant Lecturer in modern languages,[96] as various mentions in College magazine, *The Caian*, attest.[97] In 1897, *The Caian* reported that "Mr W. Rippmann was been appointed Lecturer in German language and literature at Bedford College, London. This appointment, together with the similar post which he holds at Queen's College, will necessitate his permanent residence in London."[98] The appointment at Queen's was to the post of Professor of German, a post to which the 27-year-old had beaten 39 other applicants in 1896 (Kaye 1972: 127), and which he held until 1912. These two appointments put Rippmann at the heart of pioneering educational developments: Queen's College, where Bernays had also lectured,[99] founded in 1848 and given a royal charter in 1853, was the first British institution to give academic qualifications to girls; Bedford College (which became part of the University of London in 1900) had been founded in 1849 as the first higher education college for the education of women in the UK.[100] By this stage in his career, Rippmann was already won to the cause of the reformists; he joined the International Phonetic Association in 1897, and he was one of 26 teachers from England who attended the first modern languages holiday course in that year, established at the University of Marburg by Eduard Koschwitz (1851–1904), Professor of French at Marburg, and in which Wilhelm Viëtor was also heavily involved from 1898 onwards. (The course ran for French and German in the first year; English was added in 1898 when Viëtor moved to Marburg, although he and Koschwitz did not see eye to eye. The holiday courses still run in Marburg. See Nail (2000). In 1897, the 26 English teachers were among 68 foreign teachers and a total of 363 participants.) When in 1901, a special course for foreign students was established at Queen's, Rippmann began it with a series of lectures on the pronunciation of English (Kaye 1972: 141–142).

---

96 *Biographical History of Gonville & Caius*, vol. II (1713–1899), p. 492.
97 In 1893–4, he was active in preparing a "Dramatic Performance" (*The Caian* III, p. 123); in 1894–1895 he was one of the organizers of the May Ball (*The Caian* IV, p. 127); in 1896–1897 he made a donation to the College Cricket Pavilion fund (*The Caian* VI, p. 60, 87, 91, 163).
98 *The Caian* VI, p. 163.
99 Cf. his introductory lecture, discussed above (Bernays 1849).
100 Rippmann was chosen from among 40 applicants for the position (Kaye 1972: 127). Incidentally, the author Katherine Mansfield attended Queens' College 1903–1906, and encountered Rippmann through the College magazine, in which he took a keen interest. The Katherine Mansfield Society calls Rippmann – young and ardent, unlike many of the other professors – her "first literary mentor", for whom she developed a schoolgirl passion. She wrote to her cousin Sylvia Payne after two terms at Queen's, "I am ashamed at the way in which I long for German. I simply can't help it. It is dreadful. And when I go into class I feel I must just stare at him the whole time.' (Kaye 1972: 135; see also the timeline prepared by Linda Lappin at http://www.katherinemansfieldsociety.org/timeline/); Woods (2007).

Rippmann was a prolific author throughout his life, whose publications generally ran to multiple editions. Other textbooks of German by him include *A Rapid German Course* (1921); *Easy Free Composition in German* (1911); *An easy German course* (1935); *Elementary German Composition* (1935); as well as numerous readers and anthologies. His continued belief in the need for explicit grammar instruction was put into practice with the publication in 1909, "after some not unnatural hesitation", of a volume of *Exercises in German Grammar and Word Formation*, in which he "tried to avoid foolish sentences" (1913 ed., p. v), but certainly covered grammar in the usual way – though he refrained from referring to any particular reference grammar of German "because the teacher can easily supply such help as his pupils require, and because I know of no grammar written in German that is sufficiently clear and well expressed for the use of English pupils" (p. vi), and instead compressed the essentials into twenty pages (in German).

At the University of London, Rippmann took on his share of duties, as Secretary to the Moderators for Matriculation, and inspector of schools offering candidates for the London University General Schools examinations. He also ran the University's counterpart to the Marburg modern language courses, as the University's Director of Holiday Courses for Foreigners. As part of this course, Rippmann also taught English phonetics (as advertised for example in *Modern Language Teaching* 13 (1917), pp. 104–105); he also offered to teach French and German phonetics if this was in demand. As his courses in English phonetics for foreign teachers indicate, Rippmann's interests increasingly extended beyond the teaching of German and French to English speakers, to embrace the teaching of English, to foreigners, but also to English children, an interest reflected in his *The sounds of spoken English* (1910) and *English sounds; a book for English boys and girls* (1911); *A first English book for boys and girls whose mother-tongue is not English* (1920); and *Good Speech* (1924). He was a committed member of the Simplified Spelling Society, the editor of its journal from 1911, and the author too of *A dictionary of new spelling* (1941) and *New spelling; being proposals for simplifying the spelling of English without the introduction of new letters* (1948). He probably influenced the phonetician Daniel Jones (1881–1967), and certainly helped him with his *Phonetic Dictionary of the English Language* and *Pronouncing Dictionary* (Jones 1913, 1917; see Flood 2000: 248, citing Collins & Mees 1999).

Rippmann, a key figure in the modern languages scene for two or three decades from the 1890s, may serve as an illustration of the earlier statement that the reform movement was a broad church, and accordingly not without its internal disagreements. Two examples may serve. The first concerned the question of the right age at which to start learning a language. While many within reform circles advocated starting early – and some of the simple primers, picture-books and object lessons discussed above, such as Lowe (1903), were aimed at very young children – Rippmann was reported to have said at the General Meeting of the Modern Language Association in 1917 that "no foreign language should be attempted before (the age of) twelve", prompting a heated response in the Correspondence pages of *Modern Language Teaching* (1917: 109) from a certain "D. F. K.":

Dear Sir, – I notice that at the meeting following the annual meeting (reported February), a member, Mr. Ripman, said that 'No foreign language should be attempted before (the age of) twelve,' and that this sweeping declaration was not controverted by any experienced teacher present. In this, some important considerations seem forgotten. It has been truly said, I think by Goethe, that he who knows only one language does not know that one. A glimpse into the possibilities of another tongue is of much psychological value. Foreign language teaching is best begun in object and picture lessons, which are not [*sic*, but presumably in error for *more?*] suitably given earlier than the elaborate tasks laid upon pupils in their teens. These, together with reading lively foreign nursery-tales, are comparatively restful lessons for children, who are compelled to do so much hard work in school, and give them a pleasant beginning to what should be an interesting study. That knowledge of a second language should be more widespread among English people is surely too obviously important to need urging at the present time. D. F. K.

A second controversy – no doubt in part fuelled by the sad fact of World War I, though a Modern Languages Association sub-committee had already been appointed to look into the matter in 1913 – concerned whether teachers and university professors of modern languages ought, by preference, to be British nationals (Bayley 1991: 16). The MLA inquiry found that only 8 of 23 modern language professors in English universities were British. Symptomatic of the atmosphere was the resolution proposed to the General Meeting of the Modern Language Association on January 11, 1918, and reported in *Modern Language Teaching* 14 (1918: 22–25) under the heading, "Who shall teach modern languages?" Mr. A Hargreaves had proposed that "in the interests of education" (under which he also included "the formation of character") it was better to have modern languages taught "by persons of British nationality". Not surprisingly, Rippmann (British born, but of German parents, and having clearly found it advisable to anglicise the spelling of his name) considered the resolution "inopportune" and likely to cause resentment. The exchange between Hargreaves and Rippmann (now Ripman) continued through the issues of *Modern Language Teaching* 14 (pp. 133, 151, 198).[107]

Walter Rippmann died on February 5th, 1947. According to the obituary in *Modern Language Teaching*, "his last years were clouded by an insidious illness which left him physically helpless, though his lively intelligence was never dimmed. The patience with which he bore this suffering was the only comfort he could give to his friends." He was survived by his wife.

---

107 See Bayley (1991: 14, 16–17) for further consideration of the controversy, also addressed by the Leathes Report on Modern Languages (1918), which called for all heads of university modern language departments to be British. At the time, the report found, nine of the eleven professors of German were foreigners.

3.10.2 Otto Siepmann (1861–1947)[108]

By contrast with Rippmann, Siepmann was a pragmatist, keen to learn from new ideas, but firmly rooted in the old public school ethos, and certainly far from abandoning the translation of constructed sentences, as the pure reformers advocated. Born in Germany, Otto Siepmann moved in 1885 to Britain to a teaching post in Kent, then Inverness, before settling at Clifton College, Bristol, in 1890, where he spent the next 31 years; he was naturalized as a British citizen in 1905. He became the founding head of modern languages in Clifton in 1900, where, according to Whitehead (2004), he reformed the curriculum radically, such that pupils had an hour of French and an hour of German daily, and "This unusual arrangement produced a steady stream of modern languages scholars destined for the universities of Oxford and Cambridge." Siepmann was involved in the founding of the Modern Language Association in London in 1892. In 1917 Siepmann gave evidence to the national committee of inquiry into the teaching of modern languages, under the chairmanship of Stanley Leathes (1861–1938), and was appointed reviser to the Northern Universities' Joint Matriculation Board language examinations. He retired in 1921, though he continued to act as an examiner for civil service and Oxford and Cambridge school examinations, and as an inspector for the Board of Education until 1932.

Seeing both the strengths and the weaknesses of the direct method of language teaching, Siepmann developed in his teaching and in his highly successful series of language textbooks a *via media* which kept the grammatical training and practice that had characterized language teaching in schools to that time, but based teaching on the spoken language. As Siepmann put it in his *Public School German Primer*, aimed at "boys or girls of about fourteen" (1900: vii; 1st ed. 1896), he sought "to treat the language as a living thing and at the same time draw from it some mental discipline and general culture" (1900: viii). Many elements of the *Neuere Richtung* are obvious in that volume, which Siepmann described as "an attempt to apply the principle of the *Neuere Richtung* to the teaching of German in Public Schools, *so far as this is feasible under existing circumstances*" (Siepmann 1900: viii; my emphasis). On the one hand, Siepmann believed that "Pronunciation and speaking deserve greater attention" and supported the principle of "Living practice before abstract rules" (p. viii, p. x). The introduction to German sounds in this volume was "largely based on Professor Viëtor's excellent little book on German phonetics" (p. viii), and Siepmann was clearly steeped in these new developments, as he took the trouble to include a list of "Leading Publications on the Method advocated by the Neure Richtung and on Phonetics", a list which included Henry Sweet, Viëtor, Eduard Sievers, Paul Passy and Michel Bréal (p. xiv). Years later, Siepmann's novel series of twenty-four German language gramophone records, released by His Master's Voice in 1932–3, underscored his belief in the importance of phonetics; in 1930, the BBC also used his *Primary German Course* for pioneering language education broadcasts. (Ironically, Siepmann himself, who had moved to Britain aged 24, apparently retained a strong German accent in English to the end of his life: Whitehead 2004). Whitehead

---

108 I follow here Whitehead (2004) for the biographical details of Siepmann's life.

(2004) also considered that Siepmann's advocacy of "the systematic use of topical news-paper articles to support language teaching, then unheeded, was seventy years ahead of its time" (Whitehead 2004).[109] On the other hand, however, Siepmann retained "Lists of exceptions", "for the convenience of masters who attach importance to their being learnt at an early stage" (p. xi), presumably those with a neogrammarian leaning; and incorporated philological insights such as the strong and weak categorizations of nouns and verbs (p. x, xi).

For younger learners, Siepmann's *Primary German Course* (1st ed. 1912) also included object lessons of the kind we have already seen, though again with pragmatism rather than zealotry: "In naming the things represented in the illustrations, there can be no harm giving the English of the object if there is the slightest doubt as to what is meant. But when once everything is made clear, the lesson proceeds in German" (p. vi). The grammar, on the other hand, is set out in English (unlike in Ungoed's 1912 uncom-promising Direct Method). Despite such pragmatism, Siepmann's expectations surely required either an inspirational teacher or a fairly stoical group of pupils, since he recom-mended that the first *month* of instruction should be devoted to the preliminary chapter on pronunciation and handwriting,

> so as to enable the pupils to acquire a good pronunciation from the outset. It is not difficult to arouse considerable interest in the formation of sounds; and it is much easier to be obtain good results if each sound is taken separately and practised until every pupil can reproduce it without effort.

After a month, pupils reached some carefully constructed reading passages on p. xlii, where the large number of cognates meant that they "will be pleasantly surprised to find that they can read and understand a connected piece of German without having first to learn any words or grammar" (Siepmann 1912: v–vi).

As editor of the Macmillan Modern Language series,[110] Siepmann presided over spe-cially prepared editions of classics for pupils, typically edited by practising teachers, and following a common pattern: an introduction to the material, and appendices contain-ing German-English vocabularies, and "Words and Phrases for Viva Voce drill", as well as sentences on syntax and idioms to translate into German (also deemed suitable for Viva Voce drill), and finally whole passages for translation. Besides literary works, some volumes dealt with historical topics or admirable characters (the Humanists, Frederick the Great, Walther von der Vogelweide).[111] Siepmann was both a conservative and a re-former. On the one hand, he wrote in his general preface to the series, "It is hoped that

---

109 Earlier textbook authors had also used newspapers as sources: Bachmair (1751) is the earliest example I am aware of, see Figure 3.2; in the nineteenth century, Bacon (1879: 212) also recom-mended reading German newspapers, "which afford a useful and interesting means of practising reading".

110 Siepmann's offer in 1916 to remove his name from the series in view of anti-German feeling was refused by Macmillan. Siepmann did, however, withdraw from the Modern Language Associa-tion (Whitehead 2004).

111 E.g. Zastrow, ed. Ash 1902 on Emperor Wilhelm; Ebner, ed. North, 1906; Hansjakob ed. Dixon,

pronunciation, recall that in his *Primary German Course* for slightly younger pupils, he advised that the first *month* of instruction should be devoted to the preliminary chapter on pronunciation and handwriting (Siepmann 1912: v); and his *Primary French Course* did use phonetic script (Siepmann 1902a, b).

While Siepmann evidently did not consider the use of the phonetic script helpful in his German primer, Rippmann provided a complete phonetic transcription of the passages from lessons 1–10 at the back of the book, likewise all new words introduced in lessons 11–44 (pp. 139–161), for "If a pronunciation is to be learnt at all, it should be learnt in a scientific fashion," i.e. using phonetic symbols (Rippmann 1921: v). No effort is made to introduce pupils to the script, nor is there any description of the sounds, and one wonders how useful pages of script would have been to the average pupil in the hands of the average teacher. The author of another *First German Book*, for the publishers Bell, wrote in his preface that "Pages to elucidate pronunciation, though once written, have been cut out, since experience seems to show that pupils do not look at them" (Chaffey 1907: vii), though a few other authors after Rippmann did include phonetics in one form or another. In Ungoed's text aimed at "pupils who begin to study German at an early age" (Ungoed 1912: v), several lessons were reproduced at the back in phonetic script, with specific references to the pronunciation norms set by Viëtor and Theodor Siebs (1898); Meyer (1912) likewise used phonetic script, on the facing page to the text (Meyer 1912). Althaus's *First German Book* for A. & C. Black assumed that only the teacher needed the phonetic script; a separate edition of the first thirty lessons in script was "strongly recommended to the notice of the teacher" (Althaus 1916: iii).

Speaking the foreign language

Both authors sought to promote the use of the spoken language in the classroom. Siepmann recommended that great attention be paid to "the correct reading of the passages", both individually and in chorus; in addition, questions at the end of each passage were for oral practice (cf. also the viva voce materials in Siepmann's series of German classics, noted above). Siepmann observed that experience suggested that "it is essential for beginners to have exactly the same questions asked in exactly the same form" (pp. viii–ix); for a change, a boy can be asked to "catechise the others" (p. ix); the teacher may also ask other questions, "but I believe that if those in the text, if practised until the answers are given with absolute fluency, sufficiently ensure such training of ear and tongue as should lead to a ready understanding of spoken German and the power of speaking it fluently" (p. x). Rippmann, following Alge's model, used set questions too. However, whereas for Siepmann, the questions were a follow-up on the passages given in the Reader, Rippmann made conversation in the classroom the starting point, as the teacher and pupils together explored wall-pictures. The lessons proceed gradually from single words (the very first lesson consists of a long list of names to listen to and repeat), to very simple sentences (*Das ist der Vater. Hier ist der Knabe*, etc.), into which new vocabulary and structures were gradually introduced, building up to longer passages. Rippmann also drip-fed relevant classroom language to facilitate the use of German in the classroom as a matter of course (e.g. *Öffnet die Bücher, Schließt die Bücher!*, p. 5). With grammar presented – rather than explained – in German, with classroom language in German, and with the concrete stimuli of Hölzel's four seasons pictures, Rippmann thus remained true to the ideal of keeping the use of English in the classroom to a minimum, although he conceded that with large classes and limited time, some time-saving use of English rather than the target language was acceptable (Rippmann 1899: 11). In his later *Rapid German Course* "for the use of evening classes and private students", which aimed "to make learners familiar, as expeditiously as possible, with a useful (though necessarily limited) vocabulary and with the essentials of the grammar" (Rippmann 1921: v), Rippmann used footnotes to translate new vocabulary, a device which avoided the need either for time-consuming explanations by the teacher or recourse to English. As we have seen, Siepmann was less rigid, writing in his *Primary German Course* for younger pupils, "In naming the things represented in the illustrations, there can be no harm giving the English of the object if there is the slightest doubt as to what is meant. But when once everything is made clear, the lesson proceeds in German" (Siepmann 1912: vi).

The primacy that Rippmann ascribed to the spoken language is also evident in the fact that his textbook is in Roman script, with no trace of the still widely-used *Fraktur*. Siepmann, in contrast, placed value on the ability to read German in a number of different formats. He devoted a section to German handwriting (as had many textbooks since Wendeborn 1797), and the first passage was given in handwriting, in Roman type, and in *Fraktur*. After the first few lessons, reading passages are in *Fraktur* only.

Also relevant in the context of teaching the real spoken language is the urgency or otherwise of introducing the *Sie* polite form of address that would be used by pupils addressing a teacher. Rippmann introduced it relatively early, on p. 25, as one might expect of a book where pupils and teacher are intended to spend the whole lesson speaking to one another. Siepmann's text, however, does not tackle the question until much later; second-person pronouns do not feature at all until passage 17 (p. 17), and *Sie* is introduced in passage 19 (p. 19); it is discussed in the grammar on p. 171.

The presentation of grammar
Although both authors adhered to the principle of illustrating the grammar before explicitly teaching it, their books differ markedly in approach. For Siepmann, "the nucleus of the book" was the Reader (p. vii), with passages designed to illustrate the grammatical points in context. From the outset, Siepmann's pupils were exposed to coherent texts that contained far more complex language than they were expected to produce: the very first passage, for example, ends *Wir versuchen in der Klasse und auf dem Spielplatz zu den Ersten zu gehören* ('In class and in the playground we try to be amongst the best, lit. to belong to the first', p. 1), which contains a *zu* + infinitive construction, an adjective acting as noun, and the dative case after three different prepositions. Grammatical points illustrated in the Reader are then presented in English in the substantial Grammar part of the book (pp. 101–188), where full paradigms ("living practice", p. x) precede description of the abstract rules. A good deal of grammar is dealt with very swiftly indeed: the first lesson, about school, introduces the present *and* preterite tenses of regular verbs, singular and plural; the Grammar then presents "simple tenses of weak verbs" in all per-

129

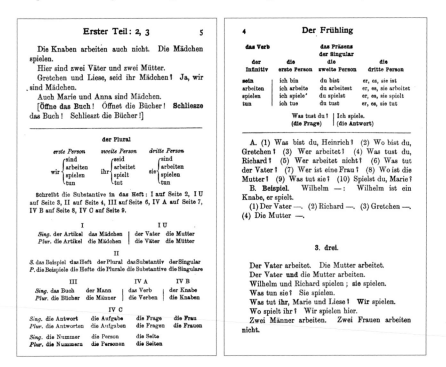

Figure 3.23: Ripman et al. (1917: 4–5)

sons, and the first drill in the Exercises is to give the Present Indicative of *lehren, lernen, schreiben, zeichnen, antworten* (p. 192). By lesson 2, on page 2, in a passage of 66 words, Siepmann's pupils are already presented with the future, perfect, and pluperfect tenses.

Rippmann's statement of principles, cited under 2. above, valued "grammar drill", and his American colleague Walter H. Buell wrote in the preface to the American edition of the *First German Book* (1901: vi) that "The constant grammatical drill which the book requires cannot fail to yield good results. Grammar is the loom by which words are manipulated to form the warp and woof of the spoken sentence".[115] Unlike Siepmann, however, Rippmann, presented grammar in German only, and gave only what Siepmann called the "living practice", with no exposition of the rules in words (see Figure 3.23) – it is assumed that learners will already know the necessary grammatical concepts.[116] Although there is a 28-page grammar booklet, the grammar presentation is

---

115 The American edition was published by Newson, for whom Rippmann was also modern languages editor, together with Buell. Rippmann's recognition of the need for explicit grammar instruction yielded in 1909, "after some not unnatural hesitation", a volume of *Exercises in German Grammar and Word Formation*, in which he at least "tried to avoid foolish sentences" (1913 ed., p. v).

116 Similarly, Siepmann presupposes his pupils already know Latin grammar, writing that "There are only four cases in German" (p. 145).

integrated into the main text, interspersed between model questions to be asked about the pictures. Rippmann also proceeds much more slowly, with a delay between the first introduction of forms orally and the first drills on them. For example, Lessons 2 and 3 present the present tense of verbs, singular first, then plural (see Figure 3.23), but not until lesson 7 (p. 13) are pupils required to undertake a drill of verb conjugation – and even then only in the present. Unlike Siepmann's input, the input in Rippmann's textbook does not go beyond patterns that pupils are expected to reproduce.

Most interestingly, the two authors's texts tackle grammar from reverse directions. Siepmann begins with all the grammar relating to the verb; even the passive (in all tenses!) has been dealt with by the end of lesson four (p. 5). Only two areas of the verb phrase are saved until later: compound verbs (i. e. separable and inseparable verbs, lesson 29), and the subjunctive.[117] Rippmann does the very reverse. Although we have seen that he introduces basic verb conjugation early on, the focus in the first of the three sections of the book is on *noun* phrase morphology rather than the verb; verb conjugation beyond the present tense is not dealt with until the second section, beginning on p. 62 of 126 pages. In beginning with the noun, Rippmann is the more traditional grammarian here, for grammars of German have begun with the noun phrase since the very first ones in the late sixteenth century, following Latin models (cf. McLelland 2009). Siepmann does not comment on his choice to introduce verbal morphology first, and I have been unable to find a model. It might signal a recognition of the centrality of the verb and verbal bracket in the structure of the German sentence, though it should be noted that his *Public School French Primer* (1906), published after the German primer, likewise begins with the simple and compound verb tenses.

Keeping learners interested

Both Rippmann and Siepmann sought to make their material of direct relevance to learners. Although Siepmann's text includes narrative and literary texts too (the first poem comes on p. 3 already), many of his passages relate to pupils' daily lives: early lessons deal with school, holidays, and a description of a room that reads like an object lesson, as the different features of the room are named (p. 6).[118] Rippmann relied on Hölzel's wall-pictures to provide the direct link to real-life experience. Rippmann's questions and statements about the pictures are, however, not inherently interesting, and almost all take the form of asking questions to which everyone already knows the answer and where the answers are to be given in full sentences. One would need a lively teacher indeed to animate pupils with *Das Dach ist auf dem Hause. Was ist auf dem Dache?* Or *Wer hat einen Pflug? Wer zieht ihn? Wer leitet ihn?* ('The roof is on the house. What is on the roof? Who has a plough? Who is pulling it? Who is leading it? pp. 14, 97), especially if the pupils – having already learnt French by a similar method – were already familiar

---

117 The subjunctive is dealt with in the last lesson, immediately following the introduction of subordinating conjunctions: "The Subjunctive of Verbs is given in the Dependent Order, because it occurs nine times out of ten in this order in actual language" (p. xi).

118 Siepmann later used object lessons in his *German Primary Course* for younger pupils (1912). The earliest book of object lessons for German known to me is Trotter (1898).

On the other hand, the report very reasonably pointed out that other languages should not be neglected either. Spanish was (or should be) important for commerce, Italy was a "pillar of European civilization" (Bayley 1991: 14), and even though Russian was not considered suitable for schools, the committee's suggestion that 55 new university Chairs of Modern Languages be funded envisaged treating all four "other" European languages equally, with ten Chairs for each. Needless to say, the report's plans were never implemented, for each of the other reports, published in 1922, came with their own "shopping lists" too, and all in the face of major cuts to the education budget in 1922 (Bayley 1991: 19). Still, some universities did extend the range of modern languages, and "at last European languages other than French and German began to emerge as university subjects" (Bayley 1991: 18).

In essence, the pre-eminence of French in a context where the case for (only) one foreign language was accepted set the points for the rest of the twentieth century. Repeated efforts in official and subject association reports and initiatives to promote what came to be known as LOTF (Languages Other Than French – the very invention of such acronym speaks volumes) did not greatly change the situation. The title of the study by Phillips & Filmer-Sankey (1993), *Diversification in modern language teaching*, might equally be – as far as its historical chapters are concerned – *Rather little diversification in modern language teaching*.

In sum, then, the effect of the first couple of decades of the twentieth century was to put German on the back foot, as the effect of the logic of making French the first foreign language was joined by the negative impact of World War I. Between 1912 and 1918, 38 schools gave up German as subject, 13 of them in the two years before the war. Still, in 1918, 65 of the most important private schools still taught it. In 1908, according to a report in *Modern Language Teaching* (1908), 40.4% of schools offered German, but this sank steadily to 27.3% in 1929; in 1929, of 48 counties, 17 offered no German at all; ditto in 18 of 79 boroughs (Ortmanns 1993: 95–96). In her "Plea for the Study of German", Marion Saunders noted in 1919–20 that there had certainly been a reaction against German after the outbreak of war (Saunders noted falls of 26% and 18% in two large, but unnamed, girls' schools between 1914 and 1919), and that this reaction was exacerbated by the shortage of teachers as many German nationals had to leave England, "and their places were only slowly filled by British-born teachers".[16] In addition to the dismal figures for German in secondary schools, Saunders also noted that the common Public Schools examination for the preceding year had included no German paper, indicating that it was barely being taught in preparatory schools; at Sandhurst there was "not a solitary cadet" learning German, and only 12% of naval cadets at the Royal Navy College Osborne (Saunders 1919–1920: 178–179).

The perception that the future of German in schools was at risk is evident in the frequency of publications with titles like "German?" (O'Grady 1906), "The place of German in the curriculum of secondary schools" (Stoy 1907), "The position of German

---

16 Cf. also Ortmanns (1993: 116). Like Saunders, Ortmanns (1993: 116) suggests that the drop-off in numbers during the war might have less to do with aversion to German, and more to do with the availability of teachers, who were involved in the war itself. On French and German in competition in British schools, see McLelland (2014).

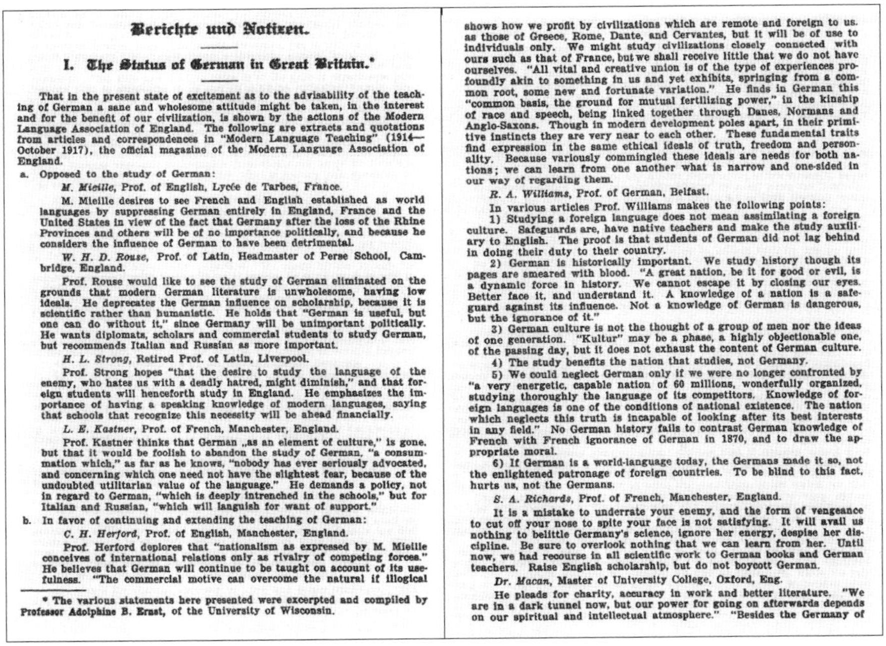

Berichte und Notizen.

I. The Status of German in Great Britain.*

That in the present state of excitement as to the advisability of the teaching of German a sane and wholesome attitude might be taken, in the interest and for the benefit of our civilization, is shown by the actions of the Modern Language Association of England. The following are extracts and quotations from articles and correspondences in "Modern Language Teaching" (1914—October 1917), the official magazine of the Modern Language Association of England.

a. Opposed to the study of German:

M. Mielle, Prof. of English, Lycée de Tarbes, France.

M. Mielle desires to see French and German established as world languages by suppressing German entirely in England, France and the United States in view of the fact that Germany after the loss of the Rhine Provinces and others will be of no importance politically, and because he considers the influence of German to have been detrimental.

W. H. D. Rouse, Prof. of Latin, Headmaster of Perse School, Cambridge, England.

Prof. Rouse would like to see the study of German eliminated on the grounds that modern German literature is unwholesome, having low ideals. He deprecates the German influence on scholarship, because it is scientific rather than humanistic. He holds that "German is useful, but one can do without it," since Germany will be unimportant politically. He wants diplomats, scholars and commercial students to study German, but recommends Italian and Russian as more important.

H. L. Strong, Retired Prof. of Latin, Liverpool.

Prof. Strong hopes "that the desire to study the language of the enemy, who hates us with a deadly hatred, might diminish," and that foreign students will henceforth study in England. He emphasizes the importance of having a speaking knowledge of modern languages, saying that schools that recognize this necessity will be ahead financially.

L. E. Kastner, Prof. of French, Manchester, England.

Prof. Kastner thinks that German ,as an element of culture," is gone, but that it would be foolish to abandon the study of German, "a consummation which," as far as he knows, "nobody has ever seriously advocated, and concerning which one need not have the slightest fear, because of the undoubted utilitarian value of the language." He demands a policy, not in regard to German, "which is deeply intrenched in the schools," but for Italian and Russian, "which will languish for want of support."

b. In favor of continuing and extending the teaching of German:

C. H. Herford, Prof. of English, Manchester, England.

Prof. Herford deplores that "nationalism as expressed by M. Mielle conceives of international relations only as rivalry of competing forces." He believes that German will continue to be taught on account of its usefulness. "The commercial motive can overcome the natural if illogical

* The various statements here presented were excerpted and compiled by Professor Adolphine B. Ernst, of the University of Wisconsin.

shows how we profit by civilizations which are remote and foreign to us, as those of Greece, Rome, Dante, and Cervantes, but it will be of use to individuals only. We might study civilizations closely connected with ours such as that of France, but we shall receive little that we do not have ourselves. "All vital and creative union is of the type of experiences profoundly akin to something in us and yet exhibits, springing from a common root, some new and fortunate variation." He finds in German this "common basis, the ground for mutual fertilizing power," in the kinship of race and speech, being linked together through Danes, Normans and Anglo-Saxons. Though in modern development poles apart, in their primitive instincts they are very near to each other. These fundamental traits find expression in the same ethical ideals of truth, freedom and personality. Because variously commingled these ideals are needs for both nations; we can learn from one another what is narrow and one-sided in our way of regarding them.

R. A. Williams, Prof. of German, Belfast.

In various articles Prof. Williams makes the following points:

1) Studying a foreign language does not mean assimilating a foreign culture. Safeguards are, have native teachers and make the study auxiliary to English. The proof is that students of German did not lag behind in doing their duty to their country.

2) German is historically important. We study history though its pages are smeared with blood. "A great nation, be it for good or evil, is a dynamic force in history. We cannot escape it by closing our eyes. Better face it, and understand it. A knowledge of a nation is a safeguard against its influence. Not a knowledge of German is dangerous, but the ignorance of it."

3) German culture is not the thought of a group of men nor the ideas of one generation. "Kultur" may be a phase, a highly objectionable one, of the passing day, but it does not exhaust the content of German culture.

4) The study benefits the nation that studies, not Germany.

5) We could neglect German only if we were no longer confronted by "a very energetic, capable nation of 60 millions, wonderfully organized, studying thoroughly the language of its competitors. Knowledge of foreign languages is one of the conditions of national existence. The nation which neglects this truth is incapable of looking after its best interests in any field." No German history fails to contrast German knowledge of French with French ignorance of German in 1870, and to draw the appropriate moral.

6) If German is a world-language today, the Germans made it so, not the enlightened patronage of foreign countries. To be blind to this fact, hurts us, not the Germans.

S. A. Richards, Prof. of French, Manchester, England.

It is a mistake to underrate your enemy, and the form of vengeance to cut off your nose to spite your face is not satisfying. It will avail us nothing to belittle Germany's science, ignore her energy, despise her discipline. Be sure to overlook nothing that we can learn from her. Until now, we had recourse in all scientific work to German books and German teachers. Raise English scholarship, but do not boycott German.

Dr. Macan, Master of University College, Oxford, Eng.

We work for charity, accuracy in work and better literature. "We are in a dark tunnel now, but our power for going on afterwards depends on our spiritual and intellectual atmosphere." "Besides the Germany of

Figure 4.1: Voices for and against German during World War I, from Ernst (1918: 110, 111)

in English schools" (Milner-Barry 1908), "Position of German in Grant-Aided Secondary Schools in England" (Board of Education 1929), and – as World War I drew to an end – "The study of German after the war" (Isaacs 1917); "The status of German in Great Britain" (Ernst 1918); "Should we teach German?" (anon. 1919); "A plea for the study of German" (Saunders 1919–1920). Ernst (1918) makes interesting reading: the author assembled extracts from correspondence to *Modern Language Teaching* over the years 1914–1917 on the subject of whether or not learning "the language of the enemy" should be encouraged (see Figure 4.1); perhaps unsurprisingly, the majority of space is given to those arguments made in favour of German.

Symptomatic of what was clearly happening across the country in the second decade of the twentieth century is the decision recorded in the minutes of the Masters' Meeting at Rugby of November 22, 1918, that in Upper Middle 1, "German will be dropped, two of the periods being devoted to Latin and two to French"; while German did not completely disappear from Rugby, it lost ground to French; Latin remained secure because it was still a requirement for university admission.[17] By 1929, only eight of 512

---

17 Cambridge did not drop the requirement for one of Greek or Latin until 1960, requiring instead any two languages (dropped to one in 1967). The requirement for foreign languages was dropped entirely by universities from the late 1960s onwards.

schools teaching a foreign language were offering German; another report stated that in 1925–26, of 1250 grant-aided schools (i. e. private schools that received some government funding), 872 provided only French; in 1928 at the Secondary School Certificate examination, 54273 students offered French, and only 3837 German (Spanish, with 719 entrants, was small but growing) (Phillips & Filmer-Sankey 1993: 15–16). In Ireland, only 7.4 % of examination candidates took German (down from the high-point of 18,4 % in 1912); in 1927 there were only 33 candidates (Fischer 2000: 465).[18]

Over and over again in the first half of the twentieth century, reports on modern languages earnestly pointed out that there was no reason why German should not be taught as the first foreign language in some schools at least, from the 1912 Circular 797, to the Leathes Report of 1918, to the 1929 report on the *Position of German in Grant-Aided Secondary Schools in England* (Board of Education 1929), to the Norwood Report of 1943 and a 1949 report by the Incorporated Association of Assistant Masters[19] (see Ortmanns 1993: 92–94; Phillips & Filmer-Sankey 1993: 12–19). By the second half of the century, small steps were being taken in some places to encourage diversity in language learning. In some schools, year groups alternated from year to year between starting either French or German as a first foreign language (Sidwell 1976: 26; Reeves 1986: 10); and although Sheppard & Turner lamented in 1976 that "only" 16 of 70 secondary schools in Norfolk offered German as the *first* foreign language (1976: 15), that was probably quite an advance.[20] So, while the proportion of candidates taking German appears to have declined slightly up to about the mid-1920s compared to other subjects (though there was a rise in absolute terms, as the overall number of examination candidates increased), from the late 1920s onwards (perhaps as the public view of Germany came closer to the picture of post-war Germany conjured up by the Leathes Report, cited above), German grew again in popularity, both measured against the overall number of candidates and compared to other foreign languages.[21] In grant-maintained secondary schools, the number of pupils learning German in 1928 was 18430 (out of about 426000 pupils, so a very respectable 23 %), well over half of them boys; there were about five hundred teachers of German. At the Second Certificate Examination (taken by about 10 % of pupils only), German had been taken by only 90 candidates in 1920, but this jumped to nearly 900 by 1938 (Ortmanns 1993: 100–01, 103).

---

18 There are interesting gender differences here. From 1933 to 1945, the number of boys taking German examinations in Ireland sank and remained under 30; but in 1936 there were 134 girls taking the examinations, all coming from five convent schools. In Ireland, Fischer suggests, German was a subject for girls from the outset, in contrast to French, which was long predominantly perceived as a boys' subject (Fischer 2000: 465–466). Incidentally, Fischer cites some examples of teacher and pupil exchanges between Irish convent schools and their German counterparts in the very late nineteenth century.

19 This document was an update on the original 1929 *Memorandum on the Teaching of Languages*. As Stern notes, "The regular re-writing of this work every ten or twenty years [i. e. 1949, 1956, 1967, 1979] provides an interesting record of the views of language teachers in the classroom" (Stern 1983: 101).

20 Tumber's paper "German as first foreign language" (Tumber 1986) describes her own experience in a school where German was – unusually – first foreign language, taken by all pupils for three years.

21 See Ortmanns (1993: 101).

4.4 Why German?

The status of German began to recover in the late 1920s, but an element of the siege mentality, of the need to defend and justify German, is evident in the tendency in the first decades of the century to devote space in textbooks to making the case explicitly for German, with sections on "why I should learn German". The earliest example I know of is that given in the last lesson of Beresford Webb's *Second German Book* (1900: 46), Lesson 34, "Warum ich die deutsche Sprache lernen sollte".[22] Seven reasons were given in German (paraphrased here in English):

1. The number of speakers: 50 million in Germany, over 13 million in Austria, Switzerland and Russia, and seven million in North America, and ten million or so in the rest of the world combined, yielding about 80 million people with German as their mother tongue;

---

22 Similarly, Kron's 1916 textbook for advanced learners of German, opened with a programmatic passage "Warum lernen wir Deutsch?" (Kron 1923 [1916]: 7):

"Die Erzeugnisse deutscher Literatur, Wissenschaft, Kunst und Industrie werden in allen Weltteilen geschätzt. Das Ausland sendet seine besten Söhne und Töchter nach Deutschland, damit sie aud deutschen Bildungsanstalten, wie Universitäten, Gymnasien, Realanstalten, Mädchen- und Fachschulen die Errungenschaften der deutschen Kultur aus eigener Anschauung kennen lernen.

Die landschaftlichen Reize und Sommerfrischen, wie sie der Rhein, der Harz, der Thüringer Wald, die Sächsische Schweiz, der Schwarzwald, die Eifel und das Riesengebirge in Hülle und Fülle bieten, sowie die zahlreichen weltbekannten Badeorte (wie Wiesbaden, Baden-Baden, Homburg, Ems, Kissingen, Wildbad) locken aus aller Herren Ländern Vergnügungsreisende, Sommerfrischler und Kurgäste nach Deutschland.

Nun versuchen es zwar viele, ja wohl die meiesten Ausländer, sich ohne Kenntnis der deutschen Sprache in den deutschen Landen notdürftig durchzuwinden. Sie suchen die deutschen Leistungen auf wissenschaftlichem, literarischem, künstlerischem, industriellem und technischem Gebiete aus Übersetzungen kennen zu lernen, um auf diesem Wege neue Eindrücke und Anregungen zu gewinnen, ihren Gesichtskreis zu erweitern und ihren Erfahrungsschatz zu bereichern. Aber abgesehen davon, daß die wenigsten neueren Werke in Übersetzungen zugänglich sind, bietet auch eine vorhandene Übertragung keinen vollständigen Ersatz für das deutsche Werk; denn jede Übersetzung ist und bleibt nur ein mehr oder weniger verzerrtes Abbild des Originals.

Wie anders aber steht derjenige da, welcher der deutschen Sprache in Wort und Bild mächtig ist! Wird der wissenschaftliche Forscher nicht weit größeren Gewinn von der Lektüre des deutschen Urtextes haben, als von einer mangelhaften Übertragung? Wird nicht der Vergnügungsreisende einen ganz anderen Einblick in Land und Volk tun, wenn er, anstatt stumme Betrachtungen an der Hand seines gedruckten Reiseführers anzustellen, mit den Leuten plaudern, Fragen an sie richten, kurzum, seine Gedanken austauschen und seine trockene Baedeker-Weisheit durch das gesprochene Wort der deutschen Landesbewohner beleben und vertiefen kann?

Um also die geistigen Errungenschaften der deutschen Denker, Künstler und Erfinder an der Quelle studieren zu können, um im persönlichen und schrtiftlichen Verkehr mit den Deutschen möglichst unabhängig von fremder Beihilfe zu sein, um Genuß und Erholung von einer Reise nach den landschaftlichen Perlen und Kurorten des deutschen Landes zu ernten, um sich endlich gegen etwaige Ausbeutungen oder Übervorteilungen durch gewissenslose Leute zu sichern, ist eine Fertigkeit im praktischen Gebrauch der deutschen Schrift- und Umgangssprache eine unabweisbare Vorbedingung" Kron (1923: 7–8).

2. Literature: Germany possesses a literature which is the equal of the other "civilized peoples";
3. Part of a good English education: "Because as an English person, I do not want to give other peoples precedence, and therefore don't want to fall behind them in my knowledge of languages";
4. Travel: "Because it is very probable that I will one day travel to Germany, Austria or Switzerland, and I would like to be able to converse with the inhabitants there who do not speak English";
5. Linguistic and cultural affinity: "Because the German language is of particular interest to an Englishman, since our ancestors and those of the Germans spoke the same language, and a comparison of these two related languages offers a most interesting study";
6. Mental exercise: "Because the study of any language is an extremely useful mental exercise and makes it easier to learn other living and dead languages";
7. Utility in professional life: "Because in any profession, whether it be in trade, in art and science, in civil or military service, or in diplomacy, knowledge of the German language is extremely useful and will significantly contribute to my success in these subject areas".

Out of the seven reasons, two (3. and 6.) were generic; the others made the case for German in particular. Teachers and lecturers of German today will be familiar with the general tenor of the arguments, which are still put at parents' evenings and university open days. Eighty years later, Nigel Reeves – Professor of German at Aston University and member of the National Congress on Languages in Education at the time – opening CILT's 1986 German in the United Kingdom conference, re-stated both the idealistic and the utilitarian arguments (Reeves 1986, "Why German?"). Reeves began by staking out the territory of literary worth, citing Heine, but he swiftly moved to "the industrial and commercial necessity for an emphasis in British education on foreign languages and on German in particular" (p. 4), and it was to this that he devoted the majority of his speech.[23] Even the "moral" case for German as part of the "intellectual portfolio of an educated Briton as a European and as a citizen of the world" Reeves exemplified with an economist's argument: the need to understand the country that produced Marx, and hence capitalism. By the 1980s, Reeves – well aware that the Under-Secretary for Education Peter Brooke was in his audience – evidently judged that it was the economic case that had the greatest chance of a sympathetic hearing. Utilitarian arguments notwithstanding, however, the difficulty remains that teachers tend, by virtue of having chosen the profession, to be in the subject for the love of it; pupils or future students are largely motivated by vague feelings of what they like or feel they are good at. Ortmanns argued that the increase in the study of German in particular (rather than of modern languag-

---

23 Note the similar optimism of Keith Emmans, a modern languages advisor, at a similar CILT event a decade earlier, that with Britain's membership of the EEC and with Germany's economic strength, "The need to learn German is becoming more apparent" (Emmans 1976: 28).

es in general) is above all attributable to economic factors, which he saw as being of "fundamental importance" (p. 231, my translation), while cultural or linguistic factors played at best a secondary role. I would dispute this conclusion. On the contrary, while arguments about its utility were made from the outset, German rose to prominence in the late eighteenth century above all for cultural factors, as we have seen. Once second to French, it stayed there. In the last twenty years or so has it clearly lost ground to Spanish, for which the strong economic argument had admittedly been being made at least since the Leathes Report of 1918, but which seems to have grown in popularity only once cultural familiarity had been achieved, as from the 1960s Spain became an affordable and popular holiday destination (joined much more recently by growing interest in South America too).

As the second half of the twentieth century dawned, the argument in favour of intercultural encounters grew in prominence. It was already implicit in Beresford Webb, and more explicit in Kron (1916: 7):

> Wie anders aber steht derjenige da, welcher der deutschen Sprache in Wort und Bild mächtig ist! Wird der wissenschaftliche Forscher nicht weit größeren Gewinn von der Lektüre des deutschen Urtextes haben, als von einer mangelhaften Übertragung? Wird nicht der Vergnügungsreisende einen ganz anderen Einblick in Land und Volk tun, wenn er, anstatt stumme Betrachtungen an der Hand seines gedruckten Reiseführers anzustellen, mit den Leuten plaudern, Fragen an sie richten, kurzum, seine Gedanken austauschen und seine trockene Baedeker-Weisheit durch das gesprochene Wort der deutschen Landesbewohner beleben und vertiefen kann?

> How different it is for those who have mastered German in word and image! Won't academic researchers profit far more from reading the German original text than an inadequate translation? Won't tourists have a quite different insight into land and people if, instead of making dumb observations on the basis of their printed travel guide, they can chat to the people, ask them questions, and, in short, exchange their thoughts and so bring to life and deepen the dry wisdom of the Baedeker guide by means of the spoken word of the German inhabitants?

But in the 1950s Fenn & Fangl (1954) now stated unequivocally that "The main purpose in learning any foreign language is to be able to make contact with the peoples of the countries concerned" (Fenn & Fangl 1954: 6).[24] Language learning as intercultural encounter was to become a strong theme in the second half, and especially last quarter, of the twentieth century.

---

24 Fenn & Fangl place unusual emphasis on Austria and Switzerland. Cf. the discussion in Wegner (1999: 145–148); see also Chapter 6.

in schools and universities.[31] These included focussing on a basic vocabulary, and using language laboratories to "drill" learners, as well as other new technologies (radio, film and television, tape-recorders), which together inspired the 'audiovisual' and 'audiolingual' approaches. School programmes for learners of German began to broadcast after the war – in the late 1950s there was one twenty-minute BBC radio programme in German of moderate difficulty, featuring poetry, dramatized stories, features about famous composers, and German songs (noted by Greatwood 1959: 63, 65). Other stand-alone productions on radio and television followed (e.g. CILT & BBC 1987), and increasingly whole courses consisting of BBC radio and television programmes and accompanying materials followed, including Oldnall, Baer et al. (1968); Kanocz (1970; 1972, 1975), BBC (1974, 1975), Schneider (1975), Trim (1985, 1987), Parker, Hawkin et al. (1986); Kohl & Carrington-Windo (1993, 1997); Matthews & Wood (1998), Schicker (1998), and Tenberg (1993, 1996). The first audiovisual approach in Britain – in essence presenting new language "and (within severe limits) show[ing] its meaning graphically and entertainingly" – was first tried down the road from where I write now, in Beeston, near Nottingham, based on a course developed for NATO forces, Teachers' Audio-Visual Oral Course (TAVOR) (Hawkins 1987: 173–174; see also Reinfried 2004 for a history of the method). Two years later, teachers at East Ham wrote up their experience of using the approach in *Modern Languages* (Ingram & Mace 1959), leading to wider imitation. The great hopes of this new "method" were reflected in the founding of the Audio-Visual Language Association, later re-named the British Association for Language Teaching.

Another important foundation in the 1960s was the national languages institute CILT (the Centre for Information on Language Teaching and Research), founded in 1965, though abolished in 2011 by the new Conservative-Liberal Democrat government in their "bonfire" of QUANGOs.[32] There were also experiments in different types of settings, including intensive courses for adults (see 4.8 below) and primary language education. The experiments in early (primary school) language learning settled on French, because it was the only one for which sufficient teachers would be found. The result was a "sorry outcome", to cite Phillips & Filmer-Sankey (1993: 22), although both Phillips & Filmer-Sankey and Hawkins (1987: 180–189) argue strenuously that the widely perceived view that the experiment "failed" was unmerited.[33] At least some voices in German studies were pleased to see primary French fail, for, in the words of Alan Horney, a teacher-trainer at the Institute of Education, "As long as French continues in the primary schools, the other languages will be endangered" (Horney 1976: 20). The impact may not have been wholly negative, however, as at least some secondary schools

---

31 Michael Byram tells me that he began learning Danish in the Cambridge University language laboratory in 1967 with an American army course, for example.

32 QUANGOs are "Quasi Non-Governmental Organizations".

33 Hawkins points to the attempt by Hoy (1977) to counter the negative assessment in the final report (Burstall et al. 1974), pointing out pupils did emerge with a more positive attitude to language learning and better listening comprehension than those who started French later. This, evidently, was not enough, although – in a country like ours – one cannot help feel that a measurable improvement in attitudes to language learning would be the most important outcome of all.

switched to German precisely because of the introduction of French to primary schools, fearing that "children had been 'messed up' for French by its being taught so badly at primary".[34] A second development was the explosion of new branches of linguistics and a renewed interest in applying linguistic theories in order to improve the quality of language learning and teaching. Finally, more pupils than ever were getting the chance to learn a language, particularly as the result of comprehensivization.[35]

4.6.1 Facts and Figures after World War II

As Tables 4.3 and 4.5 show, the raw numbers of pupils taking German at age 16 increased more than sevenfold between 1938 and 1985, and the number taking it at age 18 increased even more, by nearly ninefold. However, the increase in raw figures says much about the increasing numbers of pupils continuing with school, but little else. In fact, the number of entries for German at age 16 as a proportion of all subject entries declined steadily (from 1.9% in 1938, to 1.2% in 1985, calculated on the figures given in Table 4.3). At age 18, the equivalent percentage change was from 2.4% to 1.9% in 1965, 1.3% in 1985, and 0.6% by 2005 – a 75% proportional loss of "market share" over three-quarters of a century years (cf. Table 4.4).[36] Hawkins noted in 1987 that

two-thirds of pupils starting a foreign language at 11[+] dropped it "at the earliest opportunity". Following a consultative paper in 1983, a report in 1987 and a policy document in 1988 (DES/Welsh Office 1983; DES 1987; DES/Welsh Office 1988), the Education Reform Act of 1988 made one modern foreign language a "foundation" subject of the new National Curriculum, to be taken up to the end of compulsory schooling – but with the second foreign language not being made available until Year 4. In 2004 it ceased to be compulsory to take a language from aged 14 to GCSE or equivalent.

The 1977 DES report *Modern Languages in Comprehensive Schools* found that while roughly three-quarters of pupils were learning French in the first three years of secondary school, German reached a high point of 18% in the third year – a proportion completely in line with figures earlier in the century, although the population being sampled was now much broader (Phillips & Filmer-Sankey 1993: 27, Table 1.2). Similarly, in 1983, a survey of Welsh secondary schools found that about 120,000 pupils took French, while numbers taking German were up from 10,000 a decade earlier to 17,000 – about 12% of all those taking a modern foreign language (excluding Welsh) (Welsh Office 1983: 12, cited Phillips & Filmer-Sankey (1993: 32). In 1987, 47% of

---

34 I cite here Colin Wringe, a teacher-trainer at the University of Keele at the time.
35 Comprehensivation refers to the introduction of "comprehensive" state-funded schools to replace the tri-partite system of grammar, technical and secondary schools from the late 1950s. In those areas of the country where full comprehensivizataion was implemented, this meant the abolition of entrance examinations (known as the "11-plus") to select the most academically able pupils for grammar schools. See Gillard (2011).
36 The figures presented by Hawkins (1987: 14) also highlight the disproportionately low number of boys pursuing modern languages, and of men training to be teachers (see Carr & Pauwels 2009 for a comprehensive study).

pupils in state-funded schools were studying a foreign language, but in a survey of 22 schools where French was a core subject (with 97 % take-up), a lower percentage of pupils took up a second foreign language, because the other languages had to compete with other non-core options for the scant remaining space in the curriculum (Phillips & Filmer-Sankey 1993: 37). In 1987, grants were awarded to ten Local Education Authorities to promote the take-up of languages other than French, and a 1991 evaluation found a significant increase in those learning German (HMI 1991; cf. Phillips & Filmer-Sankey (1993: 43, 47).

There was palpable frustration in the second half of the twentieth century, just as there had been in the first half, that German – as the first of the "LOTF" – remained so far behind French. The Incorporated Association of Head Masters wrote in 1966 that "The disparity between the numbers studying French and those studying the other European languages is indefensible" (IAHM 1966: 50), and the same frustration was still evident in the work of Phillips & Filmer-Sankey (1993) thirty years later. Hawkins (1987: 16) expressed concern at the drop in numbers taking O-level French between 1965 (when the Certificate of School Education or CSE was introduced alongside the General Certificate of Education Ordinary Level or O-level) and 1985, and that there was a large drop precisely amongst the most able pupils. Yet German saw an increase of about a third during the same period, alongside very strong growth indeed in the less demanding CSE (cf. Table 4.3; on the CSE, see 4.6.4 below).

To dissect such figures and to advise on current language policy on the basis of them has been, and will continue to be, the work of MFL education experts, and falls beyond the scope of this book. Still, I cannot help but note that the 2011 figures for GCSE German had slumped to well below the 1985 figures, and even to below the 1965 figures in the case of French. At A-level, both languages were far below 1965 figures in 2011. Even with the growth of Spanish – long looked-for, at least since the Leathes Report of 1918, and now outstripping German – the total number of entries for the three major languages at A-level was lower in 2011 than it was in 1965, and far lower at age 16 than it was in 1985, though not yet at 1965 levels. For the purposes of this study, nevertheless, it is important to be aware that the numbers of people exposed to the German language at school increased massively in the twentieth century, even if there was a sharp decline as an overall proportion of subjects studied. In the second half of the twentieth century, textbooks of German – or, increasingly, *courses*, including audio and visual material – had by far the largest audience they had ever had.

Table 4.3 Entrants for German, French and Spanish at age 16 in 1938, 1965, 1985, 1995, 1997, 2003, 2007, 2011[37]

	Total no. of subject entries (each pupil entered for several subjects)	German	French	Spanish	Total German, French, Spanish
1938	531,445	9,935	72,466	1,338	83,739
1965 GCE O-level	2,170,019	32 737	163,651	9,776	
CSE	+ 230,977	+ 986	+ 8,345	+ 235	
Total	2,400,996	33,723	171,996	10 011	205,719
1985 GCE O-level	3,066,764	42,616	147,657	11,749	
CSE	+ 3,231,017	+ 31,855	+ 163,626	+6,020	
Total*	6,297,781	74,471	311,283	17,769	403,523
1995 GCSE		129,386	350,027		
1997 GCSE		136,000	*338,000	*45,000	519,000
2003 GCSE		125,851	331,890	61,490	519,231
2007 GCSE		81,061	216,718	63,978	361,757
2011 GCSE		60,887	154,221	66,021	281,129

* Both the GCE and CSE figures for French in 1985 include candidates entered for the combined GCE/CSE examination, so they are somewhat inflated; from 1988 the combined GCSE replaced separate O-level and CSE examinations.[38]

---

37 Figures from Hawkins 1987: 66; 1995 figures from Guardian, October 6ᵗʰ, 2011, "Fears languages in schools 'close to extinction'" by Jessica Shepherd); 1997 rounded figures from Moys (1998: 36); 2003, 2007 and 2011 figures from the Joint Council of Qualifications (http://www.jcq.org.uk/national_results/gcses/). Cf. also Canning (2007).

38 For an overview of changes to German syllabi 1985–1990 in the light of these developments, see Rock (1993).

Table 4.4 A-level French & German entries as percent of all A-levels[39]

	1938	1965	1975	1985	1995	2005
French	12.8	6.9	4.8	3.6	3.7	1.8
German	2.4	1.9	1.5	1.3	1.4	0.6

Table 4.5 A-level entries for French, German and Spanish (1938–2010)[40]

Year	French	German	Spanish	Total of French, German, Spanish
1938	4752	899 (= 19%)	138	5789
1965	25599	7107 (= 28%)	2213	34919
1975	24421	7810 (= 32%)	2581	34812
1985	22140	7949 (= 35%)	2615	32704
1990	27245	9476 (= 35%)	3832	40553
1995	27563	10632 (= 39%)	4,837	43032
2000	18,341	8,718 (= 48%)	5,702	32761
2005	14,248	5,834 (= 41%)	5,702	26255
2009	14,452	5,810 (= 40%)	7,385	27647
2010	13,850	5,548 (= 40%)	7,629	27027

39 Source: Richard Hudson, Trends in Language Education in England, http://www.phon.ucl.ac.uk/home/dick/ec/stats.htm#alfg)

40 Source: Richard Hudson, Trends in Language Education in England, http://www.phon.ucl.ac.uk/home/dick/ec/stats.htm#alfg). For comparison, % figures in brackets indicate German entrants as a proportion of the number of candidates for French. The figures here for 1985 and 1990 differ slightly from those given by Tenberg & Jones (1993: 45), who give 8358 rather than 7949 for the year 1985, and 9425 rather than 9476 for the year 1990.

4.6.2 Linguistics, general and applied, and language teaching

There was an explosion of research after World War II in new areas of linguistics. Behaviourist theories of language were applied with great enthusiasm to language acquisition, in accordance with the belief that language, like any behaviour, consisted of patterns that needed to be learnt by imitation and practice – some examples of how this theory was applied to teaching practice are discussed below in 4.6.3 as well as in 4.9. However, behaviourist views were also countered from the late 1950s onwards, when Noam Chomsky attacked Skinner's *Verbal Behaviour* (1957), and published his own *Syntactic Structures* (1957). Chomsky hypothesized that first language acquisition was in the hands of an innate language acquisition device that was pre-primed with certain universal properties of language. What that meant for *second* language acquisition was a question that would concern applied linguistics for the next half-century. However, the other central innovation of Chomsky – the view of syntax as structures "generated" according to set rules, and where some structures were generated by "transforming" other underlying structures by moving constituents – bore rapid fruit.[41]

Marchand's German section of *Applied Linguistics. A Guide for Teachers* (1961) exemplifies the influence of these two competing mid-twentieth-century linguistic theories, behaviourism and generative grammar, on early 1960s teaching of German, but also the influence of contrastive linguistics, for which Robert Lado's study – also published in 1957 – was a seminal text.[42] The generative grammar approach was obvious in the way Marchand set out the elements of a German "normal" clause "remembering always that this is not a description but a generation model" (p. 1), with up to 18 possible "slots". For teaching word order in the normal clause,

> Excellent examples of the transformation type may be devised: 'Insert *gestern* or *vor einigen Tagen* in the following sentences (making the necessary changes): 1. *Ich mache Einkäufe*; 2. *Wir besuchen Onkel Karl*, etc.'

(Marchand 1961: 7)

The behaviourist concern with establishing good habits, and avoiding errors, is obvious in the warning that followed: "These must be very carefully chosen and controlled, however." As for the passive,

---

41 The above is a highly simplified summary of these linguistic theories. Seuren (1998) and Allan (2007) both provide historical overviews of the development of twentieth-century linguistics.

42 For a good summary of Contrastive Analysis approaches see Larsen-Freeman & Long (1985: 52–56). Worthy of note here is the small book (87 pages) *fehler-abc English-German*, which – though published by Klett in Germany in 1975 (Zindler & Barry 1975, 2nd ed. 1980) – is aimed at English-speaking learners of German. It is arranged alphabetically by English-headword, and highlights instances where one word in English has more than one possible translation in German, e.g. *different* (*anders als* vs. *verschieden*). There follow a number of sentences with the correct German translations supplied adjacent in a red field, where the text only becomes visible once a piece of red plastic (supplied in a flap at the back of the book) is held over the red field – an ingenious way of concealing answers until ready to be checked, without flipping to cumbersome answer pages.

> The passive should be presented as a transform of the active [...] Transformation drill from active to passive and vice versa are especially recommended.[43]

The contrastive approach was evident as Marchand continued:

> In discussing the passive concept the method of forming the passive in English should first be recalled. Then one may point out similarities and differences with German

(Marchand 1961: 15).

It was somewhat later in the twentieth century that the Chomskyan view of how language acquisition worked made itself felt in language teaching, as for the first time in the entire history of German learning materials aimed at English-speaking learners, the centrality of grammar was challenged. Research on language acquisition within a broadly Chomskyan framework had shown from the 1970s onwards that just as in first language acquisition, second language learners appear to progress through relatively fixed stages of morphological and syntactical development in their spontaneous production, regardless of whether or not they "know" the grammar explicitly. If that is the case, and if the primary aim of language instruction is to enable students to communicate, then there is little point in placing heavy emphasis on grammar because, even once it is "learnt", many or most students will not be able to produce it in spontaneous speech anyway. The most explicit response to this view in a German course-book is the American *Kontakte* series aimed at students beginning German at university (Terrell et al. 1988, 1992). Here the authors followed the idea of Stephen Krashen that there was a distinction to be made between learning – conscious knowledge that could be consciously applied, for example in carefully planned writing – and acquired knowledge, "normally used unconsciously and automatically to understand and produce language" (p. xviii).[44] Acquisition, as opposed to learning, takes place in some as yet poorly understood way, in response to comprehensible input in the target language; and, as learners progress through fixed stages, their language (or "interlanguage", their emergent version of the target language) is characterized by predictable errors. For German, an obvious example was word order, where – research by Pienemann and others showed (e.g. Pienemann 1984) – learners regularly and predictably acquire the ability to "front" constituents such as adverbs into first position in main clauses *before* they acquire the rule that the main verb must come second. This leads inevitably to ungrammatical utterances of the form *Heute ich gehe in die Stadt*, which, rather than being alarming mistakes, are to be viewed as successful communication in a regular acquisition process.[45] In this light, communicative language teaching – with grammar taking a supporting role – made good sense.

---

43 On the emergence of the idea of the passive as a transform of the active – which predates Chomsky – see 5.8, especially note 34.

44 For a brief overview of Stephen Krashen's so-called monitor model, see Lightbown & Spada (2006: 36–38). See Krashen (1982).

45 In other words, systematic errors could usefully be analysed as indicators of the process of acquisi-

The call for "communicative" language teaching (e.g. Mitchell 1988) thus survived the disappointments of audiolingual and audiovisual approaches (see 4.6.3 below), in which the limitations of the Skinnerian approach to language teaching had become evident. One result was the *Deutsch Heute* series written by a languages advisor for Leicestershire, Duncan Sidwell, and Penny Capoore (Sidwell & Capoore 1983). Sidwell had felt – as he put it in his own words when interviewed – that the audiovisual course *Vorwärts* "left out meaning and motivation".[46] Even its table of contents – a bare list of *Lektion* 1–28, with no further information – would give grounds for that complaint, as learners could surely have had little sense from the textbook of where their learning was heading or why. *Deutsch Heute* was a response to that lack. The authors, conscious that what the communicative method was asking teachers to do was something new and unfamiliar to them, produced a Teachers' Resource Book to accompany the series – unwittingly repeating the act of Rippmann in writing his *Hints* to promulgate the reform movement in 1898.[47] Recognizing that many teachers would not be comfortable with the necessary vocabulary for using the target language for "real communication" in the classroom, Sidwell & Capoore (1983: 24–28) included several pages of vocabulary, including for example "Praising or criticising students" (from *Hervorragend – Excellent* to *Ihr habt es nicht versucht! – You haven't tried.*). The resource book begins:

> Modern language teaching has tended to teach students about a language rather than how to use it [...] This seems a denial of the primary reason why people learn a language which, clearly, is in order to use it. [...] *Deutsch Heute* has been written in response to this need for materials which are communicative in intent and which will enable students to achieve clearly specified goals.

(Sidwell & Capoore 1984: 2)

The "clearly" here assumed general agreement, but the validity of the assertion would *not* have been recognized by most classroom teachers of German through history, at least from the 1770s onwards. Before the 1770s some English speakers had learned German for practical purposes, but this was a tiny minority; after that period, a slightly larger minority learnt it, whether for trade or as part of a more or less formal liberal, humanist education. Now, in a world on the way to globalization, where people were becoming increasingly aware of the millions of people worldwide who were bilingual or multilingual as a matter of course, where Britain had joined the European Union (then the European Economic Community) in 1973, and where travel abroad was becoming more affordable, it might seem obvious that a large number of English speakers might indeed

---

tion. On error analysis, see for example, Lightbown & Spada (2006: 36–38) and the classic study by Corder (1967).

46 My thanks to Duncan Sidwell for giving up his time to be interviewed for this project. Alongside other subject advisors, language advisors like him had begun to appointed in the 1960s; there were over 30 by 1969 and over 150 in 1987 (Hawkins 1987: 8).

47 The *Vorwärts* series (discussed in 4.6.3 below) also included teachers' books, and these became increasingly common in the later twentieth century.

learn a language to *use* it. It was the first time in history, however, that such an assertion could have seemed plausible.

4.6.3 New technologies, new methodologies

New developments in teaching methods, classroom settings and technologies in the second half of the twentieth century were all, in their own way, a continuation of the attempt to overcome the problem first raised by Viëtor in 1882, the *Überbürdungsfrage* – the overburdening of learners – whether by restricting the vocabulary to a basic set (e.g. Hagboldt 1936. Barratt 1937), or to that needed by specialist users (e.g. Bithell & Dunstan's 1925 *German for scientists* and 1928 German course "for students of history, geography, economics and literature"),[48] or by limiting oneself to a subset of grammar, or to a limited purpose, such as reading only, or speaking only. For example, Louis (1954) focussed primarily on reading knowledge of German. Working with an "active vocabulary of 712 words", based on word-frequency studies (Morgan 1928; Hauch 1929), Louis also adopted a different prioritization of grammar topics. In the 24 chapters of Louis's book,

> modal auxiliaries are treated in Chapter 3; separable prefixes in Chapter 4; ablaut, in Chapters 7–11; dependent word order, in Chapter 10; the subjunctive in Chapters 16–19, etc. Those elements of grammar and syntax not essential for early reading are relegated to the end of the book: numerals, the declension of adjectives, noun plurals, etc.

Anderson's *German for the Technologist* (1960) was intended for students at technical colleges building on their school German in a one-year course; unlike Louis (1954), Anderson made no effort at all to restrict vocabulary – for the science student "will always rely on his dictionary for the meaning of words" – but aimed "to cover a number of those aspects of idiom and constructions which so often baffle the science student" (p. 5). By the 1990s, a Teach Yourself *Speak German with Confidence* course, which consisted only of tapes, was one of many courses promising learners only oral and aural competence (although a full transcript was eventually added in 2010, in response to demand: Coggle & Schenke 2010).

---

48 Other examples of textbooks of German for scientists up to 1966 are Moffatt (1907), Haltenhoff (1911), Phillips (1915), Greenfield (1918), Osborne & Osborne (1919), Fiedler (1921, 1924), Barker (1933), Wild (1937a, b), Fotos et al. (1938), Weiner (1943), Horne (1948, 1960), Eichner & Hein (1957), Cunningham (1958), Radcliffe (1961), Reeves (1965), and Eaton et al. (1966). Manton (1973) was in introduction to "theological German", Shaw (1994) to legal German. Among introductions to scientific German for the American market was Van de Luyster & Curts (1955), based on their own experience of teaching scientific German to undergraduates and postgraduates at The Citadel Military College and Wesleyan University (Luyster & Curts 195: vii). As well as including a list of vocabulary that was intended to assist both learners and "the beginning teacher of scientific German, whose knowledge of technical words may be limited" (p. viii), the authors included in each chapter a section on word formation, since "reading scientific German with ease presupposes an understanding of word composition" (pp. viii–ix). From chapter XI onwards, each chapter contains not just a reading passage, but also a passage for "sight" translation.

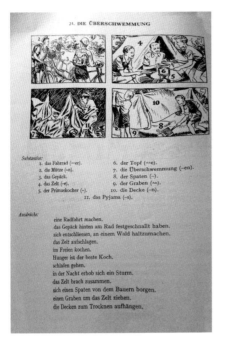

Figure 4.3:
A "storyboard" from Gilbertson (1950: 28)

The germ of the audiovisual method, already alluded to above, can already be found in a text like Gilbertson's *Picture Book of Free Composition* (1950), in retrospect a half-way house between the picture-based object-lesson (as in Trotter 1898, discussed in the previous chapter) and the fully blown audiovisual method (of which some examples follow). In the early parts of the book, single pictures are labelled so that new vocabulary may be introduced. As the book proceeds, short 'storyboards' or sequences of pictures are introduced (see Figure 4.3); the language should be worked on orally in class with the teacher *before* the pupil attempts to write out a "fair copy of his own" (Gilbertson 1950: 1):

The audiovisual movement had a concrete outcome in a Foreign Languages Materials project which began work in 1963 with pump-priming from the Nuffield Foundation and which then continued at York, to develop four audiovisual language courses (*En avant, Vorwärts, Adelante, Vpered*). As a former pupil recalled of using the German course *Vorwärts*, the starting point was a film-strip, and aural work, followed by oral work: "We learnt from watching their adventures on the overhead projector as the teacher turned the handle on the side to produce a very slow moving story and then she'd move it back a scene and we'd all 'do it again', in other words we read the 'script' in German out loud (with Isle of Wight accents) and we plodded our way through stories of going to the park, going to the shops and visiting things and other people."[49] *Grundstoff* (new grammatical points and new expressions) and *Zum Schreiben* – written work – concluded the lesson. In other words, language was treated as primarily spoken, only secondarily written, reflecting the recognition in twentieth-century linguistics that language is essentially spoken, as well as the insight that first language acquisition is initially oral-aural only. The textbook was entirely in the target language. The behaviourist stimulus-response approach to language learning is evident in exercises of the pattern:

Du hörst: Schau! Das ist Hans
Du sagst: Guten Abend, Hans! Wohin gehst du denn?

(*Vorwärts*, Nuffield Foundation 1974: 46)

---

49 The comment was posted under the name Biblins on a Sausage.net Nostalgia forum on August 22nd, 2005: http://www.sausagenet.org/nph-YaBB.pl?num=1124735531 (accessed October 2011).

Vorwärts also followed a functional approach – language structures were introduced to fulfil particular functions. For example, in the last lesson of the book, the perfect tense was introduced as a means of "talking about the past":

So kannst du über die Vergangenheit sprechen
(Verben mit *haben*)

Frage

Was	hast du	heute	gemacht?
	hat er	gestern	

Antwort

Ich habe	gestern heute	vor dem Fernsehturm gewartet Limonade getrunken Schokolade gekauft ein Buch gelesen einen Ring gefunden Fußball gespielt bei Renate getanzt
Er hat		

Vorwärts Kurzfassung (Nuffield Foundation 1974: 160)

Wir lernen Deutsch (Paxton & Brake 1970–72) was another audiovisual course designed to take pupils to O-level; the vocabulary of the first volume was restricted to 870 words, so as to place the course "within the reach of slower-moving classes" (preface, no page number), and is discussed in more detail in Chapter 6. *Fortbildung in der deutschen Sprache* (Hammond 1969, reprinted four times up to 1975) was a language laboratory course intended to be of use to learners ranging from GCE pupils to first year university students, as well as to adults preparing for examinations such as those offered by the London Chamber of Commerce. It subscribed to the stimulus-response method (cf. p. x; and cf. Figure 4.10 for a photograph of a German school language laboratory included in this text), but also used the possibilities of the language laboratory to expose learners to authentic speech extracts "covering the whole of the Bundesrepublik [...] typical of the speech regions", with non-standard features and without editing out "slips of the tongue" (pp. v, vi).[50]

Another reaction to the availability of a language laboratory and the absence of suitable materials – in this case for students at the new Monash University, which had been founded in 1959 in suburban Melbourne, Australia – was produced by Rainer Taeni and Michael Clyne (who went on to a distinguished career as a German sociolinguist).[51] It

---

50 Another language laboratory based book for German is Lavy (1965).
51 Cf. Clyne (1984, 1995). For the record, other textbooks of German produced for the relatively small Australian market are Kosler (1965), whose author was Senior German Master at Brisbane Grammar School, and Reed (1971), whose author author was "Modern Languages/ Classics Mistress" at the Sir Joseph Banks High School, Revesby, NSW (now an outer suburb of Sydney). Both were intended for school pupils rather than university students, as was Taeni & Clyne's *Efficient German*.

Figure 4.4 (left): Lino-cut by Hertha Kluge-Pott in Taeni & Clyne (1965: 62)
Figure 4.5 (right): Lino-cut for learning to tell the time by Hertha Kluge-Pott in Taeni & Clyne (1965: 79)

is worth noting here for its title alone, which sums up the hopes of its authors in a new technological age: *Efficient German* (Taeni & Clyne 1965). Its rather dry layout – full of tables of substitution drills – was enlivened by striking original lino-cuts by the artist Hertha Kluge-Pott (born 1934 in Berlin, emigrated to Australia in 1958), of which two examples are given in Figures 4.4 and 4.5. Figure 4.5 is graphic reminder of when to use *vor* (to) and *nach* (after) in telling the time.

Sprich Mal Deutsch (Rowlinson 1967), with its memorable striped cover in the colours of the German flag, was another landmark in the teaching of German of the 1960s. Like *Vorwärts*, it relied on some of the principles of the audiovisual approach – "it is suggested that the *Bildvokabeln* be presented first, by teacher or tape plus teacher" (p. 5; cf. Figure 4.6), but beyond this, it was one of the earliest textbooks to present the goal of teaching German as developing four, implicitly equally weighted "skills":

> This three-book course aims to teach the skills of understanding, speaking, reading and writing German, in that order, to twelve- to fourteen-year-old beginners. [...] The course aims above all to be lively and stimulating, encouraging the pupil's interest in Germany and at the same time teaching him to understand and communicate in German.

(Rowlinson 1967: 5)

The title, then – *Speak German*, or, with the particle *mal*, more encouraging *Go, on, speak German!* – was programmatic. As in *Vorwärts*, understanding and speaking now

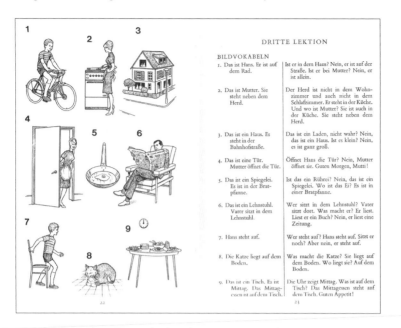

Figure 4.6: *Sprich Mal Deutsch* I (Rowlinson 1967: 22–23)

came first. Explicit grammatical knowledge, while covered in explanations that "have purposely been kept as simple and non-technical as possible", was not one of the stated goals at all. Figure 4.7 illustrates the "non-technical" presentation of grammar. Topic 1 deals with subject-verb agreement and conjugation of the verb in the first, second, and third person singular, but no grammatical terms are used. Note, however, that the example shows that basic grammatical categories such as verb, adjective and adverb are still assumed knowledge. Despite its apparently advanced approach, many "end-users" appear to have disliked *Sprich Mal Deutsch* – a "dreadful book", in the words of former Leicestershire language advisor Duncan Sidwell. While Sidwell's objections were in part based on matters of language teaching theory, his assessment is similar to many I encountered from "naive" learners in gathering reminiscences for this project.

Sprich Mal Deutsch was, alongside *Vorwärts* and its ilk, an early response to the call, made in a 1963 pamphlet – produced by a working party of teachers, and to which Eric Hawkins was a key contributor – that "communication" should be recognized as the main aim of foreign language study (Incorporated Association of Head Masters 1963: 50):

> The aim of communication should underlie discussion of method, teacher training, etc. (paragraph 41). This will help us define the kind of language we teach and the nature of the tests we use in assessing progress.

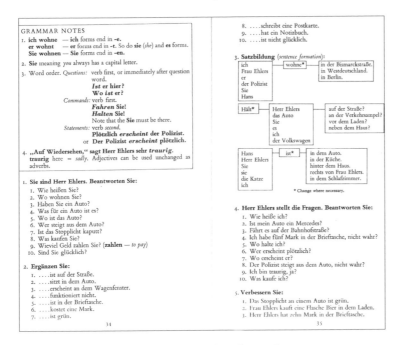

Figure 4.7: Grammar presentation in *Sprich Mal Deutsch*
(Rowlinson 1967: 34–35)

The relevant paragraph 41 – one of eleven paragraphs under the heading *The Need to Communicate* (pp. 12–14) – begins:

> Now that we are no longer mesmerised by the necessity to imitate the Latin textbooks […] we can see that languages are for us to use, for the purpose of *communication*. This is an aim which requires no justification to young minds whose natural curiosity can willingly be harnessed to the study of a foreign language. The fact that some pupils often fail to reach a high standard of accomplishment is no reason for giving up the attempt. As much might be said of many other subjects. It is worth noting that real ability to communicate is quickly and drastically tested by the most exacting of examinations – as soon as the pupil meets a foreigner. […] This puts a great responsibility on modern language teachers […]

(Incorporated Association of Head Masters 1963: 13)

While eleven paragraphs were given over to need to communicate, only one addressed "The Place of Literature" (paragraph 47, p. 14), where the authors emphasized that communication could include pupils "making direct contact with the classical writers of a great literature, or their contemporary counterparts […] *when they reach appropriate ma-*

turity" (emphasis in original). This cautious attitude to literature is worth bearing in mind when – in 4.10 below – we return to the place of literature in modern languages education.

4.6.4 Languages for all

> Given even the most ideal conditions, it must be remembered that German is a difficult language. [...] Given even the best teachers, the study of German requires, though it also repays, a strenuous educational effort.
>
> M. B. S. (1921: 698) (One is reminded of Sir Philip Sidney's complaint in 1574 of the "difficulties" of German; see 4.1 above)

An emergent theme in twentieth-century reflections on the teaching of German, and of modern languages more widely, was the recognition of different levels of ability, ultimately yielding serious research on meeting the needs of the 'average' or 'lesser ability' language learner (e.g. CILT 1972; Lee et al. 1998; Ainslie 2001; cf. also Richards 1976). The germ of recognition is already in Benson's anecdote of big boys of "little intellectual capacity," which he told to support his view that German should be reserved as a second foreign language to those "with linguistic gifts" (Benson 1907: 11). Collins, writing in the *Yearbook of Education* (1934), judged that a strict application of the Reform method required "bright pupils" and consequently preferred a "rational method" for the "average pupil" (Collins 1934: 419). Alexander Blades was the first textbook author to take into account explicitly the needs of "the more slowly moving pupil as well as [for] the average student and the intensive solo worker" in his *Modern German Course* (Blades 1935: v).[52] From the late 1950s onwards, comprehensivization of education broadened out the constituency of language learners considerably, who had largely been restricted to independent and grammar schools. French (or another foreign language) had only rarely been taught in secondary modern schools, but now a grammar-school type education became a possibility for all pupils in the comprehensive schools that replaced the tri-partite system of grammar, secondary modern and technical schools. After early experiments in comprehensivization in the 1950s, there was rapid growth in the number of pupils attending comprehensive schools in the 1960s, especially after the Labour government came to power in 1964, and continuing even once the Conservatives took over in 1970 and effectively reversed the policy to require Local Education Authorities to reorganize their provision (Crook 2002). In the context of optimism about the feasibility of teaching languages to large numbers, in part fuelled post-war by news of Armed Forces language training programmes where average learners were apparently successful (Angiolillo 1947; Lind 1948; cf. Stern 1983: 102, 104), the Newsom Report on education for average and lesser ability pupils, *Half Our Future* (1963), argued strongly that pupils of all abilities should have the opportunity to learn a foreign language (Phillips & Filmer-Sankey 1993: 24). O-levels introduced alternative syllabuses (though

---

52 Wegner (1999: 135–136) provides a brief description of this book from the point of view of its coverage of *Landeskunde*.

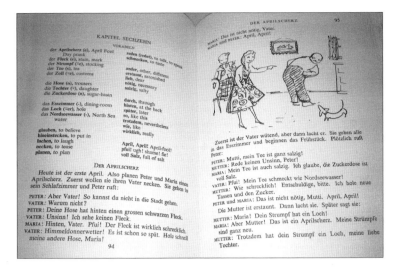

Figure 4.8: Orton (1959: 94–95)

Cambridge Local Examinations in fact did not offer alternatives available for German, only for French).

Eric Orton's *Auf deutsch, bitte!* (1959) was specially written "for use in Comprehensive and Secondary Modern Schools" with the ambition "to establish German as an exciting and rewarding new subject" for this new constituency of pupils.[53] Orton followed "the recommendations on the teaching of modern languages to non-academic pupils as given by the IAHM in their book *The Teaching of Modern Languages*", including selecting vocabulary according to frequency of use, "only a minimum of carefully presented grammar", plenty of repetition, an overall slower pace than in "the usual Grammar School course", and material chosen with the aim of "giving a lively and amusing picture of Germany and the Germans" (Orton 1959: 5, 6).[54] Figure 4.8 may serve as an illustration of what this looked like in practice. It is taken from Chapter 16, relatively near the end of Orton's book, where every fifth chapter was for revision, and where the dative was only introduced in Chapter 19. Note the very simple syntax, with the complete avoidance of subordinate clauses, and the avoidance of the dative and genitive cases (quite a feat over sixteen chapters). The intention to provide a "lively and amusing" impression of Germany is realized through the (shared) custom of April Fool.

If Orton was careful not to expose pupils to grammatical forms they had not yet learnt, Richards (1976: 57), writing on "Teaching children of moderate ability" in the CILT round-up of the state of German (*German in the United Kingdom: Problems and*

---

53 Cf. Wegner (1999: 144).
54 Orton himself was a teacher at Royal Grammar School, Worcester. Later publications of his are Orton (1960, 1972).

Contents

N.B. Language items for understanding only, rather than for active use, are shown in italics.

A   Grüß Gott! Personal information 1

Language use: Exchanging greetings and saying goodbye. ● Understanding requests for, and giving, your name, age and date of birth. ● Cardinal and ordinal numbers, days, months and dates. ● Saying where you live or where you are staying. ● Stating that you cannot find your hotel etc. ● Spelling aloud. ● Filling in a form with personal details.

Main language forms: Grüß Gott! Guten Morgen/Tag/Abend! ● Auf Wiedersehen! ● Nos 1–20. ● *Nos 21–299.* ● Alphabet (a-be-tse etc). ● Entschuldigen Sie bitte! ● Ich kann [mein Hotel] nicht finden. ● Wie bitte? ● Bitte/danke schön ● *Wie heißt du?/Dein Name?* ● Ich heiße [Michael]. ● *Wie alt sind Sie?* ● Ich bin [17] Jahre alt. ● *Woher kommst du?* ● Ich komme aus [England]. ● *Wo wohnen Sie?* ● Ich wohne in [Preston]. ● *Wann hast du Geburtstag?* Ich habe am [sechzehnten März] Geburtstag.

B   Immer geradeaus Finding the way

Language use: Politely asking for, and understanding, directions in a town. ● Giving directions. ● Asking for clarification or repetition, where necessary. ● Understanding signs in a town.

Main language forms: Wo ist [der Dom]? ● *[Du nimmst] die [erste] Straße [links].* ● *Gehen Sie immer geradeaus.* ● *[Der Zoo] ist da/dort drüben.* ● *[Das Kino] ist auf der [linken] Seite.* ● *[Der Zoo] liegt [der Post] gegenüber.* ● *Gehen Sie [am Dom] vorbei.* ● *Du gehst [links] um die Ecke.* ● *Geh die Straße entlang/hinauf/hinunter.* ● Ich weiß es nicht. ● Verstehen Sie? ● Nein, das habe ich nicht verstanden. ● Bitte langsamer.

C   Spaß mit Geld Money

Language use: Understanding and using the currencies of the four German-speaking countries. ● Asking the price and calculating prices.

Main language forms: Was kostet das? *Das kostet [50] Pfennig. Das macht [10] Mark.*

D   Guten Appetit! Food and drink

Language use: Ordering items of food and drink in a Konditorei, Schnell-Imbiß and Gasthof. ● Calling the waiter or waitress. ● Settling the bill. ● Understanding a simple menu and relevant signs.

Main language forms: *Was möchten Sie?* ● Ich möchte [ein Glas Tee] mit/ohne [Milch] bitte. ● *Guten Appetit!* ● *Was für [ein Eis?]*   [Fräulein!] Zahlen bitte! ● *Bitte an der Kasse zahlen!* ● *Sie wünschen?* ● *Und zu [trinken]?* ● *Sonst noch etwas?* ● Ich möchte [einmal] [Bratwurst] bitte.

E   Bitte schön Shopping 1

Language use: Asking for items on a market, in a Konditorei, supermarket and post office. ● Specifying quantities and ascertaining prices. ● Understanding related signs and recognising shop names.

Main language forms: Haben Sie [eine Erdbeertorte]? ● Was kostet [der Schokoladenkuchen]? ● *[Eine Mark achtzig] das Stück.* ● Haben Sie kein Kleingeld? ● Nein, es tut mir leid. ● Was kosten [zwei] Kilo [Äpfel]? ● *Was hätten Sie gern?* ● *Werden Sie schon bedient?* ● *Was darf es sein?* ● *Kann ich Ihnen helfen?* ● Haben Sie noch einen Wunsch? ● Ich möchte eine Flasche/Dose [Cola]. ● Eine Briefmarke für eine Postkarte nach England. ● Numbers above 20.

F   Spaß mit der Uhrzeit Time

Language use: Asking for, understanding and telling the time (including 24 hour clock).

Main language forms: Wie spät ist es? Wann fährt der Bus ab? *Es ist/um [zwei Uhr].*

G   Gute Reise! Travelling by public transport

Language use: Asking for and understanding information about buses, trams, trains, U-Bahn and S-Bahn. ● Buying tickets, stating type of journey, ascertaining and understanding prices and times. ● Changing money for ticket machines. ● Understanding relevant signs and information on timetables.

Main language forms: Ich möchte [nach Essen] (fahren). ● *Welcher [Zug] fährt [nach Essen]?* ● *Fahr (am besten) [mit der S-Bahn] Linie [3].* ● Wo ist [die Haltestelle]? ● Wann fährt [der Bus] [zum Bahnhof]? ● Wo muß ich [aus] steigen? ● *Du mußt [am Marienplatz] [aus] steigen.* ● Wieviel kostet [die Fahrkarte]? ● Können Sie bitte wechseln? ● Haben Sie [ein Markstück]? ● [Einmal] nach [Hamburg] einfach/hin und zurück. ● Fährt [dieser Zug] (direkt) nach [Köln]? ● Von welchem Gleis fährt der Zug nach [Köln]? ● Wann fährt der [nächste] Zug ab? ● Wann kommt der Zug in [München] an? ● *Der Zug fährt/kommt um neun Uhr nach [Köln] ab/in [Köln] an.*

Figure 4.9: The contents page of *Einfach Toll* 1 (Smith 1985)

Prospects) went even further in his assertion that "Teaching grammar to moderate-ability classes is largely a waste of time." Even if persistence could get them to learn the rules, "their limited capacity for conceptual thought does not allow them to use what they have learned in order to understand or compose meaningful utterances in German." Richards (1976: 57) also reported that "it is now widely recognized that the skill of translation is beyond [the] capacities" of "moderate-ability classes".

The concern to provide opportunities for less academic learners was of course not unique to modern languages. It bore fruit in the introduction of CSE (Certificate of Secondary Education) examinations for less academically able pupils, which ran alongside the GCE O-level (General Certificate of Education Ordinary Level) from 1967 until 1988 (when both were replaced by the General Certificate of Secondary Education or GCSE). Between 0.5 and 1 % of pupils taking these examinations took German, and pass rates were generally high: 90 % and above, compared to around 60 % for GCE (Ortmanns 1993: 163–169; 179–182), although a CSE, unless passed with the highest Grade 1, was not a suitable foundation for continuing with the language (Grade 1 was equated with a low O-level pass, though the same standard was probably not reached; Hawkins 1987: 15).

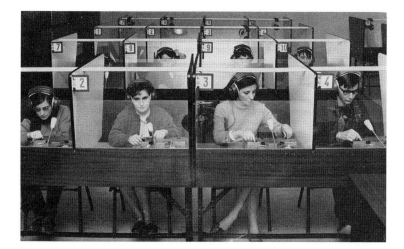

Figure 4.10: Hammond (1969: 96) showing a language laboratory in a German school

The late 1970s and early 1980s saw another adjustment to less academic pupils, with Graded Objectives in Modern Languages (cf. Page 1983; cf. Hawkins 1987: 15, 169), which broke the syllabus down into a "series of short-term goals, each building on the one before, so that the pupil advances in knowledge and skill" (Page 1983: 292). In part under the influence of the Council of Europe, whose workshops teacher trainers were now attending, the movement yielded, for German, textbooks such as *Einfach toll!* (Smith 1985), developed by a team from Lancashire and Cumbria, which broke the task of learning German down into functions, to which particular language forms were tied (see Figure 4.9). *Deutsch Jetzt* (McNab 1988) included explicit *Lernzielkontrollen* and *Zwischentests* (checking progress on the learning goals, formulated in the form *Kannst du…?*). The logical consequence of this step was the introduction of continuous assessment into the public examinations. As CILT's Derek Hewitt announced in 1986, "Gone are the days when German groups were selected in years 2 and 3 on the sole criterion of pupils being considered able to complete an often rigorous course […] over three to four years." The philosophy behind the Graded Objectives movement ultimately produced the Council of Europe's Common European Framework of Reference for Languages, being worked on from 1989 and finally published in 2001, which identified six reference levels, expressed in terms of what the learner can do, from A1 to C2.[55]

55 For example: A1: Can understand and use familiar everyday expressions and very basic phrases aimed at the satisfaction of needs of a concrete type. Can introduce him/herself and others and can ask and answer questions about personal details such as where he/she lives, people he/she knows and things he/she has. Can interact in a simple way provided the other person talks slowly and clearly and is prepared to help.
C2: Can understand with ease virtually everything heard or read. Can summarise information from different spoken and written sources, reconstructing arguments and accounts in a coherent

The career of German (and French) teacher Paul Coggle over several decades may serve as an example of an enthusiastic supporter of language learning for all, embracing the possibilities offered by new technologies. Coggle was a teacher of German at the first Greater London comprehensive, Holland Park Comprehensive, with over 2000 pupils and where the first language laboratory in London was introduced in 1962 ("It made the papers", Coggle recalls, though by the end of the 1960s there over 500 in the UK).[56] French was taken by all pupils; German was an option. Coggle recalls writing large numbers of laboratory exercises, recorded with the help of a German language assistant. Coggle later had the opportunity to make explicit his precepts for preparing language materials suitable for all when, in the early 1980s, he was hired by Hodder to produce a set of guidelines for authors for the *Teach Yourself* series. His precepts included focussing on everyday needs; using language close to spoken language; proceeding by listing situations and the functions needed for them; and basing materials on a pre-determined 'basic' vocabulary (cf. Pfeffer 1964; Oehler 1966). Coggle also went on to update the *Teach Yourself German* "course" (1989) and recalls that the publishers of the *Teach Yourself* series, Hodder, were originally very resistant to the idea of incorporating tapes, for the purely practical reason that tapes, but not books, were subject to VAT (value-added tax) and so would have to be packaged separately. Coggle was equally adamant that tapes were essential to what he insisted be referred to as a Course (not just a "book"). In a career that kept pace with technological developments, Coggle was also involved in the development of the BBC's *Deutsch Plus* (cf. Tenberg 1996), one of many radio and television courses in German produced by the BBC over the years.[57]

4.7 Examining German

> It is obviously of little use advocating, as we have done elsewhere in our Report, an active, oral approach to teaching, with the aim of enabling our pupils to communicate in the foreign language, and urging a bolder policy regarding reading, closer contacts with the foreign country, and full use of audio-visual techniques, so long as the G. C. E. Boards continue to encourage quite a different approach to the whole process.
>
> (Incorporated Association of Head Masters 1966: 40)

Despite discussions of the potential of oral examination (e.g. Brigstocke 1905) and the widespread agreement at a theoretical level about the importance of spoken German,

---

presentation. Can express him/herself spontaneously, very fluently and precisely, differentiating finer shades of meaning even in the most complex situations.

56 The first school language laboratory in the country was installed earlier in the same year, at Chorley Grammar School in Lancashire (Hawkins 1987: 4). Stack (1960) was an important text encouraging the use of language laboratories, but Keating (1963) already signalled a note of caution; Dakin (1973) argued that language laboratories had their place, but only a place.

57 I am grateful to Paul Coggle for allowing me to interview him for the purposes of this book.

examination boards were very slow to change.[58] The inertia is evident in the succession of sample examinations to prepare pupils for examination in prose composition which were published in the first half of the century by Wanstall (1922, 1926, 1934, 1935–1937, 1946), Midgley (1926, 1927), Macpherson (1929, rpt. 1931), Rivers (1935), Florian (1933, 1936), Wells (1938) and others. Still, as early as 1901, an optional element of examination in the spoken language (which had already been possible in the short-lived commercial examinations in the late 1880s and early 1890s; cf. 3.6.1) was introduced to the Cambridge Local Examinations; the following year, more conversational sentences for translation were introduced as an alternative to grammatical questions (*Modern Language Teaching* 1905: 84). The optional oral examination consisted of reading aloud, writing a dictation, and holding a short conversation, which would relate to one of the set books for the written examinations. However, the examination cost extra, and it did not contribute towards the final mark unless the candidate would not obtain a distinction without it; and at least some commentators considered it an impractical expectation, in the face of a shortage of teachers willing to teach according to new methods; the majority urged that "they cannot speak themselves, and therefore cannot teach others to speak" (Brigstocke 1905: 110). The tension between the two schools of thought is eloquently expressed in *Modern Language Teaching* (1909: 282), which carried two reviews on the same page, one of a book "frankly intended for translating English into German" (Pope 1909) and one of a *First Book of German Oral Teaching* (Florian 1909).

Despite the objections to these conditions in a Board of Education 1928 *Report on the position of French in the First School Certificate*, which recommended that a quarter of the marks should be reserved for the oral components (Hawkins 1987: 149), examinations for many decades failed to match the increased importance that had been ascribed to the spoken language in all discussions of classroom practice since the turn of the century. Finally, with the introduction of O-levels, the oral component gained some status: 1961 O-level candidates were required both to sit an aural paper (including re-telling a story that they had heard read aloud) *and* an oral examination; the dictation and oral examination now counted, although failing them could not, on its own, cause a candidate to fail overall.[59]

Likewise, on the matter of translation into German, examining boards were slow to change. Translation into German – as one half of Paper I, called "Composition" – remained compulsory at A-level for the whole of the twentieth century in the Cambridge board at least; even at O-level, a paper without prose translation was only set for the first time by any board in the 1960s (by the Associated Examining Board in 1964), and other boards followed (Hawkins 1987: 6; cf. also IAHM 1966: 40, where the case against translation before A-level is compellingly put). In the early years, the Junior (O-level

---

58 Wegner (1999: 121–126) also discusses changes to examinations between 1900 and 1960; Greatwood (1959) investigated examination papers of the eight examination boards of England and Wales at the time, from 1947 to 1956, from the perspective of what they required pupils to know about Germany and German culture.

59 At A-level, the Welsh Joint Examining Board required a conversation test from 1954, with other boards following slowly (Wegner 1999: 126).

or GCSE equivalent) examination required translation of a carefully constructed text, while the Senior examination (A-level equivalent) included a passage of authentic prose for translation into German (the passage was from John Locke in 1858). By the 1960s, however, the A-level prose translation was also carefully constructed. It is interesting to compare the opening sentence of the senior, higher or A-level passage for translation into German across the years (Table 4.3):

Table 4.3: Opening sentences of the passage for translation into German Cambridge Syndicate Senior/Higher/A-level examinations for selected years, 1858–1994

1858 Seniors:	"He that would seriously set upon the search of truth ought in the first place to prepare his mind with a love of it: for he that loves it not, will not take much pains to get it, nor be much concerned when he misses it."
1916 Seniors:	"At last the condition of affairs became so intolerable that the German princes assembled to elect a new emperor who would restore the peace of the Empire."
1919 Seniors:	"King William the Third being on a march, for some secret undertaking, was asked by a general to tell him what his purpose was."[59]
1948 Higher School Certificate:	"A few months after my great-grandfather had gone to Germany, the neighbouring farmers began to complain about inexplicable losses of sheep from among the flocks browsing in the quiet meadows."
1967 A-level:	"Mary opened her handbag and made sure that her handkerchief, purse, keys and all the other important things were in it."
1970 A-level:	"Richard and his wife were travelling along the motorway from Frankfurt to Munich."
1987 A-level:	"It was a fine evening in May when the station taxi drove her to the gate of the house."
1994 A-level:	"When we reopened conversation we talked about what we had done since school."[60]

While it might be tempting to conclude from a cursory comparison of the samples given in Table 4.3 that standards fell over the course of the twentieth century (with perhaps a noticeable step-change in the type of language tested occurring in the 1960s), it should be remembered that a passage is only ever as easy or difficult as the marking scheme makes it. Here the examiners' reports can provide an insight, though reports are

---

60 This examination also contained, as a separate task, some short, non-literary sentences for translation, "Did you know that Ford is my cousin? Do you know him? Yes, I have known him for two years."

61 This is the opening of the fourth paragraph for translation, rather than the start of the passage. It is cited in the 1995 examiners' report, p. 86.

unfortunately not available for every year.[62] The examiners wrote in their 1878 report that "The translations from English into German were in general very disappointing, shewing in many cases an entire ignorance of the commonest rules and of the structure of the simplest sentences"; "many attempted it and failed from their apparent ignorance of the ordinary rules of German, a few did it remarkably well (1878 Report, German Juniors p. 11, Seniors, p. 12). For 1950, the report reads that "in the composition work [i.e. translation into German] there was a marked improvement in German vocabulary [...] there were however many mistakes in the forms of strong verbs [...] *könnte* was used for *konnte* and vice versa". Of the 1960 A-level examination, the examiners wrote in their report: "Though there was no appreciable increase in the 'very good' band, there were few disastrously bad versions, and the proportion of fairly good and competent work was higher than in recent years", though this overall achievement was "marred by bad errors in elementary grammar, especially in accidence and in verb forms. Even the best candidates made occasional startling blunders. Many appeared to have no realization that meticulous accuracy is the *sine qua non* of all linguistic work. Distortion of the tense-forms of strong verbs was epidemic [...]" (numerous examples follow, including *laufte* and *läufte* for *lief*). In 1987, the next year for when a report is available, the examiners wrote "Candidates' performance on this question was disappointing this year, particularly as the examiners felt that the vocabulary required was straightforward and the grammatical structures far from complex. [...] On the whole it would be true to say that grammatical errors of the most basic kind prevented many candidates from achieving reasonable marks" (1987 Report, p. 30). Finally, of the 1994 prose translation, the examiners wrote (p. 16) that "Knowledge of vocabulary was mixed [...] accuracy was again a problem. Use of Umlaut was again poor, so that tenses were often unclear, strong verbs (*bekommen, bestehen*) were not well-known"; one might compare the remark about Umlaut with the comment in a report 99 years earlier, "The great inaccuracy in the use of modified and unmodified vowels seemed to shew that this essential point is not sufficiently attended to in teaching" (1895 Report: xl).

To judge by the examiners' reports, including the examples they cite, candidates throughout the whole period from the 1870s to 1990s made the same kinds of errors. The examiners' expectation of excellence was repeatedly disappointed – consider the 1960 report, where it does not appear to have entered the sheltered examiners' heads that a pupil might *aspire* to "meticulous accuracy" and yet not deliver it. One clear change over the course of the twentieth century that can be identified, however, is the shift in the type of language that is being tested, away from elevated language to language that – whilst still being narrative prose – is of a more everyday style (cf. Chapter 5). The early reports do not suggest that pupils faced with the more elevated style of the earlier papers necessarily rose to the challenge – though another common theme is that there were always a small number of excellent candidates.[63]

---

62 Between the 1930s and 1980s, reports on each subject were no longer produced annually, but only sporadically.

63 I cannot chart here in full the changes to examinations in German through the twentieth century.

4.8 Evening courses and adult learners

The 1930s – a period of resurgence for German in schools – also saw rapid growth in evening course enrolments for German. Given that the number of children aged 15–16 who were still at school around the turn of the twentieth century was extremely low (0.9 % in 1893; Ortmanns 1993: 36), evening courses had long been an important form of further education, and remained so until World War II. German evening courses were on offer at 188 colleges in 1902, increasing to between 280 and 300 in the pre-war years (1912–13), but evidently declining steeply during the war, for the next available statistics show German taught at only 78 institutions, a low-point from which German once again increased to 130 by 1926. On a different measure – the number of German courses on offer in evening schools – German likewise grew fairly steadily from just over 200 in 1920 to 1677 in 1938, an increase from 6 % of all foreign language courses offered to 36.1 % (Ortmanns 1993: 110–113). Most tellingly, the number of *individual* enrolments in German courses at evening schools also increased massively in the decade between 1927 and 1938: it nearly doubled in three years, from 4703 in 1927 to 8004 in 1930, and reached nearly 23000 in 1938. That growth is very considerable given that the numbers taking foreign languages altogether increased by only about 7000 between 1927 (50749) and 1938 (57155) Ortmanns (1993: 114–155). A similar pattern is evident in the Evening Colleges (the designation used between 1927 and 1938 to differentiate institutions where teaching was at a higher level than in the Institutes, according to Ortmanns 1993: 109). Here too the numbers enrolling for German increased more than fourfold from 3548 in 1927 to 15380 in 1938, again far outstripping the overall growth in foreign language enrolments (which increased from 26355 to 36684).[64]

The growth in the market for evening courses in German can be traced too in text-book production. Florence Ellis's *Introduction to German for Upper Forms and Evening Classes* (1913), "strictly on reform lines", is the earliest text that I am aware of that specifically included evening students in its target readership; it included "a few commercial words in common use" as well as exercises in calculating German money, weights and measures (Ellis 1913: v). Several years later, Rippmann's *Rapid German Course* "for the use of evening classes and private students" aimed "to make learners familiar, as expeditiously as possible, with a useful (though necessarily limited) vocabulary and with the essentials of the grammar" (Rippmann 1921: v). Rippmann's recognition that time was at a premium for such students led him to make some compromises that would "come as a shock to some rigid adherents of the reform method" (p. vi), including the use of footnotes to translate new vocabulary (see Figure 4.11), a device which avoided the need either for time-consuming explanations by the teacher or recourse to English.

See Rock (1993) and Jones (1993) for overviews of O-level/CSE/GCSE and A-level syllabi in the late 1980s and early 1990s, including the introduction of the new GCSE syllabus and discussion of examiners' reports.

64 For Spanish – which would later compete with German for status as the principal "LOTF", enrolments declined from 4,849 (at Institutes) and 3,457 (at Colleges) in 1927 to 2,451 (at Institutes) and 2,396 (at Colleges) in 1938.

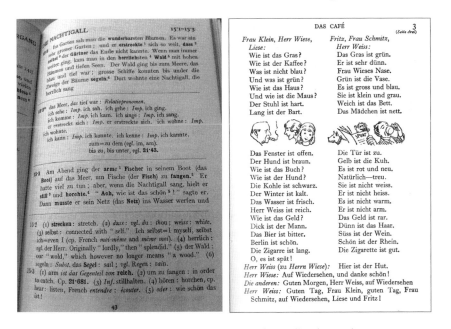

Figure 4.11 (left): Ripman (1921: 43), Figure 4.12 (right): Kelber (1938: 3)

Rapid progress in grammar was indeed envisaged, with the preterite tense introduced on page 43 in a book of 156 pages. Rippmann's presentation of grammar and exercises was "on the concentric plan", revisiting topics in slightly greater depth each time, "so that no Part of the knowledge may become rusty". Magda Kelber, in her appropriately named evening course *Heute Abend!* (1938),[65] had fewer qualms than Rippmann on the use of English: "The grammar has been explained in English as it seems a waste of time, especially for the evening student, to be burdened with the unnecessary difficulties involved in a rigid use of the direct method" (Kelber 1938: iii–iv). Every fifth chapter consisted of revision. Kelber, who later produced a separate reader for adult learners (*So einfach!*, 1943) laid great emphasis on reading – by which she meant that each lesson should be "read, translated, re-read, repeated after the teacher with books closed, retold from memory and perhaps dictated in parts", after which "the relevant grammar will not need very much more explaining." Like Rippmann, Kelber's book introduced grammar rapidly: the preterite came in Chapter 7 of 20 (p. 79 of 303), for example. Kelber made heavy use of rhymed lessons (well, doggerel) as an aide-memoire: "They do not claim to be poetry, but the great ease with which they impress themselves on the memory should justify them, and even make for the occasional unavoidable poetic licence in grammat-

---

65 Note also from the same year Faulk (1938), *A common-sense German course. For the use of Evening Institutes and Commercial Schools, and for Adult Students.*

ical construction." Figure 4.11 provides an example of the effect produced – the kind of thing to make advocates of authentic language shudder.

It was also in the 1930s that the evergreen *Teach Yourself* series began. *Teach Yourself German* was one of the first in the series to appear, in 1938 (Adams & Wells, 1938, based on Adams 1901), and has been running every since. Grundy's *Brush Up Your German* (1ˢᵗ ed. 1931) also surfed the wave of strong interest in German amongst adult learners, in this case primarily "those who have already made some slight acquaintance with the language and its grammar", though "its bi-lingual feature [the fact that all conversations were provided with facing-page translations in English] and general simplicity should also make it of use to the novice" (Grundy 1931: vi). In a sense Grundy's *Brush Up Your German* (which followed the success of a *Brush Up Your French*) was a throwback to the dialogues in parallel translation of eighteenth-century textbooks, though unlike those, Grundy's textbook contained no grammar at all; it is "neither a 'text', nor a 'course', nor a 'primer', but a series of conversations about modern things in the words and phrases of to-day" (p. vi). In his aim to use "the words and phrases of today", Grundy certainly succeeded: the conversations – of which recordings could be obtained separately from the Linguaphone Institute (p. vi) – are impressively authentic-sounding. The opening lines of the first dialogue are indicative – note the use of particles like *ja, doch, wohl*, and Frau Meyer's colloquial omission of the verb of travel after the modal *können*:

— Endlich, Ilschen, ist dieser elende Schmidtprozeß erledigt! Jetzt können wir unsere Ferienreise anfangen!
— Wie schön! Gratuliere, Helmuth. Du hast furchtbar viel Geld verdient, und jetzt könnnen wir wirklich los nach Süddeutschland!
— Süddeutschland? Norddeutschland meinst du wohl, meine Liebste.
— Du weißt ja doch, Helmuth, daß man unmöglich acht Wochen in deinem garstigen alten Berlin zubringen kann. Und sonst ist in Norddeutschland ja nichts zu sehen.

(Grundy 1931: 3)

An undoubted added attraction were the lively and witty line drawings by Phyllis R. Ward,[66] although much of the dialogue content and the drawings would fail absymally today's tests of political correctness (see 6.3 and 6.11 below). To take a comparatively anodyne example, conversation 20 depicts Frau Meyer bothering the importantly busy Herr Meyer to ask his opinion as to which summer dress to buy (Figure 4.13). Only after she has obtained his approval for her choice does she reveal that she already bought it the previous day. Despite the light-hearted approach, the intention behind the series was a serious one: Grundy noted that "largely owing to old methods and lack of initiative, we are curiously backward in our knowledge of German as it is spoken to-day", and even cited the words of the Leathes Report of 1918 that "The knowledge of German by specialists alone will not suffice; it must be widespread through the people; … it is of

66 Ward also illustrated Rosenberg's *Living Languages – How to Speak German* (1938).

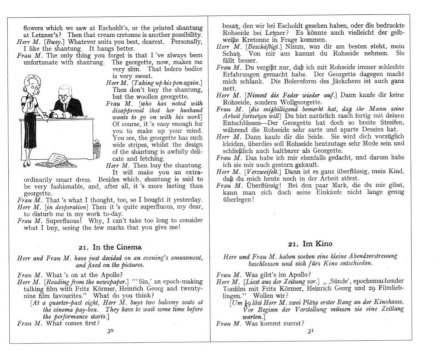

Figure 4.13: Grundy 1931: 30–31

essential importance that the study of the German language should be not only maintained but extended" (Grundy 1931: v.). The *Brush Up Your German* series (with two sequels, *The Second Brush up Your German*, and *Brush Up Your German Again*, as well as a revised edition: 1939, 1950, 1961) is discussed in more detail in Chapter 6.

The democratization of language learning after World War II – evident in the introduction of languages to learners of all abilities in comprehensive schools – was also palpable in strong support for language teaching in adult education, at least in some parts of the country. In Leicestershire – which counted itself as amongst the more progressive education authorities with its model of "Community Colleges" – language advisors were appointed to "enthuse" and to "promote excellence" in language teaching (in the words of Duncan Sidwell, a principal languages advisor in Leicestershire in the 1970s and 1980s), and their remit explicitly included supporting language tutors working in adult education in the county's Community Colleges. All adult education tutors working in the colleges were required to undertake training, and specialized training materials were produced (cf. Sidwell 1987a; Sidwell 1987b). The predominantly communicative approach endorsed is reflected in the relative lack of importance accorded to explicit grammatical knowledge in the notes for tutor trainers, which suggest that if any tutors-to-be appear "shaky", then "it may be useful to go through the main categories of verb, tense, noun, adjective and adverb" – a very elementary level of grammatical knowledge

181

indeed, which does not even cover all the main parts of speech (Sidwell 1987a: 7). Adult education also extended in the post-war years to offering German lessons in prisons: German-born Katherine Eichstaedt Lunn, herself later the author of a German reader (Lunn 1967), began her teaching career by teaching prisoners in the local prison, Camp Hill on the Isle of Wight, in the 1950s, before being employed – although without a formal teaching qualification – by the local grammar school, Carisbrooke, from 1963.[67]

4.9 Excursus: Language education in the Armed Forces, and the Joint Services School for Linguists (1951–1960)

German had been taught to at least some members of the armed forces since at least the mid-nineteenth century, even if it was moribund in the early twentieth century (cf. 3.6, 4.3). The Cold War meant that even after the end of World War II, German remained a strategic military priority, but it was now joined by Russian. The strategic case for Russian in schools was energetically made in the Annan Report of 1962 (Hawkins 1987: 70–71), but its importance had already been recognized a decade earlier with the formation of the Joint Services School for Linguists. The experience of one of my informants for this project, who completed his National Service in the RAF signals section in 1957–1958, may serve as an illustration. Having learnt French and German at school and intending to progress to university, he was one of those selected – after eight weeks of basic training – for eight months of intensive instruction in Russian at the Joint Services School for Linguists (JSSL), which had been established in 1951, in direct response to the Cold War, to supply personnel for interception and interpretation. It moved to a joint site in Crail, near St. Andrews in 1956, and until it closed in 1960 when conscription ended, some 5000 men were trained in Russian (cf. Elliott & Shukman 2003: 11; cf. also Boiling 2005).[68] Batches of between 300 and 400 uniformed conscripts at a time learned Russian in eight-hour days where, in my informant's experience, the instruction alternated between traditional grammar-presentation in classes of about 25 (taught by

---

67 Katherine Eichstaedt (b. 1913) left Germany after meeting her husband, who had been on a touring holiday, at an English-speaking club in Frankfurt in 1937. In August 1939, she arrived in England for a two-week holiday, but – when war was declared on September 3 – she stayed, marrying Fred Lunn, who had already been called up, during his 24-hour leave. Living near Leeds, Eichstaedt Lunn was one of many who, in the post-war years, invited German prisoners-of-war from the local camp into their homes for meals; her daughter Karen recalls German butchers helping with the slaughter of their pig. My thanks to Karin Reekie, Katherine's daughter, for these details.

68 Selection criteria, probably drafted by Dame Elizabeth Hill, Professor of Slavonic Studies and Cambridge and Director of the JSSL Russian course at Cambridge, began with "The WILL to learn the language", followed by powers of concentration, good memory, accuracy, good health, age under twenty-five ("the younger the better"), a background in grammatical terminology, and a School Certificate in Latin or another foreign language (Elliott & Shukman 2003: 47). Thomas (2003: 5), who learnt Russian there himself, wrote that "The JSSL was created for a practical military purpose [...] but ultimately of far greater significance was that it created a generation of young and influential Britons who had generous, respectful and affectionate feelings for Russia – the eternal Russia of Tolstoy, Pushkin and Pasternak."

teachers who were typically English Russianists) and so-called Groups of six to eight, in which the grammar presentation was followed up by small-group teaching with a native Russian speaker. "Men at JSSL were examined every week, had regular progress tests, and could be 'returned to unit' if they failed repeatedly. The courses began with intensive work to come up to O-level standard in about eight weeks, and to A-level in 4–6 months. Students considered suitable after a progress test for the more advanced courses leading to interpretation work were sent to either SSEES [University College London's School of Slavonic and East European Studies] or Cambridge, each of which developed its own teaching style. The courses consisted of sessions for the spoken word and for grammar, with dictation, reading and vocabulary learning every evening" (Lee 1999, no pagination; a more detailed account of the instruction is given in Elliott & Shukman 2002: 69–72; see also the reminiscences gathered in Boiling 2005: 89–116). Beginning at Crail in September, my informant and his fellows passed in the following July both A-level Russian and a Civil Service examination of equivalent standing. According to Boiling (2005: 93–94), conscripts had to learn between 500 and 700 words each week (listed in alphabetical order), adding up to a vocabulary of several thousand words by the end of the course. The top ten in each intake went on to Cambridge and, after two years of Russian there, became officer cadets; those who did not pass the weekly tests were "returned to unit", although my informant's impression was that once it came to the final examination, "a blind eye was turned to cheating". The final examination consisted of an oral examination, translation both ways, and *written interpretorship,* where the cadets listened to a Russian news bulletin and were required to write an English translation (the recording being paused to allow time for this). After passing this examination, the RAF signals conscripts then undertook to a two-month course at RAF Pucklechurch, near Bristol, on operating a radio and on "logging", i.e. listening in to communications and writing down what was heard. Here specialist vocabulary for listening to military communications "between Soviet tank commanders and infantry officers, aircraft and their ground controllers, and ships and their bases, and submarines and their home ports" (Elliott & Shukman 2002: 9) and ground control was taught. After 12 months' training, my informant then spent nine months in Berlin monitoring broadcasts (as other units elsewhere monitored East German communications). All the information logged was passed on to Government Communications Headquarters (GCHQ), where analysts sought to deduce from call signals and other details the location and extent of military exercises.

Troops and their families stationed in Germany were also taught German (and presumably still are). Alison Maclaine, who was in the Royal Army Educational Corps from 1977 to 1984, recalls teaching intensive two-week Basic German courses and four-week Colloquial German courses to all ranks plus spouses. The courses were not compulsory, but units were supposed to have a certain proportion who had qualified at the Basic level. Those who completed the four weeks' "Colloquial" course wore a little badge on their arm. Though some qualified officers taught German, most of the instructors were native speakers employed locally, but the Army used its own materials. The German was quite specific to the context, e.g. *Wir sind britische Soldaten und wohnen und arbeiten in Dortmund* 'We are British soldiers and live and work in Dortmund'. At the Colloquial level, the language could become quite technical, e.g. *Wo sind die Ersatzteile für die Panzer?* 'Where are the replacement parts for the tanks'?

There is growing interest in Europe in the history of language education in the armed forces, as a conference held in June 2013 in Bamberg on "Foreign language learning and foreign language communication by officers and soldiers: historical and linguistic perspectives" attests *(Fremdsprachenlernen und fremdsprachliche Kommunikation von Offizieren und Soldaten in historischer und sprachwissenschaftlicher Perspektive)*. It is important in the wider context of understanding the role played by languages in conflict. (See http://www.languageinconflict.org/.) The above notes do not go beyond anecdote, but indicate that the area is worthy of further study.

4.10 German for business and intensive courses

The perceived inherent difficulty of the German language teacher's task, noted for example by M. B. S. (1921) in the passage cited under 4.6.4 above, was particularly acute in the teaching of commercial German. In an article on the teaching of Commercial German for the *Encyclopaedia and dictionary of education*, Jethro Bithell[69] wrote in 1921, "Commercial German being a language in itself, those who teach it must make a detailed study of it." Bithell emphasized that the vocabulary was highly technical, and that each branch of trade had its own technical terms. It also varied in vocabulary and idiom according to locality, such that Austrian, Polish, and South American merchants "have strongly marked peculiarities of their own". A further difficulty was that of reading German handwritten letters, though the spread of typewriters was starting to reduce the difficulty. "The practice may begin with letters carefully written and pass on to scrawls and scribble" (Bithell 1921: 693). The truth of the matter is that the genuinely great difficulty of the task, already acknowledged by Coverley Smith in 1892 (cf. 3.6.1 above), was forever destined to undercut the arguments made about the utility of German for commercial purposes. A review of Dutton's *Practical Course in Commercial German* (Dutton 1929), while positive, noted that it was "hardly a book for young beginners" (*Modern Languages* 1930: 57). While an anonymous item in the *Educational Times* of 1919 repeated with evident pleasure the view expressed in a recent issue of the *Liverpool Journal of Commerce* that "Commerce calls for a study of German", the final sentence quoted from the original piece contained the sting in the tail – the double challenge of the need for a very high standard in a very specialized language variety: "If British commerce is to penetrate into and seek to displace German commerce in Europe, or in any part of the

---

69 Jethro Bithell (1878–1962) was a lecturer in German at Salford, then Manchester, and was ultimately Reader in German at Birkbeck College, London. He wrote a number of texts for the study of commercial German (1908, 1912, 1922), as well as German for scientists: Bithell 1925). Bithell's *Germany* (1932) is discussed in Chapter 6.3 below. For biography, see the entry in *Who was Who* (online at http://www.ukwhoswho.com/). Accessed September 27, 2011. See also the entry for Bithell in AIM25 Archives in London and the M25 area, online at http://www.aim25.ac.uk/cgi-bin/vcdf/detail?coll_id=5736&inst_id=31. Accessed July 2014.

globe, a perfect knowledge, technical and commercial, of German is a first essential to success". Such "perfection" was – and remains – a tall order.

Nevertheless, there was renewed optimism after World War II. News spread of the perceived success of intensive "audiolingual"-style US Armed Forces language training programmes, which used pre-recorded materials in language laboratories to present materials and drills to learners, emphasizing hearing and speaking ahead of reading and writing (Angiolillo 1947; Lind 1948; cf. Stern 1983: 102, 104; see Byram 2004 for a useful summary). Wightwick & Strubelt's *Audio-Lingual German* (1974) is an example of this audiolingual approach applied to German. After a decade of very intensive courses in Russian at the JSSL, Ealing Technical College (incorporated in the early 1990s into Thames Valley University), London, was the first civilian institution to experiment, beginning in 1962, with army-style intensive "crash" courses using language laboratories. The Nuffield foundation funded intensive courses for business people in Spanish and German, languages which it was felt needed more promotion than French, under the leadership of Mabel Sculthorp, with the first language laboratory in the UK (Hawkins 1987: 156). The result was the *Ealing Course in German* (1969), written by Una McNab with the assistance of Paul Coggle, and the course was trialled with learners from businesses including Bosch, Lloyds Bank, and United Biscuits (see p. vi). (There was an equivalent *Ealing Course in Spanish*). Various more or less diluted versions of "intensive" language were soon introduced in other colleges too. As an example of the more dilute end of the scale, Colin Wringe (later a teacher-trainer: cf. Wringe 1976, 1989) was asked by Tottenham Technical College to run eight-week "intensive" courses for local businessmen in French and German. These ran between 1964 and 1966; up to eight students per course attended for three hours on a Wednesday afternoon. Wringe developed his own materials for these, including material suitable for the new language laboratory, later published as Wringe (1972). At three hours once a week, such courses were not, in fact, particularly "intensive".

The *Ealing Course in German* illustrates well the new approaches to teaching being tried at the time. The setting – intensive teaching – was new. Heavy use of new technologies – tape-recordings and films-strips – was made; that too was new. It also drew on recent linguistic theories. First, it was very much under the influence of behaviourist theories of language learning: students should practise "behaving" in a given situation, until the appropriate "stimulus-response bond has been formed" (p. xv – see Figure 4.14), with the concomitant fear of allowing errors to creep in: "If there is not instant recognition of a mistake, it will be learned" (p. xvii). Second, the course took a functionalist linguistic approach. That is, although grammar was explicitly presented, the chapters worked through situations, supplying the language needed to fulfil the functions required (e.g. "At the bank"; "Looking for a flat" – see Figure 4.15 for an example). Third, the authors made use of "contrastive linguistics", making teachers aware of the differences between English and German – which, in turn, it was believed would identify areas likely to be more or less difficult for learners (Kufner 1962). Finally, the assumption that the purpose of language learning was to enable communication reflects the thinking of the 1960s. The course is also the most extreme version of a utilitarian

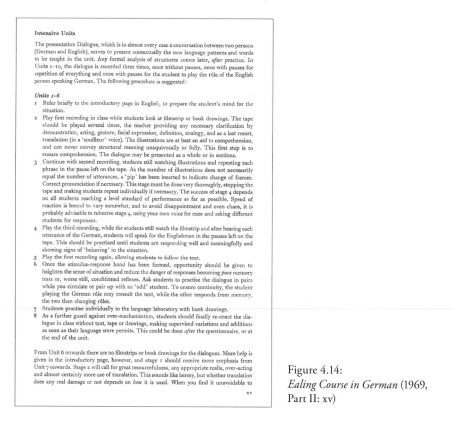

Intensive Units

The presentation Dialogue, which is in almost every case a conversation between two persons (German and English), serves to present contextually the new language patterns and words to be taught in the unit. Any formal analysis of structures comes later, *after* practice. In Units 1–10, the dialogue is recorded three times, once without pauses, once with pauses for repetition of everything and once with pauses for the student to play the rôle of the English person speaking German. The following procedure is suggested:

Units 1–6

1 Refer briefly to the introductory page in English, to prepare the student's mind for the situation.

2 Play first recording in class while students look at filmstrip or book drawings. The tape should be played several times, the teacher providing any necessary clarification by demonstration, acting, gesture, facial expression, definition, analogy, and as a last resort, translation (in a 'souffleur' voice). The illustrations are at best an *aid* to comprehension, and can never convey structural meaning unequivocally or fully. This first step is to ensure comprehension. The dialogue may be presented as a whole or in sections.

3 Continue with second recording, students still watching illustrations and repeating each phrase in the pause left on the tape. As the number of illustrations does not necessarily equal the number of utterances, a 'pip' has been inserted to indicate change of frames. Correct pronunciation if necessary. This stage must be done very thoroughly, stopping the tape and making students repeat individually if necessary. The success of stage 4 depends on all students reaching a level standard of performance as far as possible. Speed of reaction is bound to vary somewhat, and to avoid disappointment and even chaos, it is probably advisable to rehearse stage 4, using your own voice for cues and asking different students for responses.

4 Play the third recording, while the students still watch the filmstrip and after hearing each utterance of the German, students will speak for the Englishman in the pauses left on the tape. This should be practised until students are responding well and meaningfully and showing signs of 'behaving' in the situation.

5 Play the first recording again, allowing students to follow the text.

6 Once the stimulus-response bond has been formed, opportunity should be given to heighten the sense of situation and reduce the danger of responses becoming *pure* memory tests or, worse still, conditioned reflexes. Ask students to practise the dialogue in pairs while you circulate or pair up with an 'odd' student. To ensure continuity, the student playing the German rôle may consult the text, while the other responds from memory, the two then changing rôles.

7 Students practise individually in the language laboratory with book drawings.

8 As a further guard against over-mechanization, students should finally re-enact the dialogue in class without text, tape or drawings, making supervised variations and additions as soon as their language store permits. This could be done *after* the questionnaire, or at the end of the unit.

From Unit 6 onwards there are no filmstrips or book drawings for the dialogues. More help is given in the introductory page, however, and stage 1 should receive more emphasis from Unit 7 onwards. Stage 2 will call for great resourcefulness, any appropriate realia, over-acting and almost certainly more use of translation. This sounds like heresy, but whether translation does any real damage or not depends on *how* it is used. When you find it unavoidable to

xv

Figure 4.14:
Ealing Course in German (1969, Part II: xv)

approach to learning German that I have encountered. In the preface "To the student", the authors wrote:

> The course is directed to the purposeful use of German, and not to intellectual examination of its systems as a formal study. Resist the temptation, then, to ponder on the reasons for particular forms or usage, as the digression from the task in hand, however interesting, will add nothing to your skill in learning the language.
> [...]
> Concentrate on the use of the language rather than knowledge about it. Once can crack the code of a language and learn a few hundred words in a week or two. But this will not lead to real communication. The constant use of structural forms in living language is required and one must be required to devote the time to it. There is no substitute for practice.

Rather,

> Learning a foreign language, then, can be described as the formation of a new set of language habits under conditions of controlled intensive practice. [...] It is

186

Eine Bewerbung um eine Stellung 21
An application for a job

Mr Blake has just returned from another visit to England – rather later than expected, as he had so much to do. His visit had two main purposes: to inspect the progress of the building of the new English branch, and to follow up a complaint about inadequate sales service in the North of England. After discussion with area representatives, Mr Blake reports that they considered it necessary to employ 3 more technicians in the northern area. There were no complaints about orders or delivery. Mr Blake visited the new factory, spoke to the master of works and ascertained that all was going according to plan. The matter will be taken up with Herr Dietz. Herr König now proceeds to inform Mr Blake of the arrangements being made for him for the next 4 or 5 months. He has put everything in the hands of Herr Korff, his personal assistant. He has already advertised for a secretary with appropriate qualifications, and will advertise for a suitable flat for Mr and Mrs Blake, after consulting with Mr Blake. He will see that an office is furnished and fully equipped immediately. Applications for the secretary's job have already been received, and one in particular appealed to the personnel manager, who proposes to interview applicants the day after tomorrow, if Mr Blake can be present. Herr König tells Mr Blake of the details of the kind of flat he wants and let Herr Korff know at once.

The *Expansion* deals with one of the applications and will show you how to give a good account of yourself, how to describe in the imperfect tense the course of your career and to give the relevant information briefly, modestly and sensibly.

In the first *Conversation*, 2 students play the rôles of Herr König and Herr Korff, discussing the arrangements for Mr Blake referred to in the dialogue, with the help of printed clues. In the second conversation, Herr Korff consults Mr Blake about these matters and the student plays the rôle of Mr Blake. In the last exercise you are asked to give an account of your own career up to the present time, covering both business and private events. Use the printed reminders to help you get going, but your final performance should be given without referring to them or to your teacher for assistance.

This unit introduces the imperfect tense of *haben* and of strong verbs. Although certain patterns are distinguishable, as with the past participles of strong verbs, they simply have to be learned by practice. The use of the imperfect in the spoken language varies considerably. Apart from the imperfect of *haben*, *sein* and the modal auxiliaries, it is hardly ever used in speech in southern Germany, Switzerland and Austria. In north Germany, it is heard quite often as an alternative to the perfect, so it must be learned. There is really only one situation in the past which the perfect cannot possibly convey – the description of an action which was going on and was interrupted by another action before the first was completed, e.g. 'He was reading the letter when the telephone rang.' In the written language, the imperfect is widely used in description of all kinds of action and situation in the past. German verb forms in the past and perfect tenses have no such subtle distinctions as English past and perfect forms.

Dialog 21
Mr Blake kommt von einer Englandreise zürck

1. HERR KÖNIG Ah, guten Morgen, Mr Blake! Sie sind gestern abend zurückgekommen, habe ich gehört. Ich dachte, Sie wollten nur bis zum 16. in England bleiben.
2. MR BLAKE Ja, aber ich mußte etwas länger bleiben. Es gab so viel zu tun, es war einfach unmöglich, früher wegzukommen.
3. HERR KÖNIG Wie war die Englandreise?
4. MR BLAKE Recht anstrengend. Ich hatte sehr viel zu erledigen.
5. HERR KÖNIG Und der Kundendienst?
6. MR BLAKE Ich stellte fest, daß die Kunden im Norden nicht ganz zufrieden sind.
7. HERR KÖNIG Was sagten die Vertreter dazu?
8. MR BLAKE Sie hielten es für nötig, noch drei Techniker im Norden anzustellen. Die Kunden beklagten sich nur über den Kundendienst. Mit der Bestellung und der Spedition schien alles in Ordnung zu sein.
9. HERR KÖNIG Das müssen wir mit Herrn Dietz besprechen. Hatten Sie Gelegenheit, das neue Werk zu sehen?
10. MR BLAKE Ich fuhr gestern dorthin. Als ich dort war, sprach ich mit dem Baumeister. Soviel ich sah, ging alles wie geplant.
11. HERR KÖNIG Gut. Nun, zu Ihrem weiteren Aufenthalt bei uns. Ich erzähle Herrn Korff, daß Sie auf 4 bis 5 Monate bei uns bleiben. Sie haben Herrn Korff schon kennengelernt, nicht wahr?
12. MR BLAKE Jawohl. Wir verstanden uns sehr gut.
13. HERR KÖNIG Das freut mich. Denn ich will, daß er Sie betreut, während Sie bei uns sind. Ich habe ihm alle nötigen Anweisungen gegeben. Alle Vorbereitungen möchte ich ihm überlassen.
14. MR BLAKE Das wußte ich nicht, aber ich bin damit völlig einverstanden.
15. HERR KÖNIG Ich sagte ihm, Sie brauchten ein Büro und alles, was dazu gehört. Sie brauchen auch eine Sekretärin mit perfekten Englischkenntnissen, guter Stenographie und Schreibmaschine.
16. MR BLAKE Kann er vielleicht eine Anzeige in der „Frankfurter Allgemeinen" aufgeben?
17. HERR KÖNIG Das tat er vor einigen Tagen. Gestern bekamen wir schon einige Bewerbungen. Es gab eine, die dem Personalchef gut gefiel. Der Personalchef fängt übermorgen mit den Interviews an. Können Sie dabeisein?
18. MR BLAKE Augenblick, bitte. Ich muß im Vormerkbuch nachsehen. Ja, übermorgen bin ich ab 14.30 frei. Übrigens, inserierte er auch für eine Wohnung?
19. HERR KÖNIG Noch nicht. Sagen Sie ihm nur, was Sie brauchen, sobald Sie sich entschlossen haben. Er sorgt dafür.
20. MR BLAKE Vielen Dank, Herr König. Ich bin Ihnen und Herrn Korff sehr dankbar.

Figure 4.15: *Ealing Course in German* (1969, Part II: 260–261)

therefore absolutely essential to nullify the effect of the old system by referring to English as little as possible.

(*Ealing Course in German*, 1969: Part 2, pp. xxii, xxiii)

The idea of German for business remained attractive in the second half of the twentieth century, and German was increasingly made available as an adjunct to vocationally-oriented courses in further and higher education. The 1980s and 1990s correspondingly saw a flurry of textbooks in business German, to the point that a book on how to choose the right business course was even produced: *The beginner's guide to business German: how to choose a German business language course and use it successfully* (Vandevelde 1995). Textbooks (often accompanied by audio and/or video material) ranged from those promising quick results on the time invested (*Get by in Business German. A quick beginner's course for business people* (Tenberg 1993, a BBC course, revised ed. by Kothe & Spranking 1995) to more in-depth courses such as *German for business and economics* by Paulsell et al. (1999, published in the USA). *German for Business* (Paxton & Whelan 1986) was intended for learners starting with at least a CSE in German, whether they be pupils working towards examinations such as the AO level in German for Business Studies or students taking German as part of a post-secondary

vocational course or evening course.[70] Other textbooks of business German written for
the German-for-business market included *Vertrag in der Tasche* (Herde & Royce 1989),
whose authors trialled their material at Buckingham College, *Working with German*
(Lupson, Embleton & Eggington 1989, 1990; one of the co-authors, Doug Embleton, is
described on the title page as "Senior Linguist at ICI"), *Talking Business German* (1992,
by Yeomans & Yeomans in addition to the team that produced *Working with German*),
Nicholson & Estill (1992, a course specifically in telephone skills), as well as Malcolm & Farr (1991), Göricke-Driver (1991, Wessels (1992), Kohl & Carrington-Windo
(1993, a "multi-media" course with the BBC), Clarke (1993), Howarth (1994), Clay
(1995), Paulsell et al. (1999).

4.11 Literature and German learning

> Goethe's world-famous ballad of 'Erlkönig' [...] will go straight to the heart of
> any school-boy or girl.
>
> (Saunders, "A Plea for German" 1919–20: 179)

The twentieth century is in one sense a history of the banishment of literature from the
core of the school German curriculum to, at best, its fringes and upper reaches (at A-level the literature syllabus remained). Reading German no longer automatically meant
reading literature – and Seidmann's compilation of extracts from the newspaper *Die Zeit*
is an early example of attempts to provide authentic, but non-literary reading material
for more advanced learners: *Spiegel der 'Zeit': an introduction to current affairs based
on extracts from 'Die Zeit'*: Seidmann, 1969).[71] To document the teaching of German
literature during that process – whether through the history of "set books" for examinations, in excerpts found in textbooks of passages for translation or for reading, or indeed
through books seeking to give an overview of German literature for English learners –
would be a large undertaking far beyond the scope of this book.[72] This section is limited

---

70 My copy was donated by Bootham School, York, an independent school where a slip in the flyleaf
indicates that the book was used by a pupil in 1989.
71 Using newspapers as authentic materials for reading practice had had earlier advocates, as noted
in Chapter 3.10.2 above, including Bachmair (1751), Bacon (1879) and Otto Siepmann. See also
Porter (1959).
72 See, however, the substantial study of the role of literature in German teaching materials for English speakers in the *Goethezeit* (i. e. 1770–1830) by Guthke (2011). Any such study of the twentieth
century would also need to consider the emergence of new genres and expressions of German culture in the curriculum, such as radio plays, films, and pop songs. Some examples of introductions
to German literature for English speakers are Robertson (1902, 1913, 1950); Thomas (1939, 1965);
Fiedler (1916); Willoughy (1926); Breul (1927); Vrijdaghs & Rippmann (1931); Wanstall (1931, a
book of German prose and poetry "for recitation"); Bain (1902, 1932); Barker (1941, discussed
in Chapter 6.3 below); Bithell (1946, 1947, 1951, 1959); Southwell (1946); Waterhouse (1942);
Brockie (1950); Martin (1953); Closs & Williams (1957); Tymms (1955); Schulz (1961); Hamburger & Middleton (1963), Krausmann (1977).

to showing how literature teaching could continue "under the radar" into the late twentieth century. Notwithstanding the commitment to language skills for communication in the second half of the twentieth century, even as staunch a supporter as Paul Coggle, the contributing author to the *Ealing German Course*, reports that he introduced simple poems in his teaching of French and German. And even as the syllabi for German clearly moved away from a predominantly literary syllabus in the twentieth century, it should be emphasized that every teacher still had considerable freedom to shape the learning experiences of their pupils, and especially so in the independent sector. The career of Richard Stokes, for many years the Head of Modern Languages at Westminster School (a leading and academically selective boys' Public School) from 1975 to 2005 is an eloquent illustration.[73] Stokes himself was taught at Repton in 1959–1960 with *Deutsches Leben*, but had already been won to German through music, in particular through Schubert's *Lieder*. At Westminster, the language teaching was generously timetabled – starting German aged 14, in classes of 15 to 20 pupils, pupils received six 40-minutes lessons in their first year, and four in their second year, such that, teaching these "intelligent kids", Stokes felt able to cover all the grammar (including subjunctive) in "a year and a half, two years certainly […] You can't really tell me that you need a whole year, and 250 pages, to master the present tense, you know, in books like *ZickZack* [i. e. Goodman Stephens et al. 1987–89] […]." Stokes' own account of his use of literature in the classroom deserves quoting verbatim, beginning with how to use Goethe's *Erlkönig*:

> I found if you pursued the grammar really methodically, and tested them, and then chose bits of literature that really illustrated those points, I mean, like say *Erlkönig* – present tense, accusative, dative *Wer reitet so spät durch Nacht und Wind? Es ist der Vater <u>mit</u> <u>seinem</u> Kind.*[74] *Er hat den Knaben* – weak noun – *wohl in dem Arm. Er faßt ihn sicher, er hält ihn warm.*
>
> *Mein Sohn, was birgst du* – Well, that's a bit odd, *was <u>birgst</u> du so bang dein Gesicht?*
> *Siehst Vater, du <u>den</u>* – accusative – *Erlkönig nicht!*
> *Den Erlenkönig mit Kron' und Schweif?*
> *Mein Sohn, es ist ein Nebelstreif.* – Verb to be can't take an accusative
>
> *Du liebes Kind, komm geh' mit mir!* – so, imperative
> *Gar schöne Spiele, spiel ich mit dir,* – so strong ending in the plural, and so on, it's an absolute gift.
>
> […] I mean, I taught through music. I would play them the Schubert setting […] and then we would all sing along to it […] the result is, they got not just in their head, but in their fibre an idea of how German rhythm works.

---

73 I am very grateful to Richard Stokes for consenting to be interviewed for this book. A published account of some of his recollections of his German learning and teaching can be found in Stokes (2011).

74 My underlinings indicate special emphasis placed on individual words and endings by Richard Stokes.

But you know there's so much in German literature that's easy early on [...] I mean, kids of 14, 15, they don't want to be treated like little boys and girls. If you give them some Kafka, for example, twentieth century, nightmare, alienation, not belonging, outsider, they can relate to it. So if you do… I mean there's an anecdote, unpublished, that Max Brodt entitled *Gib's auf*. I mean just listen to it, it's just so easy.

Es war sehr früh am Morgen, die Straßen rein und leer, ich ging zum Bahnhof. Really simple. *Als ich meine Uhr mit der Turmuhr verglich, sah ich, dass es schon viel später war, als ich geglaubt hatte.* Full stop. *Der Schrecken dieser Entdeckung ließ mich im Weg unsicher werden. Ich kannte mich in dieser Stadt noch nicht sehr gut aus.* So simple. *Glücklicherweise war ein Schutzmann,* – well, all right, *Polizist* – *war ein Schutzmann in der Nähe, ich lief zu ihm und fragte ihn atemlos nach dem Weg.* There's a huge sentence. Full stop. *Er lächelte und sagte Von mir willst den den Weg erfahren? Ja, sagte ich, da ich ihn selbst nicht finden kann. Gib's auf, gib's auf, sagte er und wandte sich mit einem großen Schwunge ab, so wie Leute, die mit ihrem Lachen allein sein wollen.*

Well, that grammar is just so dead easy. You've got relatives, you've got subordinates, you've got adjectival endings, you've got inversion, you've got the verb going to the end, and they learn it. Why do they learn it? Not because you're a good teacher, but because this is adult, utterly memorable literature.

[...]

And you know, students like to laugh. I mean, slightly more difficult, but Christian Morgenstern wrote this piece called *Der Werwolf* and he mocks pedants. Because the Werewolf, he pretends it declines. You can see why kids like it.

Ein Werwolf eines Nachts entwich
von Weib und Kind, und sich begab
an eines Dorfschullehrers Grab
und bat ihn: Bitte, beuge mich! – Extraordinary!

Der Dorfschulmeister stieg hinauf
auf seines Blechschilds Messingknauf – Difficult!
und sprach zum Wolf, der seine Pfoten
geduldig kreuzte vor dem Toten:

And then it goes "*Der Werwolf*", – *sprach der gute Mann,* this pedant, the schoolmaster – we talk about schoolmasters – gets up and lectures the werewolf
"*Der Werwolf*", – *sprach der gute Mann* "*des Weswolfs*"- *Genitiv sodann,*
"*dem Wemwolf*" – *Dativ, wie man's nennt,*
"*den Wenwolf*" – *damit hat's ein End.'*

Dem Werwolf schmeichelten die Fälle,
er rollte seine Augenbälle.
Indessen, bat er, füge doch
zur Einzahl auch die Mehrzahl noch!

And then you get the point of the poem, add the plural to the singular:[75]

Der Dorfschulmeister aber mußte
gestehn, daß er von ihr nichts wußte.
Zwar Wölfe gäb's in großer Schar,
doch "Wer" gäb's nur im Singular.

And then – used to have the boys and girls crying, this:

Der Wolf erhob sich tränenblind –
er hatte ja doch Weib und Kind!!
Doch da er kein Gelehrter eben,
so schied er dankend und ergeben.
[...] My point is that. If it moves you, it's wonderful. The kids will love it".

Here Stokes unconsciously echoes the view of M. B. S. (1921) that literature can and should be introduced early on.[76] The extract from my interview with Stokes is given here at such length because it illustrates the difference that the individual teacher can make, at least in some classroom settings. For Stokes, it is as if most of the developments in twentieth-century MFL educational theory never happened. Yet one can have little doubt about his effectiveness in his classroom.

4.12 The status quo in the last quarter of the twentieth century

The communicative textbook *Deutsch Heute*, in its explicit statement of its approach, illustrates very well the sum of developments in language teaching from the eighteenth to the late twentieth century. The authors explicitly adhered to a number of precepts for effective language teaching, citing Sanderson (1982) (cf. Sidwell & Capoore 1984: 3):

- Material should be presented in small manageable learning units;
- Learning goals should be specific, clearly specified and attainable;
- Use of visual clues and of the OHP should be important parts of the teaching process;
- There should be ample student involvement and activity in class;
- There should be a variety of activities used within each lesson;

---

75 The point of the poem is that the werewolf, or *who-wolf*, to follow the German pun (since *wer* means *who*), is devastated to discover that there can be no more than a who- in the singular because, grammatically, *who* has no plural. Yet he has a wife and child.

76 Stokes published an anthology of complete literary texts (not extracts) with which he had had success in class, *Gefunden* (Stokes 1982).

- The foreign language should be extensively used in class;
- The use of language should be graded in difficulty so as to allow a maximum sense of success for students.

Two of these precepts – the desirability of using the target language in the classroom and the value of using visual aids – had returned to prominence after World War II with the advent of new technologies and with the behaviourist approach to language learning, but really dated to the reform movement (which in turn re-invented them after Comenius; cf. 3.10 above). Others are even older, if not always explicitly formulated. As we saw in Chapter 3, the need for carefully graded material was understood at least since Rowbotham (1823), although it is true that notional-functional syllabuses now dictated a different sequencing to some extent. Meanwhile, the view that "material should be presented in small manageable learning units" dates to the so-called practical grammars from the late eighteenth century onwards, beginning with Meidinger (1783); Ollendorf (1838) was an early exponent in German for English learners. That there should be "ample student involvement and activity in class" had been recognized from the second half of the nineteenth century onwards by at least some practitioners such as Emil Otto, when pair work began to rate a mention in some texts (cf. Chapter 3). A phenomenon new to the second half of the twentieth century, however, was the requirement that "learning goals should be specific, clearly specified and attainable" (see 4.6.4 above). It is worth noting here that the graded objectives approach took its inspiration from domains such as music, swimming and gymnastics (Page 1983). In other words, the assumption was made that proficiency in a language was a *skill* (or set of skills) to be attained by careful training and practice.

In keeping with communicative approaches and particularly in the light of the fact that it was impossible to predict when any given learner would "acquire" a given grammatical form, Sidwell & Capoore relegated grammar to the end of chapters, where it was presented in summary "i-boxes" (information boxes) with little or no explicit grammatical vocabulary. "The learning of grammar", Sidwell & Capoore summarized the views of communicative language teachers, "should be a means to more effective communication and not an academic end in itself." It was also accepted that more able students "will obviously assimilate grammatical points of considerable complexity", while others would be "sufficiently stretched" by the i-boxes. In other words, the relative lack of attention paid to grammar was in part a function of the wider ability range – and here, one is again reminded both of Benson's big boys "of little intellectual capacity" (Benson 1907: 11) and of Richards' (1976: 57) assertion that "Teaching grammar to moderate-ability classes is largely a waste of time."

It is interesting to ponder how early twentieth-century reformers would have reacted to the late twentieth-century revolution that yielded communicative language teaching; presumably they would have been delighted and appalled in equal measure. The emphasis on target language, on visual and aural stimuli, on the spoken language in the first instance and on meaningful interaction in class would have delighted them. The limiting of the goal to "mere" communication to be attained by the development of key skills, on the other hand, would probably have horrified them, for while recognizing the usefulness of language in society, it robbed languages at a stroke of their hard-won status as worthy subjects in academe.[77] It is perhaps not surprising that the discussions of Sheppard & Turner (1976: 15) with language teachers in East Anglia, as the last quarter of the twentieth century began, identified as a problem "the low status of German in our culture" compared with subjects like English and History. It is also noteworthy that a rare comparative historical study suggests that the adoption of the communicative approach in teaching German in England seems not to have been mirrored in the teaching of German in France, where MFL teaching returned to "traditional" methods (Wegner 1999: 326).[78]

Another echo of the reform movement in the last decades of the twentieth century was a return to reflection on what the reform movement had called realia, that is: teaching about the target culture and (increasingly) providing deliberately *intercultural* encounters. *Vorwärts* (1974) included regular pages – which stand out in a different colour – of explicit *Deutschlandkunde*. *Deutsch Heute* (1983) presented an early chapter about German life and culture in English; later chapters included short texts on the various *Bundesländer* introduced in turn – not a whisper about the DDR. With that, we approach the subject of Chapter 6: the changing representations of German culture and history in language textbooks for British learners.

4.13 Conclusion

The twentieth century is a century of much upheaval but – despite the perceptions of the participants in the drama – many continuities. German began the century firmly established as a bona fide Modern Languages subject, which had in turn won a place in the curriculum as supplying all (or at least much, cf. Bridge 1921) that the Classics used to supply; its adherents could make credible claims of relevance to other modern studies subjects and to permitting meaningful encounters with literature. Unlike the Classics, modern languages could also lay claim to economic importance; and the object of study had the additional advantage of being a living language. There were, however, still unresolved tensions between the differing needs of these different claims as to value, in particular between the utilitarian credo and the desire to educate the child. German was, furthermore, firmly entrenched as the "second" language, a long way behind French, with all the attendant difficulties of the optional subject of winning pupils in the face of competition from other options, as well as the tedious but often decisive problems of

---

77 Needless to say, the reduced importance of grammar would have surprised them, for they believed that, as Buell, Rippmann's collaborator wrote (Kron et. al. 1901: vi), "The constant grammatical drill [...] cannot fail to yield good results. Grammar is the loom by which words are manipulated to form the warp and woof of the spoken sentence." (Cited under 3.10.1 above.)

78 Comparative historical studies of modern foreign language teaching and learning like Wegner's remain a rarity, but her finding that the teaching of German in England and France was determined, even in the late twentieth century, by national discourses rather than by converging European visions, demonstrates the importance of making such comparisons (Wegner 1999: 333).

how to staff it adequately if take-up was erratic, and how to fit it into the curriculum and timetable. German was felt to be in crisis, and in need of urgent support.

At the end of the twentieth century, those practical difficulties facing German as an optional subject remained. In addition, it now faced competition from Spanish. German was at the end of the twentieth century still second to French, but about to fall into third place in the first decade of the twenty-first century (cf. Tables 4.3 and 4.5), as Spanish at last fulfilled the potential the Leathes report had identified for it in 1918, though probably winning more pupils for its status as a useful "holiday language" than on the basis of the solid economic case made for it by the Leathes report. Similarly, while many like Reeves (1986) increasingly make the 'savvy' economic case for German as a language for business (cf. also Hagen & CILT 1988), that argument alone probably sways relatively few to take German and even fewer to continue with it. Meanwhile, the economic, utilitarian arguments for German; the change to viewing language proficiency as a useful set of *skills*; and the opening out of German language learning, at least for a time, to a much wider constituency of schoolchildren and adults, socially and in terms of ability range – all of these undercut the prestige case for modern languages – so hard-won in the early twentieth century.

Chapter 5 –
Rules for the neighbours:
The German language presented to English-speaking learners

5.1 Introduction[1]

A key question in any study of the history of teaching and learning German is that of just *what* language variety or varieties pupils were being exposed to in their German lessons. Precisely what any individual assumes to be representative of "the" German language is a very loaded question, to which the answers have changed considerably over time. As Chapter 3 already showed, for example, one aim of the Reform Movement was to ensure that "the" German language included a good deal of spoken language. Unconsciously, reformers were reverting to the primary aim of the earliest German language learning manuals, after a century or so of increased focus on learning *about* the language and on translating into and out of the *written* language. Now, it would be impossible, and in any case dull, to provide here a comprehensive examination of what varieties, registers, styles, which pronunciations, spellings, and grammatical features have been taught over the centuries. Yet in each of these areas, what was taught changed considerably over time in ways that reflected changing views, not just of what language learning should be about but also of the German language and its linguistic make-up. In this chapter, therefore, I explore each of these themes by means of selected aspects of language description and prescription: defining and accepting standard or non-standard varieties (5.2), type-faces, hand-writing and spelling (5.3 and 5.4), some aspects of pronunciation, including intonation (5.5 and 5.6), the pragmatics of forms of address (5.7), word order (5.8), and some aspects of noun and verb inflection (5.9).

Research into codifying rules about language use has generally focussed on prescriptions aimed (implicitly, and predominantly, if not exclusively) at native speakers, and indeed there is a strong relationship in modern nation-states between national or regional *languages* and the construction and maintenance of national or regional *identities*. A good illustration of that relationship is the language purism that was one key outlet of seventeenth-century German cultural patriotism. Such purism – especially the aversion to borrowed vocabulary – has continued to feature, more or less prominently, in the centuries since, culminating most recently in the purist efforts of the *Verein Deutsche Sprache* (VDS, 'Society for the German language'), founded in 1997 'in order to pre-

---

1 Some sections of this chapter – parts of the introduction, conclusion, and section 5.9 – appeared in McLelland (2012a).

serve it [the German language] as an autonomous language of culture and language of science, and to protect it from being supplanted by English' (*[u]m sie [=die deutsche Sprache] als eigenständige Kultur- und Wissenschaftssprache zu erhalten und vor dem Verdrängen durch das Englische zu schützen*; cf. McLelland 2009, Stukenbrock 2005). The VDS claims to have a membership of over 31,000. Significantly, it also boasts on its website (http://www.vds-ev.de/) that one third of that total consists of members from Asia and Africa. That high proportion should draw our attention to the relevance of linguistic prescriptions for *non*-native speakers of a language, who learn and use the language in other countries, and who, after all, can neither rely on their native speaker intuition, nor enjoy the immediate and full access to the 'target' culture that might allow them to form their own judgements with confidence.

Advanced non-native speakers can make use of the same reference works in which the language is codified as native speakers (and for the German context, one thinks first of the Duden series of dictionaries, spelling guides, grammars). However, the vast majority of learners of a foreign language (certainly in the UK) do not attain that standard, and remain at the level of school learners who will be mainly or solely reliant on pedagogical materials. Examining representations of the target language in these foreign language-textbooks can offer an illuminating comparison with textbooks aimed at native speakers, contributing to the history of German grammatography (cf. e.g. Langer 2002, 2004; McLelland 2005a, 2008, 2009). At the very least, 'the effectiveness of prescriptive grammarians might […] be measured on the basis of their success in influencing or convincing language teachers to use their, rather than somebody else's variety of German' (Langer 2002: 79). We already know, for instance, that the leading seventeenth-century German language theoretician Justus-Georg Schottelius (1612–1676) had a direct influence on the very first German grammar for English speakers, Aedler (1680) (see 2.2 above; cf. Van der Lubbe 2007a). When, nearly a century later, Gebhardt Friedrich August Wendeborn, the Minister of the German Chapel in Ludgate Hill, London, published *The Elements of German Grammar* (1774), his work – which ran to eleven editions – was in effect an abridgement of Johann Christoph Gottsched's grammar for native speakers (1748) (11th edition 1849; cf. Carr 1935: 481). As we saw in Chapter 3 above, later in the eighteenth century, Johann Christoph Adelung's school grammar for German pupils (Adelung 1781, 1782) was in turn an influence on George Henry Noehden's *German Grammar. Adapted to the use of Englishmen* (1800). Finally, in the nineteenth century, W. G. Klattowsky's *Deutsches Handbuch* (1831) is, according to Carr, a 'slavish copy' of a grammar widely used in German schools of the nineteenth century, Heyse (1816) (Carr 1935: 483). Foreign language grammar-writers are not always slavish imitators, however, and foreign language grammars may even anticipate innovations in the native-speaker grammatical description. The syntax of the adverb in German is one such example (cf. McLelland 2008: 51), and I shall give some others below. For all these reasons, it is both legitimate and important to study foreign language grammars and textbooks in linguistic historiography, as Carr (1935, 1937), Blamires (1990), Langer (2002) and Van der Lubbe (2007a, 2007b, 2008) have done to some degree for the period up to the nineteenth century. Textbooks of German as a Foreign Language of the later nineteenth and of the twentieth century have received virtually no attention to date in German linguistic historiography, despite the fact that they too contain more or less full grammatical descriptions of German. One notable exception is Durrell's examination of how language variation is represented in four twentieth-century textbooks of German for British learners (Durrell, 2005). A borderline case is Langer (2008), whose corpus consists chiefly of schoolbooks aimed at the immigrant German community in the USA, 1800–1918, and whose focus lies on cultural rather than linguistic issues.

In this chapter, I attempt to draw some comparisons in two dimensions: both over time within the British textbooks tradition, and between the parallel British and native-speaker traditions. Before I turn to language description and prescription, however, it is worth noting that foreign language textbooks and teaching often 'prescribe' (at least strongly encourage) not just certain grammatical forms, but also a certain *attitude* to the target language. Already Martin Aedler asserted 'the Excellency of the Highdutch most *Copious and Significant, Majestick and Sweet, Perfect and Pure, Easie and Usefull, Antient and Universal* Toung' (Aedler 1680: first page of Contents, unnumbered). More recently, a positive attitude towards the target culture even became an explicitly desired outcome of foreign language instruction in the 1990s. The 'National Curriculum' for England, Wales and Northern Ireland[2] has for some years prescribed the development of 'cultural awareness' (Qualifications and Curriculum Authority 1999, Modern Foreign Languages: 8) or 'intercultural understanding' (Qualifications and Curriculum Authority 2007, Modern Foreign Languages: 3). Using the National Curriculum as their basis, the separate examining boards devise their own syllabi which teachers preparing pupils for their examinations will follow,[3] and the 2008 syllabus for the largest of these, the Assessment and Qualifications Alliance (AQA), specified as one aim for AS/ A-level students (i. e. pupils in the last two years of high school) that the course should 'develop positive attitudes to foreign language learning' (AQA 2006: 10). Particularly in the light of European history and politics, the tendency to encourage positive views of the target language (and culture) merits close attention, and it is one of the concerns of Chapter 6 below.

5.2 What is 'the' German language as it is represented to English learners?

In Russon & Russon's *Advanced German Course* (1965), a handful of passages for translation into English make assertions about the German language. *Die deutsche Sprache* ('The German language'), a passage from the autobiographical *Aus jungen Tagen* (1928) by Heinrich Federer (1866–1928), presents German as a 'virtual jungle' by comparison with the noble park of French and the bright colourful woodland of Italian (Russon & Russon 1965: 218):

---

2   Under devolution, Scotland is responsible for its own school curriculum.

3   There are seven boards in total. The three largest are AQA (Assessment and Qualifications Alliance); Edexcel (Pearson Edexcel as of April 2013); and OCR (Oxford, Cambridge and RSA Examinations).

Französisch ist ein edler Park, Italienisch ein großer, heller, bunter Wald. Aber Deutsch ist beinahe noch wie ein Urwald, so dicht und geheimnisvoll, so ohne großen Durchgang und doch tausendpfadig. Im Park kann man sich nicht verirren, in der italienischen Waldhelle nicht so leicht und gefährlich; aber im Deutsch kann einer in vier, fünf Minuten im Dickicht verschwinden. Darum, weil der Weg so schwierig scheint, suchen die meisten möglichst gradlinig hindurchzumarschieren, was eigentlich gegen die Natur dieser Sprache ist. Sie will gewiß eine Hauptrichtung, aber ladet durch hundert Pfade und Pfädchen nach links und rechts bald aus ihr heraus, bald wieder in sie hinein.

'French is a noble park, Italian a large, light, colourful wood. But German is still nearly like a jungle, so dense and mysterious, so impenetrable and yet with a thousand paths. In the park one cannot get lost, nor can one so easily and dangerously in the brightness of the Italian wood; but in German one can vanish in the thicket within four or five minutes. Because the way seems so difficult, most try to march through in as straight a line as possible, which is actually contrary to the nature of this language. It seeks a main direction, certainly, but its hundred paths and little trails to left and right now lead one out, now draw one in.' (translation NMcL)

A passage by Julius Petersen (1878–1941), headed *Wort und Begriff* ('Word and Concept') and taken from *Aus der Goethezeit* (1932) makes the point that every language conceptualizes the world differently, citing Goethe's famous aphorism *Wer fremde Sprachen nicht kennt, weiß nichts von seiner eigenen* 'He who knows no foreign languages, knows not his own' (Russon & Russon 1965: 227). Ludwig Reiners (1896–1957), in a passage headed *Die Eigenschaften der deutschen Sprache* 'the characteristics of the German language' and taken from his *Deutsche Stilkunst* (1943), presents German as a work ever in progress, and as less splendid than Italian, less clear than French and less handy than English, yet full of secrets (Russon & Russon 1965: 229). The comparisons with other languages in all these passages chosen by Russon & Russon assume that German takes its place (albeit seemingly a relatively lowly place!) amongst the major languages of European literature. Unquestioned in any case in all these passages is the Romantic belief in the meaningfulness of talking about *the* German language in the first place. Of course the reality is more complex, and choices about which features of 'the' language to prescribe, describe, or present to learners, and what to ignore and exclude, have changed according to the prevailing ideas about what language teaching was aiming to achieve.

As we have seen in previous chapters, the first grammars of German in the late seventeenth century were aimed at those seeking a practical spoken knowledge of the language. Just under a third of Aedler's work (1680: 177–254) consisted of a list of everyday idioms, English and German, included by Aedler '[so] that we do not commit either a Soloecisme, or a Germanisme and Anglicisme' (fourth page of list of contents, unnumbered). Offelen (1687) presented German as a practical spoken language for the traveller. Neither Aedler nor Offelen offered longer prose reading passages, and, as we have seen, it was not until the 1730s that Beiler (1731) recommended reading German literature and plays. Bachmair (1771: 302ff.) included passages for reading and translation practice, but only with Wendeborn (1774), who included a list of recommended works for reading, did the portrayal of German as a literary language become established (Van der Lubbe 2007a). By 1800, we find Noehden including examples from the contemporary writers Christoph Martin Wieland (1733–1813), Johann Gottfried Herder (1744–1803), Johann Wolfgang von Goethe (1749–1813), and Friedrich Schiller (1759–1805).

Up to this point, it had been assumed that the learner of German was an adult, or at least a youth, perhaps preparing for travel around Europe (and, indeed, the first Chair of German in the world, endowed at Trinity College, Dublin, in 1775, was founded to save young men the expense of the educational grand tour; see Raraty, 1966). When, in the mid-nineteenth century, German became established as a subject for children in British schools, it was established as such in its relatively new guise (to English speakers) of a *literary* language. As we saw in 3.8 above, the papers from 1858 included translation passages from Goethe and Schiller for the Seniors and Gotthold Ephraim Lessing (1729–1781) and Gottfried August Bürger (1747–1794) for the Juniors. Presenting a German language to be spoken in everyday situations, the aim which had characterized the seventeenth-century grammars, yielded, then, in the nineteenth century to teaching *literary* German – but also increasingly to the *philological* analysis of German and its history, alongside Latin and Greek (see Chapters 3 and 4 above). By the 1890s, however, Europe was becoming caught up in the Reform Movement (beginning with the manifesto of Viëtor 1882), which demanded a greater focus on teaching modern foreign languages as living languages. It took some considerable time for such pleas for more attention to the spoken language to be heard. Indeed, as I suggested in Chapter 4, the story of twentieth-century foreign language teaching methodology is, in large part, the story of the slow shift back towards greater emphasis on the spoken language. While Russon's *Complete German Course for First Examinations* (1948) still relied chiefly on prose passages for reading and translation to teach secondary pupils German, the German-published textbook *Deutsch 2000* (Luscher & Schäpers 1973), a series that I used as a learner in 1980s Australia, expressed the paradigm shift in its programmatic subtitle *Eine Einführung in die moderne Umgangssprache* 'an introduction to the modern everyday language' (Luscher & Schäpers 1973); similarly *Sprich Mal Deutsch!* 'Speak German!' (Rowlinson 1969).

As literature waned in importance in the eyes of textbook authors in the second half of the twentieth century, correspondingly greater prominence began to be given to dialects and non-standard forms of German. In itself this attention was not new. Already in 1800 Noehden had given a detailed account of the dialects of German and their pronunciation (Noehden 1800: 28–78), though this was intended to help distinguish the norm, rather than to celebrate diversity. From Noehden onwards, various textbooks of the nineteenth century included information about the history of the German language, and presented dialect variation as the outcome of that history (e.g. Brandt 1884; Theilkuhl 1940: 72–79) One relatively late development in the representation of 'the' German language, however, was the attention paid in school textbooks of German, especially since about 1990, to varieties of German spoken *outside* Germany, in line with the requirements of the examination board specifications, e.g. that of the AQA (2006: 9) which specifies 'knowledge about the contemporary culture and society of Germany and countries or communities where German is spoken.' Hammond (1969: vi) was already a pioneer in this respect, after the emphasis in the first half of the century on inculcating *das beste Deutsch*: "The speech extracts, covering the whole of the Bundesrepublik, are considered typical of the speech regions; they should enable the student to become familiar with the main regional speech differences". Typical of the late twentieth-century celebration of linguistic plurality is *Einfach toll* 1 (Smith 1985: 92), which told learners that people speak German in the BRD, the DDR, Switzerland and Austria (similarly Hermann et al. 1992 Vol. 1: 115); the greetings introduced on the first page of the first unit in *Einfach toll* include the characteristically southern German *Grüß Gott!* alongside *Guten Tag!* and *Hallo!* (Smith 1985: 6). Hermann et al. (1992: 115) presented German as one of many Germanic languages, and gave the greetings 'Good morning' and 'Good night' in Dutch, Danish, Norwegian and Swedish to show the relatedness of the languages. *Neue Aussichten Etappen* (a course for AS-level students, McNeill et al. 2000) went further still, including in its first chapter a map of where in the world – not just Europe – the *Weltsprache* 'world language' German is spoken, complete with a short feature on the Amish communities of the USA and Pennsylvania Dutch:

> Sie haben weder Telefon noch fließendes Wasser, sie sprechen 'Deitsch' … Obowohl die Amisch sowohl aus dem Rheinland und der Schweiz als auch aus dem frz. Lothringen und dem Elsass nach Amerika gekommen sind, stammen sie doch aus demselben – deutschen – Sprachraum …[sie] unterhalten sich untereinander in 'Pennsylvania German' oder 'Pennsylvania Dutch'.

> 'They have neither telephone nor running water, they speak *Deitsch* … Although the Amish came to America both from the Rhineland and Switzerland and from French Lorraine and Alsace, they originate from the same – German – language area … [they] talk amongst themselves in 'Pennsylvania German' or 'Pennsylvania Dutch'.

> (McNeill et al. 2000: 8)

More commonly, late twentieth-century textbooks explored sociolinguistic variation within German by offering dialogue samples of northern and southern German, or Austrian dialects (e.g Rowlinson et. al. 1993), or 'youth language'. *Schauplatz* (Brien et al. 2000), for example, included a focus on *Umgangssprache* with a listening exercise that required pupils to match highly colloquial phrases and terms to their English translations: *das hängt mir zum Hals heraus* 'I've had it up to here', *Weicheier* 'wimps', *er hat es voll drauf* 'he's really cool', *geil* 'cool, wicked', *Klamotten* 'clothes, gear', and *Speck ansetzen* 'to put on weight' (perhaps better 'to pile on the pounds') (Brien et al. 2000: 198). The German of migrants also became a theme: learners were presented with an ironic treatment of the case of an asylum-seeker (taken from DIE ZEIT, 6.11.1992 Nr. 46) and asked to correct the (fictional) imperfect German of the asylum-seeker, which includes phrases such as *ich heißen Aki Slaso. Ich nix verstehen, ich niemand verletzt, über Grenze mit Bus* (Brien et al. 2000: 113). Hermann et al. (1992, Vol. 1: 171) even took the trouble to note the 'many different languages' besides German that pupils would be likely to encounter in Germany.

This dual shift in the course of the twentieth century, both towards valuing the spoken language, and towards recognizing variation,[4] might have led us to expect a corresponding shift at the level of grammatical description towards *describing* norms and alternatives rather than pure prescription of a uniform language. However, such toler-ance of variation clashes with the usual purpose of the textbook, which is to distil the subject area into digestible gobbets of certain knowledge. We shall return to this tension in sections 5.8 and 5.9 below.

5.3 Typeface & handwriting

The first hurdle to confront many learners of German up to the mid-twentieth century was the very appearance of the letters on the page. At the time the first German manuals for English learners were being produced – in the seventeenth century – it was normal to use black letter (often also called Gothic type; some examples are given below), and, as Flood (1993) has shown, there were good patriotic reasons for doing so, even though no other major European languages used it.[5] At a time when German could not yet compete with the prestigious literary languages of French and Italian, at least black letter meant that it was possible to say that German – like the three 'sacred' languages Latin, Greek and Hebrew – had its own distinct script, something that advocates of German could then use as one of many reasons to argue that German should be ranked alongside Latin, Greek and Hebrew (and ahead of French and Italian) as a 'cardinal' language.[6]

---

4 These shifts reflect wider changes in attitudes and in social policy, recognizing cultural diversity, and the research programme since the 1960s, with the emergence of sociolinguistics, and the rec-ognition of German as a pluricentric language (cf. Clyne 1984). Durrell (2004, 2005) reflects on the introducing learners to linguistic variation in German as a Foreign Language in the UK. For the status of national varieties of German in teaching German as a Foreign Language teaching see Hägi (2006) and (at tertiary level) Ransmayr (2006). Watts (2000) considers the need to expose UK university students to 'real' (non-standard) German in the new century.

5 German had an image problem: the late sixteenth century saw the very first attempts to produce grammars of German, and those first grammarians found it difficult to accommodate the German language to "grammar", which equated with the grammar of Latin and Greek, the ancestral lan-guages of European cultural heritage. For example, the Germanic system of strong and weak verbs, the relative lack of distinct cases (no vocative or ablative), the strong and weak noun group endings, and the difficulty of identifying three or four obvious noun declensions all caused grammarians of German no end of difficulty (I give some examples of how such problems were recognized and resolved over the centuries in McLelland 2009).

6 These three languages were considered sacred because it was believed that the words 'King of the Jews' had been written the Cross at Jesus's crucifixion in each of the three languages. They were also all important in the transmission of the Bible, and German reformers sometimes pointed to the pre-eminence of German, particularly Luther's Bible translation, in continuing that transmission to the faithful. For this reason too, then, German could be ranked alongside Latin, Greek and Hebrew. As scholars now sought to reconcile what they were discovering about the kinship of lan-

Indeed, Aedler's *High Dutch Minerva* did put the case that German was a *Hauptquelle* ('headspring' or 'main source') of other languages, alongside Latin, Greek and Hebrew (see Van der Lubbe 2007a: 146–147). Nevertheless, as teachers of German right into the twentieth century had cause to know, learning to read black letter – while not on the same scale as learning a whole new scripts such as Greek, Russian or Hebrew – presented the learner with an additional hurdle, especially in the early stages. Aedler, who had a re-formist agenda for German spelling anyway, did *not* use German type, but chose instead to use Roman type (i. e. our 'normal' typeface).[7] Offelen (1687), however, used German type throughout for the simple reason that that was what learners would have to read: "I have also, for habituating and accustoming thee the better to read German Authors, caused this Grammar to receive the black Impression, which most German Authors and Books are of" (Offelen 1687: "To the English Reader", before p. 1 of the second part of the work; cf. Van der Lubbe 2007a: 201).

Textbook authors over the following decades were divided between following Of-felen in using German type (including Beiler (1731), Bachmair (1771) and Noehden (1800), or using the more familiar Roman type. König (1715) and Wendeborn (1774) used Roman type, Wendeborn giving only a specimen of black letter type at the end of his *Elements* (1774: 149–152). Wendeborn did, however, issue a revised edition in 1790 in which he now used German type: "as I have found that it was the wish of many, to have the German of this grammar printed with the common German types, I have, after some hesitation, thought it proper to submit to it" (Wendeborn 1790: *2, preface). His own feeling that the German type was a hurdle to his learners is clear in the fact that he made a point in his recommendations for reading (1774: [153]-[156]) of indicat-ing which works were printed in Roman type. Noehden (1800: 24) explained that the Gothic characters were the product of the twelfth and thirteenth centuries, and were characteristically "pointed and angular" (like the Gothic architecture of the same era, NMcL); they "have maintained themselves in Germany, where they have been much improved. Yet they still want the simplicity and elegance of their original [i. e. the medi-eval 'Gothic' script? NMcL]. For this reason, many German works have, in later times, been printed in the Roman type; that practice is however not become general", and "the greatest number of publications" still use Gothic type. Accordingly Noehden used it in his grammar in order to familiarize the student with it. Schade (1828: 3) only slightly paraphrased Noehden's paragraph about the angular Gothic type in his own grammar, but himself chose to use Roman type, stating, "Also the author of the present German grammar, has employed the Roman characters in the German words, which occur in it,

---

guages with the Biblical account of Babel as the source of linguistic diversity, these languages were often said to be the languages which had resulted from the confusion of tongues at Babel, from which others had subsequently been derived over generations. See Borst (1995, originally 1960) for a famously comprehensive treatment of the story of Babel in the European tradition; Eco (1995, particularly Chapters 1 and 5) is a very readable account for the lay reader.

7 Yet for the predominantly scholarly readership that Aedler seems to have envisaged, interested in, say, comparison with, say, Old English, German type was hardly a hindrance, since Old English was written in a very similar script.

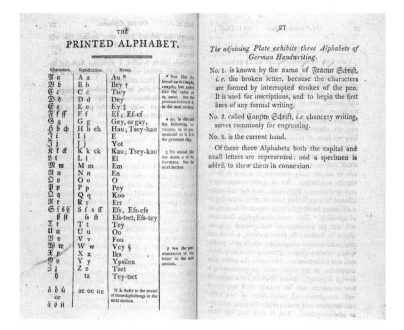

Figure 5.1: Noehden (1800: 27 and adjoining plate)

as the English are used to them. They must, however, also use their eye to the German characters, because the greatest number of publications continue to appear in them".

Noehden (1800) was one of many authors who also presented the reader with three different variants of German handwriting, as shown in Figure 5.1. Indeed, it is an indication of the intensifying contact between Germans and English-speakers by the late eighteenth century that textbook authors increasingly felt that it was necessary to introduce learners to German handwriting as well as to black letter. Beiler had introduced the individual "Manuscript Characters which you see in the Copper Plate" alongside the print characters (Beiler 1736: 2), but Bachmair (1771) and Wendeborn (1774) were the first, I believe, to include a specimen of German handwriting, Bachmair showing two slightly different hands (Bachmair 1771: unnumbered page facing p. 1). As shown in Figure 5.2, Wendeborn's specimen began *Die Deutschen haben bisher, die alten gotischen Buchstaben noch beibehalten. Die Dänen, Schweden, Preußen, Böhmen, Polen, Ungarn und Schweitzer, bedienen sich deroselben ebenfalls [...]* ('The Germans have up to now still kept the old Gothic letters. The Danes, Swedes, Prussians, Bohemians, Poles, Hungarians and Swiss also use the same'). Wendeborn's sample text continued that in recent times people had begun to print some German books in Roman type, but that it would be difficult to establish this practice generally. For now, all German school pupils had to learn two scripts, German and Latin, which meant that they were unable to attain such a fine hand as the English, who only needed to concentrate on one handwriting style. Ren-

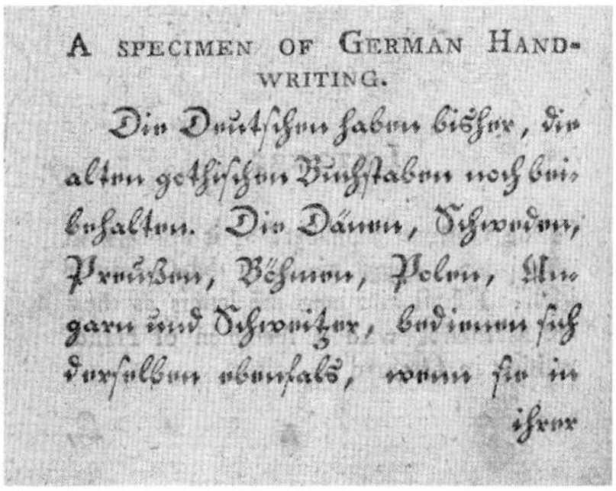

A SPECIMEN OF GERMAN HAND-
WRITING.

Figure 5.2:
Wendeborn (1797 *Exercises*: 2)

The near resemblance of several of the letters
is a cause of difficulty, which might be easily ob-
viated by a slight alteration in their form.

AMONG THE CAPITAL LETTERS:

B, instead B, (or vice versa)
W, ... M, ...
R, ... N, ...
C, ... C, ...
S, ... G, ...
K, ... N, ...

AMONG THE SMALL LETTERS.

r, instead of v, (or vice versa)
k, ... r, ...
v, ... p, are those, which I have
universally found my scholars most frequently mistake for each other.

Figure 5.3:
Render (1799: 11) on letters that can
easily be confused in German script and
type; interestingly, *f* and the long *s*, often
confused by today's readers of this script,
are not listed.

der (1799: 11), besides providing a short sample of German handwriting, also pointed out
those letters that were particularly liable to
be confused by his learners; see Figure 5.3.

Such samples seem to have been a common feature of textbooks in the nineteenth
century, especially up to about 1850. Schade
(1828: 35–39) provided a longish passage to
read in German script; Tiarks (1834b) included copies for practising German handwriting
on four leaves bound between pp. 168 and
169; Ollendorff (1850: 3) devoted several
pages to detailed explanations of how each
letter was to be formed (Figure 5.4). Later
in the nineteenth century, the short-lived
Cambridge Commercial Certificate German
examination included a handwritten letter to
be translated (see Figure 3.5 in Chapter 3). As
I noted in the previous chapter, the need to
be able to decipher German handwriting remained a genuine obstacle in efforts to train
British pupils for work in commercial German – recall Bithell's remark that practice
might "begin with letters carefully written
and pass on to scrawls and scribble" (Bithell
1921: 693). Otto Siepmann's *Public School
German Primer* (1896) still introduced German handwriting, and Oswald (1940: 10)
presented three short samples of handwriting
of decreasing size and hence decreasing legi-
bility. Koischwitz's *Deutsche Fibel* (1938) gave
a specimen of German handwriting with the
added challenge of an error to be spotted by
the pupils (Figure 5.5[8]). Beyond the Second
World War, however, any efforts to teach

---

8   The word *Deutsch* in the first three phrases should have a capital *D* rather than *d* – compare these
    lower case forms with the capitals after the full stops in the word *Die*. Upper and lower case *d* are
    distinguished by the different initial upstrokes: lower case letter *d* has a full upstroke. The omission
    of -e- in *geschriebnen* in the printed text is also a candidate for an error, but I am told that "the
    elision of -e- is typical nationalistic German of the 1930s; a famous example is Emanuel Hirsch's
    Geschichte der neuern evangelischen Theologie; he threw the e's out together with the Jewish roots of
    Protestantism" (Henrike Lähnemann, p.c.).

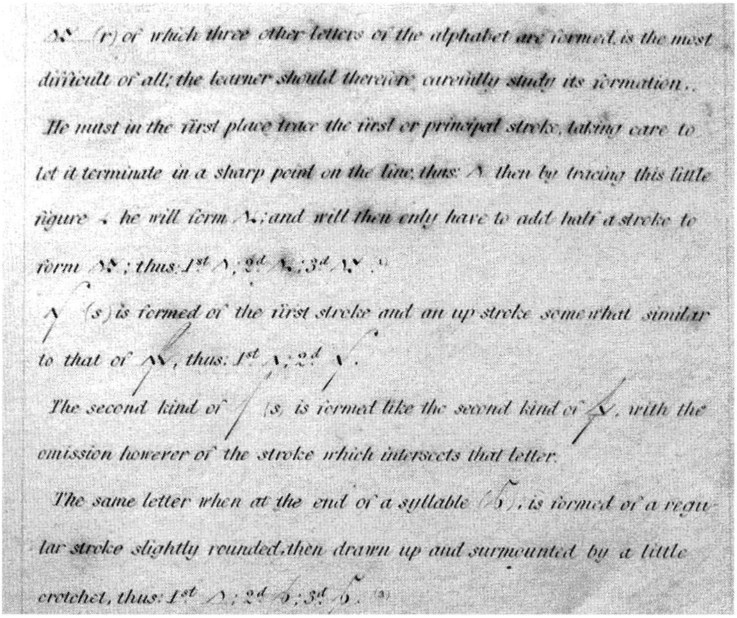
(r) of which three other letters of the alphabet are formed, is the most difficult of all; the learner should therefore carefully study its formation.

He must in the first place trace the first or principal stroke, taking care to let it terminate in a sharp point on the line, thus: then by tracing this little figure he will form ; and will then only have to add half a stroke to form ; thus: 1st ; 2d ; 3d .

(s) is formed of the first stroke and an up stroke somewhat similar to that of , thus: 1st ; 2d .

The second kind of (s) is formed like the second kind of , with the omission however of the stroke which intersects that letter.

The same letter when at the end of a syllable ( ), is formed of a regular stroke slightly rounded, then drawn up and surmounted by a little crotchet, thus: 1st ; 2d ; 3d .

Figure 5.4: Ollendorff (1850: 3): How to form the letters *r* and *s*

German script (which, to judge by Cambridge Local Examinations, had never been obligatory in examinations) were abandoned.

By the late nineteenth century, there was an increasing expectation that German type would soon be replaced completely by Roman type. In his *Grammar of the German Language for High Schools and Colleges,* Brandt pointed out acerbically that German type – which had by now been dropped in Switzerland and was rarely used for scientific publications – had only survived in Germany after the 1876 Spelling Conference thanks to "the personal prejudice of the Chancellor of the German Empire" [i. e. Bismarck], and so "German children still continue to learn to read eight alphabets and to write in four, viz. capital and small Latin scripts, and capital and small German script" (Brandt 1888: 157). A 1921 encyclopaedia entry on 'German Language, how to teach the' (M. B. S. 1921: 698) observed that "The continued use of German characters is something of an obstacle".

Efforts to introduce pupils more gradually to German type become apparent in the twentieth century, for example in Chaffey's *First German Course* (1907), which did not introduce German type till last few stories; and in Dyson's decision to print the first chapter of his *Class Book of German Conversation and Free Composition* in both Roman and Gothic typefaces "to enable those who are not thoroughly acquainted with the latter type to learn it by comparison – the easiest method" (Dyson 1913: 7). After the official switch away from Gothic type by the Nazis in 1941, textbooks were reprinted post-war in Roman type, the *Deutsches Leben* series by Macpherson & Strömer being a good ex-

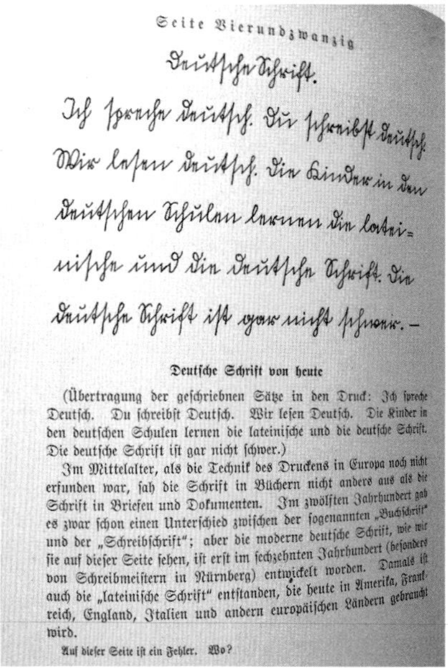
Seite Vierundzwanzig

Deutsche Schrift von heute

(Übertragung der geschriebnen Sätze in den Druck: Ich spreche Deutsch. Du schreibst Deutsch. Wir lesen Deutsch. Die Kinder in den deutschen Schulen lernen die lateinische und die deutsche Schrift. Die deutsche Schrift ist gar nicht schwer.)

Im Mittelalter, als die Technik des Druckens in Europa noch nicht erfunden war, sah die Schrift in Büchern nicht anders aus als die Schrift in Briefen und Dokumenten. Im zwölften Jahrhundert gab es zwar schon einen Unterschied zwischen der sogenannten „Buchschrift" und der „Schreibschrift"; aber die moderne deutsche Schrift, wie wir sie auf dieser Seite sehen, ist erst im sechzehnten Jahrhundert (besonders von Schreibmeistern in Nürnberg) entwickelt worden. Damals ist auch die „lateinische Schrift" entstanden, die heute in Amerika, Frankreich, England, Italien und andern europäischen Ländern gebraucht wird.

Auf dieser Seite ist ein Fehler. Wo?

Figure 5.5:
Koischwitz (1938: 24), complete with deliberate mistake in the German script

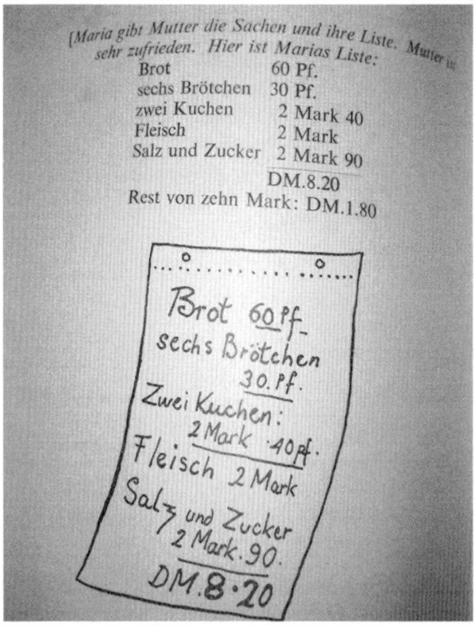
[Maria gibt Mutter die Sachen und ihre Liste. Mutter ist sehr zufrieden. Hier ist Marias Liste:

Brot	60 Pf.
sechs Brötchen	30 Pf.
zwei Kuchen	2 Mark 40
Fleisch	2 Mark
Salz und Zucker	2 Mark 90
	DM.8.20

Rest von zehn Mark: DM.1.80

Figure 5.6:
Orton (1959: 64)

ample. The first edition of Russon's *Complete German Course* (1948) used Gothic type for German passages, but not for the grammar notes, since "learners at this stage still have a certain amount of difficulty in reading German type, with the result that a grammar so printed would only put an extra burden on them" (Russon 1948: vi); but in the second edition of 1967, Russon switched to Roman type throughout: "As no books or newspapers are now printed in Gothic it seemed pointless to preserve this feature of the earlier edition". However, since many older books were still in Gothic type, students would still need to be able to read it, and "to help them do this, a passage in Gothic is printed in this edition with a line-by-line equivalent in Roman on the page opposite" (Russon 1967: preface). Similarly, the third edition of Greenfield's *German Grammar* (1968; 1st ed. 1940, 2nd ed. 1944), printed the last eight lessons in Roman and Gothic type, and Jackson & Geiger (1965: 186–188) introduced pupils to German type in one late chapter only.

In the later twentieth century, most learners of German were barely exposed to the old German type, and even most university students today remain unfamiliar with it, skirting their way around the old library books that are printed in it. As for the handwriting, even today's university lecturers, if I may count myself as a typical example, can read only the most simple examples of the 'old' German handwriting, and that with extreme difficulty. Orton (1959: 64) is the earliest example I have encountered of a sample of "modern" German handwriting in a textbook for English learners (see Figure 5.6). As Jackson & Geiger (1965: 2) noted, "German script has been almost completely superseded by a script style of writing very similar to our English script".

5.4 Spelling

To the learner who might have thought that once the question of the German typeface and script had been resolved, the matter of how to write German was straightforward, grammarians' pronouncements on German spelling would have come as a rude disappointment. Equally, the modern teacher of German – wearied by coming to terms with the much-contested 1998–2005 spelling reform – might be comforted to learn that the controversy is far from new. On the contrary, dissatisfaction with the orthography is one of the constants in the history of teaching German, from the very first grammar of German for English speakers onwards. The *High Dutch Minerva*, published in 1680, was written in the context of several decades of heated discussions about German orthography in German language societies, especially within the Fruitbearing Society (*Fruchtbringende Gesellschaft*), to which Aedler seems to have applied for membership before leaving Germany (Van der Lubbe 2007a: 74–75; see Chapter 2 above; for fuller discussion of Aedler's views on spelling, see Van der Lubbe 2007a: 160–165). The spelling that Aedler used was an ideological statement about the need for a rational, economical spelling system; it was certainly not the spelling most widely used in German texts at the time. Particularly striking was the use of <-h> rather than <-ch> for the fricatives /ç, x/ (e.g *ih* rather than *ich*) and <sh> or <s> rather than <sch> for /ʃ/, for example. *snauze dih* for *schnauze dich* 'blow your nose' (Aedler 1680: 185).

Offelen (1687), who in other ways was influenced by Aedler (cf. Van der Lubbe 2007a: 201–202), took no notice of Aedler's spelling at all, nor did any of his successors. In his own brief discussion of spelling, Offelen observed that "Our Punctuation is like the English, adding only that "our comma is a stroke (/) made in the midst of a Line, from the Right hand towards the Left" (Offelen 1687: 137). But this *Virgel* "/" – despite being the very first punctuation mark that the seventeenth-century German grammarian Schottelius (1663: 669) had listed in his authoritative account – was on its last legs. Offelen made no use of it himself, and in the German native grammatical tradition, Freyer (1721) was the first to omit it (instead using the comma ",").[9] Already Beiler (1731: 10–11), only ten years after Freyer, omitted it entirely in his grammar for English learners. Beiler is noteworthy too for the fact that his rules about spelling show clearly the influence of the rootword principle of Schottelius (1663) in stating that nouns and verb forms must be written with a double consonant at the end if other forms of the noun or verb require it, e.g. *Mann* rather than *Man* because of plural *Männer, komm* rather than *kom* because of *kommen*. Wendeborn (1774) paid no attention to spelling rules at all. However, at the end of the century, Render (1799) was greatly exercised by the variation in German spelling, which he considered was a difficulty for foreign learners in particular – a point that Philipp von Zesen had already made about German spelling a century and a half earlier, in 1651 (cf. Van der Lubbe 2007a: 122–123):

---

9   On Hieronymus Freyer's *Anweisung zur Teutschen Orthographie* (1721), see Heinle (1982) and the introduction by Moulin-Fankhänel in the 1999 reprint. On the history of German punctuation, see Simmler (2003).

> There is scarcely a language in Europe, which has so much variety in its orthography as the German. Every author of a new book, thinks himself at liberty to follow his own caprice, and differ in his orthography from all former writers.
>
> Such inaccuracies might be of little consequence to German readers; but cause very serious difficulty and disgust to the foreign reader, especially where words occur in the book which he is reading, that are spelt differently from what they are in the dictionary [...] I have known several of my own English scholars so much discouraged with this aukward [sic] circumstance, as actually to give up learning the language. [...]
>
> [A]s it is impossible to lay down general rules for German orthography, since the exceptions to them would be too numerous, it is the business of a teacher to make his scholar acquainted with these varieties in the German orthography.

(Render 1799: 9–10)

Accordingly, Render "purposely avoided pursuing any regular system of orthography in the following sheets, that the learner may immediately perceive those variations, which would otherwise be a considerable source of difficulty" (Render 1799: 11).

The history of efforts to regulate German spelling from the seventeenth century onwards fills multiple volumes, and there is no space to rehearse it here, but from about the middle of the nineteenth century onwards, German authorities – first certain individual states, then, after German unification in 1871, jointly – sought to agree a unified spelling.[10] In 1876 the First Orthographical Conference was held in Berlin, on the basis of a suggestion prepared by Rudolf von Raumer; over the early 1880s, various states gradually adopted this proposal, including Prussia, but, though the reformed spelling was used in Prussian schools, Bismarck forbade its use in official government business, effectively stymieing the reform. In any case, since individual states worked out their own spelling lists on the basis of the agreed principles, they did not always agree on every detail. In the face of this somewhat unsatisfactory state of affairs, textbook authors nevertheless on the whole attempted to adopt the reform. For example, the publisher's preface to a new edition of Otto's *German English Conversations* in (1883) noted that "the German text has been duly corrected conformably to the new orthography, now taught in German schools" (publisher's preface). In 1887, Collar's assessment of his own effort to follow the latest prescriptions had a note of melancholy, however:

> In the effort to conform to the modern system of German orthography, I regret that some inconsistencies will be found. The spelling of German is at present in a somewhat chaotic state, and it is perhaps inevitable that one who steps out

---

10 The literature on the topic is voluminous, but see Veith (2000) for a thorough summary; see also the book series *Documenta Linguistica* published by Olms for extensive documentation, reviewed by Sitta (2006); see Johnson (2005) on the most recent reform.

of the beaten track and tries to follow the lines of reform, or supposed reform, should come to grief.

(Eysenbach rev. Collar 1887: viii)

A second Orthographical Conference, held in Berlin in 1901, did succeed in agreeing regulations that came into effect in 1903. The sixth edition of Eve's *School German Grammar* – published after that second reform – is the first textbook I have encountered that ventured to list spelling rules, including (one of the perennial bones of contention) the rules governing the distribution of <ss> and <ß> (Eve 1903).[11]

Almost exactly a century later, teachers of German went through similar discussions as a spelling reform came into force from 1998 (though with a transition period until 2005, during which the old spellings were accepted), and once again had to take into account changed rules.[12] For example, the AS-level course *Neue Aussichten – Etappen* (McNeill et al. 2000: 184) drew pupils' attention to just three key changes: the change to the distribution of <ss> and <ß>, the requirement to write certain items as two separate words rather than one (*spazieren gehen* rather than *spazierengehen* 'to go for a walk') and changes to the use of the comma. Hypenation, changes to spellings for foreign words, and capitalization (even in high-frequency items such as *auf Deutsch* rather than old *auf deutsch* 'in German') were not explicitly noted.

5.5 Pronunciation

Pronunciation is an aspect of the teaching and learning of German where changes in methods are at least as interesting as the changes of substance. In this section I shall consider both. It is worth noting at the outset that the perception of German as an "ugly" language on the ear has a long history, and German patriots were already energetically defending it in the seventeenth century (e.g. Schottelius 1663: 24–27). Aedler (1680: 42) defended German:

> when our toung is styled by some or other a Rough language, either it is ment of that, which was spoken before some hundred or thousand years ago and in respect to the childish pronunciation of an effeminate speech; or that good Gentleman did never heare speake Germans but peasants and those perhaps in a Rough dialect indeed.

Render (1799: x) likewise defended German against the charge of guttural harshness by arguing that any such impression was the result of the "improper pronunciation"

---

11 Other changes noted concerned the dropping of a superfluous <h> after <t> in words like *T(h)at, T(h)eil,* and of a superfluous <-d> in words like *tö(d)ten, Bro(d)t*; and rules governing the choice between <c> and <k>, between <c> and <z>, and between <ph> and <c>, in borrowed words. Rules for capitalization are also given.

12 The spelling reform became hugely contested and highly politicized, as changes were felt to be imposed from above. It was even challenged (unsuccessfully) at Germany's constitutional court. See Johnson (2000, 2005), Johnson & Stenschke (2005), Langer (2001).

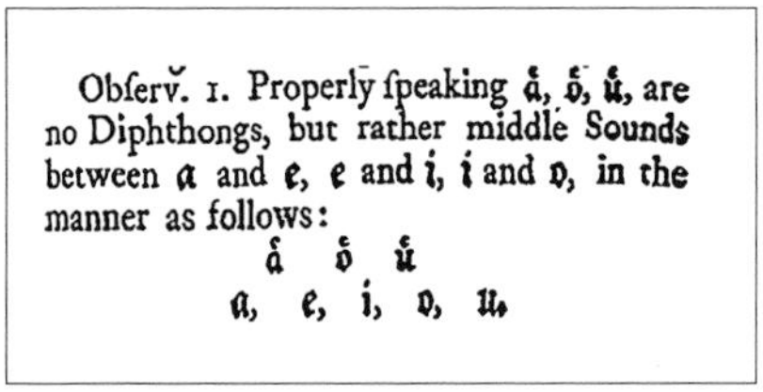

Obſerv. 1. Properly ſpeaking ä̆, ö̆, ü̆, are no Diphthongs, but rather middle Sounds between a and e, e and i, i and o, in the manner as follows:

ä̆ ö̆ ü̆

a, e, i, o, u.

Figure 5.7:
Beiler (1731: 3)

of some "illiterate individuals" rather than a defect of the language itself. Albrecht (1786: 16–17) advised the learner on how to tackle the challenging sounds of German:

"the German language delights particularly in full, broad Hissing and Guttural sounds [...] which require a strong effort of a full breath to be uttered [...] To pronounce German words perfectly right therefore your mouth generally must be open'd wider than is required for uttering English sounds, and the sounds must be begun already even in your very throat; your whole mouth and all your breath must be taken up to utter them. This is no light task indeed for any man not born in Germany; but without using your organs of speech to it it is impossible to attain that readiness in throwing as it were without a moments featching a breath a whole concert of hissing and guttural sounds, of whose harshness the clearest vowels in the German language must partake".

Certain sounds were found particularly offensive by individual authors. Albrecht (1786: 11) called the *r* "this very hard and disagreeable letter", which "has the same sound in all languages. Only in some it is sometimes a little softened, when joined to softer consonants or vowels" (German is apparently not one of those languages). Noehden (1800: 53–54) implicitly equated gutturality with backwardness: "After the German language had begun to be cultivated, it seems to have been one of the successive improvements, to divest it of many of its rough, and guttural sounds" (for example older *das Viech* is now *das Vieh* 'cattle').

For Render the *pf* affricate was unattractive:

the sound of *pf* is one of the harshest in the German language, and unknown to the English. To utter it, the lips must be pressed together with the greatest effort. The harshness of this sound is increased to a most offensive degree when it is followed by an *r*; and it becomes still worse when the same sound occurs again in the next syllable, as may be seen in the word *pfropfen*, to graft

(Render 1799: 8; the wording is very similar to that of Berg 1798: 15)

While ostensibly talking about letters, Render here recognized the *pf* phoneme as a single sound, albeit represented by two consonant graphemes. However, this apparent insight did not extend to the vowels, where Render (1799: 6) followed common practice of the time in calling the umlauted vowels diphthongs because they consist of two graphemes; they are in fact properly monophthongs, i. e. single sounds. Beiler (1731: 3) was, therefore, unusual in recognizing that "Properly speaking ä, ö, are no diphthongs, but rather middle Sounds between a and e, e and i, and i and o" (although the second half of the claim is not accurate) (see Figure 5.7). Noehden, who devoted pp. 28–66 of his work to detailed guidance on how to produce the German sounds, by means of comparison both with English and other European languages, correctly observed that the sounds represented by *Ch* are both "guttural" and "palatick", and are in complementary distribution: the "guttural" (i. e. velar [x]) occurs after a, o, u and au, while the "palatick" (i. e. palatal [ç]) occurs in conjunction with e, i, ä, ö, ü, äu.

Besides the practical difficulty of describing and producing the right sounds, an important ideological question was that of which pronunciation should be taught as the target. The study by Van der Lubbe (2008) of thirteen early textbooks of German for English learners indicates that the first nine, up to Noehden (1800), all followed the norm of Saxony (*Sachsen*) – that is, the East Central German variety of German that, owing to a number of factors, enjoyed considerable prestige in the seventeenth and eighteenth centuries (see Josten 1976). Four of these thirteen – Aedler (1680), Offelen (1687), Beiler (1731) and Albrecht (1786) – explicitly referred to Saxony as the home of the prestige variety. A key identifier of Saxon as the target variety was giving the pronunciation of <a> as *aw* rather than as a long *a* as in a*h!*. For example, Aedler rendered *an* 'to, at' as *aun* in his attempted phonetic version of the Lord's Prayer (*ig ghlòu-wey aun Gut dane vaùter, oll-magh'-e-ghen* for *ich glaube an Gott den Vater allmächtigen* 'I believe in God the father almighty', Aedler 1680: 43); similarly Wendeborn (1774: 3). For Albrecht, "The only standard for Pronunciation there is in Germany, is the Dialect of the genteel and refined order of inhabitants in Superior Saxony. A deviation from that may be excused sometimes, but cannot be defended" (Albrecht 1786: 13). Aedler (1680: 35) called the city of Halle in Saxony the Athens of Germany, for Athens had been the home of the prestige variety of Greek, the Attic dialect. Carr (1935: 486) found all the grammars except Noehden's "very faulty" in their pronunciation, and considered the fact that their authors were not native speakers of English a possible explanation. For instance, Carr singled out Wendeborn's indication that short *i* should be pronounced as *ea* in *eat* or *ee* in *eel*; presumably Carr expected *i* as in *ship*, but in fact Wendeborn's reference to *eat, eel* is a reasonable indication of the vowel *quality* of German *i*, ensuring the vowel is not pronounced as open as the English *i*, even if the length is wrong. Similarly, Wendeborn's indication of *s* as in *singer* and *six* is not wrong, although to use the voiceless *s* word-initially (rather than /z/ as in *is*) would be South German. On the other hand, his describing German *z* (/ts/) as like *z* in English *zone* would indeed suggest an imperfect knowledge of either English or German pronunciation.

From the end of the eighteenth century onwards, textbook authors shifted away from advocating Saxon German to recommending a North German pronunciation, beginning with Render (1799: 2), who now gave the pronunciation for *a* as in *ah!* and explicitly criticized "most grammarians", who indicated that *a* should be pronounced as *aw* according to the Saxon norm. Crabb (1800a: 1) and Noehden (1800: 13–14) followed suit, though Noehden – who gave a very detailed account of the dialects of German and their pronunciation (pp. 28–78) – still recommended the pronunciation of Saxony alongside the North German towns of Hamburg, Brunswick, Hanover and Göttingen.[13]

---

13 Noehden (1800: 18) did, however, criticize the "want of discrimination between [...] B and P, D

In the early decades of the nineteenth century, the two traditions – the Saxon norm epit-omized by *aw* and the North German norm with *ah* – continued to co-exist in materials for English speakers. Schade (1805, 4ᵗʰ ed. 1828) still indicated *aw* for German long *a* in words like *Vater* 'father' (though short *a* as in *hat*); but a remark by the Harvard profes-sor Charles (Karl) Follen (1835: xi), who left Germany in 1819 (see 3.3.1 above), makes it clear that the distinctive broad *aw* had by his day ceased to be a characteristic of good standard German pronunciation, and had become instead a dialectal feature:

> English students of the German language, as well as German students of the English, may be surprised to find, that the only sound which Walker, in his Critical Pronouncing Dictionary, characterizes as a German sound (I mean the *broad German a,* as he calls it), does not exist in the German language; that this sound is confined to some dialects, and is never heard from the mouth of a wellbred German.

> Follen (1835: xi, with reference to Walker [1824: 4])

A reading passage in Kron (1923: 174–175) tackled the question of *Das Beste Deutsch* 'the best German' head on, stating that no one dialect could be claimed as a model, *auch das hannöversche Deutsch nicht* 'not even Hanoverian German' – a reference to the notion, till prevalent today, that Hanover is the home of the purest German.[14] Rather, Kron wrote, the best German is that spoken by those who have lost their local dialect to the point that one can no longer hear what part of the country they come from; such a pronunciation is likely to be found most amongst well-educated people. Viëtor had already taken issue with the supposed Hanoverian ideal, saying that English students of German had asked "the Germans they had nearest at hand, viz. the Hanoverians, and, naturally, they have just as many times been told that the best German is spoken in Hanover. Yet it is a fact worth knowing that in Germany this belief is held only by the Hanoverians themselves" (Viëtor 1884, 5ᵗʰ ed. 1913: 3–4). Viëtor instead advocated the language of the stage (a belief acted upon by Theodor Siebs in his *Bühnenaussprache* 'Pronunciation of the Stage' of 1898, which was the earliest guide to 'standard' German pronunciation for native speakers). Nevertheless, Viëtor still considered that 'the com-mon German speech' amounted to 'High German word-forms pronounced with Low German speech-sounds" – by which he meant specifically a pronunciation that adopted the Low German voiced/voiceless distinction between consonants (*b-p; d-t; g-k*) rather than the southern consonant contrasts that he characterized as 'hard and soft'.[15] So 'Hanoverian German is no doubt better than that of e.g. Munich or Stuttgart. A Hano-

---

and T, G and K" as one of the "provincial aberrances in the Upper Saxon manner of speaking", so that these speakers might say *Paum, Tienen, Kott* for *Baum, Dienen, Gott* 'tree, serve, god'. In fact the distinction exists, but it is one of aspiration and force of articulation, rather than voice; non-native speakers therefore have trouble discriminating the sounds. See note 15. below.

14 See Eichinger et al. (2009). See also Stevenson (2002: 181–185).

15 This territory is rather difficult for the non-specialist, but in some southern areas, the consonant contrast rests not on voice, but either on aspiration and "force of articulation", or on force of

verian who should carefully avoid everything that is peculiarly Hanoverian in his speech would be as good a model as any other' (Viëtor 1913: 5–6).[16] By the twentieth century, the Hanoverian norm was established, though with attempts in later decades at least to expose learners to a wider range of varieties of German, including non-standard ones (as noted in 5.2 above).

If the early nineteenth century saw a marked shift in *what* pronunciation was taught – shifting from a Saxon to a North German norm – then the later nineteenth century witnessed a revolution in *how* pronunciation was taught, a revolution that was made possible by the emergence of the science of phonetics. Earlier generations of teachers like Albrecht (1786: 5) had emphasized that it was "absolutely impossible" to learn the correct sounds without hearing them correctly pronounced and that any written description could be only very approximate (similarly Noehden 1800: 28–30). Now, the emergence of the new science of phonetics and its application to German was signalled by key publications such as Sievers' *Grundzüge der Lautphysiologie* (1876) and Sweet's *Handbook of Phonetics* (1877), and was didacticized in Viëtor's *Kleine Phonetik* (1897) and in Rippmann's translation and adaptation of it, *Elements of Phonetics* (1899). These developments offered hope of a scientific approach to describing sounds accurately, as we already saw in Chapter 3 (especially 3.10) in the context of the Reform Movement. An increased focus on pronunciation began to be evident in a number of dictionaries published around this time: a review of German-English/English-German dictionaries in 1892 noted Muret's *Encyclopaedic English-German and German-English Dictionary: Giving the Pronunciation according to the Phonetic System*, of which only the English-German part was available to the reviewer, who commented on its "elaborate system, carried out with bewildering thoroughness, of typographical devices [...] together with a large number of general and special orthoëpic symbols" (White 1892: col. 172).[17] As we saw in Chapter 3, by the dawn of the twentieth century textbook authors – beginning with Rippmann's *First German Book* (1899) – began to include phonetic training and even phonetic script to varying degrees: Scholle & Smith (1903) provided *Elementary Phonetics, English, French, German. Their theory and practical application in the classroom.* Ungoed (1912) reproduced some lessons in phonetic script at the back of the book; Meyer (1912) gave texts in phonetics on the facing page to the text, although Althaus (1916) deemed the script unnecessary except for teachers, for whom she made available a separate edition of her *First German Book* (Althaus 1916: iv); Findlay (1930), writing

---

articulation alone (see e.g. Newton's clear account of the phenomenon with reference to Central Franconian: Newton 1990: 162, in Russ 1990).

16 In my copy of this text, heavily annotated by its owner, clearly a practising teacher or perhaps even lecturer, K. A. Bryden-Brown, the words "as good a model" have been struck through and the words "a better" written in.

17 There is no space to consider the history of German lexicography here, but note the 2012 special issue of *Language & History* (55.1) devoted to English "pronouncing dictionaries", ed. Joan Beal and Massimo Sturiale. Other German pronouncing dictionaries before Muret's are Oehlschläger (1861) and Cassell (1888). Other German-English dictionaries of the nineteenth century include: Rabenhorst (1800, revised by Noehden 1814, 1829), Lloyd & Noehden (1827, revd. 1836), Kaltschmidt (1837), Elwell (1855), Christoph (1880). See also Tafel (189[0?]).

Kaufen Sie drei Gold-Minen-Aktien zu 37 !
kow-*fén zee drī* golt-*mee-nén-*ak-*tsyen* tsoo zee-*bén- öönt-*dri-*sich*
Buy three Gold-mine shares at 37 !

Figure 5.8:
Rosenberg (1938: 62)

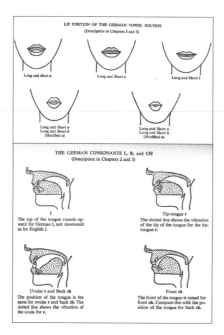

Figure 5.9:
Jackson & Geiger (1965: 11)

for fellow-teachers in *Modern Languages*, energetically advocated teaching phonetic notation to pupils from the outset. Others again, such as Chaffey (1903: vii), considered a detailed scientific approach to pronunciation to be of little practical use to learners. *Living Languages. How to Speak German* (Rosenberg 1938) is an example of the attempt to render German pronunciation in English spelling with no reference to phonetics at all, as is still found in many phrasebooks today; see Figure 5.8).[18] *German Made Simple* (Jackson & Geiger 1965: 4–6) seems to be unusual amongst textbooks in the second half of the century in including phonetic detail: that the descriptions of the sounds give IPA notation, without dwelling on it, is not uncommon, but more unusual are the diagrams illustrating the lip position for certain vowels, and even cross-sections of the vocal tract to show the tongue position for light l, alveolar trilled and uvular r, and "front and back ch" (note the authors choose *not* to use the symbols /x/ and /ç/ here) (see Figure 5.9).

By the late 1920s at the latest, at least some teachers were able to use grammophone recordings of German with their pupils (Findlay 1930: 23). When a new edition of the *Linguaphone Conversational Course: German* appeared in 1930 (Menzerath 1930; the earlier edition had been produced in 1925), it included recordings spoken by no less an authority than Theodor Siebs (author of the first guide to German standard pronunciation noted above, the *Bühnenaussprache* of 1898). That course and others like it marked the beginning of the end of the stand-alone textbook and the beginning of

---

18 Aimed at a similar class of reader as Grundy's *Brush Up Your German* series (c.f. 4.8 above), but absolute beginners rather than those seeking to 'brush up' their knowledge, the book featured similarly distinctive illustrations by the same artist, Phyllis Ward, of a harassed businessman and his dress-buying wife.

course 'packages'; and advances in technology continued from then on to allow teachers and pupils ever easier access to German spoken by native speakers (cf. 4.6.3 above).

5.6 Stress and intonation

Menzerath's *Linguaphone* course in German, noted above, was reviewed by a certain F. R. in *Modern Language Notes* (1930), where F. R. noted Menzerath's claim that his course was "the first attempt to treat colloquial German as a subject of study". F. R. also cited Menzerath's remark that "The meaning of a sentence is to be found in the intonation, not in its grammatical construction", adding "Would not teachers and examiners do well to ponder the implications of this statement?" (F. R. 1930: 57–58). This section turns to precisely that question: how textbook authors dealt with sress and intonation. Attempts to describe German prosody (word and sentence stress) can be found from early on in the tradition of language learning materials for English speakers. Attempts to formulate the rules of German prosody had begun in the seventeenth century, in the context of poetics, but were hamstrung by the confusion of quantity (short or long syllables) with stress, resulting in the need to declare that certain syllables could be short or long depending on their position in the verse (or utterance).[19] In works for English speakers, Beiler (1731) shared the confusion, for example stating that *un-* is "commonly long, and must always be so before a short syllable, e.g. *ungebühr* 'indecency'", but that it may often be short before a long syllable in compound words, as in *unwandelbahrer Gott* 'immutable God' (Beiler 1731: 7). The same system – according to which a great many syllables might be deemed either long or short – is still found in Berg (1798: 27) and Noehden (1800: 79). On the other hand, Beiler does appear capable of distinguishing length and stress in the observation that the derivative suffix *-ey* or *-ei* "is always long, and has commonly the Accent, e.g. *Abtey* 'an abbey'".

The study of intonation is commonly said in the historiography of linguistics to begin with Joshua Steele in 1775 (see Kemp 2001: 1469), but it was a century earlier that the first manual of German for English learners referred to "Accents, that make 'em [i. e. syllables and words] either rise or fall in pronouncing" (Aedler 1680: 29). In fact, Aedler's reference to syllables which "we must lift up and which suppress" (p. 30) seems on closer inspection to be only a metaphor for stress (which does include an element of pitch, besides volume and length) rather than to the pitch changes of intonation patterns. Aedler, did, however, manage to distinguish stress from quantity in effect, when he stated, correctly, that every native German rootword (*Radix*)

> has its tonick accent (and that either soft when the syllable is long or sharp when the syllable is short) in the first syllable, where it still remains both in derivates and compounds

---

19 This was the problem with Schottelius's meticulously worked out system (Schottelius 1663), for example (cf. McLelland 2011: 146–147).

Likewise the "tonick accen't falls on the first syllable in the compounds of certain particles" (in effect the separable prefixes),

> which for emphasis-sake draw upon themselves the accent from those words [...]
> but the other inseparable particles leave the tonick accent to the first syllable of
> the words, which they are compounded with.

(Aedler 1680: 30)[20]

Aedler also noted that long compounds "seem to have more than one such accent"
(p. 32), and took care to explain that borrowed words or suffixes often have different
stress patterns; Offelen largely followed Aedler in his (rather briefer) account. Albrecht
(1786) had nothing to say about stress and intonation.

Wendeborn is an interesting case. He included in his Exercises (1797: 4–6) a passage
taken "from the German original of my *Views of England*" in which he indicated the
primary stress using an acute accent (see Figure 5.10), though using the circumflex on
ê, apparently to be pronounced as in French *être, meme* [sic] "to distinguish it from [...]
English *e* in words, such as *end, elm, ere*, etc. (a distinction that is not fully clear to me).
Noehden (1800) acknowledged, with reference to Adelung, the by then well-established
principle "that the accent is placed on a radical syllable", but did not consider it helpful
for the beginning learner.[21] Still, he built on the observation already made by Aedler that
some longer compounds have more than one stress, and identified both a "full" and a
"half" accent, noting for example that "vowels at the ends of words [...] except *e*, which
is unaccented", have a demi-accent, as in *Uhù, àlsó, dèró, jètzó* – here, he presumably
hears the final vowel as carrying less emphasis than that carrying the main stress of the
word. *Uhù* 'owl' is a good example of the perceived contrast, where the initial syllable
U- carries the word-stress.

Noehden also made a significant advance by tackling stress across a whole phrase or
sentence, pointing out that in a phrase like *das Kind*, the article and noun "constitute,
as it were, one word; and the accent is fixed to the latter, being greater in signification"
(Noehden 1800: 68), unless the *das* were being used "pointedly". Likewise, the sentence *Er ist hier* could be "looked upon as a word of three syllables, and may therefore
receive the full accent: but where it is to be placed, depends upon the intention of the
person speaking", according to what is "the principal object of the speaker" (pp. 68–69).
Schade (1828) presented four general rules for the accent of German words, and at last
distinguished vowel length (or "quantity") from stress.[22] He stated that "The accent

---

20 That is, Aedler contrasts words like *'aufstehen* 'to stand' with *be'steigen* 'to climb', which have separable and inseparable prefixes respectively.

21 He claims it is "too abstruse and far-fetched for the incipient scholar (Noehden 1800: 67). Render
   (1804: 42–44) appears indebted to Noehden on this topic.

22 The confusion – which in effect meant assuming that the *a* in *Vater* was long when stressed, but
   would become short when unstressed – dates back to the seventeenth century. See McLelland
   (2011: 146–147) for a summary with reference to the problem in the thinking of the German
   grammarian Schottelius.

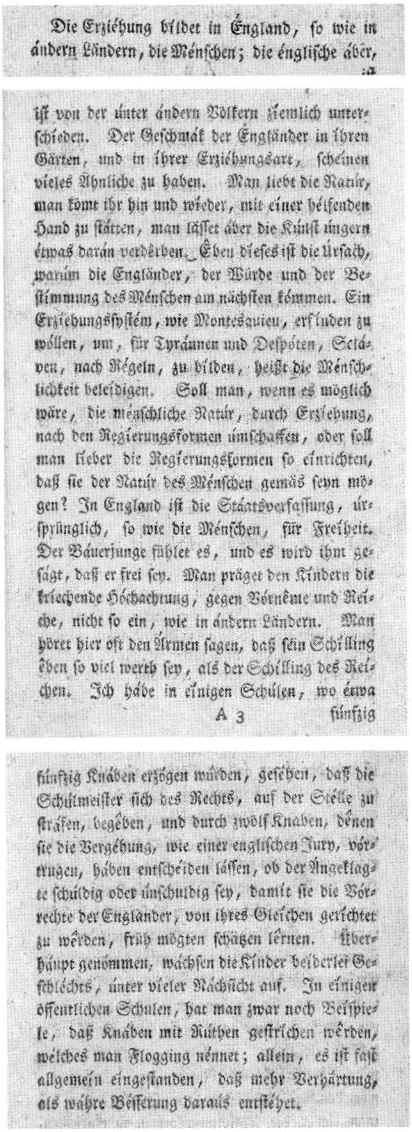

Die Erziehung bildet in England, so wie in andern Ländern, die Menschen; die englische aber,

ist von der unter andern Völkern ziemlich unterschieden. Der Geschmack der Engländer in ihren Gärten, und in ihrer Erziehungsart, scheinen vieles Ähnliche zu haben. Man liebt die Natur, man kömmt ihr hin und wieder, mit einer helfenden Hand zu statten, man lässet aber die Kunst ungern etwas daran verderben. Eben dieses ist die Ursach, warum die Engländer, der Würde und der Bestimmung des Menschen am nächsten kommen. Ein Erziehungssystem, wie Montesquieu, erfinden zu wollen, um, für Tyrannen und Despoten, Sclaven, nach Regeln, zu bilden, heißt die Menschlichkeit beleidigen. Soll man, wenn es möglich wäre, die menschliche Natur, durch Erziehung, nach den Regierungsformen umschaffen, oder soll man lieber die Regierungsformen so einrichten, daß sie der Natur des Menschen gemäß seyn mögen? In England ist die Staatsverfassung, ursprünglich, so wie die Menschen, für Freiheit. Der Bauerjunge fühlet es, und es wird ihm gesagt, daß er frei sey. Man präget den Kindern die kriechende Hochachtung, gegen Vornehme und Reiche, nicht so ein, wie in andern Ländern. Man höret hier oft den Armen sagen, daß sein Schilling eben so viel werth sey, als der Schilling des Reichen. Ich habe in einigen Schulen, wo etwa

A 3   fünfzig

fünfzig Knaben erzögen würden, gesehen, daß die Schulmeister sich des Rechts, auf der Stelle zu strafen, begeben, und durch zwölf Knaben, denen sie die Vergebung, wie einer englischen Jury, vortrugen, haben entscheiden lassen, ob der Angeklagte schuldig oder unschuldig sey, damit sie die Vorrechte der Engländer, von ihres Gleichen gerichtet zu werden, früh mögten schätzen lernen. Überhaupt genommen, wachsen die Kinder beiderlei Geschlechts, unter vieler Nachsicht auf. In einigen öffentlichen Schulen, hat man zwar noch Beispiele, daß Knaben mit Ruthen gestrichen werden, welches man Flogging nennet; allein, es ist fast allgemein eingestanden, daß mehr Verhärtung, als wahre Besserung daraus entstehet.

Figure 5.10:
Wendeborn (1797 Exercises: 4–6)

is not to be confounded with the quantity, by which is meant the measure of time in pronouncing a syllable. *Accent (der Accent)* is called that stronger percussion of voice, by which one syllable of a word is pronounced with more force than other syllables." Importantly, Schade was also able to distinguish word stress or "verbal accent" (der *Wortaccent*) from "the oratorical or declamatory accent" (*der Redeaccent*, i.e. sentence stress), "by which the tone of whole sentences is commanded" (Schade 1828: 20), although no more is said about the latter.[23]

With the advent of textbooks more clearly aimed at school pupils from the mid-nineteenth century, discussions of German prosody seem largely to disappear again. A noteworthy exception was Conrad Witter's *Drittes Lesebuch für deutsch-amerikanische Schulen: Schlussstufe* (1865), which not only contained some brief observations about stress, identifying three levels of stress (*stark, stärkere, stärkste*, i.e. 'strong, stronger, strongest' (Witter 1865: iii), but also talked explicitly about intonation, (where ' indicates rising intonation, ' indicates falling intonation):

"6. Erhebung und Senkung der Stimme bei Fragen und Antworten
Fragen, auf welche man mit Ja und Nein antworten kann, werden so gelesen, daß die Stimme immer höher steigt, und die Schlußsilbe den höchsten Ton erhält, auch wenn sie sonst nicht von Wichtigkeit ist. [...] die Antwort erfordert die Senkung der Stimme, z.B. Habt ihr noch nichts erfahren '? Nein'

7. Erhebung der Stimme
Alle Sätze, welche mehrere Nennwörter hinter einander enthalten, oder wenn der erste Satz eine Behauptung vorbereiten soll, die

---

23 Like some of his predecessors, Schade also distinguished between a full accent, half accent, and no accent.

217

der Nachsatz näher bestimmt, müssen so gelesen werden, daß die Erwartung
des Hörenden gespannt wird; daher muß die Stimme gleichsam in der Schwebe
gehalten werden. [...]
Der Hirsch', das Reh', der Hase' nähren sich von Pflanzen.
Wer sich auf seinen Gott verläßt', deß Hoffnung stehet felsenfest."

(Witter 1865: iv–v)

'6. Raising and lowering the [tone of] voice in questions and answers
Questions to which one can answer with Yes and No are read such that the voice
rises higher and higher, and the final syllable receives the highest pitch, even if
it is not otherwise important. [...] the answer requires a lowering of the [tone
of] voice, e.g. Habt ihr noch nichts erfahren '? Nein' [Have you not yet heard
anything '? No']
All sentences which contain several nouns one after the other, or when the first
clause should prepare an assertion which is more closely defined in the following
clause, must be read such that the expectation of the listener is heightened; so the
voice must be held hovering, as it were. [...]
Der Hirsch', das Reh', der Hase' nähren sich von Pflanzen. [The red deer', the
roe deer', the hare' eat plants]
Wer sich auf seinen Gott verläßt', deß Hoffnung stehet felsenfest [Whoever puts
their trust in God, his hope is rocksolid]'

Here Witter succeeded in identifying three of the five main intonation patterns in German and some of the contexts in which they are used: the rise (for some questions), the fall (for statements), and the relatively high level pitch used in non-final tone groups (where, as Witter puts it, the expectation of the listener must be aroused, and the voice is held *gleichsam in der Schwebe* 'as if hovering'.[24] This is an impressive achievement, though it seems to have had no influence on later authors. Brandt (1884) similarly identified three degrees of stress (weak, medium and strong), and also allowed for further degrees of differentiation using a numbering system (as in Figure 5.11), but even he – fully aware of developments in the study of German phonetics and phonology – had nothing whatever to say about intonation patterns. Even *Viëtor's German Pronunciation: Practice and Theory* (1st ed. 1884, 5th ed. 1913) devoted a little over a page to intonation, identifying "three simple, or primary, inflections of tone", level, rising and falling, for which he noted that he was indebted to Henry Sweet's *Handbook of Phonetics*. No mention is made there of the use of the level tone, only that the rise is "employed in questions and antecedents, the falling tone in answers and statements of facts" (Viëtor 1913: 112–113). Despite Daniel Jones' plea for the importance of intonation in language learning (Jones 1914), as far as I am aware, no school textbook after Brandt and Viëtor dealt with intonation at all. According to Russ (2010) the area of German intonation was not seriously studied even in Germany until a study by Otto von Essen in 1964. Only those Eng-

---

24 For a clear account of German intonation patterns see Hall (2003: 116–137).

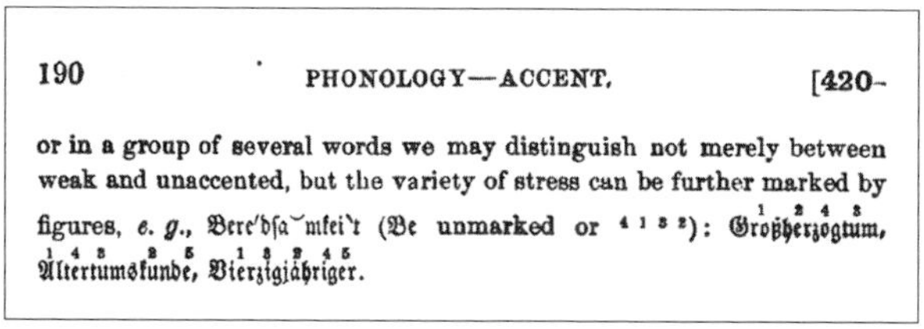

190 · PHONOLOGY—ACCENT. [420-

or in a group of several words we may distinguish not merely between weak and unaccented, but the variety of stress can be further marked by figures, *e. g.*, Berre'bſa⁓mſei't (Be unmarked or ⁴¹⁸²): Großherzogtum, Altertumskunde, Vierzigjähriger.

Figure 5.11: Brandt (1888: 190)

lish-speaking learners who go on to take a course in the linguistics of German at university are likely to be exposed to any description of German intonation (as in Fox 1984; Hall 1992, 2nd ed. 2003). All this makes the level of detail in Witter's primer, aimed at the children of German-speaking migrants in Missouri,[25] all the more striking. Not for the first time, it was a teacher outside Germany who made the first advance in describing this feature of the German language.

Given the dearth of attention paid to intonation in twentieth-century textbooks, it is worth pausing over one exception, even though the textbook in question is aimed principally at North American university beginners – its authors were at Stanford University. *German: A Structural Approach* systematically taught intonation patterns for new syntactical patterns as they were introduced, "[s]ince sentence intonation is closely linked with syntax" (Lohnes & Strothmann 1973: xxxiv; 1st ed. 1967). The authors – who did not state whose account they followed – stated that German, like English, "is spoken on three basic levels of pitch" (p. xxxiv), indicated in their book by three horizontal lines; there are symbols for rising and falling pitch, and they present intonation patterns for assertions, 'word-questions', yes-no questions and dependent clauses (see Figure 5.12). The attempt to link intonation to syntax was not wholly successful, as multiple patterns are possible for each structure, and the lack of the notions of tone group, nucleus and head made the analysis less clear. Still, the analysis did allow the authors to demonstrate that intonation alone could change a statement to a question (see "Questions structured like assertions" in Figure 5.12); and the fall, rise, rise-fall, and high-level patterns are all recognizable. Of the five German intonation patterns commonly recognized today (e.g. Hall 2003: 129–131), only the fall-rise that may be used for emphasis in questions, or for friendly warnings (e.g. *Vorsicht!*), was missing.

---

25 For the history of German migration to Missouri see Olson (1980), Burnett & Luebbering (1996), and van Ravenswaay (1997). My thanks to Dr Julia Moses at the University of Sheffield for drawing my attention to these studies. Note also, on the wider matter of German in the United States, the recent themed issue of the *Journal of Germanic Linguistics* (2011) on 'Germanic Languages and Migration in North America' (Horner 2011).

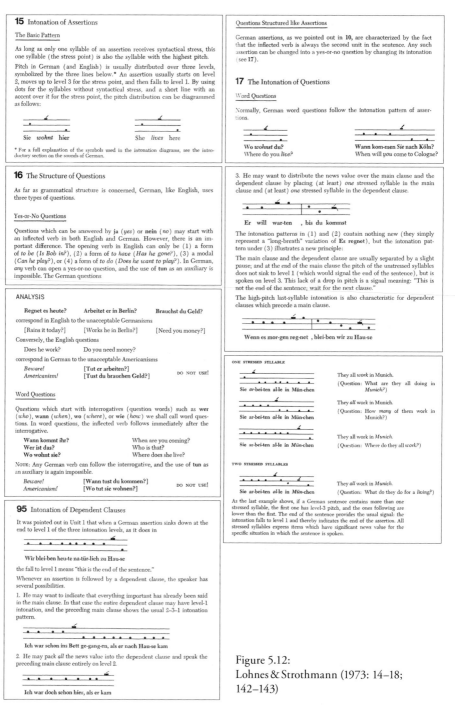

15 Intonation of Assertions

The Basic Pattern

As long as only one syllable of an assertion receives syntactical stress, this one syllable (the stress point) is also the syllable with the highest pitch.

Pitch in German (and English) is usually distributed over three levels, symbolized by the three lines below.* An assertion usually starts on level 2, moves up to level 3 for the stress point, and then falls to level 1. By using dots for the syllables without syntactical stress, and a short line with an accent over it for the stress point, the pitch distribution can be diagrammed as follows:

Sie *wohnt* hier   She *lives* here

* For a full explanation of the symbols used in the intonation diagrams, see the introductory section on the sounds of German.

16 The Structure of Questions

As far as grammatical structure is concerned, German, like English, uses three types of questions.

Yes-or-No Questions

Questions which can be answered by **ja** (*yes*) or **nein** (*no*) may start with an inflected verb in both English and German. However, there is an important difference. The opening verb in English can only be (1) a form of *to be* (*Is Bob in?*), (2) a form of *to have* (*Has he gone?*), (3) a modal (*Can he play?*), or (4) a form of *to do* (*Does he want to play?*). In German, *any* verb can open a yes-or-no question, and the use of **tun** as an auxiliary is impossible. The German questions

ANALYSIS

Regnet es heute?   Arbeitet er in Berlin?   Brauchst du Geld?

correspond in English to the unacceptable Germanisms

[Rains it today?]   [Works he in Berlin?]   [Need you money?]

Conversely, the English questions

Does he work?   Do you need money?

correspond in German to the unacceptable Americanisms

Beware!   [Tut er arbeiten?]
Americanism!   [Tust du brauchen Geld?]   DO NOT USE!

Word Questions

Questions which start with interrogatives (question words) such as **wer** (*who*), **wann** (*when*), **wo** (*where*), or **wie** (*how*) we shall call word questions. In word questions, the inflected verb follows immediately after the interrogative.

Wann kommt ihr?   When are you coming?
Wer ist das?   Who is that?
Wo wohnt sie?   Where does she live?

Note: Any German verb can follow the interrogative, and the use of **tun** as an auxiliary is again impossible.

Beware!   [Wann tust du kommen?]
Americanism!   [Wo tut sie wohnen?]   DO NOT USE!

95 Intonation of Dependent Clauses

It was pointed out in Unit 1 that when a German assertion sinks down at the end to level 1 of the three intonation levels, as it does in

Wir blei-ben heu-te na-tür-lich zu Hau-se

the fall to level 1 means "this is the end of the sentence."

Whenever an assertion is followed by a dependent clause, the speaker has several possibilities.

1. He may want to indicate that everything important has already been said in the main clause. In that case the entire dependent clause may have level-1 intonation, and the preceding main clause shows the usual 2–3–1 intonation pattern.

Ich war schon ins Bett ge-gang-en, als er nach Hau-se kam

2. He may pack *all* the news value into the dependent clause and speak the preceding main clause entirely on level 2.

Ich war doch schon hier, als er kam

Questions Structured like Assertions

German assertions, as we pointed out in **10**, are characterized by the fact that the inflected verb is always the second unit in the sentence. Any such assertion can be changed into a yes-or-no question by changing its intonation (see **17**).

17 The Intonation of Questions

Word Questions

Normally, German word questions follow the intonation pattern of assertions.

Wo wohnst du?   **Wann kom-men Sie nach Köln?**
Where do you *live*?   When will *you* come to Cologne?

3. He may want to distribute the news value over the main clause and the dependent clause by placing (at least) *one* stressed syllable in the main clause and (at least) *one* stressed syllable in the dependent clause.

Er will war-ten , bis du kommst

The intonation patterns in (1) and (2) contain nothing new (they simply represent a "long-breath" variation of *Es regnet*), but the intonation pattern under (3) illustrates a new principle:

The main clause and the dependent clause are usually separated by a slight pause; and at the end of the main clause the pitch of the unstressed syllables does not sink to level 1 (which would signal the end of the sentence), but is spoken on level 3. This lack of a drop in pitch is a signal meaning: "This is not the end of the sentence; wait for the next clause."

The high-pitch last-syllable intonation is also characteristic for dependent clauses which precede a main clause.

Wenn es mor-gen reg-net , blei-ben wir zu Hau-se

ONE STRESSED SYLLABLE

Sie ar-bei-ten al-le in Mün-chen   They all *work* in Munich.
(Question: What are they all doing in *Munich*?)

Sie ar-bei-ten *al*-le in Mün-chen   They *all* work in Munich.
(Question: How *many* of them work in Munich?)

Sie ar-bei-ten al-le in *Mün*-chen   They all work in *Munich*.
(Question: Where do they all *work*?)

TWO STRESSED SYLLABLES

Sie ar-bei-ten *al*-le in *Mün*-chen   They *all* work in Munich.
(Question: What do they do for a *living*?)

As the last example shows, if a German sentence contains more than one stressed syllable, the first one has level-3 pitch, and the ones following are lower than the first. The end of the sentence provides the usual signal: the intonation falls to level 1 and thereby indicates the end of the assertion. All stressed syllables express items which have significant news value for the specific situation in which the sentence is spoken.

Figure 5.12:
Lohnes & Strothmann (1973: 14–18; 142–143)

5.7 Forms of address

The question of how forms of address have been treated in textbooks of German is an interesting one for three reasons. First, how the German system of address was presented in textbooks is linked to changes in the importance attributed to authentic communication over the centuries;[26] second, the conventions for using those forms of address themselves changed considerably in the period we are considering; and, third, it may be revealing to compare what is said in our textbook corpus with what Germans themselves were doing at the time. For while twentieth-century authors are unanimous in making the only distinction between *du* and *ihr* one of singular and plural, that was not the case earlier on in the history of the language, where *ihr* could function as a polite singular. As noted in 2.2.2, Aedler (1680) made a three-way distinction between *du, ihr* and *Sie*:

> Children and our own servants, as well as beasts: second person singular; for the servants of others, and other common sort of people as peasants and tradesmen are 2nd ps. Pl [i. e. *ihr*]; to a Gentleman or Gentlewoman and upwards, in the third person singular, and a magistrate of authority (though a single person) in the third person plural [i. e. *Sie*]
>
> (Aedler 1680: 169)

As an explicit statement of the conventions governing the use of German personal pronouns, Aedler's remarks were already in advance of that found in the 'native' German grammatical tradition of the time, for example in Stieler (1691: 118–119), which is a purely grammatical account of singular and plural, first, second and third person; similarly Heynatz (1803). Aedler also took the trouble to list various titles to be used in addressing different persons of rank. The question of appropriate forms of address became increasingly ideologically charged in the eighteenth century, linked to the acute awareness of *politesse*, one example of the influence of French manners on the rest of Europe (cf. Polenz 1999: 60–61, 383– 387 and further references there). Wendeborn made explicit reference to this new concern with politeness when he observed that the "plain and simple" system of address found in Latin and Greek had become more complicated in Europe thanks to a tendency of "an affected politeness", which led to the use of the *Ihr* form to any single person; the Germans then went further, addressing a "person of distinction in the third person, which is now the prevailing custom; as in *Wie befinden sie [sic] sich?* How do THEY do? instead of, *Wie befindet ihr euch?* How do YOU do?" (Wendeborn 1774: 34). In fact, the binary (*Sie vs. du* and *ihr*) system presented as the 'prevailing custom' by Wendeborn – who had little time for "affected politeness" – did not become firmly established in Germany until the nineteenth century (Polenz 1999: 383),[27] and contemporary with Wendeborn, Bachmair (1771: 53) still made a

---

26 An early consideration of the authenticity or otherwise of GFL materials is Weijenberg (1979).

27 On the history of forms of address in German, and in comparison with other countries, see Glück (1998), Besch (1996).

four-way distinction, adding to the *du, ihr* and *Sie* listed by Aedler a fourth possibility, that of *er* or *sie*:

1. Husbands and Wives, Parents to their Children, Brothers and Sisters, or very good Friends, by way of Familiarity, make use of the second Person singular; *du, thou* [...]
2. To Servants, and the meaner sort of people, we say *ihr* [...]
3. Common Trade, People speaking to each other make use of the third Person of the Singular, *er, he,* to a Man; and *sie, she,* to a Woman; yet the Meaning is *you.* This is also done by great People speaking to any Person of a much inferior Station. [...]
4. In the polite Way of writing and speaking we use always the third Person of the Plural, *sie,* they, but the Meaning is *you.* [sic: *Sie* is not capitalized here]
5. Yet *du* and *ihr* are used in Poetry and from the Pulpit; *du* for the Singular, or to one Person; *ihr* for the Plural, or to many Persons.

As Bachmair pointed out, according to context, *Er ist mein Freund* could thus mean either 'he is my friend' or 'you are my friend'. His account is in essence the same as that given by Gottsched, who allowed for four different forms of address, as in Table 5.1:

Table 5.1: Forms of address according to Gotthsched (according to Polenz 1999: 384)

Du	'you', second person singular, informal	*natürlich* 'natural'
ihr	'you', second person plural, informal	*althöflich* 'old-style polite'
er or *sie* singular	'he' or 'she', third person singular	*mittelhöflich* 'medium polite'
Sie	'they', third person plural [capitalized]	*neuhöflich* 'new-style polite' and *überhöflich* 'overly polite'

Crabb (1800a: 99–100) also presented the same four possible forms of address, with *du* for "the deity, children and families", while it was "not uncommon to use *ihr* to tradesmen", and *er/sie* to male or female domestics; *sie* was "usual" in addressing "your equals and superiors". A memory of this four-way distinction is still found in the late nineteenth century, in Huss's *System of Oral Instruction in German* (1884), even though Huss himself now offered only a two-way distinction between *Sie* and *du* or *ihr* (the latter two differing only in whether the addressees are singular or plural) that Wendeborn had already adopted much earlier. Huss also explained that the use of the third person

> came in at the beginning of the seventeenth century. Persons of rank were then indirectly addressed by their title, most commonly by *Herr* or *Frau*, with the verb in the third person singular (Compare: how *is* your Lordship?). For the title was then naturally substituted the pronoun *er* (for *Herr*), or *sie* (for *Frau*). During the first half of the eighteenth century, the third person plural was considered

more polite than the singular, and has remained in use up to the present day, while *er* and *sie* (singular) are no longer used, except in certain parts of Germany, and only by superiors to their inferiors.

(Huss 1884: 72)

By the late nineteenth century, the binary system was established (e.g. Ahn 1868: 46); what is interesting over the next century or so is how the teaching of the system was then didacticized in what were now school coursebooks. Alge, Hamburger & Rippmann's strictly reformist *Leitfaden* (1916) introduced the *du*-form very early, as one might expect of a book emphasizing classroom talk: the possessive *dein* comes on p. 11, the full verb paradigm (with *du, ihr* and *Sie*) on p. 15. Russon's *Complete German Course* (1948) implicitly exposed pupils to *du* and *Sie* forms from early on, as both feature in examples in Section 1 of the book, the Grammar, from p. 5 onwards, but their use is not explained in the grammar itself until the 'Notes on the Personal Pronouns' (p. 63). Most striking in the first half of the twentieth century is *Deutsches Leben* 1 (Macpherson 1931). Although the author assumed "that German will be the language normally used in class" (p. iii), the textbook introduced only the *Sie* form from the outset, and also modelled children using the *Sie* form and being addressed using *Sie*, including in class, even though this would not have been normal usage, e.g. *Ich bin ein Junge; Sie sind ein Junge; Was tue ich? Sie heben die rechte Hand. [...] Elisabeth, nehmen Sie den Bleistift!* 'I am a boy; You are a boy; What am I doing? You are raising your right hand [...] Elisabeth, take the pencil!]' (Macpherson 1931: 6, 11; cf. also p. 67 *Im Schulzimmer*). In the verb paradigm given by Macpherson on p. 12, *du* and *ihr*-forms are missing, and they are also systematically excluded in subsequent chapters from the grammatical accounts of pronouns, reflexives, and modals. Not until chapter 33 (p. 163), the third-last chapter in the first volume of the textbook, did pupils encounter the *du*-form, where it was introduced in a conversation between a mother and young son, and the reader was referred to a grammatical note on p. 190 stating that *du* is "used to the members of one's family, to young children, to very intimate friends, to animals and among school-fellows". The very late introduction of *du* in spite of the fact that it is to be used among school-fellows and that the language of the classroom is intended to be German is odd, particularly given that works from the nineteenth century such as Otto (1864, e.g. p. 22; cf. Figure 3.8 in Chapter 3) were already modelling the use of *du* amongst pupils in class. Macpherson's choice was clearly a principled pedagogical decision, breaking with previous tradition – after all, Siepmann's widely used *Public School German Primer* (1896 and later editions), which *Deutsches Leben* could be said to have replaced as the 'standard' textbook, introduced the *du* and *ihr*-forms in verb paradigms from the outset.[28] Interestingly, the revised edition of *Deutsches Leben* 1, published in 1956, reverses this decision: Macpherson now introduced the *du*-form from the outset. Instructions to pupils used it (*Gib die Antwort* in Lesson 1, p. 12), and its conjugation was likewise given from the start (p. 17). However,

---

28 For Siepmann, the *du* and *ihr* forms are used "in addressing God, members of one's own family, intimate friends, children, and animals" (Siepmann 1900: 171).

as late as 1967, *Sprich Mal Deutsch* (Rowlinson 1967) – despite being groundbreaking at the time in its emphasis on teaching language for communication – introduced the *Sie*-form only in the fourth lesson (p. 31), and notably *before* introducing the *du*-form in the seventh lesson (p. 53) – pupils were, somewhat counter-intuitively, introduced to dialogues between adults before encountering any children speaking or being spoken to. By the later twentieth-century 'communicative' textbooks of German, however, the different forms of address (*du, Sie, ihr*) are routinely introduced very early on indeed. To take one example of many, *Gute Reise 1* (Hermann et al. 1992) introduces the *du*-form of greetings and verbs in the first chapter (*Grüß dich, Wie heißt du?*) and the formal *Sie* forms in Chapter 2 (*Wie heißen Sie bitte?*).

5.8 Word order

I turn now to how textbooks of German have dealt with word order rules. Once again it would be well beyond the scope of this chapter to provide a comprehensive history of the topic (in particular, the emergence and influence of valency grammar and transformational grammar would warrant thorough study). However, although this section cannot do the topic justice, the first foray presented here is of interest for two reasons. First, word order is an area where foreign-language grammars may have led the way ahead of the native German grammatical tradition. Second, it is interesting to see how textbook authors met the challenge posed by the lack of the concept of the constituent;[29] and then how they reacted to the rapid strides made in describing syntax in the twentieth century in particular. I shall also illustrate these points with reference to some of the most salient aspects of German word order: the position of the verb in main clauses and subordinate clauses, the position of the negator *nicht*, and the order of nominal and adverbial elements in the so-called central field or *Mittelfeld*. I shall also consider the emergence of the notion of constituent structure and the growing recognition of the verb as the key to word order (with the notion of the verbal bracket). My approach is a somewhat anachronistic one – examining past accounts in terms of current notions – but for the purposes of this brief survey here, it is perhaps the most useful.

5.8.1 Early accounts, up to ca. 1850

Until the very late seventeenth century, grammars did not even provide systematic overviews of word order rules. Rather, in the native German grammatical tradition at the time, syntax was still tackled for each part of speech separately, a parallel structure to the *etymologia* part of the grammar that dealt with inflection and word-formation. This seemingly logical structure – which came from the Latin grammatical tradition – was very resistant to change throughout Europe, but it left very little space to tackle general questions of word order at the clause level which, for a language like German, were of considerable importance. The first grammar in the native grammatical tradition to tack-

---

29 But note Noehden's observation that in a phrase like *das Kind*, the article and noun constitute 'as it were one word' (Noehden 1800: 68); see 5.6 *Stress and intonation* above.

le general word order rules was Stieler (1691), and it has been plausibly suggested that Stieler in fact took the idea from a grammar for foreign learners of German, since he mentions that such an approach could be useful for this group of learners (cf. McLelland 2008: 51, Jellinek 1914: 373; see Stieler 1691: 196). And indeed, the earliest grammar of German for foreign learners to do this predates Stieler's work: it is an anonymous French grammar (Anon. 1682), which gave eight sentence types recognizing (implicitly, at least) different patterns for main clauses, interrogatives, subordinate and relative clauses, and indirect questions. Only a few years later, in the tradition for English learners, Offelen (1687) also identified eight sentence types: affirmative, negative, interrogative, and negative interrogative, each in the present and prefect tenses. Offelen's is a less sophisticated analysis than that in the anonymous French grammar, for Offelen makes no mention of subordinate clauses as a type, but even this was a considerable advance on what was available in Germany in the 1680s. For example, Schottelius (1663: 691–790), despite being the leading grammar of the century, was still mired in the dependency-grammar approach, and any further remarks he made on word order tended to be more of a celebration of the potential for stylistic variation than a clear statement of rules (cf. McLelland 2011: 177–179).

Offelen's categorization of sentence types was still used half a century later by Beiler (1731: 201–205): affirmative, negative, interrogative, and negative interrogative. Beiler also adopted word-for-word Offelen's explanation of inversion, i.e. the rule in German that the subject, if not in first position, must immediately follow the main verb, which must be in second position, as in *Heute arbeite ich* 'Today work I':

> The *Accusative* goes regularly after the *Verb*, but sometimes before the *Verb* in this Language; and then the *Nominative* must go after the *Verb*, especially if we speak of a thing with *Emphasis*. As, Wen liebt ihr? who do you love? R. Ich liebe meinen Bruder, or Meinen Bruder liebe ich, I love my Brother.

> (Offelen 1687: 96; cf. Beiler 1731: 208; an example follows where the first element is an adverb rather than an accusative).

Bachmair (1771: 130) presented three rules on 'The Placing of the Verb':

> There is no Transposition of any Part of Speech but of the Verb, which frequently occupies quite another Place in the German Language than it does in the English. The whole may be comprehended in *three* Rules.

The first of Bachmair's three "Rules" specified that non-finite verbal elements must come last:

> Rule 1.
> Participles and Infinitives occupy the last Place of a Sentence, *as*:
> ich bin gestern sehr spät nach Hause gekommen. I did *come* home very late yesterday.

While the example above is with *sein* 'to be' as the auxiliary verb to form the perfect tense, examples with other auxiliary verbs are given too: *haben* 'to have' for perfect tense and *werden* 'to become' for future are given too. The fact that the future consists of *werden* + infinitive (rather than participle) is noted, while the perfect, pluperfect and "the whole Passive Conjugation" consist of auxiliary plus participle. Bachmair also noted that if a past participle and infinitive come together in a sentence, the infinitive comes last, as in *ich werde meine Arbeit in einer Stunde getahn haben*, 'I shall have done my Work in an Hour'.

Bachmair's second rule dealt with 'relative' clauses – in effect, subordinate clauses, since 'relatives' for Bachmair included relative pronouns, relative adverbs *wo* and *da*, and 'relative conjunctions: *ob wenn, als, da, indem, nachdem, demnach, sintemal, weil, daß, auf daß, damit* and all conditional Particles':

> Rule II.
> All Relatives govern the Verb in the last Place of the Sentence, in every Tense of the Conjugation, *as:*
> *Der Mann, welcher hier in London ist,* the Man who *is* here in London

Bachmair's third and final rule dealt with word order in main clauses and with inversion. (The implicit assumption that the verb otherwise comes second is nowhere made explicit):

> Rule III.
> The Nominative and Verb change Places, 1) in Questions; 2) if the Sentence begins with an Adverb of Time or Place; 3.) if it being with a Preposition, or any Case but the Nominative; 4.) after the Words *auch, vielleicht, daher* and other Words answering the Idea of therefore, if they begin a Sentence.

> (Bachmair 1771: 131–132)[30]

Crabb (1800a) still presents syntax strictly by part of speech. In other ways, however, he makes observations that go beyond his predecessors. Besides pointing out that separable prefixes come last, but are united with the verb if "transposing" words "throw the verb to the end of the sentence" (*Sie hielten mich zu lange auf* but *Wenn ich nicht weggienge* Crabb 1800: 110), Crabb's book also contains scattered hints about the ordering of the elements after the main verb (see below).

---

30 The author of the anonymous *True Guide* (1758) copied this account from Bachmair, though elsewhere he followed Gottsched very closely (Carr 1937: 472).

5.8.2 'Natural' word order?

By the late eighteenth century, then, we find general rules given for German word order that deal with verb placement in various sentence types. Around this time – the start of the nineteenth century – the influence of universal grammar (cf. Naumann 2000) on German grammar can be detected, in particular the assumption that there is a 'natural' word order that accords with the ordering of our thought-propositions. While Noehden's (1800) syntax section also began with the familiar approach to syntax by each part of speech, just as in Crabb's work from the same year, Noehden's final sub-section on syntax offered the most detailed discussion of German word order to date. Noehden considered that German was unique amongst the European languages:

> The Germans alone have a settled method of arranging the parts of speech in a sentence: which is, at present, so incorporated with the genius of the language, that any deviation from it may be regarded as a grammatical offence. It is, therefore, very essential to be acquainted with this subject.

(Noehden 1800: 392)

In Noehden's opinion's, the leading principle in the position of words is to give expression to the sentence, and to render it interesting to the attention of the hearer. "For this reason, the *natural* construction has been abandoned; and the words are placed in such a manner, as is calculated to produce that effect" (Noehden 1800: 393, my emphasis). Noehden added that this arrangement "favours the fluence of the language", and "frequently proves of advantage" for versification (Noehden 1800: 393).

Noehden tackles the word order of each of the parts of speech in turn, in a rather long-winded approach with a good deal of redundancy. For example, he begins with the general rule that the subject precedes the verb, but immediately follows with a lengthy listing of other elements that might be placed first, requiring the subject to come after the verb – the implicit generalization about inversion is not made. His account is not concise, but it does have the virtue of thoroughness. For example, amongst the pre-posed elements that require the subject to follow the verb, Noehden noted that with *auch* and *zwar* this was possible but not obligatory, depending on the intended effect (*Auch rief das Volk* and *Auch das Volk rief*), and suggested that "in old and formal" language, *und* could also require the subject to shift to after the verb: *Und hat Beklagter erwiesen,* and the defendant has proved' (p. 397). He also deals with clauses within clauses, distinguishing principal and subordinate "members": *Da ich den Mann, welcher so edel gedacht, ehre und liebe.* Here, *welcher so edel gedacht* is a "subordinate member" – the verbs of the principal member may or may note precede it: "Sometimes one way and sometimes the other may be preferable: it depends upon sound and perspicuity" (p. 406).

Bernays (1832: 48–53) seems to have been indebted to Noehden, but provided a far more concise summary of the same facts (see Figure 5.13); like Noehden, Bernays pointed out that *auch* may or may not require inversion. He also provided a clear summary of the conditions under which the main verb occurs in last position, as well as the greatest detail to date on the order of elements after the verb: genitive, dative and accusative ob-

Figure 5.13: Word order in Bernays (1832: 48–49)

jects occur after the verb, with dative preceding accusative, except that an accusative pronoun will come first; dative in turn precedes genitive; all generally precede prepositional objects (p. 50). Adverbs are placed after one object, or if, there is more than one, between the two, and at any rate before a prepositional object: *Wir sehen ihn oft,* but *Ich schrieb ihm gestern einen Brief* (Bernays 1832: 50). *Nicht* is "mostly placed after all the cases governed by a verb, and in comp.[ound] tenses immediately before the part.[iciple] or inf.[initive]", as in *Wir gaben ihm das Buch nicht* 'We did not give him the book' and *Wir haben es ihm nicht gegeben* 'We have not given it to him' (Bernays 1832: 51).

The existence of a 'natural' word order was also assumed by the author of a battered, undated text entitled *Ollendorff's German Method* (Ollendorff? n. d: 372[31]). The author of the work added to his presentation of word order, as shown in Figure 5.14, that "These considerations regard only the natural order of ideas; but one may sometimes transgress it by way of those inversions which are numerous in the German language, and where one wishes

---

31 On Ollendorff, see 3.7 above. Ollendorff's works spawned many imitations, as noted there (note 61). At any rate the undated text referred to here must be later that Ollendorff's first edition of 1838.

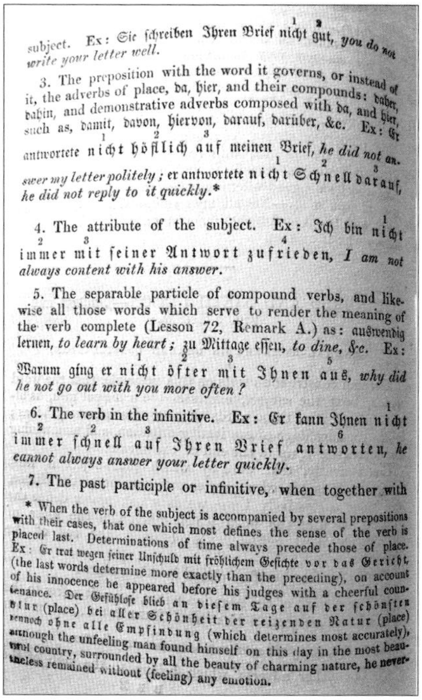

to render a certain word more prominent" (Ollendorff? n.d: 373). Placing the dative after the accusative renders it "still more prominent", as in *Er erzählte die ganze Geschichte seiner Frau* 'he told the whole story to his wife'. By now the generalized rule underlying inversion of verb and subject is clear:

"Whenever a phrase [sic!] commences by any other word but the subject or nominative, an inversion takes place, and the subject or nominative is placed after its verb, (in compound tenses after the auxiliary)."

(Ollendorff? n.d.: 376)

Ollendorff took it as a general premise that the main idea comes after accessory ideas, in effect dealing with the order of elements in the central field (*Mittelfeld*) within the verbal bracket (i.e. between the two underlined verbal elements in a sentence such as *Ich habe ihr heute das neue Buch in die Tasche gesteckt*, lit. 'I have her today the new book in her bag put)':

subject. Ex: Sie schreiben Ihren Brief nicht gut, *you do not write your letter well.*

3. The preposition with the word it governs, or instead of it, the adverbs of place, da, hier, and their compounds: dober, dahin, and demonstrative adverbs composed with da, and hier, such as, damit, davon, hiervon, darauf, darüber, &c. Ex: Er antwortete nicht höflich auf meinen Brief, *he did not answer my letter politely;* er antwortete nicht schnell darauf, *he did not reply to it quickly.* *

4. The attribute of the subject. Ex: Ich bin nicht immer mit seiner Antwort zufrieden, *I am not always content with his answer.*

5. The separable particle of compound verbs, and likewise all those words which serve to render the meaning of the verb complete (Lesson 72, Remark A.) as: auswendig lernen, *to learn by heart;* zu Mittage essen, *to dine, &c.* Ex: Warum ging er nicht öfter mit Ihnen aus, *why did he not go out with you more often?*

6. The verb in the infinitive. Ex: Er kann Ihnen nicht immer schnell auf Ihren Brief antworten, *he cannot always answer your letter quickly.*

7. The past participle or infinitive, when together with

* When the verb of the subject is accompanied by several prepositions with their cases, that one which most defines the sense of the verb is placed last. Determinations of time always precede those of place. Ex: Er trat wegen seiner Unschuld mit fröhlichem Gesichte vor das Gericht (the last words determine more exactly than the preceding), on account of his innocence he appeared before his judges with a cheerful countenance. Der Gefühllose blieb an diesem Tage auf der schönsten Flur (place) bei aller Schönheit der reizenden Natur (place) (which determines most accurately), although the unfeeling man found himself on this day in the most beautiful country, surrounded by all the beauty of charming nature, he nevertheless remained without (feeling) any emotion.

Figure 5.14:
Ollendorff? (n.d.: 372)

"German rests on this principle, that the word which, next to the subject, expresses the principal idea, is always placed after those words that express accessory ideas; it has the advantage of captivating attention, and maintaining and increasing it up to the end of the phrase.

Consequently, that word by which the subject is least determined, is placed at the commencement of the phrase, and then successively those words which nearer define the subject, so that the word which determines the sense of the phrase most definitely, is placed at the end of the phrase.

The words are there placed in this manner:

1. The adverb of the negation *nicht*, when it refers to the verb of the subject.

Ex: Sein Vater beantwortet den Brief nicht, his father does not answer my letter

2. The other adverbs which belong to the verb of the subject.

Ex: Sie schreiben Ihren Brief nicht gut, you do not write your letter well."

229

5.8.3 Word order in textbooks from ca. 1850 onwards:
the order of elements within the verbal bracket

From about the mid-nineteenth century, word order began to be tackled not just in general terms of natural order, but with somewhat more theoretical rigour, by the use of the notions of subject and predicate from propositional logic, as in Woodbury (1851), the earliest example of such usage that I have encountered. Woodbury (1851: 412) explained that "The essential parts of every sentence are the *subject*, which is that of which something is affirmed, and the *predicate*, which is that which contains the affirmation, as in *God exists*"; that which links the subject and predicate is the *copula*; when given in "the natural order", they appear in the order subject – copula – predicate, as in *Die Blume ist schön* 'the flower is beautiful' (Woodbury 1851: 441). Often, as in the case of simple tenses, "the copula and the predicate are contained in a single word; that word holds the place of the copula, while the place of the predicate either remains vacant, or is occupied by the object of the verb", as in *Die Blume blüht; Wir lesen das Buch* 'the flower is blooming; we are reading the book'. In compound tenses, the auxiliary takes the place of the copula, the place of the predicate being occupied by the infinitive or participle, as in *Ich habe gelesen* 'I have read'. Significantly, Woodbury here assumes that there is an abstract representational level of syntax (including at least the copula and predicate) which may or may not be realized at the 'surface' level (to use Chomskyan terms). While *subject – copula – predicate* constitutes the "natural order", "for the sake of giving special emphasis to words, that order is often inverted" (Woodbury 1851: 444).

Woodbury also made a clear distinction between principal sentences ("one that expresses by itself an independent proposition") and subordinate sentences – an advance on Noehden, whose example of a subordinate member was contained in a 'principal' member that was in fact a subordinate clause (*da ich den Mann ehre und liebe*). In the natural order, Woodbury tells his readers, the principal precedes the subordinate, which is usually connected with the principal one "by means of some conjunctive word" (Woodbury 1851: 445).

The text by Aue (1888: 7–11), who also described word order in terms of subject and predicate, seems indicative of a turning point in the discussion of word order. First, it is the first textbook of German for English speakers to place the information about sentence construction *first* in the grammar. Second, Aue's examples are presented in such a way as to imply that there are particular "slots" in a sentence which may or may not be filled. These slots are no longer just the subject, copula and predicate, but also break down the area after the main verb into slots. Earlier grammarians had long used the device of numbering elements in the sentence (see Figure 5.14 for an example from Ollendorff, n. d.) to discuss word order, a device which can be found in the native German discussions of word order too (see Leweling 2005: 213–216 on Elias Caspar Reichard's use of it in the mid-eighteenth century, for example) and ultimately goes right back to vernacular glosses of Latin in the early middle ages. Woodbury had got as far as labelling sentence slots and allowing for them to be empty (cf. Figure 5.15). Earlier grammarians had also made various scattered statements about the order of adjuncts and objects in a clause. For example, Noehden (1800: 400) noted that the dative follows the verb but precedes the accusative: *Er gibt dem Manne das Buch* 'he gives the man the book'; Crabb (1800: 120) noted that adverbs of time are placed before all other adverbs – the earliest mention I have found of this rule (similarly in Woodbury 1851: 443). Negators like *nicht* are generally last, but before the participle or infinitive if there is one (Crabb 1800: 120). In Aue's work of 1888 we now find this information concisely summarized, much of it in tabular form (see Table 5.2). The object of the verb comes between the copula and the predicate; objects of person precede objects of things: *Er hat den Sohn einer Sünde beschuldigt* 'he accused the son of a sin' (a different version, in effect, of the 'dative-before-accusative and both of these before genitive' rule given by Noehden).

Table 5.2: Aue (1888: 9, selected examples only)

Subject	Assertion	Object	Adverbial expression	Negative	Predicate
Das Buch The book	ist is			nicht not	leicht. easy.
Der Vogel The bird	kann can			nicht not	singen. sing.
Wir We	haben have	den Brief the letter		nicht not	erhalten. Received
Ich I	habe have	ihn him	seit einer Woche for a week	nicht not	gesehen. see

This tabular manner of presentation established itself and has continued to be used – with or without numbering of certain elements – ever since. Some examples from the course of the twentieth century are given in Figures 5.16 to 5.19, from Rippmann (1913: 135), Oswald (1940: 93), Russon (1948: 1), Buckley (1966: 286–287). An evolution of it is found in the type of presentation used in *Sprich Mal Deutsch* I (Rowlinson 1967: 35) (see Figure 5.20), where the layout encourages the notion of patterns where certain elements – subject nouns and pronouns, or various types of prepositional phrase – may be substituted for each other, a legacy of the pattern practice drills of the 1950s and 1960s. Such a layout is still found, for example, in the fourth edition of *Hammer's German Grammar and Usage* (Durrell 2002: 369)

Contemporary with Aue's work, Brandt (1884) – who we have elsewhere see was at the cutting edge of German philological studies – was perhaps surprisingly traditional in his presentation of syntax. The section on syntax still comes second, after declension and conjugation, and Brandt still begins with the "special syntax", i. e. that syntax relating to each part of speech in turn, only coming to the basic word order patterns on page 131. Brandt makes no use of tables, and much of his attention is taken up with identifying various types of clauses on semantic criteria (modal, final, intentional, concessive, etc.). However, on page 151 he does turn to general rules on the position of elements in the sentence besides the subject and verb, stating that "the adjuncts of the predicate, such as objects, adverbs, stand between the verb and the predicate". As one might expect from a trained philologist, Brandt provided the greatest number of prescriptions to date about the order of elements in this mid-field (not a term he uses, however): case of a person before case of a thing; case of a pronoun before a noun. His statement that the order of adverbs should be time-manner-place (Brandt 1884: 158) is the earliest statement of this rule that has since become a mainstay of textbooks in the twentieth century (e.g. Russon 1948: 4).[32]

Besides the layout of word order elements in Rowlinson's *Sprich Mal Deutsch* I (1967), another peculiarity is worthy of note. It is the first occurrence that I have found in a textbook of what teachers call the *verb-comma-verb* rule (Rowlinson 1967: 96). The rule relates to something that grammarians had been aware of for centuries, instances where a dependent clause precedes the main clause, as in *Wenn der Wecker läutet, steht man auf* 'When the alarm clock goes off, you get up'. Since the dependent clause – whose verb is in final position – fills the first slot in the main clause, the next element must be the main verb, such that two main verbs occur separated only by a comma, hence *verb-comma-verb*. The rule – well-established in twentieth-century textbooks since Rowlinson,[33] and certainly still used by my students today – is arguably an oddity in a textbook called *Sprich Mal Deutsch* because it depends entirely on *written* punctuation to work.

The above remarks have offered a very incomplete study of the history of German word order in textbooks of German. For example, I have not examined two changes which replaced the subject-predicate as the theory underlying rules about word order: the emergence of valency grammar from the 1950s onwards, a key development intended to capture the centrality of the verb in German syntax (see Eroms 2006); and the changing treatment of the passive in the light of transformational grammar approaches.[34] Another area worthy of greater study would be the changing attitudes to how strictly the verb-last in subordinate clauses should be observed. I already noted above Noehden's remarks on cases where a subordinate clause contains a further subordinate

---

32 One textbook extends the rule of thumb to include the giving of a reason: *time-reason-manner-place*, with the example *Wir sind gestern wegen des Regens schnell nach Hause zurückgekommen* 'We came home quickly yesterday because of the rain' (Paxton & Brentnall 1975: 117). I have not found this in other textbooks.

33 For example: Yeomans et al. (1992: 199); Stocker & Saunders (1995: 295), Esser at al. (1999: 169).

34 In practice, a preliminary inspection suggests that a new underlying theory had little impact on the presentation of the passive. Marchand's German section of *Applied Linguistics. A Guide for Teachers* (1961), clearly under the influence of the then new transformational grammar, did emphasize that "[t]he passive should be presented as a transform of the active" and that "Transformation drill from active to passive and vice versa are especially recommended" (Marchand 1961: 15; cf. 4.6.2), but the recognition that "the direct object of the active verb becomes the subject of the passive verb" (Russon 1948: 110) predates Chomsky, even if the word "transformational" is not used. However, the insight into the relationship between active and passive is not found in Siepmann (1900: 118), nor in Macpherson & Strömer (1931 vol. II: 49). It is implicit in Bithell (1929; I cite the 1943 ed. unchanged in substance here, p. 42): "There is a good rule by which a student may know when to use the German Passive Voice [...] It is this: if the subject of the English clause can be turned into the object by inverting the clause and finding a new subject, it is a clear case for *werden*".

442   COLLOCATION OF WORDS. § 158.

Subject.	Copula.	Predicate.
Ich	habe	gelesen.
I	have	read.
Wir	sind	gewesen.
We	have	been.
Er	kann	schreiben.
He	can	write.
Sie	wurden	gesehen.
They	were	seen.
Er	geht	aus.
He	goes	out.

(5) When any of those verbs which assume the place of the copula are employed in the compound form, the Participle or Infinitive belonging to them stands *after* the proper predicate. Examples:

Subject.	Copula.	Predicate.
Er	ist	thöricht gewesen.
He	has	foolish been.
Er	wird	gelesen haben.
He	will	read have.
Sie	hätten	schreiben sollen.
Sie	sind	gehört worden.
Er	wird	gesehen worden sein.
Er	ist	ausgegangen.

(6) The object of a sentence comes between the copula and the Predicate; and, if there be two objects, that of the person precedes that of the thing. Examples:

Subject.	Copula.	1st Object.	2d Object.	Predicate.
Er	hat	einen Brief	—	geschrieben.
Er	schreibt	meinen Brief	—	ab.
Er	ist	seinem Freunde	—	gewogen.
Sie	sind	eines Verbrechens	—	beschuldigt worden.
Ich	habe	dem Knaben	ein Buch	gegeben.
Er	hat	den Sohn	einer Sünde	beschuldigt.
Ich	habe	meinen Freund	—	um Rath* gefragt.

* Um Rath with fragen forms a phrase, (um Rath fragen, to ask for advice,) which belongs to a class of phrases in German, in which a noun or adjective is made to play the same part in respect to a verb, that is contained by a separable particle. This will account for the position of um Rath in the sentence: it being treated just like a separable prefix. Other phrases belonging to this class are:

Wortfolge im Hauptsatz

A. GERADE WORTFOLGE: Subjekt zuerst.

Subjekt	finites Verb		
Der Hund	bellt	laut	
Er	hat	laut	gebellt
Er	wird	laut	bellen
Wer	hat	das	getan?

NB und, aber (allein), sondern, *oder* denn *darf vorangehen*
Ich bin alt, aber du bist jung.
Er kam nicht, denn er war krank.

B. INVERSION: finites Verb vor Subjekt.

	fin. Verb	Subjekt	
	Habt	ihr	ihn gesehen?
	Gehst	du,	so bleibe ich.
	Käme	er	doch!
	Ist	das	ein dummer Mensch!
Wo	war	er	gestern?
Das	weisz	ich	nicht.
Gestern	kam	er	zu uns.
Als er kam,	war	ich	zuhause.
"Dort,"	sagte	ich,	"war ich oft."

NB Der Hund bellte = Es bellte der Hund.

Wortfolge im Nebensatz

	Nebensatz	(fin. Verb)	
Ich sah,	dasz er krank	war.	
	Als er	ankam,	säh ich ihn.
	Weil er uns gesehen	hatte,	grüszte er.

NB Ich glaube nicht, dasz ich das werde tun können.
Es ist das erste Mal, dasz ich ihn habe singen hören.

Objekte:
Er gab | dem Armen[1] | Brot.
Er gab | ihm | Brot.
aber Er gab es[2] | ihm.

[1] Das persönliche Objekt vor
[2] dem sachlichen Objekt, wenn dieses nicht ein Personal-Pronomen ist.

Adverbien: 1. Zeit 2. Ort
Ich kam spät nach Hause.

135

Figure 5.15: Woodbury (1851: 442), Figure 5.16: Rippmann (1913: 135)

clause, as to whether any finite verbs should precede another dependent clause, or follow it (*Da ich den Mann, welcher so edel gedacht, ehre und liebe* or *Da ich den Man ehre und liebe, welcher so edel gedacht*); Witte (1937: 7–11) noted a tendency to freer word order particularly in the tendency towards *Ausklammerung*, or allowing an element to follow the final verb (e.g. *Ich bin heute einkaufen gegangen mit Lukas und Ute* rather than *Ich bin heute mit Lukas und Ute einkaufen gegangen* 'Today I went shopping with Lukas and Ute', as described by Durrell 1992: 238). The same observation can be found occasionally in textbooks since then: Paxton & Brentnall (1975: 181) noted that such a structure "is possible in colloquial German" but considered that "it is not to be recommended"; Rowlinson (1993: 244) noted more tolerantly that "Subordinate order is not always adhered to in spoken German: phrases tend to be added after the verb".

One other, virtually notorious, instance where a change to the verb-last rule is underway is worth noting in conclusion: the word order after the conjunction *weil* 'because'. Main clause word order rather than subordinate clause order has been noted in spoken language since the late nineteenth century: verb-second *weil ich habe Hunger* rather than verb-last *weil ich Hunger habe* 'because I am hungry'. It has been much noted by popular linguistic commentators such as Bastian Sick (2005); from criticizing it as

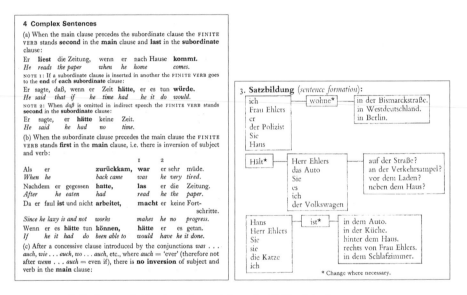

Figure 5.17 (left): Oswald (1940: 93), Figure 5.18 (right): Buckley (1967: 286)

Figure 5.19 (left): Russon (1967: 3, unchanged from the 1948 edition)
Figure 5.20 (right): Rowlinson (1967: 35)

wrong, German linguists have in recent years begun to examine its usage more closely and to observe that it may fulfil specific pragmatic functions; there is evidence that the same tendency may now be found with other conjunctions too (see Ziegler 2009 for a short and very readable summary). In the British tradition, the earliest note I found of the occurrence of *weil* with main clause word order dates from 1991, in the authoritative German grammar by Durrell (1991: 394). I found only one school-level textbook from the twentieth century that allowed for the possibility that students might encounter *weil* with non-verb-final word order (and, in fact, *weil* sometimes still served as *the* example of a subordinating conjunction, e.g Brien et al. 2000: 262). That exception is in the A-level coursebook *Sprungbrett* (Bonnyman & Oberheid 1990: 12), where readers are

234

informed *Beim spontanen Sprechen wird nicht immer auf grammatische Regeln geachtet* 'Grammar rules are not always followed in spontaneous speech', and are invited to note down the exact word order following *weil* in a listening exercise, where they will indeed hear *weil* with the verb in second position in the conversation.[35]

5.9 Some aspects of noun and verb inflection

I concluded the preceding section with some remarks on whether textbooks note (or in most cases choose not to note) ongoing changes in word order that result in language variation. In this section, I continue to explore the prescription and description in textbooks of some other areas of German grammar where there is variation, and, therefore, uncertainty amongst native speakers about what is correct. I consider an example of changes to verb conjugation, the verb *backen* 'to bake' (5.9.1); the formation of the informal imperative singular (5.9.2), and the case governed by *wegen* and *trotz* (5.9.3). This last area is particularly interesting because it is an instance where there is not just variation in usage, and corresponding uncertainty, but also strong stigmatization of certain forms deemed incorrect.[36]

5.9.1 Verb conjugation I: *backen* 'to bake'

In German (as in English), there is a general tendency that originally strong (irregular) verbs move, over time, into the class of weak verbs – something similar is happening today in the case of verbs like *strive, thrive* – increasingly we hear regularized forms like *strived* rather than *strove* and *striven*.[37] One such verb that appears to be moving classes in German is *backen* 'to bake'. Already by the early years of the nineteenth century, Heynatz (1803, *Wortforschung*: 191) listed *backen* as the first of the irregular verbs, but suggested that the regular forms in the present were 'more usual' (*gewöhnlicher*):

> *backen. bäckst, bäckt (oder gewöhnlicher backst, backt), buk (nicht buch), aber häufig auch backte. backe (nicht back). gebacken.*

> '*backen. bäckst, bäckt* (or more usually *backst, backt), buk* (not *buch*), but frequently also *backte. backe* (not *back*). *gebacken*.'

---

35 It is worth noting that *Sprungbrett* is progressive elsewhere in its focus on colloquial language, on the presence of other (migrant) languages besides German in Germany, and on the nature of German national identity; see Chapter 6.

36 Pragmatically, in the face of such variation, the textbook author need only present the learner with forms that will not be wrong, rather than with all possible forms (and indeed Ölinger (1573) already did just that for foreign, particularly French, learners of German for adjective declension and comparison, at a time when the German noun phrase was a sea of variants; cf. McLelland (2001).

37 So-called 'strong' verbs are not, technically, the same as irregular verbs, but for the reader here the distinction is not crucial. I shall use the terms interchangeably here, by contrast with "regular" and "weak".

In the mid-twentieth century, the language 'bible' for native speakers of German, the Duden (1956, s.v. *backen*) presented the strong preterite *buk* as the secondary, 'older' form:

> *Unsere Mutter backte, (älter) buk jede Woche Kuchen*
>
> 'Our mother *backte* (older) *buk* cakes every week'.[38]

Thirty years later, Duden (1985: 98) stated that strong *buk* had been "almost totally replaced" (*fast völlig verdrängt*) by the regular form, while in the present tense, the non-umlauted *du backst, er backt* are "increasingly frequent" (*immer häufiger*). A full one hundred and eighty years after Heynatz had already listed these non-umlauted forms as the "usual" ones, the Duden (1985: 98) went out on a limb to state that "this development is so far advanced, that the non-umlauted forms must also be recognized" (*Diese Entwicklung ist so weit fortgeschritten, daß auch die nicht umgelauteten Formen anerkannt werden müssen*). This seems rather conservative measured against Heynatz nearly two centuries earlier. Still, such accounts in the native-speaker tradition are presumably the basis for one common way of presenting *backen* in verb-lists for British learners: regular, non-umlauted *backte* is acknowledged as the norm in the preterite (though *buk* is often listed too, for after all it may be needed for recognition purposes when reading older works), but regular, non-umlauted *backt* in the present is still viewed only as a secondary, alternative form in Durrell (2002: 254), a reference grammar in English.

School textbooks for English learners go further, however. They continue to list the strong forms first (though this may be the natural consequence of dealing with the verb in a table of strong and irregular verbs), but add that the regular forms are "commonly used in N. Germany" (Macpherson & Strömer 1934: 120),[39] are "usual in conversation" (Clarke 1936: 173), or are "now much more common" (Tudor & Heydorn 1956: 226). Yet it is striking that there is no agreement about what factors influence the variation: is it regional variation, a question of register, or diachronic change? One is tempted to conclude that these are no more than three different educated guesses to account for the discrepancy between the native-speaker codex and the usage to which the textbook writers were exposed.

Freda Kellett (1964: 148) was the first to present the regular forms as the norm, listing *backen, backte (buk), gebacken*. In the absence of any entry in her table for the 2ⁿᵈ/ 3ʳᵈ person present singular, the learner will assume that the forms are regular, non-umlauted. This example raises the interesting question of the *selection* of the 'facts' that will be included in any textbook. While it is reasonable to expect advanced users of a grammar like Borgert & Nyhan (1976) or Durrell (2002), both aimed at university students, to cope with a full account of the range of options available (including, for both these works, the alleged subjunctive *büke* before *backte*, a form I have never yet encountered),

---

38 The entry does not discuss the present tense, although the un-umlauted forms (only) are used to illustrate *backen* in intransitive use: *der Schnee backte, backte (klebt(e)) and den Schuhen.*

39 This explanatory footnote is dropped in the 1939 edition.

the school textbook author must simplify. Such simplification may take the form of presenting not the codified prescription norm, but instead abstracting a subsistent or implicit norm from the *usus* of a language community.[40] Beginning with Kellett (1964), this is increasingly the case for *backen*. By the early 1990s Rowlinson et al. (1993) list *gebacken* as the *only* irregular form in what is otherwise treated as a regular verb. The strong preterite *buk* and strong present tense forms are ignored.

In our first example of German grammar through British eyes, then, the textbooks for non-native learners in the later twentieth century give an account of contemporary common usage, with no mention of alternative forms, and so give further 'official' sanction to the newer forms against the obsolescent ones (see Table 5.3).

Table 5.3: backen *in selected grammars and textbooks of German (1803–2002)*

Works for German native speakers	Heynatz (1803)	Weak forms in the present 'more usual' (*gewöhnlicher*). Preterite *buk aber häufig auch* ['but frequently also'] *backte*.
	Duden (1956)	Preterite *buk* as the secondary, older form.
	Duden (1985)	Weak forms in the present 'increasingly frequent'; these non-umlauted forms 'must now be recognized'. Preterite *buk* almost totally replaced by *backte*.
Works for English-speaking learners of German (school)	Macpherson & Strömer (1934)	Weak forms (present and preterite) are 'commonly used in N. Germany'.
	Clarke (1936)	Weak forms are 'usual in conversation''
	Tudor & Heydorn (1956)	Weak forms are 'now much more common'
	Kellett (1964)	Weak forms are assumed to be the primary forms: preterite *buk* is given in parentheses, and only the past participle *gebacken* is presented as normally strong.
	Rowlinson et al. (1993)	Treats *backen* as entirely weak (regular) except for the past participle *gebacken*.
Works for English-speaking learners of German (university)	Borgert & Nyhan (1976)	Conservative: even gives the alleged subjunctive *büke* before weak *backte*
	Durrell (2002)	Gives full range of forms, including subjunctive *büke* before weak *backte*, as above.

---

40 See Bartsch (1987), Gloy (2004, 2010) on explicit vs. implicit or subsistent norms.

5.9.2 Verb conjugation II: The imperative singular

If *backen* is a well-understood case of alternative regular and irregular forms, a second area of German grammar where there is considerable variation is the second person singular imperative of verbs, where one can find, for instance, both *geh*! and *gehe*! 'go!' for *gehen* 'to go'. In this case, the variation means that there is prescriptive uncertainty, but no real stigmatization of either form. The variation depends in part on whether the verb is strong or weak (which was the historical basis for the distinction): strong verbs generally have no *-e*. Hence Heynatz (1803)'s stipulation that the imperative of the historically strong *backen* (which he viewed as more usually weak) must be *backe!*, not *back*! (a belief faithfully preserved in Borgert & Nyhan 1976: 262). Weak verbs do have an *-e*, historically, at least, but many lose their *-e* in some, many or all contexts, though with some morphological or phonological constraints (e.g. for verbs with a stem ending in *-t*, the *-e* is required, hence *arbeite!*, not *arbeit!* 'work!'). Finally, strong verbs can also be found *with* an *-e*, e.g. *gehe!* Duden (1985: 347) states:

> [a]bgesehen von der gehobenen Sprache [...] wird heute bei den meisten Verben die Formen ohne Endungs-e bevorzugt

> 'apart from in elevated language, today for most verbs the forms without the *-e* ending are preferred'

This statement, with its various caveats *(apart from, today, most, preferred)*, is indicative of how complicated the picture is, and of the scope for variation. Now, it is once again the task of the textbook-writer to offer maximum clarity for the learner. In practical terms, here the learner only needs to be presented with forms that will be not be wrong, rather than with all possible forms (unlike where one might argue the need to recognize the odd-looking *buk* as a form of *backen*). What, then, do we find? Table 5.4 summarizes the results of my 'straw poll' of twentieth-century textbooks from the 1930s onwards.

What this sample shows is that in the earliest textbook, Macpherson & Strömer (1934), the learner is told, in essence, to add the *-e* for all verbs except one subgroup of strong verbs like *sieh, lies* 'see, read!' In contrast, in the three most recent textbooks examined here – all 1988 to 1993 – the learner is told in essence that leaving out the *-e* will never be wrong, at least not in speech. This advice is *similar* to that of Duden (1985) for native speakers. However, for Duden the distinction is between elevated and general language usage, i.e. register, rather than a distinction between written and spoken language (i.e. a distinction according to medium), as two British textbooks suggest (*Zickzack* by Goodman-Stephens et al. 1989: 184; *Deutschland hier und jetzt* by Rowlinson et al. 1993: 232). *Neue Perspektiven* (Della Gana 1988) goes furthest, making no mention of *-e* forms at all, and yet the text itself supplies many counter-examples, with its repeated instruction to pupils *Suche...* ('Look for...').

In this case too, then, mainstream textbooks for British learners simplify their accounts compared to native-speaker accounts – and again in the direction of colloquial, spoken rather than literary usage; and one simply passes silently over the existence of the variation.

Table 5.4: The imperative singular in selected textbooks of German (1934–1993)

Deutsches Leben III (Macpherson & Strömer 1934)	Prescribes forms with -e except for strong verbs with vowel change
Heute Abend (Kelber 1938, revised, 1955)	Lists *sag(e)* as model for weak verbs; no explicit discussion of imperative
Russon's Advanced German Course (Russon 1965)	Describes the existence of forms with -e or without, prescribes forms without -e for strong verbs with vowel change, AND with -e for verbs with unstressed syllable at end of stem -*er*, -*el*, -*ig*
Neue Perspektiven (Della Gana 1988)	Prescriptive, simplifying: *du* form without -*st*, i.e. without -e; no mention of -e forms at all. Presence of -e forms in the text (e.g. the frequent instruction *Suche an Hand des Textes…*, where a weak verb imperative ends in -e) contradicts the prescription
Zickzack, vol. 3 (GCSE level) (Goodman-Stephens et al. 1989)	Descriptive: -e forms clearly considered possible for some verbs, but no explicit guidance about where it is not possible / where it is usual; -e 'not usually heard when speaking'
Deutschland hier und jetzt (Rowlinson et al. 1993)	-e 'often omitted, especially in speech'; -e not possible in verbs with full vowel change

5.9.3 Case after prepositions

I turn now to case after prepositions. German prepositions govern the accusative, the dative, or the genitive, or take either the accusative or dative depending on function. A significant group, however, can occur with the dative *or* the genitive, depending on region, register, and specific grammatical context (cf. Durrell 2002 for an up-to-date account of these factors for advanced English-speaking learners). In this section, I examine the treatment of these vacillating prepositions in British textbooks by comparison with the native grammatical tradition. By the 1960s, a group of four prepositions had come to be treated together in materials for English-speaking learners, where a consensus appears to have emerged that there are four 'common' prepositions governing the genitive: *(an)statt* 'instead of', *trotz* 'in spite of', *während* 'during', and *wegen* 'because of'. These four tend to be presented first amongst those taking the genitive, or, depending on the level, they are the *only* four presented (as in *Sprich Mal Deutsch*, Rowlinson 1968: 126). For example, these four are listed first in the reference grammar of Durrell (1991, 1996, 2002), and are the *only* four given in *Deutschland hier und jetzt* (Rowlinson et al. 1993), a textbook aimed at learners of German preparing for A-level.[41] In the following dis-

---

41 Twentieth-century materials invariably begin with the accusative and dative prepositions; lower level textbooks may not cover prepositions governing the genitive at all. It is worth noting by con-

cussion, I shall examine the treatment of just two of these four 'common' prepositions governing the genitive, *wegen* and *trotz*, to demonstrate how these two – now grouped together – have quite different histories in grammatography, and different treatments too, in the German and British codifications of German grammar.

5.9.3.1 *wegen + genitive or dative*

The preposition *wegen* 'because of' has a history of considerable native-speaker uncertainty, analysed by Davies & Langer (2006: 197–211) in their study of language stigmatizations in German. *Wegen* + dative is now stigmatized, but studies of contemporary native-speaker usage and judgements suggest that *wegen* + dative is nevertheless at least an established usage norm alongside the genitive, especially in southern Germany, where Davies (2005: 331) found that 43 % of her informants – teachers in south-western Germany – did not correct *wegen* + dative. Wagner (2009: 150–51) also reports that a striking 67 % of pupils aged 12–14 in her sample (and still 57.2 % of pupils in *Gymnasien*, or grammar schools, the most 'academic' of German secondary schools), did not correct *wegen* + dative. As early as 1937, a scholarly study of modern German usage claimed that "The dative after *wegen* is becoming very common in the spoken language, indeed one might almost say the rule", something Witte took as indicative of "the decline of the inflexional genitive" (Witte 1937: 36). Davies & Langer (2006) note that from the 1980s onward, *wegen* + dative is considered acceptable by grammatical authorities under certain conditions: in particular, with a plural noun where the genitive would not be explicitly marked: contrast *Probleme, wegen Probleme* (genitive, no visible marking) vs. *wegen Problemen* (dative -n marking on the noun) (Duden 1985: 749–50). In other contexts, although the dative is noted as *häufig* 'frequent' in colloquial and regional German, Duden (1985: 750) states that it *gilt nicht als korrekt* 'is considered not correct'. The resulting uncertainty amongst native speakers is reflected in the fact that *wegen* was, in one year at least, the subject of the most queries to the Duden's language advice centre (cf. Russ 1993, reported in Davies & Langer 2006: 197). All this makes *wegen* an interesting case for the study of prescriptivism for non-native speakers. On the one hand, there is strong evidence that it is widely used with the dative. On the other hand, the pre-eminent authority for native speakers, the *Duden*, continues to insist in its guide to good usage that, beyond certain narrowly defined exceptions, *wegen* with the dative is 'not correct'. How, then, have the authors of British textbooks, aiming at presenting the German language as clearly as possible to non-native speakers, dealt with this uncertainty? To what extent are they governed by native-speaker authorities, to what extent by established native-speaker usage? In this case, I shall consider seventeenth- and eighteenth-century textbooks as well as a selection of twentieth-century ones. The findings discussed below are summarized in Table 5.5.

---

trast that earlier works for British learners presented prepositions taking the genitive first, because that was, traditionally, the 'second case' after the nominative (Aedler 1680: 174), with dative as third case, and accusative in fourth place. (in Aedler 1680, Wendeborn 1774, Noehden 1800, Crabb 1800). Offelen listed the prepositions in alphabetical order.

Table 5.5: wegen *in selected grammars and textbooks of German, 1641–2000*

German grammarians	Gueintz (1641)	*wegen* requires the dative
	Schottelius (1663)	*wegen* requires the genitive
	Stieler (1691)	*wegen* described as taking the dative; but examples include *wegen* + genitive
	Heynatz (1777)	*wegen* with dative is *unrichtig* 'incorrect'
	Adelung (1793)	*wegen* with dative *fehlerhaft* 'faulty, a mistake', and something often done in Upper (i. e. southern) German.
Textbooks for English learners of German 1680–1800	Aedler (1680) Offelen (1687) Wendeborn (1774) Noehden (1800) Crabb (1800)	All state that *wegen* requires the genitive, although Aedler and Wendeborn both observe that some other prepositions may govern more than one case.
Textbooks for English learners of German 1930–1800	Macpherson & Strömer (1934) Russon (1948) Russon & Russon (1965) Kellett (1964) Johnson (1971)	All state that *wegen* requires genitive
	Clarke (1936)	First stigmatization of *wegen* + dative in British tradition: 'The use of the dative is a provincialism, and should be avoided.'
	Dickins (1963)	'*wegen* is often found governing the dative in S. German'
	Borgert & Nyhan (1976)	comment on all *trotz, wegen* and *während* that '[t]hese are also found with the dative, but this is considered less correct'
	Goodman-Stephens et al. vol. 3 (1989),	'[i]n speech people sometimes use the Dative with *wegen*'
	Rowlinson et al. (1993)	*wegen* takes the dative but 'may also be found with the dative'
	Fischer (2000)	*wegen* with the dative is 'colloquial, but generally accepted in standard German'

In the native German grammatical tradition, uncertainty over *wegen* goes at least as far back as the seventeenth century, as Davies & Langer (2006: 197–202) have demonstrated. Gueintz (1641 [1978]: 92) listed *wegen* as taking the dative, whereas Schottelius (1663) stated that it required the genitive. Stieler (1691 [1968]: 237 of Vol. III) hardly helped matters when he stated that *wegen* took the dative, but included a number of examples where the noun phrase could only be genitive (and others that could be either dative or genitive). By the eighteenth century, however, *wegen* + genitive appears to have emerged as the prescribed standard. *Wegen* with the dative was first stigmatized by Heynatz (1777: 245), who called it *unrichtig* 'incorrect'; Adelung (1793: 1428) considered it *fehlerhaft* 'faulty, a mistake', and something often done in Upper (i. e. southern) German. Yet in the tradition of German grammars for English learners, Crabb, in his a self-proclaimed translation of Adelung's grammar "arranged and adapted to the English learner" (Crabb 1800, title page), lists *wegen* without further comment as a preposition governing the genitive (Crabb 1800: 61–62). One might assume that the omission in Crabb (1800) of such detail compared to Adelung (1793) reflects Crabb's desire to meet the needs of the non-native speaker audience, if it were not for the fact that he does have a section for "[t]he prepositions governing the genitive and the dative". Rather than *wegen*, though, Crabb includes under this heading *längs* 'along' as "generally with the dative, sometimes with the genitive" (Crabb 1800: 62).[42]

Some of Crabb's predecessors in the English tradition of German grammar-writing were equally open to the idea of prepositions that regularly governed the dative or the genitive. According to Aedler (1680: 174), who here followed Schottelius (1663), *wegen* took the genitive.[43] But if *wegen* had no variant case requirements in Aedler's view, other prepositions did:

> some [prepositions] require the third case, as *aus* out, *beseit* or *beseits* beside or besides, *binnen* within, […]. *binnen* and *innerhalb* seem to govern also the second case e.g. *binnen (innerhalb) zweyen jaren* and *zweyer jare* within two years &c. where we may understand the word *frist* or *zeit*'

(Aedler 1680: 175)

This observation of variant usage in the case of these prepositions, without any prescription, appears to be Aedler's own. It does not feature in Schottelius (1663), nor in any of his predecessors as far as I am aware; Schottelius (1663: 768) lists *binnen* with the "ablative", i. e. dative, only. Neither Offelen (1687), nor Noehden (1800), contemporary with Crabb, allowed for any such variation in their grammars, but like Aedler, Wendeborn (1774: 114) noted *innerhalb* 'within' (and indeed *außerhalb, oberhalb* and *unterhalb* too) in the group of prepositions that "admit of two cases": "[t]he following have sometimes the GENITVE, sometimes the DATIVE". The examples Wendeborn gives are *Außer-*

---

42 This description of the use of *längs* is the reverse, incidentally, of at least two authoritative twentieth-century accounts. Helbig & Buscha (1994: 408) note it as "G (D)", i. e. with the genitive as the usual case, while Durrell (2002: 463) lists it as taking the genitive and only "less frequently" the dative.

43 In fact, Aedler emphasized that *wegen* was not properly speaking a preposition at all: *wegen* or *von wegen* "are used as prepositions with the same [i. e. genitive] case; but (to speak accurately) these are nouns [derived from *Weg* 'way', NMcL], as in Latin *causa, gratia* […]" (likewise *halben, halb,* or *halben, willen* or *um-willen, vermittelst, vermeoge, kraft, laut,* […]). This corresponds to a long-running reluctance in German grammatography to acknowledge the existence of 'proper' prepositions governing the genitive, and to treat such words that precede a noun and govern the genitive case instead as adverbs, or as here, nouns (Jellinek 1914: 359–366).

halb, innerhalb des Königreichs 'outside, inside the kingdom' and *Außerhalb, innerhalb dem Hause* 'outside, inside the house'. This is the latest mention that I have encountered of variation between genitive and dative with this group of *-halb* prepositions. Later accounts note, instead, the tendency to use *innerhalb von* etc. governing the dative in instances where the genitive would not be explicitly marked (e.g. *innerhalb von zwei Stunden* 'within two hours').

So much for case variation after German prepositions in grammars for English learners in the period 1680–1800. Variation might be noted, but was not stigmatized – and *wegen* was in any case not included among those with varying case governance (and nor, indeed was *trotz*, to which I turn below). Let us take up the tale again in the twentieth century, beginning with the 1930s. In *Deutsches Leben* III (Macpherson & Strömer 1934), we find *wegen* listed only with the genitive – and likewise in Russon (1948: 76), Russon & Russon (1965: 56), Kellett (1964: 94), and Johnson (1971: 291–292). But just two years after Macpherson & Strömer's textbook, Clarke's grammar (1936: 124) stigmatized *wegen* + dative for the first time in the British tradition: "The use of the dative is a provincialism, and should be avoided." In a grammar written for Australian Year 1 university students, Borgert & Nyhan (1976: 200) comment on all three of *trotz, wegen* and *während* that "[t]hese are also found with the dative, but this is considered less correct." [44] These are, however, the only two instances I have found to date where *wegen* + dative is mentioned in order to be stigmatized. Rather, from at least the 1960s onwards, textbook authors show a readiness to note *wegen* + dative as an alternative, *without* stigmatization – in complete contrast to the discourse about *wegen* in codifications for German native speakers. Dickens (1963: 16) simply observes that "*wegen* is often found governing the dative in S. German"; Rowlinson et al. (1993: 243) lists *wegen* as taking the genitive but adds that "the four listed above may also be found with the dative". Even in a work for pupils at the lower GCSE level (examinations taken aged 16), there is room for the observation (without stigmatization) "in speech people sometimes use the Dative with *wegen*" (Goodman-Stephens et al. 1989, vol. 3: 189). Perhaps most tellingly of all, Fischer (2000: 340), a textbook written for tertiary level students in Ireland by a native speaker of German, comments that *wegen* with the dative is "colloquial, but generally accepted in standard German". "Standard German" here clearly does not mean what the Duden stipulates! Once again, as with the regularizing of most forms of *backen*, there appears to be a readiness in the tradition of German grammar-teaching for English speakers to present as a *fait accompli* forms that are frequent in the spoken language, even as native speaker reference works still regard them as variants not yet fully established or accepted.

---

44 While some may balk at the possibility of such gradations of correctness, speakers do work with grades of acceptability; see Hundt (2008).

5.9.3.2 trotz + *genitive or dative*

Given the salience in the British tradition of *trotz* 'in spite of' as one of "four common prepositions" governing the genitive, it may seem surprising that *trotz* did not rate a mention as a preposition at all in the grammars discussed above for the time-frame 1680–1800, which tended to give an exhaustive listing of prepositions in alphabetical order. Just how and when *trotz* 'made it' as a preposition at all in both the native and the English-speaking traditions of German grammar-writing is beyond the scope of this paper. At any rate, the shift in how it has been described since its emergence offers an interesting case study. According to Grimm's *Deutsches Wörterbuch*, the preposition *trotz* emerged in the sixteenth century from prepositional use of the interjection. It was still rare in the seventeenth century, and in the nineteenth century its roots as an interjection were still evident in the punctuation. Originally governing the dative, *trotz* in constructions with the genitive emerged in the mid-eighteenth century, and were judged incorrect by both Adelung and Campe. However, since then *bis in die gegenwart läszt sich das nebeneinander von dativ und genitiv bei demselben schriftsteller beobachten* 'the use of dative and genitive may be observed side by side in the same author, right up to the present day', as Bernhard Beckmann wrote in his entry for *trotz* in the *Deutsches Wörterbuch* in the 1930s (after *Mein Kampf*, 1933, cited as an example). The *Duden Stilwörterbuch* of 1956 (Duden 1956: 614) lists *trotz dem Regen, trotz des Regens* in that order without further comment, while Duden's *Richtiges und Gutes Deutsch* (Duden 1985: 665) states that the dative is common with *trotz* in Austria, but that elsewhere the genitive is usual (cf. Table 5.5).

This apparent tolerance in the native-speaker tradition of either dative or genitive (with some regional preferences) has a more heated history, however. Within the genre of the usage guide for native speakers that blossomed in the latter nineteenth century, Matthias conceded in his volume *Sprachleben und Sprachschäden* ('Language Life and Language Damages', Matthias 1897: 138) that the genitive is the *häufigere* 'more frequent', but maintained that the dative is the *besser* though *thatsächlich jetzt seltenere* 'the better' but 'actually now more rare' form. Wustmann took the same view in his book of *Sprachdummheiten* ('Language Howlers', Wustmann 1896: 233). With heavy irony he wrote,

> *da sind wir jetzt glücklich so weit, daß der richtige Dativ für einen Fehler und der falsche Genitiv für das Richtige und Feine erklärt wird*
> 'luckily we have now reached the point where the correct dative is taken to be an error, and the incorrect genitive is taken to be the correct and elegant form.'

Beckmann, in his entry for *trotz* for the *Deutsches Wörterbuch*, observed that by his day [i. e. at least in the 1930s], the genitive had 'almost fully supplanted the dative' *(den dativ fast ganz verdrängt)*. *Deutsches Leben* is proof of just this point, as here we find British learners warned against the (historically original) dative with *trotz*: "*Trotz* and *während* are sometimes found with the dative; this is not very good German, and should not be imitated" (Macpherson & Strömer 1934: 101; cf. also the 1962 printing of the 1939 revised edition: 115). Similarly, in their grammar for Australian students, Borgert & Nyhan (1976: 200) commented on all three of *trotz*, *wegen* and *während* that "[t]hese are also found with the dative, but this is considered less correct." More commonly, though, the variation is noted without stigmatization. Clarke (1936: 123), a grammar for British learners written around the same time as Beckmann's *Deutsches Wörterbuch* entry, allows *trotz* with either genitive or dative without stigmatization: "*Trotz* may govern the genitive or, less often, the dative." Dickins (1963: 16) observes that "*trotz* (in spite of) usually governs the genitive, but is also found with the dative"; ditto Russon & Russon (1965: 50), who have a footnote to *trotz*, "also with dative" without further comment. *Harrap's New German Grammar* (Johnson 1971: 292–93 lists *trotz* under "Prepositions with varying case" as governing the "dative or (more commonly) genitive: *trotz dem Regen* or *trotz des Regens*." For all of these, *trotz* + genitive is given first (Russon & Russon 1965), or occurs 'more commonly' (Johnson 1971) or 'usually' (Dickins 1963).

These authors all follow the observations in the native-speaker tradition, then, according to which the genitive has become the norm but the dative may be found too. An exception to this is Freda Kellett, who remarked in her grammar for advanced school pupils that the genitive after *trotz* was "less common now" (Kellett 1964: 93).[45] Kellett is at odds with the consensus here, for she evidently believed that the genitive was the form on the way out, rather than the innovation. In short, with Kellett's account, the preposition *trotz* had come full circle. Originally it governed the dative; it came to be used frequently with the genitive; but it was now perceived to be shifting *out* of the class of genitive prepositions, along with *wegen* and others, to frequent use with the dative. Although I am not aware of any other authors who go as far as Kellett did, it is true that in the codex of German for English speakers, the line between *trotz,* as a properly (or at least originally) dative preposition, and *während, statt* and *wegen* as properly genitive prepositions has blurred, and has ultimately been lost. This even extends to Durrell's authoritative revision of *Hammer's German Grammar* (Durrell 1991; cf. Hammer, 1971), the fullest reference grammar of German in English, where we read that all four prepositions *(an)statt, trotz, während* and *wegen* are "commonly used with a dative in everyday colloquial speech. [...] This usage is regarded as substandard, but it is by no means unknown in writing" (Durrell 1991: 446).

Here, in the British tradition, then, a logical conclusion based on observations of current usage – that *trotz* and *wegen* are on a par – has been drawn which does not yet appear in the native-speaker codifications, where there is still a distinction between *trotz* (where variation in case governance is tolerated) and *wegen* (where it is not). Here, once again, the British codifications of German are arguably closer to majority contemporary native speaker *usage* than are those of the native speaker tradition.

---

45 On the other hand, *wegen* is listed only under genitive with no mention of the dative (Kellett 1964: 94).

Table 5.5: trotz *in selected grammars, style guides and textbooks of German from the beginnings to 1991*

pre-1890	not discussed at all as a preposition before 1800; Adelung and Campe both consider *trotz* + genitive incorrect	
1890–1985 German style guides (and dictionary)	Wustmann 1896	Laments that the correct dative is held to be a mistake, and that the faulty genitive is declared correct
	Matthias 1897	*trotz* + genitive is more frequent, dative less common but "better"
	Beckmann [1930s]	*trotz* is used both with genitive and dative up to the present-day; genitive has "nowadays" largely replaced the dative
	Duden 1956	Examples with both dative and genitive after *trotz* are listed without comment
	Duden 1985	*trotz* + dative common in Austria; elsewhere the genitive is usual
textbooks and grammars for British learners of German 1930–	Macpherson & Strömer 1934	*trotz* with the dative is "not very good German"
	Dickins 1963	*trotz* "usually" governs genitive, but also found with dative
	Kellett 1964	Genitive after *trotz* is "less common now"
	Johnson 1971	*trotz* occurs with dative or "more commonly" genitive
	Borgert & Nyhan 1976	*trotz* is "also" found with the dative, considered "less correct"
	Durrell 1991	*trotz* is "commonly used with a dative in everyday colloquial speech" but this is "regarded as substandard"

5.10 Conclusion

This chapter has provided a preliminary exploration of the history of how the German language has been presented to English-speaking learners, and does no more than illustrate some directions for further research. However, some tentative conclusions can be drawn. First, it is clear that what 'learning German' means has changed greatly from century to century and indeed from decade to decade. Varying importance has been paid to the goal of real communication, and with varying imagined interlocutors or correspondents; such changes are reflected in whether, when and how forms of address, but also typefaces and handwriting, are presented to pupils. Our examination of pronunciation and word order revealed how textbook authors' understanding of the sound system and grammatical structures to be taught has changed too in the light of evolving linguistic theory, and sometimes even ahead of it: Witter (1865) was certainly ahead of his time in describing three of the five German sentence intonation patterns in his primer for German migrant children in the USA. Finally, the language itself has never ceased to change. And while discussions about the codification, prescription and maintenance of national standard languages have tended to focus on those processes within the nation state itself, we have seen here that similar, parallel codification takes place beyond its borders too, for the benefit of foreign learners.[46] For a global language like English, indeed, whose non-native speakers outnumber native speakers, such codification is arguably as important the "native" tradition itself. We cannot make that claim for German. Nevertheless, as an example of such a 'parallel' tradition – British textbooks of German – this chapter has demonstrated how studying foreign-language textbooks can offer an additional perspective on the relationship between developments in a national (and in this case also plurinational) language and their codification. As we have seen, authors of materials for foreign learners, untroubled by historical loyalties to a national standard variety, do not always slavishly follow the codex as set out by native-speaker tradition. The evidence here does suggest that while advanced reference grammars like that of Durrell (1991, 1996, 2002) are, with exceptions, generally close to native-speaker codifications and descriptions, many textbook authors offer simpler accounts that reflect widespread but not yet definitively codified native-speaker usage. Fischer's (2000) account of *wegen* + dative as "generally accepted in standard German", even though *wegen* + genitive remains the shibboleth of the educated German native speaker's loyalty to the standard language, is one such example, though admittedly an isolated one. Another example is Wendeborn's early adoption of the simple binary *du/Sie* system in forms of address. More recent examples are the increasing tendency over the course of the twentieth century to present weak forms of *backen* rather than strong, and to teach imperative formation without *-e*. Perhaps the most interesting finding concerns the preposition *trotz*. While accounts for native speakers still distinguish between *wegen* and *trotz* – two cases are acceptable for *trotz*, but only the genitive is acceptable for *wegen* – the accounts for British learners, even those given in advanced reference grammars, have since the 1930s unanimously presented the two as members of the same category: properly genitive prepositions that may be found governing the dative. This is all the more striking given the history of *trotz* as a preposition that, in fact, took the dative and whose use with the genitive was (unsuccessfully) stigmatized in the later nineteenth century. 'Parallel' prescriptions do not always run quite parallel.

---

46 For a still-dominant theory of language standardization, see Milroy (1999; 1st ed. 1985). On language prescription as a national or patriotic task, see Percy & Davidson (2012), which includes McLelland (2012a), where the section 5.9 and some other small sections of this chapter were first published. On standardization in German and other Germanic languages, see, for example, Linn & McLelland (2002), and Deumert & Vandenbussche (2003).

Chapter 6 –
Don't mention the war? German culture and history in the teaching of German, 1900–2000

6.1. Introduction: the "hidden curriculum"

> *In teaching Modern Languages we aim at teaching the principal features of the life, character and thought of great foreign nations*

(Breul 1899: 8, emphasis in original)

Language teaching is never just about language. There is always, in Byram's words, a "hidden curriculum", the part of language teaching that conveys "information, attitudes, images, and perhaps even prejudice about the people and countries where the particular language is spoken" (Byram 1989: 1).[1] It is evident already in the front covers of two different editions of the same series, *Teach Yourself German* (Figure 6.1) – the cover of the Romanian edition, shown on the left, peddles cosy images of pre-modern towns, Lederhosen, and beer, perhaps intended to appeal to Romanians with German heritage who may respond to a romanticised, folkloric representation of the "home" German culture;[2] in the latest British edition, meanwhile, the photo of the German *Bundestag* dome – a conscious architectural symbol of transparent democracy – is an equally deliberate choice. The history of that hidden curriculum is the subject of this chapter, which is, it should be made clear at the outset, no more than a first staking out of some of the territory, with some illustrations of possible approaches to the material.[3] It will become clear, however, that the teaching of a foreign language is inseparable from the teaching of culture, and that the teaching of culture (however understood) is in turn always ideologically determined.

---

1 On the notion of the "hidden curriculum" in education more generally, see Apple (1979, 4th ed. 2004).

2 Carl & Stevenson (2007: 100) report that members of German minority communities in Central Europe (Hungary, in the instance cited) may "have an emotional allegiance to traditional cultural practices", though this is likely to be less true of the younger generation. I return to the question of stereotypes of German culture in 6.9 below.

3 I have limited the discussion here to textbooks, but of course other materials such as the films produced by CILT and BBC School Television (1987), not to mention the multimedia materials accompanying coursebooks, became increasingly important in the second half of the twentieth century.

Figure 6.1: The front covers of Coggle & Schenke, transl. Dumitru (2009) and Coggle & Schenke (2003)

6.1.1. The twentieth century:
from aping the native speaker to creating world citizens

Textbooks of German have always taught culture, more or less implicitly – whether it be through crude stereotypes in tenth-century glosses; in model dialogues on negotiating a deal for the late-medieval cloth-merchant; or the art of complimenting modelled in eighteenth-century textbooks for those about to embark on their Grand Tour; or in introductions to German literature and thinking from the eighteenth century onwards.[4] But it was only with the Reform Movement that teachers began to reflect explicitly on how culture should be taught. In essence, the progression in approaches to teaching culture in the twentieth century can be summed up in two statements of aspirations, from opposite ends of the century. Kron (1916: 3) stated in his preface to *Der Kleine Deutsche* that his criterion in selecting material from "the virtually immeasurable field of

---

4   Van der Lubbe (2008) traces the construction of the notion of Germany in eighteenth-century grammars of German for English learners. Germany is consistently represented as a cultured nation with a prestige tongue: "particularly certain authors are esteemed and certain towns; it is associated firstly with the power and longevity of the Holy Roman Empire and then with the nobility of the Hannoverians; […] and the profile and status of German as a literary language is raised to that of French, so that the learner is brought to look at Germany as a whole as a refined, cultivated civilization" (p. 70). Langer (2008) examined German language and identity in America through school grammars over the period 1860–1918.

250

German cultural life" (*schier unermeßliche Gebiet des deutschen Kulturlebens*) was to cover only "what a German of a good average education must know and indeed does know, i. e. what counts as general education" (*was ein Deutscher von guter Durchschnittsbildung wissen muß und wohl auch weiß, also das, was in den Rahmen allgemeiner Bildung gehört*). At the other end of the century stands Michael Byram's aspiration for language teaching that it should develop intercultural speakers with certain attributes – not just knowledge and skills of the kind Kron had in mind, but also attitudes (including "curiosity and openness, readiness to suspend disbelief" in the face of the unexpected), and critical cultural awareness (Byram 1997, summarized by Risager 2007: 224–225). For, as the title of Risager's book suggests (*Language and Culture Pedagogy. From a National to a Transnational Paradigm*), the aspirations of MFL educationalists shifted in the twentieth century from seeking to produce learners who would successfully imitate the cultural attributes of the native speaker of a specific national language, to developing learners with *inter*cultural competences that were not language-specific and that would be transferable to new contexts – Risager wrote of developing "world citizens". The reasons for this shift are complex, but they include a shift away from emphasis on national philologies and literatures, increasing globalization, and, arguably, the search for a new justification of the importance of languages in the curriculum. Accordingly, early in the twenty-first century, in the National Curriculum document for modern foreign languages at Key Stage 3, the summary of the importance of foreign language learning to the National Curriculum begins:

> Through the study of a foreign language, pupils understand and appreciate different countries, cultures, people and communities – and as they do so, begin to think of themselves as citizens of the world as well as of the United Kingdom.

(The National Curriculum for England www.qca.org.uk/nc, revised 2004, p. 14)

In between these two statements came the *Kulturkunde* movement of the 1920s and 1930s – the search for the essence of a particular national culture and character (see 6.3 below) – and, after World War II, the reaction to that movement in the desire to query the kind of stereotypes that it had encouraged. I return to both of these points below, although, as in the preceding chapters, my focus is not on developments in pedagogical thinking per se, but rather on the consequences for how German culture is represented – or constructed – in textbooks.

The representation of "culture" in textbooks has, compared to other aspects of the history of modern foreign language textbooks in Europe, received a good degree of attention. (The very notion of *culture* is itself problematic, but here I use it as a short-hand to refer to the "hidden curriculum" defined by Byram above, and that has variously been called *culture, Landeskunde, civilization, background studies, area studies* and *cultural studies*. Byram used the term Cultural Studies (Byram 1987: 3), a term I prefer to avoid in this historical survey since it risks confusion with specific movements, whether it be the ideologically loaded German *Kulturkunde* up to 1945, or the later tradition of British (critical) Cultural Studies.) That analysing the representation of culture is a

251

highly ideological undertaking is illustrated by the earliest such study of textbooks of German, undertaken by Stöbe (1939). Stöbe's chief concern was the representation of contemporary National Socialism in English textbooks of German; he declared himself on the whole satisfied with the positive representation of National Socialist Germany in the 35 English textbooks he examined, but was concerned to find Jewish, Communist and other writers *dem deutschen Wesen fremd* 'foreign to the German essence' receiving attention (Stöbe 1939: 52; cf. Wegner 1999: 19).[5] In recognition of this ideologically weighted nature of textbook writing, comparative studies aimed at improving textbooks, according to their own ideological lights, were already taking place after World War I, at least as far as history textbooks were concerned, and again in the aftermath of World War II as Part of a UN initiative for bilateral textbook exchange (cf. Dance 1955, UNESCO 1953 and other references there); and such comparisons remained a focus of the Braunschweig Institute for International Textbook Research (now the Georg Eckert Institute), including the studies of representations of France and Germany in a collection published in 1954 (Internationales Schulbuchinstitut 1954, including Salewsky 1954). Other French-German comparisons include Minder (1953) on French and German readers, and Diehl (1975) on Germany in readers for French learners (1879–1970); Krauskopf (1985) on the reciprocal images of Germany and France in MFL language materials; and Lißmann (1983) on French books for learning German. The articles in the volume *Perceptions of History* (Berghahn & Schissler 1987a) compare perceptions of history in Germany, Britain and the United States, as do those in Schissler & Soysal (2005), especially Soysal et al. (2005), on projections of identity in French and German History and Civics textbooks, and Anklam & Grindel (2010) on French, German and Polish history books. But it is only comparatively recently that systematic comparative study of textbooks has begun to extend to language textbooks, as Ernst Hinrichs observed in his foreword to the first collected volume of such studies (Doyé 1991: 7). There have been more or less recent studies of the "image of Germany" (the *Deutschlandbild*) in German textbooks in the USA, France, the Netherlands, Denmark, Sweden, Poland, and Finland,[6] as well as Ammer's comparison of German textbooks produced in West and East Germany between 1955 and the mid-1980s (Ammer 1988). The treatment of German history in recent textbooks of German was considered by Thimme (1996) and Maijala (2004 and 2006, examining books for French, Norwegian, Finnish, Estonian and British learners).[7] Exceptionally, even the history of teaching German culture

---

5   For the majority of the 35 textbooks that Stöbe examined, Stöbe had attestations of their use from different parts of England; for older books (1920s and earlier), he took the number of editions or reprints as an indication of their popularity (Stöbe 1939: 9). The texts are listed on pp. 10–18 of his dissertation.

6   See for the USA Krampikowski (1991), for France Krauskopf (1985), for the Netherlands Becher & Hartung (1996), for Denmark Fink (2003), for Sweden Sörensen & Thunander (1980), for Poland Gierlak (2001, 2003 for the years 1933–1945), and for Finland Maijala (2007).

7   Maijala's corpus of British textbooks consisted of *Durchblick* (Hares et al. 1994), *Überblick* (Hares & Timm 1994, 2nd ed. 2001), *Brennpunkt* (Sandry et al. 1994, 2000), and *Zeitgeist* 1 & 2 (McCrorie et al. 2001a, b).

in England has received serious attention. Studies that have dealt specifically with the "image of Germany" (*Deutschlandbild*) in materials for *English* learners of German include Stöbe (1939), Lütkens (1959a), Hierl (1972, a diachronic study covering the years 1945–1969),[8] Johnson (1973),[9] Doerk (1990), and Maijala (2007, on German "everyday life" in British and Finnish textbooks).

A substantial comparative historical study by Anke Wegner (1999) compared the teaching of German culture in France and England in the twentieth century and concluded that teaching in both countries was largely determined by distinct national discourses, with France emphasizing the *citoyenneté nationale*, while British textbooks increasingly moved towards inculcating a "sense of European identity" (Wegner 1999: 333). Wegner's finding is the very reverse of what one might have expected in the light of the two countries' historical and current attitudes to the EEC and then the EU – it is France, after all, that has been committed to increasing European integration, with Britain keeping a sceptical distance. Indeed, we shall see below that textbooks authors may seek to offer to some extent a counterbalance to prevailing policy and social attitudes, something which makes their study as social and cultural artefacts particularly rewarding. As well as complementing studies like those just cited, of how home and foreign cultures and their histories are treated in civics, geography and historiography in critical textbook analysis, examining cultural representations in language textbooks is a part of social history in its own right (the approach taken by Buttjes 1991: 31), taking its place alongside examinations of representations in the mass media (Hughes 1994, Theobald 1999) or wider historical comparisons of British and German education such as that of Weber (2008), for example.

6.1.2 An interpretation of interpretations?

How can we study the history of cultural representations in textbooks, the "interpretation of an interpretation", to paraphrase Mennecke (1991: 39), or, to use another paradigm, the construction of knowledge through discourse (or rather through images *and* discourse)? To date, such studies have generally been undertaken from the perspective

---

8 Hierl examined American and British readers, as well as readers produced by both German states, over the time period 1945–1969. He examined 64 "*Lesebücher*" (actually a very diverse group including course books and literary anthologies as well as "readers") that he described as intended for "grammar" schools, plus a further eighteen for students or adults (all listed by Hierl 1972: 248–252). Many of the books listed are older, often decades older, than the dates given by Hierl suggest (he seems to have given only the reprint date of the copy he used), and there are numerous errors in bibliography (e.g. the *Ealing Course in German* is not by W. Ealing!) and categorization (for example, Grundy's *Brush Up Your German* is hardly a grammar-school reader).

9 The textbooks investigated listed by Johnson (1973: 44–45) are the *Deutsches Leben* series, *Deutsches Land und Deutsches Volk* (Tudor & Heydorn 1956–1959, 5th reprint 1967), *Fahrt ins Blaue* (Sutcliffe 1960, 1961, 2nd ed. 1964), *Heute Abend* (Kelber 1938, 1948), *Ich lerne Deutsch* (Fenn & Fangl 1954, 5th reprint 1968), *Living German* (Buckley 3rd ed. 1972), *Lustiges Lernen* (Jones 1965–1967), *Das Schöne Deutschland* (Anderson 1956, 1960), *Wir Lernen Deutsch* 1 (Paxton 1970), *Modern German for Adults* (Cook 1962). In addition, Johnson included 23 readers in his corpus (listed in Johnson 1973: 52–54).

of the MFL didactician. That is the approach of Risager (2007), whose excellent nuanced historical survey, tracing a shift from a national to a "transnational" focus, must be seen in the context of her work on the pedagogical aim of developing "intercultural competence".[10] Reinfried's history of visual material in French language learning materials for German pupils (1992) is, between the lines, implicitly also a history of the teaching of culture (and indeed a history of methodologies more broadly). It is also possible to critique the source material as a Foucaultian archaeology of knowledge (thus Wegner 1999, nominally at least: p. 13), or from the framework of Critical Discourse Analysis (as applied by Theobald 1999 to British media representations of Germany) in order examine how notions such as nation, gender, or class are constructed, for instance. International comparisons such as that by Maijala (2004) can be instructive; Wegner's comparison of French and English representations of German culture through time was already noted (Wegner 1999), while the joint project resulting in the volumes edited by Doyé (1991) and Byram (1993) exemplifies a synchronic and reciprocal approach: Doyé (1991) presented studies on how Britain was represented in eight 1980s textbook series of English for German learners, while Byram (1993) published the results of the opposite perspective: representations of German culture in five textbook series of German for English learners form the 1980s and early 1990s.[11] Further possible comparative dimensions are possible: representations of Germany as self and as other, by comparing textbooks of German for foreign learners with those for native speakers, or indeed by comparing GFL textbooks produced in Germany (or the Germanys: Ammer 1988) with those produced abroad.[12]

The methodology adopted varies according to the purpose of the undertaking. If one is explicit about the ultimate purpose of the analysis, one may have more or less explicit standards according to which textbooks are to be judged. Such was the approach taken by the contributors to the volumes edited by Byram and Doyé, where the desirability of developing "intercultural competence/ political education/ tertiary socialization" (thus Doyé's formulation in Doyé 1993: 25) was explicitly stated, and where the editors accordingly agreed a list of desirable "minimum content", such that "a book which fails to include a substantial part of this 'critical content' has to be considered deficient" (Byram 1993: 36–40, here p. 36). Alternatively, the approach may be a critical "close reading", more or less informed by an explicit theoretical framework such as Critical Discourse Analysis (e.g. Theobald 1999, noted above), or merely by measuring *against a priori* ideals such as accuracy, representativeness, realism and educational potential (as in Doyé 1991 and Byram 1993), though of course each of these is open to challenge as

---

10 A brief historical overview is also given in Friz (1991: 6–13); Apelt (1967) is a detailed study of the so-called *Kulturkunde* movement (to which I return below).

11 The textbook series examined are *Deutsch konkret* (Neuner 1983, 1984, published in Germany), *Los geht's* (Aufderstrasse 1986–1988), *Deutsch Heute* (Sidwell & Capoore 1983–1985), *ZickZack* (Goodman-Stephens et al., 1987–1989), and *Einfach toll* (Smith 1985–1991, Bates & Smith 1992). The last three are discussed at various points in the chapter below.

12 For two recent examinations of Nazi era German primers for native speakers, from quite different perspectives, see Pfalzgraf (2011) and (with a much smaller sample of texts) McLelland (2012b).

subjective. It can prove useful to describe textbook content according to a number of thematic categories, as did Johnson (1973), Krauskopf (1985) and Doerk (1990).[13] Reinfried's history of the use of images in the teaching of French to German speakers was, in contrast, deliberately limited to a "positivist stock-taking" (Reinfried 1992: 7, *eine solche positivistische Bestandaufnahme*), as a necessary first step towards reflecting on methods of using visual material in MFL teaching. In the light of such a diversity of approaches, given the multitude of possible comparative dimensions and the many possible purposes with which such a historical study might be written and read, my own approach in the following is deliberately eclectic. It seeks to demonstrate fruitful lines of enquiry rather than to offer the last word on any one of them. In the main, I have followed Reinfried's "stock-taking" chronological approach, but have also sought to demonstrate the value of paying attention to different aspects at different points in that history: the newly important role of images in the early part of the twentieth century (6.2); the treatment of contemporary Germany in the 1930s (6.3); the treatment of German history and of Germany's position in Europe after World War II and after reunification (6.4, 6.6, 6.7); teaching "memory" (6.5), including what maps say about the remembering or forgetting of changing borders (6.8); and confronting stereotypes (6.9). Finally, sections 6.10 and 6.11 provide an analysis of the theme of sport and a critical analysis of constructions of gender in textbooks of German.

6.2 The early twentieth century: pictures speak volumes

Some pedagogues had been advocating the systematic use of pictures in language teaching since the seventeenth century at least, as Reinfried (1992) has carefully documented: Comenius in the seventeenth century, the so-called Philanthropists in the eighteenth century; and many in the Reform Movement of the late nineteenth century (cf. 3.10 above). Nevertheless, the *widespread* use of pictures typifies twentieth-century textbooks by contrast with earlier centuries, for the twentieth century was the first in which it was technically straightforward to use images in a systematic way; photographs also became available, and their increasing availability facilitated the inclusion of realia in teaching German from the turn of the century onwards, even though – as Breul (1899: 81) lamented, drawing a comparision with Germany – there was no statutory requirement to do so. Pictures speak volumes, as the adage has it, and the selection of pictures – even a small number – arguably has a disproportionate impact on how a book is received and on the world-view that it encourages learners to construct, something that recent re-

---

13 Johnson's "themes" were the geography of Germany, "The German people: external characteristics" (including surnames, physical appearance, and dress), family life, school and university, town and village life, social life and leisure (including "the German Sunday"), police and crime, newspapers and politics, history of Germany, and the GDR. Krauskopf calculated the coverage of topics such as family, history, leisure, literature, school, politics, and landscape; Doerk described the selected textbooks according to their coverage of the following headings: politics, history, economy, geography, family, work, school, leisure and holidays, festivals, food and drink, manners and politeness, sport, fashion, transport, criminality, literature and music, and the media.

search in the field of foreign language didactics has begun to reflect (Hecke & Surkamp 2010, Skorge 2006, 2008).[14] I therefore begin this historical survey by considering the impact of images in early twentieth-century textbooks of German.

The very earliest pictures in textbooks of German pre-date the *Realien* movement and the notion of conveying something about the culture of the language to be learnt. Some, aimed at young children, took the form of object lessons, where a lesson was based around a familiar object (cf. Trotter 1898, Lowe 1903, both discussed in Chapter 3); others reflect nineteenth-century British notions of character-building education. Some of the images in Beresford Webb (1903; originally published 1896), illustrating little stories, are explicitly colonial: the tale of the courageous white hunter who shoots a lion, despite being wounded by it (p. 20–21); two white children who get lost in the Australian bush are rescued thanks to the tracking skills of an Aborigine (Lesson XVII, pp. 24–27):

> Nun sind bekanntlich die Eingeborenen sehr scharfsichtig und können oft Spuren finden, welche für uns Europäer unmerkbar sind.
> Zufällig wohnte einer von diesen Eingeborenen auf meinem Gute.
> Ich ließ ihn sogleich zu mir kommen und versprach ihm eine gute Belohnung, wenn er die Kinder finden sollte.

> 'Now it is well-known that the natives are very sharp-eyed and can often find traces that we Europeans can't detect.
> Coincidentally one of these natives lived on my property.
> I had him come to me at once and promised him a good reward if he found the children.'

These few sentences exemplify both the unreflecting relaying of stereotypes and the total absence of critical cultural awareness that educationalists like Byram and Risager were working to address in the later twentieth century. In Beresford Webb (1903), it is a well-known fact (*bekanntlich*) that the "natives" have very keen eyes; but also that such people must be offered a good reward in order to act to help children in danger. The statement that one of these natives "coincidentally" lived on the narrator's property makes breathtaking assumptions measured by today's sensibilities, for it is far from coincidence that an Aborigine lives on the white man's property, since the white man simply arrived on land that Aborigines had long occupied, and declared it "his". In the illustration, the Aborigine is crouched low, as he looks for tracks, but the pose also makes him appear subservient; he brandishes a totally superfluous boomerang to indicate his primitive status (cf. Figure 6.2). In the same volume, Lesson XXVIII narrates a conversation between two white colonials in India. The illustration shows a young Indian boy astride an elephant, while the text has one colonist lamenting to another that day-labourers get lazier the better one treats them; elephants make better workers than do the Indians, for they

---

14 I have been unable to obtain Dietrich Sturm's 1990 Kassel dissertation, *Zur Visualisierung von Lehrwerken für Deutsch als Fremdsprache – historische und kulturkontrastive Aspekte* (Diss. Kassel, 1990, available on microfiche).

Figure 6.2: Beresford Webb (1903: 26 & 38)

are the most obedient and most useful animals there are, if you train them well (*die folg-samsten und nützlichsten Tiere, die es giebt*, p. 39). Again, one is struck by the stereotyping of Indians as lazy and ungrateful, the implication that Indian workers and animals are virtually interchangeable as long as the work gets done, and the total absence of critical reflection on the power relationships of colonial India. Otto & Wright (1889) likewise adhered to inculcating the ideals of Empire (cf. Weber 2008) with a series of texts in English for translation into German which narrate the voyages of Captain James Cook, highlighting both the dangers that Cook bravely faced ("the New Zealanders were very thievish and unfriendly", p. 106), and the paternalistic care of the English captain for the men under his command.[15] These examples – some of which seem crass by today's standards – illustrate well how foreign language textbooks contribute to the overall socialization of children and inculcation of their society's norms and values.

The *Pictorial German Course* (Baumann 1910 10th ed., 1st ed. 1902) followed a modified direct method, adapting David Rees's earlier French pictorial course. Each chapter opens with a pictorial scene, with numbers corresponding to superscript numbering in the matching text on the facing page.[16] The influence of the Reform Movement is evident in the series of four pictures depicting the four seasons (cf. Hölzel's series; see 3.10); the majority of drawings, however, depict everyday upper middle-class scenes of home life that arguably reflected the background of the learners (see Figure 6.3): going to school, visiting the post-office, barber, tailor, tobacconist, dress-maker, jeweller, etc., as

---

15 Brenkmann (1909?) also alludes to Britain's colonial ties to India; cf. Wegner (1999: 132–133); Wegner dates the book to 1909, citing Rowlinson (1986: 93); Rowlinson himself points out that the work was "still in print" then, but was "apparently published some decades earlier". In fact it was first published in 1885, and it is not clear to what extent the section cited by Wegner, which refers to Queen Victoria inspecting troops in 1882, differs from the original edition.

16 The identification of items by the pictures alone is not always unambiguous, however. In lesson 2, for example, a gentleman entering the living room is labelled not as "man", or "father", but rather *der Onkel*. Explaining this in the target language might haven been tricky.

Figure 6.3: Baumann (1910: 2, 18)

Figure 6.4: Colour illustrations of Nuremberg and Berlin
in Black's *First German Book* (Althaus 1916)

well as dining out and attending the theatre – a revival, *mutatis mutandis*, of such scenes found in manuals from the seventeenth century onwards (cf. Chapters 2 and 3).

It is worth noting that the *Pictorial German Course* includes two photos – one a Berlin streetscape, the other an unnamed port city. Other early examples of photos – illustrations of German coins in Ungoed (1912) and German tennis and football teams in Chaffey (1907) – were discussed in 3.10. Althaus's *First German Book* (1916) contains the earliest colour pictures in a textbook that I am aware of: paintings of the market in

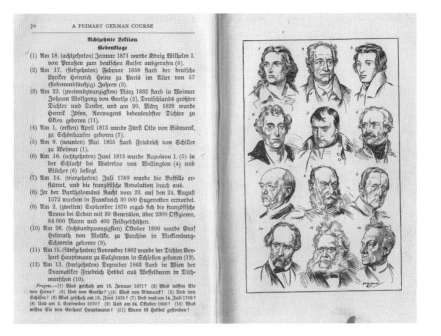

Figure 6.5: Siepmann (1913: 70–71)

Nuremberg and of Unter den Linden in Berlin (see Figure 6.4) – the modest beginnings of efforts ever since to make textbooks ever more visually appealing.

In the earliest texts, even once the shift was made from inculcating values to serve the British Empire, part of the overall goal of British Public Schools in the nineteenth century (cf. Weber 2008) to focussing on realia of German culture, the emphasis on the great white males and their achievements remained. Siepmann's full page of famous heads in his *Primary German Course* (1913) is a visually striking case in point (cf. Figure 6.5). The twelve heads featured (not all German) are: (top row) Schiller, Goethe, and Heine, (second row) Wellington, Napoleon and Blucher, (third row) Bismarck, Emperor Wilhelm I, and Count Moltke, and (bottom row) Ibsen, the Austrian playwright Friedrich Hebbel, and Gerhart Hauptmann. In sum, the great heads thematicize German(ic) military might sandwiched between older and more recent literary greatness – an interesting selection given that this is the only explicit treatment of German realia in this text.[17] The Anglophile Siepmann's faith in the achievements of Empire is evident in the fact that the only other passage with real-world relevance in his volume describes the Crystal

---

17 The list of memorable dates on the facing page also includes important historical events that have neither a direct German connection, nor a direct link to the illustrations, notably the St Bartholomew's Day massacre of the Huguenots (1572) and the French revolution and (1789).

Figure 6.6:
Siepmann (1913: 51 Crystal Palace)

Palace, built for the 1851 Exhibition and still used at the time for concerts and shows (see Figure 6.6).

Contemporary with Siepmann's *Primary German Course*, Mutschmann – who was my predecessor by a century at Nottingham (then University College Nottingham) – arranged his collection of passages for prose translation into German so as "to have in every second passage some reference to German or to things German." He had initially intended to compile a book entirely made up of such extracts, but had found that in English, "literature dealing with German is rather scarce" (Mutschmann 1914: 3). As can be seen from the list of Mutschmann's German-related passages below, his criteria for inclusion were very similar to Siepmann's: literature and literary figures (Luther, Wieland, Goethe, Schiller), history, especially great battles (Waterloo, Sedan) and emperors (Charles V, Frederic I and II) predominate, as well as some nods to the experiences of the gentleman tourist in German-speaking lands. The passages are:[18]

Goethe commences his Collegiate life at Leipzig (G. H. Lewes); Through the North German Plain (Bayard Taylor); Walter Scott and German poetry (George L. Craik); Nuremberg (Anna Jameson); The Ballad in Germany (*Edinburgh Review*); Charles the Fifth's Escape from Inspruck [sic] (W. Robertson); Schiller's 'Robbers' (Thomas de Quincy); A vision of the Rhine (Walter Scott); Winckelmann (Walter Pater); The German *Limes* or *Pfahlgraben* (E. Gibbon); The Theatre at Weimar (Henry Crabb Robinson); A Model German Country Hausfrau (Author of 'Elizabeth and her German Garden'); Goethe's Conversation with Gillies (R. P. Gillies); Frederic I and Frederic II (E. Gibbon); Wieland (G. Moir); The *Hofbräuhaus* (E. V. Lucas); On Pastoral Poetry (Hugh Blair); Frederic the Great and Voltaire (Lord Macaulay); Goethe's Minor Poems (Thomas Carlyle); Tramping Through Bohemia (Bayard Taylor); English and German Ideals of Freedom (C. H. Herford); *Frau Professor* (Author of 'Elizabeth and her German Garden');

---

18 Eggeling's *Advanced German Prose Composition* (1933) is beyond the scope of this study, because it is explicitly intended for College and University use – Eggeling was a Reader in German at the University of Edinburgh. It should be noted, however, that Eggeling drew on many of the same authors as Mutschmann (Carlyle, de Quincy, Lewes, Hazlitt, Gissing, Lucas, Pater) and likewise made sure that figures like Goethe, Schiller and Luther were covered.

Waterloo (J. R. Green); Luther's Sense of Satanic Presence (W. E. H. Lecky); The Extent of Germany and the Origin of its Inhabitants (A. Murphy's 'Tacitus'); Goethe and Schiller (G. H. Lewes); Effects of Frederic the Great's Victory at Rossbach (Lord Macaulay); Student Life at Jena in 1820 (John Russell); Sedan ('Daily News'); From Luther's 'Table-Talk' (William Hazlitt)

(Mutschmann 1914: selected list of contents – all those with a reference "to German or to things German")

6.3 Contemporary Germany in 1930s textbooks

After a lull in the 1920s, a significant landmark in the renewed wave of German study in the 1930s was *Germany. A Companion to German Studies* (ed. Bithell 1932). Even though it was not primarily intended for use in schools,[19] it deserves attention here as the first comprehensive introduction to Germany written by specialists from British universities, being intended to express "the British view of German subjects" and to give a "picture of British scholarship as a whole in the field of German" (p. v). It thus marked the growing strength of German Studies as a discipline in British universities, although Bithell was at pains to emphasize that both German-born colleagues in the UK and colleagues in Germany had been carefully consulted (p. v). Bithell's preface acknowledged the importance of realia, commenting that "The intensive study of medieval texts as a philological exercise is yielding to a more practical concern with the Realien of the modern period" (p. vii), but his optimism that it was possible to pin down the essence of Germanness also bore the influence of the new, racially-tinged *Kulturkunde* movement that had gained momentum in the 1920s in Germany, led by figures such as Eduard Schön (1925, 1926). The *Kulturkunde* movement (lit. 'knowledge of culture', hence loosely, "cultural studies", analogous to *Erdkunde*, *Geschichtskunde* for geography and history) expressed the belief that it was possible to 'get at' the essence of the culture of any given ethnic group or race.[20] It was in part a reaction to the shortcomings perceived in the realia approach, in particular the danger of imparting only very superficial and fragmentary cultural knowledge; one must seek instead to understand the underlying essence of a people. As Bithell noted,

---

19 It followed the success of a similar volume on *Spain* edited by Allison Peers (1929), published at a time when the numbers taking Spanish at school were tiny. The book was presumably intended primarily for students and other well-educated readers. I also note here in the context of teaching German culture in the 1930s Steinhauer (1939), though I have not had the opportunity to inspect it.

20 How this approach worked in practice in foreign language classrooms is illustrated by Raddatz in his study of *Englandkunde* in German schools up to 1945 (Raddatz 1977). For a detailed critique of the movement see Apelt (1967); Reinfried (1992: 210–214) gives a very useful sketch of the key features of the movement; cf. also Risager (2007: 31).

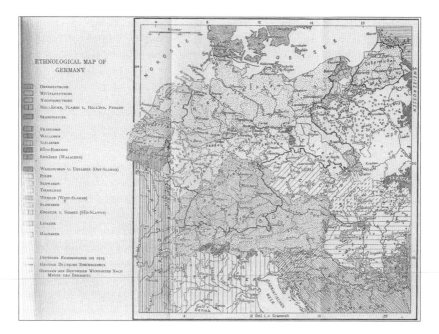

Figure 6.7: Fold-out Ethnological Map of Germany (Bithell 1932)

> The hoary past we reverenced we are now asked to regard as interesting only in so far as it explains the present. We know now that we must study Germany, not merely German; we must follow the Germans themselves and busy ourselves with Deutschkunde; fortunately that is, racially considered, part and parcel of Englischkunde, so that we may harmonize our study of Germany with the conviction we should all have that the first of all studies is for us the study of our own race.

> (Bithell 1932: viii)

Here Bithell consciously echoed very closely the slogan of the German *Kulturkunde* movement that *Alle Kulturkunde ist Deutschkunde* – lit. "all cultural study is German study", i.e. the cultural study of any culture is the study of one's own (cf. Risager 2007: 31, Reinfried 1992: 213). With two chapters on history, four on literature, and one each on painting and music (and none on geography, economics, or social conditions), the culture that Bithell's volume presented was Culture with a capital C. Bithell's attention to *Deutschkunde* here – and, indeed, already in his earlier volume *Advanced Prose Composition* (Bithell 1929), aimed at students working towards a degree – was in keeping with the general mood among British educationalists concerned with German in the late 1920s and in the 1930s, as the numerous attestations gathered by Stöbe (1939: 5–7) from textbook prefaces and from teachers show. These include such comments as "I think it is safe to say there is a great amount of Deutschlandkunde in the English schools where German is taught" (Mr Bird, Hitching, Hertfordshire, cited Stöbe 1939: 7); "The subject matter of these passages has been drawn from the field of German history, topography, and legend; it is thus thoroughly national in character, dealing with 'Land und Leute'" (Fiedler 1928: 6, cited Stöbe 1939: 6).

A reflection of the tendency of the time to identify peoples on racial lines (not just in Nazi Gemany) is Bithell's inclusion, alongside physical and political maps of Germany, of an "ethnological map" of central Europe showing various Germanic, Romance, Slav and other peoples (implicitly grouped as such in the key on the left), as well as the German linguistic boundaries (Figure 6.7).

In Bithell's opening chapter on "The Country: its peoples, its language and its thought", he asserts that *Deutsch* is the name for a number of tribes (*Stämme*) "which have to a large extent retained their special characteristics to this day" (p. 14). This statement is followed by four pages of generalizations about the different regions of Germany (or ethnicities, for Bithell), concluding that "One characteristic is common to all German tribes: unmitigated honesty" (p. 17), and that "A German takes his time with a thing, but he exhausts it" (p. 18), although Bithell does take issue with the physical stereotype of the German ("the pot-bellied, bushy-bearded, blob-nosed, rubicund German", p. 17).[21] As for German thought, "there are two parallel phases which represent the two tendencies of the German mind: one to truth and the application of truth, that is, to logic and practical science; and the other to an imaginative and emotional illumination of truth" (p. 26). Despite this apparently uncritical catalogue of Germanness, Bithell reverted to the influence of the *Kulturkunde* movement at the end of his opening chapter with slightly more critical distance, and even hinted at what such essentialist views of Germanness might lead to:

> [...] This new education aims at shaping the man; but the sum and substance of education is culture. *Kulturkunde* is one of the main aspects of contemporary German education; in studying a language, for instance, not the language itself is the thing, but the culture of which the language is the expression. There is a marked tendency, however, to regard the study of all culture other than German culture as a help to the intelligence of German culture: the most vital of all sciences to a German, the Germans think, is *Deutschkunde*.

(Bithell 1932: 33).

Bithell went on to hint at fears that Germany might in the near future seek to dominate Europe, and it is on that note that the chapter ends:

> The quickening of mental life by defeat in war has thus led, not to humiliation, but to an intensification of German culture and to heightened race-consciousness. The fiery gospel of a new humanity proclaimed by the expressionists burns less fierce than the gospel of a new Germanism. If this gospel welds the Germans together, as it is intended to do, a German or Germanic hegemony of Europe is

---

21 It is interesting that while a physical stereotype still exists today, it is not the same as that cited by Bithell, but instead tall and muscular, blond, blue-eyed and beardless.

possible, because of the victory of cultured personality over races still floundering in a medley of ideas and with no clear vision of development.

(Bithell 1932: 33)

If Bithell gave an implicit warning that Germany might in the future be a country for Europe to fear, his (relative) note of caution stands in contrast to a number of other textbooks produced for German learners in the 1930s, even once Hitler had come to power in 1933. By far the most extreme example of pro-Nazism is the 1934 edition of Meyer & Nauck's reader for third-year boys, *Das neue Deutschland*. Dr Nauck was a teacher at the Gymnasium Francisceum in Zerbst, and indeed his pupils there contributed some of the reading passages in the book; Meyer taught German at Wygeston Grammar School in Leicester. In its second edition of 1934, Meyer & Nauck's book was characterized by English teachers at the time as "Nazi" (Stöbe 1939: 14), and it had indeed been thoroughly Nazified compared to the first edition (1931). *Guten Morgen* had become *Heil Hitler!* (p. 12); a section on how schoolboys spend their afternoons (when British children would still be in lessons) turned into a description of the Hitler Youth (p. 15). A visiting English teacher expressed his concern that the Hitler Youth was "quite military. You know we don't like that in England", but a German pupil replied with an eager account of the HJ as being just like the Boy Scouts, except that "we Germans like strong military discipline more" than the English, who "prefer their freedom" (p. 16). According to the world-view expressed here, while the English had been democratic for centuries, the fourteen years since the First World War had "shown that a democratic spirit does not suit Germany [...] and so we have given our education a different form" (p. 16). (With hindsight, one is reminded of Erich Fromm's famous analysis of Hitler's rise to power as the result of Germans' "fear of freedom"; Fromm 1942). Chapter 2 – which in the first edition had described the youth movement and the hiking *Wandervögel* – instead described a Hitler Youth hike. Chapter 7 – which in the first edition had included selected articles from the constitution of the Weimar Republic – "has been left out altogether", as the authors laconically noted in their preface (p. vi). The last chapter of the book – which in the first edition bore the title "German leaders" and concluded with a paeon of praise to President von Hindenburg for having had the courage to sign up to the Young Plan in 1929, complete with its 58 years of reparations – was substantially re-written. Hindenburg's signing of the Young Plan was now portrayed as a mistake, a mistake which had been revealed as such by the economic collapse of 1932; Hindenburg had lost much sympathy "through his support for [Germany's] democratic governments" (p. 163). Hitler was portrayed as the young leader naturally succeeding the elderly Hindenburg, a great leader who had now lost his way:

> Der alte Marschall konnte den jungen Revolutionär nicht verstehen und wollte nicht glauben, daß des jungen Führers Pläne zum Wohle Deutschlands wäre. [...] Hitler hat zu jeder Zeit, auch als er als politischer Gegner Hindenburgs auftreten mußte, immer seiner Verehrung für den großen Feldmarschall und Präsidenten Ausdruck gegeben

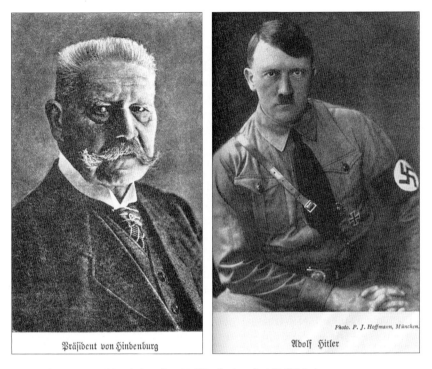

Präsident von Hindenburg   Adolf Hitler

Photo. P. J. Hoffmann, München.

Figure 6.8: Meyer & Nauck (1934): 159 (Hindenburg), 165 (Hitler)

'The old marshal could not understand the young revolutionary and did not believe that the young Hitler's plans were for the good of Germany. […] At all times Hitler, even when forced into the role of Hindenburg's political opponent, always showed his esteem for the great field-marshal'

(Meyer & Nauck 1934: 163)

The supposed natural kinship between Hindenburg and Hitler, both great leaders, was also suggested by the inclusion of photo portraits of each of them, the only such portraits in the book (Figure 6.8).

Another 1930s contribution to teaching German culture by a German author was *Deutsches Land und Deutsches Leben* (Theilkuhl 1936; 1st ed. 1932). The work, whose author was an Assistant at King's College London,[22] showed somewhat more critical distance than Meyer & Nauck. Theilkuhl's second, 1936 edition included "minor alterations" updating recent history, chiefly that "The chapter on Constitution has been replaced by a chapter on History", where, "as throughout the book, the author has tried

---

22 Wolfgang Theilkuhl was Lektor at King's College London from 1928 to 1933, when he was succeeded by Hans Galinsky. My thanks to John Flood for this information.

to state the main facts in an unbiassed [sic] way". Theilkuhl observed coolly, "A German reader may find that it [the book] lacks enthusiasm; enthusiasm would have made it impossible for the book to have been used in English schools" (preface to the second edition, p. vii). Theilkuhl's lack of enthusiasm is, I think, palpable, in his account of German history 1919–1933, which foregrounds negatives rather than listing achievements, as the following extract illustrates:

> After repeated negotiations, Hindenburg recognized a national-socialist cabinet with Hitler as Reichskanzler in January 1933. To secure the new order, political gatherings and demonstrations were forbidden, press censorship introduced, and several thousand communists arrested […] Amongst the most important goals of the national movement are to defend German honour, to reunite Germans living outside the borders with the Reich, to eliminate Jews from public life, and to make Germany economically independent.

(Theilkuhl 1936: 48–49)

Theilkuhl stood firmly in the *Deutschkunde* tradition, for he included a chapter on *Volkskunde* where, like Bithell, he was quite comfortable identifying differences between different Germanic tribes (*Stämme*) which – "despite railway and industry" – still exist today (Theilkuhl 1936: 50). Nevertheless, Stöbe (1939: 16) – loyal to the new regime in his dissertation on the image of Germany in English textbooks – felt that the revisions made did not do justice to the new Germany. To Stöbe's annoyance, Theilkuhl made a point of mentioning that three million emigrants had recently left Germany (Theilkuhl 1936: 48), and Stöbe also criticized the inclusion of Jews and Communists in the chapter on literature. That criticism had evidently already been made of the first edition, for Theilkuhl responded robustly in the preface to the second edition (though perhaps not quite as robustly as he might have):

> That is nonsense. Among the sixty-one writers mentioned there are, as far as the author is aware, six Jews and two communists. And in a chapter dealing with literature, and not with race or politics, it was not advisable to omit entirely writers well known and much appreciated in England.

As the contrasting instances of Nauck & Meyer and Theilkuhl show, attitudes to Nazism in textbooks did not necessarily go along the lines of nationality. Indeed, two other, very popular, textbook series first published in the 1930s were, despite having English authors, largely uncritical in their representation of Nazi Germany, something which might surprise us now but which needs to be seen in the context of the time. There were close ties between Fascist Germany and the English elite at the time, and the British long underestimated Hitler – after all, Chamberlain signed the Munich Agreement with Hitler in September, 1938. The series in question are *Deutsches Leben* (Macpherson 1931, Macpherson & Strömer 1934, 1939, and reader 1937; also revised editions 1940, 1941, 1946, and 1956–1965), and *Brush Up Your German* (Grundy 1931, 1939; also 1950, 1961), originally written for adults but of which at least the first volume was adapted for schools as *Meyers Reisen nach Deutschland* (Grundy 1932), intended as an addition "to the existing works on German *Realien*" (Grundy 1932: v). *Deutsches Leben*, one of the longest-lived twentieth-century textbooks of German,[23] signalled a programmatic shift which the title reflected. For one thing, the title was in German. For most of the history of learning German, textbook titles had been in English and were straightforwardly descriptive, with, if anything, an indication of the method adopted, and – as such differentiations come to be made in the second half of the nineteenth century – the type and level of learner for whom they were intended (e.g. Siepmann 1912, *A primary German course comprising object lessons, a first reader, grammar and exercises*; Osborne & Osborne 1919 *German grammar for science students*). The Reform Movement brought a minor change, as first titles in German appear, such as Alge's *Leitfaden für den ersten Unterricht* (1905), or Kron's *Der Kleine Deutsche* (1916), and Bishop & McKinley's *Ausführliche Deutsche Grammatik in gedrängter Form* (1921). Not only was the title of *Deutsches Leben* in German, however, but the authors aspired to "make a useful and attractive blend of things ancient and modern, which shall justify the title of 'Deutsches Leben'" (Macpherson & Strömer 1931: v). Anke Wegner summed up the approach taken in this series as "everyday topics and all parts of Germany"[24], and also noted the relatively generous attention paid to matters of commerce and industry. Most striking, however, as Wegner also noted, is the uncritical portrayal of National Socialist Germany, though in fact Wegner did not have access to the far more explicitly pro-Nazi first edition (1934), and based her discussion instead on the second, 1939, edition. Wegner singled out a letter describing a parade in Passau, Austria, where *Auslandsdeutsche* from all over the world "brought their greetings" to the *Reichsdeutsche* (1939: 16); accounts of school life and of the 1936 Olympic games in the 1937 reader emphasize physical exercise, strength, discipline, and competitive sport (Wegner 1999: 140), themes which could, incidentally,

---

23 Stöbe (1939: 12) cited a Mr Pask from Great Shelford, Cambridgeshire, who had told him "This course is now widely used in English schools." *Deutsches Leben* was ranked 22nd out of the top 49 texts in a list compiled by Lütkens (1959: 155), and – with 17 "mentions" – it was the highest ranked textbook of all (the first 21 items being literary texts or anthologies; Lütkens' list combined lists of set books from the various examining boards and lists of texts that German teachers known to Lütkens had been using in higher classes). Timms (2011: 40) reminisces about using a pre-war edition of *Deutsches Leben* at school in the early 1950s. *Deutsches Leben* continued to be used – with two revised editions – well into the 1960s (1970 saw the 36th impression of the first volume and 32nd of the second volume), and even in some cases into the 1990s: at least one volume of an edition of *Deutsches Leben* was used at St Ambrose College, Hale Barns, Altrincham in Cheshire, for GCSE preparation in the years 1994–1996 (John Bellamy, former pupil of the school, p.c.). I am very grateful to several members of the public who kindly donated their copies of various editions of *Deutsches Leben*, including Bruce Perkins, who was able to pass on two copies owned by the original authors, A. Macpherson and (for the second and third parts of the revised edition) H. C. Howlett-Jones (Howlett-Bones to his pupils) and used by them in their teaching at Dulwich College. Perkins reported that the German co-author of the second and third parts, Paul Strömer, who taught at a *Gymnasium* in Schwerin, was granted special permission to travel out of the DDR in 1956 to visit Macpherson to work on the revision of the series. Macpherson retired in the same year, and the last two volumes were revised by Howlett-Jones with Strömer.

24 Thus the sub-heading of her section (Wegner 1999: 137, my translation).

also be very prominent in Nazi-era textbooks of English.[25] However, it is the short-lived 1934 edition of the third volume of *Deutsches Leben* that contained the most strikingly pro-Nazi material, with three chapters on life in a labour camp, the Hitler Youth, and the formation of the Nazi stormtroopers (*Sturmabteiling* or S. A.). The preface stated that

> the authors have tried to give a picture representative of all parts of Germany. It is hoped that no one will regard the chapters dealing with contemporary German life as in any sense a form of political propaganda. Any such purpose is far from the authors' thoughts; their one aim to arouse an intelligent and sympathetic interest in the conditions and problems of present-day Germany (p. v).

Despite these hopes, all three chapters were quietly removed in a second edition in 1939 with the laconic comment that "experience showed that in its original form certain material in the third volume was not satisfactory" (Macpherson & Strömer 1939: v). The first of the three problematic chapters dealt with life in a labour-camp, and came complete with two illustrations labelled *Freiwilliger Arbeitsdienst* ('voluntary labour'; cf. Figure 6.9). The majority of the description of the labour camp is quoted verbatim from a German newspaper report. Though it needs to be considered in the context of the time, the opening of the text is astonishing for today's readers, aware of the brutal reality of the labour camps, for it gives the impression of a happy social mix and a healthy lifestyle mixing work and pleasure. Translated into English the opening lines read as follows (see Figure 6.9):

> Um die Zahl de Arbeitslosen zu reduzieren, sind an vielen Stellen Deutschlands Arbeitslager eingerichtet worden. Männer aller Berufe: Arbeiter, Handwerker und Kaufleute wohnen zusammen in einfachen Baracken, Schuppen, Zelten. Sie bauen Straßen oder machen unfruchtbares Land urbar. Oft wird in diesen Lagern neben der regelmäßigen Arbeit auch Sport getrieben.

> 'In order to reduce the number of unemployed, labour camps have been set up in many places in Germany. Men of all professions, workers, tradesmen and businessmen, live together in simple barracks, barns, tents. They build roads or clear uncultivated land. Besides the regular work, there are often also sporting activities in these camps.'[26]

This account is strikingly similar to those given in 1930s textbooks of German for Polish learners described by Gierlak (2001: 360, 362), where unemployed people who would otherwise starve are housed in labour camps, and where mention is likewise made of cheery "voluntary" labourers clearing land. Gierlak (2001: 340) is of the opinion that

---

25 For example, a textbook of English for German girls (Salewsky 1941), highlights Scouts and Girl Guides as a parallel to the Hitler Youth. See also Gierlak (2001: 362, 365) for the 1936 Olympic Games in Polish textbooks of German.

26 See also the passage in English for translation, pp. 146–147.

the authors of Polish textbooks were constrained by the non-aggression pact that Poland and Germany had signed in 1934.[27]

The chapter on labour camps is followed by one on the Hitler Youth,[28] complete with a breathless account of the excitement of attending the Nuremberg rally in September 1933, where "the air trembles with the thundering cries of the men and boys, all thanking the 'Führer' for uniting their riven land" (Macpherson & Strömer 1934: 23, my translation). Again, there are strong similarities here with the enthusiasm of the Hitler Youth at the 1936 Nuremberg rally presented in a 1937 Polish textbook (described by Gierlak 2001: 363), suggesting that these "set pieces" of propaganda made their way quite effectively not just into textbooks for German pupils but also into those for learners of German abroad.[29] The narration of how Hitler's *Sturmabteilung* (stormtroopers) came to be so called is also very sympathetic, portraying Hitler's supporters as having heroically defeated an overwhelming opposition when a meeting at the Hofbräuhaus in Munich on November 4, 1921 got out of hand. The passage concludes:

> Heute soll die S.A. vor allem den Geist der Disziplin und der Kameradschaft pflegen und dadurch die Klassenunterschiede überwinden. Mit wehenden Fahnen ziehen sie aus und gehen waffenlos neben einander: Männer und Jünglinge, Kaufmann und Bauer, Arbeiter und Gelehrter.

> 'Nowadays the S.A. is above all intended to cultivate a spirit of discipline and camaraderie and so to overcome class differences. With flags waving, they parade, walking unarmed alongside one another: men and youths, businessman and farmer, worker and scholar' (p. 33).

Note the strong similarity to a 1938 German textbook of English cited by Macht, with the emphasis on overcoming class differences through the various Nazi organizations:

> In the Hitler-Jugend, in the Reich Labour Service, and in the Army, the German youth does not care for class or position, profession and education, birth and money. It is thus that the unified National Socialist nation is being constructed.

> Heinrich Fischer's *Englisches Unterrichtswerk* (Breslau/Bielefeld/Leipzig, 1938), cited by Macht (1994: n. p.)

Taken together, the three chapters in Macpherson & Strömer (1934) suggest that the authors gave sympathetic credence to the apparently socialist aspects of National Socialism, and had not grasped either its fascism or racism.

If Macpherson & Strömer (1934) represented a naive faith in National Socialism – as both socialist and promoting national unity – the second, 1939, volume of Grundy's

---

27 However, some Polish textbooks from 1937 onwards did invite criticism of National Socialist ideology (Gierlak 2001: 365–367).
28 See also the English passage for translation, pp. 154–155, discussed by Stöbe (1939: 48).
29 The Polish textbooks of the period make greater use of extracts from textbooks that were used in Germany than do the British, however; see Gierlak (2001: 361).

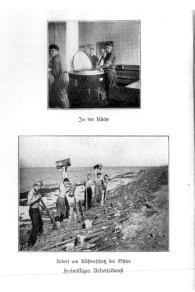

Figure 6.9: Macpherson & Strömer (1934: 12–13)

Brush up Your German series is more ambiguous. As already noted in Chapter 4, the language of the series is lively, and is supported by equally lively and expressive line drawings by Phyllis (Phil) R. Ward. The scenes are full of humour (albeit now dated). The light, humorous touch was very successful, but it was more difficult to sustain in the second volume, published in 1939 under the title *The Second Brush Up Your German. Conversations about the New Germany – on and off parade*, with an appendix that included not just German road signs but also a key to German military and paramilitary uniforms (see Figure 6.10). The volume approaches the awkward aspects of contemporary Germany fairly gently: in general Herr Meyer is more sceptical, Frau Meyer more inclined to warm to the New Germany. After several chapters about the Meyer family's journey from England to Germany, the family spend three scenes in the car on one of the newly-built autobahns, including a run-in with a traffic policeman, before a scene titled "Propaganda upsets Appetite", which takes place in a café where – the stage directions tell us – one lady is plainly wearing ear plugs:

Figure 6.10: front cover and pp. 104–105 of Grundy (1939)

Herr Meyer:	What's all this infernal row? What's going on?
Waitress:	To-day there's another speech from the Ministry of Air Raid Precautions.
Herr Meyer:	How long is it going to go on for?
Waitress:	I've only just come on duty and I don't know exactly. They mostly last two or three hours.
Herr Meyer:	The devil they do!

A young man, obviously displeased at the interruption, comes over to them.

| The Young Man: | Heil Hitler! May I point out to you that you are disturbing our reception of the great cultural speech of the Chief of the Captive Balloon Service, Professor von Goebbling? I must insist on quiet. |

[...]

| Herr Meyer: | By Jove! It's enough to drive you crazy. I've never heard such a shindy [i.e. commotion, NMcL]. |
| Frau Meyer: | Sh! The Nazi chap has his eye on us. Besides, it's our duty. |

[As Werner's ears are hurting, the family are about to leave but] *at this very moment the orator ends his speech and 'Deutschland über alles' sounds forth. The Meyers and the other guests are obliged to stand to attention and give the Nazi salute.*

(Grundy 1939: 19–20; I cite only the English version of the bilingual conversations)

Similarly, on May 1ˢᵗ (the Festival of the German People), the Meyers find that "there won't be a single spot in the country where you can't hear Hitler's speech" (p. 74). Press censorship is alluded to when Herr and Frau Meyer compare the contents of the Nazi party paper the *Völkischer Beobachter* and the Berlin *Illustrierte* and find that the wording of a political piece is identical in both. (It begins "In view of the unaccountably cool attitude of the English press, unquestionably influenced by its Jewish and Communist paymasters…"; p. 84.) The Meyers' friends the Paulis discuss – superficially, but warmly – Hitler's *Mein Kampf*, which, as Frau Meyer has learned, is given to all newly married couples. Herr Pauli also recommends Alfred Rosenberg's *Mythus des zwanzigsten Jahrhunderts* (1930) (the second-most influential Nazi text of the time, presenting the racial and political ideologies of Nazism).

In a chapter about the Hitler Youth, a young lad waxes lyrical about summer camping and sport, until the boys all line up "looking very earnest" and Werner "stands on one side gazing longingly at them" (p. 24). There are further encounters with strict traffic police, before Herr and Frau Meyer take their son to the Napola, Nazi boarding-school (*NAtional-POLitische ErziehungsAnstalt*), where the boys all wear the Hitler Youth uniform. A temporary anxiety arises when the headmaster explains that they must be able to give "proof of your ancestors back to the third generation", but Herr Meyer's maternal great-grandmother's uncle's Jewish wife is too remote a relation to be considered a problem, and Frau Meyer whispers delightedly "you wouldn't believe me when I said that we should get away with great-great aunt Rebecca" (p. 40). At the swimming pool, Herr Meyer sees the sign *Juden ist der Zutritt streng verboten* ('Strictly no entry for Jews') and jokes "waggishly" about whether anyone will detect their connection to the unacceptable great-aunt Rebecca (p. 86).

Some of the hardships of daily life are hinted at in other chapters. Herr Meyer's scepticism about the lottery to raise money for the Nazi-run charity *Winterhilfe* ('Winter Relief Fund')[30] – he criticizes his wife for believing everything she sees printed – is undercut when the family do at least win ten marks with one of their tickets. Nevertheless, Herr Meyer's critical distance stands in stark contrast to the jubilant statistic in *Das Neue Deutschland* that over 300 million marks were collected from "voluntary donations" in the winter of 1933/1934 (Meyer & Nauck 1936: 181). On *Eintopfsonntag*, the family find the restaurant menu limited to two simple dishes, and that 30% of the final bill goes to support the *Winterhilfswerk*. Frau Meyer reproaches her husband when he objects to the limited choice: "Helmut, how can you go on like that? Just suppose the waiter goes to his manager and says there's a grouser sitting over there. Then you may well have your next one-course meal in a concentration camp" (p. 26). Scrap iron is collected to be made into guns (p. 90); and there is an air-raid practice during the Meyers' stay (p. 74–77). Staying with their friends the Paulis, they find that butter is rationed to 200g per person per week, although Frau Meyer unveils the two pounds of butter she has secretly brought from England. A brownshirt (i.e. a Nazi storm-trooper) becomes unpleasant when someone is heard complaining about the shortage of butter on the tram (cf. Figure 6.11).

---

30 "Winter Relief Fund was a Nazi-organized charity collected during the winter months. Pressure to contribute was considerable, and armbands and bins were distributed for public display to identify donors – and thus, non-donors. Much of the money was siphoned off by the Party, and scholars have noted that it kept the populace short of extra cash and acclimated to the idea of privation." (This lucid note appears in Michael Hofman's translation of Hans Fallada's *Jeder stirbt für sich allein* (1947), *Alone in Berlin* (Berlin: Aufbau-Verlagsgruppe 1994: 19).

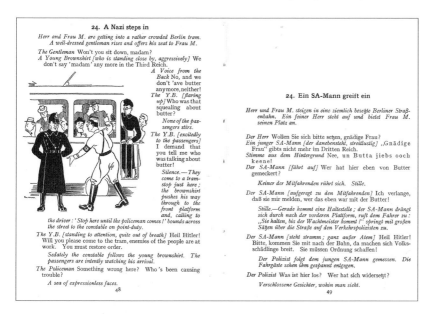

Figure 6.11: A Nazi steps in (Grundy 1939: 48–49)

Nazi expansionism is also thematicized. During a brief trip to Vienna, the Meyers hear a waiter grumble that "it's not the same dear old Vienna [...] they had to 'bring us into line'". When Frau Meyer inadvertently refers to "beer from Czechoslovakia", she is berated by an outraged stranger: "Pilsen beer! From Czechoslovakia, did the lady say? [...] German territory, German soil, German blood, and German tongue." Her husband mildly explains to his wife, "You remember, the Sudetenland has come back to the Reich, and Pilsen has become German too". But again the stranger expostulates, "*Become* German? My dear sir, ruthless desperadoes had ravished German land from its mother-country. And now the prodigal son is back home. Our great Führer has achieved his task" (pp. 70–72).

In sum, Grundy's little book highlights and gently mocks much that was troubling about contemporary German life. However, the humorous tone means that Grundy always stops short of straightforward condemnation, and instead depicts Germans under Nazism as ordinary people too busy getting on with their own lives to be inclined to question the wisdom of their leaders. While Frau Meyer represents naive credulity, Herr Meyer openly dislikes much of Nazism, but both want their son to have the education they believe that the Napola offers, and are not really interested in the ideology behind Nazism (they decide to donate their unread copies of *Mein Kampf* and *Mythus des zwanzigsten Jahrhunderts* to the *Winterhilfswerk*). They are aware of the danger of open criticism, and, when it comes to it, Meyer is content to joke about banning Jews from public swimming pools. As the couple sail back, the band play *Deutschland über alles* and the Horst-Wessel hymn (also known as *Die Fahne hoch*, the Nazi party anthem and joint

273

national anthem alongside the first verse of *Deutschland über alles* between 1933 and 1945). The book ends as "Both the people standing on the quayside and the passengers raise their arms. Involuntarily Herr and Frau M. follow suit" (p. 100).

I have no evidence that the second volume of *Brush Up Your German* was ever used in schools. Grundy's depiction of the Germans under Nazism through the Meyers – broadly critical of Nazism, but not demonizing Germans, for the Meyers are full of human foibles, distracted by their own concerns, rather than evil – reflected public and official discourse about the "two Germanys" that was characteristic of Britain both during World War I and right up to the outbreak of World War II in 1939. There was the Germany with which Britain was at war, and the Germany of the ordinary people with whom Britain had no quarrel. Liberal MP J. C. Wedgwood had said in 1914, "I wish the country would remember that there are two Germanys, and not one. We are fighting the Yunkers and the Hohenzollerns […] But there is another Germany – a lovable, peaceful Germany. […] That Germany […] has nothing to do with this war". Lloyd George similarly stated, "We are not fighting the German people. The German people are under the heel of this military cast, and it will be a day of rejoicing for the German peasant, artisan and trader, when the military cast is broken". Even at the outbreak of World War II, Neville Chamberlain still said "We have no quarrel with the German people except that they allow themselves to be governed by a Nazi government"; Labour politician Stanley Cripps wrote, "Our enemy is Hitler and the Nazi system, and not the German people" (Brechtken 2000: 28). The President of the Modern Language Association, W. W. Vaughan, spoke in a very similar vein of the "other" Germans in 1915 in his address to the Association (printed in *Modern Language Teaching* vol. 11, 1915):[31]

> Let us then recognize the need to bear witness, even before the conflict is over, to the fact that besides the Germany with which the newspapers have made us so sadly familiar, there is another Germany; that besides the German soldiers or officers, there are the German people up and down the country who love their homes as we love ours: people who have been kind to us in daily life and tended us in sickness, people for whom we feel, maybe, that special affection that we have for those we have laughed at and with […].

Brush Up Your German and *Deutsches Leben* are exceptions amongst textbooks with British authorship in the 1930s in dealing with contemporary Germany at all. *German for Sixth-Form and Adult Beginners* by Marie Louise Barker (1941) is more typical. According to the author – incidentally surely one of the first women to gain a PhD and lecture in German[32] – the book's aim was:

---

31 The digitized text may be found at http://www.archive.org/stream/modernlanguagete11modeuoft/
modernlanguagete11modeuoft_djvu.txt, but page numbers are not clear.

32 The author was lecturer in German at the University of Edinburgh, and had already published *Basic German for Science Students* (1933). Thanks to Bruce Perkins for lending me his copy of this work.

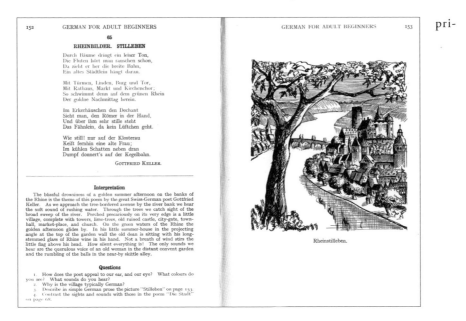

Figure 6.12: Barker (1941: 152–153)

marily cultural. It is not merely an introduction to German language, but also to German literature and landscape [...] Part II deals exclusively with 'Deutsches Land und deutsches Volk' – North, Central and South Germany [including] a 'cultural' knowledge of the literature associated with the various districts: e.g. the treeless, wind-swept North Sea Coast of Schleswig Holstein and the poetry of Theodor Storm; the forests of Silesia and Eichendorff's songs (p. vii).

In essence, we travel around Germany through its literature; a further innovation is Barker's inclusion of short paragraphs of interpretation accompanying the literary texts (see Figure 6.12 for an example). Writing in 1938, Barker ended with the remark that students who worked through the book would have "obtained an insight into and a love for the *real* Germany, the Germany that will always be there, the Germany of the great poets" (p. viii). Beyond this very oblique allusion (not to be mistaken for the *real* Germany), there is virtually no reference to present-day Nazi Germany at all, although minor adjustments of content allowed for changes post-*Anschluss*, including an illustration (uncommented) of a *Reichsautobahn* cut through Bavarian countryside, with a swastika flag visible waving from a flagpole (Figure 6.13). Austria was included in the section on South Germany as *Die Ostmark (Österreich)* (pp. 247ff.), and on Lore Holtz's pictorial map (on the endpapers), a swastika flag leant symbolically from Germany's Alps into Austria. A footnote on p. 237 pointed out that "Since the *Anschluss* [in March 1938] Germany's tallest mountain is no longer the Zugspitze [in the Bavarian Alps],

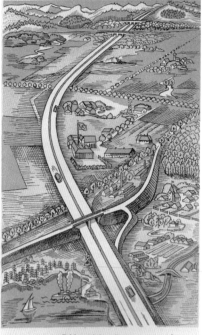

Reichsautobahn. Bayern.

Figure 6.13:
Barker (1941: illustration facing p. 236)

but the Grossglockner [in Austria]" (Barker 1941: 237, my translation).

Another early 1930s textbook with a title *in* German was the *Deutsche Fibel* ('German primer') of Koischwitz (1933), a reader which was, in the author's eyes, pioneering, having been "developed through research, experience and trial", making "practical classroom use of some of the theories of contemporary philologists, language teachers, and educators here and abroad".[33] The work was influenced by those who advocated "visual instruction, flexibility of curricula and methods, intensive word-study and extensive vocabulary-building, application of materials relating to the land, life and social conditions of the foreign country" (p. v). Stöbe was disappointed to find that "the new conditions in Germany" were not mentioned by Koischwitz at all, but in his *Bilderlesebuch* of 1934 Koischwitz referred explicitly to *Kulturkunde* as an underlying principle (Koischwitz 1934, Introduction, cited by Stöbe 1939: 17); and the *Kulturkunde* approach is obvious in the contents of the primer, which includes several folk tales (e.g. Till Eulenspiegel, the Bremen *Stadtmusikanten*), nursery rhymes, descriptions of a German village and a medieval town, as well as "the Germans' three favourite trees", the fir, oak and linden, illustrations of wall-signs bearing German proverbs, and of the sixth-century Silver Bible, a manuscript of the Bible in Gothic (a now defunct East Germanic language). Here the common Germanic past – of which folk tales, proverbs, the Gothic Bible, and the ancient Germanic veneration of the oak were all prominent examples – is foregrounded in much the same way as was done in contemporary primers for German native speakers (cf. McLelland 2012b). A certain positive bias towards the achievements of modern Germany is also evident in Koischwitz's illustrations: the front cover shows an aeroplane flying over village rooftops, and other illustrations show the Berlin airport, radio tower, the underground, and modernist architecture.

---

33 "Here" is New York, where the work was first published in 1932, and where it had been trialled in schools and colleges "partly under the auspices and supervision of the Institute of School Experimentation of Teachers College, New York" (p. v). Further research would be needed to confirm whether this author is identical with Max Oscar Otto Koischwitz (February 19, 1902 – August 31, 1944), a naturalized American of German origin who directed and broadcast Nazi propaganda during World War II.

Magda Kelber's *Heute Abend* (1938) included only very limited reference to Nazi Germany. When the weekly newsreel is played at the cinema her character Herr Kaufmann is heard to complain that young people these days are obsessed with sport, to which Frau Kaufmann responds, "Military and nothing but military. Parades, manoeuvres, navy manoeuvres, marches and heaven knows what. I'm really sick of the uniforms" (Kelber 1938: 188–189, my translation).

6.4 *Don't mention the war?*
Representations of Germany and German History after World War II

> Why German? Because for most of my conscious childhood Germany had been the rogue elephant in the drawing room. Germans were murderous fellows. They had bombed one of my schools (which I did not entirely take amiss); they had bombed my grandparents' tennis court, which was very serious, and I was terrified of them.
>
> But in my rebellious adolescent state, a country that had been so thoroughly bad was also by definition worth examining.
>
> [...] I had a teacher who not only loved the language but was always at pains to remind his pupils that there was another Germany, a decent one, far removed from the one we thought we knew about, and that was the Germany we would be able to explore once we understood its language.
>
> John le Carré, keynote speech to an audience of teachers, academics and others at a *Think German* event, on 25 June 2010.

In this section I turn to an area of teaching "culture" that came to prominence in the late twentieth century: the treatment of history in textbooks for learners of German as a foreign language. Three monographs have been devoted to the topic since the 1990s, by Koreik (1995), Thimme (1996), and Maijala (2004; cf. also 2006). Koreik's focus was not on language textbooks themselves, but on overviews of German history written either for teachers of German as a foreign language, or for advanced GFL learners such as those preparing to study in Germany; none was written by an English-speaking author, nor intended for English-speaking learners, so that his small sample differs from mine. Thimme, meanwhile, compared textbooks for adult learners of French and German as a foreign language.[34] Maijala's work compared the treatment of history in textbooks of German for British school pupils with those of other European countries and will be referred to below. My brief section here cannot hope to provide the theoretical rigour and coverage of such book-length studies, but aims to complement them with a historical perspective on their analyses of contemporary practice (though some of the materials Koreik examined date to the 1970s) and by focussing on textbooks for the British context. It would be desirable to compare treatments of German history in language

---

34 I have, despite my best efforts, been unable to locate a copy of Thimme's book.

textbooks with the history of teaching German history in Britain over the same period, but unfortunately very little is known about that history.[35]

Perhaps surprisingly, Frau Kaufmann's expostulation in Kelber's *Heute Abend* (1938), cited at the end of 6.3, about all the uniforms and military activity in the German news, was left unchanged in the revised edition of 1955 – a detail, it is true, but one that is at odds with the majority of texts that appeared in the first fifteen years after World War II, which on the whole signally ignore the recent German past altogether. The single most widely used textbook of German after the war was probably Russon's *Complete German Course for First Examinations* (1948; rpt. 1950, 1953, 1962, 2nd ed. 1967) (described briefly by Wegner 1999: 156).[36] In its revised version, it was used in to the 1980s at least – in the flyleaf of my copy, from North Berwick High School, the girls using it each year have faithfully entered their names annually from 1974 to 1981. With no illustrations at all, and with no passages from contemporary Germany, there are nothing more than scattered allusions to the past in the isolated sentences for translation (including such gems as "All these short sentences are very easy to translate", Russon 1948: 161) such as those listed below:

> In this century we have already had two World Wars. (p. 158)
> The USA, Russia, England [sic!], France and China were the Great Powers which fought against Germany in the Second World War. (p. 159)
> Many Germans live in London. (p. 161)
> My sister has several German friends. (p. 167)
> The First World War broke out in the reign of William the Second. (p. 168)
> The Russians won a great victory over the Germans. (p. 171)
> Germany attacked Russia in June 1941. (p. 172)
> The Germans invaded Russia. (p. 181)
> Ebert was elected President of Germany in 1919. (p. 181)[37]

In contrast to Russon, the authors of several other post-war textbooks followed the example set by Macpherson's *Deutsches Leben* and gave their books more or less programmatic German titles. Already before the Second World War, titles like *Ferien in Deutschland* (Dutton 1932), *Meyers reisen nach Deutschland* (Grundy 1932) and *Bob lebt sich in Deutschland ein* (Güntsch 1934) had developed the theme of getting to know Germany by going there, and post-War publications continued that trend: *Aufenthalt*

---

35 A project at the Institute for Historical Research on History in Education largely focuses on the teaching of British history (http://www.history.ac.uk/projects/digital/history-in-education; accessed July 2014), and the absence of a national curriculum for most of the century means that it is difficult to reconstruct what learners of German would have been exposed to in their history lessons. I am grateful to the postdoctoral researchers on the project, Dr Jenny Keating and Dr Nicola Sheldon, for their assistance.

36 See also the later textbooks by the Russons, also widely used, listed under Russon (1948) in the chronological bibliography below.

37 All these examples are from the 1967 edition. Passages for translation also include anecdotes about Bismarck (pp. 189–90) and Richard Strauss (pp. 190–91), but otherwise there is no historical matter at all.

in Deutschland (Anderson 1949), *John erlebt Deutschland* (Gretton 1955) and *Fahrt ins Blaue* (Sutcliffe 1960, 1961). Many of these read like exercises in positive thinking about Germany in the face of recent events, and generally avoid any reference to the past at all – thus making the occasional isolated sentence in Russon (1948) seem positively confronting by comparison. Given the comparatively nuanced picture of Nazi Germany in Grundy's characterization of the Meyers (Grundy 1939), this lack of engagement with Nazism in textbooks after the War may seem surprising, but it is borne out by a number of analyses, including those of Hierl (1972), Krauskopf (1985), and Ammer (1988). In his study of the *Deutschlandbild* in French textbooks Krauskopf found for textbooks of the 1950s that "The French authors are visibly trying to keep the concentrations camps, the mass exterminations, the wars of aggression and the economic expansion out of schoolbooks [...] The French authors endeavour to show the good Germany, the Germany of Goethe, Heine and Wagner, that is the Germany of interior life [*Innerlichkeit*]" (Krauskopf 1985: 249, my translation).[38] Nazism and the Holocaust were effectively taboo.

Not until 1969 – in Baber et al.'s *Mach Mit!* 3 – do we see a renewed attempt in British textbooks to address the question of how ordinary Germans could have allowed Hitler to lead them into the atrocities perpetrated in the name of Nazism. In *Mach Mit!* 3 a son attacks his father and his generation for not seeing "what an idiot Hitler was". The father explains that at first things really did seem better under Hitler, insists that though of course people knew that things were "not good" for Jews, people did not realize all that was happening until after the War; and concludes that "back then everything looked different" (*was für ein Idiot Hitler war*, p. 53, *damals sah alles anders aus* p. 54, cited Johnson 1973: 183–184; see also Johnson's discussion p. 193–195).

Broadly speaking, two images have dominated British views of Germany since the eighteenth century. Prior to 1871 the view had been a romanticized one, "based on an uncritical admiration of its literature, music, philosophy and sciences" (a view that some of the eighteenth-century textbooks discussed in Chapter 3 certainly support). After the founding of the German *Reich* in 1871 under the leadership of Prussia's Chancellor Otto von Bismarck, however, the British view of Germany had become one of "an authoritarian and militaristic society" (Brechtken 2000: 15). After World War II, textbook authors retreated with one accord in to the older, romanticized view of Germany, emphasizing the beautiful landscape and folklore. The grammar-school course *Fahrt ins Blaue* (Sutcliffe 1960, 1961), for example, carried pupils to O-level through

---

38 Hierl (1972: 288) summarizes his similar finding for British and American "readers" for learners of German: "'Germany' and the Germans are without exception positively portrayed. There are barely the beginnings of a critical analysis, and there is only seldom reference to the atrocities of the Third Reich" (*'Deutschland' und die Deutschen werden durchwegs positiv geschildert. Es finden sich kaum Ansätze einer kritischen Analyse, auch auf die Untaten des Dritten Reiches wird nur selten hingewiesen*). Likewise Ammer (1988) in his analysis of textbooks of German produced in Germany: "Characteristic of the textbooks of the 1950s is that mainly the positive side of the FRG is emphasized" (*Charakteristisch für das Lehrwerk der fünfziger Jahre ist, daß hauptsächlich das Positive an der Bundesrepublik Deutschland herausgestrichen wird*, Ammer 1988: 272).

idyllic travels along the Rhine. Meanwhile the two-volume O-level course *Aufenthalt in Deutschland* – published in 1949, at the time of the Berlin blockade and airlift – can be justly summed up in the dry comment of Wegner (1999: 142) that "Alles ist nett". As the title indicates (it means *A Stay in Germany*), the two volumes are based around the visit of English schoolboy Robert to the Weber family in a village called Rheindorf (lit. "Rhine-village"; there is more than one place of that name in Germany); not a word of the war which had ended only four years earlier. Kelber & Freudenberger's *Heute und Morgen* (1955) was, in its title (*Today and Tomorrow*), firmly forward-looking,[39] while in the same year Anderson's still more affirmatively titled *Das schöne Deutschland* for older pupils or adult students (Anderson 1955) glossed over the inner-German division with its opening sentence:

> Deutschland ist ein Staat in Westeuropa. Wir reden aber heute von Deutschland und meinen damit Westdeutschland, denn Ostdeutschland hat eine eigene Regierung.

> 'Germany is a state in Western Europe. Today we talk about Germany and mean West Germany, for East Germany has its own government.'

(Anderson 1955: 11)[40]

Perhaps surprisingly, given how the *Kulturkunde* movement was discredited after its adoption by National Socialism to serve its chauvinist-nationalistic ends (Apelt 1967: 90–155), several textbooks after World War II still seem to reflect a faith drawn from the *Kulturkunde* movement that it was possible to give a definitive account of "the" Germans to British learners; certainly that is what is implied by post-War titles such as *Deutschland und die Deutschen* and *Deutsches Land und deutsches Volk* (*Germany and the Germans*, Baier 1956; *German land and the German people*, Tudor & Heydorn 1956). As for the contexts of such works, the chapters in Tudor & Heydorn, for example, limited themselves to daily life interspersed with Germanic mythology (with the stories of Siegfried, Gudrun, and Lohengrin). This tendency to reproduce German folk tales, myths and legends (the pied piper of Hamelin, the Nibelungs and the Lorelei are stalwarts), was on one level a hangover from the *Kulturkunde* movement (which did not necessarily bear any relation to Nazism), but equally reflected a deliberate strategy to avoid the "awkward" topic of the War. For example, even in the 1950s Lütkens criticized "a certain harmlessness"

---

39 The title also indicates that the work is a development for schools of the text *Heute Abend*, originally developed as an evening course by Magda Kelber (1938) (cf. Chapter 4.8).

40 Anderson was a lecturer in German at Bradford Technical College in 1949; he later became head of the Department of Arts and Languages at Manchester Polytechnic. Although in his 1950s textbooks Anderson avoided dealing with the two World Wars and the Cold War, in the sixties his *Das heutige Deutschland* (1964) addressed the matter head on: "The very title of this book is to some extent a misnomer, since we are in fact faced not with one Germany but two" (Anderson 1964: 7). His chapter on *Betrachtungen zum deutschen Volkscharakter* also addressed the atrocities perpetrated in the name of Nazism (see below). Anderson also published *German for the Technologist* (1960), where, besides a technical passage in each lesson, Anderson also included a second passage "dealing with some aspect of German life and institutions", the first of which was, tellingly, on "the atomic age" (p. 15).

in Baier's *Deutschland und die Deutschen* (Baier 1952, 1956), a book inspired by Jethro Bithell (cf. p. v), which was for some years a set text for the Cambridge Board, making it the second most-mentioned work in Lütkens's survey (Lütkens 1959: 149, 153).[41] It is indeed very striking, for example, that the photos in Baier's post-War volume (all credited to the West German Tourist Information Bureau) show nothing of post-War or even post-agrarian Germany. They show two views of the Lüneburg Heath (one with sheep, one without!), views of the Rhine and the Alps; a traditional North German farmhouse; three "old people" (thus the caption!) outside a Frisian fisherman's cottage; Mainz Cathedral; musicians in Swabian costume; the house of Schiller's birth, with horse and cart out the front; and a painting of Schiller in Stuttgart. Hierl concluded from his analysis of textbooks used between 1945 and 1969 that "If one only knew Germany from these pictures, it would seem like a country that belonged to the Middle Ages rather than to the twentieth century" ('Würde man Deutschland nur aus diesen Bildern kennen, so erschiene es als ein Land, das eher dem Mittelalter als dem 20. Jahrhundert zuzuordnen ist'; Hierl 1972: 235).

Lütkens' charge of "harmlessness" is not dissimilar to that made fifteen years later by Johnson (1973: 225–232) that textbooks showed a "lack of balance, social bias, political commitment". Both "harmlessless" and – more extreme – lack of balance are explained, however, by another of Johnson's observations, "the tendency to germanophilism". Textbooks authors who do *not* try to win readers over to their subject must surely be rare (for most have spent years trying to win over their pupils in the classroom). Even before World War II, it is hardly surprising that textbooks sought to portray a sympathetic picture of Germany; Stöbe was struck in 1939 by the strong emphasis on the beauty of the German landscape (Stöbe 1939: 51). In the second half of the century, at first in the face of recent history (as in the case of Le Carré's teacher), and then – as we shall see – in the face of pervasive stereotypes, textbooks still tended to germanophilism. As already noted in Chapter 4, Orton (1959: 6) stated that he chose his material with the aim of "giving a lively and amusing picture of Germany and the Germans". Greatwood – the author of a *School German Course* (1958) that, like Anderson's *Aufenthalt in Deutschland*, depicted travels around Germany – made explicit the desire to counteract negative views of the Germans, stating that:

> The inherited image of German militarism of the Bismarck era shaped the basic conception of Germany in people's heads before 1914, and the same image has been preserved up to the present day – strengthened in war, but also changed. This image is not openly nourished by the press, indeed it is rarely directly addressed at all, but such firmly rooted thoughts die hard. We attach a great deal of importance to eradicating such uncritical thinking and adoption of such traditional prejudices.

(Greatwood 1958: 58, my translation)

---

41 The book was the second-highest non-literary text in the ranking of Lütkens (1959: 155) (though still 29th out of 49 books); cf. note 23 above for how the ranking was arrived at.

Such positive bias has continued. Maijala (2006: 17) has noted in her comparative study of British, Finnish, French, and Norwegian textbooks of German that "on the whole authors strive for a positive [freundlich] look at German history, despite its dark sides" (my translation). In the second half of the century, that bias towards developing in pupils a positive attitude towards the target culture, or to other cultures generally, was ultimately inscribed by language educators into the ideology of the National Curriculum. Byram (1993: 15) wrote of "the development of insight into the foreign culture and positive attitudes towards foreign people" (cf. Byram 1993: 15). The Modern Foreign Languages National Curriculum for England (1999: 10) included a slightly weaker formulation: "*cultural development,* through providing pupils with insights into cultural differences and opportunities to relate these to their own experience and to consider different cultural and linguistic traditions, attitudes and behaviours". Under the heading of responding to "pupils' diverse needs", the document recommended "using materials which reflect social and cultural diversity and provide positive images of race, gender and disability" (p. 22).

Beyond teachers' natural bias towards their subject and the ultimately formally encoded bias in favour of foreign cultures, however, textbooks of German in particular had to respond to changes in public attitudes towards Germany after World War II. Right up to the start of World War II, German people were – notwithstanding militaristic clichés noted by Greatwood above – not judged by the policies and acts of their governments. However, during World War II, attitudes gradually hardened. The British historian Nicholls cites Robert Vansittart, from the Foreign Office, clearly taking issue with the earlier "two Germanys" rhetoric in the early months of the War: "We are fighting the German army and the German people on whom the army is based. We are fighting the *real* and not the accidental Germany", a view that "gained ground steadily" through the War (Nicholls 1997: 31). After World War II, thinking in absolutes about "the" German character (of which detailed analyses had been made during the War, of the kind for which the *Kulturkunde* movement would be so criticized), was strong, and statements like those of MP Mavis Tate in *The Spectator* were common: "There is undubitably [sic] a deep streak of evil and sadism in the German race" (*Spectator*, May 4, 1945, p. 402, cited by Brechtken 2000: 35). It is these highly negative views that the champions of German studies sought to counterbalance with their "germanophilic" post-war textbooks.

In the 1960s, *Heute und Morgen* III (Freudenberger 1964) has three passages on "Germans who are known abroad" (*Deutsche, die man im Ausland kennt*). One is Carl Schurz (1829–1906), one of the German liberals and nationalists who supported the failed 1848 revolution, and later American statesman; another is Albert Einstein (1879–1955), who "had to" (*musste*) leave Germany during the *Hitler-Zeit* and who emigrated to America. Most striking, however, is the presentation of Daniel Gabriel Fahrenheit (b. 1686), born in Danzig/Gdansk, as *Ein großer Sohn der Stadt Danzig* (pp. 25–27). The chapter includes two short passages about the city (pp. 30–32), but there is no mention anywhere of the fact that Danzig had – since it lay east of the Oder-Neisse line – been made (provisionally) part of Poland at the Potsdam Conference of 1945.[42] The one German whose name would truly have been universally known – Hitler – was now mentioned, at least, unlike in earlier texts, but only as the name of an era, in the compound *Hitler-Zeit*.

Freudenberger seems to be the last of the post-War textbook authors who turned a blind eye to the recent German past and to the resulting changes to present-day Germany. Surveying his corpus of textbooks used in the 1960s, Johnson (1973: 212) still commented that "The majority of textbooks ignore the existence of the GDR, while those which do acknowledge it often dismiss it in a few sentences". Indeed, only three of the 19 textbooks in his corpus furnished him with any material for his chapter on treatments of the GDR.[43] However, from the late 1960s onwards, a clear change is noticeable, presumably triggered by the new German *Ostpolitik*, and the related, wider, normalization of relations between East Germany and the West, which had been in the air since a speech given by Egon Bahr in 1963 and a series of speeches by J. F. Kennedy in 1963 (see below). Already contemporaneous with Freudenberger's text, Anderson's *Das heutige Deutschland* addressed the matter of a divided Germany head on (in contrast to his *Das schöne Deutschland* of nine years earlier): "The writer of a book on German life and institutions is, however, very conscious of the existence of a second Germany, the German Democratic Republic. [...] The very title of this book is to some extent a misnomer, since we are in fact faced not with one Germany but two" (Anderson 1964: 7). For the first time in such a textbook, Anderson recounted the growing separation between the Soviet sector and the other Allied sectors, and how it resulted in the blockade and air-lift of 1948–1949 and, ultimately, the building of the Berlin Wall on August 13, 1961. He also presented a statistic according to which almost a quarter of GDR inhabitants had left the country since 1945, leaving the GDR without the workforce it needed to develop. The book concluded with the words of President J. F. Kennedy, who had been assassinated in November 1963, presumably just as Anderson was finishing his book:

> Let us re-examine our attitude toward the Cold War, remembering that we are not engaged in a debate, seeking to pile up debating points. We are not here distributing blame or pointing the finger of judgement. We must deal with the world as it is, and not as it might have been had the history of the last eighteen years been different.
>
> J. F. Kennedy, Address at American University, Washington, D. C., 10 June 1963[44]
>
> (Anderson 1964: 301; I cite the original here; Anderson presented a German translation.)

---

42 In the Treaty of Warsaw of 1970, the BRD recognized the Oder-Neisse line, and it became definitive in 1990, after German reunification. On the representation of German borders in twentieth-century textbooks, see section 6.8 below.

43 They are *Lustiges Lernen* 2 and 3, and *Mach Mit*! 3 (Jones 1964–1967, and Baber et al. 1969). In addition, three of the 23 readers are discussed.

44 Original cited from http://www.jfklibrary.org, accessed July 2014.

True to the spirit of Kennedy's speech, Anderson devoted the final chapter of the book to describing life *hinter dem eisernen Vorhang* 'behind the Iron Curtain', with sections on Berlin and the GDR more generally (pp. 267–301). He ex[plained that "The GDR calls itself a workers' and farmers' state, which emerged from a socialist revolution" (p. 283, my translation, as in all citations which follow, unless otherwise indicated). Anderson described collectivization, the FDJ (*Freie Deutsche Jugend*, Free German Youth, the youth arm of the SED [*Sozialisitische Einheitspartei*, i. e. Socialist Unity Party]), the school system, and attitudes to religion. The account is sober in tone:

> This chapter on the GDR seeks to portray matters as free from prejudice as possible. Objectivity and insight into the true situation are prerequisites for solving any question, and precisely in the problems of the "German question", of the relationship between the Federal Republic and the GDR, reunification, and the whole complex of east and west, any subjective heat or lack of accuracy in discussion only delays and perhaps renders impossible the solution.

(Anderson 1964: 301)

Nevertheless, Anderson described the GDR as a "totalitarian" system in contrast to the "democratic" system of the West; its ruling party was bound to "a rigid Marxism and Leninism" (pp. 281, 291). Anderson also raised the "adaptation of language":

> Words which thus far had a traditional, if not always completely clear, meaning (freedom, democracy, science, peace) are given a new interpretation by the SED [*Sozialisitische Einheitspartei*, i. e. Socialist Unity Party]. By individual freedom for example, the German idealism of Kant, Schiller and Goethe understood the capacity to decide according to one's conscience. In the party jargon of the SED freedom means "insight into necessity" (according to a pronouncement by Fr[ie-drich] Engels). Freedom in the old civic sense exists, according to the Marxist view, only for the capitalists in "bourgeois" society.

(Anderson 1964: 292)

It is striking that Anderson was here much more explicit in identifying the ideological problems with the GDR than were any of the 1930s authors dealing with contemporary Nazi Germany. Whereas Theilkuhl simply removed his chapter on the Weimar constitution once Hitler took power, Anderson spelled out how the GDR state contravened its own constitution, by contrasting passages from the constitution about freedom of speech, freedom to choose where to live, and freedom to strike, with GDR press statements explicitly denying those freedoms (pp. 293, 296–297).

After Anderson (1964), other textbook authors also readily engaged with the GDR, and, again, this finding for the 1960s coincides with a similar tendency identified by Krauskopf for French textbooks of German of the same period. Krauskopf (1985: 257) does not take into account the changed political context, however, and attributes the willingness to address the recent past and contemporary developments to intensifying contacts between France and Germany through student and teacher exchanges, which no doubt also played a role in revealing that modern Germany, including a divided Berlin, did exist.

It is instructive to compare with Anderson's (1964) reasoned criticism of the GDR the treatment of the GDR in the two 1960s textbook series discussed in the tenth chapter of Johnson's dissertation (Johnson 1973). On the one hand, Johnson reproduced a passage from *Lustiges Lernen* 2 (Jones 1965, rpt. 1971: 115), which in his view "comes close to the style of political propaganda", and was "designed to strengthen prejudice and to create misunderstanding (Johnson 1973: 213–214). For example, Johnson points out the "simplified and misleading contrast" in "*Die DDR ist keineswegs demokratisch, sondern kommunistisch*". On the other hand, he found that *Mach Mit!* 3 (Baber et al. 1969: 109–110) "presents its criticism in the form of a discussion of divergent opinions [and] presents the arguments fairly and leaves the student to make up his own mind", a format that was also used for the question of how Germans could have allowed the atrocities of Nazism under Hitler. Another example of engagement with the GDR is provided by Rowlinson's *Sprich mal Deutsch* series (cf. Chapter 4.6.3). The third volume (Rowlinson 1969: 62–73) included a chapter on young people in the GDR which begins with a conversation about the GDR – or the "so-called" (*sogenannte*) GDR, as one boy corrects the other (p. 62), signalling that the GDR was not at this time recognized by the Federal Republic (that recognition came in 1972). In the chapter, Anna relates how she and her family left East Berlin shortly before the wall was built, when it was still possible to travel between the two zones by tram and U-Bahn, something one could scarcely credit these days (*Das würde man heute nicht mehr glauben*, p. 63); the conversation concludes, "Well, it's a serious matter, the Zone" (*Naja, das ist schon eine ernste Sache, die Zone*, p. 63), and the first item of vocabulary preparing pupils for the next passage is, complete with illustration, *Stacheldraht* ('barbed wire'). Despite this, the portrayal of the GDR overall is less negative than Anderson's:

> Die DDR, die so lange der verlorene Winkel von Mitteleuropa war, unzugänglich, verschlossen, ein primitives, rückschrittliches Land mit Ackerbau als Mittelpunkt des Lebens, hat jetzt ihr eigenes Wirtschaftswunder erlebt, ist jetzt zu einem blühenden Industriestaat aufgebaut worden.

> 'The GDR, which was for so long the lost corner of Central Europe, inaccessible, closed, a primitive, backward country with agriculture at the centre of life, has now experienced its own economic miracle, has now been built up to new, flourishing industrial state' (p. 64).

Sprich mal Deutsch was later supplemented by readers (*Lies mal Deutsch*, Rowlinson 1973–1976); Pack 2 was divided into three: 2a. ten booklets based around life in Bonn; 2b. ten booklets split between Austria and Switzerland; and 2c. ten booklets set in the GDR, including East Berlin – a clear recognition of the GDR as a state requiring separate treatment, even if it did not yet have political recognition. On the whole, the ten booklets on the GDR steered away from difficult topics, dealing rather with minor dramas in everyday family life, but included snippets of basic, if somewhat superficial information, for example about collective farming, the prominent role of unions in everyday life, the allocation of living space on the basis of one room per inhabitant, and GDR-specific vocabulary like *Volkspolizist, Spartakiade* (biennial youth games), and *VEB* (*Volkseigener Betrieb*, glossed simply as a "state-owned concern" in 2c *Eisenacher Phantasien*, p. 5). Tensions between East and West were hinted at, but at the same time trivialized, in a plot-line that had a young GDR boy "fantasizing" about Federal German Republic spies finding their way to Eisenach from the border, which ran only five kilometres to the west (*Eisenacher Phantasien*, p. 7).[45] In contrast, a 1969 German reader discussed by Johnson (1973: 201–205) characterized East Germans in a way that evokes the stereotypical enemy of war films and spy thrillers[46] – the local population "withdrawn and passive", the policeman with "steel-blue eyes" and "iron in his voice", albeit also intelligent and capable of humour (Johnson 1973: 204, discussing *Ferien mit Schuss*, i. e. Königsberg 1969; see also Johnson 1973: 218).

Krauskopf (1985: 258) found that French textbooks of German became distinctly "more sober", as "the hard realities of the economy, society and politics" gained in prominence; again a similar development can be found in British textbooks from 1970 onwards. Paxton & Brake's *Wir lernen Deutsch* (1970–1972) broke consciously with the post-war tendency to focus on the beauties of the German landscape, for it dealt with "everyday topics in a typical German industrial town, for which purpose we have chosen Essen, as being more representative of modern Germany than more romantic places which might suggest themselves" (Paxton & Brake 1970: Preface, no page no.). The series also dealt with the realities of two Germanys. Chapter IV of the second book opened with the Berlin Wall, which "we Berliners call the *Schandmauer*" (*Wir Berliner nennen sie die Schandmauer*), and had a German remark:

> es gibt immer große politische Schwierigkeiten zwischen der DDR und der Bundesrepublik […] In einigen Jahren werden die Westberliner die Ostberliner als Fremde betrachten.

> 'there are always great difficulties between the GDR and the Federal Republic […] in a few years, West Berliners will view East Berliners as foreigners.'

> (Paxton & Brake 1971 [vol. II]: p. 8)[47]

---

45 More soberly, in *Lies mal Deutsch* 1, the story *Barfuß auf der Brücke* alludes briefly to an elderly man's memory of fleeing the Russians in 1945. Maijala (2006: 17) observed that in French schoolbooks of German, literature may serve to introduce the "difficult and problematic topics of German history" *(schwierigen und problematischen Themen der deutschen Geschichte)* to pupils, and that "the authenticity of literary texts gives learners the chance to form their own opinion about the historical events" *(Die Authenzitität literarischer Texte gibt den Lernenden die Chance, sich selbst eine Meinung über die geschichtlichen Ereignisse zu bilden)*. Arguably this potential can be found in the carefully constructed texts in *Lies mal Deutsch* too, especially in this case, as the man's war memory is triggered by the sight of a young runaway on a bridge, someone the same age as the pupils.

46 Johnson (1973: 218) makes the point by citing from John Le Carré's *The Spy Who Came in From the Cold* (1963).

47 The passage appears to have been re-written, as two sentences appear in a slightly different type-

Figure 6.14: Photo of GDR guard at the Berlin Wall,
Paxton & Brake (1971, vol. 2: p. 30)

The *Schandmauer* is mentioned again on p. 25, and a full-page photo showed a guard on the Wall looking through binoculars at the no-man's land of the Brandenburg Gate (p. 30), the weapon at his side clearly visible (Figure 6.14). Volume III devoted two of its eighteen chapters to the GDR: the first sets out the basic political situation;[48] the second concentrates on daily life for children. Both present a fairly sympathetic picture:

> Dank dem Fleiß ihrer Bevölkerung zählt jetzt die DDR trotz ihrer großen, wirtschaftlichen Schwierigkeiten auch außerhalb des Ostblocks zu einer der führenden Industriemächte.

> 'Thanks to the hard work of its population, despite its considerable economic difficulties, the GDR now counts, thanks to the industry of its population, as one of the leading industrial powers, also outside the Eastern Bloc.'

> (Paxton & Brake 1972 [vol. III]: 60)

The other chapter describes the everyday life of a GDR schoolboy, including a lesson in which his teacher asks pupils to compare the daily life of workers in the GDR, and *versucht zu erklären, wie die Bürger der DDR au einer echten Gemeinschaft zusammenwachsen* ('tries to explain how the citizens of the GDR are growing together to a real community', p. 66) – this in contrast to the West, where workers have no time to get to know and support each other. For homework, the teacher sets pupils the task of comparing the two states, deciding in which state they think people can be happier, and in which state they

---

face, as if amended at the stage of proofs.

48 Again differences in type-face in my copy (a 1974 reprint) suggest some amendments to the text here.

would rather live (p. 66). The idealistic-sounding oath of the *Jugendweihe* is given in full, without comment, on p. 69.

An unusual book representing German culture to British learners is *Introducing Germany*, which – written entirely in English – was presumably written to supplement information that pupils would find in their German language textbooks; the simple language would have made it accessible to pupils just beginning German at secondary school (Wightman 1974).[49] The bulk of Part III, devoted to East Germany, presents the GDR from the relatively non-ideologized geographical perspective, with short texts and photos introducing the regions, towns and cities, including a giant bust of Karl Marx in Karl-Marx-Stadt (since 1990 known as Chemnitz once more). In the section on "How East Germany is governed", however, Wightman states:

> The German Democratic Republic is not 'democratic' in the same way as Britain, America or West Germany. In an East German election there is only one list of candidates to vote for. The people therefore have no chance to vote for a change of policy. The SED claims that everyone in the country is working for the victory of Socialism.

(Wightman 1974: 109)

Life in East Germany is summarized (not inaccurately, but incompletely) as follows:

> Most towns and villages in East Germany are drab and dirty because the country is short of money and has not enough money to brighten them up. There is also a shortage of building and cleaning materials. Very few houses have sparkling windows, gay window boxes and neat gardens, as in West Germany. [...] East Germany does not look like a rich country.

(Wightman 1974: 121)

Similarly, Johnson (1973: 206) noted that vocabulary evoking the drabness of East Germany was "fundamental" in his corpus of 1960s and early 1970s textbooks and readers: *abgetreten, baufällig, ohne Farbe, ohne Leben, schäbig, trüb, verrostet* ('worn out, derelict, colourless, lifeless, shabby, gloomy, rusty'). Socialism is implicitly criticized against the benchmark of capitalism in Wightman's following statement:

> The East Germans are always looking for new ways to increase production, but they insist that new ideas must fit in with the teachings of Karl Marx. They plan five or seven years ahead, but rarely finish what they plan in the time allowed; spare parts for machines are often not available and building materials are usual-

---

49 There is no preface or introduction. Wightman later wrote the materials for a BBC radio and television course, *Deutsch Direkt* (Wightman 1985).

ly in short supply. It seems that many of the people are not prepared to work their hardest under a system which prevents anyone from making a personal fortune.

(Wightman 1974: 122)

Krauskopf (1985: 258) was struck that French textbooks of German dealt much more freely with the GDR and the Oder-Neisse line than did Federal German schoolbooks of the same period, which still tended to refer to the GDR in quotation marks, and to label maps with the Oder-Neisse line, rather than as the border between the GDR and Poland. Rowlinson (1969: 64) wrote of the "Polish border, which has been formed by the Oder-Neisse line since 1945". One British textbook of German that did use quotation marks for the GDR, however, was *Panorama* (Shotter 1975: 232). By 1988, a certain sense of normality is implicit in *Zickzack 2,* where the GDR is presented neither through the lens of its history and politics (admittedly, its history had been treated in Vol. 1 of *ZickZack*), nor as the "required" chapter alongside similar chapters on Austria and Switzerland. Instead, the textbook opens with the theme of a group of young Britons visiting the GDR (Goodman-Stephens et al. 1988: 4–7), something which is arguably presented as more normal than it was. We read that *Die FDJ ist eine politische Organisation für die Jugend in der DDR. Das Ziel der FDJ ist, die junge Generation zu guten Sozialisten zu erziehen* ('The FDJ is a political organization for young people in the GDR. The goal of the FDJ is to raise the young generation to be good Socialists', p. 7), but it is nonetheless striking that the GDR serves here chiefly as the backdrop for exploring the universal theme of how young people spend their free time. Similarly in *Sprungbrett* (Bonnyman & Oberheid 1990), where the second half of one chapter clearly had to be re-written as events in 1989 rendered the material outdated, the first half significantly included a passage by Richard von Weizsäcker to the effect that it was, after all, "quite all right to admire the truly impressive achievements of the GDR footballers [...]". Clearly, by the late 1980s, textbook authors were reflecting a degree of normalization in East-West relationships.

6.5 Teaching memory?

Memory studies have become one of the dominant paradigms in cultural studies over the past fifteen years or so,[50] but already in 1995 Uwe Koreik pointed out the relevance of theories of memorialisation to analysing the teaching of history to learners of German as a foreign language (Koreik 1995: 63–70); more recently Schmenk & Hamann (2007) have also drawn attention to the importance of acknowledging cultural memory in language teaching, something that has always been there – note, for example, the illustration of the Niederwald Monument, which commemorates the 1871 founding of the

---

50 Foundation texts are the articles collected in Assmann & Hölscher (1988), and Assmann & Harth (1991), building on Halbwachs's *On collective memory* (1992, but first published, after his death, as *La mémoire collective* in 1950; he had died in Buchenwald in concentration camp in 1945). It is impossible to do justice to the vast field of German memory studies here, but see as a starting point Erll (2008).

Das Niederwald-Denkmal.
157

Figure 6.15:
Scholle & Smith (1909: 157), showing
the Niederwald monument, constructed
to commemorate the foundation of the
German Empire in 1871 (construction
began in 1881; it was inaugurated in 1883)

German Empire, in Scholle & Smith's reader (1909; see Figure 6.15).[51] Citing Claire
Kramsch's definition of a culture as "a discourse community that shares a common social space and history" (Kramsch 1998: 10),
the authors plead for reconceptualizing
culture as "something teachable that has
been and continues to be constructed", thus
avoiding the risk either of "essentializing"
either culture(s) (as with the *Landeskunde*
approach) or cultural differences (a risk they
see in more recent intercultural approaches)
(Schmenk & Hamman 2007: 374). Teaching
culture could thus still legitimately include
teaching "factual knowledge about German-speaking discourse communities […]
whose members share, inter alia, a cultural
memory", allowing learners "to encounter
the cultural memory of another discourse
community" (p. 382). While such an approach to teaching culture has only recently
been explicitly theorized (Schmenk & Hamann illustrate it with regard to "teaching
Divided Germany, the Berlin Wall, and
German Unification"), the question of how
German cultural memory has been represented or constructed can be usefully asked
of textbooks of any era, and is perhaps particularly interesting for textbooks produced
after World War II. The following remarks
are a small step in that direction.

Wightman's *Introducing Germany* (1974: 80) observed drily that "The Germans like
to remember Germany's past – except for the years of Nazi rule". As we have seen, however, the same could also have been said of English textbooks of German until the very
late 1960s. Rowlinson's *Sprich mal Deutsch* (vol. III, published in 1969, at a time when
serious efforts were being made to "come to terms with the past"), thematicizes the topic
of remembering – or choosing not to remember – in a discussion between three young
people deciding on a topic for their next youth radio programme:

---

51 In Siepmann (1900: 17) a group of boys are keen to be photographed in front of the Monument. On
the importance of the Niederwald Monument as a – not wholly successful – exercise in collective
memorialization, see Horan (2012).

Peter: [...] Wollen die jungen Leute noch mehr von dieser Nazizeit hören? Ich finde, wir sollten die ganze scheußliche Sache endlich mal ruhen lassen.

Anna: Und vergessen?

Peter: Ja, und vergessen – nein, vielleicht nicht vergessen, aber nicht mehr davon reden.

Anna: Ich bin nicht deiner Meinung. Ich finde es doch noch nötig, die jungen Leute davor zu warnen, wozu der Mensch fähig ist.

[...]

Fritz: Man kann nicht einfach wegsehen, vergessen.

'Peter: Do young people want to hear even more about this Nazi era? I think we should finally just let the whole dreadful matter rest.

Anna: And forget it?

Peter: Yes, and forget it – no, perhaps not forget it, but not talk about it any more.

Anna: I don't agree. I think it's still necessary to warn young people what humans are capable of.

[...]

Fritz: You can't just ignore it, forget it.'

(Rowlinson 1969: 133–134)

What follows is a historical overview of Hitler's rise to power, culminating in his Thousand-Year Reich, which "came to an end after the murder of six million Jews and the devastation of Europe with Hitler's suicide" (Rowlinson 1969: 138). Contemporary with this is the son's challenge to his father in *Mach Mit! 3* (Baber et al. 1969: 53–54, discussed above) about how people could have supported Hitler and have remained unaware of what was happening in the concentration camps. These are, as far as I am aware, the earliest references to the murder of Jews in post-War German textbooks; the closest previous effort was Anderson's references in 1964 to "Nazi atrocities" and "all the awful events of the years 1933–1945" (*Greuel des Nazismus, alle schrecklichen Ereignisse der Jahre 1933–1945*, p. 17). Illustrations in the same *Sprich mal Deutsch* chapter include a Nazi rally in Berlin, and ruins in Berlin after the War (Figure 6.16). Exercises in the same chapter require pupils to re-tell Hitler's rise to power after 1920, to write essays in pairs about the events in Germany between 1933 and 1945 – explicitly including library research – and to translate a scenario where "you are interpreting for your friend, who speaks no German, in a rather heated though still fairly polite argument with a neo-Nazi". The passage for translation ends, "And last of all remind him of six million murdered Jews..." (p. 143). A few years later, Wightman (1974) stated, "In his desire to keep the German race pure, he [Hitler] persecuted the Jews, and little by little took away from them their rights as citizens. Many were sent to concentration camps along with his political opponents. Later he tried to kill as many Jews as possible (1942–1945)." The same page shows a photo of a Jewish bookshop marked with a star and the word *Jude* on its window (Wightman 1974: 15).

Berlin: *Nachkriegsruinen*

Figure 6.16: Rowlinson (1969: 140, 141)

A byword for memorialisation is Dresden, as a 2c booklet *Putzi*, in the *Lies mal Deutsch* series (Rowlinson 1976), begins by reminding readers:

> Dresden. Bis 1945 eine der schönsten Städte Europas. Am Ende des Krieges wurde sie durch englische Bombenangriffe total vernichtet, eine grausame Rache für die Zerstörung von Coventry durch die deutsche Luftwaffe kurz vorher. Dresden – für die Sinnlosigkeit des Krieges fast zu einem Begriff geworden.

> 'Dresden. Until 1945 one of the most beautiful cities in Europe. At the end of the War it was totally annihilated by English bombardments, a cruel revenge for the destruction of Coventry by the German air force a little earlier. Dresden – it has become almost a byword for the pointlessness of war.' (Rowlinson 1976, 2c: 3)[52]

Paxton & Brake (1971, vol. 2, p. 8) has a West Berliner explain to visitors that the street *Straße des 17. Juni* is named in memory of the East Berlin uprising against the government in 1953. Two photos on p. 13 show the *Kaiser-Wilhelm-Gedächtniskirche* on the Kurfürstendamm ('Kaiser Wilhelm Memorial Church'), left in its war-damaged state

---

52 Wightman (1974: 16) also shows a photo of Dresden in 1945, though the text makes no reference to its status as a special focus of remembrance.

as a memorial, though the memorializing name of the church is only stated in the list of photos at the front of the book.

One of many cartoons featured in Paxton & Brentnall's *Zielpunkt Deutsch* (1975: 84) is that shown in Figure 6.17, whose caption reads, "I know it's historically wrong, but how else are we going to make a musical out of it?", first published in *Stern* magazine. The cartoon alludes to the so-called *Hitler-Welle* ('Hitler wave'), a wave of books and productions in the late 1960s and early 1970s that took Hitler the personality (rather than the Nazi system as a whole) for their topic, and exemplified by Joachim Fest's biography of Hitler (1973).[53] The cartoon – complete with a harp-playing Hitler, a fallen swastika, and the historically loaded Brandenburg gate – suggests that remembering and reconstructing the National Socialist past had, by the 1970s, become part of mainstream public discourse, and, accordingly, also something which it was possible to satirize.[54]

In the context of current discussions in German cultural studies about the importance of the *archive,* as first-hand memories of World War II will be lost, *Deutsch Jetzt* 2 (McNab 1988), aimed at GCSE pupils, is worthy of a mention. The textbook begins with an odd selection of six photos purporting to be *Aus dem Familienalbum* 'from the family album'. All six photos are dated between 1932 and 1933; while one shows a chartered bus on the *Münsterplatz* in Bonn, one a group photo (labelled "school trip to Germany 1933") and one a family group, the fourth shows two policemen complete with the Prussian-style pointed *Pickelhauben* that long dominated as a German stereotype (on such stereotypes, see below), and two others show the Halle-Leipzig airport. Although the teacher was presumably intended to guide discussion based on these photos, the silence about Hitler's takeover in March 1933 in this "family album" – an archive for when memory fails – is, in the absence of any further context in the volume, very striking.[55] With German reunification and the fall of the Berlin Wall, the two-state phase in German twentieth-century history became ripe for commemoration or forgetting too.

---

53 Specifically, the cartoon alludes to the 1951 film *Quo Vadis,* in which Peter Ustinov played the brutal tyrannical emperor Nero, including singing "Oh lodernd Feuer…" and burning down Rome – a scene that, I am told, would have been triggered by the collocation of a harp, a city aflame, and music. In the cartoon, Hitler in Berlin is seen doing more or less the same as Nero/Ustinov did in Rome. Hitler's orders for "scorched earth policy" from March 1945 were also called *Nero-Befehle* ('Nero-commands'), strengthening the basis for the allusion. My thanks to Magnus Brechtken for reconstructing this historical context for me.

54 Rimrott et al. (1978) is interesting for encouraging 'memory' in a quite different context: it is aimed at heritage speakers of German in Canada, with funding from the Canadian federal government. Its programmatic title, *Was du ererbt,* is from Goethe's *Faust I,* l.682–3: *Was Du ererbt von Deinen Vätern hast, erwirb es, um es zu besitzen* 'What you have inherited from your fathers, acquire it, in order to possess it!' The authors – a total of 22 contributors – put together a book of reading passages on topics relating to the history of prominent German migrants and their families in Canada. My thanks to Matthias Schulze (University of Waterloo, Canada), for drawing my attention to this work.

55 The *Teacher's Resource Pack* accompanying the textbook (McNab 1988) states merely "This introductory page sets the scene for Book 2, introducing the themes of the family, past and present, and the school trip" (p. 6).

293

"Ich weiß, es ist historisch falsch, aber wie sollen wir denn sonst ein Musical daraus machen?"

Figure 6.17 (left): Paxton & Brentnall (1975: 84) showing a cartoon first published in the *Stern* magazine
Figure 6.18 (right): Rowlinson (1993: front cover)

The front cover of Rowlinson (1993), for example, shows the Berlin Wall become a memorial recalling divided Germany (see Figure 6.18), but – as we shall see under section 6.8 – there was a great deal of implicit forgetting too.

6.6 Germany(s) and Europe

The mid-seventies mark another break in representations of the German past and present, as the GDR seems once again to move down the agenda of textbook authors, probably as a result of the normalization of relations between East and West.[56] In Paxton & Brentnall's *Zielpunkt Deutsch* (leading to A-level) (1975), the emphasis was on using authentic texts (a great many of them from the women's magazine *Brigitte*, but also extracts from literary texts). The authentic passage chosen for the chapter on East Germany is as uncontroversial as possible. Extracted from a GDR publication, the *DDR-Revue*, it presented the state as a tourist destination, parallel to similar chapters on Austria and Switzerland. Rather than East-West tensions, the new geopolitical context which authors now began to take into account was the European Community (which Britain had joined in 1973). *Panorama* (Shotter & Ahrens 1981) may serve as an example. The

---

56 The BRD recognized the GDR in 1972, swiftly followed by the UK and many other states; the USA did so in 1974.

text devoted several pages to the history of the relationship between the BRD and the GDR (pp. 232–235), but situated that history less in the context of the Cold War than in that of Western European integration, as the section was one of 14 under the broad heading of "Germany, Britain and Europe." Other sections compared the British political system with that of the Federal Republic, addressed current British issues (the Northern Ireland question, Scottish nationalism and North Sea oil, and unions), before Chapter 30, headed *Mut zu Europa,* dealt with Britain's accession to the European community in 1973, from a clearly pro-European standpoint. For example, the opening sentence, "People have now recognized that the United States of Europe can only be achieved step by step", assumed that a United States of Europe would be the ultimate outcome, and viewed the European Community as a "promising start" (*hoffnungsvoller Anfang,* p. 248) towards that goal, a view that, despite being far from uncontroversial, is not challenged elsewhere in the chapter. A second passage likewise noted the "grounds for hope" that the next generation would be more European-minded than the current one (p. 250).

In *Deutsch Heute* (Sidwell & Capoor 1983) sections of information on the country (at the end of chapters 12, and 14–18 in Part I) dealt only with the *Bundesländer.* The text featured characters from East as well as West Germany, but now also from Austria and Switzerland – again, then, the German language was portrayed as a European phenomenon. A chapter in *Brennpunkt* headed *Europa! Europa!* included a passage on *Deutschland in Europa* (Sandry et al. 2000: 212–213), and it would be easy to multiply the examples. Even at the level of beginners, *Einfach toll* 1, takes a wider perspective than just Germany West and East, by including illustrations not just of Federal Republic currency, but also of those of Austria, Switzerland and the GDR (Smith 1985: 32, 35). Similarly, a map of the whole of Europe in Chapter 1 of the beginner-level *Zickzack* 1 (Goodman-Stephens et al. 1987: 11) places the study of German in a European context from the word go, and speakers of German from all four German states are introduced on p. 13. Overall, the inspection of my corpus of textbooks supports Wegner's finding in her study that British textbook authors increasingly moved towards creating a "sense of European identity" (Wegner 1999: 333).

6.7 After Reunification[57]

We have thus far seen that the history of dealing with Germany's past in textbooks after World War II falls into three phases: a first phase, roughly up to the end of the fifties, when it was on the whole as if the War had never been; a second phase in the sixties and early seventies, in which the GDR was acknowledged as a state with which it was necessary to engage and about which pupils of German should be informed; and a third phase from about the mid-seventies onwards, during which there was greater focus on the

---

57 Some prefer to refer to German "Unification" rather than "Reunification", as the newly created state is very different, both politically and territorially, from what had gone before the division into two states. For clarity, I use the term "Reunification" here.

German language and its cultures within the wider context of Europe. The final phase of the twentieth century is the one in which, following German reunification, textbook authors seem at last to have found it possible to present German history as a completed narrative with a beginning and an ending. So, while just before unification we find a textbook like *Zickzack* 1 (volume 1 of a course leading to GCSE, Goodman-Stephens et al. 1987) still beginning a three-page spread in English on the history of Germany with the "End of World War II" (1987: 208–11), and ending with the "first twenty-five years" of the Berlin Wall, textbooks a few years later encompass a more complete historical overview. *Überblick* (Hares et al. 1994) stretches from the first attestation of the word *deutsch* (or rather the Latin form *theodisce*) in 786 right up to 1990, concluding, *Nun leben die Deutschen wieder in Einheit* 'Now the Germans live in unity again' (Hares et al. 1994, vol. 2: 123–24). Similarly, *Brennpunkt* (Sandry et al. 2000: v) presents a *Zeittafel* from 800 (the crowning of Charlemagne as Holy Roman Emperor) to 1990 (*Wiedervereinigung Deutschlands* 'the reunification of Germany'). Where before the story felt incomplete, history is implicitly presented as teleological: despite many divisions on the way, Germany is now, ultimately, united.

Sprungbrett (Bonnyman & Oberheid 1990) was evidently being (re)written *nur [...] wenige Wochen nach dem Beginn der 'neuen Ära' der detuschen Geschichte* 'only a few weeks after the start of the "new era" of German history' (p. 113, my translation; the latest news on reunification is contained in newspaper articles from late April 1990). Its chapter titled *BRDDR* contains the earliest attempt in a textbook of German to address the new situation. It does not shy away from representing the concerns of many, including many British people, that the creation of a new German state resulted in a state so large as to be "incompatible" with the institutions of the EU, for the EU rested on the assumption of relative equilibrium between the various European powers; the opinion of the French president Giscard d'Estaing to this effect is cited on p. 131. The same fear – one which was a very real fear among some British politicians, especially in the Conservative government of the time (cf. Nicholls 2000: 17–21) – is also represented in an article from the *Spiegel* in the programmatically titled *Deutschland Hier und Jetzt* ("Germany here and now", Rowlinson 1993: 212, complete with front cover showing the Berlin Wall become a memorial, rather than a barrier; see Figure 6.18). Gradually, through the 1990s, a tendency is noticeable to place recent German history in a larger historical context. So *Einfach toll!* 5 (Bates & Smith 1992) – where the Brandenburg Gate, with pedestrians once again milling through it, has iconic status on the front cover, as it had earlier in the century (see Figure 6.19) – is the earliest example I have found post-1945 of a textbook that places German history since 1933 in a wider historical context. There, the timeline for the history of Berlin starts not with World War II, but with the first mention of the city in documents in 1237.

It is interesting to note a difference identified by Maijala (2004) between the treatment of German history in the seven British A-level textbooks and the equivalent texts used in the other European countries that she studied. Whereas other countries' textbooks of this period treat German history in the context of introductions to major cities and tourist "sights", the British textbooks (Hares et al. 1994, Hares & Timm 1994,

Figure 6.19: Twentieth-century photos of the Brandenburg Gate
in textbooks of German: Scholle & Smith (1909: 13); Wightman (1974: frontispiece);
Bates & Smith (1992: front cover)

2nd ed. 2001; Sandry et al. 1994, 2000, and McCrorie et al. 2001) instead treat it variously under the headings of the economy, *Heimat*, art, Europe, transport, and racism: German history is not something to be consumed like a tourist, but remains relevant to current problems and constructions of national and regional identities today.

6.8. *Was ist Deutschland?* Remembering and forgetting borders

The political geography of Germany underwent more changes in the twentieth century than that of a great many other countries, and presenting up-to-date information not just in text form but also in maps was a challenge which textbooks did not always meet successfully. Kron (1916, 1923) was perhaps the first of many twentieth-century authors forced to take into account changes to German borders in the light of the Treaty of Versailles, which was explicitly discussed in the 1923 edition. In contrast, *Harrap's Modern German Grammar* (Van der Smissen & Fraser 1911) included in 1911 a map on which Germany's borders were detectable as a dash-and-dot line, but where the four kingdoms that made up the Empire alongside the smaller states were far more prominent: Prussia, Saxony, Bavaria and Württemberg (cf. Figure 6.20). Both the map and the information accompanying it (Figure 6.21) still appeared, unchanged, in the 1927 issue, by which time they were hopelessly out of date.

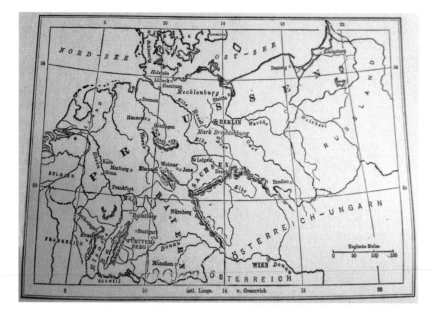

Figure 6.20: Van der Smissen & Fraser (1911, 1927: [xxvi])

Keeping up with Germany's changing borders and political status did not become easier after World War II. The question "What is Germany?" was answered by the post-war textbook *Das schöne Deutschland* (Anderson 1955: 11) as follows, as cited in 6.4 above – note the implicit ideological position of the "we" who "mean" West Germany, brushing aside any meaning that East Germany might lay claim to:

> Lektion Eins
> Was ist Deutschland?
> Deutschland ist ein Staat in Westeuropa. Wir reden aber heute von Deutschland und meinen damit Westdeutschland, denn Ostdeutschland hat eine eigene Regierung.

> 'What is Germany? Germany is a state in Western Europe. But we talk about Germany today and mean West Germany, for East Germany has its own government.'

Sixteen years later Jones (1971) effectively undid this explicit exclusion of the GDR from consideration, however:

> Wenn wir Deutschland sagen, denken wir an die Bundesrepublik, aber es gibt ein zweites Deutschland – die sogenannte DDR… – ein Land hinter Stacheldraht und Mauer.

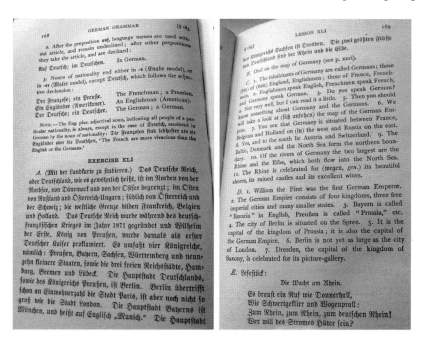

Figure 6.21: Van der Smissen & Fraser (1927: 168–169)

'When we say Germany, we think of the Federal Republic, but there is a second Germany, the so-called GDR – a country behind barbed wire and wall.'

(Jones 1971: 115, cited by Johnson 1973: 196)

Likewise, the opening words in Wightman (1974: 4) gave rather greater weight to the existence of the GDR:

> What is Germany?
> There is no longer just one country called Germany; there are two separate states, usually called East and West Germany. They were both founded in 1949, and are very different.
> [The official names of the two states are explained.]
>
> In this book Part I deals with Germany's past [pp. 5–34], Part II deals with West Germany [pp. 35–93], and Part III deals with East Germany [pp. 94–127].

Given the constantly changing state of the German state(s) in the twentieth century, the history of how Germany's place in Europe and indeed the world was defined in twentieth-century school textbooks and maps is worth tracing in brief, for maps, too, are about remembering and forgetting. In *Brush up Your German* and *Meyers reisen nach Deutschland* (Grundy1931, 1932), the fortunate Herr Meyer's route criss-crossed Germa-

299

Figure 6.22: Grundy (1931, 1932: map on the endpapers)

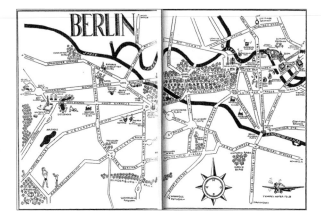

Figure 6.23: *Heute Abend* 1 map of Berlin (Kelber 1938: 258–259, but also still in the eleventh impression, 1953)

ny in a way that would be unthinkable just a decade later, as the maps on the endpapers indicate (Figure 6.22).[58]

In Kelber's *Heute Abend* textbook of 1938 (pp. 258–259), there is no map of Germany, but there is a map of pre-war Berlin (the same map also appears in one of the *Deutsches Leben* texts). It shows an attractive undivided city, with good shopping, theatres, and many parks to relax (Figure 6.23). The image survived until the eleventh impression of

---

58 The back of the book in *Brush Up Your German* showed a map detailing the costs of the different stages of the journey; this was evidently not considered suitable for school use, so that *Meyers reisen nach Deutschland* has an identical map front and back.

Figure 6.24: U.S. Special Services map of Berlin (top from Hill 2008: 212), and Kosler (1965) map of Berlin, appearing as in inset on the map of Germany on the page facing the title page, showing clearly the four sectors and (less clear in this reproduction) the crossing-points between the Soviet and Allied sectors

the book in 1953 – by which point it is interesting to compare it with the very different map handed to Allied Forces stationed in early 1950s Berlin, clearly showing Berlin as a city of four sectors (Figure 6.24). It was eventually removed from the revised edition of 1960 and replaced with a plan of a flat's interior instead. Kosler (1965) is the only textbook I am aware of that marked the four sectors in Berlin, complete with crossing-points points between the Soviet and Allied sectors.[59]

---

59 Kritsch (1961) similarly included a map showing the occupation zones of Germany. Perhaps to Kritsch, in the USA, and Kosler, an Australian teacher, the plain facts of the occupation of Germany after World War II seemed a less delicate matter than they did to textbook authors working in Europe.

301

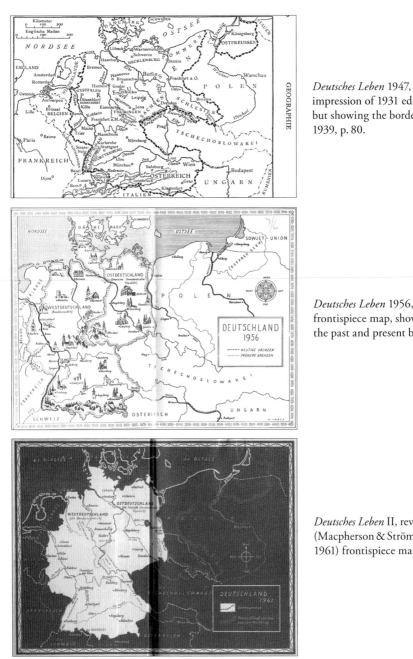

Deutsches Leben 1947, impression of 1931 edition, but showing the borders of 1939, p. 80.

Deutsches Leben 1956, frontispiece map, showing the past and present borders

Deutsches Leben II, revised ed. (Macpherson & Strömer 1961) frontispiece map

Figure 6.25: maps of Germany in three editions of *Deutsches Leben* (Macpherson & Strömer 1947, 1956, 1961)

In 1949, the map of the politically aware duo Macpherson & Strömer in their *Deutsches Leben* text shows Germany with the borders of 1939 – post-*Anschluss*, so with Austria still named, but included, but still pre-War. In 1956, this was updated to show the "old" and "present-day" borders of Germany. Finally, in 1961, the map still shows the old borders, but highlighted is the outline of what we would consider present-day Germany, both East and West, though this map, too, was rapidly going to become outdated, with 'East Germany' (*Ostdeutschland*) acknowledged as a separate entity. In Marthe Freudenberger's *Heute und Morgen* (1955; also in the 1965 impression, Figure 6.26), the frontispiece map shows Germany, but also with shaded areas showing the extent of Germany before the Second World War, right into East Prussia, with Königsberg, now Kaliningrad, areas that I doubt many pupils today suspect of ever having belonged to Germany. It is striking, by contrast with current textbooks, that these historical territories are given more prominence than German-speaking Austria, which is not shown in full. Anderson's *Aufenthalt in Deutschland* (1949) – predicated on the idea of an exchange visit to West Germany, so very much in the post-War spirit of rebuilding relations through youth exchanges – includes (and excludes) the same areas, though the illustrations guide the eye more to the culture of present-day Germany (Figure 6.27). Anderson's next textbook, *Das schöne Deutschland* (1955), which targeted adults in "continuation schools of all types," including evening students, was cited at the outset for its answer to the question *Was ist Deutschland?* The answer given in the frontispiece map differs from that given in the text, where Germany is West Germany, with its eleven *Bundesländer*. The map, in contrast, marks the eastern *Länder* off from the west with a dotted line, but the cities east of that line are nevertheless marked. Berlin appears as a black spot (literally!), with another dotted line down the middle. R. W. Buckley's *Living German* (first published in 1957, still going strong in a fifth edition in 1994) included no map of Germany at all, despite having a whole section devoted to travelling to Germany. This was still the case in 1982, but post-reunification, the fifth edition did finally include a map showing Germany with each of the (newly configured) *Länder* and their capitals marked. Austria and Switzerland are not marked – indeed none of the countries with which Germany shares a border are indicated. Fenn & Fangl (1954) in part avoided the awkward question of what Germany was by innovatively including cultural material about Austria and Switzerland (Fenn & Fangl 1954: 6; cf. Wagner 1999: 145–149), although the map on the endpapers shows both the "old" and "new" borders (Figure 6.29).

In the 1960 textbook *Fahrt ins Blaue* (Sutcliffe 1960), the embarrassment about Germany's borders was circumvented altogether by a map showing the stops along the journey of the book's title: these meander along the Rhine (a prime destination for early package holidays to Germany) and then into southern Germany and to Lake Constance, safely removed from any eastern borders (cf. Figure 6.29). By the later 1960s, we find *Sprich mal Deutsch* perhaps the first to accept the political reality of the separation of Germany into two states, with its map showing West Germany – under the proud banner of *Die Bundesrepublik* – as if it were an island (Figure 6.30). Not even Berlin rates a mention on this map. The map is accompanied by statements which pupils are to complete – one wonders just what constituted the correct completion of sentence 6.

303

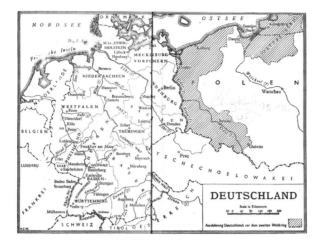

Figure 6.26: *Heute und Morgen* (Freudenberger 1955–1956)
map in front endpapers, also in 1965)

Figure 6.27: *Aufenthalt in Deutschland* endpapers map
(Anderson 1949 (-1965))

Ostdeutschland ist … Is what, indeed?[60] Contemporary with this map, however, was the 1967 reprint of the textbooks *Deutsches Land und deutsches Volk* I & II (Tudor & Heydorn 1956, 1959), whose map still shows Germany stretching right into East Prussia and

---

60 Similarly, Hammond (1969: xiv) showed West Germany – enough of East Germany was shown to put Berlin on the map, but the eastern border of East Germany was not shown, nor any GDR cities other than Berlin (compared to 20 marked in West Germany).

Figure 6.28: *Das schöne Deutschland* map (Anderson 1955)

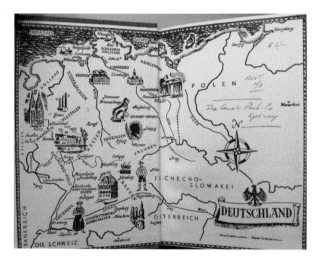

Figure 6.29: Fenn & Fangl (1954: front endpapers)

into Silesia, territory that had been agreed since the Potsdam conference of 1945 to belong (albeit provisionally, until 1990) to the south of Poland (Figure 6.33). It is possible that this is simply an error – the undated map is reproduced courtesy of Esso Petroleum Company, and one wonders if it was selected in haste for its eye-catching illustrations of the "sights", without sufficient attention to its eastern extent – but perhaps not. After all, a chapter in the second volume about a class excursion from Bremen to Braunschweig, then on into the Harz – through which the border between East and West ran – made no mention of such matters at all.

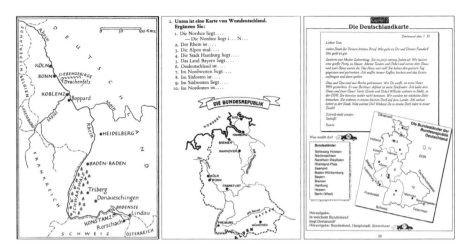

Figure 6.30 (left): *Fahrt ins Blaue* II (Sutcliffe 1961), map facing title page
Figure 6.31 (centre): *Sprich mal Deutsch* I (Rowlinson 1967: 57); the border to the East is marked with the West German terminology of *Zonengrenze* 'zone border'; the GDR, asserting its status as an independent state, referred to the *Staatsgrenze* 'state border'.
Figure 6.32 (right): *Deutsch Jetzt* 2 (McNab 1988: 38); Berlin, was de facto in many ways an eleventh *Bundesland*, as it is marked here, but was not officially a *Bundesland*.

Figure 6.33: *Deutsches Land und deutsches Volk*
(Tudor & Heydorn 1956, rpt. 1967: map on endpapers)

The map shown in *Sprich mal Deutsch* is the kind of map that I was familiar with when I was learning German at school in the early 1980s, and it is still there in *Deutsch Jetzt* 2, a textbook that had the misfortune to be published the year before the Wall fell in 1989. Berlin (West) appears in an island of apparently completely uninhabited territory (Figure 6.32), although other textbooks in the 1980s did at least show East Germany, as in

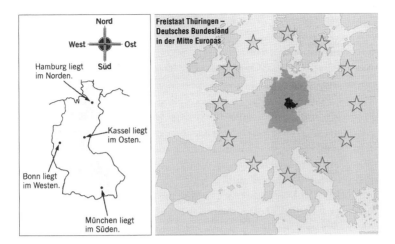

Figure 6.34 (left): *ZickZack* (Goodman-Stephens et al. 1987: 12) –
note the description of Kassel as "in the east"
Figure 6.35 (right): *Durchblick* feature on Thuringia as the heart of Germany
and Europe (Hares et al. 2000: 154)

Figure 6.36:
Alle einsteigen! 1 (Saunders 1992: 38) – note
the description of Kassel as in the centre of
Germany

Einfach toll (vol. I 1985: 92) and *ZickZack* 1
(1987: 12; Figure 6.34). Note the pedagogically motivated but otherwise rather strange
statement in *ZickZack* (1987: 12) that *Kassel
liegt im Osten*; five years later, after German
reunification, in *Alle einsteigen*, we find that
Kassel liegt in der Mitte Deutschlands (Saunders 1992: 38). The unified German map
there (Figure 6.36) shows not a hint of former divisions, quite unlike many of the post-
World War II maps, a difference that recalls
the need to reflect on the teaching of memory
(see above). The astonishing mobility of Kassel – and of a great many other places – sums
up nicely the difficulties of teaching basic
German geography in the twentieth century.
Finally a feature in *Durchblick* (Hares et al.
2000: 154–155, an A-level course tailored
to the OCR examining board A-level) on
Thuringia as the "green heart of Germany"
both reclaims this difficult border territory
and, through the map, places it and therefore Germany as a whole, symbolically at the
heart of the European Union (Figure 6.35).

6.9 Textbooks and stereotypes

Education influences children's constructions of self and other, including constructions of national identities (cf. Barrett 2007, Oppenheimer & Barrett 2011). Foreign language education – where teaching children about a specific out-group, a specific language community, is actually part of the task – is no exception. This section therefore examines how textbooks of German have constructed what it means to be "German" for English-speaking learners. Of course, representations in textbooks of German-speaking people and countries must be seen in the context of the troubled relationship between the UK and Germany in the twentieth century. In the late nineteenth century, it was still accepted that the Germans and the English were essentially the same. "The English were undoubtedly Teutons", and the Bishop of London, preaching before Queen Victoria in 1897, could safely assert that "the Teutonic race has the same fundamental ideas" (Robbins 1999: 20). Such views also found their way into the teaching of pupils. When an essay question for the 1890 Queen's Medal Preliminary examination at Rugby asked *What is the distinction observable between the Teutonic and Latin races with regard to the treatment of native populations?*, candidates would certainly have been expected to contrast the British and German treatment of native populations with those of the French and Spanish. In 1907, Stoy (1907) wrote in the *Modern Language Teaching* journal, on the topic of "The place of German in the curriculum of secondary schools":

> From the earliest times to the present, German and English thought have coincided; it is remarkable how, in all progress, English and German minds have marched in the same groove and supported and supplemented one another.

(Stoy 1907: 147)

That perspective, emphasizing affinities between the Germans and British (or English) rather than difference, would, however, disappear in the course of the twentieth century. The title of one historian's reflection on the history of that relationship already says much about it: "Always good neighbours, never good friends?" (Nicholls 2005), and the negative portrayal of Germany in the British media – especially the tabloid press – was a cause for concern throughout the twentieth century, beginning with O'Grady in the *Modern Language Teaching* journal of 1906, who bemoaned the "ten thousand devils in the guise of a cheap daily paper" fanning the flames of negative attitudes to Germany. Negative portrayals of Germany in the media continued even after German reunification, and such was the concern in the early 1990s that the Goethe Institute in London devoted a two-day British-German seminar to the topic of German national stereotypes in the British media (Hughes 1994; cf. also Theobald 1999, Krampikowski 1990), though Krönig (1999) remained equally aghast at the depiction of Germany in the British media five years later.[61] The historian Brechtken (2000: 17) has observed

---

61 There has been, perhaps, a perceptible shift just in the last few years, with a number of high-profile productions that take the long view of German history and attempt to present an insider's view to

that public images of Germany "are transformed with a certain 'delay' compared to the changes in political reality and bilateral relations" (Brechtken appears to be thinking of a delay of a couple of decades). Certainly the British view of Germans as highly patriotic, militaristic anti-Semites found by Keller (1986) to prevail in the 1980s would seem to support that view, even if Brechtken himself applied it to changing Anglo-German relations in the first half of the twentieth century too. Furthermore, Doerk (1990, cited Wegner 1999: 27), who examined representations of Germany in English schoolbooks from 1968–1986, found a time-lag of between five and ten years between the *Zeitgeist* and its finding its way into textbooks. With two levels of delay – first from actual political relations to an appropriately adjusted "image" or *Zeitgeist*, and then from the changed *Zeitgeist* to its being detectable in textbooks – we might expect to find textbooks of German some considerable way "behind the times" in the stereotypes they perpetuate or – later in the twentieth century – seek to confront. We should also bear in mind that textbook authors will not necessarily be balanced or objective in their representations of German-speaking people and their cultures; a certain germanophilism is to be expected (cf. section 6.4).

By the late twentieth century, challenging stereotypes was inscribed in the national curriculum (albeit only with the force of a suggestion of good practice):

> [S]tereotypical views are challenged and pupils learn to appreciate and view positively differences in others, whether arising from race, gender, ability or disability.

(Modern Foreign Languages National Curriculum 1999: 21)

The stereotype of German militarism, noted in MFL circles by Greatwood (1959: 58, cited earlier in this chapter), was one that Anderson had attempted to address in 1964, but Anderson was himself steeped in the essentialist thinking that generated such stereotypes. His answer to the charge that German militarism had caused two World Wars was that it was not militarism, but the "incapacity of the masses to think objectively and above all independently" (*diese Unfähigkeit der Masse, sachlich und vor allem selbständig zu denken*, p. 19) which had allowed "despotic" leaders to come to the fore, thus merely replacing one stereotype with another stereotype. Another common stereotype – the most frequent according to Hierl (1972: 174–175) in his analysis – is that of German humourlessness, which he finds mentioned in seven books in his corpus and countered either by counter-assertion, by narration of personal experience of humorous Germans, or with amusing

---

win over a sceptical British public. They include journalist Simon Winder's bestselling *Germania. A Personal History of Germans Ancient and Modern* (2010), BBC 4's television Germany Season (April 2011), including *Al Murray's German Adventure*, in which the comedian "embarks on a journey to discover the real Germany", and Misha Glenny's three-part BBC Radio 4 series *The Invention of Germany* which "aims to tackle British lack of knowledge about the country before the two world wars" (October 2011). The 2006 football World Cup, which Germany hosted, also yielded a great deal of positive coverage of Germany in the media and brought many British people to discover the modern Germany first-hand.

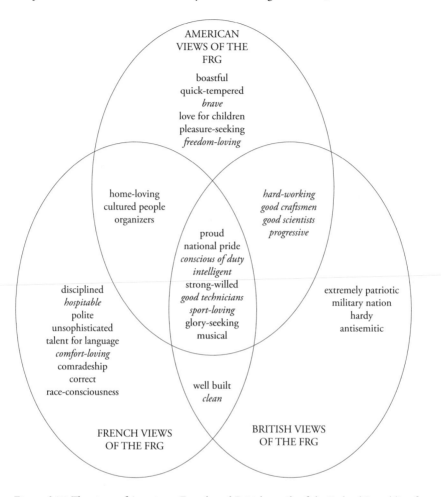

Figure 6.37: The views of American, French and British pupils of the Federal Republic of Germany in the mid-1980s (illustration following Keller 1986: 211, also presented in Friz 1991: 87). Characteristics in italics are those that were also found to be Part of (West-)Germans' views of themselves

anecdotes or literary references (e.g. Anderson 1964: 28, 1967: 41, Kelber 1951: 60). Garret's *Modern German Humour* (1969) was intended to counteract the view that German literature is "humourless, abstract, boring, in short Teutonic" (Garret 1969: 2).

A decade after Anderson, Paxton & Brentnall (1975) addressed not the substance of the stereotype, but the stereotypical thinking itself. Reflecting changing fashions in language teaching, the chapters in their *Zielpunkt Deutsch* were structured around topical "issues", also found in similar courses for A-level students, such as *Panorama* (Shotter 1981, volume four of a series that began in 1973) and *Neue Perspektiven* (Della

Gana 1988): the environment, women's rights, unemployment, generational conflicts, consumerism. One such issue was now that of stereotyping. By this stage, the German past had passed from being taboo to being endlessly present in popular British culture, whether in war dramas like the BBC's *Colditz* (1972–1974), or in popular comedies such as the BBC's *Dad's Army* (1968–1977) and the US film *The Producers* (1968). The result was growing stereotyping, which – with a certain delay – now focussed very strongly on World War II. In 1976, Keith Emmans, of the National Association of Language Advisors, lamented: "British TV seems to find rerunning the last war – through films or programmes such as *Colditz* – a necessary part of entertainment. This gives an entirely erroneous picture of the Federal Republic of Germany" (Emmans 1976: 28). Keller's (1986) comparative study of German-learning pupils' views of Germany is revealing (Figure 6.37). Note in particular two negative assessments held only by British pupils: "military nation", and "anti-Semitic" (as well as "hardy", but perhaps "tough"?, and "extremely patriotic"). Keller's finding should perhaps be viewed alongside the fact that British pupils in the late 1980s were heavily reliant on television as a source of information about Germany. It was named by 71 % of pupils as one of the top three sources of information about Germany, second only to German lessons – and recall that those learning German were only ever a minority. In the USA, the percentage listing television was only 48 %; see Friz (1991: 57). Such concerns no doubt contributed to the move to challenge stereotypes through foreign language education from the 1970s onwards. Indeed, the authors of the *Vorwärts* textbook series – which, with its sections explicitly labelled *Deutschlandkunde*, Wegner (1999: 290) described as *Deuschlandkunde intensiv* – explicitly stated that they sought to provide "an antidote to the inaccurate generalizations which might otherwise be made about Germany as a whole" (Nuffield Foundation 1971: 7, i. e. *Vorwärts* Stage 2B, cited by Wegner 1999: 291). Even as Wightman (1974: 29) continued the pre-war essentialist tradition of describing "the" Germans (e.g. "The Germans have always been a very musical people [...] The Germans obviously have a wonderful feeling for sounds and rhythms, and it is natural for them to express their feelings in music"), Paxton & Brentnall (1975: 209–219), devoted one of their 72 chapters to "what others think of us Germans" (*Was die anderen von uns Deutschen halten*), reporting research from 1966–1968 that showed foreigners associated Germans with uniforms and goosestepping soldiers, but also with Bavarian Lederhosen. The discussion is then widened to gender stereotypes (in France and Germany), asking "what such sweeping assumptions are good for", and explaining that they help us deal with the anxiety of not knowing what to expect from the unknown (p. 212). The textbook *Panorama* (Shotter 1981) dealt briefly with the question of race and racial stereotyping, which, it noted, had been particularly strongly associated with German Nazism, though for the first time Nazism was set alongside Mosley's Blackshirts in the UK, and Franco's and Mussolini's Fascism in Spain, and Italy. *Neue Perspektiven* (Della Gana 1988) devoted one of 14 units (three of 42 chapters) to the wider theme of prejudices, though it dealt not with prejudices about Germany but with typical gender roles, *Gastarbeiter* and xenophobia in Germany. In a *Sprungbrett* chapter on national identity (Bonnyman & Oberheid 1990: 135–136), the opening section, on *Deutschland-Klischees*, began

311

with an anecdote of the kind of thing such teachers and authors were trying to combat: a young German visiting England in 1986 being astonished to be greeted with a *Heil Hitler*. The focus is on the young German's surprise at the persistence of such *uralte* 'ancient' clichés, which are then contrasted with what the German pupils associated with being German (including descriptions such as *fortschrittlich, ein sozial[er] und menschenfreundlich[er] Staat, eine ganze normale Industrienation* 'progressive, a social and humane state, a perfectly normal industrialized nation', p. 137).

A somewhat courageous decision in the context of combating national stereotypes was that made by the authors of the *Einfach toll* series (Smith 1985–1991, Bates & Smith 1992) to base the illustrations around a cartoon sausage, *Würstchen* (Willy Würstchen, as some of my informants tell me he was inevitably known in their classes). The figure was presumably intended to avoid any particular stereotype of physical appearance for the "typical" German. However, besides positively inviting graffiti from pubescent learners (something that the first name Willy would further have encouraged amongst British learners, at least), the figure pandered to the stereotype of Germans as sausage-eaters. Perhaps the authors became aware of the problem, as the later volumes feature a bear rather than a sausage (cf. Figure 6.19 above).

A different way of avoiding stereotyping German speakers was that adopted by *Deutsch Heute* I (Sidwell & Capoore 1983), in which photographs of the characters showed not only white-skinned people, but also black individuals and a family whose names and appearance suggest roots in the Indian sub-continent (front inside cover and p. 119) – this a counterbalance to Johnson's finding for textbooks used in the 1960s that the most common adjectives for the physical appearance of Germans were *groß* and *blond* (Johnson 1973: 85, 88), even if in fact the images arguably reflect the profile of British rather than German ethnic minorities. In *Deutsch Heute* Germans eat not only sausages but also *Schaschlik* (marinated kebab of Turkish origin).[62] By the very end of the twentieth century, the first volume of the A-level course *Neue Aussichten* (McNeill et al. 2000) begins with a '*Kulturspot*' on *Deutschland – ein multikulturelles Land* ('Germany – a multicultural country'), a montage of photos with the question "Which of these people and scenes are typically German? Answer: all of them!" (p. 12; see Figure 6.38). Accounts by four individuals from France, Turkey, Canada and Taiwan of what strikes each of them about Germany offer an opportunity to discuss both positive and negative first impressions. "Discussing stereotypes" is one of the communicative foci listed for Chapter 4, which begins with an invitation to consider whether the people shown in the photos are *typisch deutsch* ('typically German', p. 80). Multiculturalism is clearly valued, as one section heading reads *Ein deutsches Deutschland? Nein, danke!* ('A German Germany? No thanks!' p. 90); and the textbook also reflects the wider concern since the 1990s, formulated for example in Fritzsche (1993: 55), that pupils' language learning experiences should attune them to the "multiperspectivity" of the world, that is:

---

62 Nevertheless, Byram & Baumgardt (1993) found that the textbook fell short of their requirements of intercultural approaches to learning.

Figure 6.38: McNeill (2000: 12)

"eine Vielheit und Verschiedenartigkeit von Traditionen, Weltanschauungen, Sinndeutungen, Lebensweisen und Werten. Genau genommen ist Multiperspektivität eine Qualität historischen und gesellschaftlichen Lebens überhaupt: die Unterschiedlichkeit der Abstammung, Herkunft und Klasse, der Religion, Kultur und Ideologie. [...] Die Welt ist multiperspektivisch (geworden)."

'a multitude and variety of traditions, worldviews, interpretations, lifestyles and values. To be precise, mulitperspectivity is a quality of all historical and social life: the variation in ancestry, origin and class, in religion, culture and ideology. [...] The world is (or has become) multiperspectivist.'

Of course, reflecting multiple perspectives is not limited to the matter of representing identities, including self and other, but is also addressed in late-twentieth-century textbooks showing a range of views on controversial issues such as political preferences (e.g. Stocker & Saunders 1988: 66) and abortion (Brien et al. 2000).

Though it is not our concern here, it is worth noting that the success of explicit attempts to challenge British stereotypes of Germany in the last quarter of the twentieth century seems at best qualified, for both Coleman (1999) and Price (1999) found that even university students returning from a period of study abroad ascribed positive and negative attributes to Germans, some of which at least seem to perpetuate long-held steretoypes (e.g. "disciplined", "lacking in humour" in Price 1999: 139), and some of which seem to become *more* entrenched after the period of residence abroad, such as "arrogant", a finding which Coleman attriuted to "incomplete intercultural competence". It is also worth reminding ourselves that even as textbooks have followed the stipulations of the National Curriculum since 1988 about positive images of cultural and racial difference (cited earlier), they are still in effect imposing a British agenda on pupils' familarization with a non-British language and culture.

6.10 Thematic analysis:
sport and fitness in twentieth-century textbooks of German

> – Do they divert themselves well in England?
> – Very well. There's Tennis, Bowling, Billiards, Nine-pins, Tables, Cards, and Dice.

(Offelen 1687: 216, "The fifteenth Dialogue. Of England")

> "'What do German boys want to know about English football, etc.?'

(Brebner 1898: 34)

Studies such as those of Johnson (1973), Krauskopf (1985), and Doerk (1990) have provided – each for their defined time-frames – studies of a wide range of themes in textbooks of German, including family life, school and university, work, fashion, literature, music and media (cf. footnote 13). In this section, I have chosen for exemplary analysis just one recurrent theme in twentieth-century textbooks of German, which may serve as an illustration of the potential for taking the long view of such themes: that of sport and physical fitness. The importance of sports as a pastime in British life was already acknowledged by Offelen (1687: 216, above), but sport became virtually ubiquitous in textbooks for young foreign language learners from the late nineteenth century onwards. Despite the scepticism that Mary Brebner heard some German teachers of English express in the late nineteenth century (cited above), sport has clearly been seen by textbook authors as being both appealing and relevant to young people: "sporty" Germans almost always feature in textbooks of German (as Price 1999 has noted). But sport is also the locus of social anxieties. It is one avenue through which cultural historians can analyse "the production of identity in modern societies" (Schiller & Young 2009: 319). It is something through which "conflicts of class, gender and ethnicity can be acted out" (Schiller & Young 2009: 319). In addition, sport can "act as an imaginative space and sphere of experience for emerging national identities" (Schiller & Young 2009: 320), perhaps particularly so for Germany and Britain. Sport has a strong ideological tradition in Britain, in particular as a part of the education of young men in Public Schools for their destiny as servants of Empire (Holt 1989). In Germany, meanwhile, sport (or at least certain forms of it) was closely associated with nationalism from the early nineteenth century onwards (when Ludwig Jahn's championing of gymnastics had a nationalistic agenda; see 6.10.2 below), and, in the twentieth century, with National Socialist and Communist ideologies.[63] Yet the only analysis to date of the treatment of sport in twentieth-century textbooks does not engage with this ideological burden at all. Johnson (1973) merely observes:

---

63 For bibliography on sport under Nazism, see Peiffer (2009); for bibliography on sport in the GDR, see Peiffer & Fink (2003). I follow here the overview of German sports history provided by Schiller & Young (2009) in the introduction to their themed issue of *German History* on sport in German history.

Germany emerges as a relative newcomer to professional sport, particularly football. The latter developed much later in Germany than in England, when the Germans borrowed a good deal. It is implied that Germans are basically less interested in sport than the English, perhaps because there is less emphasis placed on competitive team games at school. Other sports, such as canoeing, are mainly pursued for private recreation or to get to know the country better.

(Johnson 1973: 153–154).

Johnson's summary reflects the contents of the three textbooks he cited as representative examples,[64] but his narrow selection (and narrow time-frame, limited to the 1950s and 1960s) conceals the fact that sport and fitness become, in the twentieth century, a locus where considerable, though changing, social anxieties were played out.

6.10.1 Which sports?

The question of which sports are popular in Germany was of enduring interest throughout the twentieth century. Theilkuhl (1940) observed that walking and running were popular; so too was cycling; likewise horse and dog-racing, on which bets might be laid, but *lange nicht so viel wie in England* 'not nearly as much as in England' (Theilkuhl 1940: 182); Theilkuhl also noted motor racing and flying as German strengths; winter sports were much more popular than in England. Amongst ball sports, tennis was reported to be the most popular, with 1000 clubs with a total of 100,000 members. There was, Theilkuhl stated, little general interest in football (*Für Fußball interessiert sich die Allgemeinheit wenig*, p. 183); rugby was rarely played and was considered *roh* 'rough'. In keeping with the tenets of the dominant *Kulturkunde* paradigm of the time, Theilkuhl emphasized the differences between German and British attitudes to sport, in a section headed *Vergnügungen und Sport* ('Pastimes and Sport') in a chapter on *Öffentliches Leben* ('Public Life'):

---

64 The three passages cited by Johnson are: *Im allgemeinen zeigen die Deutschen noch heutzutage weniger Interesse für Sport als die Engländer und Schotten, doch ist es nötig, dies weiter zu erklären. Die vielen Ligen, die für die Kirchen- und Fabrikmannschaften und für allerlei Amateurvereine in Großbritannien so weit verbreitet sind, waren vor einigen Jahren in Deutschland so gut wie unbekannt, kommen aber heute zum Vorschein. Zweitens spielen die Schulen nicht gegeneinander, obgleich sie auch jetzt besonders in Norddeutschland mit Ausscheidungs- und Meisterschaftskämpfen beginnen. Erst 1920 haben die Deutschen begonnen, ernsthaft Fußball zu spielen, sodaß heutzutage fast jede Stadt mindestens eine Mannschaft besitzt.* (*Modern German for Adults*, i. e. Cook 1962: 51, cited by Johnson 1973: 152–53) – *Dann kann man sagen, dass die Faltboote ein Vergnügen bereiten, dass die Studenten und alle jungen Leute lieben. Sehr viele können in ihren Jugendjahren, danke den Faltbooten und dem Kanalsystem, ihr Land gut kennenlernen. Überhaupt ist die ganze Sportjugend sehr stolz, eine Rhein-, Donau- und Oderfahrt gemacht zu haben, und für die Jungen und Mädels, die nicht so stark sind, gibt es immer die Kanäle als Ersatz.* (Cook 1962: 52, cited by Johnson 1973: 153) – *Fußball ... ist das beliebteste Spiel ... Rugby wird nur sehr wenig gespielt. Jeden Samstag und Sonntag finden Fußballspiele statt, und zu diesen Spielen kommen Tausende von Zuschauern ... Lange Berichte erscheinen in den Zeitungen, und die großen Spiele hört man im Radio, oder man sieht sie im Fernsehen. Alles ist genau wie in England, aber in Deutschland spielen fast nur Amateure, es gibt weniger 'Profis' als in England.* (*Deutsches Leben* 2 1961, 2nd ed., 1970 impression: 47–48, cited by Johnson 1973: 153)

> Das Interesse für Sport hat seit dem Kriege in Deutschland sehr zugenommen. Immerhin ist es lange nicht so groß und allgemein wie in England.

> 'The interest in sport has greatly increased since the [First World] War. Still, it is not nearly so great or general as in England.'

> Theilkuhl (1940: 182).

Also in keeping with the ideals of the *Kulturkunde* movement, two textbooks drew attention to German sports not well known in Britain. The 1934 edition of *Deutsches Leben* 3, presented a dialogue explaining the rules of *Schlagball*, a version of rounders, complete with diagram of the pitch (Macpherson & Strömer 1934: 24–27). Meyer & Nauck's *Das Neue Deutschland* (1931) featured a report from an older pupil in Germany in which the rules of handball, described as the favourite sport of most older pupils, were minutely explained, complete with a diagram of the pitch and players' positions, and right down to the off-side rule (Meyer & Nauck 1931: 32–35). Natan (1955) also singled out handball as a specifically German contribution to sport: played according to football rules, it is a sort of German equivalent of English cricket and American baseball. By 1965, however, Buckley (1965: 200) considered in *Living German* that handball 'used to be played a lot, especially by schoolboys' but was less played now (*Handball ist auch früher viel gespielt worden, besonders von den Schuljungen*).

In Buckley's *Living German*'s chapter on *Deutscher Sport* (Buckley 3rd ed. 1965: 200–201), Herr Jones learns in conversation that the most popular sports are swimming and boating; winter sports are also popular; football is played too; tennis is not much played because of the expense. In the latter decades of the century, information about popular sports is often presented not through conversation, but through survey data which provide a springboard for classroom discussions. According to the *Neue Aussichten* chapter on *Sportnation Deutschland?*, swimming, gymnastics, cycling, jogging and table tennis were the top five sports practised by Germans (McNeill et al. 2000: 37). Football was in seventh place, behind cross-country skiing. According to the data presented in *Brennpunkt* (Sandry et al. 2000: 23), water sports (including swimming) had the highest participation rates among young people, followed by football for boys; for girls, volleyball was in second place.

While the textbooks of the 1930s and 1940s tended – in keeping with the principles of *Kulturkunde* – to focus on the differences between the sporting cultures of Germany and Britain, later textbooks more or less explicitly attended to shared interests, increasingly with a focus on football. Fifteen years after Theilkuhl's assessment that football was of relatively minor interest, Natan (1955) judged that 'Germany's most popular sport is football' (*Deutschland's* [sic] *populärster Sport ist der Fussball*), noting that Germany had won the World Cup in 1954. In second place was athletics, followed by handball. Hockey and rugby were, Natan stated, particularly popular in those cities with historical ties to England: Heidelberg, Frankfurt, Hamburg and Hannover (p. 141). Wightman (1974: 87) noted that "Football, athletics, gymnastics and several ball games are all popular", and pointed out that "there are always huge crowds at professional football matches". Paxton & Brake vol. 2 (1971: 62–63), writing in the aftermath of two world-cup finals between Germany and England (1966, 1970), is the only textbook that I am aware of to devote a chapter to football: the double-page spread of *Fußball in Deutschland* opens with a table summarizing the results of the two recent World Cup finals, both of which ended with penalty shoot-outs:

1966 London	1970 Mexiko
England 4	Westdeutschland 3
Westdeutschland 2	England 2

The 1954 German World Cup victory over Hungary is also noted. Nevertheless, the main text of the chapter still begins with the observation that 'football perhaps does not have the same fascination for Germans as for the English' (*Fußball hat vielleicht für die Deutschen nicht genau denselben Reiz wie für die Engländer*). In *Neue Perspektiven*, football hooliganism in England, rather than football itself, is the topic of a passage for translation into German. However, this is characteristic of the earnest, problem-based approach to all topics in *Neue Perspektiven* – in the same chapter, young offenders are required to attend gymnastics club as an alternative to prison, for example (Della Gana 1987: 110, 111).

6.10.2 Why sport?

Despite Paxton & Brake's focus in *Lernen wir Deutsch* on the competition between German and British footballers in two World Cup showdowns, on the whole textbook treatments of sport bear out Johnson's observation that sports in Germany are portrayed in textbooks as more about taking an active part, and less about competition (whether direct competition, or vicarious competition through spectating). In Buckley's *Living German* Herr Jones comes to the enthusiastic conclusion that Germans participate more than spectate, by implicit contrast with the British: *Hier sind Sie richtige Sportsmänner: alle Teilnehmer und keine Zuschauer!* ('Here you are real sportsmen: all participants and no spectators!' Buckley 1965: 201). Even when Paxton & Brake devote a chapter in the third volume to the 1972 Munich Olympics (Paxton & Brake vol. 3, 1972), the focus is not on elite competition. Instead, the reader is presented with facts and figures about the building of the Olympic village; we are reminded of Hitler's refusal at the 1936 Berlin Olympics to present the gold medal to Jesse Owens because he was black (p. 81); and we learn that more than half of the workers involved in building the Olympic village were *Gastarbeiter* from Italy, Yugoslavia and Turkey. The Olympics are here used to comment on demographic change, rather than to highlight sporting achievements. *Sprungbrett* (Bonnyman & Overheid 1990: 24–25) reproduces a billboard poster of the German Sports Federation (*Deutscher Sportbund*), showing two tennis players relaxing after a game (one holds a long drink in his hand), proclaiming that 'Sport is nicest in a club … because here we forget everyday stress from the word go' (*mit einem Schlag*)[65]

---

65 There is an untranslateable play on words here: *mit einem Schlag* means 'with one strike, in one fell swoop', but *schlagen* is also the verb used for hitting a ball in sport.

Im Verein ist Sport am schönsten

...weil wir hier den Alltagsärger mit einem Schlag vergessen!

Bei uns im Verein ist die Entspannung so wichtig wie die Spannung beim Spiel. Sie werden überrascht sein, was die Vereine auch bei Ihnen für den Feierabend so zu bieten haben.

Deutscher Sportbund

Figure 6.39:
Sprungbrett (Bonnymann & Overheid 1990: 24)

(Figure 6.39). Even club sport, then, is represented as recreational rather than competitive, although the textbook does ask pupils to analyse the advertisement critically.

In Britain, in contrast, sport had won its ideological value in the Public School education system as a means of promoting fair play, team spirit and healthy competition amongst the young elite in the nineteenth century (Holt 1989). Two of the very earliest photos in a textbook of German are used to picture tennis and football teams (and it is no coincidence that the author of that text was Assistant Master at the leading Public School Eton, where sports had a key role: Chaffey 1907: 4, 16; cf. 3.10 above). At the dawn of the twentieth century, Siepmann's *German Public School Primer* recognized on the very first page of the first lesson the central importance of sports for encouraging competition:

"Die Spiele spielen eine wichtige Rolle im englischen Schulleben. Wir versuchen, in der Klasse und auf dem Spielplatz, zu den Ersten zu gehören"

'Games play an important role in English school life. We try to be among the first, in the classroom and on the pitch'

(Siepmann 1900: 1)[66]

Thirty years later, Meyer & Nauck, the German authors of *Das Neue Deutschland* (1931), now also acknowledged the importance of sport as part of children's education. In their first chapter, on education, a third-year class at a *Gymnasium* reports that they have sport three times a week, plus a break for sports of 45 minutes every day (Meyer & Nauck 1931: 11). Still, German and British attitudes to sport in education are contrasted explicitly, as a German and English teacher exchange views. The German teacher comments that for the British, school sport is part of the aim to educate 'the whole person at school. Hence

---

66 On the other hand, reading passage 17, headed "Sport in den Ferien" does not deal with competitive sport at all, but with going fishing (Siepmann 1900: 17). Notwithstanding this representation of fishing as a sport for the holidays, Theilkuhl (1940: 183) considered fishing *eine ziemlich seltene Liebhaberei* 'a relatively rare passion'.

the large role that sport plays for you, much more than for us' (*den ganzen Menschen auf der Schule. Daher auch die große Rolle, die Sport bei Ihnen spielt, viel mehr also bei uns*). In contrast, 'in Germany we particularly want to train the spirit and reason' (*In Deutschland will man besonders den Geist und Verstand ausbilden*, Meyer & Nauck 1931: 15).

Two further chapters – Chapters 2 and 3 – of the eight chapters in *Das Neue Deutschland* are also devoted to sport: *Sport und Spiel*, and the book also contains a chapter on the *Jugendbewegung*, the German youth hiking and hostelling movement that emerged around 1900. Theilkuhl (1940: 148) laid bare the political tensions inherent in this youth movement, pointing out that after a short-lived umbrella organization was founded in 1919, the movement split again into a more working class grouping that became an organ of the Communist party, and a larger grouping that ultimately became incorporated into the Hitler Youth, founded in 1926 as the youth branch of the National Socialist Party.

Anxiety about such ideological harnessing of sport in Germany is very obvious in Natan's post-War textbook *Neues Deutschland*, a reader for "students of advanced German studies" published in 1955 (Natan 1955: v). The ideological dimension of sport is explicit in the opening sentence of Chapter XVIII, *Sport*:

> Die Leibesübungen sind zu einem Kult geworden, dem im nationalen Leben Deutschlands eine grössere Rolle zugefallen ist als in anderen Ländern.

> 'Physical fitness has become a cult, which has taken on a greater role in the national life of Germany than in other countries.'

(Natan 1955: 137)

Natan's account of sport in Germany begins with the gymnastics movement of Friedrich Ludwig Jahn (1778–1852), known as *Turnvater Jahn* (Father of Gymnastics). During the Napoleonic occupation of Prussia, he writes, the nationalist Jahn viewed gymnastic exercises as 'ideological schooling against the hated arch-enemy Napoleon. Jahn belonged to those Teutomaniacs who abhorred everything foreign and who preached a return to the customs and practices of the ancient Germanic people' (*ideologische Schulung gegen den verhassten Erbfeind Napoleon. Jahn gehörte zu jenen Teutomanen, die alles Fremdländische verabscheuten und die Rückkehr zu den Sitten und Gebräuchen der alten Germanen predigten*, Natan 1955: 137), but Jahn was not, Natan remarks, taken very seriously after the liberation of Germany from Napoleon.[67] Nevertheless, the always somewhat nationalistic gymnastics movement later came to be associated closely with National Socialism, part of the cultivation of a mighty Germanic race. Natan wrote that after World War I, as sports fell in the 1920s into the hands of former army officers, sporting excellence came to be seen as a means of overcoming a sense of inferiority: every German victory was a re-assertion of German greatness after the humiliation of World War I, a view which reached its highpoint in the 1936 Olympics hosted by the National Socialists

---

67 See Schiller & Young (2009) for a recent assessment of Jahn's place in the history of German sport and German nationalism, against which Natan's summary appears to be reasonable accurate.

in Berlin. Natan summarized, 'Under the leadership of narrow-minded nationalists, the German sportsman had lost the art of being able to lose with a smile' (*Unter der Führung engstirniger Nationalisten hatte der deutsche Sportsmann die Lebenskunst verlernt, mit einem Lächeln verlieren zu können*, Natan 1955: 139).

Natan's final words on sport – which are also the final words of his book – expressed the fear that sport could once again become an outlet and rallying point for excessive nationalism:

> Die Überbewertung allerdings, die der Sport ganz allgemein in Deutschland ge-
> niesst, birgt die Gefahr neuer nationalistischer Exzesse in sich. Deswegen würde
> es auch nicht überraschen, wenn ein Rückschlag in politischer oder wirtschaft-
> licher Hinsicht zu einer Flucht vor der Realität führen würde, hinein in den
> Sport, der durch seine billigen Erfolgsmöglichkeiten einer enttäuschten Jugend
> so leicht zu einem künstlichen Rausch verhelfen kann.

> 'However, the excessive value accorded sport in general in Germany conceals
> a danger of new nationalistic excesses. It would therefore not be surprising if a
> political or economic set-back led to a flight from reality into sport, which, with
> the possibilities of cheap success, can so easily cause an artificial intoxication in
> disaffected youth.'

(Natan 1955: 142–143)

This "Reader for students of advanced German studies" thus ends on a strikingly down-beat note, especially compared with the determinedly positive representations of Germans and Germany in 1950s school textbooks (cf. 6.4). The book also serves to illustrate the importance of an author's personal biography to understanding their choice of material. Heinz Alex Natan (1906–1971) (originally Nathan) had competed in the 1928 Olympics and was part of the team that broke the world record for the 100m relay in 1929. However, because he was deemed by the Nazi authorities to be a Jew, Natan's name was removed from the list of record-holders. He moved to England in 1933, where he taught History at the King's School, Worcester, but also taught the Sixth Form German literature. One can hardly wonder that he paid so much attention to the topic of sport, nor that he was particularly alert to its susceptibility to ideology.[68]

The overtly political dimension of sport is not addressed again in textbooks after Natan, and indeed 1960s and 1970s textbooks have relatively little to say about sport at all. When sport returns to prominence as a topic in the 1980s, it is because it once again becomes ideological territory – this time not along political lines, but reflecting societal pressure to keep fit and healthy. If Wightman (1974: 87) had observed that in West Germany, "A surprising number of people take part in sports just to keep fit" and that in the German Democratic Republic, "There are sports facilities in public parks to encourage even middle aged people to keep fit" (Wightman 1974: 126), such attitudes had ceased

---

68 I am grateful to Professor Nicholas Boyle, Cambridge, who was taught by Natan and who alerted
  me to his sporting background. See Amrhein (2005), s.v. Natan.

to surprise by the 1980s. In *Neue Perspektiven*, keeping the population fit is presented as a societal concern, and, indeed, more specifically as a concern of the medical insurance companies who finance medical care; and an article presents cycling as an ideal form of keeping fit. The frequency of the deontic form *sollte* 'should' is striking (and it is not a language focus for the chapter). People 'should' *(sollten)* use cycling to counterbalance stress at work; one 'should' *(sollte)* train daily; one's speed 'should' *(sollte)* be such that one can still hold a conversation. Meanwhile, in a listening exercise, expectant mothers 'should' *(sollten)* keep fit throughout their pregnancy (Della Gana 1987: 120, 121). Here, clearly, sport has attracted moral value. It is something one is supposed to do.

This moral dimension – the obligation to measure one's sport-related behaviour against a societally accepted standard – is similarly evident in the chapter *Fit werden, fit bleiben* of the 1995 AS-level textbook *Einsicht*, which opens with the challenge to readers: *Wie zufrieden sind Sie zur Zeit mit Ihrer körperlichen Fitneß?* ('How content are you at the moment with your physical fitness?' Stocker & Saunders 1995: 95). According to a survey cited on that opening page, the top sports in Germany – in terms of numbers of participants – are swimming, cycling, running, football and tennis (in that order). However, while sport is the springboard into the chapter, most of the chapter is about fitness more broadly, including good nutrition, the risks of smoking, 30 tips for good health, and a "stress-test", a survey about stress levels. Pupils are invited to write essays on the topic 'My health is my business!' (*Meine Gesundheit ist meine Sache!*), or on the pros and cons of smoking (p. 104).

In *Einsicht* (2000), an entire chapter is devoted to *Essen und Gesundheit* ('eating and health'), with features on healthy eating, reasons for wanting to lose weight, and eating disorders, including bulimia. *Schauplatz* (Brien et al. 2000: 48, 50) also tackles the question of sport and gender in its chapter on *Freizeit* ('leisure'). A feature on Andrea Spitzer, women's world champion in the quadriathlon, implicitly challenges the tendency of society to attend to successful male rather than female sports personalities, though it is striking that she is introduced in the first sentence as a *Fotomodell*, a model. The following feature tackles the question of gender roles and sports head-on: 'Ice hockey – men only?' (*Eishockey – nur Männersache?*), with an interview with a player in Cologne's female ice-hockey team, the Brownies. Likewise, *Deutschland hier und jetzt* (Rowlinson 1993: 114) features an article form the German magazine *Kicker* titled *Frauen boxen sich durch: Männerdomänen gibt es kaum noch* ('Women box their way through: there are hardly any men-only domains left in sport').

In sum, we have seen that the perennially popular topic of sport has been repeatedly angled to suit a changing ideological agenda. It has been used to promote an ideal of healthy competition, but also of participation for all; it has served to emphasize shared interests (football) or to stress cultural difference (handball); it can be a means to warn against excessive nationalism, or to highlight social dysfunction (hooliganism); and it has been used to promote healthy lifestyle choices and gender equality in line with much wider British political and educational agendas.

6.11 Gender and historical critical textbook analysis

Textbooks of German do not only perpetuate or challenge stereotypes about German speakers. As already noted, they also help construct group identities: national and regional identities, but also other categories such as gender, as some of the final examples from Section 6.10 above show. A great deal of recent work has been on the construction of gender, race and national and European identities in public discourses of various kinds (see e.g. Wodak et al. 2009, Hogan 2009); and earlier sections in this chapter have looked briefly at some aspects of the construction in textbooks of a German national or ethnic identity, as well as at the construction of a European identity. In this section, I will illustrate how a critical approach, inspired by Critical Discourse Analysis (CDA), can be used to analyse the historical construction of such key notions in textbook discourse and imagery,[69] though again with the caveat that I can offer no more than a helicopter flyover of material that would warrant closer study. While it is tempting to widen coverage beyond the twentieth century – recall the prominence of women as objects of love and desire in König (1715), for example (Chapter 2) – I shall restrict myself to the twentieth century. The analysis is to some extent the equivalent of shooting fish in a barrel, for it will come as no surprise to find that textbooks of German reflect prevailing female stereotypes and gender roles, but as documentation of the treatment of one aspect of society that underwent a revolution in the last century, it has its place.[70] Implicit in much of my discussion is the question of class – in particular the strong bias towards portraying (upper) middle class lifestyles – but space prevents me from pursuing it further. The analysis of gender stands as one example of the kind of historical thematic analysis that could be undertaken for a wealth of themes that have already been the subject of synchronic rather than diachronic textbook analyses, such as representations of family, work, ethnicity and religion.

As we saw in Chapter 4, the authors of most language textbooks early in the twentieth century assumed their users would be boys in the Public School or Grammar School system. This may partially explain – but only partially – why women and girls are barely present as actors outside the home in textbooks of this era. In Trotter's book of Object Lessons, for example (1898), a picture labelled "The kitchen" shows the female cook busy "preparing the meals", while the text beneath tells us that the female servant cleans the house and the nursemaid looks after the children (Figure 6.40). In the upper

---

69 As Van Dijk (2003: 352) defines it, Critical Discourse Analysis is a "type of discourse analytical research that primarily studies the way social power abuse, dominance, and inequality are enacted, reproduced and resisted by text and talk in the social and political context". See also Wodak et al. (2009: Chapter 2).

70 It should also be remembered that it is male rather female learners who are now tending to be under-represented in the foreign language classroom. See Carr & Pauwels (2009), Jones et al. (2001). On the history of the feminization of the pursuit of language education see Cohen (1999, 2001, 2002); Bayley & Yaworsky Ronish (1992) on gender and modern languages in Victorian England; and Doff (2002) on the teaching of English in girls' schools in nineteenth-century Germany. On sexual identity and the teaching of French in the Low Countries, see Kok Escalle & van Strien-Chardonneau (2011). On the history of 'finding' gender differences between learners, see Schmenk (2001).

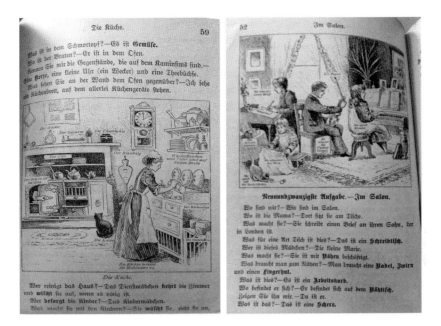

Figure 6.40 (left): Trotter (1898: 59), Figure 6.41 (right): Trotter (1898: 52)

middle-class living room, meanwhile, the women are in subservient roles too: *Im Salon* shows a mother writing a letter to her son in London, Marie busy sewing, and an older sister playing the piano, ready to accompany her brother. It is he who occupies the centre of the picture, tuning his violin. Around him the two older female figures are engaged in supporting males, the third, sewing, is practising a skill she will need for such a role when she is older (Figure 6.41). In another image of the living room in the same volume (cf. Figure 6.3 above), three of the four females are again relegated to the peripheral space: two are at the piano, the youngest is nursing a doll. In contrast her brother rolls a ball towards the central space, which is occupied by the grandfather and father. In deference to age, the fourth female, the grandmother, sits in an armchair reading, but it is the grandfather, not she, who has the warm spot by the fire. Here as in the dining-room image (also shown in Figure 6.3 above), the fashionable dress of the lady of the house strikes the eye, with its corseted wasp waist that precludes much action. In Siepmann (1913), also already discussed, the predominance of "white male heads" was already noted (Figure 6.5); in the only other image in that book, that of Crystal Palace, in contrast, women outnumber and are more prominent than men, but it is their nostalgically drawn elaborate crinolines that strike the eye (Figure 6.6). Like the wasp-waisted women in the Trotter volume, the women are here to be admired; the one male in the foreground gesticulates authoritatively with his walking cane.

(34)
9.—DIE SCHULE.

1. Eine Schule.   2. Die Knabenklasse.   3. Die Mädchenschule.
4. Der Lehrer.   5. Ein Zögling.   6. Die Schultafel.   7. Das Pult.
8. Die Mädchen.   9. Die Lehrerin.   10. Das Gerüst.   11. Die Landkarte.
12. Das Bild   13. Die Wand.   14. Das Schultafelgestell.
15. Die Feder.   16. Das Papier.   17. Das Buch.   18. Der Bleistift.

Figure 6.42:
Baumann (1910: 34)

Figure 6.43:
Grundy (1931: 2)

Despite the persistence of gender-specific titles like *Bob lebt sich in Deutschland ein* ('Bob gets used to living in Germany', Güntsch 1934) and *John erlebt Deutschland* ('John experiences Germany', Gretton 1955), some girls *were* of course learning German, and Baumann's course (1910) conscientiously reflects that, showing both a girls' classroom and a boys' classroom (Figure 6.41). Even here, though, there are strong gender differences. The boys are drawn facing the viewer, watching the teacher, who stands tall and – like Siepmann's male visitor at the Great Exhibition – gesticulates with his cane. In contrast, the girls are facing away from the viewer, their heads bowed meekly over their work; their teacher too has her head bowed to speak to a pupil at her desk. Established gender roles – men act and control, women are subservient – are here reinforced.

One way that women could feature in roles beyond the home was through the selection of prose composition passages for more advanced learners. Here too, however, women are not strongly represented, neither as authors nor – to judge by my analysis of one textbook presented below – as figures in the passages chosen. In Mutschmann's 1914 collection of prose passages for translation, discussed in 6.2 above, just over ten per cent of the passages (seven out of sixty) are by women: Charlotte Brontë, Jane Austen, George Eliot, Elizabeth Gaskell, Elizabeth von Arnim (two passages), and Anne Jameson. Besides two fictional passages about children – Brontë's Jane Eyre and Eliot's Tom and Maggie Tulliver, there only two passages about females. Both are from Elizabeth von Arnim's anonymously published *Elizabeth and her German Garden* (1898), and although that is a work where the question of the equality of the sexes is

324

Figure 6.44: Frau Meyer's fashions in Grundy (1931: 10, 14, 20, 30, 34)

explicitly raised,[71] the titles that Mutschmann assigned to the two extracts serve to stereotype the women respectively as a "Frau Professor" (the male professor's helpmeet) and "A Model German Country Hausfrau". In the second of the two passages, the narrator describes her neighbour as "the pattern of what a German country lady should be [...] not only a pretty one but an energetic and practical one, and the combination is, to say the least, effective" (Mutschmann 1914: 34). The woman's busy life is described with a mixture of admiration and gentle ridicule; for example, the woman apparently enjoys the legal privilege of being able to punish her servants, "standing on tiptoe to box the ears of some strapping girl big enough to eat her". On the other hand, the possible frustration of an intelligent woman in her closely circumscribed domestic role is alluded to: "The making of cheese and butter and sausages excellently well is a work which requires brains [...] entirely worthy of the attention of the intelligent" (p. 64). Such a life has "no room for those listless moments of depression and boredom, and of wondering what you

---

71 For example: "What nonsense it is to talk about the equality of the sexes when the women have the babies!"; "I wish with all my heart I were a man". (I have used the text at Project Gutenberg: http://www.gutenberg.org/files/1327/1327-h/1327-h.htm, accessed July 2014).

Figure 6.45:
Hammond (1969: front cover, also p. 154)

will do next, that leaves [*sic*] wrinkles around a pretty woman's eyes" (pp. 64–65) – a statement suggesting that the narrator/author herself, an intelligent lady of leisure, *is* prone to such boredom-induced wrinkles. The prettiness of the intelligent neighbour is invoked three times in the passage.

The idea that women are chiefly an adornment for the benefit of men is strong in the 1930s *Brush Up Your German* series, already discussed at some length in this chapter and in Chapter 4 (Figure 4.12). As we have seen, Frau Meyer is portrayed as a sweetly scheming flibbertigibbet, who tricks her husband into approving of her new dress, for example; as a loving mother who wants the best for her son; and as someone with no interest at all in contemporary politics. The illustrations – wonderful though they are – reinforce the infantilization of the woman. Frau Meyer is first introduced to us by the illustrator on page 2, where she sits at her husband's feet, with a winning smile on her face; her overly large head and eyes give her the proportions of a child (Figure 6.43). Her gown here is followed by a succession of strikingly fashionable clothes in later images (Figure 6.44 shows some examples); her role is limited to that of attractive and sometimes distracting accessory for Herr Meyer as he conducts his business affairs.

Grundy's series is certainly an extreme example of the stereotyping of (upper middle class) women, and of course to some extent it is a deliberate caricature on which much of the humour of the series depends. What is perhaps more surprising is to find an image that objectifies women on the front cover of a textbook nearly six decades later: Hammond (1969) (Figure 6.45). The image is credited to the German Embassy, and is harmlessly titled "newspaper kiosk" where it recurs in the main text (p. 155): *Zeitungskiosk*. Clearly some thought has gone in to the selection of images – "The pictures are intended not only to illuminate the background to the extracts, but also to serve as material for description or discussion" (Preface, p. vi) – and the construction of female gender in this prominent cover image evidently did not seem problematic. The image shows a young woman, well dressed and with her blond hair beautifully styled, standing at a kiosk. Three magazine front covers are visible in the kiosk display, and all show women in sexualized poses – on the left, the woman sucks suggestively on her fingers, while the second and third gaze at the camera from under their lashes.

Less visually striking than images such as those discussed thus far, but still significant in delineating gender roles, is the selection of passages in the many books of prose passages for translation in the third quarter of the twentieth century, to which I now turn. In Kolisko & Yuill (1956), out of 150 English passages for translation into German, sixteen, or just over 10 %, are by women writers (Naomi Mitchison, Naomi Royde-

Smith (4), Jane Austen, Eileen Wedgwood, Amy Cruse, Ngaio Marsh, Margaret Cole, Caroline A. Lejeune, George Eliot (2), and Dorothy L. Sayers (3)). In Russon & Russon's *Advanced German Course* (1965), the representation of women writers is just under 10%, at 19 out of 120 passages in English (Virginia Woolf (4), Elizabeth Bowen (2), Ivy Compton-Burnett (3), Doris Lessing, Iris Murdoch (3), L. Susan Stebbing, F. Tennyson Jesse, C. Veronica Wedgwood (2), Margaret Mare, Victoria Sackville-West). Freda Kellett – a woman who was prominent in girls' education, ending her career as Headmistress of the independent girls' Birkenhead High School (1971–1986) – managed double that rate in her selection of English passages in Kellett (1964), with 18 out of 70 passages by women (just over a quarter), without even drawing on the old standbys of Jane Austen and George Eliot. Kellett's choices included Katherine Mansfield, Pamela Hansford Johnson, Muriel Spark, Vita Sackville-West, Rosamund Lehmann, Daphne du Maurier, Gwen Raverat, Dorothy Sayers, Honor Tracy, Emma Smith (2), Nancy Mitford, Marghanta Laski, Iris Murdoch, Ann Bridge, Elspeth Huxley (2), and Rebecca West. Brookes & Fraenkel (1958) – a duo of female compilers – featured 24 passages by women out of 110, or about 22% (Jean Ingelow, Helen Keller, Mrs Molesworth, Dorothy Sayers, Edith Nesbit, Elizabeth Bowen (2), Sylvia Warner Townsend, Queen Victoria, Flora Thompson, Jane Austen, Rebecca West, Anne Brontë, Freya Stark, Jacquetta Hawkes, Elizabeth Gaskell, Virginia Woolf (2), Gertrude Bell, C. Veronica Wedgwood, Agnes Arber, Katherine Mansfield, and Ivy Compton-Burnett (2)). Judging compilers by the number of women writers represented in composition textbooks like this is crude, for it does not allow for the fact that the compilers sought to cover a range of subject areas, including many where women were underrepresented. So, while the textbook with the lowest proportion of passages by women is Russon & Russon (1965), it is noteworthy that the book does include writing by the analytical philosopher Susan Stebbing and the historian C. Veronica Wedgwood. It is also worth noting that of the sixty passages in Fehrke (1903), none is identifiably by a woman. Clearly the difference between 0 and 10% – between invisibility and visibility – covered in the first half of the twentieth century is more significant than the variation between 10 and 20% in the mid-twentieth century.[72] Nevertheless the difference between male or mixed compilers (hovering around 10% representation of women) – and female compilers (22 and 25% respectively) is striking, and suggests that some sort of gender bias is in play, one way or the other. It would take a more detailed analysis than I have scope for here to determine whether positive or negative discrimination, or indeed both, are at work.

Turning to the topic coverage in textbooks, up to about the last quarter of the twentieth century, females feature relatively rarely – they are not the movers and shakers of history, nor the literary greats who were often selected as suitably edifying topics. If women do feature, it is often in faintly humorous or satirical contexts, or in relation to marriage with a man. As an example, the collection of 140 prose composition passages in

---

72 It would, however, be untrue to say that no women featured in early prose composition manuals. For comparison, Buchheim (1890) included four female authors in his 99 passages: George Eliot, Elizabeth Gaskell, Harriet Martineau, and Agnes Strickland.

Fowler et al. (1966) was chosen at random for closer analysis. Women feature in around 30 of them (cf. Table 6.1), and are generally explicitly dependent on a man in some way, or feature as mothers. Where they feature in their own right, they are often faintly laughable: Alice at the Mad Hatter's tea party, a girl whose head is turned by reading novelettes, Catherine applying her knowledge of Gothic novels to real life in *Northanger Abbey*, females performing at a humorously described benefit concert. One elderly woman is victim of a burglary; more women are caught shoplifting more than men. There are a few notable exceptions to this prevailing portrayal of women as subjugated and/or silly: a mother who declares to her family that she has spent half her life raising her children, and that now it's time to do what she wants to do (Doris Lessing), a shopkeeper (Irish Murdoch), and a woman trying to motivate herself to work on her doctoral thesis on Donne (C. S. Lewis). But in sum: women feature in only about 20 % of the passages at all; and in nearly all of those they are either subjugated to a man, silly, or both.

Table 6.1 Female figures in Fowler et al. (1966), with chapter numbers

1.	A Berlin landlady – faintly ridiculous in her fear of losing her male permanent lodger, and jealous of the "lucky woman" with whom he goes to the opera
7.	A servant girl who welcomes a male to wait for her mistress with the words "I am lonely enough, I can tell you, and you do not look as though you would eat a girl"
9.	Women waiting anxiously for a brother to return
13. & 14.	A woman being taken to lunch by a man and choosing caviar and champagne that he can ill afford
17.	Alice at the Mad Hatter's tea party
21.	A woman trying to motivate herself to work on her doctoral thesis on Donne (C. S. Lewis, *That Hideous Strength*)
24.	A woman announcing her engagement in a letter to a female friend
26.	An Italian war-widow
28.	A woman wakening next to her husband (whom she had left but has returned to)
29.	A little girl watching her father, a mechanic, at work
30.	The "sweet" mother of Little Lord Fauntleroy
31.	A flirtatious conversation between a man and a woman
35.	A woman caught sleeping in the sun by a man – "she felt sick. And he was angry with her"
37.	"A perfect wife" from a social satire by Samuel Butler, beginning "Her principal duty was, as she said, to him her husband"
45.	An elderly woman is the victim of a burglary
47.	A mother and daughter whose "gets her head turned reading those penny novelettes"

54.	A mother who says she's spent half her life raising her children, now it's time to do what she wants to do (Doris Lessing, *Each His Own Wilderness*)
59.	A lady who finds an escaped convict under her bed
65.	Women discussing an old inn sign
69.	A woman brings tea to a man in bed
75.	A humorous family circle. "All virtuous and handsome and intelligent men like onions"; only "paragons among women" like onions.
76.	More women are convicted of shoplifting than men.
79.	Mr Collins's description of the marriageable heiress Miss de Bourgh (Jane Austen, *Pride and Prejudice*)
80.	Myrtle Wilson killed in a car accident (rushing out believing her lover is in the car) (F. Scott Fitzgerald, *The Great Gatsby*)
104.	Catherine, inspired by Gothic novels, excitedly searching a room looking for a hidden manuscript, heart fluttering, cheek alternately flushed and pale (*Austen, Northanger Abbey*)
111.	Charlotte the object of Goethe's love and inspiration for his love poetry
123.	Mrs Tinckham, a shopkeeping chain-smoker and the owner of many cats (Iris Murdoch, *Under the Net*)
126. & 127.	A faintly ridiculous Frau Obelehrer sings at a benefit performance; a young girl acts a poison scene and a girl plays a lullaby

In many textbooks and readers, the portrayal of women is skewed by the focus on the "family" as an accessible and relevant topic for young language learners, as Johnson has demonstrated for textbooks and readers in use in the 1960s and early 1970s. Although it would be desirable to expand the chronological scope of Johnson's investigation (Johnson 1973: 112, 99–100), there is no scope for that here, so it is worth repeating in full his summary of his analysis of the role of women in textbooks in use in the 1960s (which says as much as it does about class bias as it does about gender):

> The mother is a housewife; her educational background and any professional training she may have had, are not mentioned [by contrast with the father, who is by far most likely to be a "businessman", followed by other white collar professions; cf. Johnson (1973: 92–93)]
> [...]
> While her husband goes out into the world, the German wife and mother stays at home and runs the household. As she has no household help, she is mainly concerned with cooking in her well equipped kitchen, cleaning and shopping. She regards the kitchen as her personal domain which the other members of the family are rarely allowed to enter. She is a conscientious housewife who does not like to spend her time idly. When the family is listening to the radio or watching television, she usually has some knitting or darning to do. Of all the members

329

of the family circle, she works the longest hours. She also has the strongest personality: the rules she lays down are observed, and she criticizes the others when they displease her. She is a good cook and can always be relied upon to provide an attractive meal for guests or friends of the children. Although she is devoted to her husband, she does not take him too seriously, especially when he makes unrealistic plans or launches into boring speeches. While her life is chiefly centred on the home, she does not exclude herself completely from other company. She has a friend, another housewife like herself, with whom she goes shopping, to cafes, the cinema and the theatre. Sometime she takes the children shopping with her, and then they can expect to be treated to an ice cream. She is also fashion conscious, and tries to keep her figure by dieting in order to be able to wear fashionable clothes. Her tastes in literature are conservative: when she goes to the theatre, she prefers to see Goethe's *Götz* rather than the works of modern authors which demand a closer study of the text. For her private reading she prefers love stories and the *Novellen* of Theodor Storm. No information is given about her educational background. She is described as being *sentimental*, and her attitude towards her children, even when they are grown up, is protective, with an admixture of pride.

An early challenge to the model of females as wives and mothers (only) is offered by Magda Kelber in her reader *So Einfach!* (1943), though it should be noted that it was intended for adult learners rather than children. Chapter XV features a passage where children discuss what they want to be when they grow up, and here the girls do at least voice a choice. Nevertheless their choices are highly stereotyped by gender. The boys want variously to be a landlord, an explorer in Africa, a photographer, a train conductor, a sea captain. The girls want to sell nice clothes in a city department store or be a cinema usherette; a third wants to stay at home and have many children. At this, one of the boys responds, "You're just a girl. [...] Men have to go out into the world and experience a lot, and you women sit at home and sew" *Dafür bist du ja auch nur ein Mädchen [...] Männer müssen in die Welt und viel erleben, und ihr Frauen bleibt zu Haus und kocht und näht*, p. 105). Interestingly, this statement is not challenged by the girls. Rather, it is the male stereotype that is undermined by the reported thoughts of the male teacher, who says to himself that he, too, once thought he wanted to go out and have adventures, but now finds himself quite happy as a teacher in this small place. (One wonders whether the fact that this book was published during World War II might account in part for the desire for a quiet life at home.)

While Paxton & Brentnall (1975: 211) already query American stereotypes of French and German women, it is not until the 1980s that the theme of women's issues features in textbooks (incidentally some twenty years later than I had intuitively anticipated). Dickins (1963) is a course in *German for Advanced Students* with a second edition in 1973 and a third in 1984, with several reprints along the way. In the third edition (1984), Dickins wrote that "much of the material has been updated in style and content to keep it attractive and relevant at the present time" (p. iv). One of those changes was the introduction of a passage headed "Women's Lib" – its German title was *Die Töchter der Emanzen* ('the daughters of the women's libbers') from *Zeit-Magazin* (1983). The passage describes this generation of daughters as being "against oppression", but having "nothing against men"; only a minority are willing to call themselves "feminists", a label they associate with women who are anti-men. Dickins's inclusion of the topic of feminism in 1984 (and not, for instance, at the time of the second edition in 1973) matches the development I find in other German textbooks, namely that "feminist" topics do not make it onto the agenda until the 1980s.

Questions of gender roles are addressed repeatedly in *Neue Perspektiven* (Della Gana 1987), an A-level textbook based around "issues". For example, it features the regrets of a single (divorced) mother who left her children to their own devices so she could go to work, and who presents this as the direct cause for her daughter's drug addiction (Della Gana 1987: 114–115). The text does not seem to query at all the woman's self-blame and belief that everything would have been all right if she had been content to be there for her children by depending on welfare rather than working. Rather, the textbook asks "What mistakes did she make?" (*Welche waren aber die Fehler, die sie gemacht hat*? p. 115). On the other hand, later in the same book, a chapter on "prejudices" addresses traditional roles head on, taking issue with the entire idea that men should "help" women with the housework: why should housework still be considered a *Frauensache* in which men at most "help", so that working women must be superwomen (cf. Figure 6.46)? Yet, the text tells us, 12–14-year old boys in English schools still seem to hold the prejudice that "women are hardly capable of anything anyway" (*Frauen seien sowieso kaum zu etwas fähig*, p. 188). The text ends, "Why does no one think to ask women whether they want to help with the housework?" A passage on the following page considers the lot of house-husbands (*Hausmann*, p. 190; see Figure 6.47): some are glad to get out of the rat race; others are anxious about how they will be regarded when they try to return to work, for "people are more inclined to forgive it [a career break] in women" (*Einer Frau verzeiht man das schon eher*). Overall, *Neue Perspektiven* certainly suggests that the negotiation of gender roles is a pressing issue – but also difficult territory.

For a period from the late 1980s onwards, women's rights are a staple topic in A-level textbooks such as *Durchblick*, which, with twenty pages on the topic, is the most detailed treatment (Hares et al. 1994 Unit 6 *Frauen – wie geht's am Arbeitsplatz?* pp. 86–106). *Einsicht* (Stocker & Saunders 1988: 124–125) invites readers to compare how men and women are presented in advertising. In the same book, Chapter 4A is devoted to the roles of men and women in family and home life. It begins by asking pupils to fill out a table of which tasks are predominantly or exclusively done by the man or woman in their household; an article headed 'Men still bone idle' (*Männer immer noch stinkfaul*) then presents statistics on 'what men (don't) do in the house' (*Was Männer im Haushalt (nicht) machen*). The section concludes by asking pupils to agree or disagree with ten statements of the type "Bringing up children is women's work", "The father must have the last word in the family" (p. 37). The topic is given similar, though briefer, treatment, in *Brennpunkt* (Sandry et al. 2000: 124–125) as part of the larger topic of equal rights (Chapter 10, pp. 117–128). In *Deutschland hier und jetzt* (Rowlinson 1993: 110–118) a

331

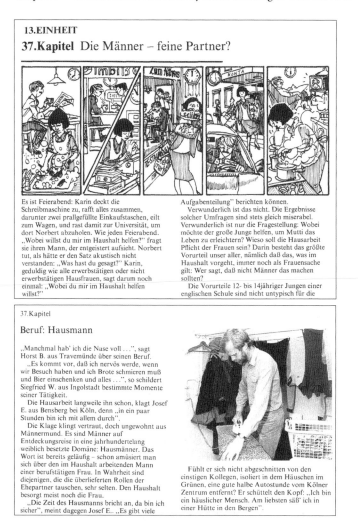

13.EINHEIT

37.Kapitel Die Männer – feine Partner?

Es ist Feierabend: Karin deckt die Schreibmaschine zu, rafft alles zusammen, darunter zwei prallgefüllte Einkaufstaschen, eilt zum Wagen, und rast damit zur Universität, um dort Norbert abzuholen. Wie jeden Feierabend. „Wobei willst du mir im Haushalt helfen?" fragt sie ihren Mann, der entgeistert aufsieht. Norbert tut, als hätte er den Satz akustisch nicht verstanden: „Was hast du gesagt?" Karin, geduldig wie alle erwerbstätigen oder nicht erwerbstätigen Hausfrauen, sagt darum noch einmal: „Wobei du mir im Haushalt helfen willst?"

Aufgabenteilung" berichten können. Verwunderlich ist das nicht. Die Ergebnisse solcher Umfragen sind stets gleich miserabel. Verwunderlich ist nur die Fragestellung: Wobei möchte der große Junge helfen, um Mutti das Leben zu erleichtern? Wieso soll die Hausarbeit Pflicht der Frauen sein? Darin besteht das größte Vorurteil unser aller, nämlich daß das, was im Haushalt vorgeht, immer noch als Frauensache gilt: Wer sagt, daß nicht Männer das machen sollten?

Die Vorurteile 12- bis 14jähriger Jungen einer englischen Schule sind nicht untypisch für die

37.Kapitel

Beruf: Hausmann

„Manchmal hab' ich die Nase voll ...", sagt Horst B. aus Travemünde über seinen Beruf.

„Es kommt vor, daß ich nervös werde, wenn wir Besuch haben und ich Brote schmieren muß und Bier einschenken und alles ...", so schildert Siegfried W. aus Ingolstadt bestimmte Momente seiner Tätigkeit.

Die Hausarbeit langweile ihn schon, klagt Josef E. aus Bensberg bei Köln, denn „in ein paar Stunden bin ich mit allem durch".

Die Klage klingt vertraut, doch ungewohnt aus Männermund. Es sind Männer auf Entdeckungsreise in eine jahrhundertelang weiblich besetzte Domäne: Hausmänner. Das Wort ist bereits geläufig – schon amüsiert man sich über den im Haushalt arbeitenden Mann einer berufstätigen Frau. In Wahrheit sind diejenigen, die die überlieferten Rollen der Ehepartner tauschen, sehr selten. Den Haushalt besorgt meist noch die Frau.

„Die Zeit des Hausmanns bricht an, da bin ich sicher", meint dagegen Josef E.. „Es gibt viele

Fühlt er sich nicht abgeschnitten von den einstigen Kollegen, isoliert in dem Häuschen im Grünen, eine gute halbe Autostunde vom Kölner Zentrum entfernt? Er schüttelt den Kopf: „Ich bin ein häuslicher Mensch. Am liebsten säß' ich in einer Hütte in den Bergen".

Figure 6.46: (above) Della Gana (1987: 188)
Figure 6.47 (below): Della Gana (1989: 190)

chapter on "women in Germany" invites pupils to consider the requirement in Germany that married couples decide on one common surname, and the finding that 97 % of the time the man's surname is chosen. The point is made that with generous state childcare provision in the former GDR, 90 % of women worked, in contrast to the Federal Republic (p. 115). The division of labour in the home is again a topic (men still don't do enough, according to the newspaper item featured, p. 111; a similar finding is still presented in the year 2000 in *Brennpunkt*, Sandry et al. 2000: 124)! Pupils are also asked to consider case studies of women in typically male jobs: a plasterer, electrician,

Figure 6.48:
Alle Einsteigen! 1 (Saunders et al. 1992: 232)

IT specialist, and TV camerawoman/editor (pp. 112–113). For younger pupils, *Alle Einsteigen* 1 (Saunders et al. 1992: 232) offers another update on the gender-specific treatment of job prospects in Kelber (1943). Here (Figure 6.48) a female nurse is shown, but also a female doctor, police officer and lorry-driver. A male teacher and vet are shown as well as a male businessman, mechanic, engineer and lawyer. The message is clear, and in stark contrast to half a century earlier: any job is open to either gender (and, indeed, irrespective of skin colour).

In sum, the representation of gender roles has, predictably, followed developments in British society at large. Representations in the first three-quarters of the twentieth century reflect the established sexism of the society of the time, and Johnson's (1973) summary finds that women are in essence represented as wives and mothers. The 1980s see the first challenges to this view: *Neue Perspektiven* (Della Gana 1987), for example, tackles many of the conflicts caused by the re-negotiation of gender roles. The difficulties women face in sharing the burden of work in the home remain topical right up to 2000, but from the 1990s onwards, decidedly "up-beat" representations of the opportunities for women and girls become more frequent: they are often shown succeeding in sports and professions that were not open to them a few decades earlier (e.g. the boxer, the smiling lorry-driver), thus supporting the now prevailing ideology of equal opportunities irrespective of gender. Not surprisingly, then, this sample analysis reveals that even textbooks of *foreign* languages contribute to advancing the prevailing ideologies of *British* education.

6.12 Conclusion

The teaching of modern languages is ideological territory. In the case of German for English learners, the ground has been particularly tricky over the past century or so, and the representation of the German present and past has been constantly re-negotiated. The first half of this chapter, has, then, in effect been a contribution to the history of Anglo-German relations. We have seen how authors long clung to the historical sense of an affinity with the Germans, even to the extent of Macpherson & Strömer's desire in 1934 to awaken "sympathetic interest" in Nazi Germany, not excepting its labour camps (p. v). After World War II, textbook authors retreated (along with their counterparts elsewhere in Europe) into rose-tinted, romanticized representations of the "other" Germany, with no mention at all of Germany's recent past. The problem of East Germany was dealt with largely by ignoring it, at least until the 1960s and early 1970s, when relations with East Germany eased and then full diplomatic relations were established. East Germany could now be talked about – but generally critically, more critically than British authors had talked about Nazism at the time. Anderson's learners were shown first-hand from press reports how East Germany denied its inhabitants freedom of speech (Anderson 1964); Wightman's readers learnt that East Germany was "drab and dirty" (Wightman 1974: 121). In the late 1960s, the collective amnesia about World War II and of the Holocaust was overcome in textbooks at last, as in wider society, and the obligation to remember began to be addressed: recall Rowlinson's task of translating a "heated though still fairly polite argument" that ends with the speaker's demand, "And last of all remind him of six million murdered Jews…" (Rowlinson 1969: 143). Finally, after German (re)unification in 1990, textbook authors seem to have felt able to take the long view of German history (not just since 1945), for that history now had a satisfyingly tidy ending: a united, democratic Germany at the heart of Europe.

Throughout this history of representations of Germany past and present, one point emerges very clearly. No textbook tells the truth, the whole truth and nothing but the truth, whether about ourselves or about the "other"; authors can only select a tiny fraction of the culture of the language being taught. The impossibility of telling "the truth" was addressed towards the end of the twentieth century by encouraging multiperspectivity in teaching materials: pupils had already been learning to recognize and challenge national stereotypes since the 1970s, but now they should be shown that there are multiple views on the world (Fritzsche 1993) – that, too, is an ideology. We should recognize, above all, that our sense of what pupils *ought* to be taught about the culture(s) of the language they are studying is largely determined by the prevailing educational ideology of the "home" culture, not the culture(s) of the language being taught. That is perhaps most obvious in the treatment of gender roles and fitness in later twentieth-century textbooks, where we find, for example, that healthy lifestyles and equality of opportunity for females and ethnic minorities are energetically promoted.

This chapter, examining the question of *what* has been taught in German language textbooks, has provided another opportunity to reflect on the fundamental question of why we teach a language, as it lays bare the decisions made about what is important for pupils to know about the "culture". Taking "the long view" to examine how culture has been handled in twentieth-century textbooks of German, makes it easier to recognize the reasons why certain topics and approaches have been preferred, others sidelined. It should, therefore, make us more sensitive to the choices we make – more or less consciously – about our how we treat culture in our classrooms and in our teaching materials today.

Chapter 7 – Outlook

This book is largely a history of language education "from below" – it has concentrated not on abstract pronouncements about what *should* be done in language education (of which there are precious few before the second half of the nineteenth century), but has examined the textbooks used in practice. It is intended as a contribution to the history of German Studies in Britain, to the history of Anglo-German relations, and, more widely, to the history of linguistic ideas and of applied linguistics (*avant la lettre*) as well as to the history of education.

Most urgently, the book provides some of the raw material and analysis that teachers, trainee-teachers, educationalists and policy-makers need in order to reflect on the goals, methods and challenges of language teaching and learning today, by allowing them to compare the present with what has been tried in the past. Why, where and how do we teach language, and what, precisely, do we teach? Such questions are most pressing in the UK, where foreign language education seems to be in a permanent state of crisis. (That is one comfort, in fact: no matter how badly things stand with German today, its proponents at the start of the twentieth century were just as worried, as we saw in Chapter 4.3). However, the themes tackled in this book are common to the task of language education everywhere. The following brings these strands together from the preceding chapters. I end with some indications of where research could go from here.

7.1 Why?

Over the past five chapters we have seen *why* German was taught: how, from the late seventeenth century onwards, the learning of German – initially the preserve of merchants travelling Europe – attracted the interest first of English scholars and then of travellers, not just for trade but, increasingly, as a valuable tool for participating in the socially prestigious Grand Tour of Europe. By the eighteenth century, interest had grown sufficiently to warrant more than one edition of some manuals. By the end of that century, learning German had additionally been recognized as the gateway to great literary works of Goethe, Schiller, Lessing, Wieland and many others: German was now a language enjoying prestige in Britain on a par with the other major languages of Europe. In the course of the nineteenth century, and with the help of school grammars and exercises, this newly prestigious language was incorporated into the school curriculum, albeit the curriculum of a still tiny elite at British Public Schools and Grammar Schools, and only ever second to French. Its importance to military and commercial careers was also recognized. The twentieth century saw massive expansion of foreign language study beyond the elite who had traditionally had access to it.

We have also looked at how the case has been made for learning German and other foreign languages. Arguably, German was most desirable when it enjoyed intellectual prestige; utilitarian arguments, which have been put for centuries, in various forms, but which have increasingly dominated arguments in the twentieth century, may have value when putting the case to policy-makers; they do not seem to be effective in swaying individuals to devote time and effort to learning a language beyond the elementary level. After all, the arguments made about the commercial value of Spanish in the Leathes Report of 1918 (see 4.4) bore no fruit until Spain (and now South America) became a holiday destination, a place with which learners had a personal relationship. Today, we continue to make the case for the usefulness of foreign languages, but seemingly to little avail.

7.2 Where and how?

Advocates of the modern languages fought hard from the late nineteenth century for their place in formal education, emphasizing the academic challenge and the edificatory potential of philological study and literary appreciation. The result was, ultimately, the victory of modern languages over Latin and Greek in the early twentieth century. But this growth in curricular prestige had been matched by a sharp decrease in the interest in German as a living, spoken language of practical use, even if the rhetoric about the practical value of German in the military and commercial spheres never let up, and even if various "conversational methods" continued to appear regularly. Across Europe, however, a newly professionalized body of increasingly formally qualified teachers had begun to reflect on the best methods for teaching modern languages, and a critical mass of opinion began to support the Reform Movement, which – amongst other things – brought teachers' attention firmly back to the importance of teaching the language as a living practical language – not just because oral skills were useful, but because they believed it to be a more effective pedagogy for teaching languages full stop. Experiments in teaching phonetics in the early twentieth century had variable outcomes. Rippmann was a firm advocate, but others found phonetics less useful in the classroom, and the crucial contribution that phonetics could make was in any case superseded by the 1930s as gramophones, radio broadcasts and the many technologies that succeeded those early efforts made it ever easier to gain direct access to the sounds of the language as spoken by native speakers. In the early decades of the twentieth century, although the numbers of pupils in education were steadily increasing, German in schools had been under pressure both from the structural inertia of French as the first modern language and from the 'bad publicity' of the First World War, but it was newly resurgent in the 1930s as many new textbooks appeared after a relative hiatus. The teaching of German became more ideologically charged than it had ever been in that decade, with authors manoeuvring more or less consciously and more or less critically around the realities of Nazi Germany. The Second World War itself triggered two key, but very different, developments. First, large-scale intensive language learning programmes in the armed forces, taking advantage of new technologies, opened civilian instructors' eyes both to the potential of democratizing language learning and to new ways of teaching and learning foreign languages, resulting in audiolingual and audiovisual methods, out of which evolved the communicative methods that dominated the last quarter of the century. Second, to put it crudely, if the First World War had been a PR problem for German, the Second World War was a PR disaster. In common with authors of textbooks of German across Europe, British textbook authors were at pains to overcome the German image problem, first by completely ignoring the awkward past and often also the equally awkward present that it had yielded, then by gradually undertaking their own process of *Vergangenheitsbewäl-tigung*, the Germans' term for the "coming to terms with the past" that began, at least in West Germany, in the late 1960s. That challenge continued to be a concern right up to the end of the twentieth century and arguably remains today.

7.3 What?

The last two chapters of this book have considered the often overlooked question of what, precisely, we teach in the classroom, both with regard to the language variety presented, and to the question of what culture is taught in the process. The book is far from the last word on the subject. For one thing, my study has, despite my best intentions at the outset, been largely limited to England, with only very occasional nods to the specifics of Scotland, Wales and Ireland. More fundamentally, virtually all of the themes touched on would warrant much more thorough treatment than I have been able to give them, and I could have written a book on any one of them. Nevertheless, the range of topics I have explored here – from gender construction to the teaching of German word order, from Anglo-German relations to the history of teaching intonation – give an indication of the *kinds* of things we can learn from studying the history of teaching and learning modern foreign languages. Much of what we can learn transcends the narrow field of educational history and reaches into language history and history of linguistics, social history and sociology.

7.4 *Quo vadis?* Where to now?

This book is one of a tiny number devoted to the history of language education in Britain (see Chapter 1). As I come to the end of this study, the following stand out as potentially very rewarding avenues of further investigation, besides the obvious need for more comparative studies like that of Wegner (1999), especially within Europe, where there are both many similarities and significant differences:

1. More work on the **history of teaching culture**, for example the history of changes to teaching literature (cf. Guthke 2011 for the period up to 1830), alongside the rise of teaching other cultural outputs such as film and popular music. Anecdotally, many of those who continue with a language to an advanced level do so not for "reasons of the head" but because they have formed a lasting bond with some aspect of its culture (Richard Stokes is a case in point, coming to German through music; (see 4.11),

so that what and how we teach matters not just for the formation of interculturally competent citizens, but in order to win learners to languages.

2. More work on **gender and the history of language education**. The emergence of females both as textbook authors and as learners is a story that is implicit in the authors and titles of some of the textbooks in the chronological bibliography given in 8., and it would be rewarding to examine their contribution to language education. In addition, the hints that it was easier to innovate in language education for girls in the nineteenth century than in that for boys (3.6.3, 3.10.1) warrant further investigation.

3. **The history of pupil, student and staff exchanges**. The history of exchanges goes back at least as far as the Hanseatic League (see 2.1); summer courses in Germany played a key role in the training of reform-minded language teachers (see 3.10.1); it was the model around which Walter Anderson's *Aufenthalt in Deutschland* (1949) was based (6.8), and has become essential to the study of languages at university. My impression as a lecturer at the University of Nottingham is that many of those who continue with a language do so because of some kind of relationship with the country where it is spoken, or with its culture, so the history of these relationships is worth studying.

4. Related to the previous point is a methodological one: the potential of telling the history of language education through oral history and **personal narrative**. For the history of language learning in the armed forces, such personal narratives (as collected, for example, in Elliott & Shukman 2003 and Boiling 2005) are the only published sources to date, for example, and show the contribution that such a systematic study based on such histories could make to social history and the history of education.

5. Not just first-hand accounts of teachers and learners, but also the **biographies of textbook authors** are important. For the authors of the German textbooks examined in this study, one interesting strand is the considerable importance played by German emigrants and refugees in the teaching of their language: the history of German grammars in England begins with a German emigrant (Martin Aedler, cf. 2.2.2), and they continue to play a key role in language education to the present day. The contribution of many of them would warrant further study: the nineteenth century radical Karl Follen in the USA (3.11), to the reformer and Anglophile Otto Siepmann (3.10.2), to the Jewish Olympic athlete Alex Natan (6.10), but also those about whom we currently know very little, such as Magda Kelber, author of a 1938 textbook (4.8).

6. **Language education in the armed forces**. As already hinted above and in 4.9, the armed forces have played a key role in language education, from the early modern period, to the examinations in modern languages set for admission to military academies in the nineteenth century (3.6) to the intensive methods trialled in the USA in the 1940s (4.6.4). There are likely to be rich archives to be investigated.

7. **Language history**: As Chapter 5 showed, foreign language textbooks are important sources for the history of language description and use, whether it be advances in the

description of word order or evidence for changing attitudes to forms of address. The description and prescription of languages as *foreign* languages – where accounts may be less conservative than in the national tradition – therefore merits further study.

8. More work on the **history of methodology, as part of the history of applied linguistics**. The textbooks examined here have allowed us to revisit some of the familiar stories of the history of language education methodologies offering a much more differentiated picture of the nineteenth century than just "grammar-translation", for example, as well as identifying the different ways in which the tenets of the Reform Movement were tried out in the classroom (see Chapter 3). However, much, much more remains to be done, for example in the history of teach-yourself materials (cf. Sørensen 2010, 2011), the history of many of the "methods" developed in the nineteenth century (Emil Otto's survived from the 1850s to a last reprint in the 1970s (see 8.), the history of quirkier methods that promised to teach German while you sing, act or play (Lapper 1943, Kallmann 1939, Wayne 1950), or on the history of language education for specific purposes. The evolution of multimedia course packages in the face of ever accelerating technological change (cf. Hill 1989, Hagen 1993, Rendall 1991 and Townshend 1997), which I have done no more than allude to occasionally in this study, also comes under this heading.

9. Related to methodology is the **history of assessment**, which, for world languages like English, at least, is increasingly big business; and examinations are often barriers to change in teaching and learning practices (cf. 3.8).

10. **Book history and bibliography**. As indicated there, the bibliography in 8., though it gives full references as far as possible, is not a bibliographer's bibliography, merely a starting-point for further work. There is much more to be done to establish the distribution and popularity of the textbooks listed there.

Much remains to be done.

Chapter 8 – Bibliography
A chronological bibliography of German textbooks for English speakers, 1600–2000 (and some other related sources)

The bibliography is arranged in chronological order by year; within years, entries are in alphabetical order. The chronology runs by year of first publication, or of the earliest edition that I have been able to identify. Later editions or impressions, where known, are indicated too, but this information is certainly very incomplete.

The bibliography contains all the textbooks of German referenced in this book. In addition, it lists many further textbooks of German published in the UK (and some in the USA) that I have become aware of in the course of working on the book. However, it is not a comprehensive bibliography on the level of, for example, Moulin-Fankhänel's bibliographies of German grammars to 1700 (1994, 1997) or Görlach's bibliography of nineteenth-century grammars of English (Görlach 1998), nor Schröder's bibliographies of foreign language teaching materials in German (Schröder 1975, 1987–1999). Especially for the latter half of the century, is probably best described as "indicative" of the kind of texts published. In the latter years of the twentieth century, textbooks increasingly have multiple elements (pupil's book, teacher's book, workbook, transcripts, etc.), but I have not even attempted to give details of all these, but have simply listed the "main" text. I have not listed online resources at all, with one exception (based on Gschossmann-Hendershot 1976, but published in 2000). Library catalogues will supply details of the accompanying materials. It does not, on the whole, include dictionaries of German, except a handful of early dictionaries and others whose authors are mentioned in this book. The bibliography contains a small number of works published outside the British Isles where they have been discussed in the book. It also includes texts that are intended for the study of other languages, if they are discussed in the text, e.g. Anon. (1715), which has similarities with König (1715). Other texts are also included where they shed light on the biography and other activities of textbook authors, e.g. Lange & Klemm (1890), Strauss (1883), and the many publications of Walter Rippmann (Ripman).

Where I am aware that a copy is available online (generally through EEBO, ECCO or through the Hathi Trust), I have indicated this, but I have not checked systematically for online availability. "Taylor Collection" indicates that I consulted a copy held in the Taylor Collection (a collection of books donated by Brian Taylor, formerly of the University of Sydney), at the Centre for German as a Foreign Language, University of Bamberg.

Evidence of when and where the book was used is also given, where available. I have provided cross-references to works by the same author – in general, the earliest reference to a work by the author contains the full list of other relevant works in the bibliography, and other entries refer back to this entry.

Full names of authors and editors have been given wherever known. I have supplied the place of publication and publisher wherever I have been able to identify them. Walter Rippmann's name is spelled *Rippmann* for works known to have been published before he anglicized his name at the outbreak of World War I, *Ripman* thereafter. Library catalogues are not consistent in this matter, however.

1500–1599

1576. Anon. *Colloquia ou Dialogues avec un Dictionaire en six langues: Flamen, Anglois, Alleman, François, Espaignol, & Italien.* Antwerp: H. Heyndrickx. Cited by Flood (1991: 258) as earliest such manual to include English at all.

1599. Dufflau, Cornelius Killian. *Dictionarium Latino-Germanicum.* Antwerp: Plantijn.

1600–1649

1616. Ritter, Stephan. *Grammatica Germanica Nova [...]* Marburg: Hutwelcker.

1617. Minsheu, John. *The guide into the tongues: with their agreement and consent one with another, as also their etymologies, that is, the reasons and deriuations of all or the most Part of wordes, in these eleuen languages, viz. 1. English. 2. British or Welsh. 3. Low Dutch. 4. High Dutch. 5. French. 6. Italian. 7. Spanish. 8. Portuguez. 9. Latine. 10. Greeke. 11. Hebrew, &c.: which are so laid together (for the helpe of memory) that any one with ease and facilitie, may not only remember 4. 5. or more of these languages so laid together... / by the industrie, studie, labour, and at the charges of Iohn Minsheu published and printed. anno 1617. Cum gratia & priuilegio Regiae Maiestatis, & vendibles extant Londini: Apud Ioannem Browne Bibliopolam in vico vocato little Brittaine..., 1617.*

1637. Berlemont, Noël de. *The English, Latine, French, Dutch, Schole-master. Or, an Introduction to teach young Gentlemen and Merchants to travell or trade. Being the onely helpe to attaine to those languages, etc.* London: A. G. for Michael Sparke. EEBO.

1641. Gueintz, Christian. *Deutscher Sprachlehre Entwurf.* Reprint in Documenta linguistica, Reihe 5: Deutsche Grammatiken des 16. bis 18. Jahrhunderts. Hildesheim: Olms, 1978.

1650–1699

1663. Schottelius, Justus Georg. *Ausführliche Arbeit von der teutschen Haubtsprache.* Braunschweig: Zilliger. Rpt. ed. Wolfgang Hecht. Tübingen: Niemeyer, 1967.

1664. Duez, Nathanael. *Dictionarium Germanico-Gallico-Latinum = Teutsch-Franzosisch- und Lateinisch ... durch Nathanael Dvez. In diesem dritten Truck widerum ubersehen, verbessert und weit vermehrt.* Amsterdam: Ben Ludwig und Daniel Elzevier.

1680 (1685). [Aedler, Martin, published anonymously]. *The Hig [sic] Dutch Minerva // a-la-mode// or // A Perfect Grammar // never extant before // whereby // The English // may both // easily and exactly// learne // the Neatest Dialect of the German // Mother-Language // used throughout all Europe; // most humbly dedicated.* [1685 edition:

under the name Higgs, Daniel. *The high Dutch Minerva a-la-mode or a.perfect. grammar never extant before, whereby the English may both easily and exactly learne the neatest dialect of the German mother-language used thoroughout all.Europe; most humbly dedicated to.His.Royal.Highness Prince Rupert Count.Palatine.of.the Rhine Duke.of.Bavaria.and.Cumberland Vice-Admiral.of.all.England Knight.of.the.most. noble Order.of.the.Garter Constable.of His.Majesties castle.and.honour.of Windsor and.one.of His.Majesties most.honourable Privie-Council &c. by his.most.illustrious highnesses most humble and most obedient servant, the author.*]. See Carr (1937), Glück (2002), Guthke (2011), and (in most detail) Van der Lubbe (2007a).

1682. Anon. *La véritable et unique Grammaire alemande … Exactement corrigée et aug- mentée de plus d'un tiers dans cette nouvelle édition.* Strasbourg: Schmuck.

1687. Offelen, Heinrich. *A double grammar for Germans to learn English, and for Eng- lish-men to learn the German-tongue: wherein all Latine words, belonging to the grammar, are translated both into the German and English tongue: treating besides of the derivation of the English tongue, with all grammatical rules: and dialogues, treating of all necessary matters that daily may be spoken of: and, especially what is to be seen for a stranger, at Versailles in France and England, with a compendium of the estate of the German empire / composed and set forth by Henry Offelen…* London: Old Spring Garden by Charing Cross. EEBO.

1691. Stieler, Kaspar. *Der Teutschen Sprache Stammbaum und Fortwachs […].* Nürnberg: Johann Hoffmann. Rpt. with afterword by Stefan Sonderegger. Munich: Kösel, 1968.

1693. Gonzaga, Luigi. *The eloquent master of languages.* Hamburg, Gedruckt und verlegt durch Thomas von Wiering.. und… bey Zacharias Herteln zu bekommen. See Van der Lubbe (2007b).

1694. Kramer, Matthias. *Die richtige Grund-Festen Der Teutschen Sprache: Hauptsächlich eröffnet Der Italiänischen Nation Welche Da begierig seye diese herrliche Sprache zu erlernen; Ein neues auch denen Teutschen selbst zu beyder Sprachen Beförderung sehr ersprießliches … Werck.* Nuremburg: Endter.

1700–1749

1702. Pastorius, Franz Daniel. *New All-German Primer.* For information on the author of this book in Germantown, Pennsylvania, see Glück (2002: 332). I have been unable to trace publication details for the book, noted by Glück.

1715. König, Johann. *A royal compleat grammar, English and High-German = Das ist: Eine Königliche vollkommene grammatica, in Englisch-und Hochteütscher Sprach… Durch John King,…* Londen, gedruckt for Wilhelm Frieman, und bey B. Barker und Charl. King, 1715. Schaible (1885: 341) mentions this grammar but with wrong date; Carr (1937: 469) says "This is not a German grammar at all but an English one with the examples translated into German" Author says in preface that his *Englischer Wegweiser* from some years ago is now out of print – Carr (1937: 470) has identified it as 1706; German ed. then 1716 and reprinted tenth time 1782, and notes he is a German who's lived in London for about 30 years. "Both of these works [ie the

German and the English grammars] contain a description of the sights of London which reappears word for word in *The True Guide* 1758 (cf. Carr 1937: 472–3).

1720. Anon. (König?). *The Royal French GRAMMAR; By which One may In a Short Time Attain the FRENCH TONGUE in Perfection […]*. London: Printed for M. Wellingoton, and sold by J. Darby, A. Betterworth, F. Clay, P. Varenne, P. Vaillant, P. Dunoyer, H. Ribotteau, and J. Moetiens.

1721. Freyer, Hieronymus (1675–1747). *Anweisung zur Teutschen Orthographie*. Rpt. of the Halle/Saale 1722 edition, ed. Moulin (1999). Hildesheim: Olms.

1731 (2ⁿᵈ ed. 1736). Beiler, Benedictus. *A NEW German Grammar. Whereby an ENGLISHMAN May easily attain to the KNOWLEDGE of the German Language, especially useful for MERCHANTS and TRAVELLERS. To which are added, Several useful and familiar DIALOGUES* [2ⁿᵈ edition 1736]. London: J. Downing for the Author. See Van der Lubbe (2007b). ECCO.

1750–1759

1751, 1771, 1772 (USA 1752, 1793, 1811). Bachmair, John James. *A complete German grammar... To which are added... several pieces of news, German letters, and some moral pieces both in prose and verse. Together with an ample vocabulary in alphabetical order*. See Carr (1937: 470), who considers that "the system of grammar it presents is much closer to Schottel's than the other grammars of the time which derive from Gottsched. Bachmair is therefore a century behind the times and depsite its popularity his grammar is woefully inadequate". 1793 ed. ECCO: "The second American edition. To which are prefixed rules for pronunciation and spelling."

1754. Aichinger, Carl Friedrich. *Versuch einer teutschen Sprachlehre, anfänglich nur zu eignem Gebrauche unternommen, endlich aber, um den Gelehrten zu fernerer Untersuchung Anlaß zu geben, ans Liecht gestellt*. Frankfurt und Leipzig: Kraus.

1757. Prussian Army, Infantry. *New regulations for the Prussian infantry: containing an exact detail of the present field-service: ...translated from the original German manuscript, and illustrated with various representations of the exercise in sixteen copper-plates*. London: printed for J. Rivington and J. Fletcher, Alinde, and Thomas Pote.

1758. [Anon.]. *The true guide to the German language. In three parts... Together with a description of the city of London:...* London: J. Nourse. See Van der Lubbe (2007b: 100) years...; see Carr (1937: 472–474). Carr writes, p. 473, that "The greater Part of this grammar, as indicated in the Preface, follows Gottsched very closely but in parts of the Etymologia and the whole of the Syntax the author has not hesitated to copy from Bachmair".

1760–1769

1762. Gottsched, Johann Christoph. *Vollständigere und neuerläuterte deutsche Sprachkunst: nach den Mustern der besten Schriftsteller*. Leipzig: verlegts Bernh. Christ. Breitkopf und Sohn.

1765. Ludwig, Christian. *Teutsch-Englisches Lexicon, worinne nicht allein die Wörter, samt den Nenn- Bey- und Sprich-Wörtern, sondern auch sowol die eigentliche als verblümte Redens-Arten verzeichnet sind… Dritte verbesserte Auflage.* Leipzig.

1768, 1st ed. 1736. Arnold, Theodor. *Theodor Arnolds Grammatica anglicana concentrata: oder kurzgefaßte Englische grammatik, worinnen die richtige pronunciation, und alle zur Erlernung dieser Sprache unumgänglich nöthigen Grundsätze aufs deutlichste und leichteste abgehandelt sind.* Leipzig und Züllichau, in der Buchhandlung des Waysenhauses, bey Nathanael Sigism. Frommann. See Klippel (1994: 168ff).

1770–1779

1770. Arnold, Theodor. *Neues deutsch-englisches Wörter-Buch: worinnen nicht nur die Wörter, und deren verschiedene Bedeutung; sondern auch die nöthigsten Redensarten, idiotismi… nach der… reinsten deutschen und englischen Mund- und Schreibart,… zusammen getragen von Theodor Arnold.* Leipzig und Züllichau, in der Buchhandlung des Waysenhauses, bey Nathanael Sigism. Frommann. ECCO.

1770. Arnold, Theodor. *Vollständiges Englisch-Französisch- und Deutsches Wörterbuch; a compleat English, French and German, and German and English Dictionary. 2 vol. 8vo.* Züllichau.

1774. Wendeborn, Gebhard Friedrich August. *The elements of German grammar, by the Rev. Mr. Wendeborn.* Described by Carr (1937) as "an abridgement of Gottsched's Grundlegung einer deutschen Sprachkunst".

1777. Heynatz, Johann Friedrich. *Deutsche Sprachlehre zum Gebrauch der Schulen.* Berlin: Mylius.

1780–1789

1781. Adelung, Johann Christoph. *Johann Christoph Adelungs Deutsche Sprachlehre. Zum Gebrauche der Schulen in den Königl. Preuß. Landen.* Berlin: Bey Christian Friedrich Voß und Sohn.

1782. Adelung, Johann Christoph. *Umständliches Lehrgebäude der Deutschen Sprache, zur Erläuterung der Deutschen Sprachlehre für Schulen. Von Joh. Christoph Adelung.* Leipzig: verlegts Johann Gottlob Immanuel Breitkopf.

1783. Bailey, Nathan, Anton Ernst Klausing, et al. *A compleat English dictionary; oder, Vollständiges englisch-deutsches Wörterbuch.* Leipzig: Waysenhaus- und Frommannische Buchhandlung. Vol. 2 has the title *Vollständiges deutsch-englisches Wörterbuch, ehemals mit vielem Fleisse zusammen getragen von Theodor Arnold und jetzt aufs neue verb. und verm. von Anton Ernst Klausing.* Hathi Trust.

1783 (1st ed.; 1799). Meidinger, Johann Valentin. *Praktische französische Grammatik, wodurch man diese Sprache auf eine ganz neue und sehr leichte Art in kurzer Zeit gründlich erlernen kann.* [Frankfurt?]: self-published. Hathi Trust.

1786. Albrecht, Heinrich Christoph. *A short grammar of the German tongue by Henry Christopher Albrecht.* Hamburgh: B. G. Hoffmann. ECCO.

1790–1799

1793. Adelung, Johann Christoph. *Grammatisch-kritisches Wörterbuch der hochdeutschen Mundart: mit beständiger Vergleichung der übrigen Mundarten, besonders aber der oberdeutschen.* Leipzig: bey Johann Gottlob Immanuel Breitkopf und Comp.

1793. Ebers, Johannes. *Vollständiges Wörterbuch der englischen Sprache für die Deutschen: Nach den neuesten und besten Hülfsmitteln mit richtig bezeichneter Aussprache eines jeden Wortes bearbeitet von Johannes Ebers.* Leipzig: bey Johann Gottlob Immanuel Breitkopf, Sohn und Compagnie. ECCO.

1794. Hesse, E. *A German and English Vocabulary.* London: Thomas Boosey. Advertised in the back of Crabb (1800c).

1796. Uttiv, John. *A complete practical German grammar, according to the best German grammarians, containing true, plain, and easy instructions for acquiring fondamentally* [sic] *and expeditiously a clear knowledge of the language, both in speaking and writing.* Göttingen: Vandenhoek and Ruprecht. Reviewed in *Allgemeine Literaritsche Zeitung* September 1797, p. 632: The reviewer says the exercises are "ganz nach der Meidingerschen Manier" – "fade[n]" – and would have preferred materials containing historical, moral or factual matter.

1797a. Wendeborn, Gebhard Friedrich August. *An introduction to German grammar, by the Rev. Dr. Wendeborn. The third edition with additions and improvements.* [London]: Printed for the author… G. G. J. Robinson's, [etc.]. ECCO.

1797b. Wendeborn, Gebhard Friedrich August. *Exercises to Dr. Wendeborn's Introduction to German Grammar, written by himself. A copious vocabulary, and a catalogue of some of the best modern german books are added.* ECCO.

1798. Berg, Franz Christopher August. *A concise grammar of the German language by Franz Christopher August Berg.* Hamburg: B. G. Hoffmann.

1799. 5th ed. 1817. Render, William. *A concise practical grammar of the German tongue. By the Rev. IV. Render, teacher of the German language in the University of Cambridge.* See Carr (1935: 481–2). Carr, p. 482 says, "Render in 1799 is independent in his presentation of the noun, but the section on the verb simply repeats Wendeborn. This is seen particularly in the treatment of the compound verb where both use *aufhalten* as model and both give *hielte auf*". Van der Lubbe (2007b: 152) notes a 6th ed. London: Printed by C. Whittingham for H. D. Symonds, 1810. See Render (1804).

1800–1809

1800a. Crabb, George. *A complete introduction to the knowledge of the German language; or, a translation from Adelung: arranged and adapted to the English learner… To which is affixed, a dictionary.* London: Printed for the author, by C. Whittingham. See Van der Lubbe (2007b). See Crabb (1800b, 1800c, 1801, 1803, 1811, 1828).

1800b. Crabb, George. *An easy and entertaining selection of German prose and poetry. With a small dictionary, and other aids for translating.* London: printed for the author, by C. Whittingham, and sold by J. Johnson; T. Boosey; C. Geisweiler; De Boffe, and Esher; and Wilson and Spence, York. See Van der Lubbe (2007b). See Crabb (1800a).

1800c. Crabb, George. *Elements of German conversation;: upon the plan of Perrin's Elements.* London: Printed by C. Whittingham, for T. Boosey. See Van der Lubbe (2007b). Later editions, revised by Adolphus Bernays: 1836, 1840, 1849, 1852, 1856. See Crabb & Bernays (1828) below. See Crabb (1800a).

1800 (2nd ed. 1807, 8th ed. 1838). Noehden, Georg Heinrich. *German grammar, adapted to the use of Englishmen.* London: Printed by C. Whittingham. Carr (1935: 483) considers that "this was the most popular grammar of the period". Carr finds the "unmistakeable" influence of Adelung (1782), though Noehden often quotes him in an attempt to refute him. See also Noehden (1814, 1816, 1818, 1830, 1842), and Noehden & Lloyd (1827, 1829). See 3.3 above.

1800. Rabenhorst, C. *The new pocket-dictionary of the German and English languages.* Leipsic: Printed for C.T. Rabenhorst [etc., etc.]. Hathi Trust. See also Noehden (1814), Noehden & Lloyd (1827, 1829).

1801. Crabb, George. *The order and method of instructing children, with strictures on the modern system of education: by George Crabb.* London: printed by M. and S. Brooke, for T.N. Longman and O. Rees, Paternoster-Row. See Crabb (1800a).

1803. Crabb, George. *Neue practische englische Grammatik for German learners.* Frankfurt. See Klippel (1994). See Crabb (1800a).

1803. Heynatz, Johann Friedrich. *Deutsche Sprachlehre zum Gebrauch der Schulen. Fünfte vermehrte und verbesserte Auflage (1803). Die Lehre von der Interpunktion. Zweite, durchgängig verbesserte Auflage (1782).* Rpt. ed. Petra Ewald. Hildesheim: Olms, 2006.

1804. Render, William. *A complete analysis of the German language, or A philological and grammatical view of its construction, analogies, and various properties.* London: H.D. Symonds. Hathi Trust. See Render (1799).

1805. Müller, G.A. *A new German grammar: or, a concise and easy introduction to the German language, adapted to the use of Englishmen.* n.p.: n. p.

1805 (2nd ed. 1817, 3rd ed. 1822, 4th ed. 1828). Schade, Carl Benjamin. *A New Grammar of the German Language for the use of Englishmen.* London and Leipzig: J.C. Hinrichs. See Schade (1828) below.

1808. P.A.R. (= Weston, Stephen). *A supplement to the Grammar: for the use of Students in the German Language.* [S. I.]: [s. n.].

1810–1819

1811 (= 2nd ed.). Crabb, George. *German Extracts from the Best Authors with the English words at the Bottom of the Page, and a Dictionary at the End, for Tranlsating into English. Auswahl vorzueglicher Stellen: aus den besten deutschen Schriftstellern zusammengetragen, und mit einer englischen Erklärung der darin vorkommenden Wörter und Redensarten begleitet.* London: Gedruckt bei Hamblin and Seyfang… und bei T. Boosey… Mentioned by Watson (1921: 694), following Schaible (1885). See Crabb (1800a).

1814. Noehden, Georg Heinrich. *Rabenhorst's dictionary of the German and English languages: in two parts.* London: Printed for Longman, Hurst, Rees, Orme and Brown; Cadell and Davies; T. Boosey, and J. Mawman. Hathi Trust. See Noehden (1800).

1816. Heyse, Johann Christian August. *Kleine theoretisch-praktische deutsche Grammatik.* Hanover.

1816. Noehden, Georg Heinrich. *A grammar of the German language.* London: Mawman. Hathi Trust. See Noehden (1800).

1818. Noehden, Georg Heinrich. *A grammar of the German language.* London: J. H. Bohte. Hathi Trust. See Noehden (1800).

1819. Fischer, J. J. G. *A new classification of the nouns substantive in the German language.* London: [Printed by Schulze and Dean]. See Carr (1935).

1820–1829

1820 (1840, 1843). Boileau, Daniel. *The nature and genius of the German language displayed: in a more extended review of its grammatical forms than is to be found in any grammar extant, and elucidated by quotations from the best writers.* London: T. Boosey & Sons; Treuttel & Würtz. Carr (1935: 481) writes, "This is not a formal grammar but deals more with questions of German style by means of quotations from contemporary authors". 1840 ed. London: Jonathan Wacey. 1843 ed. London: D. Nutt. [Google books]. See Boileau (1827, 1837, 1840), Wendeborn & Boileau (1837).

1820. Jehring, Ernst. *A grammar of the German language.* Glasgow: n. p. Carr (1935: 481) states that "this appears to be the first German Grammar published in Scotland. Jehring was a lieutenant in the York Light Infantry, resident in Glasgow." Jehring is notable chiefly for his "many mistakes and inaccuracies", which "it would be risky to [attribute] to any reputable German grammarian" (Carr 1935: 483).

1822. Heyse, Johann Christian August. *Theoretisch-praktische deutsche Grammatik oder Lesebuch eines reinen und richtigen Sprechen, Lesen und Schreiben der deutschen Sprache.* 3rd ed. Hannover: Hahn.

1824. (2nd, revised ed. London 1832). Rowbotham, John. *A practical German grammar.* London: printed for Baldwin, Cradock and Joy; Harvey and Darton; and Boosey and Sons. Listed by Carr (1935: 481). See also Rowbotham (1829, 1833, 1839).

1824. Walker, John. *Walker's critical pronouncing dictionary: and expositor of the English language. Abridged for the use of schools. To which is annexed, an abridgment of Walker's key to the pronunciation of Greek, Latin, and scripture proper names.* London: Blake, Cutler & Co.

1826. Williams, Thomas Sidney. *Modern English and German Dialogues and elementary Phrases adapted to the use of learners in both languages.* London: Hamburg: n. p. Revised eds. 1856, 1860, published London: Williams & Norgate. Discussed by Macht (1994). See also Williams & Crueger (1856).

1827. Boileau, Daniel, and C. Will. *A Key to the German Language and Conversation… With an easy introduction to German grammar… Revised and enlarged by C. Will.* Francfort on the Main: Charles Jugel. The British Library record states that Will was an English teacher in Frankfurt am Main. Later eds: 2nd ed., revised and enlarged by W. Howe. Frankfort: Charles Jugel. 1837; 3rd ed. (also rev. Howe) London: Jonathan Wacey, 1839. Besides the other works listed here, Boileau was author of: *A Few Remarks on Mr. Hayward's English Prose Translation of Goethe's*

Faust, with additional observations on the difficulty of translating German works in general. London: Treuttel, Würtz & Richter, 1834. See Boileau (1820).

1827 (2ⁿᵈ ed. revised C. W. Asher 1836). Lloyd, Hannibal Evans, and Georg Heinrich Noehden. *A new dictionary of the English and German languages*. Hamburgh: A. Campe. Hathi Trust. See Noehden (1800).

1828 (1836, 1840, 1849, 1852, 1856). Crabb, George, and Adolphus Bernays. *Elements of German and English conversation*. London: n. p. Based on Crabb (1800c) above. See Crabb (1800a).

1828. Follen, Charles. *A practical grammar of the German language*. Boston: Hilliard, Gray, Little, and Wilkins. Hathis Trust. See Follen (1835, 1836).

1828. Schade, Karl Benjamin. *A complete practical grammar of the German language. 4ᵗʰ ed., thoroughly altered and improved in every Part of speech by many additions*. Leipsic: Printed for J. C. Hinrichs. Hathi Trust. See Schade (1805) above.

1829. Becker, Carl Ferdinand. *Deutsche Grammatik*. Frankfurt: Joh. Christ. Hermann'sche Buchhandlung. See Becker (1830), also Apel (1844, 1857).

1829 (1831, 1837). Bernays, Adolphus. *German poetical anthology. Preceded by a concise history of German poetry, and short notices of the authors selected*. On Bernays, who held the first Chair of German at King's College, London, see Flood (1999) and discussion in 3.6.2. See also Bernays (1831, 1833, 1835, 1837, 1847, 1849, 1852a,b,c, 1851, 1855.)

1829. Noehden, Georg Heinrich, and Hannibal Evans Lloyd. *Rabenhorst's Pocket dictionary of the German and English languages*. Hathi Trust. See Noehden (1800).

1829. Rowbotham, John. *Deutsches Lesebuch; or, lessons in German Literature, being a… collection of… pieces, in prose and verse, selected from… German authors*. London. See Rowbotham (1824).

1829. Wendeborn, Gebhard Friedrich August, and Daniel Boileau. *Wendeborn's practical German Grammar. The eighth edition… enlarged and improved by D. Boileau*. London. See also 11ᵗʰ ed. 1849 "entirely remodelled by A. [Adolph] Heimann." See also Wendeborn (1797a), Boileau (1820).

1830–1839

1830 (2ⁿᵈ ed. 1845 "greatly improved, edited by Bernhard Becker, 3ʳᵈ ed. 1855). Becker, Carl Ferdinand. *A grammar of the German language*. London: John Murray. Carr (1935: 482–3) writes, "this is an adapation of the author's Deutsche Grammatik, Frankfurt, 1829. It is not intended for beginners, and even the advanced student must have found Becker's terminology difficult, if he were not philosophically minded." Second edition, "greatly improved", edited by Bernhard Becker. London: Longman & Co, 1845. Third ed. "carefully revised and adapted to the use of English students, by J. W[ilhlem]. Fraedersorf." London: Williams & Norgate, 1855. Carr (1935: 484) says Becker is the first grammar of German for English to show influece of Grimm and philology, e.g. attempting to group strong verbs by original vowel of infinitive. "Becker's grammar never seems to have been very popular" but influenced others including Skene, Bernays, and – less so – Tiarks. See Becker (1829).

1830 (1832, 1837, 1859). Bernays, Adolphus. *A compendious German grammar*. London: Treuttel & Co. 1832 ed. 1832. Bernays, Adolphus and Hermann Bokum. *Bernay's Compendious German grammar: with a dictionary of prefixes and affixes, and with alterations, additions, and references to an "Introduction to the study of the German language*. Philadelphia: Hogan and Thompson. Hathi Trust. See Bernays (1829).

1830. Mayo, Elizabeth, and Charles L. L. D. Mayo. *Lessons on objects as given in a Pestalozzian school at Cheam, Surrey*. London: R. B. Seeley & W. Burnside. [By Elizabeth Mayo. The preface signed: C. M., i. e. Charles Mayo.].

1830. Mühlenfels, Ludwig von. *An introduction to a course of German literature*. London: [s. n.].

1830. Noehden, Georg Heinrich. *A grammar of the German language*. London: Longman, Rees, Orme, Brown, and Green. Hathi Trust. See Noehden (1800).

1830. Schoeler, Georg. *New Concise Grammar of the German Tongue*. Berlin.

1831a. Bernays, Adolphus. *Familiar German Exercises; or, Practice on the German language, adapted to the "Compendious German Grammar." With an appendix*. London: Treuttel & Co. See Bernays (1829).

1831b. Bernays, Adolphus. *An introductory lecture, delivered in King's College, London: November 2, 1831*. London: B. Fellowes. See Bernays (1829).

1831. Klauer-Klattowsky, Wilhelm G. *Deutsches Handbuch. le manuel de la langue allemand; the German manual for self-tuition*. 2 vols. Paris: Baudry, Bobé et Hingray...; London: Simpkin and Marshall, T. and T. Boosey... Carr (1935: 482) states that "the first volume contains extracts from German authors followed by a grammar written in German. Vol II opens with a short grammar in English and French which is followed by German extracts with an interlinear translation in French." Carr calls it a "slavish" copy of Heyne's *Kleine theoretisch-praktische deutsche Grammatik* (1816).

1831. Skene, Philip Orkney. *Die Geschichte des kleinen Jack aus dem Englischen [The History of Little Jack of Thomas Day] übersetzt von A. Mensbier; adapted for teaching and learning the German Language by means of a verbal translation [in English] on the principles of the Hamiltonian system, and an elementary grammar, by P. O. Skene*. London: Longman, Rees, Orme, Brown, and Green. Text in German, then again in German with interlinear English. Mentioned by Carr (1935).

1832. Bernays, Adolphus, and Hermann Bokum. *Bernay's Compendious German grammar: with a dictionary of prefixes and affixes, and with alterations, additions, and references to an "Introduction to the study of the German language"*. Philadelphia: Hogan and Thompson.

1832. Rowbotham, John. *A practical German grammar*. London: Effingham Wilson. Second ed. of Rowbotham (1824), above.

1833. Bernays, Adolphus. *The German Reader, a selection from the most popular writers, with literal and free translations, grammatical and other notes, etc*. London: Treuttel, Wurtz & Richter. See Bernays (1829).

1833. Rowbotham, John. *An Abridgment of German Grammar, etc*. London. See Rowbotham (1824).

1834. Ahn, (Johann) Franz. (1796–1865). *Praktischer Lehrgang zur schnellen und leichten Erlernung der französischen Sprache.* Cologne. Macht (1994) writes "His book was a stupendous success: in fifty years it was re-edited and reprinted 207 times". See Ahn (1849, 1856, 1867, 1869, 1875, 1876), Ahn & Oehlschläger (1857, 1860, 1862, 1880), Ahn & Pfeiffer (1868), Grauert & Ahn (1871), Ahn & Fischer (1873), Ahn & Henn (1876, 1888), Weisse (1888). See 3.7 above.

1834. Bramsen, John. *A guide to the German language.* London: Adolphus Richter, and Co. … [and 12 others]. See Carr (1935: 482).

1834. Klauer-Klattowsky, Wilhelm, and Friedrich Ludwig Zacharias. Werner. *Der vierundzwanzigste februar. A tragedy by Ludwig Zacharias Werner. With explanatory notes, and a translation of all difficult words and phrases by Wilhelm Klauer-Klattowsky.* London: Simpkin and Marshall [etc.]. Hathi Trust. See Klauer-Klattowsky (1837).

1834a (1845, 1847, 1852, 1864 = 15th ed.). Tiarks, Johann Gerhard. *A practical grammar of the German language.* London. See also Tiarks & Schmidt (1835).

1834b (1837, 1839, 1847, 1852, 1873). Tiarks, Johann Gerhard. *Exercises for writing German, etc.* London: Also. 1846 (1849, 1852):*A Key to Dr. J. G. Tiarks's Exercises for Writing German.* London. Tiarks was PhD, and Minister of the German Reformed Church, London. He also published a description in German of Cambridge in 1852; and *The Conjugation of the Greek Verb… according to Professor Thiersch's System* (1833); and *Sacred German Poetry, or a Selection of hymns on the most important truths of the Gospel. Arranged and edited by the Rev. J. G. Tiarks* (1838).

1835. Bernays, Adolphus. *German Historical Anthology; being a sequel to the German Reader.* London: J. W. Parker. See Bernays (1829).

1835. Follen, Charles. *A practical grammar of the German language [preface to 1st ed. is dated 1828].* Boston: Hilliard, Gray, and Company. Hathi Trust. See also Follen (1828).

1835. Tiarks, Johann Gerhard and O. Schmidt, Professor of German. *A Progressive German Reader.* London: J. Wacey. See also Tiarks (1834a,b).

1836. Follen, Charles. *German reader for beginners.* Boston, Mass.. Hathi Trust. See also Follen (1828).

1836 (2nd ed.; 1st ed. 1827). Lloyd, Hannibal Evans, and Georg Heinrich Noehden. *A new dictionary of the English and German languages.* Hamburgh: A. Campe.

1836 (later eds. 1839, 1849 = "fourth, enlarged ed."). Troppaneger, Albert. *The grammatical forms of the German language and the construction of sentences, with reading lessons and exercises.* London. See Carr (1935: 482).

1837. Bernays, Adolphus. *German poetry for beginners.* London. See Bernays (1829).

1837. Boileau, Daniel. *The Linguist. A complete course of instructions in the German language. New edition, etc.* London: J. Wacey. See Boileau (1820).

1837. Kaltschmidt, J. H. *A new and complete dictionary of the english and german languages: with two sketches of grammar, english and german.* Leipsic, printed for C. Tauchnitz. Hathi Trust.

1837. Klauer-Klattowsky, Wilhelm. *Ballads and romances, poetical tales, legends and idylls of the Germans. With a translation of all unusual words and difficult passages and with explanatory notes.* London: Simpkin, Marshall and Co., etc. etc. Hathi Trust. Klauer-Klattowsky (1834).

1837 (1847, 1848, 1849, 1855, 1873). Rowbotham, John. *A New Guide to German and English Conversation, etc.* London. Rowbotham had published a similar guide to Spanish and English conversation in 1835.

1838. Bernays, Adolphus. *A key to the difficulties, philological and historical, of the first book of Schiller's Thirty years' war.* London. See Bernays (1829).

1838. Ollendorff, Heinrich Gottfried. *A new method of learning to read, write, and speak a language in six months: adapted to the German: for the use of schools and private teachers.* London: Whittaker. See also Ollendorff (1844, n.d. after 1844?) and Gands (1841). See 3.7 in this book.

1839 (1844, 1863). Eulenstein, Charles (Professor of German). *An easy introduction to the German language.* London: C.&H. Senior…

1839. Rowbotham, John. *A New Derivative Spelling-Book, in which not only the origin of each word is given from the Greek, Latin, Saxon, German, Teutonic, Dutch, French, Spanish, and other languages; but also their present acceptation, etc.* London: n.p. Revised eds. by different authors 1855, 1858.

1840–1849

1840. Apel, Heinrich. *A grammar of the German language.* London. See also Apel (1844, 1851, 1857).

1840. Boileau, Daniel. *The linguist: a complete course of instruction in the German language: in which attention is particularly directed to peculiarities in grammatical forms and construction, exemplified by selections from the best authors. New edition, carefully revised and corrected.* London: Longman, Orme, Brown, Green, and Longmans. Hathi Trust. See Boileau (1820).

1840. Kombst, Gustaf. *A German grammar, for the use of schools and private teaching.* Edinburgh; London: Charles Smith; Whittaker&Co.; Black&Armstrong; D. Nutt (Printed at the University Press).

1841. Flügel, Johann Gottfried, et al. *Flügel's complete dictionary of the German and English languages : adapted to the English student, with great additions and improvements.* London: Whittaker.

1841. Gands, P. *The German Literary Companion, or a Guide to German literature: being a choice collection of pieces in prose and verse… With an introduction… translations and notes, and sketches of the lives of the most celebrated German writers… intended to serve as a sequel to Ollendorff's New Method of learning the German Language.* Frankfurt am Main: Charles Jugel. See Ollendorff (1838).

1842. Noehden, Georg Heinrich. *Exercises for writing German: according to the rules of grammar. Corrected and revised by C.H.F. Bialloblotzky.* London: Longman, Brown, Green and Longmans; Dulau. Hathi Trust. See Noehden (1800).

1844. Apel, Heinrich. *The formation of words of the German language, practically developed and arranged according to the views of Dr. Becker… forming a supplement to every German grammar.* London: Simpkin, Marshall & Co. See Becker (1829), Apel (1840).

1844. Ollendorff, Heinrich Godefroy. *A new method of learning to read, write and speak the German language in six months.* Translated from the fifth French edition by G. J. Bertinchamp. London: Hippolyte Baillière. Second edition, revised… by J[ames]. D. Haas. London. Other editions include New York: 1848; London: 1850. See also: *Ollendorf's German Method* (n. d., after 1844?). Copy held in the Taylor collection. Note to the teacher on p. 5–6: "Each lesson should be dictated to the pupil, who should pronounce every word, as it is dictated to him. After this, the teacher should exercise the pupil by putting questions to him in every possible way. Each lesson, with the exception of the fourth, will comprise three divisions: the Professor commences examining the pupil by putting such questions to him as are given in the exercises; next, he will dictate to him the following lesson; lastly, he will put to him new questions on all the preceding lessons. According to the different degrees of competency of the pupils, one lesson may be divided into two, two lessons into three, or three lessons combined into one…"

1846. Egestorff, Georg Heinrich Christoph. *A concise grammar of the German language, on the principles adopted in the schools in Germany: in which the declension is facilitated and simplified and the relation of prepositions pointed out and familiarized, in a series of easy and comprehensive examples.* London: Simpkin, Marshall, and Co.

1847. Bernays, Adolphus (transl.). Friedrich Schiller, *William Tell: a play.* London: John W. Parker. See Bernays (1829).

1849. Ahn, (Johann) Franz. *A New… Method of learning the German Language. First course.* Leipzig: Brockhaus & Avenarius. Ahn's *A New Practical and Easy method of learning German.* [German ed. 2 vols; English ed. Philadelphia 1859] See Ahn (1834) above. His grammar was described by Hawkins (1987: 113) as a "very popular" grammar, along with Plötz (1865). On Ahn's method, see Titone (1968: 28) and Wheeler (2013: 114–15). Many editions and revisions followed: see entries including Ahn under (1849, 1856, 1857, 1859 (Philadelphia), 1862, 1864, 1867, 1868, 1869, 1871, 1873, 1874, 1875, 1876, 1880, 1888) below, and Weisse (1888). An American edition (New York: American Book Co.) is available through the Hathi Trust.

1849. Bernays, Adolphus. On the German Language. *Introductory Lectures delivered at Queen's College, London.* London. See Bernays (1829).

1849, 1852, 1854. Eichhorn, Karl (Charles). *The practical German grammar; or, a natural method of learning to read, write and speak the German language.* 1854 3rd ed., revised and corrected [original preface dated 1849]. New York: D. Appleton & Co. Hathi Trust.

1849, 1850, 1856, 12th ed. 1879; (1898 edited by Mary C. Rothwell). Rothwell, J. S. S. *Neue englische und deutsche Gespräche.* Munich. Mentioned by Macht (1994).

1849. Woodbury, W. H. *Woodbury's kurzgefasste englische Grammatik, besonders für Anfänger welche die englische Sprache in möglichst kurzer Zeit zu erlernen wünschen.* New York: M. H. Newman & Co. Hathi Trust. See Woodbury (1851, 1854, 1857a, b) and Fasquelle & Woodbury (1854) below.

1850–1859

1850. Ollendorff. 7th ed. of Ollendorff (1838), q. v.

1851. Apel, Heinrich. *A grammar of the German language, on Dr. Berker's system: with copious examples, exercises, and explanations for the use of schools and for self-tuition.* London: Williams and Norgate. See Apel (1840).

1851. Woodbury, W. H. *A new method of learning the German language: embracing both the analytic and synthetic modes of instruction being a plain and practical way of acquiring the art of reading, speaking, and composing German.* New York: Mark H. Newman & Co. Hathi Trust. See Woodbury (1849) above.

1852a. Bernays, Adolphus. *German Examples, illustrating the author's German Grammar... Sixth edition.* London: J. W. Parker & Son. See Bernays (1829).

1852b. Bernays, Adolphus. *German Phrase Book; a guide to the formation of sentences for conversation and composition, etc.* London: J. W. Parker & Son. See Bernays (1829).

1852c. Bernays, Adolphus. *German word-book: a comparative vocabulary displaying the close affinity between the German and English languages.* London: J. W. Parker. See Bernays (1829).

1852. Eichhorn, Charles. *The practical German Grammar: or, a natural method of learning to read, write, and speak the German language.* New York: D. Appleton and Company. See Eichhorn (1849).

1852. Oehlschlaeger, James C. *A method of learning to read and understand the GErman langauge, WITH OR WITHOUT A TEACHER.* New York: D. Appleton & Co. Author described on title page as "Professor of Modern Languatges in Philadelphia and author of a pronoucning dictionary of the English and German languages." See Oehlschlaeger (1861) below – I have been unable to identify an earlier edition. See Ahn & Oehlschlaeger (1857, 1860, 1862, 1880).

1852 (also 1853, 1856). Strauss, G. L. M. *A grammar of the German language. Adapted for the use of English students from Heyse's Theoretical and Practical German grammar.* London: J. Weale. Hathi Trust. See Strauss (1859, 1883).

1853. Bernays, Adolphus. *German conversation book; being a selection from German prose dramatists, with a free translation and notes.* London. See Bernays (1829).

1854. Fasquelle, Louis, and W. H. Woodbury. *A new method of learning the French language; embracing both the analytic and synthetic modes of instruction.* New York: Ivison & Phinney. Hathi Trust.

1854. Woodbury, W. H. *Woodbury's elementary German reader: consisting of selections in prose and poetry, chiefly from standard German writers; with a full vocabulary, copious references to the author's German grammars, and a series of explanatory notes; designed for schools, colleges and private students.* New York: Ivison & Phinney. Hathi Trust.

1855. Bernays, Adolphus. *Queen's College: Introductory lecture delivered at the commencement of the academical year 1854–1855.* London: John W. Parker and Son. See Bernays (1829).

1855. Bernays, Adolphus (ed.). Schiller, Friedrich. *Maria Stuart, ein Trauerspiel [in five acts and in verse].* With an introduction and explanatory notes by Adolphus Bernays. London. See Bernays (1829).

1855. Elwell, Wm Odell. *A new and complete dictionary of the English and German languages. For general use. Containing a concise grammar of either language, dialogues with reference to grammatical forms and rules on pronunciation.* Brunswick: G. Westermann. Hathi Trust.

1856. (6ᵗʰ ed.). Ahn, (Johann) Franz. *A new, practical and easy method of learning the German language... Second course. With a pronounciation, arranged according to J. C. Oehlschlager's recently published pronouncing German dictionary.* Philadelphia: Hathi Trust. See Ahn (1834, 1849), see Oehlschlaeger (1852), Ahn & Oehlschlaeger (1860, 1862, 1880).

1856. Moncriff, Bernard. *A German Grammar, on a new and simplified method.* London, Liverpool printed: 1856.

1856. Williams, Thomas Sidney, and Carl Crueger. *Modern German and English Dialogues, and elementary phrases: adapted to the use of learners in both languages... The German revised and corrected by C. Crüger... The fourteenth enlarged edition [of "Modern English and German Dialogues"].* London & Edinburgh: Williams & Norgate. See also Williams (1826).

1857. Ahn, (Johann) Franz, and James C. Oehlschläger. *A new, practical and easy method of learning the German language. With a pronounciation, arranged according to J. C. Oehlschläger's recently published pronouncing German dictionary. First course.* Philadelphia: J. Weik. Hathi Trust. See Ahn (1849).

1857. Apel, Heinrich. *A School Grammar of the German Language, according to Dr. Becker's Views; with a complete course of exercises... Fourth edition, thoroughly revised and embodying a new method.* London & Edinburgh: Williams & Norgate. See Becker (1829), Apel (1840, 1844).

1857. Oswald, Eugene. *A German reading-book: with notes.* London. On Oswald, see Flood (2001, 2005). See Oswald (1870a,b, 1911).

1857. Otto, Emil. *German Conversation-Grammar...* Second edition. London; Heidelberg [printed]: D. Nutt. See Otto (1864, 1866, 1889, 1890), Otto & Mauron (1883), Otto & Wright (1889), and Otto & Mennie (1937). See 3.7 above.

1857a. Woodbury, W. H. *A shorter course with the German language.* New York: Phinney. Hathi Trust.

1857b. Woodbury, W. H. *Woodbury's Elementary German Reader: Consisting of Selections of Prose and Poetry, Chiefly from Standard German Writers; With a full Vocabulary, Copious References to the Author's German Grammars, and a Series of Explanatory Notes; Designed for Schools, Colleges and Private Students.* New York. Discussed by Langer (2008).

1857. (later eds. 1867, 1875, revised ed. 1878, 1902). Sonnenschein, A. and James Steven Stallybrass. *German for the English... 1st reading book; easy poems with interlinear translations & ill. by notes and tables chiefly etymological.* London: David Nutt. Hathi Trust. Cited by Eve (1880: vii) as "a book which no teacher can read without pleasure and profit". See also Heimann (1889), who acknowledges the help of these two men in preparing his own volume.

1858. Tiarks, Johann Gerhard. *An introductory grammar of the German language with an introductory reader and introductory exercises.* London: David Nutt (Wertheimer and co., printers).

1859. Strauss, G. L. M. *The German reader: consisting of selections from the following German writers: L. Börne, Engel, Garve, Göthe, W. Hauff, H. Heine,…: for the use of English students.* London: J. Weale. Hathi Trust. See Strauss (1852).

1860–1969

1860 (11th & 12th eds.). Ahn, (Johann) Franz and James C. Oehlschläger. *A new, practical and easy method of learning the German language.* Philadelphia: John Weik & Co. Each course has a separate title page. First course. 12th ed. – Second course. 11th ed. See Ahn (1834, 1849). See Oehlschlaeger (1852).

1861, 1863. Oehlschlaeger, James C. *English German and German-English Pocket-Dictionary, with the Pronunciation of the English Words in German Sounds and Signs. AND English German and German-English Pocket-Dictionary, with the Pronunciation of the German Part in English Characters and English Sounds.* (Since the title page of Oehlschlaeger (1852) above already refers to the author's pronoucning dictionary, there was presuambly also an earlier edition.) New York: K. Steiger.

1862. Ahn, (Johann) Franz, and James C. Oehschläger. *Ahn's introductory practical course to acquire the French language, by a short and easy method.* New York: D. Appleton. Hathi Trust, where the record calls it "A translation of his Praktischer lehrgang zur schnellen und leichten erlernung der französischen Sprache, erster cursus." See Ahn (1849), Oehlschläger (1852).

1864. Ahn, (Johann) Franz *Ahn's new practical and easy method of learning the German language, with a pronunciation numerous corrections… and a remodelling of the whole of the exercises and reading lessons in the practical Part by J. C. Oehlschlager. Second course.* New York: J. Wieck. Hathi Trust. See Ahn (1849).

1864. Otto, Emil. *German conversation-grammar: a new and practical method of learning the German language.* New York; Boston: Holt and Williams; S. R. Urbino. Hathi Trust. See Otto (1857).

1865. Witter, Conrad. *Witters drittes Lesebuch für deutsch-amerikanische Schulen: Schlussstufe.* St. Louis, Mo.: Conrad Witter. Hathi Trust. At head of title: *Third German reader.* See Witter (1881a,b).

1866. Otto, Emil. *Materials for translating English into French, etc.* Heidelberg.

1867. Ahn, (Johann) Franz. *A new practical and easy method of learning the German language… Course 1–2.* New York: D. Appleton and Co. Hathi Trust. See Ahn (1849).

1868. Ahn, (Johann) Franz, and Pfeiffer, Johann. *New, Practical and Easy Method of Learning the German Language. New edition, considerably enlarged and improved upon from the original French edition by Johann Pfeiffer, P. D..* London: T. J. Allman. See Ahn (1849).

1868, 1871. Prendergast, Thomas. *The Mastery Series. German. 5th edn. London: Longmans, Green & co.* [1st edn., 1868] London: Longmans, Green & co. On Prendergast, see Atherton (2010), Wheeler (2013: 121–124).

1869. Ahn, (Johann) Franz. *Ahn's New, practical and easy method of learning the German language.* New York: E. Steiger. Hathi Trust. First course: Practical part. Second course: Theoretical part. See Ahn (1849).

1869 (1873, 1877, 1880, 1882, 1900). Whitney, William Dwight. *A Compendious German Grammar.* [S. I.]: Macmillan and co. Carr (1935: 493) refers to Whitney (1869) as acknowledging Heyse as an influence. See Klemm & Whitney (1883).

1870–1879

1870. Eve, Henry Weston, and F. de Baudiss. *The Wellington College French primer.* London: David Nutt. See Eve (1880, 1884, 1887, 1894, 1903) and Eve et al. (1883).

1870. Helfenstein, James. *A comparative grammar of the Teutonic languages: being at the same time a historical grammar of the English language, and comprising Gothic, Anglo-Saxon, Early English, Modern English, Icelandic (Old Norse), Danish, Swedish, Old High German, Middle High German, Modern German, Old Saxon, Old Frisian, Dutch.* London: Macmillan.

1870a. Oswald, Eugene. *Early German courtesy-books: an account of The Italian Guest by Thomasin von Zirclaria, of 'how the Knight of Winsbeke taught his son, and the Lady of Winsbeke her daughter', the German Cato, and Tannhaeuser's courtly breeding.* [London?]: John Childs. See Oswald (1857).

1870b. Oswald, Eugene. *German poetry for schools, and home circle: with English notes, &c.* London: T. J. Allman. See Oswald (1857).

1871. Grauert, William and (Johann) Franz Ahn. *Ahn's manual of German conversation.* New York: E. Steiger. Hathi Trust. See Ahn (1834, 1849).

1871. Keetels, Jean Gustave. *Oral method with German.* New York: H. Holt & Co. Hathi Trust.

1871. Wrage, Hermann D. *A practical grammar of the German language.* New York: Appleton. Hathi Trust.

1872. Anon. *Buchstabir- und Lesebuch zum ersten Unterricht der Kinder.* Amana. Discussed by Langer (2008: 509).

1872. Preu. *Preu's German Primer: being an introduction to first steps in German. Second edition. With engravings from designs by G. B. Bowlend, etc.* London.

1873. Ahn, (Johann) Franz, and Gustavus Fischer. *Ahn's method of learning the German language.* New York: E. Steiger. Hathi Trust. Second (theoretical) course: 2nd ed., 1871 has separate title page. See Ahn (1849).

1873. Keane, Augustus Henry. *True Theory of the German Declensions and Conjugations* London. Mentioned by Carr (1935).

1873a (10th ed.). Worman, James Henry. *An elementary grammar of the German language: with exercises, readings, conversations, paradigms, and a vocabulary.* New York: Chicago, American Book Company. Hathi Trust. See Worman (1873b, c, 1880, 1881).

1873b. Worman, James Henry. *A collegiate German reader in prose and verse: with copious explanatory notes and references to Worman's "Complete" and "Elementary" German grammars, and Campbell's "New German course", and a complete vocabulary.* New York: A. S. Barnes & Co. Hathi Trust.

1873c. Worman, James Henry. *An elementary German reader in prose and verse: with copious explanatory notes and references to the editors German grammars, and a complete vocabulary.* New York: A. S. Barnes & Co. Hathi Trust.

1874. Quick, Robert Herbert. *A German primer: giving the essentials of German grammar, with a selection of proverbs, poems etc for learning by heart: also easy exercises in the use of common German words.* Harrow: Samuel Clarke.

1874. Roehrig, Frederic Louis Otto. *The Shortest Road to German.* Ithaca, N. Y.: Andrus, Mochain & Lyons. Cited by Kelly (1969: 55).

1875. Ahn, (Johann) Franz. *Ahn's first [-second] German reader, with footnotes and vocabulary.* New York: E. Steiger. Hathi Trust. See Ahn (1834, 1849).

1875. Heness, Theophilus [Gottlieb]. *Introduction to the Leitfaden. A guide for instruction to German without grammar or dictionary.* Reprint 2009: Kessinger Publishing Company. See Titone (1968: 32) on Heness's biography: he started a small private school of modern languages at New Haven, 1866. Together with Sauveur, he founded a school in Cambridge, Mass., and opened summer schools for modern languages, largely attended by modern languages teachers. See Heness (1884).

1876. Ahn, (Johann) Franz. *Ahn's fourth German book. Being the fourth division of Ahn's Rudiments of the German language.* New York: E. Steiger. Hathi Trust. See Ahn (1834, 1849).

1876. Ahn, (Johann) Franz and P. Henn. *Ahn's complete method of the German language.* New York: E. Steiger. Hathi Trust. See Ahn (1834, 1849).

1876, 1877a. Klemm, Louis Richard. *Lese- und sprachbuch für deutsch-amerikanische schüler. Uebungen im lesen, sprechen, schreiben und uebersetzen mit berücksichtigung der deutschen grammatik in concentrischen kreisen geordnet [...] Von L. R. Klemm... Erster[-siebenter] kreis. Erstes[-siebentes] schuljahr. Fibel nach der analytisch-synthetischen methode.* New York: Boston: H. Holt und company [etc.]; Schönhof & Möller. Hathi Trust. See Klemm (1877b, 1878, 1881, 1888, 1889, 1911), also Klemm & Whitney (1883), Lange & Klemm (1890), Hughes & Klemm (1907).

1877. Apel, Heinrich. *A short and practical German Grammar for Beginners with copious examples and exercises.* London: Williams and Norgate. See Apel (1840).

1877b. Klemm, Louis Richard. *Lese= und Sprachbuch für die amerikanische Jugend. Uebungen im Lesen, Sprechen, Schreiben und Uebersetzen mit Berücksichtigung der deutschen Grammatik in concentrischen Kreisen geordnet. Sechster Kreis. – Sechstes Schuljahr.* New York. Discussed by Langer (2008). See Klemm (1876).

1878. Eugène-Fasnacht, G. *Macmillan's Progressive German Course. I. First Year. Containing easy lessons on the regular accidence.* London: Macmillan. Title page describes author as Senior master of modern languages, Harpur Foundation Modern School, Bedford. Author of the "Progressive French Course", etc. The copy I inspected belonged to Emil Trechmann (see Trechmann 1891), who taught German at the University of Sydney.

1878. Klemm, Louis Richard. *Abriss der geschichte der deutschen literatur.* New York: Boston: H. Holt und company [etc.] Schonhof & Moller. Hathi Trust. See Klemm (1876, 1877a, b).

1879. Bacon, Edwin F., and Magnus Schoeder. *One thousand German nouns, being those in common use, classified upon a new plan and employed in a variety of familiar sentences, stories and dialogues; constituting a complete introduction to German reading and conversation. With a synopsis of German grammar, and a vocabulary of 2000 words. By Edwin F. Bacon, PH. D. Rev. by Magnus Schoeder...* New York: Baker, Pratt & Co. Hathi Trust.

1880–1889

1880. Ahn, (Johann) Franz, and James C. Oehlschlaeger. *Ahn-Oehlschlaeger's pronouncing method of the German language: designed for instruction in schools and for private study.* New York: E. Steiger. Hathi Trust. Spine title: German method. See Ahn (1849).

1880. Christoph, Friedrich. *Dictionary of the English and German languages. To which is added a synopsis of English words differently pronounced by different ortoëpists.* Stuttgart: P. Neff. Hathi Trust.

1880. Eve, Henry Weston. *A School German Grammar.* London: David Nutt. Online at: http://www.archive.org/stream/aschoolgermangr00evegoog#page/n7/mode/1up. See Eve (1870).

1880, 1882, 1888, 1894 ("3rd, thoroughly revised edition"). Sachs, H. *German conversational grammar. A complete grammar of pure modern High German. By H. Sachs. On the principles of his improved system of teaching languages.* London: W. B. Whittingham & Co. Later editions with various publishers.

1880. Worman, James Henry. *Erstes deutsches Buch nach der natürlichen Methode für Schule und Haus.* New York: A. S. Barnes &. co. Hathi Trust. Hathi Trust. See Worman (1873a, 1881).

1881. Klemm, Louis Richard. *Poesie für Haus und Schule. A collection of German poems for use in schools and families.* New York: G. P. Putnam's Sons. Hathi Trust. Text in German; preface in English. See Klemm (1876).

1881a. Witter, Conrad. *Witter's Deutsch=Englische Schreib- und Lese-Fibel und Neues Erstes Lesebuch für Amerikanische Freischulen.* St. Louis. Discussed by Langer (2008). See Witter (1861).

1881b. Witter, Conrad. *Witter's Neues Drittes Lesebuch für Amerikanische Freischulen.* St. Louis. Discsussed by Langer (2008). See Witter (1861).

1881. Worman, James Henry. *Zweites deutsches Buch nach der Natürlichen methode für Schule und Haus.* New York: American Book Co. Hathi Trust. See Worman (1873a, 1880).

1882 (3rd ed.) Raysenberg, A. von. *Practical Grammar of the German language with conversational exercises, dialogues, Idiomatic expressions, a complete vocabulary for the exercises And a selection of reading lessons by a. Von Rayensberg, p. E. I. S., German master of the Royal High School and the Philosophical Institution, Edinburgh. Third edition. Carefully revised, improved and enlarged.* London & Edinburgh: Williams & Norgate.

1883. Eve, Henry Weston, Arthur Sidgwick, et al. *Three lectures on subjects connected with the practice of education; delivered in the University of Cambridge in the Easter term, 1882.* Cambridge: The University press; [etc., etc.]. Hathi Trust. Contents: On marking, by H. W. Eve. – On stimulus, by A. Sidgwick. – On the teaching of Latin verse composition, by E. A. Abbott. See Eve (1870).

1883. Klemm, Louis Richard, and William Dwight Whitney. *Elementary German reader.* New York: Boston: Henry Holt and Company, F. W. Christern; Carl Schoenhof. Hathi Trust. See Whitney (1869), see Klemm (1876).

1883 (2nd ed.). Otto, Emil, and A. Mauron. *German-English Conversations. A New Methodical Guide to Learn to Speak German.* Heidelberg: Julius Groos/ London: David Nutt/Paris: Fr Vieweg. 1883. Revised by Dr. A. Mauron., Prof. Front cover lists author as "Dr Emil Otto. Professor of modern languages, Lecturer at the University of Heidelberg. Author of the 'German conversation grammar' and some other class-books." See Otto (1857).

1883. Strauss, Gustave Louis Maurice. *Reminiscences of an old bohemian.* London: Tinsley Brothers. Hathi Trust. See Strauss (1852).

1884, 7th ed. 1888. Brandt, Herman Carl George. *A grammar of the German language for high schools and colleges, designed for beginners and advanced students. 7th Edition with an appendix containing full inflections, and a list of strong and irregular verbs. Mit Sachverzeichnis, Wortverzeichnis, deutsch-englischem Wörterverzeichnis und Anhang.* Boston and Chicago: Allyn and Bacon. New York & London: G. P. Putnam's sons. Hathi Trust.

1884. Eve, Henry Weston. *A school German grammar.* London: David Nutt. See Eve (1870).

1884. Heness, Gottlieb. *Der Leitfaden für den Unterricht in der deutschen Sprache, ohne Sprachlehre und Wörterbuch, mit einer englischen Einleitung über die Lehrmethode der Schule moderner Sprachen in Boston.* New York: Boston: H. Holt und company [etc.]; C. Schönhof. Hathi Trust. See Heness (1875).

1884. Huss, Hermann C. O. *A system of oral instruction in German by means of progressive illustrations and applications of the leading rules of grammar.* London: Macmillan. Copy owned by Emil Trechmann (see Trechmann 1891).

1884 (3rd ed. 1903; 5th ed. 1913). Viëtor, Wilhelm. *German pronunciation: practice and theory. The best German – German sounds, and how they are represented in spelling – the letters of the alphabet, and their phonetic values – German accent – specimens.* Leipzig: O. R. Reisland. See also Viëtor (1882) in secondary literature. See also Viëtor (1897).

1885. Brenkmann, Charles. *Hossfeld's new method for learning the German language. [With] Key.* London. Later (in part) revised editions listed in COPAC are: 1887, 1900, 1909, 1912, 1914, 1919 and 1957; discussed by Wegner (1999: 132), who unfortunately follows Rowlinson (1986) in dating it to 1909. Discussed by Stöbe (1939: 11) in the 1926 ed. revised by Happé.

1885. Comfort, George Fisk. *A first book in German: to precede the "German course".* New York: Harper. Hathi Trust.

1885. Lechner, Alfred.R. *German passages for practice in unseen translation.* London: Rivingtons. Lechner is described on title page as "senior master of modern languages, Modern School, Bedford". Copy belonged to Emil Trechmann (see Trechmann 1891) – an inspection copy from the publishers. Listed in Rugby School, *Books in Permanent Use in Various Parts of the School* (1903), Upper School, Modern Side.

1886 (1887, 1889, 1890). Beresford Webb, Henry S.. *A Practical German Grammar, with exercises, etc.* London: Rivingtons. A copy belonged to Emil Trechmann (see Trechmann 1891) with stamp "presented by the publisher". See also Beresford Webb (1889, 1894a,b, 1896, 1900, 1902, 1918).

1886. Lee, Jane (ed.). Goethe, Johann Wolfgang von. *Faust. Faust. by Goethe. With an Introduction and Notes. Part I. Followed by an Appendix on Part II.* London: Macmillan & Co.

1886 (Key 1887). Meissner, Albert L. *The public school German grammar. With exercises for translation, composition and conversation.* London. *Key to the Public school German grammar.* London. See Meissner (1888).

1886 (1887, 1902). Townson, Benjamin. *Easy German Stories. A First German reading book.* London: Rivingtons. Townson was Assistant Master at the High School Nottingham. Set text at Rugby School, July 1895, Upper School, Classical side, German, Set 6; 1902: Rugby School, Christmas 1902, Modern side, Upper School, German, Set 4.

1887 (1892). Beresford Webb, Henry. S. *Manual of German Composition. With passages for translation.* London: Rivingtons.

1887 (1893, 1897, 1904). Eve, Henry Weston. *A SHORT GERMAN ACCIDENCE AND MINOR SYNTAX. Abridged from the German Grammar; First German Exercises to accompany the Accidence, By H. W. Eve., and Second German Exercises, to accompany the German Grammar By H. W. Eve and P. de Baudiss.* London: David Nutt. See Eve (1870).

1887. Eysenbach, William. *A Practical Grammar of the German Language.* [S. I.]: H. Grevel & Co.; Boston: Ginn & Company. Hathi Trust. See Eysenbach (1889).

1887. Hohnfeldt, Dr. B. von. *German examination papers in grammar and idioms with notes* London: Rivingtons. Copy belonged to Emil Trechmann (see Trechmann 1891), signed by him "Univ. College Bangor".

1888. Ahn, (Johann) Franz and P. Henn. *Henn-Ahn's German grammar. In accordance with the modern German orthography.* New York: E. Steiger & Co. Hathi Trust.

1888. Aue, Carl Eduard. *Elementary German Grammar.* London & Edinburgh: W. & R. Chambers. Copy belonged to Emil Trechmann (see Trechmann 1891). Author described as "formerly German master in the High School of Edinburgh"; reverse of title page lists Chamber's German Series edited by Dr Aue, consisting of 2 readers, elementary and advanced grammar, phrase book, dictionary of German synonyms, and dictionary.

1888. Brandt. See Brandt (1884).

1888. Cassell. *German Pronouncing Dictionary in 2 parts: German-English-English-German with an appendix.* [S. I.]: Cassell.

1888. Dann, Joseph T. *German Commercial Correspondence with exercises German-English and English-German glossaries hints on letter-writing, german idioms and copious notes. For the use of schools and classes and for self-tuition.* London: Longmans, Green & Co. Author is PhD late assistant master in University College School, London. Copy belonged to Emil Trechmann (see Trechmann 1891).

1888. Glünicke, George J. Robert, and Sir [Henry] Evelyn Wood. *The new German field exercise. Part I. The portion on drill in extended order. Part II. Attack and defence – complete. Translated with the sanction of Maj.-Gen. Sir Evelyn Wood... by G. J. R. Glünicke.* Bedford: F. Hockliffe, [etc., etc.]. Pt. 1. The portion on drill in extended order. – Pt. 2. Attack and defence.

1888. Klemm, Louis Richard. *Educational topics of the day. Chips from a teacher's workshop.* Boston: Lee and Shepard. Hathi Trust. See Klemm (1876).

1888. Lange, Franz. *Intermediate German Course. Comprising the elemets of German grammar; idioms; materialis for translation; dictation; extempore, conversation; and vocabularies.* London: Whittaker and Co. See also Otto (1890).

1888. Meissner, Albert L. *Practical Lessons in German Conversation. A companion to all German Grammars and a Manual for Candidates for the Civil and Military Service Examinations.* London: Librairie Hachette. Copy belonged to Emil Trechmann (see Trechmann 1891). Author described on title page as MA PhD D Lit. "Librarian and Professor of modern languagea in Queen's College, Belfast, Mitglied der Gesellschaft für das Studium der neueren Sprachen zu Berlin". Facing page lists "by the same author: The philology of the French language, The Public School German grammar; The children's own German book; the first German reader; Pictures of German Life." See Meissner (1886).

1888 (later eds. include 1889, 13th ed. 1907 16th ed. 1919). Meyer, Kuno Edward. *A German grammar for schools, based on the principles and requirements of the Grammatical Society.* Part 1 Accidence. Part 2 Syntax. London: Swan Sonnenschein, Lowrey & Co. 16th ed. London: Kegan Paul Trench and Trubner. Author described as Ph.D., lecturer in German in University College, Liverpool.

1888, 1890, 1900. Van Der Smissen, William Henry, and Fraser, William Henry. *The high school German grammar: with appendices, exercises in composition and vocabularies.* New York: D. Appleton. Toronto: Copp; Clark. "Authorized by the Education Department of Ontario." Hathi Trust. See also the work by the same authors (1911), below.

1888. Weisse, Traugott Heinrich. *A complete practical grammar of the German language, with exercises constituting a method and reader, with a synopsis of prepositional idioms, and full directions for the proper use of Ahn's First course.* London: Williams and Norgate. Hathi Trust.

1889. Beresford Webb, Henry. S. *Key to passages for translation in Manual of German Composition.* London: Rivingtons.

1889. Eysenbach, William and William C. Collar (reviser). *Graded German lessons, being a practical German grammar.* Boston: Ginn & Company. Hathi Trust. See Eysenbach (1887).

1889 (9ᵗʰ ed. corrected and augmented). Heimann, Adolph. *Materials for Translating from English into German.* London: David Nutt. Copy sold in Sydney. Author listed as: A. Heimann, PhD. Professor of the German language and literature in University College, London. Heimann also revised Wendeborn's grammar, 11ᵗʰ ed. 1849. Preface, dated April 1851 at University College London, states: "A proficient scholar in German ought to be able to do four things well: to explain the structure of the language; to read a German book; to speak with some fluency; and to write a letter, or to translate a part of an English book into German without the assistance of Dictionary and Grammar. The greatest number of pupils master the first three points, but very few succeed in the last. It is acknowledged to be the most difficult of all. Now in order to smooth the way towards acquiring it, I have undertaken this volume. It contains a course of carefully selected and not very easy Exercises on the chief parts of Grammar, and a variety of fragments taken from good prose-writers, with notes, which both explain grammatical difficulties, and give a complete vocabulary, since it has been found that small Dictionaries afford but insufficient aid, and the large ones, on account of the great number of meanings mentioned under one word, often impede and puzzle the student instead of guiding him.

I am convinced that those who have gone through a good part of this book, will gain a facility in expression, which must ultimately not only make the task of writing a composition or rendering and English piece into German very easy, but also contributes to a greater proficiency in speaking, and to a better understanding of the classical writers in Germany.

Third ed. acknowledges "two excellent scholars of German, Mr. A. Sonnenschein, and Mr. J. S. Stallybrass" for their help – see Sonnenschein & Stallybrass (1857).

1889. Klemm, Louis Richard. *European schools; or, What I saw in the schools of Germany, France, Austria, and Switzerland.* New York: D. Appleton and company. Hathi Trust. See Klemm (1876).

1889 (6th ed). Otto, Emil, and Joseph Wright. *Materials for Translating English into German with Grammatical Notes and a Vocabulary. Revised by Dr J. Wright. First Part.* Sixth Edition. London: David Nutt – Heidelberg: Julius Groos (5ᵗʰ ed. 1882). See Otto (1857).

1890–1899

1890. Buchheim, Carl Adolf. *Materials for German Prose Composition; or, Selections from modern English writers, with grammatical notes, idiomatic renderings of difficult phrases, essentials of German syntax, preliminary chapters on punctuation and the division of words in German, and a grammatical index. Thirteenth, enlarged edition, with a list of subjects for original compositoin* [first issued in 1868, according to the preface p. vii). London: George Bell & Sons. Author is listed as Phil Doc.,

F.C.P. [Fellow of College of Preceptors], Professor of the German language and literature in King's College, London; Examiner in German to the University of London: etc. Copy owned by Emil Trechmann (see Trechmann 1891). Preface to 13th ed. says the author considers both that the utility of German may be considered "as an axiom", and the "importance of German as a discipline of the mind, and as a medium of enlightenment and refinement" are "universally admitted" (p vii). See Buchheim (1910).

1890. Lange, Helene, and Louis Richard Klemm. *Higher education of women in Europe.* New York: D. Appleton and company. Hathi Trust. See Klemm (1876).

1890 (25th edition). Otto, Emil, rev. Franz Lange. *German Conversation – Grammar. A Practical Method of Learning the German Language. Revsied by Franz Lange.* London: David Nutt; Heidelberg: Julius Groos. Lists authors as: Emil Otto, PhD Late lecturer at the unversity of Heidelberg; author of the 'French conversation-grammar', &c.; Franz Lange, PHD Professor, Royal Military Academcy, Woolwich. Examiners in the German language, and literature at the Victoria University, Manchester. In the copy held in the Taylor collection, Bamberg, p. [III] is inscribed with the name Mary Smith 29/1/94; in pencil above the title page is Nil Desperandum [!]. See Otto (1857).

Page facing preface to first edition: "The method of Gaspey-Otto-Samer is my own private property, having been acquired by purchase from the authors. The text-books made after this method are incessantly improved. All rights, especially the right of making new editions, and the right of translation for all languages are reserved. Imitations and fraudulent impressions will be persecuted according to the law. I am thankful for communications relating to these matters. Julian Groos."

189[0?]. Tafel, Leonhard, and Louis Hermann Tafel. *Neues, vollständiges englisch-deutsches und deutsch-englisches Taschen-Wörterbuch, mit der Aussprache der deutschen und der englischen Wörter, und mit besonderer Berücksichtigung der technischen Ausdrücke der Künste und Wissenschaften, für Geschäftsleute und Schulen.* Philadelphia: J.J. McVey. Hathi Trust.

1891. Becker, Anton Leopold. *First Steps in German Idioms: containing an alphabetical list of idioms, explanatory notes and examination papers.* London: Hachette.

1891. Muret, Eduard. D. *Encyclopaedic English-German and German-English Dictionary: Giving the Pronunciation according to the Phonetic System / E. D. Muret. Part 2, German-English.* Berlin: Langenscheidt Verlags-Buchhandlung.

1891. Storr, Francis. *German Declensions and Conjugations By Help of Reason and Rhyme.* London: William Rice. Cost sixpence. Author is "sometime master of modern subjects, Merchant Taylors' School". See 3.7, 3.8.

1891. Trechmann, Emil. *A short historical Grammar of the German Language.* London: MacMillan. On Trechmann, see Taylor (forthcoming), according to whom Trechmann (b. 1856?) studied at Leipzig, Heidelberg and then Oxford, and was the first lecturer in Modern Languages at University College, Bangor, a post which he left in 1888 to take up a similar position at the University of Sydney, where he was responsible for teaching German and French from 1889 to 1903.

1892. Coverley Smith, F. *Introduction to Commercial German*. London: Macmillan. Author is according to title page, BA. Assistant Master in the High School, Nottingham. Formerly scholar of Magdalene College, Cambridge. With a preface by James A. Gow, M.A. Litt.D. Headmaster of the High School, Nottingham. Copy belonged to Emil Trechmann (see Trechmann 1891).

In his preface (dated Nottingham, March 1892), Gow notes that the book's publication had been delayed by uncertainties about which schools would be allowed to teach commercial education and what and how (p. [v]); he continues (pvi–vii), "On the one hand, all boys may well gain a working knowledge of German by means of a more useful vocabulary and a less complicated grammar than are usually presented in school-books. On the other hand, we may well abandon that higher technique which, even when described in English, few boys under sixteen are able to follow. It is hoped that a book on these lines will prove accpetable at least as a temporary expedient. Certainly the examiners in recent commerical examinations hardly seem to expect more than is here given." See 3.6.1, 4.10.

1892. Wendt, Gustav. *England: seine Geschichte, Verfassung und staatlichen Einrichtungen*. Leipzig: O. R. Reisland.

1893. Anon. *Drittes Lesebuch für Evangelisch=Lutherische Schulen [published by the Missouri Synod]*. St. Louis: Concordia Pub. House. Discussed by Langer (2008).

1894 (1920). Beresford Webb, Henry. S. *A First German Book, etc.* London: Longmans & Co.

1894 (1902). Beresford Webb, Henry. S. *Primary German Translation and Exercise Book*. London: Rivington, Percival & Co.

1894 (1903). Eve, Henry Weston. *A school German Grammar. Uniform with The Wellington College French Grammar*. [S. I.]: David Nutt. See Eve (1870).

1894. Henry, Victor. *A short Comparative Grammar of English and German*. London: [s.n.].

1894. Lange, Hermann. *The Germans at Home: A practical introduction to German conversation, with an appendix containing the essentials of German grammar*. [S. I.]: Clarendon Press.

1894 ("3rd, thoroughly revised edition"; first ed. 1880). Sachs, H. *German conversational grammar. A complete grammar of pure modern High German. By H. Sachs. On the principles of his improved system of teaching languages*. London: W. B. Whittingham & Co. Later editions with various publishers.

1896 (1898, 1900, 1909). Bally, Stanislas Emile. *A manual of German commercial correspondence*. London: Methuen. The author had published a similar manual for French commercial correspondence in 1894.

1896. Beresford Webb, Henry S. *Longmans' Illustrated First German Reading Book and Grammar*. London: Longmans & Co.

1896 (later editions include 1900, 5th ed. 1916). Fiedler, Hermann Georg. *A third German reader and writer*. London. Discussed by Stöbe (1939: 11), who says "der Verfasser legt Wert darauf, durch die Auswahl seiner Übungsstücke, den Schüler mit 'Land und Leuten' vertraut zu machen (Einleitung)". See Fiedler (1900, 1916, 1921, 1924, 1928).

1896 (1900). Siepmann, Otto. *A Public School German Primer comprising a first reader, grammar, and exercises, with some remarks on German pronunciation and full vocabularies*. London: Macmillan and co., ltd. First edition 1896. Reprinted 1897, 1898, 1899 (twice), 1900. Revised edition August 1900. Author listed as "Head of the modern language department in Clifton College". See McLelland (2012c) and Chapter 3.10 above. See also (Siepmann 1902a, b, 1912) and Siepmann & Pellessier (1906).

1897. Viëtor, Wilhelm. *Kleine Phonetik des Deutschen, Englischen und Französischen*. Leipzig: O. R. Reisland. See Viëtor (1884).

1898. Alge, Sines, and Walter Rippmann. *Dent's first French book*. London: Dent. See also Alge (1902) and works with Ripman & Hamburger (1899, 1917). See Ripman (1898).

1898 (3rd ed. 1904; rpt. 1909). Brebner, Mary. *The Method of Teaching Modern Languages in Germany being the report presented to the Trustees of Gilchrist Educational Trust on a visit to Germany in 1897, as a Gilchrist Travelling Scholar*. London: C. J. Clay and Sons.

1898. Rippman, Walter. *Hints on teaching French. With a running commentary to Dent's first and second French books*. London: Dent. 1913 ed. New York: E. P. Dutton & co. Hathi Trust. See McLelland (2012c) and 3.10.1 above. See also Rippmann (1899a, b, 1906a, b, 1908, 1909, 1910, 1911), Alge & Rippmann (1898, 1899), Ripman (1920, 1921, 1922, 1929, 1935a, b, 1941), Kron & Ripman (1917), Vrijdaghs & Ripman (1930, 1931), Ripman & Archer (1948).

1898 (enlarged ed. 1904). Thimm, Carl Albert. *German self-taught. On the system of F. J. L. Thimm*. London: E. Marlborough & Co. See Weber (1913) below.

1898. Trotter, James Jeffrey. *Object Lessons in German. Based on "Object Lessons in French" by Alec Cran. Illustrated*. London-Edinburgh-New York: Thomas Nelson and Sons. The preface is by Cran – the books is a translation of his one. Copy held in Taylor Collection, Bamberg, bears the stamp of St Scholastica's training college (Sydney). Author given as M. A. German Master, Royal High School, Edinburgh.

1899a. Alge, Sines, Walter Rippmann, Sophie Hamburger. *Dent's first German book*. London: J. M. Dent & Co. (in the US: *Newson's First German Book*. New York: Newson & Co., 1901). See Rippman (1898).

1899 (2nd, revised ed. 1905, 10th ed. 1909, 24th ed. 1905.). Alge, Sines, Sophie Hamburger, and Walter Rippmann. *Leitfaden für den ersten Unterricht im Deutschen: unter Benützung von Hölzels Wandbildern für den Anschauungs- und Sprach-Unterricht: zum Gebrauche für Schüler aller Nationalitäten*. St. Gallen: Fehr'sche Buchhandlung. Hathi Trust. See Rippman (1898).

1899. Anon. *German business interviews: with correspondence, invoices, etc., each forming a complete commercial transaction, including technical terms, dialogues for travellers, and idiomatic expressions used in shipping and mercantile offices: for use in commercial and technical schools, and also for the private student*. London: Pitman.

1899a. Rippmann, Walter. *Elements of Phonetics, English, French and German.: Translated and adapted by W. Rippmann from Prof. Viëtor's "Kleine Phonetik"*. London: Dent. See Rippman (1898).

1899b. Rippmann, Walter. *Hints on teaching German, with a running commentary to Dent's First German Book and Dent's German Reader.* London: Dent. See Rippman (1898).

1899 (1905, 1921, 1935, 1948). Spanhoofd, Arnold Werner. *Lehrbuch der deutschen Sprache.* London: Heath (Harrap). 1948 reprint held in Taylor Collection.

1899 (1903?). Trechmann, Emil. *Passages for Translation into French and German for use in University and school classes.* Sydney: Angus & Robertson. Copy owned by Trechmann. Front cover gives the date of 1903, title page 1899. See Trechmann (1891), above, for his biography.

1900–1909

1900, new impression 1903 (1st ed. 1896). Beresford Webb, Henry S. *A Second German Book, with passages for translation and continuous exercises.* London: Longmans and Co. Author listed on title page as author of "A Practical German Grammar, A manual of German composition, etc., and examiner in German to the Royal Naval College, Greenwich; the University of Glasgow (Prelim.), etc." Original preface is dated 1896: "In the idea of this little book I do not lay claim to any originality. It has been written by request on the lines of Messrs. Bidgood and Harbottle's Illustrated French Reading-Book and Grammar, and I trust it will meet with the same success. The illustrations are different, and the letterpress has been specially written for the purpose. The grammatical portion comprises merely the elementary accidence, only very general rules for the declension of the nouns being given. It is best that these should, if possible, be learnt as they occur in the course of the reading.
I am indebted to Herrn T.H. Dittel, of the Royal Engineering College, Cooper's Hill, for his care in the revision of the Readings Lessons."
Preface to the new edition, 1900: "The alterations to this edition are confined to a few verbal emendations. I take this opportunity of pointing out that the vocabularies at the head of each lesson contain words only which are inserted because necessary for a continuous narrative. They are not intended to be committed to memory by a beginner, at any rate not at the earlier stages."
Listed in Rugby School's list of *Books in Permanent Use in Various Parts of the School*, 1903. Upper School, Modern Side.

1900. Fiedler, Hermann Georg. *A Key to the third German Writer in the Parallel Grammar Series.* London: Swan Sonnenschein. See Fiedler (1896).

1900 and later editions, 1914?, 192–?, 193–?]. Hugo's Institute for Teaching Foreign Languages. *German grammar simplified: an easy and rapid self-instructor: exercises and vocabulary; with the pronunciation of every word exactly imitated. With Key.* London: Institute for Teaching Foreign Languages. Copies are undated; dates according to COPAC. See also Hugo's Language Institute (193–?).

1900. Joynes, Edward S. (ed.), and Heinrich Zschokke. *Das Wirtshaus zu Cransac: Novelle,* edited with introduction, notes and vocabulary, and paraphrases for retranslation into German by Edward S. Joynes. Boston: Heath.

1900. Oswald, Alfred. *First Course of German Commercial Correspondence. for initiatory and intermediate classes or private use.* Compiled by A. Oswald. London: Blackie & Son. (With Key, published 1901). For biographical information, see Oswald (1902a), see also Oswald (1902b, 1909, 1914, 1932, 1935).

1900. Voegelin, Albert (ed.). *Isolde Kurz. Die Humanisten. Edited by A. Vægelin. Mit vierteiligem Anhang. 141 Seiten* (= Siepmann's German Series Advanced 8). Authorised edition, London: London: McMillan. Editor is A. Voegelin, M.A. (Lond.) Assistant Master at St Paul's School.

1901. Forster, E. P. Arnold (transl.). *The Poems of Schiller. Translated into English by E. P. Arnold-Forster.* London: William Heinemann.

1901. Adams, John. *The self-educator in German.* London: Hodder and Stoughton. See Adams & Wells (1938).

1901. Ehrke, Eduard. *A Guide to Advanced German Prose Composition Containing Selections from Modern English Authors Notes and a Grammatical Introduction.* Oxford: Clarendon Press.

1901. Kron, Richard, Walter Rippman, et al. *French daily life. Common words and common things. A guide for the student as well as for the traveller. Adapted by Walter Rippmann and Walter H. Buell from Dr. R Kron's "Le petit Parisien".* New York: Newson & company. Hathi Trust. See Rippman (1898), Kron (1916).

1902. Alge, Sines, and Institut Schmidt St. Gallen. *Der Anfänger im Deutschen.* Zollikofer'sche Buchdr. Google Books.

1902. Allpress, Robert Henry (ed.), and Ferdinand Schrader. *Friedrich der Grosse und der Siebenjährige Krieg. Adapted and edited by R. H. Allpress.* Authorised edition, London: Macmillan and Co., Limited (= *Siepmann's German Series Elementary 6*). Allpress is MA, Senior Modern Language Master at the City of London School. Owner's inscription on copy in Taylor Collection: "R. Challinos, Norman Creek, East Brisbane. Feb 1904".

1902. Ash, Edward Philip (ed.) and Karl Zastrow. *Wilhelm der Siegreiche. Ein Kaiser und Heldenbild aus der Neuzeit der deutschen Jugend gewidmet. Edited by E. P. Ash.* Authorised Edition, London: Macmillan and Co., Limited (= *Siepmann's German Series Elementary 9*). Taylor Collection.

1902, 1903. Atkins, Henry Gibson. *A Skeleton German Grammar.* London: Blackie & Son Ltd.

1902. Breul, Karl (ed.), and Friedrich Schiller. *Maria Stuart ein Schauspiel.* Edited K. Breul. Cambridge: Cambridge University Press. On Breul, see 3.6.2, 3.9. See also Paulin (2010), Jaworska (2010). See also Breul (1904, 1906, 1909, 1927) and Breul et al. (1936, 1957), and Breul (1898, 1911) in the bibliography of secondary literature.

1902, 1903. Cotterill, Henry Bernard (ed.). *Das Nibelungenlied* Part 1. Blackie's German texts, London: Blackie's, 1902. *Das Nibelungenlied* Part 2. Blackie's Little German Classics, London: Blackie, 1903.

1902, 1905. Latham, Albert George (transl.). *Goethe's Faust. Parts I and II translated by Albert G. Latham*. London; New York: Dent & Sons; E. P. Dutton & Co. Latham was the first lecturer of German at Newcastle University. On Latham, see 4.5 above.

1902a. Oswald, Alfred. *A Practical German Composition*. London: Blackie. With *Key*, published separately. Taylor Collection. Oswald described as "Lecturer in German at the Church of Scotland Training College; German Master at 'the Athenaeum' commercial college and at the Hutschesons' Grammar schools [sic], Glasgow Author of 'First course of German commercial correspondence', etc." In the *Key*, he is described as "FRSE [Fellow of the Royal Society of Edinburgh], Principal Lecturer and master of Method, Modern Languages Department. Provincial training college, Glasgow." In a later, undated edition of the grammar (cf. Oswald 1900 above), he is described as: "late principal lecturer and master of method, modern languages department Glasgow College for the training of teachers; Oral examiner in German to the University of London and to the Civil Service Commission, London; Member of the Scottish council of research in education (M. L. Panel)." See Oswald (1900).

1902b. Oswald, Alfred. *A Selection of German Idioms and Proverbs*. London: Blackie. Taylor Collection. See Oswald (1900).

1902. Robertson, John George. *A History of German Literature*. Edinburgh and London: William Blackwood & Sons Ltd. See Robertson (1913, 1950).

1902. Scholle, William. *A First German Grammar*. London: Blackie & Son. See Scholle & Smith (1902?), Scholle & Smith (1903, 1909).

1902? (n. d.). Scholle, William, and George Smith. *First steps in German*. London: Blackie & Sons. Authors: W. Scholle PhD Lecturer on [sic] French, Aberdeen University; G. Smith MA LL.D Director of Studies, Aberdeen Provincial Committee for the Training of Teachers. The first textbook of German of specifically Scottish provenance? Taylor Collection copy stamped Canterbury Boys High School [Sydney, Australia] 15 March 1929. Two names written in: R. Nelson 2A 1933. G. Bradshaw 2A 1945. Scholle & Smith draw on characters from Hölzel's seasons pictures (Preface, p. vi). "The language we use is that of the German child of twelve or so, and the teacher addresses his pupils with du and ihr." (Introduction, p. 3). All new words, or new forms of words, are printed in Clarendon type," p. 7; "No lesson should be without a certain amount of colloquial practice". p. 7 gives a model of how to teach. See Scholle (1902).

1902a. Siepmann, Otto. *Primary French course: First term: lessons in colloquial French based on the transcript of the Association Phonétique*. London: Macmillan. See Siepmann (1896).

1902b. Siepmann, Otto. *Primary French course [Part I.] First year. Comprising a first reader, grammar, and exercises*. London: Macmillan. See Siepmann (1896).

1902. Wickert, Ernst. *Als Verlobte empfehlen sich*. Edited with notes by G. T. Flom. London: Heath.

1902. Wesselhoeft, Edward Charles. *German composition with notes and vocabulary*. Boston: Heath.

1903. Ash, Edward Philip (ed.), and Carl Theodor Körner. *Körner, Selected poems.* London: Blackie.

1903. Beresford Webb, Henry S. *A Second German Book, with passages for translation and continuous exercises.* London: Longmans and Co.

1903. Eve. 6th editon of Eve (1887), q. v.

1903. Lowe, Lucy Augusta. *A First German Primer.* London: Blackie & Son, Limited (= *The German Picture Primers*). Cost 6d (front cover). Lowe is "certified student in honours, Girton College Cambridge. Modern Languages Mistress at Blackheath High School. Preface dated 1903 indicates that it was "intended only for very young children". Nevertheless, annotations in the copy held in the Taylor Collection show it was clearly used by someone older – it is inscribed with the name "G. Perkins, University of Sydney, 24.2.[19]11".

1903. Scholle, William, and George Smith. *Elementary Phonetics, English, French, German. Their theory and practical application in the class room… Two plates and other diagrams, etc.* London: Blackie & Son. See also Scholle (1902).

1903. Whitfield, Edward Elihu, and Carl Kaiser. *A course of commerical German. Commerical correspondence in German. Comprising sketch of grammar, systematic vocabularies, reading lessons, business dialogues and commercial letters, etc.* London: Pitman.

1904. Adams, Warren Austin. (ed.), and Johann Wolfgang von Goethe. *Goethes Hermann and Dorothea edited with introduction and notes by W. A. Adams*, Heath.

1904 (1931, 1934, 1946, 1950, 1959). Bain, Archibald Watson (ed.). *A German Poetry Book for school and home.* London: Methuen. Revised 1946 ed. revised by Jethro Bithell.

1904. Breul, Karl (ed.), and Johann Wolfgang von Goethe. *Iphigenie auf Tauris ein Schauspiel. Edited by K. Breul.* Cambridge: Cambridge University Press. See Breul (1902).

1904. Dixon, Edith. (ed.), and Heinrich Hansjakob. *Aus dem Leben eines Unglücklichen. Erzählung aus dem Schwarzwalde. Edited by E. Dixon.* Authorised edition, London: Macmillan and Co. (= *Siepmann's German Series Elementary 4*). Dixon was at Girton College, Cambridge. Formerly lecturer at Westfield College, University of London.

1904–1906. Graham, James, and George A. S. Oliver. *German commercial practice connected with the export and import trade: to and from Germany, the German colonies, and the countries where German is the recognised language of commerce.* London & New York: Macmillan and Co. Listed by Bithell (1921: 693). Graham, PhD, was inspector to the West Riding County Council.

1904 (1953, 1955, 1965, 1968). Hatfield, James Taft (ed.) and Goethe, Johann Wolfgang von. *Goethes Egmont edited with introduction and notes by James Taft Hatfield.* London: Heath.

1904. Wesselhoeft, Edward Charles. *Exercises in German Conversation and Composition. With notes and vocabularies.* London: George G. Harrap *(Heath's Modern Language Series).* The author's preface is dated University of Pennsylvania, December, 1903. The author thanks Edward S. Joynes of the University of South Carolina for "his kindly criticism and many helpful suggestions." The two collaborated on Joynes (1908).

1905. Atkins, Henry Gibson. *German exercises: specially arranged to accompany the Skeleton German grammar.* London, Glasgow, Dublin, Bombay: Blackie & Son Limited. The *Skeleton German Grammar* by Atkins is undated, but Atkins published a *Skeleton French Grammar* in 1902.

1905 (1952). Curme, George Oliver. *A grammar of the German language.* New York: Frederick Ungar.

1905. Thouaille, Albert, and E. Nonnemacher. *First steps in colloquial German* [lithographed]. Manchester: Gouin School of Languages. On Gouin, see Wheeler (2013: 124–135), also Kuiper (1961: 150–80).

1906. Breul, Karl, and Elizabeth Weir. *A new German and English Dictionary. Revised by Karl Breul.* [S.I.]: Cassell. See Breul (1902, 1909).

1906. Ebner, Theodor, and Eustace Guest North. *Herr Walther von der Vogelweide. Eine Geschichte aus der Zeit der Minnesänger für die Jugend erzählt. Adapted and Edited by E. G. North.* Authorised Edition. (= *Siepmann's German Series Elementary 1*). London & New York: Macmillan and Co., Limited.

1906. Rhoades, Lewis Addison, and Lydia Schneider. *Erstes Sprach= und Lesebuch. A German Primer.* New York. Discussed in Langer (2008). Held in Special Collections (Ellis Collection), Memorial Library, University of Wisconsin, Madison.

1906. Rippmann, Walter. *Picture Vocabulary. German* London: Dent. See Rippman (1898).

1906. Siepmann, Otto, and Eugène Pellissier. *A public school French primer. Comprising reader, grammar, and exercises with a chapter on French sounds and lists of words for practice in pronunciation and spelling.* London & New York. See Siepmann (1896).

1906 (2nd revised ed.); fourth (unchanged) ed. 1929. Rippmann, Walter. *Hints on Teaching German. With a running commentary to Dent's First New German Book and to Dent's German Reader.* London: Dent. See Rippman (1898).

1907. Chaffey, Lionel Bethell Trenchard. *Bell's First German Course.* London: G. Bell & Sons.

1907. Hughes, James L., and Louis Richard Klemm. *Progress of education in the century.* Toronto; Philadelphia: Linscott. Hathi Trust. See Klemm (1876).

1907 (rep. 1956). Lewis, Orlando Faulkland (ed.), and Gerstacker, Friedrich. *Germelshausen.* Edited, with notes and vocabulary by Orlando F. Lewis. London: Heath. (One of many editions of this work for English learners).

1907 (1910 and later eds.). Moffatt, Christopher, and William Paget. *Science German Course.* London: University Tutorial Press. See also Horne at al. (1955), Horne (1948) below.

1908. Ball, Francis Kingsley. *A German grammar for schools and colleges.* London: D. C. Heath and Company.

1908. Bithell, Jethro. *Handbook of German Commercial Correspondence.* Bithell, who was lecturer and later Reader in German, was a prolific author and editor. See Bithell (1912, 1922, 1929, 1932, 1939, 1941, 1946, 1947, 1949, 1951, 1952, 1959), Bithell & Dunstan (1925, 1928), Bithell & Eastlake (1933), and entries in the bibliography of secondary literature.

1908. Joynes, Edward S. (with the Cooperation of E. C. Wesselhoeft). *Heath's Practical German Grammar. A Complete German Grammar in Progressive Lessons.* London: D. C. Heath & Company, 1908 *(= Heath's Modern Language Series).* Taylor Collection. See also Wesselhoeft (1904). Authors listed on title page as Edward S. Joynes MA LL.D with the coöperation of E. C. Wesselhoft M. A.

1908. Lambert, Marcus B. *Alltägliches. Ein Konversations= und Lesebuch.* Boston. Discussed by Langer (2008).

1908. Mosher, William Eugene. *Willkommen in Deutschland.* Boston: Heath. Mosher was Professor of German at Oberlin College (USA). The author states in the preface (p. III), "I have sought to give something of a typical but real picture of the German people, and to introduce the student to an elementary knowledge of their political institutions and history". Stöbe (1939: 11) says it is "durchaus fortschrittlich und rückt die kulturkundliche Seite in den Vordergrund."

1908. Rippmann, Walter. *English, French and German Sound charts.* London: Dent. Reviewed by Arnold Jones, the brother of Daniel Jones, in *Le Maître phonétique* 1909 (24,7–8), pp. 104–5. See Jones (2001: 247). See Rippman (1898).

1909. Anon. *Zweites Lesebuch, Deutsch=englische Lesebücher für katholische Schulen.* New York; Cincinatti; Chicago. Discussed by Langer (2008).

1909. Breul, Karl. *Cassell's German and English Dictionary: Compiled from the best authorities in both languages / Rev. and considerably enlarged by Karl Breul.* London: Cassell. Other editions: 1928, 1939, 1941, 1945, 1947, 1964. See Breul (1902).

1909. Florian, Arthur Rudolph. *First Book of German Oral Teaching.* London: Rivingtons. Reviewed in *Modern Language Teaching* 1909. See Florian (1933, 1936).

1909 (later eds. include 1915, 9th ed. 1930). Hernan, William James. *"What you want to say and How to say it" in German.* London: Eyre and Spottiswoode. 9th, 1930 ed. (London: George Newnes Ltd.) held in Taylor Collection. Similar volumes were published form 1907 onwards for Spanish, Italian, French and Norwegian.

1909. Oswald, Alfred. *Advanced course of German commercial correspondence.* London: Blackie. See Oswald (1900).

1909. Pope, Paul R. *German composition.* London: George Bell & Sons. Reviewed in *Modern Language Teaching* 1909.

1909. Scholle, William, and George Smith. *A German Reader for Middle Forms.* London & Glasgow, Blackie & Son. Taylor Collection. Scholle listed as PhD Lecturer in French, Aberdeen University, and Smith, MA, LL. D., Director of Studies, Aberdeen Provincial Committee for the Training of Teachers; stamp of Canterbury boys High School [Sidney, Australia]; 6 different names written in and crossed out with dates from 1930 to 1940, with classes either 2A or 3A. See Scholle (1902).

1909 (2nd ed. 1913). Rippmann, Walter. *Exercises in German Grammar and Word Formation.* London: J. M. Dent & Sons, Ltd. Pp. 118–119 of the 1913 ed. gives table of German sounds in phonetic symbols and the first two sections in phonetic script. Preface says "written for the reform teacher", trying to avoid "foolish sentences". See also the "Contents, with notes" for more information on the didactic approach. Reviewed in *Modern Language Teaching* 1909. See Rippman (1898).

1910–1919

1910 (1ˢᵗ ed. 1902). Baumann, Henry (ed.). *The Pictorial German Course (with pictures, descriptions, conversations and grammar)*. London: The Modern Language Press. Baumann is described as "Fellow of the College of Preceptors; late Head Master of the Anglo-German School". It is part of the Rees Pictorial Language Series of David John Rees, London University. Page facing title page states, "The great success attending the introduction of Rees' Pictorial Language System during the past few years has induced the publishers to make more widely known the advantages of the adoption of the spoken language yet placed in the hands of teachers or the private student [...]. Each lesson deals with common surrounding, and with subjects most familiar to the Pupil, as the Family Circle, the School, Street, Railway Station, Four Seasons, etc., and is thus within the capacity of any Pupil." There are books for German, Spanish, Italian, and English (for French, Spanish and German learners), and "phonographic records of these books, giving exact pronunciation, and provided by native elocutionists" may be obtained.

1910. Buchheim, Carl Adolf. *Balladen und Romanzen selected and arranged by C A Buchheim*. London: Macmillan. See Buchheim (1890).

1910. Hirsch, Ludwig, and J. Stuart Walters. *Aus dem Leben. German scenes for the classroom*. London: Dent.

1910. Lange (not further identified). *Lange's Reader*. Listed as used at Rugby, Christmas 1910, Upper School, Classical, German, Set 5.

1910 (1913, 1914). Rippmann, Walter. *The sounds of spoken English*. London: Dent. 1913 ed. New York: E. P. Dutton. Hathi Trust. See Rippman (1898).

1910. Spanhoofd, Arnold Werner. *Erstes Lesebuch. A German reader for beginners*. London: Heath's. (According to Stöbe (1939: 11), first published 1909; rept. 1914, 1916, 1923). Stöbe (1939: 11) cites from the preface, p. IX, "German literature, social life and customs have been illustrated", but judges that this promise is not fulfilled.

1911. Ahrens, William Heinrich Carl (ed.) and Konrad Ferdinand Meyer. *Jürg Jenatsch. Eine alte Bündnergeschichte von Konrad Ferdinand Meyer. Adapted and Edited by W. Ahrens*. Authorised Edition. London: Macmillan and Co., Limited *(= Siepmann's German Series Advanced 9)*. Taylor Collection. Ahrens MA (Lond.) is Senior Modern Language Master at Elstow School, Bedford. The book is edited with notes, and abridged for the pupil with an introduction about the writer and about the historical figure Jenatsch.

1911 (1913, 1915, 2ⁿᵈ ed. 1917, 3ʳᵈ ed. 1930, 4ᵗʰ ed. 1932, 1934, 1946). Bondar, David. *Bondar's Simplified Russian Method-conversational and commercial. Compiled by D. Bondar... partly assisted by Alfred Calvert*. London: Effingham Wilson. Bondar is listed in the 1918 print of 2ⁿᵈ ed. as "D. Bondar, M. S.P. late teacher of Russian to the Manchester Municipal School of Commerce; graduate at the Academy of Commercial Sciences and Languages (Russia and Switzerland); author of "Bondar's simplified German method"; editor of "Bondar's Russian readers"."

1911 (2ⁿᵈ ed. 1916). Haltenhoff, Adolf George. *Science German course: graduated readings, specially prepared on mathematics, chemistry, physics, zoology, botany, physiolo-*

gy, psychology, political economy etc.; with grammatical rules and hints based on the text matter and questions from the German science papers recently set for the London University Examinations. London: Hachette.

1911. Kip, H. Z. (ed.) and Keller, Gottfried. *Zwei Novellen. Die drei gerechten Kammacher/Frau Regel Amrain und ihr Jüngster. Edited by H. Z. Kip.* Oxford: Oxford University Press.

1911. Klemm, Louis Richard. *Public education in Germany and in the United States.* Boston: R. G. Badger. Hathi Trust. "A collection of selected essays, lectures, and articles prepared during the last twenty years." See Klemm (1876).

1911. Oswald, Eugen. *Reminiscences of a busy life.* London: A. Moring. See Oswald (1857).

1911a (2nd ed. 1919, 1927). Rippmann, Walter. *Easy Free Composition in German.* London: J. M. Dent & Sons. Copy in Taylor Collection has a stamp on inside cover from Bathurst High School, New South Wales. See Rippman (1898).

1911b. Rippmann, Walter. *English sounds; a book for English boys and girls.* New York: E. P. Dutton & Co. Hathi Trust. See Rippman (1898).

1911 (1913, 1919, 1925, 1927, 1957). Van Der Smissen, William Henry, and William Henry Fraser *(Harrap's) Modern German Grammar with exercises and vocabularies.* London: George G. Harrap and Co. Ltd. *(Harrap's Modern Language Series).* 1927 ed. Taylor Collection. See Van der Smissen et al. (1888).

1912. Allen, Philip Schuyler. *Hints on the teaching of German conversation.* Boston: Ginn. Hathi Trust.

1912 (1929). Betz, Frederick. *Deutscher Humor aus vier Jarhunderten.* London: Heath.

1912 (1932). Bithell, Jethro. *Pitman's Commercial German Grammar.* London: Pitman. See Bithell (1908).

1912 (2nd ed.). Meyer, Ernst A. *Deutsche Gespräche. Mit phonetischer Einleitung und Umschrift.* Leipzig: O. R. Reisland. Author is "Dr Phil. Lektor der deutschen Sprache an der Handelshochschule in Stockholm". Preface of 1st ed. is dated Uppsala, February 1906. Dialogues with the phonetic transcription on facing page. The copy in the Taylor Collection shows signs of use – the text pages have marks for stress (e.g. on *Berlin, Paket*), and vocabulary written in English shows it was used by an English learner.

1912? (n. d.) Oswald, Alfred. *A Complete German Grammar.* Glasgow: Robert Gibson & Son. Revised edition. Taylor Collection. Several editions. See Oswald (1900, 1940).

1912 (1913 twice, second time with minor revisions; then unchanged 1916, 1920, 1922, 1924, 1928, 1930, 1955). Siepmann, Otto. *A primary German course comprising object lessons, a first reader, grammar and exercises, with some remarks on German pronunciation and the relation between German and English and full vocabularies.* London: Macmillan and Co. Illustrated by H. M. Brock. Author listed as "Head of the modern language department at Clifton College". See Chapter 3.10 above, also McLelland (2012c). Preface includes the following: "The book opens with a chapter of German sounds and handwriting. To this chapter the first month should be devoted so as to enable the pupils to acquire a good pronunciation from the outset.

It is not difficult to arouse considerable interest in the formation of the sounds; and it is much easier to obtain good results if each sound is taken separately and practised until every pupil can produce it without effort. The comparison between English and German which follows cannot fail to impress upon a class the close relation there is between the two languages." Taylor Collection. See Siepmann (1896).

1912. Ungoed, Gwilym Thomas. *A First German Book on the Direct Method. First Edition,* Cambridge: University Press. Author on title page: GT Ungoed, M.A. Late Exhibitioner of Trinty College, Cambridge. Assistant Master at Acton County School. Taylor Collection. Facing page to title page shows photo of German coins. Preface states the work is intended "for pupils who begin to study German at an early age". The pronunciation is said to be that of Siebs and in Viëtor for the stage(!). Stamp on flyleaf of Taylor Collection copy of Hornsby Girls' High School library (in Sydney). Lessons 1–11 are repeated in phonetic script on pp. 88–99.

1912. Wiehr, Josef. *Graded Exercises in German Prose Composition. Based on a brief Survey of Modern German History.* New York: Oxford University Press.

1912. Wilson, Archibald Edward. *Outlines of German Grammar.* London et al.: Henry Frowde Oxford University Press. Taylor Collection. Author was senior master at Winchester College. The preface states Wilson took Heyse's *Schulgrammatik* as arbiter (by now surely rather dated – it had already been cited as an authority by Strauss in 1852).

1912. Wilson, Frank William. *Free Composition in German.* London: Edward Arnold & Company. Author listed as: Frank William Wilson PhD (Leipzig). Assistant master at Clifton College [where Siepmann also taught], formerly assistant master at the royal realgymnasium Doebeln (Saxony). Author of 'Arnold's Modern German course'. The preface is in German. Aimed at pupils with at least a year of German. Begins with easy reading, then short paragraphs in German which pupils should re-tell using a skeleton outline, then complete the story, etc. Taylor Collection copy is stamped "This book is the property of the Department of Education New South Wales", and is inscribed FC Woolton for Sr BHS Petersham; signed in pencil SF Jones 1934. See also Wilson (1915).

1913. Dyson, Taylor. *A Class Book of German Conversation and Free Composition.* London: Harraps. Dyson listed as "M. A. Headmaster of Almondbury Grammar School; late modern language master at Nottingham High School." Preface, p. 5, p. 6: "It aims at supplying materials for class conversation and subject-matter for free composition. It is hoped that it may prove a help to beginners in this difficult branch of their work, and serve as a useful stepping stone to further progress." [...] "The subject is discussed in class, and, where possible, all explanations, etc., should be given in German. This creates the right atmosphere, but there should be no hesitation in using English to clear a difficulty." In his preface, Dyson thanks Mutschmann for his help – see Mutschmann (1914) below. Taylor Collection.

1913 (1927, 1938). Egan, Alfred. *A German Phonetic Reader.* London: University of London Press.

1913. Ellis, Florence. *Introduction to German for Upper Forms and Evening Classes.* London: Dent.

1913. Robertson, John George. *The Literature of Germany.* London: Thornton Butterworth Ltd. Held in the Temple Reading Room, Rugby School.

1913 (1916, 1919, revised ed.1930–31, 1939). Weber, William Edwin. *German Grammar Self Taught. By the natural method, with phonetic pronunciation. Thimm's system. Revised by W. A. Weber.* With Key. London: E Marlborough & Co Ltd. Thimm is Franz J. L. Thimm. 16th ed. (1928) has the title *Marlborough's tourist's German self-taught phrase-book: Thimm's system.* Similar "self-taught" works existed for French, Spanish, Norwegian, Italian. See Thimm (1898) above, Weber (1938) below.

1914. Bridge, George Fletcher (ed.). *Prinz Friedrich von Homburg. Ein Schauspiel von Heinrich von Kleist.* London: Macmillan and Co., Limited *(= Siepmann's German Series Advanced 13).* On Bridge, see 4.2.1. The Taylor Collection copy carries the inscription of Ralph B. Farrell (Professor of German at the University of Sydney, 1946–1974), perhaps best-known for his *Dictionary of German Synonyms* (1953, CUP).

1914. David, William Hermann (Rev.). *First steps in German composition.* Oxford: Oxford University Press.

1914. Mutschmann, Heinrich. *Passages for Translation into German.* London. Taylor Collection. Author is MA, PhD, Lecturer in German at the University College, Nottingham. See Dyson (1912).

1914. Oswald, Alfred. *Deutsches Lesebuch für Anfänger.* London: Blackie. See Oswald (1900).

1914. Seeligmann, Karl. *Altes und neues: an easy German reader for beginners.* Boston: Ginn and Company. Mentioned by Stöbe (1939: 11).

1915. Phillips, Francis C. *Chemical German: an introduction to the study of German chemical literature.* Easton, Pennsylvania: The Chemical Publishing Co.

1915. Wilson, Frank William. *Deutscher Sagenschatz.* London: Bell. See also Wilson (1912).

1916. Alge et al. Later ed. of Alge et al. *Leitfaden* (1899), q. v.

1916. Althaus, Louisa Harriet. *Black's First German Book.* London: A. & C. Black.

1916 (1927, 1929). Fiedler, Hermann Georg. *Buch Deutscher Dichtung von Luther bis Liliencron. Herausgegeben mit Einleitung, Abriss der Deutschen Verslehre und Anmerkungen von H. G. Fiedler.* [Also called 'A Book of German Verse' on front cover]. London: Oxford University Press. Copy held in Temple Reading Room, Rugby School. From Vorwort: "Dies *Buch deutscher Dichtung* ist kein bloßer Auszug aus dem *Oxforder Buche deutscher Dichtung.* Während die frühere Sammlung sich an einen weiteren Leserkreis wandte, ist die vorliegende als Hilfsmittel beim Unterricht in Schulen und Universitäten gedacht." (July 1915). 2 copies of 1927 ed. held in Temple Reading Room, Rugby School. See Fiedler (1896).

1916 (15th ed. 1923). Kron, Richard. *Der kleine Deutsche. Ein Fortbildungsmittel zur Erlernung der deutschen Umgangssprache auf allen Gebieten des täglichen Lebens, mit steter Bezugnahme auf deutsche Eigenart in Sitten, Gewohnheiten und Einrichtun-*

gen. 15th ed. Freiburg im Breisgau: J. Bielefelds Verlag, 1923. Author is Professor Dr R. Kron. Taylor Collection. See Kron (1901).

1916. Stroebe, Lilian Luise. *Deutsche Anekdoten fur die Schule.* London: Heath.

1917 (rep. 1931). Guerber, Hélène Adeline. *Märchen und Erzählungen. Erster Teil. with direct-method exercises and revised vocabulary by W. R. [= Walter Raleigh] Myers. H. A. Guerber with revisions by W. A. Myers.* New ed. London: Heath.

1917 (1928). Ripman, Walter, Sines Alge, Sophie Hamburger. *Dent's new first German book.* New York: Dutton. Hathi Trust. For the *First German Book*, see Rippmann et al. (1899). See Rippman (1898).

1918. Beresford Webb, Henry S. *A Fly-Leaf to Beresford-Webb's German Grammar. Arranged by W. H. C. [i. e. William H. Counsell.].* Sedbergh: Jackson & Son.

1918. Greenfield, Eric Viele. *An introduction to chemical German.* Boston: Heath.

1919. Osborne, William Alexander, and Ethel E. Osborne. *German Grammar for Science Students.* London: Sir Isaac Pitman & Sons, Ltd.

1920–1929

1920 (Reprinted 1925, 1929, 1934, 1935, 1937, 1939; Revised reprint 1944; second edition 1946, reprinted 1954). Keegan, John. *A new German grammar.* London: Pitman. On title page of 2nd ed, Keegan is "John Keegan, M. A. Formerly head of the modern language department in the Central Foundation School, Cowper Street, City Road, London: E. C. 2; sometime assistant teacher of English in the Royal Gymnasium, Kiel, Germany."

1920. Ripman, Walter. *A first English book for boys and girls whose mother-tongue is not English.* London & Toronto: J. M. Dent & Sons Limited. Hathi Trust.

1921. Bishop, Mabel Lovett, and Florence Mckinlay. *Ausführliche Deutsche Grammatik in gedrängter Form.* Boston: New York: etc., D. C. Heath and co. Available as a reprint (2010) from Nabu Press.

1921. Fiedler, Hermann Georg. *A Second German Course for Science Students.* Oxford: O. U. P. See Fiedler (1924) below for the *First Course.* See Fiedler (1896).

1921 (1936, 1941). Ripman, Walter. *A Rapid German Course.* London & Toronto: J. M. Dent & Sons Limited. Taylor Collection.

1922 (2nd ed. 1927). Bithell, Jethro. *Commercial German Dictionary.* London: Sir I. Pitman & Sons. See Bithell (1908).

1922 (1924, 1925, 1929, 1940). Ripman, Walter. *Good speech. An introduction to English phonetics.* London & Toronto: J. M. Dent; New York: E. P. Dutton.

1922, 1923 (1955). Wanstall, Humphrey John Boraston. *Tests in German Composition and Grammar* (1922). *Key (1923).* London: Harrap's Modern Language Series. 1955 print in Taylor Collection. Author listed as formerly of Wellington College. The preface states these tests are intended to prepare for School Certificate and for army examinations. See Wanstall (1926, 1931, 1934, 1935, 1936).

1923. Brown Hewitt, Theodore. *Intermediate German Composition With Notes and Vocabulary. Revised Edition.* Boston et al.: D. C. Heath and Company. Taylor Collection.

1923. Kron. 15th edition of Kron (1916), q. v.

1924 (= 3rd ed. 1937). Fiedler, Hermann Georg, and Francis E. Sandbach. *A first German course for science students*. London: Oxford University Press. See Fiedler (1921) above for the *Second Course*. See Fiedler (1896).

1924 (revised ed.). Greenfield, Erich Virle. *Technical and scientific German*. Boston: Heath. (Heath's modern language series).

1924. Purdie, Edna (ed.). *Von Deutscher Art und Kunst*. Oxford: Clarendon Press. Held in the Temple Reading Room, Rugby School.

1925 (1949). Bennett, Edwin Keppel (ed.). *Passages from German authors for unseen translation*. Cambridge: Cambridge University Press.

1925 (1929, 1934, 1953). Bithell, Jethro, and Arthur Cyril Dunstan. *A German Course for Science Students*. London: Methuen & Co. See Bithell (1908).

1926 (revised 1949). Cardwell, Cyril Rowland. *A German grammar simple and complete*. London & Paris: Hachette.

1926. Midgley, Harold. *Translation from and into German: a guide to German unseen translation and composition*. London: Dent. Also *Key*, 1926.

1926 (rpt. 1927, July 1929, Oct 1932, July 1935, Sept 1937, Nov 1939, Sept 1941, 1946). Wanstall, Humphrey John Boraston. *Advanced Tests in German Composition and Grammar. With a Key*. London: George G. Harrap & Company Ltd. Taylor Collection. See Wanstall (1922).

1926 (1931). Williams, John David Ellis. *Deutsch: a school-certificate course*. London: G. Bell & sons Ltd.

1926. Willoughby, Leonard Ashley. *The Classical Age of German Literature 1748–1805*. Oxford University Press. Humphrey Milford. Held in Temple Reading Room, Rugby School. Acquired Dec 1962. From Preface: "In writing this book I had in view especially two types of reader: the general public for whom this series is intended, and the young student of German literature, whether he be in his last year at school or his first year at college." (November 1925).

1927. Breul, Karl. *The Romantic Movement in German Literature. Illustrative Texts-Prose & Verse. Selected and arranged with Biographical Notices of the Authors, Introduction and Notes by Karl Breul, M.A., Litt.D., Ph.D.* Cambridge: W. Heffer & Sons Ltd. Copy held in Temple Reading Room, Rugby School. From preface: "The aim of the present anthology, the first of its kind published in this country, is to provide a selection of texts in prose and verse illustrative of the Romantic Movement in German literature. The book is intended for students of German at the Universities, but selected portions of it will also be found suitable for pupils in the higher forms of secondary schools who are reading for scholarships or are preparing for the Higher Certificate." See Breul (1902).

1927. Hayes, Lionel Charles Maclean. *German Free Composition*. London:

1927. Midgley, Harold. *Junior test papers in German*. London: Pitman.

1927. Stockton, Charles Edward (ed.). *Advanced German Unseens*. London: Methuen.

1927 (1933 revised ed. with exercises, 1936, 1939 3rd ed. with exercises and illustrations). Winter, Anton Hermann. *A progressive German Reader*. London: Pitman.

1928. Balg, G. (ed.) and Bonsels, Waldemar. *Die Biene Maja und ihre Abenteuer. Abridged and edited for schools by G. Balg.* London: Bell. Balg is "formerly of Cheltenham Ladies College".

1928. Bithell, Jethro, and Arthur Cyril Dunstan. *A Modern German Course, for students of history, geography, economics and literature.* London: Methuen & Co. Ltd. See Bithell (1908).

1928 (rpt. 1930). Fiedler, Hermann Georg. *German short stories.* Oxford: Clarendon Press. Noted by Stöbe (1939: 12). See Fiedler (1896).

1928 (1933). Tindall, Samuel. *A School Certificate German Reader.* London: Rivingtons. See Tindall (1934, 1939).

1929 (1933, 1937, 1943). Bithell, Jethro. *Advanced German Composition. [With a key by the author and Wolfgang Tehilkuhl.].* London: Methuen & Co. Stöbe (1939: 11) says "'Deutschkundlich" zu sein (Einleitung), ist das Ziel dieses Lehrbuches. Man darf sagen, daß es dem Verfasser zu einem großen Teil gelungen ist. Deutsche Sagen, Männer aus der deutschen Geschichte, wie Friedrich der Große und Bismarck, deutsche Oster- und Weihnachtssitten, Jugendherbergen usw. werden dem Schüler vertraut. [...] Im allgemeinen gibt das Buch ein einwandfreies Bild von Deutschland, wenn auch aus einigen wenigen Abschnitten das Hervorkehren einer typisch englischen Überlegenheit gegenüber deutschem Wesen herauszuspüren ist". See Bithell (1908).

1929. Dutton, S. V. *A practical course in commercial German.* London: G. Harrap.

1929. Peers, Edgar Allison. *Spain: a companion to Spanish studies.* London: Methuen. Bithell (1932) follows this model.

1929. Ripman, Walter. *Specimens of English in phonetic transcription, with notes, parallel passages and a word-list.* London: Dent. Hathi Trust.

1929 (1931, 1933). Macpherson, Arthur Stewart. *Test examinations in German.* London: Methuen. See Macpherson (1931).

1930–1939

193–? (n. d.) Hugo's Language Institute. *German Commercial Correspondence: A collection of practical business letters and commerical phrases, with full translation and explanatory notes, list of abbreviations, etc: Hugo's Simplified System.* London: Hugo's Language Institute. See also Hugo's Institute (1900).

1930–31. Clark, James Midgley. *Langenscheidt's commercial dictionary of the English and German languages.* Two parts. Berlin: Langenscheidtsche Verlagsbuchhandlung.

1930–31 (2nd ed. 1932–34,. 1936, rep. 1947). Clark, Andrew Crockett and W. O. Williams, *A Modern German Course.* Two parts. London: Hirschfeld.

1930 (1st ed. 1925). Menzerath, Paul. *Linguaphone. Conversational Course. German. [15 double-sided LPs with accompanying transcriptions and Supplementary Booklet for the Use of English Students].* Linguaphone Institute.

1930–31 (1934, 1948). Sack, Friedrich Leopold and Thompson, L. F. *A German Course. Part I. A Practical Grammar of the German Language* (1930). *Part II. A practical German reader: with grammar notes and exercises.* (1931). London: Longmans.

1930. Vrijdaghs, Paul, and Walter Ripman (eds.). *Short stories by modern German authors*. London & Toronto: Dent. See also Rippmann (1898).

1930. Weiss, Bryher, and Trude Weiss. *'The Lighthearted Student' I German*, London & Dijon: Pool Publications.

1930. Wells, Sydney W. *Einführung ins Deutsche*. London: Harrap. See Wegner (1999: 133–135). See Wells (1931).

1930 (2nd ed. 1935, 1939, 1946). Wilson, Percy George. *The student's guide to modern languages: a comparative study of English, French, German and Spanish*. London: Sir Isaac Pitman. See Wilson (1932, 1937, 1938, 1950).

1931 (1936). Gladstone, Soloman G. *Ich kann Deutsch lesen*. London: Heinemann.

1931. Grundy, John Brownsdon Clowes. *Brush up your German. Drawings by Phil Ward*. London: J M Dent & Sons Ltd. See discussion in Chapter 4 and 6 above. See Grundy (1932, 1939, 1950) below.

1931. Lieder, Frederick W. C. (ed.). *Popular German stories edited with notes by F W C Lieder*. London: Bell.

1931. Macpherson, Arthur Stewart. *Deutsches Leben*. Parts I and II (Part III appeared in 1934, see below). London: Ginn and Company Ltd. *Deutsches Leben* was very widely used. See Chapter 6.3, note 23 for evidence of the series's popularity. See discussion in chapters 4 and 6 of this book. See also Macpherson (1929, 1934, 1937, 1939, 1940, 1963), Macpherson & Schnitzler (1931), Howlett Jones & Fischer-Wollpert (1965).

1931. Macpherson, Arthur Stewart (ed.), and Arthur Schnitzler. *Zwei Tiroler Novellen. I. Der blinde Geronimo und sein Bruder. II. Die Weissagung. (From Die griechische Tänzerin.) Edited, with questions, notes, exercises and reproductions, by A. S. Macpherson*. London: Bell. See Macpherson (1931a).

1931, revised edition 1934. Meyer, Paul, and G. Nauck. *Das neue Deutschland: A German reader for middle forms on post-war Germany*. London: G. Bell & Sons Ltd. Stöbe (1939: 14) says of the 2nd ed. "Es wird von den englischen Lehrern als 'Nazi' (ein Ausdruck, der den Inhalt charkaterisieren soll), bezeichnet." See discussion in 6.3 above.

1931–1934. Pegrum, Arthur William. *The active German course*. London: University of London Press. Stöbe (1939: 14) mentions it shows "viele Züge deutschen Wesens und deutscher Landschaft". See Pegrum (1935).

1931. Vrijdaghs, Paul, and Walter Ripman (compilers). *Second German reader*. London: Dent. See also Vrijdaghs & Ripman (1930), Rippmann (1898).

1931. Wanstall, Humphrey John Boraston (ed.). *German Prose and Verse for Recitation*. London: Harrap. See Wanstall (1922).

1931. Wells, Sydney W. *Ein deutsches Aufsatzbuch*. London: Harrap. See also Wells (1930, 1937, 1938, 1945) and Adams & Wells (1938).

1932. Bain, A. Watson. *German poetry for students*. London: Macmillan.

1932 (other editions 1942, 1955, 1965, 1968). Bithell, Jethro (ed.). *Germany: a companion to German studies*. London: Methuen. See discussion in 6.3 above. See Peers (1929) and Bithell (1908).

1932. Dutton, S. V. *Ferien in Deutschland*. London: Harrap. Dutton was Lecturer at the High School of Commerce, Manchester. Stöbe (1939: 13) describes it as using *leichter Plauderstil*: "Die deutschkundliche Seite ist berücksichtigt und bietet einige für uns bemerkenswerte Gesichtspunkte". See Dutton (1948).

1932. Grundy, John Brownsdon Clowes. *Meyers reisen nach Deutschland*. Adapted from *Brush Up your German. With Vocabulary, Annotations and Materials for Free Composition*. London: Dent. See Grundy (1931) above.

1932 (1933). Leather, Charles Henry. *Common Errors in German. With rapid corrective exercises*. [With Key]. London: Dent. Leather published a parallel text for French in 1931.

1932 (1934, 1948, 1950). Oswald, Alfred. *A Complete German Grammar*. Glasgow: Robert Gibson and Sons Glasgow Ltd. See Oswald (1900).

1932. Rivers, Jack (ed.), and Berkner, Kurt. *Elf Fussballjungens. Ed. Jack Rivers*. London: Macmillan & Co. Ltd. See also Rivers (1934, 1935, 1939) and Rivers & Wilson (1935).

1932. Rose, Fred C. *Elementary German prose composition*. London: Harrap.

1932 (1946). Schücking, Elisabeth and Levin. *Deutsches Lesebuch*. London: Harrap.

1932 (revised 1936, 1938, 1940, 5th ed. 1944). Theilkuhl, Wolfgang. *Deutsches Land und deutsches Leben*. London: Methuen. Stöbe (1939: 13) says it was "viel benutzt" but criticizes the fact that the author felt it necessary to mention that three million emigrants had left Germany (Theilkuhl 1936: 48), and that he suggests *Arbeitsdienst* is mainly to keep the unemployed occupied (p. 170). Preface p. v states "It contains a large amount of reliable and up-to-date information on life in Germany." See discussion in 6.3 above.

1932 (1934, 1937). Wilson, Percy George, and Arthur Charles Smith. *Through German Eyes. Thirty-six texts in simple German on everyday subjects for intensive study*. London: Pitman. See Stöbe (1939: 17). See Wilson (1930).

1933. Bithell, Jethro, and Alice Eastlake. *A Commercial German Reader*. London: Metheun & Co. See Bithell (1908).

1933 (later eds. 1934, 1937, 1945, 1949, 1956). Barker, Marie Louise. *Basic German for science students*. Cambridge: Heffer. See also Barker (1941).

1933. Bunn, Neville Harrow Harrow [sic]. *Practical German exercises*. London: Macmillan.

1933 (revised 1935, 4th ed. 1943). Chaffer, Gladys Russell. *A first German course*. London: Pitman.

1933–34. Clark, Andrew Crockett. *A modern German commercial course*. Two parts. London: Hirschfeld.

1933a. Eggeling, Hans F. *Advanced German Prose Composition for Use in Colleges and Universities*. London: Oxford University Press. See also Eggelig (1933b, 1974).

1933b (rep. 1937). Eggeling, Hans F. (ed.). *Modern German short stories. Second series, selected and edited by H. F. Eggeling*. Oxford Univ Press. Hierl (1972) used a 1954 reprint.

1933. Florian, Arthur Rudolph. *Junior German Test Papers*. London: Rivingtons.

1933. Hagboldt, P. *Fabeln, Bk 2*. London: Heath. See Florian (1909).

1933 (1946). Horsley, Rupert Harry. *A German Course*. Cambridge: Cambridge University Press. Discussed by Wegner (1999: 131–132).

1933 (rpt Jan 1934, Aug 1935, July 1937, May 1938). Koischwitz, Otto. *Deutsche Fibel*. London: Harrap. An American edition had appeared first, in 1932: New York: F. S. Crofts. Taylor Collection. See discussion in Chapter 6 above. See Koischwitz (1934).

1933. Schulze, Kurt, and H. E. Lewington. *Auf Skiern im Harz und zwei andere Geschichten*. London. Lewington was German master at John Ruskin School, Croydon. Noted by Stöbe (1939: 14).

1933. Shirreffs, John Grant, and Percival Milne Gillan. *The beginner's German reader*. London: Rivingtons. See also Shirreffs & Gillan (1936).

1934. Güntsch, E. and W. W. Whitworth. *Bob lebt sich in Deutschland ein*. London: Dent. See Stöbe (1939: 15), who says it makes no mention of "NS-Revolution".

1934. Herborn, Otto. *Extracts for translation into French, German and Spanish. O and E Herborn. Key to the German edition*. London: Harrap.

1934 (1937, 1940). Koischwitz, Otto. *Bilderlesebuch*. London: Harrap & c. Stöbe (1939: 17) quotes preface as saying it tries to combine "Anschauungsunterricht, Arbeitsunterricht, Kulturkunde" (Einleitung p. VII) but considers that it says nothing about the "new conditions" in Germany. See Koischwitz (1933).

1934 (revised 1939, 13th impression 1962). Macpherson, Arthur Stewart, and [Studienrat] Paul Strömer. *Deutsches Leben. Dritter Teil*. London: Ginn & Company Ltd. 1962 impression in Taylor Collection. Parts I & II had appeared in 1931. See Macpherson (1931).

1934. Meyer & Nauck. New ed. of Meyer & Nauck (1931), q. v.

1934. Neumann, G. E. *A First German Vocabulary*. London: The Pitfield Publishing Company. Taylor Collection. Revised by Wells (1945).

1934. Rivers, Jack (ed.) & Durian, Wolf. *Stabusch: Die Geschichte eines Wolfes*. Edited by Jack Rivers. London: Macmillan. See Rivers (1932).

1934. Silverman, Morris. *German for business: German commercial correspondence with German-English and English-German commercial vocabularies*. London: Harrap.

1934. Strong, Pitt. *Der Doppelgänger*. Oxford: OUP.

1934. Tindall, Samuel. *Deutsches Exerzieren*. London: Rivingtons. See Tindall (1928, 1939).

1934 (rpt. Sept 1937, Dec 1940). Wanstall, Humphrey John Boraston. *Alternative Tests in German Composition and Grammar. [With a key.]*. London: Harrap. Taylor Collection. See Wanstall (1922).

1935. Atkinson, Nora, and Ivy Geraldine Anderson. *Deutsch durch das Diktat*. London: Dent.

1935 (rep. 1938, 1945). Awty, Harry. *Simplified prose in German*. London: Harrap.

1935. Blades, Alexander. *A Modern German Course*. London: University Tutorial Press. See Wegner (1999: 135).

1935. Burkhard, Oscar. *Sprechen Sie Deutsch!* London: Harrap. See Burkhard (1936) below.

1935 (1948, 1956, 1962, 1968). Corbett, John Ambrose. *Essentials of modern German grammar*. London: Harrap.

1935. Ireland, Walter Anthony Vellemann. *A Quick-Reference German Grammar*. London: Methuen. Ireland had published a similar work for French in 1932.

1935 (1946). McPhee, John, and Robert Mackenzie Jack. *Progressive German Course*. London: Pitman.

1935. Oswald, Alfred. *Graded selection of German poems, including rhymes and action songs. Arranged in three parts*. London: Blackie. See Oswald (1900).

1935. Pegrum, Arthur William. *The active German reader, etc.* London: University of London Press. See Pegrum (1931–34).

1935a. Ripman, Walter. *An easy German course*. London: Dent.

1935b. Ripman, Walter. *Elementary German Composition*, Dent.

1935. Rivers, Jack. and Wilson, Alexander. *School certificate German translation. Prose and verse passages with exercises*. London: Macmillan. See Rivers (1932).

1935 (1937). Wanstall, Humphrey John Boraston. *German Passages for Unseen Translation. Advanced. Selected by H. J. B. Wanstall*. London: Harrap. See Wanstall (1922).

1935 (rpt July 1938, Aug 1944, May 1948, April 1949, July 1955, July 1958). Wanstall, Humphrey John Boraston. *German Passages for Unseen Translation. Intermediate*. London: George G. Harrap & Co. Ltd. 1958 reprint in Taylor Collection. See Wanstall (1922).

1936, 1939. Breul, Carl Hermann, J. Heron Lepper & Rudolph Kottenhahn. *Cassell's German and English Dictionary... Revised and enlarged by J. Heron Lepper and Rudolph Kottenhahn*. London: Cassell & Co. See Breul (1902).

1936. Burkhard, Oscar C. *Lesen sie deutsch!* London: Harrap. See Burkhard (1935) above.

1936 (rpt. 1953, 1962, 1966). Clarke, Firstbrook. *German grammar for revision and reference*. London: Bell.

1936. Florian, Arthur Rudolph. *Senior German Test Papers*. London: Rivingtons. See Florian (1909).

1936. Hagboldt, Peter. *Aus deutscher Vergangenheit, Bk 12. Adding 143 words and 8 idioms of frequent occurrence to the 1528 words and 278 idioms used in the eleven previous readers. Total: 1671 words and 286 idioms...* New York: Heath and Co. The Heath-Chicago German series [book 12].

1936 (2nd ed. 1951). Proudfoot, Colin McAlpine. *Wie Schreibt man Deutsch? A practical guide to free composition in German*. London: University Tutorial Press.

1936. Shirreffs, John G. and Percival M. Gillan. *Das Buch der Jugend*. London: Rivingtons. See Stöbe (1939: 17). See also Shirreffs & Gillan (1933).

1936. Stockton, Charles Edward. *School Certificate German Composition*. London: Methuen. Stockton published an equivalent title for French in 1938. See also Stockton (1937), Stockton & Froschel (1939).

1937. Barratt, Agnes Stephanie (ed.), and Pitt Strong. *Oxford rapid-reading German texts based on word-frequency. Series B. Der Große Unbekannte* (Tom Sharp, der König der Detektive No. 170). New York: Oxford University Press.

1937 (1944, 1948, 1957). Bell, Clair Hayden (ed.) and Kästner, Erich. *Drei Manner im Schnee*. London: Harrap. Authorized school edition.

1937 (new ed. 1955, rpt. 1962). Harold, John James. *Elementary translation into German*. London: Harrap.

1937. Johannsen, Else, and Wagner, Albert Malte. *Die Abenteuer von Paula und Peter*. Ten broadcast dialogues in German. London: University of London Press.

1937 (1948, 1960 6th impression). Macpherson, Arthur Stewart and Paul Strömer. *Deutsches Leben Lesebuch*. London: Ginn. Taylor Collection. See Macpherson (1931a).

1937 (1959, 1972). Otto, Emil, and Duncan M. Mennie. *Elementary German grammar, combined with exercises, readings and conversations*. (Method Gaspey-Otto-Sauer for the study of modern languages) [11th ed.] Revised by Duncan M. Mennie. [Key... by Duncan M. Mennie.]. The last publication of this grammar in 1972 means that Otto's method lasted over a hundred years; see Otto (1857) and other editions listed above.

1937. Seydewitz, Baroness Margaret von. *Schiller: ein Lebensbild*. Cambridge: The University Press.

1937. Stockton, Charles Edward. *Graded German passages for unseen translation and diction*. London: Methuen. Noted by Stöbe (1939: 12). See Stockton (1936).

1937. Wells, Sydney William. *Notes and Exercises on German Grammar and Construction*. London et al.: George G. Harrap. Author is Senior German Master, Minchenden Secondary School, Senior instructor in German, Southgate Evening Technical Institute. Taylor Collection. See Wells (1931). See Wells (1931).

1937 (2nd ed. 1956). Wild, Jacob Henry. *An anthology of scientific German*. New York: Oxford University Press. 2nd ed. *An Introduction to scientific German*.

1937. Wilson, Percy George, and Beate Salz. *Lies und spiel: Lese und Theaterstück für Anfänger*. London: Macmillan. See Wilson (1930).

1937. Witte, William. *Modern German Prose Usage*. London: Methuen.

1938. Adams, John, and Sydney William Wells. *Teach Yourself German. A book of self-instruction in German based on the work ["The Self-Educator in German"] by Sir John Adams... Completely revised and enlarged by Sydney W. Wells*. London: English Universities Press. See Adams (1901) above, see Wells (1931).

1938. Amburger-Stuart, Hannah Stephanie M. *Intermediate German Prose. Extracts from Modern and Classical Writers for Translation into German*. London: Duckworth.

1938. Faulk, Henry. *A common-sense German course. For the use of Evening Institutes and Commercial Schools, and for Adult Students*. London: Pitman.

1938 (1947). Fotos, John Theodore, Fritz Ullmann, et al. (eds.). *Intermediate readings in chemical and technical German: with a summary of reading difficulties, a chemical German frequency list and lesson vocabularies and notes*. (Simple selections from Ullmann: *Enzyklopädie der technischen Chemie*.). New York; London: J. Wiley & Sons; Chapman & Hall.

1938 (2nd ed. 1966). Hearn, William John. *Graded German composition for School Certificate forms*. London: Macmillan.

1938. Jenner, Dorothy. *Die Ferienkolonie (German readers for beginners)*. London: Oxford University Press.

1938 (1948, 11th impression 1953, 1955–1959, 1964). Kelber, Magda. *Heute Abend*. Books 1 and 2. London: Ginn and Company Ltd. See also Kelber (1943), Kelber & Freudenberger (1955–58).

1938. Koischwitz. An edition of Koischwitz (1933), q. v.

1938. Rivers, Jack (ed.) and Dittmer, Hans. *Spiel mit Wolken und Winden. Erzählung aus einem Segelfliegerleben*. London: Macmillan & Co. Ltd. See Rivers (1932).

1938. Rosenberg, Joseph. *Living Languages. How to Speak German. Illustrated by Phyllis R. Ward*. London: Nicholson and Watson. *(German Series Book I)*. Taylor Collection.

1938 (1947). Spiero, Ella (ed.). *Passages from German authors*. London: Macmillan.

1938 (1944, 1946, 1962). Weber, William Edwin. *The Intelligent Student's Guide to Modern German: A methodical study of German Vocabulary and Grammar, based on Gerstacker's well known story "Germelshausen"*. London: Sir Isaac Pitman & Sons Ltd. For the story by Gerstacker, see Lewis & Gerstacker (1907). See Weber (1913) above.

1938. Wells, Sydney William. *School CertificateTest Papers in German*. London: University of London Press. See Wells (1931).

1938 (3rd ed. 1946–54). Wildhagen, Karl. *English-German, German-English dictionary: Entirely rewritten, enlarged and brought up-to-date with special regard to pronunciation, semantics, syntax, idiomatic usage and the most recent business, scientific, technical, and sporting expressions... Third revised and enlarged edition. (Vol. 2. By K. Wildhagen and Will Héraucourt)*. Leipzig: B. Tauchnitz. Later editions by various publishers.

1938. Williams, W. O. *German passages for translation: general and literary, commercial and technical*. London: Hirschfeld.

1938. Wilson, Percy George. *Zum Wiedererzählen. A collection of simple German anecdotes and stories for intensive reading and reproduction*. London: Macmillan. See Wilson (1930).

1939 (2nd, revised ed. 1946). Bithell, Jethro. *Modern German Literature 1880–1938*. London: Methuen & Co. Ltd. In the preface, dated March 1939, Bithell notes the difficulties of including works he considered worthy of treatment aggravated "by the insistence of Nazi propaganda, which by its very nature keeps in the limelight those writers who before 1933 had the foresight to be *volkhaft* or the prudence to be so after that date." See Bithell (1946) below for the 2nd ed. See Bithell (1908).

1939. Grundy, John Brownsdon Clowes. *The Second Brush Up Your German. Conversations about the New Germany – on and off parade. Maps, vocabularies. With 26 Drawings by Phil Ward. 3 maps and other drawings. Conversations of real use*. London: J. M. Dent & Sons. From the inside blurb: "Since the original *Brush Up Your German* appeared eight years ago 50,000 copies of it have been sold. But so much has happened in those eight years – National Socialism for one thing, and 'Greater' Germany for another. So Herr Meyer and his charming wife Ilse go back to see just what has happened, taking with them their son Werner, who is to go to Nazi boarding-school (not to mention camping with the Hitler Youth, BGH). Matters are slightly complicated by the fact that Herr Meyer has a non-Aryan great-aunt somewhere up the family tree… All the essentials of life in Germany today are here, either in sprightly conversations or in the useful vocabularies and appendices." See discussion in Chapter 6.3 above. See Grundy (1931).

1939. Kallmann, Gertrud. E. (ed.). *Learn German while you act. Sketches and short plays for beginners.* London: Pitman.

1939. Klee, Wolfhart, and Magda Gerken. *Gesprochenes Deutsch.* Leipzig: Verlag Friedrich Brandstetter, 1939. *(Deutsch für Ausländer*, produced by the Goethe-Institut der Deutschen Akademie München. *Sprachlehre I. Teil, Stufe für Anfänger).*

1939 (8ᵗʰ impression 1946). Macpherson, Arthur Stewart. *Deutsches Leben. Part 3.* London: Ginn. See Macpherson (1931a, 1934) above.

1939 (revised ed. 1948). Parker, Altham Hampton, and Robert Edward Cecil Donati. *Graduated German Free Composition.* London: G. Bell and Son.

1939. Rivers, Jack (ed.), and Leonhard Roggeveen. *Der Radio-detektiv. Eine abenteuerliche Geschichte.* London: Macmillan and Co Ltd. See Rivers (1932).

1939–41. Schröder, Anton. *Lin-Hai-Fo in Deutschland.* (Supplementary German readers). Part I 1939, Part II 1941. London: Nelson.

1939. Stansfield, Agnes. *Karin geht in die Schule.* London: University of London Press.

1939. Steinberg, Sigfrid Heinrich. *A One-Year German Course.* London: Macmillan & Co.

1939. Stirk, Samuel Dickinson (ed.). *Modern German Short Stories.* London: Pitman.

1939 (2ⁿᵈ ed. 1962). Steinhauer, Harry. *Deutsche Kultur: ein Lesebuch.* Oxford: Oxford University Press.

1939 (1ˢᵗ ed. 1935). Stockton, Charles Edward (ed.), and Georg Froschel. *Himmel, meine Schuhe!* London: Methuen. See Stockton (1936).

1939. Thomas, R. Hinton. *The Classical Ideal in German Literature 1755–1805. An Introduction and an Anthology.* Cambridge: Bowes & Bowes. From the Preface: "The aim of this book is to furnish in a convenient form a selection of passages, mainly in prose and of theoretical interest, which illustrate the chief objects and ideals of German classicism. […] In the choice of texts I have been guided by the desire to combine well-known passages with others less accessible or less familiar. I trust that this method of selection will make the book helpful both in Sixth Form and University courses." (April 1939).

1939 (1947). Tindall, Samuel. *A practical German course.* London: Rivingtons. See Tindall (1928, 1934).

1940–1949

1940 (1944, 3ʳᵈ ed. 1968, rpt. 1970). Greenfield, Eric Virle. *German Grammar.* 3ʳᵈ Edition, New York: Barnes & Noble (= College Outline Series Languages 34). Taylor Collection. A page "About the author" tells us that Greenfield studied at Colgate and Harvard Universities, then "studied intensively abroad" in Spain, France and Germany. He taught for more than 40 years at Purdue University. Author of numerous textbooks of German, French and Spanish.

1940. Kirkby, John Walter. *A shorter German grammar*. Ediburgh: Oliver & Boyd.

1940. Oswald, Alfred. *A Complete German Grammar*. Glasgow: Robert Gibson & Son. See Oswald (1900).

1940. Theilkuhl, *Deutsches Land und Deutsches Leben*. See Theilkuhl (1932) above.

1941. Barker, Marie Louise. *German for Sixth-Form and Adult Beginners. An introduction to German Language, Literature and Landscape. With illustrations by Lore Holtz*. Cambridge: W. Heffer & Sons. See also Barker (1933).

1941 (1947, 5th ed. 1951). Bithell, Jethro. *An anthology of German poetry 1830–1880*. London: Methuen. From the Preface: "The idea of compiling this Anthology came to me when I was examining Higher Certificate scripts: a book of modern verse had been set, and the candidates were asked to interpret certain poems. Reading the answers was something of a revelation: here were boys and girls who showed the liveliest interest in poetry quite different from that of (say) Longfellow, and excellent appreciation too. It was clear that what attracted them most was the social poetry (*Armeleutepoesie*) and the power-poetry of machines. German ideologies of all kinds fired them to attack or approval. How they were moved by the exiles' poetry could not be missed. [...] The more complicated symbolist and expressionist poems were handled with ingenuity, but here there was some fumbling, obviously because the pupils had not been helped to pierce the intricacies of this technique, the difficulty of which usually vanishes with practice. It seemed to me that what was needed was a selection of verse bringing in all the modern movements, with sufficient explanatory matter to help the teacher and stir the pupils to independent effort." (November 20, 1940). From Preface to Fifth Edition of 1956: [...] "The two Nazi poets who were included at the end of the first edition, with a view to making the selection completely representative of the verse of the day, have been taken out." (June 1950). See Bithell (1908).

1941. Ripman, Walter. *A dictionary of new spelling*. London: Pub. on behalf of the Simplified Spelling Society by Sir I. Pitman & sons, ltd.

1942 (1947). Waterhouse, Gilbert. *A Short History of German Literature*. London: Methuen & Co. Ltd. Held in Temple Reading Room, Rugby. From the Preface: "This *Short History of German Literature* is designed as an introduction to the subject for university students and the higher forms of schools and may not be without interest for the general reader.' [...] 'The point of view is, I hope, invariably that of an Englishman writing for English readers, for I cannot avoid the conclusion that much of our academic study of German literature during the past forty years has been coloured by a too ready acceptance of German values." (1st January 1942).

1943 (1953, 1955). Kelber, Magda. *So einfach! An elementary German reader for adult students*. London: G. G. Harrap. See also Kelber (1938), Kelber & Freudenberger (1955–58).

1943. Lapper, Georg. *Singendes Lernen. Ich lerne singend Deutsch. Methode Lapper*. Oldenbourg: published by the author. Copy held in Taylor Collection, Bamberg.

1943. Weiner, P. F. *German for the scientist (chemist and physicist)*. London: G. Bell & Sons.

1944. Bithell, Jethro. *A Modern German Course.* London: Methuen & Co. Ltd. See Bithell (1908).

1944 (2nd ed. 1949). Stott, Denis Herbert. *A School German Course using inductive and other active methods.* Two parts. London: Methuen.

1944 (1951). Witte, William. *Homespuns: 9 one-act plays for learners of German.* London: Methuen.

1945? Lentz, Emil Ernest. *A German vocabulary: the 3500 most useful words arranged in connected groups suitable for translation, conversation, and free composition in University Matriculation, Leaving Certificate, and similar examinations.* London: Blackie. COPAC lists similar texts for French and Spanish by Lentz, published in 1969 and 1972.

1945 (1946, 1948, 1956, 1959, 1967). Steinberg, Sigfrid Heinrich (ed.). *Fifteen German Poets From Hölderlin to George.* London: Macmillan.

1945. Wells, Sydney William. *A first German vocabulary.* London: Pitfield. A revision of Neumann (1934). Wells published similar vocabularies of French and Italian. See Wells (1931).

1946. Bithell, Jethro. *Modern German Literature 1880–1938.* London: Methuen & Co. Ltd. 2nd ed. of Bithell (1939), above. Preface to Second Edition, dated July 1945: "The normal procedure would have been, in the second edition, to add a chapter on whatever German literature of importance has appeared since the first edition was published. But the intervening years are those of the War, and books printed in Germany have been unobtainable. The supplementary chapter will be provided as soon as full information is available. In the meantime, corrections to the present text have been made." See Bithell (1908) and (1959) below.

1946. Macpherson, Arthur Stewart. *Deutsches Leben.* London: Ginn. See Macpherson (1931a).

1946. Richey, Margaret Fitzgerald. *An introduction to Modern German Prose.* London: University of London Press.

1946. Southwell, Kathleen A. *Signposts in German literature.* Oxford: OUP.

1947. Bithell, Jethro. *An anthology of German poetry 1830–1880.* London: Methuen.

1948 (= revised ed.). Dartington, Edward Robert Cecil, and Altham Hampton Parker. *Graduated German free composition.* London: G. Bell & sons Ltd..

1948. Dutton, Walter Martin (ed.), and Hesse, Hermann. *Kinderseele und Ladidel. Zwei Erzählungen... Edited with introduction, notes and vocabulary by W.M. Dutton.* [With a portrait.]. London: Harrap. See Dutton (1932).

1948. Ewing, Nancy Rossie. *Hie und da. Allerlei fröhliche Geschichten.* London: G. Bell & sons Ltd.

1948. Horne, Joseph. *A Complete Course of German for Science, Commerce and other Students, etc.* Birmingham: Cornish Bros. See Moffatt & Paget (1907), Betteridge & Horne (1960), Horne (1960).

1948. Ripman, Walter, and William Archer. *New spelling; being proposals for simplifying the spelling of English without the introduction of new letters.* London: Pub. on behalf of The Simplified Spelling Society by Sir I. Pitman. Hathi Trust.

1948 (2nd impression 1950, then 1951, then with minor corrections 1953, then 1955, 1957, 1959, 1967). Russon, Leslie John. *Complete German Course for first examinations.* London: Longmans, Green & Co. Author is listed as M.A. Head of the Department of Modern Languages, Winchester College. See Wegner (1999: 156), and discussion in Chapter 6.4 above. See also works by Russon or Russon & Russon (1955, 1961, 1963, 1989), and Kershaw & Russon (1971).

1948. Williams, Tom Pugh. *Advanced Modern German Unseens. Selected by T.P. Williams.* London: George G. Harrap & Co.

1949 (1954–55, 1956, 1961, 1976). Anderson, Walter Ewart. *Aufenthalt in Deutschland.* 2 vols. London: Harrap. See also Anderson (1955, 1960a,b) and Anderson & Kägeler (1967).

1949. Bithell, Jethro. *German-English and English-German dictionary.* London: Pitman. See Bithell (1908).

1949. Huggard, Eveleen M. (translator), and Meyer, Conrad Ferdinand. *Das Leiden eines Knaben. Translated by E.M. Huggard.* London et al.: George G. Harrap & Co. Ltd. *Harrap's Bilingual Series.* Bilingual, English and German. Taylor Collection.

1949 (repr. 1961, 2nd ed. 1968). Osborne, Neville Goldsmith, and M. Morgenthal. *German free composition and vocabulary.* London: Harrap.

1950–1959

1950. Brockie, Cecilia. *German Prose and Verse for comprehension.* London: Bell.

1950. Gilbertson, J.C. *Picture Book of Free Composition in German.* [London]:[Hachette]. Taylor Collection.

1950 (1961). Grundy, John Brownsdon Clowes. *Brush up your German again.* London: J.M. Dent & Sons. Front cover reads: "English translation, vocabularies, drawings by Ward. Maps and diagrams. Business letters." See Grundy (1931, 1932, 1939 above). 1961 ed. front cover reads: "42 dialogues – business letters and glossaries. German and Germany of the 'sixties'".

1950. Mare, Margaret Laura. *Bergauf! A German reader and grammar... Illustrated, etc.* London: Methuen & Co. See Mare (1953, 1954), Braddick & Mare (1952).

1950. Robertson, J.G. *Outlines of the History of German Literature.* Edinburgh and London: William Blackwood & Sons Ltd. See Roberston (1902).

1950. Wayne, Philip Arthur. *Zwanzig Fragen or German while you play.* London: Heinemann.

1950 (1954, 1958). Wilson, Percy George. *[Teach Yourself] German Grammar.* London: The English Universities Press, Ltd. (Teach Yourself Books). See Wilson (1930).

1951 (2nd ed. 1963). Asher, John Alexander. *The Framework of German.* London: Harrap.

1951. Bithell, Jethro. *An Anthology of German Poetry 1880–1940.* London: Methuen & Co. Ltd.

1951. Harold, John James. *Wo? Wie? Warum? German comprehension tests.* London: Harrap.

1951. Yandell, Bernard (ed.), and Kästner, Erich. *Emil und die drei Zwillinge. Die zweite Geschichte von Emil und den Detektiven. Adapted and edited, with vocabulary, by Bernard Yandell.* London: G. Bell & Sons.

1952. Bithell, Jethro. *German pronunciation and phonology.* London: Methuen. See Bithell (1908).

1952. Braddick, G. M., and Margaret Laura Mare. *Stimmen des deutschen Volkes. I: Um den Christbaum und in der Schule. 2: Aus alten deutschen Gauen.* London: Methuen. See Mare (1950).

1952. Huebener, Theodore, and Newmark, Maxim. *A First Course in German.* Boston: D. C. Heath & Co.

1952. Spalding, Keith (ed.). *Selections from Adalbert Stifter.* London: Macmillan & Co. Ltd. See Spalding (1958).

1952. Sperber, Milo. *Hans und Willi. Ten German one-act plays.* Notes and vocabulary by E. A. Brett-James and R. P.L. Ledésert. Illustrations by Leo Bieber. London: Harrap.

1953. Collinson, William Edward. *The German language today: its patterns and historical background.* London: Hutchinson's University Library.

1953. Forster, Leonard Wilson. *German tales of our time. Edited with an introduction and notes by Leonard Forster.* London: Harrap.

1953 (1954, 1959). Gallimore, Nancy Winifred. *German dialogues for beginners.* London: Univ. Tutorial Press.

1953. Haller, M. [pseudonym of Margarethe Meinet]. *Die Mädchen von Oberhofen.* Londond: Methuen.

1953. Huebener, Theodore, and Maxim Newmark. *A Second Course in German. [With illustrations.].* Boston: D. C. Heath & Co.

1953 (rep. 1963). Mare, Margaret Laura (ed.) and Storm, Theodor. *Der Schimmelreiter, ed. by Margaret L. Mare.* London: Methuen. See Mare (1950).

1953. Martin, Allison Archer. *German interpretation tests in prose and verse.* Edinburgh: Oliver and Boyd.

1953. Richardson, Geoffrey, and William Fletcher. *Illustrierte Geschichten*, illustrations by Barbara M. Jowett. London: Edward Arnold.

1953. Southwell, Kathleen Annie. *Aus der Heimat.* Oxford: OUP.

1953 (1969). Van de Luyster, Nelson. *German readings in science for intermediate students.* New York & London: American Book Co.

1954, 1956, 1959. Fenn, Robert William, and Walter Fangl. *Ich lerne Deutsch… Illustrated by A. Horowicz.* London: Harrap. See Wegner (1999: 145–148).

1954. Louis, Andrew. *German Grammar. An Approach to Reading.* n. p.: Henry Holt & company. Taylor Collection. Preface states that it is above all intended to achieve reading; active vocabulary of 712 words taken from 1928 German frequency word book; assumes little formal knowledge of English grammar.

1954. Mare, Margaret Laura. *Am Gipfel. A reader and grammar for the General Certificate… Illustrated by Betty Finnemore & N. E. Huggett.* London: Methuen & Co.

1955–56 (new ed. 1960). Anderson, Walter Ewart. *Das Schöne Deutschland.* Two parts. London: Harrap. See Anderson (1949).

1955. Black, Kenneth. *Specialists' German Vocabularies.* London: Pitman.

1955. Gretton, Wanda. *John erlebt Deutschland.* [A school reader. With illustrations and a map.] London: G. Bell.

1955. Harold, John James. *Deutschlernen ist ein Spiel.* London: Harrap.

1955. Horne, Joseph, and Betteridge, Harold Thomas, Moffatt, Christopher and Paget, William. *Science German course. Rev. by Joseph Horne and H. T. Betteridge.* London: University Tutorial Press. See Moffatt & Paget (1907), Betteridge & Horne (1960), Horne (1948, 1960).

1955–1958. Kelber, Magda, and Marthe Freudenberger. *Heute und Morgen.* Book One 1955 (9th impression 1964); Book Two 1955 (eighth impresssion 1965); Book Three (by Freudenberger only) 1956 (fifth impression 1974); Book Four 1958. London: Ginn. See also Kelber (1938, 1943).

1955. Natan, Heinz Alex. *Neues Deutschland. (Reader for students of advanced German studies based on a survey of Germany's development since the end of the war.).* Oxford: Basil Blackwell. See discussion in Chapter 6.10.

1955 (1969). Russon, Agatha, and L. J. Russon. *Simpler German Course for First Examinations.* London et al.: Longmans, Green & Co. 1969 ed. with Leslie John Russon. Taylor Collection. See Russon (1948).

1955. Tymms, Ralph. *German Romantic Literature.* London: Methuen & Co. Ltd.

1955. Van de Luyster, Nelson, and Paul Holroyd Curts. *German grammar for science students: a beginning course.* Boston: Heath.

1956. Baier, Clair. *Deutschland und die Deutschen.* London: Methuen.

1956. Baker, H. Howard. *A classified German vocabulary.* London: Bell.

1956 (1962 revised ed.; last reprint 1966). Cook, Herbert Frederick. *Modern German for Adults, etc.* London: J. M. Dent & Sons.

1956 (2nd ed. 1966). Macintyre, Sheila, and Edith Witte. *German-English mathematical vocabulary; with a grammatical sketch by Lilias W. Brebner.* Edinburgh: Oliver & Boyd.

1956–1959. Tudor, Leslie, and Marianne Hedwig Gertrud Heydorn. *Deutsches Land und deutsches Volk.* London: etc., Blackie. See Wegner (1999: 155–156).

1957. Atkins, Henry Gibson and Maurice O'Connell Walshe. *A skeleton German grammar.* London; Glasgow: Blackie and Son.

1957 (other editions: 1962, 1963, 1965, 1966, 1974). Betteridge, Harold Thomas, and Carl Hermann Breul. *Cassell's German & English Dictionary. Based on the editions by Karl Breul. Completely revised and re-edited by Harold T. Betteridge, etc.* London: Cassell & Co. See Breul (1902), Betteridge & Horne (1960).

1957 (1960, 1965, 1973, 1982, 1994). Buckley, Richard Woods. *Living German.* London: London University Press. See also Buckley (1966).

1957 (1965). Closs, August, and T. Pugh Williams. *The Harrap anthology of German poetry.* London: Harrap. Hierl (1972) examined a 1965 print of this.

1957. Condoyannis, George E. *Scientific German, a concise description of the structural elements of scientific and technical German.* New York: Wiley.

1957. Eichner, Hans, and Hans Hein. *Reading German: for scientists.* London: Chapman and Hall.

1957. (rpt. 1959, 1961, 1963). Kolisko, Gertrud Anna, and William Edward Yuill. *Practice in German prose. London: Macmillan.* London: Macmillan. See discussion in 4.5 above. (Key published in 1961.) Authors listed as G. Kolisko PhD Lecturer in German, University of Sheffield and W. W. Yuill MA Lecturer in German, Universtiy of Sheffield.

1957 (1960). Stopp, Frederick John. *A Manual of Modern German.* London: University Tutorial Press.

1958. Brookes, Hedwig Anna Edith French , and Charlotte Elizabeth Fraenkel. *German prose composition.* London: Heinemann. Key published separately.

1958. Cunningham, Amy Fletcher. *Science students' guide to the German language.* London: Oxford University Press.

1958. Greatwood, Edward Albert. *School German Course.* London: University Tutorial Press. See Wegner (1999: 145).

1958 (2nd ed. 1964). Spalding, Keith. *Advanced German unseens.* London: Macmillan. See Spalding (1952).

1958 (1960). Nicholson, James Alexander. *Praktisches Deutsch.* London: George G. Harrap. See Wegner (1999: 149–154).

1959 (1982). Berger, Erich W. and Dorothea. *New German self taught: the quick, practical way to reading, writing, speaking, understanding / revised by Erich W. Berger and Dorothea Berger.* New York; Cambridge: Barnes & Noble.

1959 (3rd ed.). Bithell, Jethro. *Modern German Literature 1880–1950.* London: Methuen & Co Ltd. From Preface to the Third Edition, dated September 1957: "The present edition fulfils the promise made in my last Preface [cf. Bithell 1946 above]. The text of the first edition has in the main been kept; but certain writers who in 1939 were in the forefront of interest have now passed to the rear and the space allotted to them has necessarily been shortened. [...] The writers of the Nazi period with their clamour and clangour have now only historical and symptomatic importance, except perhaps that their cult for racial reasons of *Heimatkunst* has kept the prestige it gained." (See Bithell (1908).

1959. Fletcher, Ralph Beaumont. *Treffpunkt Köln, etc.* London: Methuen. Analysed by Hierl (1972).

1959–1966. Jørgensen, Peter, and Gertrud Anna Kolisko (transl.). *German Grammar.* (3 vols.). Translated [from Danish] by G. Kolisko in consultation with the author, and with F. P. Pickering. London: Heinemann.

1959 (vol. 2 1963). Orton, Eric. *Auf deutsch, bitte!* Illustrated by Sheila Whitby. London: George G. Harrap. Taylor Collection. Author was Senior German Master, Royal Grammar School, Worcester. Written for comprehensive schools; see discussion in 4.6.4. See Orton (1972), Orton & Schuldt (1960).

1959 (1966). Porter, James Arthur. *A guide to advanced German essay-writing on topical themes. Based on extracts from "Welt am Sonntag" and "Die Welt".* London: Harrap.

1959. Savigny, William Bryan, and William Cartmer Mitchell. *Frisch auf! A German course for the 'O' level examination… Illustrated by Christopher Brooker*. London: George G. Harrap & Co. See Savigny (1962).

1959. Waidson, Herbert Morgan (ed). *German short stories, 1900–1945*. Cambridge: CUP.

1960–1969

1960a. Anderson, Walter Ewart. *Das schöne Deutschland. Erster Teil*. London: Harrap. See Anderson (1949).

1960b. Anderson, Walter Ewart. *German for the technologist*. London: Harrap. See Anderson (1949).

1960. Betteridge, Harold Thomas, and Joseph Horne. *A rapid German course*. London: Macmillan. See Betteridge & Breul (1957), Horne et al. (1955), Horne (1948).

1960 (rpt. 1967, 6th rpt. 1970). Dodkins, Evelyn M. *Die Familie Neumann*. London: Macmillan. Johnson (1973: 48) writes that it was "designed to meet the needs of less academically gifted children learning German in secondary modern schools and comprehensives". Also examined by Hierl (1972).

1960. Flehinger, Arthur. *Gesprochenes Deutsch*. London: Macmillan.

1960. Hooever, Marjorie (ed.), and Frank, Anne. *Das Tagebuch der Anne Frank*. Abridged and edited by Marjorie Hoover. London: Methuen.

1960. Horne, Joseph. *A streamlined course in scientific German*. London: Pitman. See Horne (1948).

1960. Orton, Eric, and Kolle Schuldt. *Bei Jürgen in Lübeck*. London: Harrap. See Orton (1959, 1972).

1960 (2nd ed. 1965, 3rd ed. 1967). Salamé, Sydney John William. *Deutsch für Dich*. London: Faber and Faber.

1960, 1961 (2nd ed. 1964). Sutcliffe, Kenneth Edward. *Fahrt ins Blaue. A German course for schools*. 2 vols. London: Bell.

1961. Fleck, J. C. C. H. *Deutsch für den Alltag*. Adapted with Notes and Vocabulary by Wolfgang Herman. London: University of London. Referred to by Hierl (1972).

1961. Harvard, Joseph. *Conversational German. A Course for Adults*. London: University of London Press Ltd.

1961. Kritsch, Erna. *Modernes Deutsch. Eine Wiederholung der Grammatik mit modernen Autoren*. New York: Appleton-Century-Crofts, Inc. 1961. Author is from Douglass College, Rutgers.

1961. Nicholson, James Alexander. *Parallel passages for German translation and composition*. London: Harrap Nicholson published an equivalent text for French in 1954. Author listed as M. A., Headmaster Plympton Grammar School. Taylor Collection. See Wegner (1999: 149–154).

1961 (1967, 1978). Radcliffe, Stanley. *Learn scientific German*. London: Harrap.

1961. Russon, Agatha, and Russon, Leslie John. *A second German book*. London: Longmans. See Russon (1948) and (1955).

1961 (1967). Schulz, Gerhard Ernst Otto. (ed.) *German verse: an anthology of German poetry from sixteenth to twentieth century*. London: Macmillan.

1961. Willey, Peter Robert Everard. *Guten Tag. An illustrated manual of German conversation and free composition*. London: Harrap.

1962. Cook. A later edition of Cook (1956), q. v.

1962. Fletcher, Ralph Beaumont, and Oscar Blobel. *German Idiom & Compound Verbs*. London: Methuen & Co Ltd.

1962. Johnson, Charles B. (ed.). *Deutsche Erzähler der Gegenwart: seven modern German short stories*. London: Harrap.

1962. Madrigal, Margarita, and Inge D. Halpert. *See It and Say It in German*. New York: New American Library. Taylor Collection.

1962. Savigny, William Bryan. *Sixth form German course*. London: Harrap. See Savigny & Mitchell (1959), Savigny & Scholl (1967), Mattel (1970).

1962–1975. Springer, Otto (ed.). *Langenscheidt's encyclopaedic dictionary: of the English and German languages based on the original work by E. Muret and D. Sanders; edited by Otto Springer*. Berlin: Langenscheidt. Part 1 also published, London: Methuen, 1962, 1963. Part 1: English-German. 1962, 1963. 1v. in 2, Part 2: German-English. 1974, 1975.

1963. Dickins, E[ric] P[aul]. *German for Advanced Students*. London: Oxford University Press.

1963. Hamburger, Michael, and Christopher Middleton. *Modern German poetry, 1910–1960: an anthology with verse translations*. London: MacGibbon & Kee.

1963–1974. Jones, Trevor. *Harrap's standard German and English dictionary: Part 1 German-English A–E*. London: Harrap. Eight volumes were planned; only the first three appeared.

1963. Macpherson, Arthur Stewart, Paul Strömer, et al. *Deutsches Leben*. Part Two. London: Ginn. Taylor Collection. See Macpherson (1931).

1963. Russon, Agatha, and Russon, Leslie John. *A first German reader*. London: Longmans. Aimed at first-year students [i. e. pupils] of German. See Russon (1948).

1964 (rpt. 1967, 1969). Anderson, Walter E. *Das heutige Deutschland*. London: Harrap.

1964. Buckley, Richard Woods (ed.). *Moderne Lesestücke*. London: University of London Press.

1964. Freudenberger. Later impression of *Heute und Morgen III*; see Kelber & Freudenberger (1955–58) above.

1964–1967. Jones, Geoffrey Brangwyn. *Lustiges Lernen*. Three Parts. Illustrated by Barry Cummings. London: University of London Press. See Jones (1966).

1964. Kellett, Freda. *Advanced Modern German*. London: University of London Press. Author listed on title page as "Senior German Mistress, King's Norton Grammar School for Girls, Birmingham". Kellett published specimen translations for the text in 1965.

1964. Law, Michael Haldane. *How to read German: a short-cut for non-linguists*. London: Hutchinson.

1964. Pfeffer, Alan. *Basic (Spoken) German Word List.* Englewood Cliffs, N.J.: Prentice-Hall.

1964. Malpas, Frederick John. *German unseens for 'O' level.* Selected and with a vocabulary. London: Harrap.

1964. Meiklejohn, William Hope. *Was Wissen Sie über Deutschland?* London. A volume of *Antworten* was also published.

1965. Buckley, *Living German.* See Buckley (1957) above.

1965. Burg, Marie. *A modern German reader.* London: Macmillan.

1965 (1981, rpt. 1982, 1988). Jackson, Eugene, and Adolph Geiger. *German Made Simple.* New York: Made Simple Books Doubleday & Company. Taylor Collection. Authors: Jackson, A. B. [sic] Chairman of foreign languages (ret.), Samuel J. Tilden High School, Brooklyn NY, and Adolf Geiger, M.A. Teacher of German (ret.), Thomas Jefferson High School, Brooklyn NY. See Chapters 5.3 and 5.5.

1965 (revised ed. 1973). Harvard, Joseph. *Bilingual guide to business and professional correspondence. German-English. Zweisprachen-Briefsteller für das Geschäft und den Beruf. Englisch-Deutsch.* Oxford: Pergamon.

1965. Howlett Jones, H.C., and Heinz Fischer-Wollpert. *Deutsches Leben, dritter Teil.* London: Ginn. See Macpherson (1931) for earlier editions of this work.

1965. Kosler, Gerhard. *Practical Approach to German Grammar. Complete course for secondary schools.* Brisbane – Sydney: William Brooks & Co. Taylor Collection.

1965. Moore, Charles Henry. *Advanced composition in German.* London: Methuen.

1965. Reeves, Norman Charles. *German for engineers.* London: Pitman.

1965. Russon, Agatha, and Leslie John Russon. *Advanced German course.* London: Longman. See Russon (1948).

1965. Taeni, Rainer, and Michael G. Clyne. *Efficient German.* London: Macmillan. Lino-cuts by Hertha Kluge-Pott, an artist in her own right. See 4.6.3 above.

1965 (amended ed. 1968). Thomas, Richard Hinton. *Seventeen modern German stories.* New York: Oxford University Press.

1966. Buckley, R.W. *Lesen und lernen.* London: University of London Press. Intended as a companion volume to *Living German* by the same author. See Buckley (1957) above. Part of the corpus of Johnson (1973).

1966. Creese, Kenneth John Harry, and Peter Stuart Green. *German. A Structural Approach. Book 1.* Edinburgh, Oliver & Boyd.

1966. Eaton, Richard Stanley, Herbert Sheldon Jackson, and Cyril Raymond Buxton. *German for the scientist.* London: English Universities Press.

1966. Fowler, Frank Macpherson, Brian John Kenworthy, et al. *A Manual of German Prose Composition for Advanced Students.* London: Harrap. Key published separately.

1966. Jones, G[eoffrey] Brangwyn. *Vor Jahr und Tag.* With illustrations by Barry Cummings. London: University of London Press. See Jones (1964–1967).

1966. Lavy, George Julius William. *Language laboratory pattern drills in German: basic series.* London: Pitman.

1966. Oehler, Heinz. *Grundwortschatz Deutsch. Essential German. Allemand fondamental. Bearbeitet von H. Oehler.* Stuttgart.

1966. Scherer, George A.C. (ed). *German. Reading for Meaning.* New York: Harcourt, Brace & World, Inc.

1967. Anderson, Walter Ewart, and Heid Kägeler. *Advanced Conversational Idiom in German. A Practice Book for Language Laboratory and Classroom Use.* London: Sir Isaac Pitman & Sons Ltd. See Anderson (1949).

1967 (1976). Baer, Edith Ruth. *Der arme Millionär: a radio course in everyday German, based on Erich Kästner's novel 'Drei Männer im Schnee'. Radio adaptation by Edith R. Baer; notes, grammar and general linguistic advice by L. Löb* [Dr Ladislaus Löb]. London: British Broadcasting Corporation. See also Oldnall et al. (1968), Baer & Wightman (1982).

1967. Fellner, Ernst. *Speak German: German grammar through conversation.* London: Parrish.

1967. Gilbertson, Gerard and Charles Whiting. *Spiegel-Gesprache: an English-German interpreters' course.* London: Longmans.

1967. Lunn, Katherine Johanna Eichstaedt. *Das treffende Wort. Lesestücke und Rätsel.* London: Ginn and Co.

1967. McInnes, Edward, and Anthony John Harper. *German today: a selection of contemporary German passages for translation practice.* London: Methuen.

1967–1969. Rowlinson, William. *Sprich mal Deutsch.* 3 volumes. Oxford: OUP. See also Rowlinson & Lehnigk (1973–76), Rowlinson (1993a,b,c), Prowe et al. (1995).

1967. Russon. See Russon (1948).

1967. Savigny, William Bryan (adaptor), Inge Scholl. *Die Weisse Rose. Adapted by W. B. Savigny.* London & Glasgow: Blackie & Son. See Savigny (1962).

1968 (Book 1 1969, Book 2 & 3 1969; rpt. 1970, 1971, 1984). Baber, Daniel Clement, G. Everson, et al. *Mach mit! A German course to O level.* Book 1 by Daniel Clement Baber, etc. (Book 2 by D.C. Baber... and Gilda Everson. Book 3 by Gilda Everson and Paul Coggle.). London: Nelson. Discussed by Johnson (1973).

1968. Bisset, Anna Black, and Ian M. Hendry. *German prose passages for the middle school.* Edinburgh: W. & R. Chambers.

1968. Frobenius, Lore. *Ferner als der fernste Stern.* London: Heinemann Educational.

1968. Happ, Jürgen (compiler) and Brigitte E. Schatzky. *Gestern und Heute: unsere Zeit wie Menschen sie erlebten.* English ed. revised and edited by Brigitte Schatzky. London: Longmans.

1968. Oldnall, R.M., Edith Ruth Baer, et al. *Starting German: Reisebüro Atlas: a BBC radio course for beginners.* London: BBC Publications. See Baer (1967).

1968. Pickering, Frederick. *University German: a reader for arts students.* Oxford: O U.P.

1969. Garrett, Thomas John. *Modern German humour: 20 stories.* Harlow: Longmans.

1969. Hammond, Robin T. *Fortbildung in der deutschen Sprache. Student's book.* London: Oxford University Press. See Hammond (1981).

1969. Konigsberg, Conrad Isodore, with drawings by John Holder. *Ferien mit Schuss.* London: CUP.

1969. Lederer, Herbert. *Reference grammar of the German language. Based on Grammatik der deutschen Sprache, by Dora Schulz and Heinz Griesbach.* New York: Scribner

1969. McNab, Una (et al.). *Ealing course in German produced under the direction of Una McNab at Ealing Technical College.* Two parts. Harlow: Longman.

1969. Politzer, Robert Louis. *Speaking German.* Englewood Cliffs (N. J.); Hemel Hempstead: Prentice-Hall.

1969. Rowlinson, *Sprich Mal Deutsch* III. See Rowlinson (1967–1969).

1969. Seidmann, Gertrud. *Spiegel der 'Zeit': an introduction to current affairs based on extracts from 'Die Zeit': [Compiled by] Gertrud Seidmann.* Harlow: Longmans.

1969. Waidson, Herbert Morgan. *German short stories, 1955–1965. Selected and edited by H. M. Waidson, etc.* Cambridge: University Press.

1970–1979

1970. Kanocz, Stephen. *Intermediate German: BBC Radio for schools. Autumn term 1970.* London: BBC.

1970. Mattel, Susanne. *Die Mädchen Vom Internat Rainer.* London: Blackie. GCE 'O' Level. A new title in the Elementary Grade of 'Die Moderne Lesereihe' series (General editors William B. Savigny and Marianne Heydorn). "These supplementary readers combine an interesting story line with a simple German style to assist rapid-reading. Each book has a short German-English vocabulary."

1970. Owens, Rosalie Anne (ed.), and Stephan Gräffshagen. *Zwei Krimis.* Illustrated by Gareth Floyd. Abridged ed. Edinburgh: Oliver & Boyd.

1970. Page, J. F. *Penguin German Reader.* Middlesex: Penguin.

1970–1972. Paxton, Norman, and Richard John Brake. *Wir lernen Deutsch.* 3 parts. London: English Universities Press. See Wegner (1999: 294–5) and 4.6.3. See Paxton (1986).

1971 (1975, 1996). Clapham, John. *Basic German grammar.* London: Murray. The grammar appeared in 1975 as part of *Basic German dictionary-grammar: a dictionary containing the 2500 most commonly used words, with the essentials of German grammar.* London: J. Murray (1975).

1971. Davidson, Rosemary. *Aktuell aufgenommen: 12 Interviews mit Deutschen von heute.* Harlow: Longman.

1971 (1978, and later eds. revised by Martin Durrell). Hammer, Alfred Edward. *German grammar and usage.* London: Edward Arnold.

1971 (1977, 1986). Johnson, Charles B. *Harrap's New German Grammar.* London: Harrap.

1971. Kershaw, Frank G. and Stephen Russon. *German for business studies.* Harlow: Longman. See Russon (1948).

1971. Paxton & Brake. Vol. 2 of Paxton & Brake (1970–72), q. v.

1971. Reed, Joan. *Lernen wir Deutsch!* Book 1. Sydney: Whitcombe & Tombs Pty. Ltd. Author was Modern Languages and Classics Mistress at the Sir Joseph Banks High School, Revesby, New South Wales, Australia.

1972 (1975). Kanocz, Stephen. *Frisch begonnen: German for beginners. 11.–20. programm.* London: BBC.

1972. Messinger, Heinz. *Langenscheidt's Comprehensive English-German Dictionary*. London: Hodder and Stoughton.

1972. Orton, Eric. *Sprich mit!: deutsche Strukturen in Dialograhmen*. London: Harrap. See Orton (1959).

1972. Pache, Walter. *German at work: a second stage course for adults* by W. Pache… [and others]. London: University of London Press.

1972. Werba, Henry. *Intermediate German*. New York; London: Holt, Rinehart and Winston.

1972. Wringe, Colin A. *An intensive German course for travel and business: student's manual with teacher's introduction*. London: Heinemann Educational.

1973. Kenngott, E. *Deutsche und englische Geschäftsbriefe. German and English business letters… Compiled and annotated by Dr. E. Kenngott*. London: Cassell.

1973 (1st ed. 1967; also 1989). Lohnes, Walter F. W., and Friedrich Wilhelm Strothmann. *German. A Structural Approach*. New York: W. W. Norton & Company, Inc.

1973. Manton, John Derek. *Introduction to theological German*. London: Tyndale Press.

1973–1976 (1 1973, 2a 1975, 2b 1976, 2c 1976). Rowlinson, William, and G. Lehnigk. *Lies mal Deutsch!* Oxford: Oxford University Press. See Rowlinson (1967–69).

1973–1981 (rpt. 1983, twice). Shotter, David, and Hartmut Ahrens. *Deutscher Sprachkurs. 1. Biberswald 1973; 2. Unterwegs 1974; 3. Angekommen 1975; 4. Panorama 1981*. London: Heinemann Educational. Shotter is listed as Head of the Faculty of Modern Languages at Furze Platt Comprehensive School Maidenhead, Ahrens as Oberstudienrat, Gewerbeschule, Kehl am Rhein. See Wegner (1999: 297–302).

1974. British Broadcasting Corporation (BBC). *Kontakte: a combined BBC Television and Radio course for beginners in German*. London: BBC. See BBC (1975), Utton et al. (1979).

1974. Eggeling, Hans F. *A dictionary of modern German prose usage*. Oxford: Clarendon Press. See Eggeling (1933a).

1974 (1979, 1984, 1991,…2013). Moeller, Jack, and Helmut Liedloff. *Deutsch Heute 1 & 2*. Boston: Houghton Mifflin. Used in schools for the PXPROD diversification of languages project (Phillips & Filmer-Sankey 1993: 76–77) to "reflect the trend of recent years towards 'communicative' teaching methods by providing materials which encourage pupils to use actively the language they have have learnt. They aim to give pupils clearly specified and attainable goals which they can see have relevance to everyday life, so that they feel a sense of achievement, whatever the level of their ability. Pupils are presented with the language they need in order to be able to cope in social or public situations. Thes include, for example, giving information about themselves and their families and asking others about themselves, expressing wishes, needs and preferences, performing simple transactions such as shopping, eating out and making enquiries, interpreting different sources of public information and making travel arrangements. In addition to the topical or situational approach, each course provides a structural/grammatical progression."

1974. Nuffield Foundation. *Vorwärts*. York: University of York, Language Teaching Centre. Leeds: E. J. Arnold.

1974. Wightman, Margaret. *Introducing Germany*. London: Harrap. See Baer & Wightman (1982), Wightman & BBC (1985).

1974–1979. Wightwick, Charles Christopher Brooke, and Strubelt, H. W. *Longman audio-lingual German*. London: Longman. In 3 'Stages', each consisting of a textbook and teacher's book; Stage 1 also includes a 'Workbook'. Stage 3 is co-written by N. A. L. Norman. Stage 1. Herr Körner und seine Welt. – Stage 2. Die Welt ist rund. – Stage 3. So ist eben die Welt.

1975. Apelt, Mary L. and Hans-Peter. *Reading knowledge in German: a course for art historians and archaeologists = Ein engl.-dt. Lesekurs f. Kunstgeschichte u. Archäologie*. Berlin: Schmidt

1975. British Broadcasting Corporation (BBC). *Wegweiser*: 2nd stage German; a BBC Radio course to follow *Kontakte*. Book 1 Programmes 1–10. [By British Broadcasting Corporation.] London: British Broadcasting Corporation. See BBC (1974), Utton et al. (1979).

1975. Kanocz, Stephen. *Halb gewonnen: a BBC radio course in German*. London: BBC.

1975 (1981). Paxton, Norman, and Bernard Alan Brentnall,. *Zielpunkt Deutsch: a complete course for advanced students*. London: English Universities Press. See Paxton (1986), Paxton & Brake (1970–72).

1975. Schneider, Rudolf. *Auf Deutsch gesagt 1–4*. Vol. 1 London: BBC; later volumes Bonn: Köller.

1975 (2nd ed. 1980). Zindler, Horst, and William Barry. *fehler abc [sic] English-German* Stuttgart: Klett.

1976. Borgert, Udo H. G., and Charles Anthony Nyhan. *A German reference grammar*. (2nd ed. 1991). Sydney: Sydney University Press.

1976 (1983, 2000 abridged version and online resource). Gschossmann-Hendershot, Elke. *Schaum's outline of German grammar*. New York; London: McGraw-Hill. 2000. *German / abridgement editor, Sigmund J. Barber; based on Schaum's Outline of German grammar by Elke Gschossmann-Hendershot and Lois M. Feuerle and Schaum's Outline of German vocabulary by Edda Weiss and Conrad J. Schmitt*. New York; London: McGraw-Hill.

1976. Luscher, Renate, and Roland Schäpers. *Deutsch 2000. A Grammar of Contemporary German*. Munich: Max Hueber Verlag.

1976. Rowlinson. *Lies mal Deutsch* 2c. See Rowlinson & Lehnigk (1973–76).

1977. Heron, Patricia A. *A concise German-English grammar dictionary*. Birmingham: Department of Modern Languages, University of Aston.

1977. Konrad, Rosalinde. *Essentials of German grammar in review*. New York: Harper and Row.

1977. Krausmann, Rudi. *Recent German Poetry*. Paddington, NSW, Autralia: Aspect Publications.

1977. Penner, Adrienne. *Der Gimmick. Gesprochenes Deutsch von Adrienne. German as the Germans speak it!* London: Hutchinson & Co Ltd.

1978. Crossgrove, Hannelore. *Graded German reader. Erste Stufe.* Lexington, Mass.: Heath.

1978. Rimrott, F. P. J. and W. Eichenlaub (eds., with 22 contributors). *"Was du ererbt…"*. Toronto: Deutsche Sprachschulen (Metro Toronto) Inc.

1978. Rogers, R. Max et al. *Scenes from German drama: a review grammar and reader.* New York; London: Harper and Row.

1978–1979. Todd, Keith. Series: *German grammar topic books*, including *The imperfect tense*; *The indirect object*; *Modal verbs*; *Prepositions*. (All by Todd, 1978). Also Peter Satchwell, *The perfect tense.* Leeds: E. J. Arnold.

1978. Winkler, George, and Margrit Meinel Diehl. *Unsere Freunde.* San Diego: Harcourt Brace Jovanovich.

1979. Bergethon, K. Roald. *Grammar for reading German: a second year workbook with recognition exercises.* Boston [Mass.]; London: Houghton Mifflin.

1979. Elston, Charles Sidney. *German.* Sunbury on Thames: Celtic Revision Aids.

1979. Helbling, Robert E. *First-year German.* New York; London: Holt, Rinehart and Winston.

1979 (1982). Utton, Vera, Ursula Runde, Christopher Candlin, Rodney Mantle, and Iris Sprankling. *Kein Problem. Third stage German. A BBC Radio course to follow Kontakte & Wegweiser.* London: British Broadcasting Corporation. See BBC (1974, 1975).

1980–1989

1980. Alexander, Louis George, Ingeborg Bauer, Antony Peck. *Survive in German.* London: Longman.

1980 (1984). Sevin, Dieter. *Wie geht's?: an introductory German course* by Dieter Sevin, Ingrid Sevin, Katrin T. Bean. New York; London: Holt, Rinehart and Winston.

1981. Hammond, Robin T. *A German reference grammar.* Oxford: Oxford University Press. See Hammond (1969).

1981. Shotter. *Panorama.* See Shotter & Ahrens (1973–1981).

1982. Baer, Edith Ruth, and Wightman, Margaret. *Signposts German.* Cambridge: CUP. See Baer (1967), Wightman (1974).

1982. Peck, Antony J. *Mastering German 1.* London: Macmillan.

1982. Stokes, Richard *Gefunden.* London: Heinemann. On Stokes, see 4.11 above.

1983 (1991). *German schoolmate: fast A–Z reference grammar for exams and self study* compiled by Lexus with Lesley Robertson; German consultant, Dagmar Förtsch. Edinburgh: Chambers.

1983. Moeller, Jack. *Kaleidoskop: Kultur, Literatur und Grammatik.* By Jack Moeller, Helmut Liedloff, Helen Lepke. Boston: Houghton Mifflin.

1983 (1984). Neuner, Gerd. *Deutsch konkret: ein Lehrwerk für Jugendliche.* 2 vols. Berlin: Langenscheidt.

1983 (1985). Rogers, Paul. *Alles klar: German grammar through cartoons: demonstration and practice to examination level.* Walton-on-Thames: Nelson. See also Goodman-Stephens et al. (1987–89).

1983–1985. Sidwell, Duncan and Penny Capoore. *Deutsch heute (Part 1 1983, Part 2 1984, Part 3 1985; new edition 1990–1994). With teacher's resource books, assessment papers, flashcards, and worksheets.* Walton-on-Thames etc.: Nelson.

1983. Willshaw, Isabel. *Companion German grammar.* London: Pan.

1984. Corrie, Elspeth. *The German oral examination: Certificate of Secondary Education and General Certificate of Education – ordinary level.* London: Macmillan.

1984. Fox, Anthony. *German intonation. An outline.* Oxford: Clarendon Press.

1985 (1993). Godfrey, Elke. *Deutsch, Schritt für Schritt.* New York; London: Prentice Hall.

1985. MacLean, Ilse. *German grammar.* London: Collins.

1985. Rogalla, Hanna and Willy. *Grammar handbook for reading German texts.* Berlin; New York: Langenscheidt.

1985. Smith, Patricia M. *Einfach toll! Vol. 1.* Cheltenham, Stanley Thornes. 5 vols. For other vols. see separate entries below. Series published 1985–1992.

1985. Trim, John, and British Broadcasting Corporation (BBC). *Deutsch direkt!: a BBC course for beginners in German.* London: BBC. See also Trim (1987).

1985. Wightman, Margaret, and British Broadcasting Corporation (BBC). *Deutsch direkt! a combined BBC radio and television course for beginners in German.* London: British Broadcasting Corporation. See Wightman (1974).

1986–1988. Aufderstrasse, Hartmut, Peter Lupson, et al. *Los Geht's!* Cheltenham: Thornes. 3 vols.

1986. *Harrap's "drive-in" German.* London: Harrap. Two parts. Multimedia course.

1986. Johnson, Victor. *Kernpunkte: German grammar revision.* Walton-on-Thames, Nelson Harrap

1986. Parker, Julie, Terry Hawkin, et al. *Deutsch express! Second stage BBC Radio German language course.* London: BBC.

1986. Paxton, Norman. *German grammar.* London: Hodder & Stoughton. See also Paxton (1988), Paxton & Brake (1970–72), Paxton & Brentall (1975).

1986. Paxton, Norman, and Anthony R. Whelan. *German for business.* London: Hodder and Stoughton.

1986. Smith, Patricia M. *Einfach toll! Vol. 2.* Cheltenham, Stanley Thornes. 5 vols. For other vols. see separate entries below and Smith (1985). Series published 1985–1992.

1987. Bansleben, Manfred. *Perspektiven: Übungen zur Grammatik.* New York; London: Holt, Rinehart and Winston.

1987. Centre for Information on Language Teaching and Research (CILT), and BBC School Television. *A Level German: five programmes for use as a resource with 6th forms, filmed in Austria, Bavaria, and East Berlin.* [London]: Centre for Information on Language Teaching and Research.

1987–1989. Goodman-Stephens, Bryan, Paul Rogers, et al. *Zickzack.* London: Arnold. See Wegner (1999: 302–308). See also Rogers (1983).

1987. Lockwood, William Burley. *German today: the advanced learner's guide.* Oxford: Clarendon.

1987, 1988, 1989 & 1990. McNab, Rosi. *Deutsch jetzt! 1, 2, 3& 4.* London: Heinemann Educational.

1987 (2nd ed. 1996). Turneaure, Brigitte M. *Der treffende Ausdruck. Texte, Themen, Übungen*. New York; London: Norton.

1987. Trim, John L. M. and BBC Radio. *Ganz spontan!: a third stage BBC Radio German course*. London: BBC Books. See also Trim (1985).

1988. Della Gana, David. *Neue Perspektiven*. London: Longman.

1988. Dollenmayer, David B., and Thomas S. Hansen. *Neue Horizonte. A First Course in German Language and Culture. Instructor's Annotated Edition*. Lexington, Massachusetts: D. C. Heath and Company.

1988. Goodman-Stephens et. al. See Goodman-Stephens et al. (1987–1989).

1988. James, Charles J. *German verbs and essentials of grammar: a practical guide to the mastery of German*. Lincolnwood: Passport Books.

1988. McNab. See McNab (1987 etc.).

1988. Paxton, Norman. *Basic German*. London: Teach Yourself. See Paxton (1986).

1988. Stern, Guy. *Essential German grammar*. London: Teach Yourself Books.

1988. Stocker, Paul, and Keith Saunders. *Einsicht*. London: Hodder & Stoughton. See also Saunders et al. (1992).

1988 (1992, 1996). Terrell, Tracy D., Erwin Tschirner, Brigitte Nikolai, and Herbert Genzmer. *Kontakte. A Communicative Approach*. New York: McGraw-Hill, Inc.

1989. Boaks, Peter, Ebba-Maria Dudde, et al. *Deutsch konkret for GCSE*. European Schoolbooks Publishing.

1989. Coggle, Paul. *[Teach Yourself] German*. London: Hodder and Stoughton Educational. Teach yourself books. See also Coggle (2003, 2009).

1989. Corl, Kathryn A. *Sprechen wir Deutsch!* New York; London: Holt, Rinehart and Winston.

1989. Herde, Dieter, et al. *Vertrag in der Tasche: practical business German*. London: Hodder & Stoughton.

1989, 1990. Lupson, Peter, et al. *Talking Business German*. Cheltenham, England: Stanley Thornes.

1989. Russon, Agatha, and Russon, Leslie John. *German grammar for all*. Harlow: Longman. See Russon (1948).

1990–1999

1990. Bonnyman, Douglas, and Klaus Oberheid. *Sprungbrett*. Cheltenham, Thornes. [Teacher's book 1991].

1990. Fox, Anthony. *The structure of German*. Oxford,: Clarendon.

1990 (1997). Martin, Sigrid-B. *German in three months*. London: Hugo's Language Institute.

1990. Smith, Patricia M. *Einfach toll!* vol. 3. Stanley Thornes, Cheltenham. 5 vols. For other vols. see separate entries. Series published 1985–1992.

1991. Cochran, Emory E. *Cochran's German review grammar*. Englewood Cliffs, N. J.; London: Prentice Hall.

1991 (1999). Buck, Timothy. *A concise German grammar*. Oxford: Oxford University Press.

1991 (1996). Durrell, Martin. *Hammer's German grammar and usage.* London: Edward Arnold. See also Durrell (1992, 1993, 1996, 2002), Hammer (1971).

1991. Göricke-Driver, Gisela, and Marc Ducassé. *German for business.* Cheadle: Limitcode.

1991. *Harrap's five language business dictionary: English-French-German-Italian-Spanish.* London: Harrap

1991. *Harrap's German school dictionary: plus German grammar.* London: Harrap.

1991. Malcolm, Irene, and Marilyn Farr. *German just for business.* Oxford, Oxford University Press.

1991. Neuhaus, Karsta, and Margaret Maltern. *Business the German way.* London: Cassell.

1991. Smith, Patricia M. *Einfach toll!* vol 4. Cheltenham, Stanley Thornes. 5 vols. For other vols. see separate entries. Series published 1985–1992.

1992. Barrack, Charles M., and Horst M. Rabura. *Mosaik. Deutsche Grammatik: intermediate German.* New York; London: McGraw-Hill.

1992. Bates, Maria, and Patricia M. Smith. *Einfach toll! Lehrbuch 5.* Cheltenham: Stanley Thornes. 5 vols. For other vols. see separate entries under Smith. Series published 1985–1992.

1992. Durrell, Martin. *Using German: a guide to contemporary usage.* Cambridge: Cambridge University Press. See also Durrell (1991).

1992 (1995). Eckhard-Black, Christine, and Ruth Whittle. *German: a handbook of grammar, current usage and word power.* London: Cassell.

1992. Fuhr, Gerhard. *A grammar of scientific German.* Heidelberg: Groos.

1992–1994. Hermann, Christiane, John Hill, Gwynne Pomfrett, et al. *Gute Reise!* Cheltenham: Mary Glasgow. Vol. 1 is by first three authors; vol. 2 by Anna Lise Gordon; vol. 4 is by Gordon and Harriette Lanzer. See Wegner (1999: 308–314).

1992 (2000). Jones, Alan J., and Gudrun Lawlor. *Practice in German grammar: for students starting post-16 courses.* London: Mary Glasgow.

1992. Nicholson, Sally, and Louise Estill. *German telephone skills for business.* Gerrards Cross: LETA Telephone Training.

1992 (vol. 1), 1994 (vol. 2), 1996 (vol. 3). Saunders, Keith, Mike Simpson, and Karin Ernst. *Alle einsteigen!* vol. 3 London: Hodder & Stoughton. See also Stocker & Saunders (1988).

1992. Wessels, Dieter, and Brian Hill. *Business German.* Basingstoke: Mcmillan.

1992. Yeomans, Andy, Ulrike Yeomans, et al. *Talking Business German.* Cheltenham, England: Stanley Thornes.

1992–1993. West, Jonathan. *Progressive grammar of German.* Dublin: Authentik. 4 vols.

1993. Clarke, Stephen. *Collins business German: language pack.* [S.l.], Harper Collins.

1993. Crean, John E. *Deutsche Sprache und Landeskunde.* New York; London: McGraw-Hill.

1993 (1996). Durrell, Martin. *Practising German grammer: a workbook for use with Hammer's German grammar and usage.* London: Arnold. See Durrell (1991).

1993. Hartley, Paul. *Freut mich! German for business.* Language consultants Fritz Berger and Renate Bohne-Berger. London: Pitman, 1993.

1993. Kohl, Katrin, and Tristam Carrington-Windo. *German means business: a multi-media language course in business German.* London: BBC.

1993 (1), 1994 (2), 1995 (3), 1996 (4 rot and grün). McNab, Rosi, and Alan O'Brien. *Auf Deutsch!* 5 vols. Oxford: Heinemann. See Wegner (1999: 314–315).

1993a (1994). Rowlinson, William. *German grammar.* Oxford: OUP. See Rowlinson (1967–69).

1993b. Rowlinson, William. *German verbs.* Oxford: OUP. See Rowlinson (1967–69).

1993. Rowlinson, William, Liselotte Lehnigk, et al. *Deutschland hier und jetzt.* Oxford: OUP. See Rowlinson (1967–69).

1993. Tenberg, Reinhard. *Get by in business German: a quick beginner's course for business people.* London: BBC Books. See Kothe & Sprankling (1995), Tenberg & Rings (1996), Tenberg et al. (1996).

1993. Wightwick, Charles Christopher Brooke. *German grammar handbook.* Oxford: Berlitz.

1994. Eichinger, Hubert, Maris Grinvalds and E. Barton. *German once a week. Book 1.* Guildford: Hermes.

1994. Fink, Stefan R. *Spiralen: intermediate German for proficiency.* Boston: Mass.: Heinle & Heinle.

1994 (2nd ed. 2000). Hares, Rod J., David Hood, et al. *Durchblick: Deutsch für die Oberstufe 1 / Überblick: Deutsch für die Oberstufe 2.* London: John Murray. See Hares & Timm (2001).

1994. Howarth, Marianne. *Absolute beginners' business German.* London: Hodder and Stoughton.

1994 (1995, 1999). Levick, Val, Glenise Radford, and Alasdair McKeane. *German grammar: your guide.* Malvern: Malvern Language Guides.

1994. Russ, Charles V. J. *The German language today: a linguistic introduction.* London: Routledge.

1994, 2000 (new. ed.). Sandry, Claire, et. al. *Brennpunkt.* Cheltenham: Nelson Thornes (New edition of Student's Book published by Sandry et. al. (1999)).

1994. Shaw, Gisela. *Deutsche Juristen im Gespräch: Textbuch.* Munich: Klett Edition Deutsch.

1994 (1999). Zorach, Cecile. *English grammar for students of German: the study guide for those learning German.* London: Arnold.

1995. Briggs, Jeanine, and Beate Engel-Doyle. *Alles in allem: an intermediate German course: readings & activities.* New York; London: McGraw-Hill.

1995. Clay, Gudrun. *Geschäftsdeutsch: an introduction to business German.* New York; London: McGraw-Hill.

1995. *Collins gem German grammar / [editors: Ilse MacLean, Lorna Sinclair-Knight].* Glasgow: HarperCollins.

1995 (1998). Hatherall, Glyn, and Dietlinde Hatherall. *Colloquial German: a complete language course.* London: Routledge.

1995. Kothe, Joachim, and Iris Sprankling. *Get by in German: a quick beginner's course for holidaymakers and business people* (revised ed. of Tenberg 1993). London: BBC Enterprises.

1995. Lanzer, Harriette. *The key to German grammar for Key Stages 3 and 4*. Cheltenham, MGP International.

1995. Prowe, Gunhild, Jill Schneider and William Rowlinson. *The Oxford paperback German dictionary and grammar*. Oxford: Oxford University Press. See Rowlinson (1967–69).

1995. Stocker & Saunders. 2nd ed. of Stocker & Saunders (1988), q. v.

1995. Roche, Jörg. *Für- und Wider-Sprüche: eine integriertes Text-Buch für Colleges und Universitäten*. New Haven; London: Yale University Press.

1995. Vandevelde, Helen. *The beginner's guide to business German: how to choose a German business language course and use it successfully*. Bedford, Strasbourg-Rhein (UK).

1996. Arthur, Lore, and Open University. *Café Einklang: a fresh start in German*. London: Hodder & Stoughton.

1996. Dodd, Bill [et al]. *Modern German grammar: a practical guide*. London: Routledge. See also Coles & Dodd (1998).

1996. Hartley, Paul, and Gertrud Robins. *German business correspondence*. London: Routledge.

1996. Kirk, Graeme S. F. *Grammatik ohne Panik*. St Leonards-on-Sea: Senlac Language Publications.

1996 (2000). Klapper, John, and Trudi McMahon. *Aktion grammatik!* London: Hodder & Stoughton.

1996. Tenberg, Reinhard, and Guido Rings. *BBC German grammar. Consultant Duncan Sidwell*. London: BBC Books. See Tenberg (1993).

1996. Tenberg, Reinhard, Susan Ainslie, et al. *Deutsch plus [kit]: a multi-media course for beginners learning German*. London: BBC. See Tenberg (1993).

1996. Whittaker, Helga M. *Hochdeutsch: as spoken and taught by a German*. Lanham MD; London: University Press of America.

1996. Whittle, Ruth [et al]. *Modern German grammar: a practical guide to grammar and usage*. London: Routledge.

1997. *BBC German learner's dictionary: German-English, English-German: the ideal companion for all learners of German*. London: BBC Books.

1998. Coles, Waltraud, and Bill Dodd. *Reading German: a course and reference book*. Oxford: Oxford University Press. See also Dodd et al. (1996).

1998. Johnson, Sally A. *Exploring the German language*. London: Arnold.

1998. Matthews, Judith, and Jeanne Wood. *Talk German*. London: BBC.

1998 (2000). Price, Linette, and Marjorie Semple. *Help yourself to essential German grammar: a grammar reference and workbook GCSE/Standard Grade*. Harlow: Longman.

1998. Russ, Jennifer M. *German grammar*. London: Teach Yourself Books.

1998. Schicker, Corinna. *German*. London: BBC Educational Publishing.

1999. Ashworth-Fiedler, Susan. *Beginner's German grammar*. London: Teach Yourself.

1999. Burke, Claire, et al. *Kenntnisse: an advanced German course.* By Claire Burke, Edmund Burke and Susanne Parker. London: Routledge.

1999. Esser, Martina, Michael Spencer, et al. *Aufgeschlossen.* Cheltenham, England, Mary Glasgow Publications.

1999. Paulsell, Patricia Ryan, Anne-Katrin Gramberg, et al. *German for business and economics.* East Lansing: Michigan State University Press.

1999. Rehahn, Jens Peter. *Langenscheidt's dictionary telecommunications: English-German/German-English.* Berlin: Langenscheidt; London: Routledge.

1999. Webster, Paul. *The German handbook: your guide to speaking and writing German.* Cambridge: Cambridge University Press.

2000–2010

2000. Brien, Alistair, Sharon Brien, Colin Christie, and Heike Schommartz. *Schauplatz.* Oxford: Heinemann.

2000. Fischer, Dagmar. *Deutschland erleben. Ein Lehrbuch für irische Studenten.* Dublin: Gill & Macmillan Ltd.

2000. Hares et al., *Durchblick*, 2nd ed. See Hares et al. (1994) above.

2000. McNeill, Jennie, Judith Ram Prasad, et al. *Neue Aussichten. Stage 1 Etappen. Stage 2 Ziele.* London: Hodder & Stoughton.

2000. Sandry et al. See Sandry et al. (1994) above.

2001 (1st ed. 1994). Hares, Rod J., and Alexandra Timm. *Überblick: Deutsch für die Oberstufe.* London: John Murray. See Hares et al. (1994).

2001. Hermann, Christiane, Morag McCrorie, et al. *Zeitgeist 1.* Oxford: Oxford University Press.

2001. Jones, Alan G., and Gudrun Lawlor. *Practice in German grammar: for students starting post-16 courses.* Cheltenham, Mary Glasgow.

2001. McCrorie, Morag, Dagmar Sauer, et al. *Zeitgeist.* Oxford: Oxford University Press.

2001. Tebbutt, Susan. *Klaro!: a practical guide to German grammar.* London: Arnold.

2002. Durrell, Martin. *Hammer's German grammar and usage.* London: Arnold.

2002. Fehringer, Carol. *German grammar in context: analysis and practice.* London: Arnold.

2003. Coggle, Paul, and Heiner Schenke. *[Teach Yourself] German.* London: Hodder & Stoughton.

2009. Coggle, Paul, and Heiner Schenke. *Germana fara profesor cu 2 CD* (translated by Magda Dumitru). Bucharest: Romana.

2010 (2nd ed.). Coggle, Paul, and Heiner Schenke. *Speak German with Confidence.* Audio CD. London: Teach Yourself.

Secondary Literature

Ainslie, Susan, Sue Purcell and Centre for Information on Language Teaching and Research. 2001. *Mixed-ability teaching in language learning*. London: CILT.

Allan, Keith. 2007. *The Western Classical Tradition in Linguistics*. London: Equinox.

Ammer, Reinhard. 1988. *Das Deutschlandbild in den Lehrwerken für Deutsch als Fremdsprache*. Munich: iudicium.

Amrhein, Klaus. 2005. *Biographisches Handbuch zur Geschichte der Deutschen Leichtathletik 1898–2005*. 2nd ed. vol. 2. Darmstadt: Deutsche Leichtathletik Promotion- und Projektgesellschaft.

Angiolillo, Paul F. 1947. *Armed Forces' Foreign Language Teaching: Critical Evaluation and Implications*. New York: Vanni.

Anklam, Ewa, and Grindel, Susanne. 2010. Europa im Bild – Bilder von Europa: Europarepräsentationen in deutschen, französischen und polnischen Geschichtsschulbüchern in historischer Perspektive. In: Carsten Heinze und Eva Matthes (eds.), *Das Bild im Schulbuch* (Beiträge zur historischen und systematischen Schulbuchforschung). Bad Heilbrunn: Klinkhardt, pp. 93–108.

Anon. 1797. [Review of] Uttiv, J.: *A complete practical German grammar*. Göttingen: Vandenhoeck & Ruprecht 1796. *Allgemeine Literarische Zeitung* 3, No. 285, p. 632. Accessible online at *http://zs.thulb.uni-jena.de*.

Apelt, Walter. 1967. *Die kulturkundliche Bewegung im Unterricht der neueren Sprachen in Deutschland 1886 bis 1945. Ein Irrweg deutscher Philologien*. Berlin: Volk und Wissen.

Apelt, Walter. 1991. *Lehren und Lerner fremder Sprachen. Grundorientierungen und Methoden in historischer Sicht*. Berlin: Volk und Wissen.

Apple, Michael W. 1979, 4th ed. 2004. *Ideology and curriculum*. New York; London: Routledge; Falmer.

Apple, Michael. 1992. The Text and Cultural Politics. *Educational Researcher* 21(4): 4–19.

AQA (Assessment and Qualifications Alliance). 2006. General Certificate Examination. German 5661–6661. 2008 Specification: Copyright © 2006 AQA and its licensors; was available via (www.aqa.org.uk) [but this version is no longer accessible online].

Arnauld, Antoine, and Claude Lancelot. 1660 [1966]. *Grammaire générale et raisonnée ou La Grammaire de Port-Royal*. Edition critique présentée par H. E. Brekle. Stuttgart-Bad Canstatt: Frommann-Holzboog.

Arnold, E. P., and Fabian Waren. 1900. The teaching of modern languages in preparatory schools. In *Special Reports on Educational Subjects*, Vol. 6: *Preparatory Schools for Boys: Their Place in English Secondary Education. Presented to both Houses of Parliament by Command of Her Majesty*, Cd. 418, ed. Board of Education, 231–247. London: H. M. S. O.

Arthur, Lore, & Stella Hurd (Centre for Information on Language Teaching, and Research). Eds. 1992. *The adult language learner: a guide to good teaching practice.* Illustrations by Caroline Mortlock. London: CILT.

Assmann, Aleida, and Dietrich Harth. 1991. *Kultur als Lebenswelt und Monument.* Frankfurt am Main: Fischer Taschenbuch Verlag.

Assmann, Jan, and Tonio Hölscher. 1988. *Kultur und Gedächtnis.* Frankfurt am Main: Suhrkamp.

Auroux, Sylvain, Koerner, Konrad, Hans-Josef Niederehe, and Kees Versteegh. Eds. 2000–06. *History of the Language Sciences. An International Handbook on the Evolution of the Study of Language from the Beginnings to the Present.* 3 vols. (HSK 18: 1–3). Berlin: de Gruyter

Bagster-Collins, E. W. (Elijah William). 1904; reprinted 1907, 1908, 1910, 1913, 1915, 1916. *The teaching of German in secondary schools.* New York: University of Colombia Press.

Bahlsen, Leopold. 1905, rpt. 2002. *The Teaching of Modern Languages,* translated by M. Blakemore Evans, 2ⁿᵈ ed. Boston: Ginn. Rpt. in Howatt & Smith (2002, V: 333–435).

Barrett, Martyn. 2007. *Children's Knowledge, Beliefs and Feelings about Nations and National Groups.* Hove: Psychology Press.

Bartsch, Renate. 1987. *Norms of language. Theoretical and practical aspects* (= Bartsch's translation of her *Sprachnormen. Theorie und Praxis*, Tübingen: Niemeyer, 1985). London: Longman.

Bayer-Klötzer, Eva-Suzanne. 1979. Kneller, Sir Godfrey. In: *Neue Deutsche Biographie* 12, pp. 176–77.

Bayley, Susan. 1989. 'Life is too short to learn German': Modern languages in English elementary education, 1872–1904. *History of Education* 18: 57–70.

Bayley, Susan. 1991. Modern Languages: An 'Ideal of Humane Learning': The Leathes Report of 1918. *Journal of Educational Adminstration and History* 23: 11–24.

Bayley, Susan, and Donna Yavorsky Ronish. 1992. Gender, modern languages and the curriculum in Victorian England. *History of Education* 21: 363–382.

Bayley, Susan. 1998. The Direct Method and modern language teaching in England 1880–1918. *History of Education* 27: 39–57.

Beal, Joan, Carmela Nocera and Massimo Sturiale, Eds. 2008. *Perspectives on Prescriptivism.* Frankfurt: Peter Lang.

Becher, Ursula A. J., and Matthias Hartung. Eds. 1996. *Grenzen und Ambivalenzen: Analysen zum Deutschlandbild in den Niederlanden und in niederlandischen Schulbüchern.* Frankfurt: Diesterweg.

Bell, Alexander Melville. 1867. *Visible speech: the science of universal alphabetics: or self-interpreting physiological letters, for the writing of all languages in one alphabet. Illustrated by tables, diagrams, and examples. By Alex. Melville Bell.* New York: Simpkin, Marshall & Co.; London: N. Trübner & Co.

Benson, A. C. (Arthur Christopher?). 1907. The place of modern languages in the secondary curriculum. Presidential Address to the Modern Language Association, Durham, January 4. *Modern Language Teaching* 3(1): 6–18; also in *Journal of Education* 12: 117–121.

Berghahn, Volker, and Hanna Schissler. Eds. 1987a. *Perceptions of History. International Textbook Research on Britain, Germany and the United States.* Oxford, New York & Hamburg: Berg.

Berghahn, Volker, and Hanna Schissler. 1987b. Introduction. History Textbooks and Perceptions of the Past. In *Perceptions of History. International Textbook Research on Britain, Germany and the United States,* eds. Volker Berghahn and Hanna Schissler, pp. 1–16. Oxford: Berg.

Bithell, Jethro. 1921. The Teaching of German (Commercial). In *The Encyclopaedia and Dictionary of Education,* ed. F. Watson, 692–693. London: Pitman.

Birke, Adolf M., Magnus Brechtken and Alaric Searle, Eds. 2000. *An Anglo-German Dialogue. The Munich Lectures on the History of International Relations.* Munich: K. G. Saur.

Blackall, Eric. 1959. *The emergence of German as a literary language.* Cambridge: CUP. 2nd ed. Ithaca & London: Cornell University Press, 1978.

Blackie, John Stuart. 1852. *On the Studying and Teaching of Languages.* Edinburgh: Sutherland & Knox

Blamires, David. 1990. British Knowledge of German before the High Dutch Minerva. *German Life and Letters* 43: 102–112.

Blusch, Martina, Ed. 1992. *Ein italienisch-deutsches Sprachlehrbuch des 15. Jahrhunderts. Edition der Handschrift Universitätsbibliothek Heidelberg Pal. Ger. 657 und räumlich-zeitliche Einordnung des deutschen Textes.* Frankfurt am Main: Peter Lang.

Board of Education. 1912. *Circular No. 797. Modern languages (re-issued 1925).* London: HMSO

Board of Education. 1928. *The position of French in the First School Certificate Examinations. (Educational Pamphlets 70).* London: HMSO.

Board of Education. 1929. *Position of German in Grant-Aided Secondary Schools in England. (Educational Pamphlets 77).* London: HMSO.

Board of Education. 1930a. *Memorandum on the teaching of foreign languages in certain types of schools. (Educational Pamphlets 82).* London: HMSO.

Board of Education. 1930b. *Second Interim Report of the committee of education for Salesmanship. Modern Languages.* London: HMSO.

Boehning, John. 1977. *The Reception of Classical German Literature in England, 1760–1860: a documentary history from contemporary periodicals.* New York and London: Garland Publishers.

Boiling, Graham. 2005. *Secret students on parade: cold-war memories of JSSL, Crail.* Powys: Old Station Offices.

Borst, Arno. 1995 [1960]. *Der Turmbau von Babel. Geschichte der Meinungen über Ursprung und Vielfalt der Sprachen und Völker.* Stuttgart: Hiersemann. Reprinted Munich: DTV, 1995.

Bosselmann-Cyran, Kristian. 1997. Fremdsprachen und Fremdsprachenerwerb im Mittelalter und in der frühen Neuzeit. Forschungen zum Turmbau. In *Fremdsprachen und Fremdsprachenerwerb,* ed. Kristian Bosselmann-Cyran. Berlin: Akademie Verlag.

Bourdillon, Hilary. 1992. *History and social studies: methodologies of textbook analysis: report of the educational research workshop held in Braunschweig, Germany, 11–14 September 1990.* Amsterdam: Swets & Zeitlinger.

Braune, Wilhelm, and Ernst A. Ebbinghaus. 1994. *Althochdeutsches Lesebuch.* Tübingen: Niemeyer.

Brechtken, Magnus. 2000. Personality, Image and Perception: Patterns and Problems of Anglo-German Relations in the nineteenth and twentieth Centuries. In *An Anglo-German Dialogue. The Munich Lectures on the History of International Relations,* eds. Adolf M. Birke, Magnus Brechtken and Alaric Searle, pp. 13–40. Munich: K. G. Saur.

Brereton, Cloudsley, D. L. Savory, Walter Rippmann, and F. B. Kirkman. 1908. Report on the conditions of modern (foreign) language instruction in secondary schools. *Modern Language Teaching* 4: 33–38, 65–68.

Brereton, Cloudsley. 1930. *Modern Language teaching in day and evening schools with special reference to London.* London: University of London Press.

Breul, Karl. 1898. *The teaching of modern foreign languages and the training of teachers.* Cambridge: CUP.

Breul, Karl. 1911. Aims and claims of modern languages. Presidential address by Dr Karl Breul, Schröder Professor of German in the University of Cambridge. *Modern Language Teaching* 7: 4–19.

Breymann, Hermann Wilhelm. 1895, rpt. 2002. *Die neusprachliche Reform-Literatur von 1876–1893: Eine bibiliographisch-kritische Übersicht.* Leipzig: Deichert. Rpt. in Howatt & Smith (2002, V: 1–164).

Breymann, Hermann Wilhelm. 1900, rpt. 2002. *Die neusprachliche Reform-Literatur von 1894–1899. Eine bibiliographisch-kritische Übersicht.* . Leipzig: Deichert. Rpt. in Howatt & Smith (2002, V: 165–268).

Bridge, G. F. 1921. French and German in Higher Education. *Contemporary Review* 120: 805–810.

Brigstocke, W. O. 1905. Oral Examinations. *Modern Language Teaching* 1: 110–112.

Budziak, Renata. 2010. *Deutsch als Fremdsprache in Polen. Sprachlehrbücher aus dem 16. bis 18. Jahrhundert.* Wiesbaden: Harrassowitz.

Burnett, Robyn, and Ken Luebbering. 1996. *German settlement in Missouri: new land, old ways.* Columbia & London: University of Missouri Press.

Burstall, C., M. Jamieson, S. Cohen, and M. Hargreaves 1974. *Primary French in the Balance.* NFER.

Buttjes, Dieter. 1991. Culture in German foreign language teaching: making use of an ambiguous past. In: *Mediating languages and cultures.* Ed. Dieter Buttjes and Michael Byram, pp. 47–62. Clevedon: Multilingual Matters.

Byram, Michael. 1989. *Cultural studies in foreign language education.* Clevedon: Multilingual Matters.

Byram, Michael, ed. 1993. *Germany: its representation in textbooks for teaching German in Great Britain.* Frankfurt am Main: Diesterweg.

Byram, Michael, and Christiane Baumgardt. 1993. Textbook analysis: *Deutsche Heute*. In *Germany: its representation in textbooks for teaching German in Great Britain*, ed. Michael Byram, pp. 115–139. Braunschweig: Diesterweg.

Byram, Michael. 1997. *Teaching and Assessing Intercultural Communicative Competence*. Clevedon: Multilingual Matters.

Byram, Michael, ed. 2000. *Routledge Encyclopaedia of Language Teaching and Learning*. London: Routledge. 2nd ed. ed Byram and Adelheid Hu, 2012.

Byram, Michael. 2004. Audiolingual method. *Routledge Encyclopaedia of Language Teaching and Learning*, ed. Michael Byram, pp. 58–60. London: Routledge.

Byram, Michael. 2008. *From Foreign Language Education to Education for Intercultural Citizenship. Essays and Reflection*. Clevedon: Multilingual Matters.

Cambridge Local Examinations and Lectures Syndicate Examination papers, report, syllabi, etc. since 1858. Held in Cambridge University Library, Cam.c.11.51

Canning, John. 2007. *Five years on. The language landscape in 2007*. London: CILT.

Caravolas, Jean-Antoine. 1994. *La didactique des langues. Précis d'histoire I. 1450–1700. Anthologie I. A L'ombre de Quintilien*. Tübingen: Gunter Narr.

Caravolas, Jean-Antoine. 1995. *Le point sur l'histoire de l'enseignement des langues (ca. 3000–1950)*. Anjou, Quebec: Centre Educatif et Culturel.

Caravolas, Jean. 2000a. *Histoire de la didactique des langues au siècle des Lumières: précis et anthologie thématique*. Montréal & Tübingen: Presses de l'Université de Montréal & Gunter Narr Verlag.

Caravolas, Jean. 2000b. Les origines de la didactique des langues en tant que discipline. In *History of the Language Sciences*, Vol. 1, eds. Sylvain Auroux et al., pp. 1009–1022. Berlin: de Gruyter.

Carl, Jenny, and Patrick Stevenson. 2007. Being a German-speaker in Central Europe: Language Policies and the Negotiation of Idenities. In *Standard, Variation and Language Change in Germanic Languages*, eds. Christian Fandrych and Reinier Salverda, pp. 91–112. Tübingen: Gunter Narr.

Carr, Charles. 1935. German grammars in England in the nineteenth century. *Modern Language Review* 30: 483–501.

Carr, Charles. 1937. Early German grammars in England. *Journal of English and Germanic Philology* 36: 455–474.

Carr, Jo, and Anns Pauwels. 2009. *Boys and foreign language learning: real boys don't do languages*. Basingstoke: Palgrave Macmillan.

Carter, Sarah Anne. 2010. On an Object Lesson, or Don't Eat the Evidence. *The Journal of the History of Childhood and Youth* 3: 712.

Chaney, Edward. 1998, revised ed. 2000. *The Evolution of the Grand Tour: Anglo-Italian Cultural Relations since the Renaissance*. London and Portland OR: Frank Cass; revised edition, London: Routledge.

Charlton, Kenneth. 1965. *Education in Renaissance England*. London and Toronto: Routledge and Kegan Paul; University of Toronto Press.

Chaytor, H. J. 1909. The teaching of German in middle and higher forms. *Modern Language Teaching* 5: 45–49.

Chomsky, Noam. 1957. *Syntactic structures*. The Hague & Paris: Mouton.

Christ, Herbert. 2005. Rekonstruktion von Fremdsprachenlehrmethoden um 1800. In *Sprachen der Bildung – Bildung durch Sprachen im Deutschland des 18. und 19. Jahrhunderts*, eds. Werner Hüllen and Friederike Klippel, pp. 127–152. Wiesbaden: Harrassowitz.

Christ, Herbert, and Hans-Joachim Rang. Eds. 1985. *Fremdsprachenunterricht unter staatlicher Verwaltung 1700 bis 1945. Eine Dokumentation amtlicher Richtlinien und Verordnungen*. 7 vols. Tübingen: Narr.

CILT (Centre for Information on Language Teaching and Research), ed. 1972. *Teaching modern languages across the ability range: papers from a conference on teaching a foreign language to all pupils and across the ability range, held at State House, High Holborn, London, on 27th and 28th March 1972 (CILT reports and papers 8)*. London: Centre for Information on Language Teaching and Research.

CILT (Centre for Information on Language Teaching and Research), ed. 1976. *German in the United Kingdom: problems and prospects: papers from a colloquium convened in November 1975: (CILT Reports and papers 13)*: London: Centre for Information on Language Teaching and Research.

CILT (Centre for Information on Language Teaching and Research), ed. 1986. *German in the United Kingdom. Issues and Opportunities. Papers from a conference held at Regent's College, London, 11–13 July, 1985*. London: Centre for Information on Language Teaching and Research.

CILT (Centre for Information on Language Teaching and Research). 2002. *A new landscape for languages*. London: Centre for Information on Language Teaching and Research.

CILT (Centre for Information on Language Teaching and Research). 2005. *Early language learning DVD* [videorecording]. London: CILT, the National Centre for Languages.

Clyne, Michael. 1984. *Language and society in the German-speaking countries*. Cambridge: CUP.

Clyne, Michael. 1995. *The German language in a changing Europe*. Cambridge: CUP.

Cohen, Michèle. 1999. Manliness, Effeminacy and the French: Gender and the Construction of National Character in Eighteenth Century England. In *English Masculinities 1660–1800*, eds. Tim Hitchcock and Michèle Cohen. London: Longman.

Cohen, Michèle. 2001. The Grand Tour: Language, National Identity and Masculinity. *Changing English: Studies in Reading and Culture* 8, 2:1 29–141.

Cohen, Michèle 2002. *Fashioning Masculinity. National Identity and Language in the Eighteenth Century*. London: Routledge.

Colbeck, Charles. 1887. *On the Teaching of Modern Languages in Theory and Practice*. Cambridge: CUP.

Coleman, Algernon. 1931. *The teaching of modern foreign languages in the United States. American and Candadian Committee on Modern languages*. New York: Macmillan.

Coleman, Algernon. 1934. *Experiments and studies in Modern Language teaching.* Chicago: University of Chicago Press.

Coleman, James A. (Centre for Information on Language Teaching and Research). 1996. *Studying languages: a survey of British and European students: the proficiency, background, attitudes and motivations of students of foreign languages in the United Kingdom and Europe.* London: Centre for Information on Language Teaching and Research.

Coleman, Jim. 1999. Stereotypes, objectives and the *Auslandsaufenthalt.* In *Intercultural perspectives. Images of Germany in Education and the Media,* ed. Reinhard Tenberg, pp. 145–171. Munich: iudicium.

Collins, Beverly, and Inger Mees. 1999. *The real Professor Higgins. The life and career of Daniel Jones.* Berlin & New York: Mouton de Gruyter.

Collins, Beverly, and Inger Mees, eds. 2002. *Daniel Jones. Selected Works.* London Routledge.

Collins, H. F. 1934. Modern languages. In *The Yearbook of Education 1934,* eds. Eustace Percy and M. P. Former, pp. 417–428. London: Evans.

Colombat, Bernard, and Manfred Peters. 2009. *Mithridates: (1555). Conrad Gessner. Introduction, texte latin, traduction française, annotation et index par Bernard Colombat et Manfred Peters.* Geneva: Droz.

Comenius, Johann Amos. 1658. *Orbis Sensualium Pictus […]. Die Sichtbare Welt […].* Nuremberg: Noribergae Typis et sumptibus Michaelis Endteri. [*Johannis Amos Comenii Opera Omnia.* 17. Prague: Academia, 1970].

Comenius, Johann Amos. 1670. *Janua linguarum trilinguis; sive, Johannis-Amos-Comenii Janua linguarum novissime ab ipso authore recognita, aucta, emendata: adjunctis metaphrasi Graeca et Anglicana versione.* Londini: typis J. Redmayne, & veneunt apud J. Williams.

Considine, John. 2008. *Dictionaries in Early Modern Europe. Lexicography and the Making of Heritage.* Cambridge: Cambridge University Press.

Considine, John. 2010. Why was Claude de Saumaise interested in the Scythian hypothesis? *Language and History* 53: 81–96.

Corder, S. Pit. 1967. The significance of learners' errors. *International Review of Applied Linguistics* 5: 161–169.

Crawford, Keith. 2003. The role and purpose of textbooks. *International Journal of Historical Learning, Teaching and Research* 3(2): 5–10.

Crook, David. 2002. Local authorities and comprehensivization in England and Wales, 1944–1974. *Oxford Review of Education* 28 (2–3): 247–260.

Dakin, Julian. 1973. *The Language Laboratory and Language Learning.* London: Longman.

Dance, E. H. 1955. Anglo-German Textbook exchange. The first five years. *Internationales Jahrbuch für Geschichts-Unterricht* 4: 258–259.

Davidson, J. M. C. Ed. (Centre for Information on Language Teaching and Research). 1981. *Issues in language education: papers arising from the second assembly of the National Congress on Languages in Education, 1978–80* (NCLE [National Congress on

Languages in: Education] papers and reports 3). London: Centre for Information on Language Teaching and Research.

Davies, Anna Morpurgo. 1998. *History of Linguistics* (series ed. G. Lepschy). Volume IV: *Nineteenth Century Linguistics*. London: Longman.

Davies, Winifred, and Nils Langer. 2006. *The making of bad language. Lay linguistic stigmatisations in German: past and present*. Frankfurt: Peter Lang.

del Valle, Carlos. 2000. Hebrew linguistics in Arabic. In: *HSK* 18.1 ed. Auroux et al. Berlin: de Gruyter, vol. 1: 234–239.

DES (Department of Education and Science). 1977. *Modern Languages in Comprehensive Schools* HMI Series: *Matters for Discussion* 3. London: HMSO.

DES (Department of Education and Science). Inspectorate of Schools. 1987. *An inquiry into practice in 22 comprehensive schools where a foreign language forms part of the curriculum for all or almost all pupils up to age 16*. London: Department of Education and Science/ HMSO.

DES (Department of Education and Science). 1991. National Curriculum: Draft order for modern foreign languages. London, 11 July 1991.

DES (Department of Education and Science), Welsh Office. 1983a. *Foreign languages in the school curriculum: a consultative paper*. London: DES.

DES (Department of Education and Science), Welsh Office. 1983b. *A Survey of Modern Languages in the Secondary Schools of Wales*: Education Survey 11. Cardiff: HMSO.

DES (Department of Education and Science), Welsh Office. 1988. *Foreign languages in the school curriculum: a statement of policy*. London: HMSO.

Deumert, Ana, and Wim Vandenbussche. Eds. 2003. *Germanic Standardizations. Past to Present*. IMPACT Studies in Language and Society 18. Amsterdam: Benjamins.

Diehl, Erika. 1975. *Deutsche Literatur im französischen Deutschlesebuch 1879–1970*. Wiesbaden: Athenaion.

Doerk, Gabriele. 1990. *Spracherwerb und Deutschlandkunde: Zum Deutschlandbild in englischen Deutschlehrbüchern*. Diss. Uni-Gesamthochschule Duisburg.

Doff, Sabine. 2002. *Englischlernen zwischen Tradition und Innovation: Fremdsprachenunterricht für Mädchen im 19. Jahrhundert*. Munich: Langenscheidt-Longman.

Doff, Sabine. 2007. *Englischdidaktik in der BRD 1949–1989*. Munich: Langenscheidt.

Donmall, B. Gillian. Ed. (Centre for Information on Language Teaching and Research). 1985. *Language awareness* (NCLE [National Congress on Languages in Education] papers and reports 6). London: Centre for Information on Language Teaching and Research.

Doughty, Catherine. 1991. Second Language Instruction does make a difference. *Studies in Second Language Acquisition* 19: 431–469.

Doyé, Peter. 1991. *Großbritannien: seine Darstellung in deutschen Schulbüchern für den Englischunterricht*. Frankfurt: Moritz Diesterweg.

Doyé, Peter. 1993. Neuere Konzepte der Fremdsprachenerziehung und die Bedeutung für die Schulbuchkritik. In: Germany: Its representation in textbooks for teaching German in Great Britain, ed. Michael Byram, pp. 19–29. Frankfurt am Main: Diesterweg.

Driedger, Otto. 1907. *Johann Königs (John King's) deutsch-englische Grammatiken und ihre späteren Bearbeitungen. 1706–1802. Versuch einer kritischen Behandlung.* Diss. Marburg.

Duden. 1956. *Der Große Duden. 2. Das Stilwörterbuch der deutschen Sprache.* Mannheim: Duden.

Duden. 1985, 1997, 2001, 2007, 2011. *Richtiges und gutes Deutsch. Wörterbuch der sprachlichen Zweifelsfälle. Grammatische, stilistische und rechtschreibliche Zweifelsfälle – Abkürzungen – Fremdwortfragen – Anreden und Anschriften – Bewerbungsschreiben – Lebenslauf u.a.* 3rd edition 1985; 4th edition 1997; 5th edition 2001, 7th edition 2011. Mannheim: Duden.

Durrell, Martin. 1991. *Hammer's German grammar and usage.* London: Edward Arnold.

Durrell, Martin. 1992. *Using German: a guide to contemporary usage.* Cambridge: Cambridge University Press.

Durrell, Martin. 2004. Variation im Deutschen aus der Sicht von Deutsch als Fremdsprache. *Der Deutschunterricht* 56: 69–77.

Durrell, Martin. 2005. Sprachnormen, Sprachvariation und Sprachwandel im DaF-Unterricht. In *Perspektiven der Germanistik in Europa. Tagungsbeiträge*, eds. Eva Neuland, Konrad Ehlich and Werner Roggausch, pp. 189–193. Munich: iudicium.

Eco, Umberto. 1995. *The search for the perfect language.* Oxford: Blackwell.

Education, Ministry of. 1956. *Modern Languages.* (*Pamphlet*, No. 29). London: HMSO.

Eichinger, Ludwig M., et al. 2009. *Aktuelle Spracheinstellungen in Deutschland. Erste Ergebnisse einer bundesweiten Repräsentativumfrage.* Mannheim: Institut für Deutsche Sprache/Universität Mannheim.

Elliott, Geoffrey, and Harold Shukman. 2003. *Secret classrooms: a memoir of the Cold War.* London: St Ermin's.

Emmans, Keith. 1976. The adviser's view (by Keith Emmans, National Association of Language Advisers). In *German in the United Kingdom: Problems and Prospects*, ed. CILT, pp. 27–28. London: CILT.

Erll, Astrid. 2008. Towards a conceptual foundation for Cultural Memory studies. In *Cultural Memory Studies. An international and interdisciplinary handbook*, eds. Astrid Erll and Ansgar Nünning, pp. 1–18. Berlin: de Gruyter.

Erll, Astrid, and Ansgar Nünning, Eds. 2008. *Cultural Memory Studies. An international and interdisciplinary handbook.* Berlin: de Gruyter.

Ernst, Adolphine B. (Compiler). 1918. The status of German in Great Britain. *Monatshefte für deutsche Sprache und Pädagogik* 19 (4): 110–113.

Eroms, Hans–Werner. 2006. Die Wegbereiter einer deutschen Valenzgrammatik. In: *Dependenz und Valenz.* Ed. Vilmos Ágel, pp. 159–70. Berlin: de Gruyter.

Eurviews. *Europa im Schulbuch* (http://www.eurviews.eu/en/en/start.html). Accessed July 2014.

Extermann, Blaise. 2013. *Une langue étrangère et nationale. Histoire de l'enseignement de l'allemand en Suisse romande (1790–1840).* Neuchâtel: Editions ALPHIL Presses universitaires suisses.

F. R. [not further identified]. 1930. Reviews: German Records. *Modern Languages. A Review of Foreign Lettters, Science and the Arts. Published by the Modern Language Association* 12: 58–59.

Fabian, Bernhard. 1985. Englisch als neue Fremdsprache des 18. Jahrhunderts. In *Mehrsprachigkeit in der deutschen Aufklärung*, ed. Dieter Kimpel, pp. 178–196. Hamburg: Felix Meiner.

Faulstich, Katja. 2008. *Konzepte des Hochdeutschen. Der Sprachnormierungsdiskurs im 18. Jahrhundert.* Berlin: de Gruyter.

Findlay, J. J. 1930. A note on phonetics in the classroom. *Modern Languages. A review of Foreign Letters, Science and the Arts* (October 1930): 23–26.

Fink, Matthias C. 2003. Das Deutschlandbild in dänischen Lehrwerken für den Deutschunterricht in der Folkeskole. *Info DaF* 30: 476–488.

Finkenstaedt, Thomas. 1992. Auf der Suche nach dem Göttinger Ordinarius des Englischen, John Thompson (1697–1768). In: *Fremdsprachenunterricht 1500–1800.* Ed. Konrad Schröder, pp. 57–74. Wiesbaden: Harrassowitz.

Fischer, Joachim. 2000. *Das Deutschlandbild der Iren 1890–1939.* Heidelberg: Winter.

Fischer, Joachim. 2001. Deutschunterricht und Germanistikstudium in der Republik Irland. In *Deutsch als Fremdsprache: ein internationales Handbuch*, eds. Gerhard Helbig, Lutz Götze, Gert Henrici and Hans-Jürgen Krumm, pp. 1471–1480. Berlin: de Gruyter.

Fischer, Joachim, and Manfred Schewe. 2010. Deutsch in Irland. In *Deutsch als Fremd- und Zweitsprache*, eds. Hans-Jürgen Krumm, Christian Fandrych, Britta Hufeisen and Claudia Riemer, pp. 1689–1693. Berlin de Gruyter.

Flood, John L. 1991. Fortunatus in England. In: *Reisen und Welterfahrung in der deutschen Literatur des Mittelalters.* Ed. Dietrich Huschenbett and John Margetts, pp. 240–263. Würzburg: Königshausen & Neuman.

Flood, John L. 1993. Nationalistic currents in early German typography. *The Library* 6th series, 15: 125–141.

Flood, John L. 1996. Dietrich Wilhelm von Soltau und seine Übersetzungen des 'Reynke de Vos'. Ein Beitrag zur Erforschung der deutsch-englischen Literaturbeziehungen um 1800. *Archiv für Geschichte des Buchwesens* 45: 283–336.

Flood, John L. 1999. Ginger beer and sugared cauliflower. Adolphus Bernays and language teaching in nineteenth-century London. In *German studies at the turn of the century*, eds. Rüdiger Gorner and Helen Kelly-Holmes, pp. 101–115. Munich: iudicium.

Flood, John L. 2000. German Studies and Collections since 1830. In *Handbuch historischer Buchbestände in Europa*, Vol. 10. *A guide to Collections of printed books in German-speaking countries before 1901 (or in German elsewhere) held by Libraries in Great Britain and Ireland*, eds. Graham Jefcoate, William A. Kelly and Karen Kloth, pp. 21–33. Hildeshim: Olms-Weidmann.

Flood, John L. 2001. The London branch of the Allgemeiner Deutscher Sprachverein. In *'Proper Words in Proper Places' Studies in Lexicology and Lexicography in honour of William Jervis Jones,* eds. Máire C. Davies, John L. Flood and David N. Yeandle, pp. 230–253. Stuttgart: Heinz.

Flood, John L. 2003. Die beiden Weltkriege und die Folgen für die Entwicklung der Germanistik in Großbritannien. In *Akten des X. Internationalen Germanisten-kongresses Wien 2000,* Vol. 11: *Übersetzung und Literaturwissenschaft – Aktuelle und allgemeine Fragen der germanistischen Wissenschaftsgeschichte (Jahrbuch für Internationale Germanistik, Reihe A, Bd. 63),* ed. Peter Wiesinger, pp. 251–256. Bern, etc.: Lang.

Flood, John L. 2005. Oswald, Eugene (1826–1912). In *Oxford Dictionary of National Biography,* Oxford University Press, May 2005; online edn, Jan 2008.

Flood, John L. To appear. Bernays, Adolphus. In *Oxford Dictionary of National Biography,* Oxford University Press.

Fluck, Hans-Rüdiger. 1991. *Didaktik der Fachsprachen. Aufgaben und Arbeitsfelder. Konzepte und Perspektiven im Sprachbereich Deutsch.* Tübingen: Gunter Narr.

Fox, Anthony. 1984. *German intonation. An outline.* Oxford: Clarendon Press.

Fox, Anthony. 2005. *The structure of German.* Oxford: Oxford University Press.

Fraenkel, Gerd. 1969. A chapter in the history of language study. *Linguistics* 53: 10–29.

Frank, Horst Joachim. 1973. *Geschichte des Deutschunterrichts von den Anfängen bis 1945.* Munich: Carl Hanser Verlag.

Franke, Felix. 1884. *Die praktische Spracherlernung auf Grund der Psychologie und der Physiologie der Sprache.* Leipzig: Reisland.

Franz, Jan. 2005. *Englischlernen für Amerika. Sprachführer für deutsche Auswanderer im 19. Jahrhundert.* Munich: Langenscheidt.

Fritzsche, K. Peter. 1993. Multiperspektivität – eine Strategie gegen Dogmatismus und Vorurteile. In: *Germany. Its Representation in Textbooks for Teaching German in Great Britain.* Ed. Michael Byram, pp. 55–61. Braunschweig: Moritz Diesterweg.

Friz, Susanne. 1991. *Das Bild von England, Amerika und Deutschland bei Fremdsprachenlernern und in Fremdsprachenlehrwerken. Ein Beitrag zur komparativen Landeskunde.* Munich: Tuduv-Verlagsgesellschaft.

Fromm, Erich. 1942. *The fear of freedom.* London: Kegan Paul, Trench, Trubner.

Fynes, R. C. C. 2007. Müller, Friedrich Max (1823–1900). *Oxford Dictionary of National Biography.* Oxford: Oxford University Press, 2004; online edn, May 2007 [http://www.oxforddnb.com/view/article/18394, accessed 15 June 2014].

Gabrielsson, Artur. 1932/33. Das Eindringen der hochdeutschen Sprache in die Schulen Norddeutschlands im 16. und 17. Jahrhundert. *Niederdeutsches Jahrbuch* 58/59: 1–79.

Gardner, Phil. 2003. Oral History in Education: Teachers' Memory and Teachers' History. *History of Education* 32: 175–188.

Germain, C. 1993. *Evolution de l'enseignement des langues: 5000 ans d'histoire.* Paris.

Gierlak, Maria. 2001. Das Deutschlandbild in polnischen Lehrwerken für Deutsch als Fremdsprache 1934 – 1939. *Internationale Schulbuchforschung* 23: 339–378.

Gierlak, Maria. 2003. Deutschunterricht und Politik: das Deutschlandbild in den Lehrbüchern für Deutsch als Fremdsprache in Polen (1933–1945) vor dem Hintergrund der deutsch-polnischen Beziehungen. Wyd. 1. Toruń: Wydawn. Uniw. Mikołaja Kopernika.

Gilbert, Glenn G. 1971. *The German language in America. A Symposium.* Austin, Texas: University of Texas.

Gilbert, Mark. 1953, 1954, 1955. The origins of the reform movement in Modern Language Teaching in England (parts I, II, III). Three articles in vols. 4–6. *Research Review (Institute of Education, University of Durham)/ Durham and Newcastle Research Review)* 4: 1–9; 5: 9–18; 6: 1–10.

Gillard, Derek. 2011. Education in England: a brief history. Published online at www.educationengland.org.uk/history.

Giustiniani, Vito R. 1987. *Adam von Rottweil, Deutsch-Italienischer Sprachführer.* Tübingen: Gunter Narr.

Glehn, Dr. von. 1912. [Appendix to Board of Education 1912] A brief sketch of the theory and practice of what is generally called the Direct Method which it is attempted to carry out in this school. [i. e. the Perse School, Cambridge]. In *Board of education circular 797.*

Gloy, Klaus. 2004. Norm. In: *Sociolinguistics / Soziolinguistik. 2. Auflage.* Ed. Ulrich Ammon. Berlin: de Gruyter, Vol. 1, pp. 392–398.

Gloy, Klaus. 2010. Varietäten in normentheoretischer Perspektive. In: *Variatio delectat: Empirische Evidenzen und theoretische Passungen sprachlicher Variation. Festschrift für Klaus J. Mattheier.* Ed. Peter Gilles, Joachim Scharloth and Evelyn Ziegler. Frankfurt: Lang, pp. 29–44.

Glück, Helmut. 2002. *Deutsch als Fremdsprache in Europa vom Mittelalter bis zur Barockzeit.* Berlin: de Gruyter.

Glück, Helmut. 2006. Anredekonventionen im Deutschen: Ein geschichtlicher Überblick. In *Dialogic language use,* eds. Irma Taavitsainen, Juhani Härmä and Jarmo Korhonen, 159–171. Helsinki: Société Neophilologique.

Glück, Helmut. 2011. Die Fremdsprache Frühneuhochdeutsch. In: *Frühneuhochdeutsch – Aufgaben und Probleme seiner linguistischen Beschreibung.* Ed. Anja Lobenstein-Reichmann and Oskar Reichmann. Hildesheim: Olms, pp. 97–156.

Glück, Helmut. 2013. *Die Fremdsprache Deutsch im Zeitalter von Aufklärung, Klassik und Romantik.* Wiesbaden: Harrassowitz.

Glück, Helmut. Ed. 1997. Altdeutsch als Fremdsprache. In *Grammatica ianua artium. Festschrift für Rolf Bergmann zum 60. Geburtstag,* eds. Elvira Glaser and Michael Schlaefer, pp. 251–269. Heidelberg: Winter.

Glück, Helmut. Ed. 2001. *Die Volkssprachen als Lerngegenstand im Mittelalter und der frühen Neuzeit. Akten des Bamberger Symposiums am 18. und 19. Mai 2001. (Die Geschichte des Deutschen als Fremdsprache 3).* Berlin: de Gruyter.

Glück, Helmut et al. 2002. *Deutsche Sprachbücher in Böhmen und Mähren vom 15. Jahrhundert bis 1918: eine teilkommentierte Bibliographie* (Die Geschichte des Deutschen als Fremdsprache 2). Berlin: De Gruyter.

Glück, Helmut, and Bettina Morcinek. Eds. 2006. *Ein Franke in Venedig. Das Sprachlehrbuch des Georg von Nürnberg (1424) und seine Folgen.* Wiesbaden: Harrassowitz.

Glück, Helmut, and Konrad Schröder. 2007. *Deutschlernen in den polnischen Ländern vom 15. Jahrhundert bis 1918. Eine teilkommentierte Bibliographie.* Wiesbaden: Harrassowitz.

Glück, Helmut, and Yvonne Pörzgen. 2009. *Deutschlernen in Russland und in den baltischen Ländern. Eine teilkommentierte Bibliographie.* Wiesbaden: Harrassowitz.

Glück, Helmut, Mark Häberlein, and Konrad Schröder. 2013. *Mehrsprachigkeit in der frühen Neuzeit. Die Reichstädte Augsburg und Nürnberg vom 15. bis ins frühe 19. Jahrhundert.* Wiesbaden: Harrassowitz.

Görlach, Manfred. 1998. *An Annotated Bibliography of nineteenth-Century grammars of English.* Amsterdam: Benjamins.

Gottsched, Johann Christoph. 1748. *Grundlegung der deutschen Sprachkunst, Nach den Mustern der besten Schriftsteller des vorigen und jetzigen Jahrhunderts abgefasst von Johann Christoph Gottscheden.* Leipzig: Verlegts Bernh. Christoph Breitkopf. 2nd edition 1749, 3rd 1752. From 4th ed. onwards with title: *Vollständigere und Neuerläuterte Deutsche Sprachkunst, Nach den Mustern [...],* 5th ed. 1762, 6th ed. 1776.

Greatwood, H.A. 1959. Wie trägt der Deutschunterricht in den englischen Schulen dazu bei, dem Schüler ein geistiges Bild Deutschlands zu geben? In *Das Bild vom Ausland. Fremdsprachliche Lektüre an höheren Schulen in Deutschland, England und Frankreich.*, eds. Charlotte Lütkens and Walther Karbe, pp. 56–78. Munich: R. Oldenbourg.

Guthke, Karl. 2011. Deutsche Literatur aus zweiter Hand: Englische Lehr-und Lesebücher in der Goethezeit. *Jahrbuch des Freien Deutschen Hochstifts* (2011): 163–237.

Häberlein, Mark, and Christian Kuhn. 2010. *Fremde Sprachen in frühneuzeitlichen Städten.* Wiesbaden: Harrassowitz.

Hagen, Stephen (Centre for Information on Language Teaching and Research). Eds. 1988. *Languages in British business: an analysis of current needs.* Newcastle upon Tyne: Newcastle upon Tyne Polytechnic Products in association with Centre for Information on Language Teaching and Research.

Hagen, Stephen (Centre for Information on Language Teaching and Research). Eds. 1993. *Using technology in language learning.* (*CTC Trust Publications* 7). London: City Technology Colleges Trust Limited in association with Centre for Information on Language Teaching and Research.

Hägi, Sara. 2006. *Nationale Varietäten im Unterricht Deutsch als Fremdsprache.* Frankfurt: Lang.

Halbwachs, Maurice. 1992. *On collective memory. Edited, translated, and with an introduction by Lewis A. Coser.* Chicago: University of Chicago Press.

Hall, Christopher. 2003. *Modern German Pronunciation.* Manchester: Manchester University Press.

Halliwell, Susan (Centre for Information on Language Teaching and Research). 1991. *Yes – but will they behave?: managing the interactive classroom* (*Pathfinder* 4). London: Centre for Information on Language Teaching and Research.

Halstead, J. Mark, and Monica J. Taylor. 2000. Learning and teaching about values: a review of recent research. *Cambridge Journal of education* 30: 169–202.

Hammar, Elisabeth. 1992. A track in the jungle. A need for a useful classification of language teaching material. In *Fremdsprachenunterricht 1500–1800*, ed. Konrad Schröder, pp. 99–108. Wiesbaden: Harrassowitz.

Hammer, A. E. (Alfred Edward). 1971. *German grammar and usage.* London: Edward Arnold.

Hammer, Elisabeth. 1980. *L'enseignement du français en Suède jusqu'en 1807. Méthodes et manuels.* Stockholm: Akademi-litteratur.

Hammerich, Louis Leonor, and Roman Jakobsen, eds. 1961. *Tönnie Fenne's Low German Manual of Spoken Russian. Pskow 1607.* Copenhagen: E. Munskgaard (Royal Danish Academy of Sciences and Letters).

Hardach-Pinke, Iris. 2000. German Governesses in England. In: *Prinz Albert und die Entwicklung der Bildung in England und Deutschland im 19. Jahrhundert.* Ed. Franz Bosbach, Caroline Filmer-Sankey and Hermann Hiery, pp. 23–32. Munich: K. G. Saur.

Harding, Ann, Brian Page, and Sheila Rowell (Centre for Information on Language Teaching and Research). 1980. *Graded objectives in modern languages.* London: Centre for Information on Language Teaching and Research.

Harris, Vee (Centre for Information on Language Teaching and Research). 1992. *Fair enough?: equal opportunities and modern languages (Pathfinder 14).* London: Centre for Information on Language Teaching and Research.

Hawkins, Eric. 1987. *Modern languages in the curriculum.* Revised edition. Cambridge: CUP.

Hawkins, Eric W., and George E. Perren. Eds. (Centre for Information on Language Teaching and Research). 1978. *Intensive language teaching in schools.* London: Centre for Information on Language Teaching and Research.

Hecke, Carola, and Carola Surkamp. Eds. 2010. *Bilder im Fremdsprachenunterricht. Neue Ansätze, Kompetenzen und Methoden.* Tübingen: Narr.

Heinle, Eva-Maria. 1982. *Hieronymus Freyers Anweisung zur Teutschen Orthographie. Ein Beitrag zur Sprachgeschichte des 18. Jahrhunderts.* Heidelberg: Carl Winter Universitätsverlag.

Helbig, Gerhard, Lutz Götze, Gert Henrici and Hans-Jürgen Krumm. Eds. 2001. *Deutsch als Fremdsprache: ein internationales Handbuch.* Berlin: de Gruyter.

Hellgardt, Ernst. 1996. Mehrsprachigkeit im Karolingerreich. Bemerkungen aus Anlass von Rosamond McKittericks Buch *The Carolingians and the written word. Beiträge zur Geschichte der deutschen Sprache und Literatur* 118: 1–48.

Hewitt, Derek (Centre for Information on Language Teaching and Research). 1986. Graded Objectives in Modern languages – a survey of German in GOML for 1985–86. In *German in the United Kingdom: issues and opportunities,* pp. 54–56. London: CILT.

Heynatz, Johann Friedrich. 1777. *Deutsche Sprachlehre zum Gebrauch der Schulen.* Berlin: Mylius.

Heyse, Johann Christian August. 1816. *Kleine theoretisch-praktische deutsche Grammatik.* 3rd ed. Hannover: Hahn.

Hierl, Wolfgang. 1972. *Zum Deutschlandbild in den anglo-amerikanischen Deutschlesebüchern von 1945 bis 1969.* Diss. Aachen.

Hill, Brian (Centre for Information on Language Teaching and Research). 1989. *Making the most of video.* Illustrations by Pieter Sluis. London: Centre for Information on Language Teaching and Research.

Hill, T.H.E. 2008. *Berlin in Early Cold-War Army Booklets.* n.p., [ISBN 978-1434839756].

HMI (Her Majesty's Inspectorate). 1977. *Mathematics, Science and Modern Languges in Maintained Schools in England: An appraisal of problems in some key subjects by HM Inspectorate.* London: HMSO.

HMI (Her Majesty's Inspectorate). 1991. *Diversification of the First Modern Foreign Language in a Sample of Secondary Schools. A report by HMI.* London: HMI.

Hogan-Brun, Gabrielle. Ed. 2000. *National varieties of German outside Germany.* Bern: Lang.

Hogan, Jackie. 2009. *Gender, race and national identity: nations of flesh and blood.* Abingdon, Oxon: Routledge.

Holt, Robert. 1989. *Sport and the British: A Modern History.* Oxford: OUP.

Hope Simpson, J.B. 1967. *Rugby since Arnold. A history of Rugby school since 1842.* London: Macmillan.

Horan, Geraldine. 2012. 'Not a foreign goddess': Germania, the Niederwald Monument, and Discourses of Gender and Nationalism. In *Germania Remembered 1500–2009. Commemorating and Inventing a Germanic Past*, eds. Christina Lee and Nicola McLelland, pp. 137–154. Tempe, Arizona: ACMRS.

Horner, Kristine. 2011a. Guest Editor's Preface: Germanic Languages and Migration in North America. *Journal of Germanic Linguistics* 23: 313–314.

Horner, Kristine. 2011b. Language, Place, and Heritage: Reflexive Cultural Luxembourgishness in Wisconsin. *Journal of Germanic Linguistics* 23: 375–400.

Horney, Alan. 1976. As the teacher-trainer sees them. In: *German in the United Kingdom: problems and prospects.* Ed. CILT, pp. 18–20. London: CILT.

Howatt, A.P.R. (Tony), and Henry George Widdowson. 2008. *A History of English Language Teaching.* 2nd ed. Oxford: OUP.

Howatt, A.P.R. (Tony), and Richard C. Smith, eds. 2000. *Foundations of Foreign Language Teaching: Nineteenth-century Innovators.* 6 vols. London: Routledge.

Howatt, A.P.R. (Tony), and Richard C. Smith, eds. 2002. *Modern Language Teaching: The Reform Movement, with General Introduction and volume introductions.* 5 vols. London: Routledge.

Hoy, Peter. 1977. *The early teaching of modern languages. A report on the place of language teaching in primary schools by a Nuffield Foundation Committee.* London: The Nuffield Foundation.

Höybye, Poul. 1956. Meister Jörg fra Nürnberg. Troek af middelalderens sprogundervis-ning. In *Festskrift til Christen Möller*, eds. Louis Hammerich, Max Kjaer-Hansen and Peter Skautrup, pp. 205–221. Copenhagen: Borgen.

Höybye, Poul. 1964, 1974. Glossari italiano-tedeschi del Quattrocento I, II. *Studi di Filologia Italiana* 22: 167–204, 32: 143–203.

Hudson, Richard. Trends in Language Education in England. http://www.phon.ucl.ac.uk/home/dick/ec/stats.htm#alfg. Accessed June 2014.

Hughes, Terence. Ed. 1994. *The Image Makers. National stereotypes and the media. Text based on the British-German seminar at the Goethe-Institut London, January 21–22, 1994.* London: Goethe-Institut.

Hüllen, Werner. Ed. 1990. *Understanding the Historiography of Lingusitics. Problems and Projects.* Münster: Nodus.

Hüllen, Werner. 1995. The path through an undergrowth: A *Royal Compleat Grammar, English and High German* (1715). *Paradigm* 17: n. p. http://faculty.education.illinois.edu/westbury/paradigm/hullen.html. Accessed June 2014.

Hüllen, Werner, and Friederike Klippel. Eds. 2000. *Holy and Profane Languages: The Beginnings of Foreign Language Teaching in Western Europe.* Wiesbaden: Harrassowitz in Kommission.

Hüllen, Werner. 2001. History and approaches of language typology. In *Language typology and language universals*, eds. Martin Haspelmath, Ekkehard König, Wulf Oesterreicher and Wolfgang Raible, pp. 234–249. Berlin: de Gruyter.

Hüllen, Werner. 2002a. Der *Orbis Sensualium Pictus* und die mittelalterliche Tradition des Lehrens fremder Sprachen (first published 1992). In *Collected papers on the History of Linguistic Ideas*, ed. Michael Isermann, pp. 137–158. Nodus: Münster.

Hüllen, Werner. 2002b. Schemata der Historiographie. Ein Traktat. In *Collected Papers on the History of Linguistic Ideas*, ed. Michael Isermann, pp. 16–28. Münster: Nodus.

Hüllen, Werner. 2002c. *Collected Papers on the History of Linguistic Ideas* (The Henry Sweet Society for the History of Linguistics 8). Münster: Nodus.

Hüllen, Werner. 2005a. *Kleine Geschichte des Fremdsprachenlernerns.* Berlin: Erich Schmidt.

Hüllen, Werner. 2005b. On the method of linguistic historiography. A treatise. In *Flores Grammaticae. Essays in Memory of Vivien Law*, eds. Nicola McLelland and Andrew R. Linn, pp. 9–20. Münster: Nodus. Translation of 'Schemata der Historiographie. Ein Traktat' (in Hüllen 2002c: pp. 16–28).

Hüllen, Werner, and Friederike Klippel. Eds. 2005. *Sprachen der Bildung. Bildung durch Sprachen im Deutschland des 18. und 19. Jahrhunderts. (Wolfenbüttler Forschungen* 107). Wiesbaden: Harrassowitz.

Hüllen, Werner. 2007a. The European tradition of early foreign language teaching. In *Geschichte der Sprachtheorien. 6.2 Sprachtheorien der Neuzeit III. Sprachbeschreibung und Sprachunterricht,* Teil 2, ed. Peter Schmitter, pp. 479–499. Tübingen: Narr.

Hüllen, Werner. 2007b. The presence of English in Germany. *Zeitschrift für Fremdsprachenforschung* 18: 3–26.

Hundt, Markus. 2008. Normverletzungen und neue Normen. In: *Deutsche Grammatik – Regeln, Normen, Sprachgebrauch [Jahrbuch des Instituts für deutsche Sprache.* Ed. Marek Konopka and Bruno Strecker, pp. 117–140. Berlin: de Gruyter.

Hunt, Tony. 1991. *Teaching and learning Latin in thirteenth century England.* Cambridge: Brewer.

Incorporated Association of Assistant Masters in Secondary Schools. 1929. *Memorandum on the teaching of modern languages.* London: University of London Press.

Incorporated Association of Head Masters (IAHM). 1963, revised ed. 1966. *Modern languages in the grammar school: report of a Working Party of Division XII (Lancashire and Cheshire) of I.A.H.M.* London: Incorporated Association of Head Masters.

Ingram, S. R., and J. C. Mace. 1959. An audio-visual French course. *Modern Languages* 40: 139–143.

Internationales Schulbuchinstitut. Ed. 1954. *Deutschland und Frankreich im Spiegel ihrer Schulbücher.* Braunschweig.

Ising, Erika. 1959. *Wolfgang Ratkes Schriften zur deutschen Grammatik (1612–1630).* Teil I: *Abhandlung.* Teil II: *Textausgabe.* Berlin: Akademie Verlag.

Ising, Erika. 1970. *Die Herausbildung der Grammatik der Volkssprachen in Mittel- und Osteuropa. Studien über den Einfluß der lateinischen Elementargrammatik des Aelius Donatus. De octo partibus orationis ars minor.* Berlin (Ost): Veröffentlichungen des Instituts für deutsche Sprache und Literatur.

Issitt, John. 2004. Reflections on the study of textbooks. *History of Education* 33: 683–696.

Jantz, Harald. 1952. An Elizabethan statement on the origins of the German Faust Book. *Journal of English and Germanic Philology* 51: 137–153.

Jaworska, Silvia. 2008. Where Have All the Linguists Gone? The Position of Linguistics in British German Studies from the mid-nineteenth Century until 2000. In: *Englischer Sprachkontakt in den Varietäten des Deutschen / English in Contact with Varieties of German*, ed. Falco Pflazgraf, pp. 13–33. Frankfurt: Peter Lang.

Jaworska, Silvia. 2009. *The German language in British higher education: problems, challenges, teaching and learning perspectives.* Wiesbaden: Harrassowitz.

Jaworska, Silvia. 2010. Anglo-German Academic Encounters before the First World War and the Work towards Peace: The Case of Karl Breul. *ANGERMION Yearbook for Anglo-German Literary Criticism, Intellectual History and Cultural Transfers* 3: 135–60.

Jefcoate, Graham, and John L. Flood. 2000. Libraries in the British Isles and their German Holdings (including: German Studies and Collections since 1830 by John L. Flood). In *Handbuch historischer Buchbestände in Europa.* Vol. 10. *A guide to Collections of printed books in German-speaking countries before 1901 (or in German elsewhere) held by Libraries in Great Britain and Ireland*, eds. Graham Jefcoate, William A. Kelly and Karen Kloth. Hildesheim: Olms-Weidmann.

Jellinek, Max. 1913–1914. *Geschichte der neuhochdeutschen Grammatik von den Anfängen bis auf Adelung.* Heidelberg: Carl Winter.

Jespersen, Otto. 1904. How to teach a foreign language (translated from the Danish *Sprogundervisning* by S. Yhlen-Olsen Bertelsen). London: Allen and Unwin.

Johnson, J. 1973. *The academic, psychological and didactic background to the image of Germany in English textbooks of German.* Diss. Braunschweig.

Johnson, Sally. 2000. The cultural politics of the 1998 reform of German orthography. *German Life and Letters* 53: 106–125.

Johnson, Sally. 2005. *Spelling trouble? Language, ideology and the reform of German orthography.* Clevedon: Multilingual Matters.

Johnson, Sally, and Oliver Stenschke. Eds. 2005. *'After 2005: Re-visiting German Orthography.' Special issue of German Life and Letters* 58.4. With contributions from Theodor Ickler (Universität Erlangen-Nürnberg), Horst Sitta (Universität Zürich) and Jens Sparschuh (Berlin).

Jolles, Frank. 1968. The hazard of travel in medieval Germany: an attempt at an interpretation of the altdeutsche Gespräche. *German Life and Letters* 21: 309–319.

Jones, Barry, Gwenneth Jones, Helen Demetriou, Peter Downes, Jean Rudduck. 2001. *Boys' performance in modern foreign languages: listening to learners. A project carried out by Homerton College Cambridge on behalf of the Qualifications and Curriculum Authority.* London: CILT.

Jones, Daniel. 1914. The importance of intonation in the pronunciation of foreign languages. *Modern Language Teaching* 10: 201–205.

Jones, Roger. 1993. Survey of German at A-level. In: *German Studies in the United Kingdom. A Survey of German in Schools and Universities,* ed. Reinhard Tenberg and Roger Jones, pp. 43–80. London: European Business Associates.

Jones, William J. 2000. *German lexicography in the European context: a descriptive bibliography of printed dictionaries and word lists containing German language (1600–1700).* Berlin: de Gruyter.

Josten, Dirk. 1976. *Sprachvorbild und Sprachnorm im Urteil des 16. und 17. Jahrhunderts. Sprachlandschaftliche Prioritäten. Sprachauthoritäten. Sprachimmanente Argumentationen.* Frankfurt: Lang.

Kaiser, Stefan 2000. The first Japanese attempts at describing Chinese and Korean bilingualism. In: *HSK 18.1* ed. Auroux et al. Berlin: de Gruyter, vol. 1, pp. 77–84.

Kaltz, Barbara. 1995. L'enseignement des langues étrangères au XVIe siècle. Structure globale et typologie des textes destinés à l'apprentissage des vernaculaires. *Beiträge zur Geschichte der Sprachwissenschaft* 5: 79–106.

Karnein, Alfred. 1976. Deutsch als Fremdsprache im 15. Jahrhundert. Das Sprachbuch Meister Jörgs. *Jahrbuch Deutsch als Fremdsprache. Zweites Jahrbuch des Goethe Instituts,* pp. 1–13.

Kast, B., Ed. 1994. *Zur Analyse, Begutachtung und Entwicklung von Lehrwerken für den fremdsprachlichen Deutschunterricht.* Berlin [u.a.]: Langenscheidt.

Kaye, Elaine. 1972. *A History of Queen's College.* London: Chatto & Windus.

Keating, Raymond F. 1963. *A study of the effectiveness of language laboratories (The Keating Report)*. New York: Columbia University Teachers' College, Institute of Administrative Research.

Keller, G. 1986. Das Deutschlandbild amerikanischer, britischer und französischer Schüler im kulturkundlichen Unterricht. *Neuphiloligische Mitteilungen* 39(4): 209–217.

Kelly, Louis G. 1969. *25 Centuries of Languages Teaching*. Rowley, MA: Newbury House.

Kemp, J. Alan. 2001. The development of phonetics from the late 18th to the 19th century. In: *HSK* 18.2, ed. Auroux et al., pp. 1468–1480. Berlin: de Gruyter.

Kibbee, Douglas. 1991. *For to Speke Frenche Trewely: The French Language in England, 1000–1600: Its Status, Description and Instruction*. Amsterdam/Philadelphia: John Benjamins.

Klippel, Friederike. 1994. *Englischlernen im 18. und 19. Jahrhunderts. Die Geschichte der Lehrbücher und Unterrichtsmethoden*. Münster: Nodus.

Knobloch, Clemens. 1989. Die deutsche Schulgrammatik vor dem Erscheinen von Karl Ferdinand Beckers 'Organism der Sprache' (1827). In *Satzlehre – Denkschulung – Nationalsprache. Deutsche Schulgrammatik zwischen 1800 und 1850*, eds. Hans Dieter Erlinger, Clemens Knobloch and Hartmut Mayer, pp. 63–86. Münster: Nodus.

Knobloch, Clemens, Stefan Schallenberger, and Rolf Schneider. 2005. Zur Grammatikographie des Deutschen. Vom 16. bis zur zweiten Hälfte des 20. Jahrhunderts. In *Geschichte der Sprachtheorie. 6.1 Sprachtheorien der Neuzeit* III/1, ed. Peter Schmitter, pp. 70–104. Tübingen: Narr.

Koch, Kristine. 2002. *Deutsch als Fremdsprache im Rußland des 18. Jahrhunderts (Die Geschichte des Deutschen als Fremdsprache* 1). Berlin: de Gruyter.

Kok Escalle, Marie-Christine. 1999. Le français aux Pays-Bas dans la deuxième moitié du XIXe siècle. *Documents pour l'histoire du français langue étrangère ou seconde* 23: 83–107.

Kok Escalle, Marie-Christine, and Madeleine van Strien-Chardonneau. 2007. Aspects culturels et interculturels des manuels d'apprentissage du français dans les Pays-Bas des XVIe–XIXe siècles. In: *Le manuel scolaire d'ici et d'ailleurs, d'hier à demain*, ed. Monique Lebrun. Québec: Presses de l'Université du Québec.

Kok Escalle, Marie-Christine, and Madeleine van Strien-Chardonneau. 2010. Le français aux Pays-Bas (XVIIᵉ–XIXᵉ siècles): de la langue du bilinguisme élitaire à une langue du plurilinguisme d'éducation. *Documents pour l'histoire du français langue étrangère ou seconde* 45: 123–156. Accessible at http://dhfles.revues.org/1364.

Kok Escalle, Marie-Christine, and Madeleine van Strien-Chardonneau. 2011. Moyens linguistiques et construction identitaire sexuée dans l'enseignement de la language française aux Pays-Bas XVVᵉ–XIXᵉ siecles. *Beiträge zur Geschichte der Sprachwissenschaft* 21: 219–238.

Kolb, Elisabeth. 2013. *Kultur im Englischunterricht: Deutschland, Frankreich und Schweden im Vergleich (1975–2011)*. Heidelberg: Winter.

Kolinsky, Eva. 1993. Survey of German at the "old" universities. In: *German Studies in the United Kingdom. A Survey of German in Schools and Universities*. Ed. Reinhard Tenberg and Roger Jones. London: European Business Associates, pp. 81–134.

Koreik, Uwe. 1995. *Deutschlandstudien und deutsche Geschichte: die deutsche Geschichte im Rahmen des Landeskundeunterrichts.* Baltmannsweiler: Schneider Verlag Hohengehren.

Krampikowski, Frank. 1990. *Amerikanisches Deutschlandbild und deutsches Amerikabild in Medien und Erziehung.* Baltmannsweiler: Pädagogischer Verlag Burgbücherei Schneider.

Krampikowski, Frank. 1991. *Das Deutschlandbild im Deutschunterricht am amerikanischen College: ein Beitrag zur Landeskunde und ihrer Vermittlung im Unterricht in Deutsch als Fremdsprache.* Tübingen Narr.

Kramsch, Claire J. 1998. *Language and culture.* Oxford: Oxford University Press.

Krashen, Stephen. 1982. *Principles and practice in second language acquisition.* Oxford: Pergamon.

Krauskopf, Jürgen. 1985. *Das Deutschland- und Frankreichbild in Schulbüchern. Deutsche Französischbücher und französische Deutschbücher von 1950–1980.* Frankfurt: Gunter Narr.

Krönig, Jürgen. 1999. Vergiften die Medien die deutsch-britischen Beziehungen? In: *Intercultural Perspectives. Images of Germany in Education and the Media.* Ed. Reinhard Tenberg. Munich: iudicium.

Krumm, Hans-Jürgen. 1999. Zum Stand der Lehrwerkforschung aus der Sicht des Deutschen als Fremdsprache. In *Die Erforschung von Lehr- und Lernmaterialien im Kontext des Lehrens und Lernens fremder Sprachen*, eds. Karl-Richard Bausch, Herbert Christ, Frank G. Königs and Hans-Jürgen Krumm, pp. 119–128. Tübingen: Narr.

Krumm, Hans-Jürgen, Christian Fandrych, Britta Hufeisen, and Claudia Riemer, eds. 2010. *Deutsch als Fremd- und Zweitsprache.* Berlin: de Gruyter.

Kufner, Herbert L. 1962. *The grammatical structures of English and German: a contrastive sketch.*

Kuhfuß, Walter. 2014. *Eine Kulturgeschichte des Französischunterrichts in der Frühen Neuzeit. Französischlernen am Fürstenhof, auf dem Marktplatz, und in der Schule in Deutschland.* Göttingen: V&R unipress.

Kuhn, Christian, and Mark Häberlein, eds. 2010. *Fremde Sprachen in frühneuzeitlichen Städten. Lernende, Lehrende und Lehrwerke.* Wiesbaden: Harrassowitz.

Kuhn, Elisabeth. 1981/82. Geschlechterspezifische Unterschiede in der Sprachverwendung. Linguistic Agency University Duisburg.

Kuiper, Willem. 1961. *Historisch-didactische aspecten van het onderwijs in het Duits. Beschouwingen over de ontwikkeling van het Hoogduits op de Nederlandse scholen voor voorbereidend hoger en middelbaar onderwijs.* Groningen: J. B. Wolters.

Lambley, Kathleen. 1920. *The teaching and cultivation of the French language in England during Tudor and Stuart Times.* Manchester: Manchester University Press.

Landfester, Manfred. 2012. Neo-Humanism (CT). In *Brill's New Pauly. Brill Online, 2013.* <*http://referenceworks.brillonline.com/entries/brill-s-new-pauly/neo-humanism-ct-e1508000*> Accessed June 2013.

Langer, Nils. 2001. The Rechtschreibreform: A Lesson in Linguistic Purism.' In: German as a Foreign Language. *GFL (on-line journal).* http://www.gfl-journal.de/Issue_3_2000.php. Accessed June 2014.

Langer, Nils. 2002. On the importance of foreign language grammars for a history of standard German. In *Standardization: studies from the Germanic languages*, eds. Andrew R. Linn and Nicola McLelland, pp. 67–82. Amsterdam: Benjamins.

Langer, Nils. 2004. Frühe Fremdsprachengrammatiken als Vermittlerinnen der Standardsprache. In *Sprachwandel und Gesellschaftswandel – Wurzeln des heutigen Deutsch*, eds. Klaus J. Mattheier and Haruo Nitta, pp. 223–243. Munich: iudicium.

Langer, Nils. 2008. German language and German identity in America: Evidence from School Grammars 1860–1918. *German Life and Letters* 61: 497–512.

Larsen-Freeman, Diane, and Michael Long. 1991. *An Introduction to Second Language Acquistion Research.* London: Longman.

Law, Vivien. 2003. *The History of Linguistics in Europe from Plato to 1600.* Cambridge: Cambridge University Press.

le Carré, John. 2010. The importance of the German language. Key-note address by John le Carré at the opening of the Think German Conference at Whitgift-School, Croydon, 25 June 2010 (full text was available at http://thinkgerman.org.uk/john_le_Carr%C3%A9_thinks_German, no longer accessible).

Lee, Jeff, David Buckland, Glenis Shaw and Centre for Information on Language Teaching and Research. 1998. *The invisible child: the responses and attitudes to the learning of modern foreign languages shown by year 9 pupils of average ability.* London: CILT.

Lee, Michael. 1999. The Joint Services School for Linguists *The Linguist* 38: no pagination.

Leweling, Beate. 2005. *Reichtum, Reinligkeit und Glanz – Sprachkritische Konzeptionen in der Sprachreflexion des 18. Jahrhunderts.* Frankurt am Main: Peter Lang.

Lightbown, Patsy, and Nina Spada. 2006 (3rd ed.). *How Languages are Learned.* Oxford: OUP.

Lind, Melva. 1948. Modern language learning: the intensive course as sponsored by the United States Army and implications for the undergraduate course of study. *Genetic Psychology Monographs* 32: 3–82.

Linke, Angelika. 1988. Die Kunst der 'guten Unterhaltung': Bürgertum und Gesprächskultur im 19. Jahrhundert. *Zeitschrift für Germanistische Linguistik* 16: 123–144.

Linke, Angelika. 1996. *Sprachkultur und Bürgertum. Zur Mentalitätsgeschichte des 19. Jahrhunderts.* Stuttgart: Metzler.

Linn, Andrew R., and Nicola McLelland. Eds. 2002. *Standardization. Studies from the Germanic Languages.* (*Current Issues in Linguistic Theory* 235). Amsterdam: Benjamins.

Linn, Andrew R. 2008. The birth of applied linguistics. The Anglo-Scandinavian School as discourse community. *Historiographia Linguistica* 35: 342–84.

Lißmann, H.-J. 1983. Stufe II: Analyse von Schulbüchern für den Fremdsprachenunterricht. Das Bild des Anderen in französischen Schulbüchern für den Deutschunterricht. In *Analyse von Inhalten einiger der wichtigsten Schulbücher in Deutschland und Frankreich.*, eds. DFJW and OFAJ, pp. 25–29.

Longolius, Johann Daniel. 1715. *Einleitung zur gründtlicher Erkäntniß einer ieden, insonderheit aber der Teutschen Sprache.* Budissin: Richter.

Low, Lesley et al. (Scottish CILT). 1995. *Foreign languages in primary schools: evaluation of the Scottish pilot projects 1993–1995: final report.* Stirling: Scottish CILT.

Lütkens, Charlotte. 1959a. Das Deutschlandbild englischer Oberschüler auf Grund der Schullektüre. In *Das Bild vom Ausland. Fremdsprachliche Lektüre an höheren Schulen in Deutschland, England und Frankreich,* eds. Charlotte Lütkens and Walther Karbe, pp. 144–156. Munich: R. Oldenbourg.

Lütkens, Charlotte. 1959b. Über Wesen und Funktion des Auslandbildes. In *Das Bild vom Ausland. Fremdsprachliche Lektüre an höheren Schulen in Deutschland, England und Frankreich,* eds. Charlotte Lütkens and Walther Karbe, pp. 13–32. Munich: R. Oldenbourg.

Lütkens, Charlotte, and Walther Karbe. Eds. 1959. *Das Bild vom Ausland. Fremdsprachliche Lektüre an höheren Schulen in Deutschland, England und Frankreich.* Munich: R. Oldenbourg.

M. B. S. [not further identified]. 1921. German Language, How to Teach the. In *The encyclopaedia and dictionary of education. A comprehensive, practical and authoritative guide on all matters connected with education, including education principles and practice, various types of teaching instruction and educational systems throughout the world.,* ed. Foster Watson, pp. 695–698. London: Pitman.

Macht, Konrad. 1986. *Methodengeschichte des Englischunterrichts.* Augsburg: Universität Augsburg.

Macht, Konrad. 1986–1990. *Methodengeschichte des Englischunterrichts.* Vol. 1 *1800–1880.* Vol. 2: *1880–1960.* Vol. 3: *1960–1985.* Augsburg: Universität Augsburg.

Macht, Konrad. 1992. Englischmethodik an der Schwelle zum 19. Jahrhundert zwischen Spätaufklärung und Neuhumanismus. In *Fremdsprachenunterricht 1500–1800,* ed. Konrad Schröder, pp. 109–123. Wiesbaden: Harrassowitz.

Macht, Konrad. 1994. Practical skills or mental traning? The historical dilemma of foreign language methodology in nineteenth and twentieth century Germany. *Paradigm* 14 (http://faculty.ed.uiuc.edu/westbury/paradigm/macht.html).

MacMahon, Mike. 1998. Phonology. In: *The Cambridge History of the English Language,* Vol. 4, 1776–1997. Ed. Suzanne Romaine, pp. 373–535. Cambridge: CUP.

Maijala, Minna. 2004. *Deutschland von außen gesehen: geschichtliche Inhalte in Deutschlehrbüchern ausgewählter europäischer Länder.* Frankfurt: Lang.

Maijala, Minna. 2006. Die Darstellung von Geschichte in Lehrwerken für Deutsch als Fremdsprache – am Beispiel des Nationalsozialismus. *Info DaF* 33: 13–30.

Maijala, Minna. 2007. Zum Lehrwerkalltag in britischen und finnischen Lehrwerken für das Fach Deutsch – Von Stadtmenschen, Landeiern und Mülltonnen. *GFL. German as a foreign language.* Online at http://www.gfl-journal.de/3–2007/maijala.pdf:25–48.

Marchand, James W. 1958. The teaching of German word order – a linguistic approach. *Language Learning* 8: 27–35.

Marchand, James W. 1961. *Applied linguistics, German. A guide for teachers.* Boston: Heath.

Maréchal, Raymond. 1972. *Histoire de l'enseignment et de la méthodologie des language vivantes en Belgique des origines au début du 20e siècle.* Paris: Didier.

Martin, Daniel. 1635. *Acheminement à la langue allemande.* Strassburg: Everhard Zetzner Libraire.

Mattheier, Klaus J., and Edgar Radtke. Eds. 1997. *Standardisierung und Destandardisierung europäischer Nationalsprachen.* Frankfurt: Lang.

Matthias, Theodor. 1897. *Sprachleben und Sprachschäden. Ein Führer durch die Schwankungen und Schwierigkeiten des deutschen Sprachgebrauchs. Von Dr. Theodor Matthias. Oberlehrer a. Kgl. Realgymnasium zu Zittau i. Sachsen. Zweite verbesserte und vermehrte Auflage.* Leipzig: Friedrich Brandstetter.

McLelland, Nicola. 2001. Albertus (1573) and Ölinger (1574). Creating the first grammars of German. *Historiographia Linguistica* 28: 7–38.

McLelland, Nicola. 2002. Schottelius, Language, Nature and Art. Buildings and Banyans. *Beiträge zur Geschichte der Sprachwissenschaft* 12: 65–92.

McLelland, Nicola. 2003. Die Anfänge der deutschen Grammatikschreibung im 16. Jahrhundert – und davor? In *Jahrbuch für international Germanistik. Reihe A.* Vol. 63. [= Akten des X. Internationalen Germanistenkongresses Wien 2000, vol. 11], ed. Peter Wiesinger, pp. 291–297. Bern: Peter Lang.

McLelland, Nicola. 2004. Dialogue & German language learning in the Renaissance. In *Printed Voices. The Renaissance Culture of Dialogue*, eds. Dorothea Heitsch and Jean-François Vallee, pp. 206–225. Toronto: University of Toronto Press.

McLelland, Nicola. 2005a. German as a second language for adults in the seventeenth century? Jacob Brücker's *Deutsche Grammatic* (1620). In *Flores Grammaticae. Essays in Memory of Vivien Law*, eds. Nicola McLelland and A. R. Linn, 171–185. Münster: Nodus.

McLelland, Nicola. 2005b. Authority and audience in seventeenth-century German grammatical texts. *Modern Language Review* 100: 1025–1042.

McLelland, Nicola. 2008. Approaches to the semantics and syntax of the adverb in German foreign language grammars *Beiträge zur Geschichte der Sprachwissenschaft* 18.1: 37–58 (Das Adverb in der Grammatographie – Teil II Themenheft, ed. Aino Kärna and Stephanos Matthaios).

McLelland, Nicola. 2009. Understanding German grammar takes centuries… In *Landmarks in the History of the German Language*, eds. Nils Langer, Geraldine Horan and Sheila Watts, pp. 57–84. Oxford: Lang.

McLelland, Nicola. 2010. Justus Georgius Schottelius (1612–1676) and European linguistic thought. *Historiographia Linguistica* 37.1: 1–30.

McLelland, Nicola. 2011a. *J. G. Schottelius's Ausführliche Arbeit von der Teutschen Haubtsprache (1663) and its place in early modern European vernacular language study.* Publications of the Philological Society. Oxford: Blackwell.

McLelland, Nicola. 2011b. From humanist history to linguistic theory: the case of the Germanic rootword. In *Language and History, Linguistics and Historiography Inter-*

disciplinary Approaches, eds. Nils Langer, Steffan Davies and Wim Vandenbussche, pp. 89–109. Frankfurt: Lang.

McLelland, Nicola. 2012a. Rules for the neighbours: Prescriptions of the German language for British learners. In *The Languages of Nation: Attitudes and Norms*, ed. Carol Percy, pp. 245–270. Clevedon: Multilingual Matters.

McLelland, Nicola. 2012b. Germanic virtues in linguistic discourse in Germany (1500–1945). In *Germania Remembered*, eds. Christina Lee and Nicola McLelland, pp. 75–97. Tempe, AZ: Arizona Center for Medieval and Renaissance Studies.

McLelland, Nicola. 2012c. Walter Rippmann and Otto Siepmann as Reform Movement textbook authors: A contribution to the history of teaching and learning German in the United Kingdom. *Language & History* 55: 125–145.

McLelland, Nicola. 2013a. Mittelhochdeutsch in DaF-Lehrwerken für englischsprachige Lerner des 19. und 20. Jahrhunderts. In: *Zurück zum Mittelalter. Neue Perspektiven für den Deutschunterricht*. Ed. Nine Miedema and Andrea Sieber, pp. 173–194. Frankfurt: Lang.

McLelland, Nicola. 2013b. *Des guten Gebrauchs Wegzeigere*. Du bon usage dans la tradition allemande 1200–2000. In: Bon usage et variation sociolinguistique. Perspectives diachroniques et traditions nationales, ed. Wendy Ayres-Bennett & Magali Seijido, pp. 207–220. Lyon: ENS Editions.

McLelland, Nicola. 2014. French and German in Competition in British Schools, 1850–1945. In: *Documents pour l'histoire du français langue étrangère ou seconde*, N° 53, ed. by Marcus Reinfried, pp. 125–151.

Mennecke, Arnim. 1991. Überlegungen zur Bewertung landeskundlicher Inhalte in fremdsprachlichen Lehrwerken. In: *Großbritannien: seine Darstellung in deutschen Schulbüchern für den Englischunterricht*. Ed. Peter Doyé. Frankfurt: Moritz Diesterweg.

Metcalf, George J. 1974. The Indo-European hypothesis in the sixteenth and seventeenth centuries. In: *Studies in the History of Linguistics: traditions and paradigms*. Ed. Dell Hymes. London: Bloomington.

Mikk, J. 2000. *Textbook: Research and Writing*. Frankfurt am Main: Peter Lang.

Milner-Barry, E.L. 1908. The position of German in English Schools. *Modern Language Teaching* 4: 68–81.

Milroy, James, and Lesley Milroy. 1999 [1st ed. 1985]. *Authority in language. Investigating language prescription and standardization*. London: Routledge.

Minder, Robert. 1953. Soziologie der deutsche und französischen Lesebücher. In *Die Diskussion um das deutsche Lesebuch*, ed. Hermann Helmers, pp. 1–13. Darmstadt.

Minsheu, John. 1978. *Ductor in linguas =: Guide into the tongues; and, Vocabularium hispanicolatinum = A most copious Spanish dictionary*. Delmar: Scholars' Facsimiles and Reprints.

Mitchell, Rosamond (Centre for Information on Language Teaching and Research). 1988. *Communicative language teaching in* practice. London: Centre for Information on Language Teaching and Research.

Mitchell, Rosamond. 2011. Still gardening in a gale: policy, research and practice in foreign language education in England. Fremdsprachen Lehren und Lernen 40.1: 49–67.

Modern Language Association of America. 1901 *Report of the Committee of Twelve of the Modern Language Association of America*. Boston: D.C. Heath.

Moulin-Fankhänel, Claudine. 1994. *Bibliographie der deutschen Grammatiken und Orthographielehren*. Vol. I. *Von den Anfängen der Überlieferung bis zum Ende des 16. Jahrhunderts*. Heidelberg: C. Winter.

Moulin-Fankhänel, Claudine. 1997. *Bibliographie der deutschen Grammatiken und Orthographielehren*. Vol. II. *Das 17. Jahrhundert*. Heidelberg: C. Winter.

Moulin-Fankhänel, Claudine. 2000. Deutsche Grammtikschreibung vom 16. bis 18. Jahrhundert (Article 132). In *Sprachgeschichte. Ein Handbuch zur Geschichte der deutschen Sprache und ihrer Erforschung* (2ⁿᵈ edition). Vol. II, eds. Werner Besch, Anne Betten, Oskar Reichmann and Stefan Sonderegger, pp. 1903–1911. Berlin: de Gruyter.

Moulton, William. G. 1961. Linguistics and language teaching in the United States 1940–1960. In *Trends in American Linguistics: 1930–1960*, eds. Christine Mohrmann, Alf Sommerfelt and Joshua Whatmough. Utrecht: Spectrum. Reprinted in *IRAL* 1 (1963): 21–41.

Moys, Alan. Ed. (Centre for Information on Language Teaching and Research). 1980. *Modern language examinations at sixteen plus: a critical* analysis. London: Centre for Information on Language Teaching and Research.

Moys, Alan, & Richard Townsend (Centre for Information on Language Teaching and Research. 1991. *Making the case for languages* (Pathfinder 8). London: CILT.

Moys, Alan, ed. 1998. *Where are we going with languages? (Consultative report of the Nuffield Languages Inquiry)*. London: Nuffield Foundation.

Muckle, James. 2008a. *The Russian language in Britain. A historical study of learners and teachers*. Ilkeston, Derbyshire: Bramcote Press.

Muckle, James. 2008b. Russian in the University Curriculum: A Case-study of the Impact of the First World War on Language Study in Higher Education in Britain. *History of Education* 37.3: 359–381.

Murphy, Daniel. 1995. *Comenius: A Critical Reassessment of his Life and Works* Blackrock, Co Dublin: Irish Academic Press.

Nail, Norbert. 2000. 100 Jahre Marburger Ferienkurse – Die ersten Jahrzehnte. Ein Rückblick anläßlich des Internationalen Sommerkurses vom 30. Juli bis 22. August 1996. http://www.staff.uni-marburg.de/~nail/ferienkurse.htm. First published in the newspaper "Oberhessische Presse" 30.7.1996.

Naumann, Bernd. 1986. *Grammatik der deutschen Sprache zwischen 1781 und 1856. Die Kategorien der deutschen Grammatik in der Tradition von Johann Werner Meiner und Johann Christoph Adelung*. Berlin: Schmidt.

Naumann, Bernd. 2000. Die 'allgemeine Sprachwissenschaft' um die Wende zum 19. Jahrhundert. In: Auroux et al. 2000, pp. 1044–1056.

Neis, Cordula. 2003. *Anthropologie im Sprachdenken des 18. Jahrhunderts. Die Berliner Preisfrage nach dem Ursprung der Sprache (1771)*. Berlin: de Gruyter.

Nerius, Dieter. 2010. Zur Geschichte und Bedeutung des deutschen Orthographiewörterbuchs. *Aptum* 6: 76–95.

Nerius, Dieter, and Jürgen Scharnhorst, eds. 1992. *Studien zur Geschichte der deutschen Orthographie. Germanistische Linguistik 108–109*. Hildesheim: Olms.

Neumann, Josef N. and Udo Sträter, Eds. 2000. *Das Kind in Pietismus und Aufklärung. Beiträge des Internationalen Symposions vom 12.–15. November 1997*. Tübingen: Niemeyer.

Newsom, John. 1963. *The Newsom Report. Half Our Future*. A report of the Central Advisory Council for Education (England). London: Her Majesty's Stationery Office.

Newton, Gerald. 1990. Central Franconian. In: *The Dialects of Modern German*, ed. Charles V. J. Russ, pp. 136–209. London: Routledge.

Nicholls, Anthony J. 1997. The German 'National Character' in British Perspective. In *Conditions of Surrender: Britons and Germans Witness the End of the War*, ed. Ulrike Jordan, pp. 26–39. London: Tauris Academic Studies.

Nicholls, Anthony J. 2000. *Fifty years of Anglo-German relations*. London: Institute of Germanic Studies, University of London, School of Advanced Study.

Nicholls, Jason. 2003. Methods in School Textbook Research. *International Journal of Historical Learning, Teaching and Research* 3: 11–26.

Nicholls, Anthony J. 2005. *Always good neighbours, never good friends? Anglo-German relations, 1949–2001* [Pamphlet]. London: London Historical Institute.

Norwood, Cyril. 1943. The Norwood Report. Curriculum and Examinations in Secondary Schools. Report of the Committee of the Secondary School Examinations Council appointed by the President of the Board of Education in 1941. London: HM Stationery Office.

O'Grady, Hardress. 1906. German? *Modern Language Teaching* 2: 207–210.

Olson, Audrey L. 1980. *St. Louis Germans, 1850–1920: the nature of an immigrant community and its relation to the assimilation process*. New York: Arno Press.

Oppenheimer, Louis, and Martyn Barrett. Eds. 2011. *National Identity and Ingroup-Outgroup Attitudes in Children: The Role of Socio-Historical Settings*. Special Issue of the *European Journal of Developmental Psychology*, Volume 8, Issue 1.

Ortmanns, Karl Peter. 1993. *Deutsch in Großbritannien. Die Entwicklung von Deutsch als Fremdsprache von den Anfängen bis 1985* (Deutsche Sprache in Europa und Übersee. Berichte und Forschungen, 15). Stuttgart: Franz Steiner.

Ostermeier, Christiane 2012. *Die Sprachenfolge an den höheren Schulen in Preußen (1859–1933) – ein historischer Diskurs*. Stuttgart: ibidem.

Osthoff, Hermann, and Karl Brugmann. *Morphologische Untersuchungen auf dem Gebiete der indogermanischen Sprachen*. Leipzig: S. Hirzel.

Page, Brian. 1983. Graded Objectives. *Language Teaching* 16: 292–308.

Panayi, Panikos. 1995. *German Immigrants in Britain during the Nineteenth Century, 1815–1914*. Oxford: Berg.

Panayi, Panikos. Ed. 1996. *Germans in Britain since 1500*. London: The Hambledon Press.

Parr, Harmer (Centre for Information on Language Teaching and Research). 1997. *Assessment and planning in the MFL department* (Pathfinder 29). London: CILT.

Paul, Hermann. 1880. *Principien der Sprachgeschichte*. Halle: Max Niemeyer.

Paulin, Roger. 2010. Breul, Karl Hermann (1860–1932), Oxford Dictionary of National Biography, Oxford University Press, May 2010; online edn, May 2011 [http://www.oxforddnb.com/view/article/61616, accessed 19 Oct 2011].

Pausch, Oskar. 1972. *Das älteste italienisch-deutsche Sprachbuch. Eine Überlieferung aus dem Jahre 1424 nach Georg von Nürnberg.* Vienna: Böhlhaus.

Pegrum, A.W. 1914. The oral teaching of German. *Modern Language Teaching* 10: 206–212.

Peers, Allison E. 1945 *"New" tongues or modern language teaching of the future*. London: Pitman.

Peiffer, Lorenz. 2009. *Sport im Nationalsozialismus: Zum aktuellen Stand der sporthistorischen Forschung: eine kommentierte Bibliographie* (2nd, updated edition). Göttingen: Verlag Die Werkstatt.

Peiffer, Lorenz, and Matthias Fink. 2003. *Zum aktuellen Forschungsstand der Geschichte von Körperkultur und Sport in der DDR: Eine kommentierte Bibliographie*. Cologne: Sport u. Buch Strauß.

Pellin, Tommaso. 2011. The Sweet Revolutionaries: The Chinese Revolution in Grammar Studies and Henry Sweet. *Language & History* 54: 35–57.

Penzl, Herbert. 1984. *Gimer min ros*. How German was taught in the 9th and 11th centuries. *The German Quarterly* 57: 392–401.

Percy, Carol. 2012. The king's speech: metalanguage of nation, man and class in anecdotes about George III. *English Language and Linguistics* 16: 281–299.

Percy, Carol E., and Mary Catherine Davidson. 2012. *The languages of nation: attitudes and norms*. Bristol: Multilingual Matters.

Perren, George E. (Centre for Information on Language Teaching and Research). 1979a. *Foreign languages in education* (NCLE [National Congress on Languages in Education] papers and reports 1). London: Centre for Information on Language Teaching and Research.

Perren, George E. (Centre for Information on Language Teaching and Research). 1979b. *The mother tongue and other languages in education* (NCLE [National Congress on Languages in Education] papers and reports 2. London: Centre for Information on Language Teaching and Research.

Pfalzgraf, Falco. 2011. Ausländer, Fremde(s) und Minderheiten in deutschen Fibeln 1933–1945. *Muttersprache* 2011.3: 161–192.

Pfalzgraf, Falco, and Felicity Rash. Eds. 2008. *Anglo-German linguistic relations*. Frankfurt: Lang.

Pfeffer, Alan. 1964. *Basic (Spoken) German Word List*. Englewood Cliffs, N. J.: Prentice-Hall.

Pfrehm, James. 2011. The Pluricentricity of German: Perceptions of the Standardness of Austrian and German Lexical Items. *Journal of Germanic Linguistics* 23: 37–63.

Phillips, David. 2011. *The German example: English interest in educational provision in Germany since 1800*. London: Continuum.

Phillips, David, and Caroline Filmer-Sankey. 1993. *Diversification in modern language teaching: choice and the national curriculum*. London: Routledge.

Pienemann, Manfred. 1984. Psychological Constraints on the Teachability of Languages. *Studies in Second Language Acquisition* 6 (1984), 2, pp. 186–214. Reprinted in *First and Second Languge Acquisition Processes*, Carol Pfaff, ed., pp. 103–116, Cambridge: Newbury House (1987), and *Grammar and Second Language Teaching: A Book of Readings*, eds. William Rutherford & Mike Sharwood-Smith, pp. 85–106. New York: Harper and Row (1988).

Pingel, Falk. 2010. *UNESCO Guidebook on Textbook Research and Textbook Revision.* 2nd revised edition. *(Georg Eckert Institute for International Textbook Research, 2010).*

Polenz, Peter von. 1994. *Deutsche Sprachgeschichte vom Spätmittelalter bis zur Gegenwart.* Vol. II *17. und 18. Jahrhundert.* Berlin: de Gruyter.

Polenz, Peter von. 1999. *Deutsche Sprachgeschichte vom Spätmittelalter bis zur Gegenwart.* Vol. III *19. und 20. Jahrhundert.* Berlin: de Gruyter.

Polenz, Peter von. 2000. *Deutsche Sprachgeschichte vom Spätmittelalter bis zur Gegenwart.* Vol. I *Einführung. Grundbegriffe. 14. bis 16. Jahrhundert.* Berlin: de Gruyter.

Prendergast, Thomas. 1864. *The Mastery of Languages, or, the art of speaking foreign tongues idiomatically.* London: Bentley.

Prendergast, Thomas. 1868 (1st ed.), 1871 (5th ed.). *The Mastery Series. German.* London: Longmans, Green & co.

Price, Michael H. 1986. *The Development of the secondary curriculum.* London: Croom Helm.

Price, Susan. 1999. Pride and prejudice: evidence for stereotyping on the Part of British students of German. In *Intercultural Perspectives. Images of Germany in Education and the Media.*, ed. Reinhard Tenberg, pp. 136–144. Munich: iudicium.

Proescholdt, C. W. 1991. The introduction of German language teaching into England. *German Life and Letters* 44 (2): 93–102.

Puff, Helmut. 1995. *'Von dem schlüssel aller Künsten / nemblich der Grammatica.' Deutsch im lateinischen Grammatikunterricht 1480–1560.* Tübingen: Francke Verlag.

Puff, Helmut. 1996. Exercitium grammaticale puerorum. Eine Studie zum Verhältnis von pädagogischer Innovation und Buchdruck um 1500. In: *Schule und Schüler im Mittelalter. Beiträge zur europäischen Bildungsgeschichte des 9. bis 15. Jahrhunderts.* Ed. Kintzinger et al. Cologne: Böhlau, pp. 411–439.

Puren, Christian. 1988. *Histoire des méthodologies de l'enseignement des langues.* Paris: Nathan-CLE International.

Puren, Christian. 1994. *La didactique des langues à la croisée des méthodes. Essai sur l'éclectisme.* Paris: CRÉDIF-Didier.

Quick, Robert Herbert. 1872. On the study of language: Prendergast's Mastery System. *Quarterly Journal of Education* 1872: 64–69.

Raban, Sandra. Ed. 2008. *Examining the World. A History of the University of Cambridge Examinations Syndicate.* Cambridge: CUP.

Raddatz, Volker. 1977. *Englandkunde im Wandel deutscher Erziehungsziele 1886–1945.* Kronberg/Ts.: Scriptor.

Ransmayr, Jutta. 2006. *Der Status des Österreichischen Deutsch an nicht-deutschsprachigen Universitäten. Eine empirische Untersuchung.* Frankfurt am Main: Peter Lang.

Raraty, M. M. 1966. The Chair of German at Trinity College 1775–1866. *Hermathena. A Dublin University Review* 102: 53–72.

Reershemius, Gertrud. 2010. Deutsch in Großbritannien. In *Deutsch als Fremd- und Zweitsprache*, eds. Hans-Jürgen Krumm, Christian Fandrych, Britta Hufeisen and Claudia Riemer, 1674–1680. Berlin: de Gruyter.

Reeves, Nigel B. R. 1986. Why German? In *German in the United Kingdom: Issues and opportunities*, ed. CILT, 1–12. London: CILT (Centre for Information on Language Teaching and Research).

Reid, Euan. Ed. (Centre for Information on Language Teaching and Research). 1984. *Minority community languages in school: the first of two volumes from working parties for the Third Assembly, Nottingham, 1982.* (NCLE [National Congress on Languages in Education] papers and reports 4). London: Centre for Information on Language Teaching and Research.

Reinfried, Marcus 1992. *Das Bild im Fremdsprachenunterricht: eine Geschichte der visuellen Medien am Beispiel des Französischunterrichts.* Tübingen: Narr.

Reinfried, Marcus. 2004. Audio-visual language teaching. In: *Routledge encyclopedia of language teaching and learning*, ed.Michael Byram, pp. 61–64. London: Routledge.

Rendall, Heather. 1991. *Making the most of micro-computers.* London: Centre for Information on Language Teaching and Research.

Richards, Donald (Joint Council of Language Associations). 1976. Teaching children of moderate ability. In *German in the United Kingdom: Problems and Prospects*, ed. CILT, pp. 56–59. London: CILT.

Richards, Jack C., and Theodore S. Rodgers. 1986. *Approaches and Methods in Language Teaching. A description and Analysis.* Cambridge: CUP.

Richter, Elke, et al. n. d. Johann Wolfgang Goethe. Repertorium sämtlicher Briefe 1764–1832. Hrsg. von der Klassik Stiftung Weimar / Goethe- und Schiller-Archiv. Bearbeitet von Elke Richter unter Mitarbeit von Andrea Ehlert u. a. Begründet von Paul Raabe an der Herzog August Bibliothek Wolfenbüttel. http://ora-web.weimar-klassik.de/swk-db/goerep/index.html. Accessed September 2014.

Riedl, Michael. 2004. *Hermann Breymann. Aspekte eines Gelehrtenlebens im Kontext neusprachlicher Reformdiskussion.* Munich: Pixel & Dots.

Rippmann, Walter. 1899a. Hints on Teaching German, with a Running Commentary to Dent's *First German Book & Dent's German Reade.* London: Dent

Rippmann, Walter. 1899b. *Elements of Phonetics, English, French and German. Translated and adapted by W. Rippmann from Prof. Viëtor's "Kleine Phonetik".* London: Dent.

Rippmann, Walter. 1906a. The learning of Words. *Modern Language Teaching* 2: 210–214.

Rippmann, Walter. 1906b. The gentle art of translating verse. *Modern Language Teaching* 2.

Rippmann, Walter. 1909. Typical Questions in Grammar. *Modern Language Teaching* 5: 211–215.

Rippmann, Walter. 1910. Obituary: Sines Alge. *Modern Language Teaching* 6: 27–28.

Rippmann, Walter (identified as author in index only). 1911. Written examinations in phonetics. *Modern Language Teaching* 7: 150–151.

Risager, Karen. 2006. *Language and culture: global flows and local complexity.* Clevedon: Multilingual Matters.

Risager, Karen. 2007. *Language and culture pedagogy. From a nation to a transnational perspective.* Clevendon: Multilingual Matters.

Rjéoutski, Vladislav, and Alexandre Tchoudinov, eds. 2013. *Le Précepteur francophone en Europe. XVIIe–XIXe siècles.* Paris: L'Harmattan.

Robbins, Keith. 1999. *Present and Past: British Images of Germany in the first half of the 20th century and their historical legacy.* Göttingen: Wallstein Verlag.

Robins, R. H. 1997. *A Short History of Linguistics.* London: Longman.

Rock, David. 1993. Survey of German at O-level / GCSE. In: *German Studies in the Unitied Kingdom. A Survey of German in Schools and Universities.* Ed. Reinhard Tenberg and Roger Jones. London: European Business Associates, pp. 5–42.

Rodden, John. 2006. German for the East Germans. Language, literature and ideology in the former GDR. *Paradigm* 3: 20–27.

Rodden, John. 2007. Textbook Reds? How East Germans look back on their classroom textbooks. *Paradigm* 3: 1–10.

Roelcke, Thomas. 2004. Die englische Sprache im deutschen Sprachdenken des 17. und 18. Jahrhunderts. *Beiträge zur Geschichte der Sprachwissenschaft* 13: 85–114.

Rösch, Heidi. 2011. *Deutsch als Zweit- und Fremdsprache. Studienbuch.* Berlin: Akademie Verlag.

Rösler, Dietmar. 1994. *Deutsch als Fremdsprache* Stuttgart: Sammlung Metzler.

Rösler, Dietmar. 2001. Deutschunterricht und Germanistikstudium in Großbritannien. In *Deutsch als Fremdsprache: ein internationales Handbuch*, eds. Gerhard Helbig, Lutz Götze, Gert Henrici and Hans-Jürgen Krumm, pp. 1464–1471. Berlin: de Gruyter.

Rossebastiano Bart, Alda, ed. 1983. *Vocabulari Veneto-Tedeschi del secolo XV.* Torino: L'artistica Savigliano.

Rossebastiano Bart, Alda. 1984a. *Antichi vocabolari plurilingui d'uso popolare: la tradizione del "Solenissimo vochabuolista".* Alessandria: Edizioni dell'Orsa.

Rossebastiano Bart, Alda. 1984b. *I Dialoghi di Giorgio da Norimberga: redazione veneziane, versione toscana, adattemento padavano.* Savigliano: L'artistica Savigliano.

Rowles, David, Marian Carty, Anneli McLachlan, eds. 1998. *Foreign language assistants: a guide to good practice* (Pathfinder 32). London: CILT.

Rowlinson, William. 1986. Modern languages: the retreat from reform. In *The development of the secondary curriculum*, ed. Michael H. Price, pp. 77–102. London: Croom Helm.

Ruisz, Dorottya. 2013. *Umerziehung durch Englischunterricht? US-amerikanische Reeducation-Politik, neuphilologische Orientierungsdebatte und bildungspolitische Umsetzung im nachkriegszeitlichen Bayern (1945–1955).* Münster: Waxmann.

Russ, Charles V. J. Ed. 1990. The dialects of modern German: a linguistic survey. London: Routledge.

Russ, Charles V. J. 1993. Normalization in action: the Duden and the German language. In*: 'Das unsichtbare Band der Sprache'. Studies in German Language and Linguistic*

History in memory of Leslie Seiffert, ed. John L. Flood et al., pp. 501–519. Stuttgart: Hans-Dieter Heinz Akademischer Verlag.

Russ, Charles V. J. 2010. *The Sounds of German*. Cambridge: Cambridge University Press.

Russell, Paul. 2012. An habes linguam Latinam? Non tam bene sapio: views of multilingualism from the early-medieval West. In: *Multilingualism in the Greco-Roman Worlds*. Ed. Alex Mullen and Patrick James. Cambridge: CUP, pp. 193–224.

Sagarra, Eda. 1999. Die britische Germanistik 1896 bis 1946. In *Zur Geschichte und Problematik der Nationalphilologien in Europa. 150 Jahre Erste Germanistenversammlung in Frankfurt am Main (1846–1896)*, eds. Frank Fürbeth, Pierre Krügel, Ernst E. Metzner and Olaf Müller, pp. 683–696. Tübingen: Niemeyer.

Salewsky, R. 1954. Französische Schulbücher in deutscher Sicht. In *Deutschland und Frankreich im Spiegel ihrer Schulbücher*, ed. Internationales Schulbuchinstitut, pp. 96–99. Braunschweig: Verlag Albert Limbach.

Salmon, Vivian. 1972. *The works of Francis Lodwick. A study of his writings in the intellectual context of the seventeenth century*. London: Longman.

Salmon, Vivian. 1992. Anglo-Dutch linguistic scholarship: a survey of seventeenth-century achievements. In *The history of linguistics in the Low Countries*, eds. Jan Noordegraaf, Kees Versteegh and Konrad Koerner, pp. 129–153. Amsterdam: Benjamins.

Salmon, Vivian. 2003. Some notes on the life and work of John Minsheu (1560–1627). *Historiographia Linguistica* 30: 259–272.

Salter, Michael V. Ed. (Centre for Information on Language Teaching and Research). 1989. *Languages for communication: the next stage: recommendations for action*. London: D. E. S. in association with the Centre for Information on Language Teaching and Research.

Sandbach, F. E. 1926. German studies in the British Isles since 1914. *Monatshefte für deutsche Sprache und Pädagogik. Jahrbuch* 1927: 22–37.

Sanderson, David. 1982. *Modern language teachers in action: a report for the Language Teaching Research Project, Language Teaching Centre, University of York*. [York]: Language Materials Development Unit of the University of York.

Sasse, Werner. 2000. Die traditionelle Sprachforschung in Korea. In: *HSK* 18.1 ed. Auroux et al. Berlin: de Gruyter, vol. 1, pp. 63–71.

Saunders, Alison. 2000. *The seventeenth-century French emblem: a study in diversity*. Paris: Librairie Droz.

Saunders, Marion J. 1919–20. A plea for the study of German. *Modern Languages* 1919–1920: 177–179.

Sayce, Charles. 1879. How to learn a language. *Nature*.

Schäfer, Jürgen. 1973. John Minsheu: Scholar or Charlatan? *Renaissance Quarterly* 26: 23–35.

Schäfer, Jürgen. 1978. Introduction. In: *John Minsheu Guide Into Tongues*. Ed. Jürgen Schäfer. New York: Scholars' facsimiles and reprints.

Schaible, Karl Heinrich. 1885. *Geschichte der Deutschen in England von den ersten germanischen Ansiedlungen in Britannien bis zum Ende des 18. Jahrhunderts*. Strassburg: Trübner.

Scharfe, Hartmut. 2000. Die Entwicklung der Sprachwissenschaft in Indien nach Panini. In: *HSK* 18.1 ed. Auroux et al. Berlin: de Gruyter, vol. 1, pp. 125–136.

Schiller, Kay ed. 2009. *Sport in German History* (special issue of the journal *German History*, vol. 27, issue 3).

Schiller, Kay, and Christopher Young. 2009. The History and Historiography of Sport in Germany: Social, Cultural and Political Perspectives. *Germany History* 27 (3): 313–330.

Schissler, Hanna. 1987. Perceptions of the Other and the Discovery of the Self. What pupils are supposed to learn about each other's history. In *Perceptions of History. International Textbook Research on Britain, Germany and the United States*, eds. Volker R. Berghahn and Hanna Schissler, pp. 26–37. Oxford, New York & Hamburg: Berg.

Schissler, Hanna. 2005. World History: Making Sense of the Present. In *The Nation, Europe and the World. Textbooks and Curricula in Transition*, eds. Hanna Schissler and Yasemin Nuhoğlu Soysal, pp. 228–245. New York: Berghahn.

Schissler, Hanna, and Yasemin Nuhoğlu Soysal. Eds. 2005. *The Nation, Europe, and the World. Textbooks and Curricula in Transition*. New York & Oxford: Berghahn Books.

Schlieben-Lange, Brigitte. 1989. Überlegungen zur Sprachwissenschaftsgeschichtsschreibung. In *Europäische Sprachwissenschaft um 1800* (4 vols.), ed. Brigitte Schlieben-Lange et al., pp. 11–23. Münster: Nodus.

Schmenk, Barbara. 2001. *Geschlechtsspezifisches Fremdsprachenlernen? Zur Konstruktion geschlechtstypischer Lerner- und Lernbilder in der Fremdsprachenforschung*. Tübingen: Stauffenburg Verlag.

Schmenk, Barbara, and Jessica Hamann. 2007. From history to memory: new perspectives on the teaching of culture in German. In *Interkulturelle Kompetenzen im Fremdsprachenunterricht. Intercultural Literacies and German in the classroom*, eds. Chistoph Lorey, John L. Plews and Caroline L. Rieger, pp. 373–394. Tübingen: Gunter Narr.

Schmitter, Peter. Ed. 1999, 2005. *Geschichte der Sprachtheorie. Sprachtheorien der Neuzeit III. 1. Sprachbeschreibung und Sprachunterricht,* Teil I (1999), Teil II (2005, edited posthumously by Lefteris Roussos) Tübingen: Narr.

Schmitter, Peter. 2003. *Historiographie und Narration. Metahistoriographische Aspekte der Wissenschaftsgeschichtsschreibung der Linguistik*. Tübingen: Narr.

Schnurmann, Claudia. 1991. *Kommerz und Klüngel: der Englandhandel Kölner Kaufleute im 16. Jahrhundert*. Göttingen: Vandenhoeck & Ruprecht.

Schools Council. 1969. *Development of Modern Language Teaching in Secondary Schools. Working Paper* 19. London: HMSO.

Schön, Eduard. 1925. *Sinn und Form einer Kulturkunde im französischen Unterricht der höheren Schule*. Leipzig: Teubner.

Schön, Eduard. 1926. *Vom Recht der Kulturkunde*. Leipzig: B. G. Teubner.

Schottelius, Justus Georg. 1663. *Ausführliche Arbeit von der teutschen Haubtsprache*. Braunschweig: Zilliger. Reprinted with an afterword by Wolfgang Hecht, Tübingen: Niemeyer, 1967.

Schröder, Konrad. 1969. *Die Entwicklung des Englischunterrichts an den deutschsprachigen Universitäten bis zum Jahre 1850. Mit einer Analyse zu Verbreitung und Stellung des Englischen als Schulfach an den deutschen höheren Schulen im Zeitalter des Neuhumanismus.* Diss. Saarbrücken. Ratingen: Henn.

Schröder, Konrad. 1975. *Lehrwerke für den Englischunterricht im deutschsprachigen Raum 1665–1900. Einführung und Versuch einer Bibliographie.* Darmstadt: Wissenschaftliche Buchgesellschaft.

Schröder, Konrad. 1980, 1982, 1983, 1985. *Linguarum recentium annales. Der Unterricht in den modernen europäischen Sprachen im deutschsprachigen Raum.* 4 vols. *(1500–1700; 1701–1740; 1741–1770; 1771–1800).* Augsburg: Universität Augsburg.

Schröder, Konrad. 1984. *Wilhelm Viëtor, "Der Sprachunterricht muss umkehren": ein Pamphlet aus dem 19. Jahrhundert neu gelesen.* Munich: M. Huber.

Schröder, Konrad. Ed. 1992. *Fremdsprachenunterricht 1500–1800.* Wiesbaden: Harrassowitz.

Schröder, Konrad. 2000. Die Traditionen des Sprachunterrichts im Europa des 17. und 18. Jahrhunderts In *History of the Language Sciences. An International Handbook on the Evolution of the Study of Language from the Beginnings to the Present,* ed. Sylvain Auroux et al., pp. 734–741. Berlin: de Gruyter

Schröder, Konrad. 2014. *Fremdsprachenlehrer des deutschsprachigen Raums 1500–1800. Ein bio-bibliographisches Lexikon.* Wiesbaden: Harrassowitz.

Shapiro, Michael C. 2000. The Hindi grammatical tradition. In: *HSK* 18.1 ed. Auroux et al. Berlin: de Gruyter, pp. 178–181.

Shaw, Stuart, and Gillian Cooke. 2009. The evolution of international History examinations: An analysis of History question papers for 16 year olds from 1858 to the present *Research Matters* 9: 11–19. (http://www.cambridgeassessment.org.uk/Images/109986-research-matters-09-january-2010–.pdf). Accessed July 2014.

Sheppard, R., and G. Turner. 1976. A regional view. In: *German in the United Kingdom. Problems and Prospects.* Ed. CILT, pp. 14–17. London: CILT.

Sick, Bastian. 2005. *Neues aus dem Irrgarten der deutschen Sprache.* Cologne: Kiepenheuer & Witsch.

Sidwell, Duncan. 1976. An LEA perspective. In *German in the UK: problems and prospects,* ed. CILT, pp. 23–26. London: CILT.

Sidwell, Duncan. Ed. 1987a. *Teaching languages to adults.* London: Centre for Information on Language Teaching and Research.

Sidwell, Duncan. 1987b. *Adult learning strategies and approaches. Modern Language Learning. Trainers' handbook; Tutors' handbook.* Leicester: NIACE (National Institute for adult and continuing education).

Siebs, Theodor. 1898. *Deutsche Bühnenausprache: Ergebnisse der Beratungen die [...] 1898 im Apollosaale des Königlichen Schauspielhauses zu Berlin stattgefunden haben.* Berlin: Ahn.

Sievers, Eduard. 1876. *Grundzüge der Lautphysiologie.* Leipzig: Breitkopf & Härtel.

Simmler, Franz. 2003. Geschichte der Interpunktionssysteme im Deutschen. In: *Sprachgeschichte. Ein Handbuch zur Geschichte der deutschen Sprache und ihrer Erforschung. 2., vollständig neu bearbeitete und erweiterte Auflage.* Ed. Werner Besch, Anne Betten, Oskar Reichmann and Stefan Sonderegger. Berlin: de Gruyter, vol. 3, pp. 2472–2504.

Sitta, Horst. 2006. Documenta Orthographica. Stationen des Bemühens um die deutsche Rechtschreibung vom 16. Jahrhundert bis in die Gegenwart. *Zeitschrift für deutsche Philologie* 125 (1): 91–106.

Sitta, Horst 2010. Documenta Orthographica II – ein Nachtrag. *Zeitschrift für Deutsche Philologie* 129: 49–62.

Skinner, B. F. (Burrus Frederic). 1957. *Verbal behavior.* London: Methuen.

Skorge, Patricia. 2006. *The affordances of visuals in materials for foreign language learning and teaching: Perspectives from theory and research.* Unpublished Ph.D. dissertation, University of Bielefeld.

Skorge, Patricia. 2008. Visual information in language learning and teaching. In *Bielefeld Introduction to Applied Linguistics*, eds. Stephan and Vivian Gramley, pp. 27–39. Bielefeld: Aisthesis.

Smith, David G. Ed. (Centre for Information on Language Teaching and Research). 1981. *Teaching languages in today's schools.* London: Centre for Information on Language Teaching and Research.

Smith, Richard C. 1999. *The writings of Harold E. Palmer. An Overview.* Tokyo: Hon-o-Tomosha.

Smith, Richard C. 2003. *English as a Foreign Language Teaching, 1912–1936: Pioneers of ELT.* London: Taylor & Francis.

Smith, Richard C., ed. 2005. *Teaching English as a Foreign Language, 1936–1961: Foundations of ELT*, 6 vols., with General Introduction (pp. xv–cxx). Abingdon: Routledge.

Smith, Richard C. 2009b. Claude Marcel (1793–1876): A neglected applied linguist? *Language & History* 52: 171–182.

Sörensen, Christer, and Rodolf Thunander. 1980. Das Deutschlandbild in schwedischen Deutschlehrwerken. In *LMS-Lingua 2 (LMS = Lärarna i Moderna Språk)*, pp. 78–87. Uppsala Riksföreningen för lärarna i moderna språk.

Sørensen, Louise Munch. 2010. *Teach Yourself? Language Learning Through Self-Instruction Manuals in Nineteenth-Century Scandinavia.* PhD thesis, University of Sheffield. Available online at: http://etheses.whiterose.ac.uk/904/2/SORENSEN_FINAL.pdf.

Sørensen, Louise. 2011. Popular language works and the autonomous language learner in nineteenth-century Scandinavia. *Histoire, Epistemologie, Langage* 33.1: 28–38.

Soysal, Yasemin Nuhoğlu, Teresa Bertilotti, and Sabine Mannitz. 2005. Projections of Identity in French and German History and Civics Textbooks. In *The Nation, Europe and the World. Textbooks and Curricula in Transition*, eds. Hanna Schissler and Yasemin Nuhoğlu Soysal, pp. 13–34. New York: Berghahn.

Stack, Edward M. 1960. *The language laboratory and modern language teaching.* New York & Oxford: OUP.

Stern, H. H. (Hans Heinrich). 1983. *Fundamental concepts of language teaching.* Oxford: OUP.

Stevenson, Patrick. 2002. *Language and German Disunity. A sociolinguistic history of East and West in Germany, 1945–2000.* Oxford: OUP.

Stevick, Earl. 1982. *Teaching and learning languages.* Cambridge: CUP.

Stöbe, Ernst. 1939. *Das Deutschlandbild in englischen Schulbüchern für Deutsch.* Diss. Göttingen.

Stokes, Richard. 2011. A Life in Lieder. *New Books in German* Autumn 2011: 8–9.

Stone, Margaret. 1978. *Das Deutschstudium an britischen Schulen und Hochschulen.* Munich: Minerva-Publikation.

Storch, Günther. 1999. *Deutsch als Fremdsprache, eine Didaktik: theoretische Grundlagen und praktische Unterrichtsgestaltung* Munich Fink.

Storr, Francis. 1897. The Teaching of Modern Languages (French and German). In *Teaching and Organization, with Special Reference to Secondary Schools. A Manual of Practice,* ed. Percy Arthur Barnett, pp. 261–280. London: Longmans.

Stoy, J. F. 1907. The place of German in the curriculum of secondary schools. *Modern Language Teaching* 3: 146–149.

Strasser, Gerhard F., and Mara R. Wade. Eds. 2004. *Die Domänen des Emblems,* Wiesbaden: Harrassowitz.

Streuber, Albert. 1914. Rpt. 1967. *Beiträge zur Geschichte des französischen Unterrichts im 16. bis 18. Jahrhundert.*

Streuber, Albert. 1962, 1963, 1964. Die ältesten Anleitungsschriften zur Erlernung des Französischen in England und den Niederlanden bis zum 16. Jahrhundert. *Zeitschrift für französische Sprache und Literatur* 72: 186–211; 73: 197–112, 189–209; 74: 159–176.

Sturm, Dietrich. 1990. *Zur Visualisierung von Lehrwerken für Deutsch als Fremdsprache – historische und kulturkontrastive Aspekte.* Diss. Kassel, 1990.

Sweet, Henry. 1877. *A handbook of phonetics: including a popular exposition of the principles of spelling reform.* Oxford: Clarendon Press.

Sweet, Henry. 1899. *The Practical Study of Languages: A Guide for Teachers and Learners.* London: Dent.

Taylor, Brian. Forthcoming. By their books ye may (get to) know them (3): Emil Trechmann. To appear in: *Biblionews and Australian Notes & Queries.*

Tenberg, Reinhard. 1993. Survey of German at the "new" universities. In *German Studies in the United Kingdom. A Survey of German in Schools and Universities,* eds. Reinhard Tenberg and Roger Jones, pp. 135–168. London: European Business Associates.

Tenberg, Reinhard, and Michael Byram. 1999. *Intercultural perspectives: images of Germany in education and the media.* München: Iudicium.

Tenberg, Reinhard, and Roger Jones. 1993. *German Studies in the United Kingdom. A Survey of German in Schools and Universities.* London: European Business Associates.

Theobald, John. 1999. Manufacturing Europhobia out of Germanophobia. Case studies in popularist propaganda. In: *Intercultural perspectives. Images of Germany in Education and the Media.* Ed. Reinhard Tenberg. Munich: iudicium, pp. 30–40.

Thimme, Christian. 1996. *Geschichte in Lehrwerken Deutsch als Fremdsprache und Französisch als Fremdsprache für Erwachsene: ein deutsch-französischer Lehrbuchvergleich.* Baltmannsweiler: Schneider-Verl. Hohengehren.

ThinkGerman. 2010. http://thinkgerman.org.uk/think_german_conference.

Tinsley, Teresa (British Academy). 2013. Languages: The State of the Nation. London: British Academy. http://www.britac.ac.uk/policy/State_of_the_Nation_2013.cfm (accessed May 2013).

Tintemann, Ute. 2006. *Grammatikvermittlung und Sprachreflexion. Karl Philipp Moritz' Italiänische Sprachlehre für die Deutschen.* Hannnover-Laatzen: Wehrhahn Verlag.

Titone, Renzo. 1968. *Teaching Foreign languages. An Historical Sketch.* Washington DC: Georgetown University Press.

Titone, Renzo. 2000. History: the nineteenth century. In *Routledge Encyclopaedia of Language Teaching and Learning,* ed. Michael Byram, 264–269. London: Routledge.

Townshend, Kate. 1997. *E-mail: using electronic communications in foreign language teaching.* London: Centre for Information on Language Teaching and Research.

Tumber, Margaret A. 1986. German as first foreign language. In *German in the United Kingdom: issues and opportunities,* ed. CILT, pp. 44–47. London: CILT.

UNESCO. 1953. Bilateral consultations for the improvement of history textbooks. (Educational Studies and Documents July 1953, no. IV).

Usher, H. J. K., Black-Hawkins, C. D., and Carrick, G. J. 1981. *An Angel without Wings. The history of University College School 1830–1980.* London: University College School.

Van der Lubbe, Fredericka. 2007a. *Martin Aedler and the High Dutch Minerva. The First German Grammar for the English* Duisburger Arbeiten zur Sprach- und Kulturwissenschaft. (Duisburg Papers on Research in Language and Culture 68). Frankfurt: Lang.

Van der Lubbe, Fredericka. 2007b. One hundred years of German teaching. *AUMLA* December 2007 [no vol no]: 143–152.

Van der Lubbe, Fredericka. 2008. Constructing Germany: The German nation in Anglo-German grammars of the eighteenth century. In *Anglo-German linguistic relations,* eds. Falco Pfalzgraf and Felicity Rash, pp. 63–72. Frankfurt: Lang.

Van Dijk, Teun A. 2003. Critical Discourse Analysis. In *The Handbook of Discourse Analysis,* eds. Deborah Schiffrin, Deborah Tannen and Heidi Ehernberger Hamilton, pp. 352–371. Oxford: Blackwell.

Van Hal, Toon. 2010a. *'Moedertalen en taalmoeders'. Het vroegmoderne taalvergelijkende onderzoek in de Lage Landen.* Brussel: Koninklijke Vlaamse Academie voor Wetenschappen en Kunsten.

Van Hal, Toon. 2010b. On 'the Scythian theory'. Reconstructing the outlines of Johannes Elichmann's (1601/1602–1639) planned Archaeologia harmonica. *Language & History* 52 (2): 70–80.

Veith, Werner Heinrich. 2000. Bestrebungen der Orthographiereform im 18., 19., und 20. Jahrhundert. In *Sprachgeschichte. Ein Handbuch zur Geschichte der deutschen Sprache und ihrer Erforschung. 2., vollständig neu bearbeitete und erweiterte Auflage,* eds. Werner Besch, Anne Betten, Oskar Reichmann and Stefan Sonderegger, pp. 1782–1803. Berlin: de Gruyter.

Veltman, Calvin. 1991. Theory and method in the study of language shift. In *Language and ethnicity. Focusschrift in honor of Joshua A. Fishman*, ed. James R. Dow, pp. 145–167. Amsterdam: Benjamins.

Verbaan, Eddy. 2011. *Grondslagen van de stadsbeschrijving in de zeventiende-eeuwse Republiek.* Hilversum: Uitgeverij Verloren.

Verner, Karl. 1865. Eine Ausnahme der ersten Lautverschiebung. *Zeitschrift für vergleichende Sprachforschung* 23: 97–130.

Viëtor, Wilhelm (published under the pseudonym Quousque Tandem). 1882. Der Sprachunterricht muss umkehren. Pamphlet. Heilbronn: Henninger.

Viëtor, Wilhelm. 1902, rpt. 2002. *Die Methodik des neusprachlichen Unterrichts: ein geschichtlicher Überblick in vier Vorträgen.* Leipzig: Trübner. Rpt. in Howatt & Smith (2002), vol. 5, pp. 269–332.

Vos, Frits. 2000. The influence of Dutch grammar on Japanese language research. In: *HSK* 18.1 ed. Auroux et al. Berlin: de Gruyter, vol. 1, pp. 102–103.

Wagner, Melanie. 2009. *Lay linguistics and school teaching: An empirical sociolinguistic study in the Moselle Franconian dialect area.* Stuttgart: Franz Steiner Verlag (ZDL Beihefte).

Watson, Foster. 1909. *The beginnings of the teaching modern subjects in England.* London: Pitman. Reprint Wakefield: S.R. Publishers, 1971.

Watson, F. 1921. History of the teaching of German in England. In *The encyclopaedia and dictionary of education*, ed. F. Watson, pp. 693–694. London: Pitman.

Watts, Andrew. 2008. Cambridge Local Examinations 1858–1945. In: *Examining the World*. Ed. Sandra Raban. Cambridge: CUP, pp. 36–70.

Watts, Sheila. 2000. Teaching talk: should students learn 'real' German? *German as a foreign language* 1: 64–82. Accessible at http://www.gfl-journal.de/1–2000/watts.pdf. Accessed July 2014.

Weber, Thomas. 2008. *Our friend "the enemy": elite education in Britain and Germany before World War I.* Stanford: Stanford University Press.

Wegner, Anke. 1999. *100 Jahre Deutsch als Fremdsprache in Frankreich und England. Eine vergleichende Studie von Methoden, Inhalten und Zielen.* Munich: iudicium.

Weijenberg, Jan. 1979. Wie Deutsch sind Lehrwerke für Deutsch als Fremdsprache? Zur Frage der Sprachauthentizität von Lehrwerkdialogen. In *Dortmunder Diskussionen zur Fremdsprachendidaktik*, ed. Helmut J Heuer, pp. 239–242. Dortmund: Lensing.

Weinbrenner, Peter. 1992. Methodologies of textbook analysis used to date. In *History and Social Studies – Methodologies of Textbook analysis.*, ed. Hilary Bourdillon. Amsterdam: Swets & Zeitlinger.

Westerhoff, Jan C. 2001. A world of signs: Baroque pansemioticism, the *Polyhistor* and the Early Modern *Wunderkammer. Journal of the History of Ideas* 62: 633–650.

Wheeler, Garon. 2013. *Language Teaching Through the Ages.* London: Routledge.

Whitehead, Maurice. 2004. 'Siepmann, Otto (1861–1947)', *Oxford Dictionary of National Biography*, Oxford University Press, 2004; online edn, Oct 2009. http://www.oxforddnb.com/view/article/36088, accessed July 2014.

Whitehead, Maurice, and David Hartley. 2006. *Teacher Education: Major Themes in Education* London and New York: Routledge.

Widgery, William H. 1888. *The teaching of languages in schools.* London: David Nutt.

Wierlacher, Alois ed. 1987. *Perspektiven und Verfahren interkultureller Germanistik.* Munich: iudicium.

Wierlacher, Alois. 2001. *Architektur interkultureller Germanistik.* Munich iudicium.

Wierlacher, Alois, and Andrea Bogner. 2003. *Handbuch interkultureller Germanistik* Stuttgart: Metzler.

Wodak, Ruth, ed. 1997. *Gender and discourse.* London: Sage Publications.

Wodak, Ruth. 2009. *The discursive construction of national identity.* Edinburgh: Edinburgh University Press.

Wodak, Ruth, and Michael Meyer. 2009. *Methods of critical discourse analysis.* London; Thousand Oaks [Calif.]: SAGE.

Woods, Joanna. 2007. Katherine Mansfield, 1888–1923. *Kotare 2007.* Special issue: *Essays in New Zealand Literary Biography,* Series 1. *Women Prose Writers to World War I.* https://ojs.victoria.ac.nz/kotare/article/view/776. Accessed July 2014.

Wringe, Colin. 1976. *Developments in Modern Language Teaching.* London: Open Books.

Wringe, Colin. 1989. *The Effective Teaching of Modern Languages.* London: Longman.

Wustmann, Gustav. 1896. *Allerhand Sprachdummheiten. 2nd edition. [I have second edition; first was 1891, 3rd was 1903].* Leipzig: Fr. Wilh. Grunow.

Yeandle, Peter. in prep. *Teaching "Our Island Story": Citizenship, Nation and Empire in the teachinf of history, c.1850–1925.* Manchester: Manchester University Press.

Zhang, Wenqiao. 2002. 'Lun Siweite dui Zhongguo wenfa yanjiu de yingxiang' [On the influence of Sweet on Chinese grammatical research]. Foreign Language Teaching and Research, 34 (1): 69–74.

Ziegler, Evelyn. 2009. 'Ich sag' das jetzt so, weil das steht auch so im Duden!' Sprachwandel als Sprachvariation: weil-Sätze. *Praxis Deutsch. Zeitschrift für Deutschunterricht* 215: 45–51.

Zwartjes, Otto, Ramón Arzápalo Marín and Thomas C. Smith-Stark, Eds. 2009. *Missionary Linguistics IV: Selected Papers from the Fifth International Conference on Missionary Linguistics, Merida, Yucatan, 14–17 March 2007.* Amsterdam: Benjamins.

Fremdsprachen in Geschichte und Gegenwart

Herausgegeben von Helmut Glück und Konrad Schröder

HARRASSOWITZ VERLAG · WIESBADEN

www.harrassowitz-verlag.de · verlag@harrassowitz.de

Fremdsprachen in Geschichte und Gegenwart

Herausgegeben von Helmut Glück und Konrad Schröder

13: Matthias Schulz (Hg.)

Sprachliche Aspekte des Reisens in Mittelalter und Früher Neuzeit

2014. 184 Seiten, 18 Abb., 11 Tabellen, br
ISBN 978-3-447-10050-2   € 38,– (D)

Im Mittelalter und in der Frühen Neuzeit waren Angehörige ganz verschiedener Gruppen auch über längere Distanzen hinweg unterwegs: Mönche, Händler, Adelige, Gelehrte sowie Frauen, Männer und Kinder des einfachen Volkes waren ebenso mobil wie Handwerker, Studenten, Spielleute oder Abenteurer. Auf den Straßen des Hoch- und Spätmittelalters und der Frühen Neuzeit begegneten sich Fernhandelskaufleute, Missionare, Pilger, Ritter, Kreuzfahrer, Handwerker, Söldner und Boten. Doch welche Rolle spielten die fremden Sprachen, mit denen die Reisenden in Kontakt kamen? Welche Schwierigkeiten bereiteten sprachliche Grenzen? Wie konnte man sich sprachlich auf Reisen vorbereiten? Wie wurden Sprachbücher und Grammatiken eingesetzt? Wie wird in Quellen über Sprachkontaktsituationen und über gelungene und gescheiterte Verständigung berichtet? Und nicht zuletzt: Wie beeinflussten Reisen das Wissen über fremde Sprachen?
Der Sammelband vereint die Beiträge zur gleichnamigen Tagung im November 2011 an der Universität Bamberg. Die Untersuchungen fragen, ausgehend von unterschiedlichen fachlichen Blickwinkeln und Bezugspunkten, nach Aspekten des Fremdsprachenlernens und -gebrauchs für und auf Reisen und nehmen spezifische Sprachkontaktsituationen in den Blick. Dabei werden sprachliche Bedingungen einzelner Reisetypen wie der Kavalierstour, der Bildungsreise oder der Missionsfahrt analysiert, Strukturen und Bedingungen von Sprachlehrwerken erörtert, der Wortschatz der Reiseberichte untersucht und die Rolle reisender Setzer und Drucker für den Variantenabbau im Buchdruck diskutiert. Zudem wird der Band durch die Eröffnungsvortrag der zugehörigen Ausstellung in der Staatsbibliothek Bamberg ergänzt.

14: Helmut Glück, Mark Häberlein (Hg.)

Militär und Mehrsprachigkeit im neuzeitlichen Europa

2014. 256 Seiten, 15 Abb., 3 Tabellen, br
ISBN 978-3-447-10299-5   € 58,– (D)

Obwohl Soldaten zu den besonders mobilen Gruppen der alteuropäischen Gesellschaft gehörten und Armeen des 16. bis 19. Jahrhunderts häufig multinational zusammengesetzt und mehrsprachig waren, ist das Phänomen der sprachlichen Verständigung im Militär bislang wenig untersucht. Die Beiträge dieses Sammelbandes erschließen dieses vernachlässigte Forschungsfeld anhand deutscher, österreichischer, französischer, schweizerischer und dänischer Fallbeispiele auf der Grundlage neuer Quellen und unter Anwendung sprach- und kulturgeschichtlicher sowie linguistischer Methoden. Aus Selbstzeugnissen wie Briefen und Tagebüchern erschließen sie die sprachlichen Kontaktsituationen, Verständigungsprobleme und Fremdwahrnehmungen, mit denen sich frühneuzeitliche Offiziere und Soldaten konfrontiert sahen. Sprachlehrwerke und Vokabellisten, die speziell für Militärangehörige verfasst wurden, Zeitungsinserate für Sprachunterricht und Lehrpläne von Kadettenakademien erhellen den hohen Bedarf an Fremdsprachenkompetenz im militärischen Bereich. Ein Beitrag über die Erfahrungen von Soldaten in multinationalen Verbänden in Afghanistan macht schließlich die unverminderte Aktualität des Themas deutlich.

HARRASSOWITZ VERLAG · WIESBADEN

www.harrassowitz-verlag.de · verlag@harrassowitz.de